Neue Freunde

A functional approach to proficient communication!

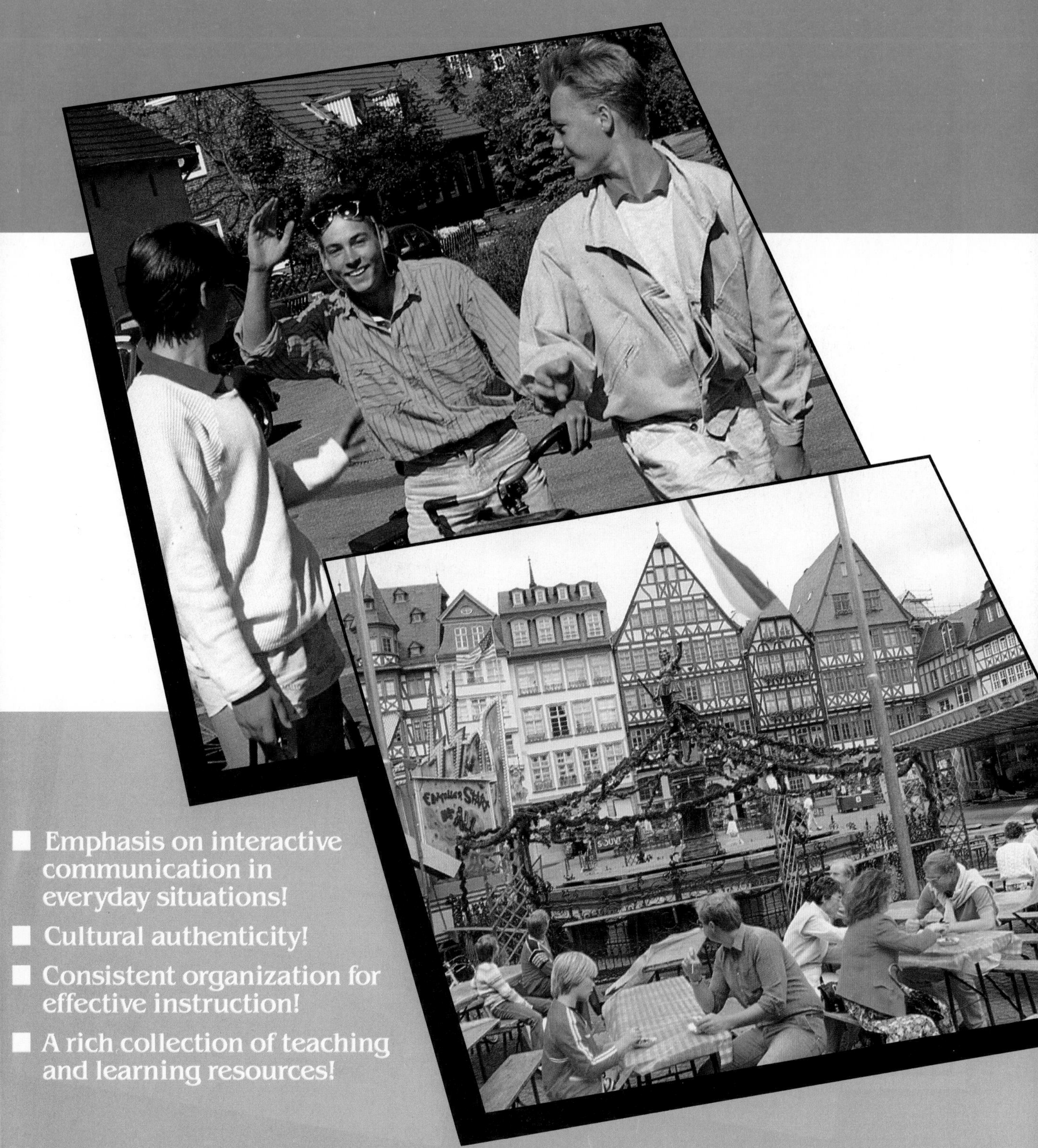

- Emphasis on interactive communication in everyday situations!
- Cultural authenticity!
- Consistent organization for effective instruction!
- A rich collection of teaching and learning resources!

Functional language for proficient communication

From greeting others to inviting friends, from seeking information to expressing opinions, ***Neue Freunde*** introduces students to the world of *real* language in *real* situations!

Learning activities that develop basic concepts

Through a variety of activities, ***Neue Freunde*** provides specific practice for basic vocabulary and grammar concepts.

Each section opens with an appealing situation rich in ideas for lively communication.

Application activities for proficient communication

Motivating activities invite students to apply what they have learned to real-life situations.

A balance of activities for learning and application helps students become proficient in listening, speaking, reading, and writing in German.

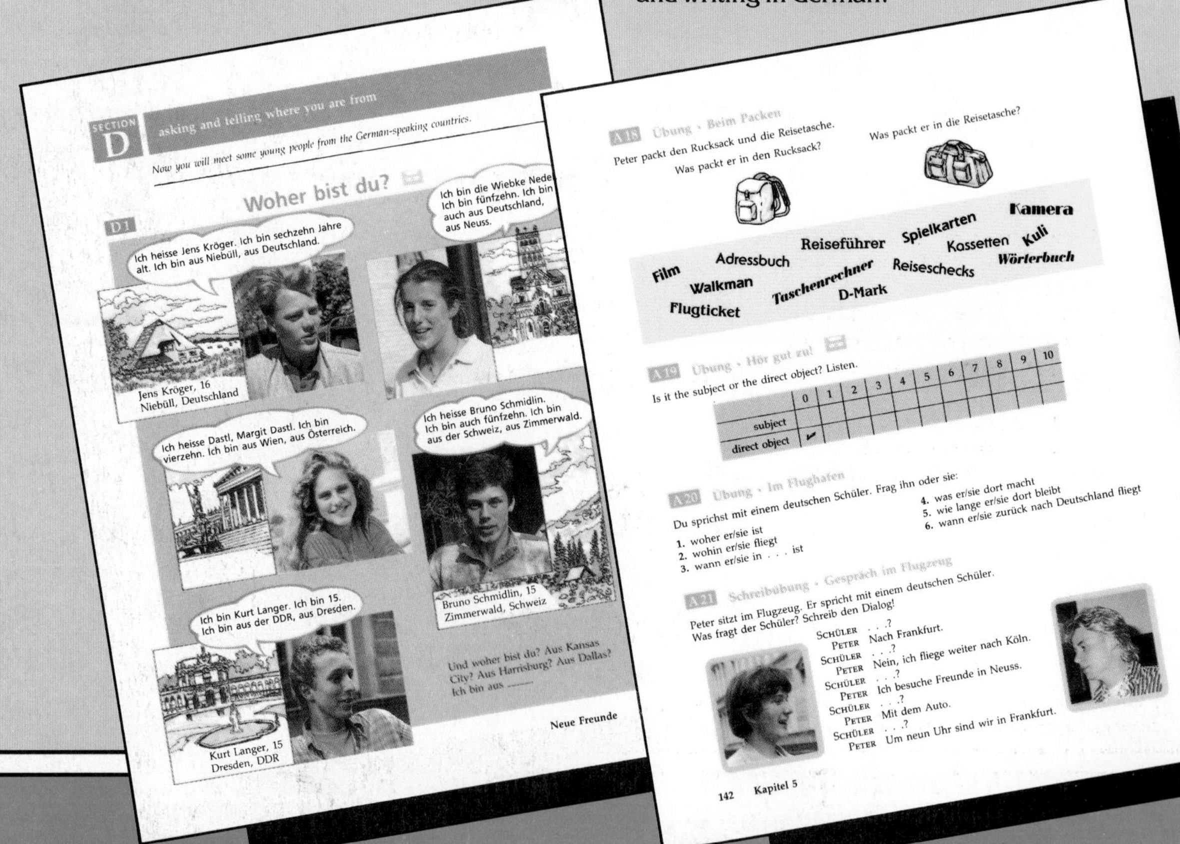

SECTION D asking and telling where you are from

Now you will meet some young people from the German-speaking countries.

D1 Woher bist du?

Ich heisse Jens Kröger. Ich bin sechzehn Jahre alt. Ich bin aus Niebüll, aus Deutschland.
Ich bin die Wiebke Nede... Ich bin fünfzehn. Ich bin auch aus Deutschland, aus Neuss.
Ich heisse Dastl, Margit Dastl. Ich bin vierzehn. Ich bin aus Wien, aus Österreich.
Ich heisse Bruno Schmidlin. Ich bin auch fünfzehn. Ich bin aus der Schweiz, aus Zimmerwald.
Ich bin Kurt Langer. Ich bin 15. Ich bin aus der DDR, aus Dresden.

Jens Kröger, 16
Niebüll, Deutschland

Bruno Schmidlin, 15
Zimmerwald, Schweiz

Kurt Langer, 15
Dresden, DDR

Und woher bist du? Aus Kansas City? Aus Harrisburg? Aus Dallas? Ich bin aus ______.

Neue Freunde

A18 Übung · Beim Packen

Peter packt den Rucksack und die Reisetasche.
Was packt er in den Rucksack? Was packt er in die Reisetasche?

Film
Adressbuch
Reiseführer
Spielkarten
Kamera
Kassetten
Kuli
Wörterbuch
Reiseschecks
Walkman
Taschenrechner
D-Mark
Flugticket

A19 Übung · Hör gut zu!

Is it the subject or the direct object? Listen.

	0	1	2	3	4	5	6	7	8	9	10
subject	✓										
direct object											

A20 Übung · Im Flughafen

Du sprichst mit einem deutschen Schüler. Frag ihn oder sie:

1. woher er/sie ist
2. wohin er/sie fliegt
3. wann er/sie in . . . ist
4. was er/sie dort macht
5. wie lange er/sie dort bleibt
6. wann er/sie zurück nach Deutschland fliegt

A21 Schreibübung · Gespräch im Flugzeug

Peter sitzt im Flugzeug. Er spricht mit einem deutschen Schüler. Was fragt der Schüler? Schreib den Dialog!

SCHÜLER . . .?
PETER Nach Frankfurt.
SCHÜLER . . .?
PETER Nein, ich fliege weiter nach Köln.
SCHÜLER . . .?
PETER Ich besuche Freunde in Neuss.
SCHÜLER . . .?
PETER Mit dem Auto.
SCHÜLER . . .?
PETER Um neun Uhr sind wir in Frankfurt.

142 Kapitel 5

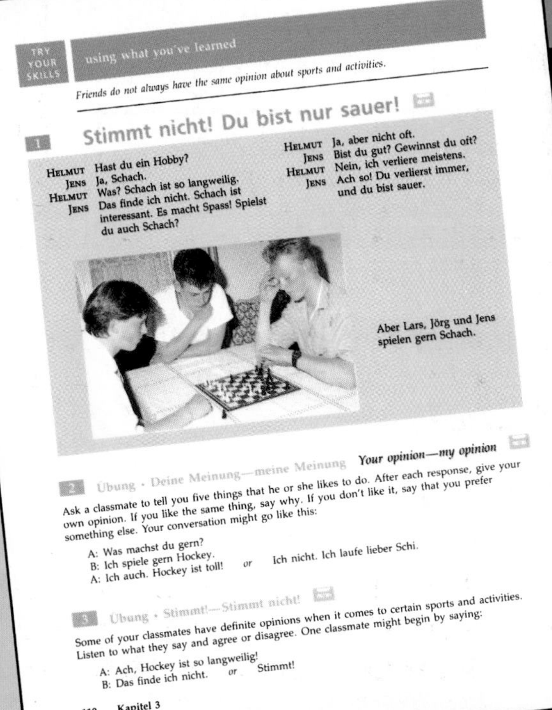

TRY YOUR SKILLS

using what you've learned

Friends do not always have the same opinion about sports and activities.

1 Stimmt nicht! Du bist nur sauer!

HELMUT Hast du ein Hobby?
JENS Ja, Schach.
HELMUT Was? Schach ist so langweilig.
JENS Das finde ich nicht. Schach ist interessant. Es macht Spass! Spielst du auch Schach?
HELMUT Ja, aber nicht oft.
JENS Bist du gut? Gewinnst du oft?
HELMUT Nein, ich verliere meistens.
JENS Ach so! Du verlierst immer, und du bist sauer.

Aber Lars, Jörg und Jens spielen gern Schach.

2 Übung · Deine Meinung—meine Meinung *Your opinion—my opinion*

Ask a classmate to tell you five things that he or she likes to do. After each response, give your own opinion. If you like the same thing, say why. If you don't like it, say that you prefer something else. Your conversation might go like this:

A: Was machst du gern?
B: Ich spiele gern Hockey.
A: Ich auch. Hockey ist toll! *or* Ich nicht. Ich laufe lieber Schi.

3 Übung · Stimmt!—Stimmt nicht!

Some of your classmates have definite opinions when it comes to certain sports and activities. Listen to what they say and agree or disagree. One classmate might begin by saying:

A: Ach, Hockey ist so langweilig!
B: Das finde ich nicht. *or* Stimmt!

110 Kapitel 3

Application activities in **Try Your Skills** provide "real-life" opportunities for students to use their new language skills.

ZUM LESEN

München

The city of Munich attracts people from all over Germany and from all over the world. What makes Munich so special?

„München mag man". Was ist diese Stadt für den Besucher? Hofbräuhaus—Oktoberfest—Theater, Oper, Kunst—„Gemütlichkeit"—oder einfach Bayern?

München ist nicht nur „deutsch", München hat auch einen südlichen Charakter: griechische Säulen, italienische Renaissance-Fassaden, barocke Kirchen.

München ist gemütlich. Wer kennt nicht den Marienplatz, „die gute Stube" Münchens?

München hat seinen Viktualienmarkt. Hier gibt es alles, was Herz und Magen begehren. Wie wär's mit einer bayrischen Brotzeit?

220 Kapitel 7

Reading selections in a variety of formats—including comic strips, letters, interviews, character sketches, and articles, as well as narratives—help students develop reading skills in German. Activities, following each selection, check comprehension and relate reading to students' personal experiences.

Sample pages are reduced.
Actual sizes are 8"x10". All pages are from *Level 1*.

Cultural awareness to broaden understanding

Positive cultural attitudes

To help students understand and appreciate German-speaking people and countries, ***Neue Freunde*** interweaves cultural insights and information. Teaching more than just the language, the program depicts everyday life, such as family and peer relations and social customs, in German culture.

Cultural authenticity

To surround students with vibrant, authentic German culture, the textbook includes such special features as an introduction to the language and culture, colorful photographic essays, and cultural notes. To ensure authenticity, the textbook was written by native speakers of German. In addition, the annotated *Teacher's Edition* and *Teacher's ResourceBank* ™ provide an abundance of cultural resources, realia, and insights to further enhance learning experiences.

INTRODUCTION

German and You

Welcome to the German-speaking world! During the coming year you will learn to understand, speak, read, and write German in a variety of situations. You will also learn more about the German-speaking world outside your classroom: daily life, customs, traditions, music, art, science, and history. As you begin your travels through the German-speaking world, here's wishing you . . .

Viel Glück!
Good luck!

In this introduction you will learn about:

1 Germany: a pictorial view
2 the German-speaking countries
3 German in the United States
4 German, English, and other languages
5 German and your future career
6 suggestions for studying German

1

Strikingly illustrated, **German and You** introduces students to German people, language, and culture.

Depicting the lifestyles of German-speaking people, colorful photo essays enhance students' understanding of German attitudes and customs.

Austria

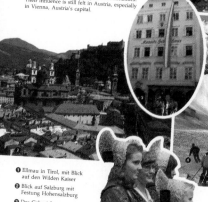

Austria is one of the smaller countries in Central Europe, mostly famous for its beautiful scenery, its music, and its culture. Two thirds of Austria is covered by the Alps, where skiing is the most popular sport. This country, with its beautiful mountains, lakes, historic cities, and picturesque villages, is a vacationer's dream. There are ancient abbeys, fairytale castles, and beautiful churches. Under the Habsburg rulers, Austria was the heart of a vast empire that included many different ethnic groups and nationalities. Their influence is still felt in Austria, especially in Vienna, Austria's capital.

1. Ellmau in Tirol, mit Blick auf den Wilden Kaiser
2. Blick auf Salzburg mit Festung Hohensalzburg
3. Das Geburtshaus von Mozart (1756–1791) in Salzburg
4. Schilaufen in Hintertux
5. Trachtengruppe aus der Wachau

232 Landeskunde 2

Each section includes a cultural note—**Ein wenig Landeskunde**—that provides interesting facts about German-speaking people to increase students' cultural awareness.

C2 Ein wenig Landeskunde

Occasions for giving gifts in German-speaking countries are pretty much the same as in the United States: birthday, Christmas, anniversary, Mother's Day, and Father's Day, to mention a few. It is also customary to give a gift when visiting someone. Flowers, which Germans are especially fond of, are often given as a gift. Some flower shops even have a vending machine outside so that people can purchase a bouquet even if the store is closed—for example, on a Sunday. Many people buy a gift box of candy or a bottle of wine. It is also customary to bring a bar of chocolate for each child in the family.

Zum Geburtstag alles Gute!

Herzliche Wünsche zum Namenstag

C3 Was sagt die Reklame?

C4 Übung • Was schenkst du?

1. Zum Geburtstag schenke ich meinem Bruder ein T-Shirt.
2. Zum Namenstag schenke ich meiner Mutter ein Buch.
3. Zu . . .

Geschenke kaufen 313

Sample pages are reduced. Actual sizes are 8″x10″. All pages are from *Level 1*.

Consistent organization for effective teaching and learning

Manageable content

Designed as a one-year course, ***Neue Freunde*** promotes active learning at a comfortable pace. Instruction progresses logically without overwhelming students, introducing a manageable amount of new grammar and vocabulary to support the communicative functions.

Clear learning objectives

Consistent unit organization with clearly defined objectives ensures success in learning. As students move through each new lesson, they build self-confidence and self-motivation.

Frequent review

Periodic review helps students apply what they have learned to new and different situations. Self-checks in each unit allow students to monitor their grasp of important concepts and skills while word-study activities help students review vocabulary effectively. Review units provide numerous activities that teachers may select to reinforce learning and satisfy special needs.

KAPITEL 2

Schule

In this unit you will meet some high school students from German-speaking countries. About 35 percent of the young people between the ages of 10 and 19 attend academic high schools, and many, though not all, will continue to a university or to another school of higher learning.

In this unit you will:

SECTION A — tell how you get to school

SECTION B — talk about school supplies and how much they cost

SECTION C — talk about your class schedule, tell time

SECTION D — talk about homework and grades

TRY YOUR SKILLS — use what you've learned

ZUM LESEN — read for practice and pleasure

61

WAS KANNST DU SCHON?

Let's review some important points that you have learned in this unit.

Can you say how to get to school?
Using the verb **kommen,** make complete sentences saying how each person comes to school. Vary the means of transportation.
1. Kristin 2. er 3. du 4. Peter und Barbara 5. ich

Can you name some school supplies?
Say the definite article and the plural form of:
Heft, Wörterbuch, Kuli, Bleistift, Schultasche, Taschenrechner, Kassette, Stundenplan

Can you buy things in a store, asking for prices and saying thank you and you're welcome?
Ask how much these items cost and give an answer. Say thank you and you're welcome.
Kuli, Heft, Schultasche, Kassetten

Can you use the right pronoun for people and things?
For each of these nouns, use the pronoun that correctly refers to it:
Schultasche, Lehrer, Mädchen, Taschenrechner, Karin, Bleistifte, Frl. Seifert, Jens, Wörterbuch, Heft

Can you talk about your class schedule?
Say what subjects you have on each day of the week.
Say the names of the days of the week.

Do you know the forms of the verb *haben*?
Write the forms of **haben** that go with these subjects:
1. ich 2. er 3. Sabine und Peter 4. Sabine 5. du 6. Peter 7. sie 8. wir 9. ihr

Can you tell time?
Say what time it is: 7.30; 9.45; 12.50; 1.30; 5.20; 8.15

Can you talk about grades?
What would you say if you got an A? an F?

Can you say whether or not a subject is easy or difficult?
Respond to the following questions:
Du hast eine Eins in Bio? Eine Fünf in Mathe?

86 Kapitel 2

Clearly delineated sections with specific communicative functions provide a "purpose" for language learning.

Cross-referenced to the communicative functions, **Was kannst du schon?** helps students monitor their progress.

Sample pages are reduced. Actual sizes are 8"x10". All pages are from *Level 1.*

A wealth of teaching resources for a range of needs

Flexible resources

Neue Freunde provides a range of resources to satisfy a variety of teaching preferences and individual learning rates and styles.

Teacher's Edition

The easy-to-use annotated *Teacher's Edition* contains numerous convenient features:

- A scope and sequence chart for each unit
- Detailed teaching suggestions—including ideas for cooperative learning—conveniently located before each unit
- Cultural background notes for each section of every unit
- Provisions for students of different abilities
- Scripts and answers for listening comprehension exercises
- Annotated pupil's pages with answers to exercises

A1–2

OBJECTIVES **To socialize:** say hello and say goodbye; greet adults

CULTURAL BACKGROUND Germans insist on a greater degree of formality than Americans do. In the United States, adults may be on a first-name basis immediately. In Germany, adults who have known one another for 30 years may still be on **Sie**-terms. Come back to this point when you cover **Sie.**

The emblems shown on page 31 are those of the four German-speaking countries: the Federal Republic of Germany, the German Democratic Repub- lic, Austria, and Switzerland.

MOTIVATING ACTIVITY Before starting on Section A, have the students list all the ways we greet one another in English and the ways we take leave of one another. Remind them to think of formal and informal expressions, of long forms and of short forms. See how many expressions they can think of. Put all suggestions on an overhead transparency or on the blackboard. Ask the students to come up with contexts for the various expressions: where might an informal expression be appropriate? A formal one?

Tell students that in German, too, there are many different ways of greeting people and of saying goodbye. They will learn the most common expressions—those that teenagers use with one another and the more formal expressions they would use with adults.

Guten Tag! Auf Wiedersehen!

Play the cassette once through or read the text aloud to introduce the three exchanges of greetings. At this point, students should just listen with their books closed. Repeat. Then, with books open, have the students listen to the cassette or to your reading of the text once more. Say the greetings in the first of the exchanges **(Steffi** and **Andreas).** Have the students repeat each phrase after you. When they can say each phrase reasonably well, turn the exchange into a dialog: you take one part and the students take the other. Repeat; then reverse roles. Follow the same procedure for the second and third sets of greetings.

Follow the same procedure for the leave-taking expressions. You may want to present the leave-taking expressions on another day, unless the stu- dents are still highly motivated.

CHALLENGE Have the students use greetings taken from one set with re- sponses taken from another set: for example, one student might say **Tag!** and the other answer with **Hallo!** They should use their own names for this, unless they have already chosen a German name for the classroom.

SLOWER–PACED LEARNING For these students, you might put off one of the sets of greetings until the next day. You might also consider introducing *one* set of greetings coupled with *one* set of farewells at a time. However, do not leave the students with the impression that any one set of farewells must always be used with the same set of greetings.

Übung

If you are planning to use German first names in the classroom, either A2 or A4 is a good place to introduce the idea. You might want to have a longer list of names on hand than the one provided in A4, especially if you have a large class. Currently popular names should predominate on your list, but include a few more traditional ones. Some other currently popular names are **Christian, Katharina,** and—surprise!—**Jennifer** and **Patrick.**

T26 Teacher's Notes Kapitel 1

Teacher's Notes provide specific strategies for each part of the unit—including basic material, activities, and reading selections. Notes include special projects, variations of textbook exercises, and suggestions for accommodating different learning styles.

Tabbed pages allow quick location of **Teacher's Notes.**

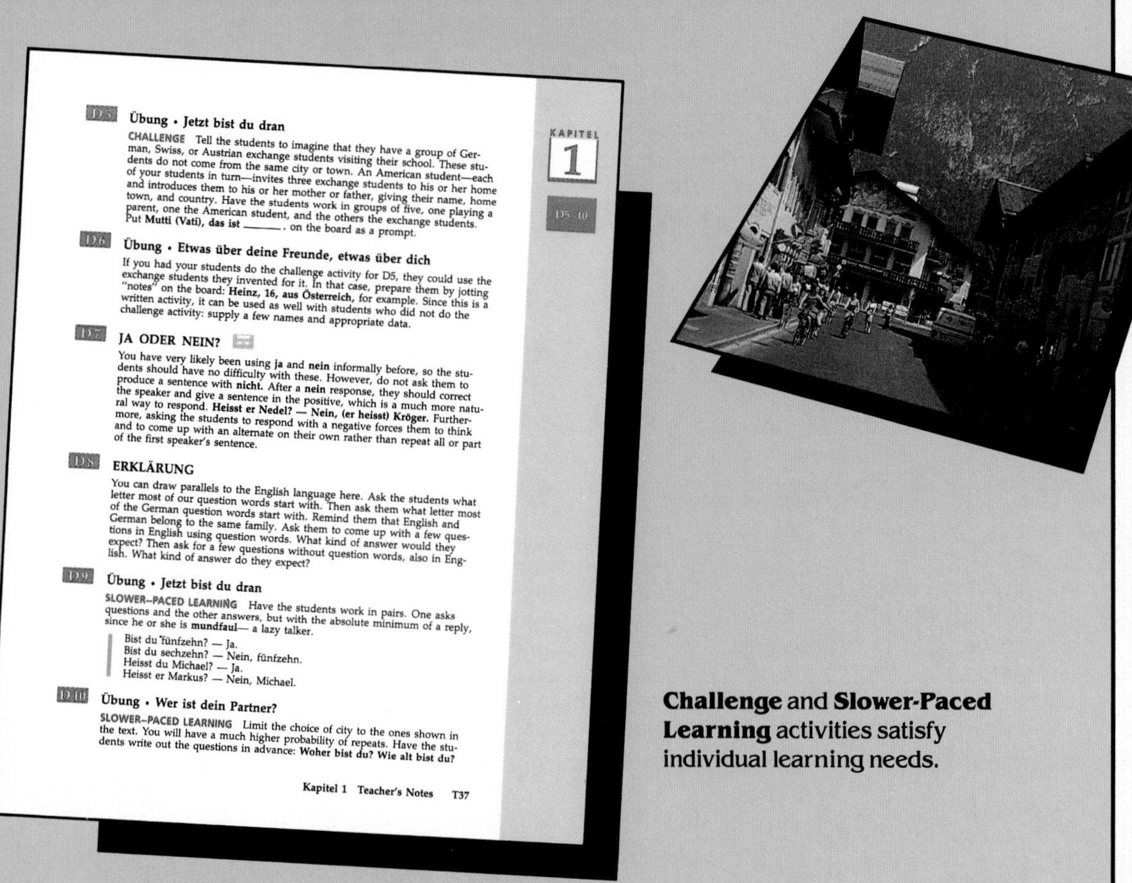

D5 **Übung • Jetzt bist du dran**

CHALLENGE Tell the students to imagine that they have a group of German, Swiss, or Austrian exchange students visiting their school. These students do not come from the same city or town. An American student—each of your students in turn—invites three exchange students to his or her home and introduces them to his or her mother or father, giving their name, home town, and country. Have the students work in groups of five, one playing a parent, one the American student, and the others the exchange students. Put **Mutti (Vati), das ist ______.** on the board as a prompt.

D6 **Übung • Etwas über deine Freunde, etwas über dich**

If you had your students do the challenge activity for D5, they could use the exchange students they invented for it. In that case, prepare them by jotting "notes" on the board: **Heinz, 16, aus Österreich,** for example. Since this is a written activity, it can be used as well with students who did not do the challenge activity: supply a few names and appropriate data.

D7 **JA ODER NEIN?**

You have very likely been using **ja** and **nein** informally before, so the students should have no difficulty with these. However, do not ask them to produce a sentence with **nicht.** After a **nein** response, they should correct the speaker and give a sentence in the positive, which is a much more natural way to respond. **Heisst er Nedel? — Nein, (er heisst) Kröger.** Furthermore, asking the students to respond with a negative forces them to think and to come up with an alternate on their own rather than repeat all or part of the first speaker's sentence.

D8 **ERKLÄRUNG**

You can draw parallels to the English language here. Ask the students what letter most of our question words start with. Then ask them what letter most of the German question words start with. Remind them that English and German belong to the same family. Ask them to come up with a few questions in English using question words. What kind of answer would they expect? Then ask for a few questions without question words, also in English. What kind of answer do they expect?

D9 **Übung • Jetzt bist du dran**

SLOWER-PACED LEARNING Have the students work in pairs. One asks questions and the other answers, but with the absolute minimum of a reply, since he or she is **mundfaul**— a lazy talker.

Bist du fünfzehn? — Ja.
Bist du sechzehn? — Nein, fünfzehn.
Heisst du Michael? — Ja.
Heisst er Markus? — Nein, Michael.

D10 **Übung • Wer ist dein Partner?**

SLOWER-PACED LEARNING Limit the choice of city to the ones shown in the text. You will have a much higher probability of repeats. Have the students write out the questions in advance: **Woher bist du? Wie alt bist du?**

KAPITEL 1

D5–10

Kapitel 1 Teacher's Notes T37

Challenge and **Slower-Paced Learning** activities satisfy individual learning needs.

Teacher's ResourceBank™

The *Teacher's ResourceBank* ™ includes useful *Teacher's Resource Materials* —proficiency practice situations, games, songs, vocabulary lists with exercises, realia, component correlation charts, a glossary of grammatical terms, and a pronunciation guide. The *Teacher's ResourceBank* ™ also contains posters; an Overhead Transparencies Sampler and Planning Guide; the *Student's Test Booklet* in copying-master form; the *Teacher's Test Guide;* and the *Unit Cassette Guide.* A three-ring binder with convenient tabbed dividers provides organized storage for these teaching resources.

Sample pages are reduced. Actual sizes are 8″x10″. Pages are from *Level 1, Teacher's Edition.*

Additional components for students and teachers

Exercise Workbook with Teacher's Edition

The *Exercise Workbook* contains activities that provide practice in grammar concepts and vocabulary. The accompanying *Teacher's Edition* contains answers for all activities.

Activity Workbook with Teacher's Edition

Rich in illustrations and realia, the *Activity Workbook* provides entertaining and challenging activities to develop communication skills. The accompanying *Teacher's Edition* contains answers for all activities.

Testing Program

The comprehensive *Testing Program*—consisting of the *Student's Test Booklet, Teacher's Test Guide,* and *Test Cassettes*—assesses both achievement and proficiency in German. The perforated *Student's Test Booklet* includes section quizzes, unit tests, review unit tests, mid-year and final examinations, and proficiency tests. The *Teacher's Test Guide* includes recording scripts for the listening portions of all quizzes and tests, speaking tests for each unit, suggestions for administering and scoring tests, and an answer key. *Test Cassettes* contain the listening portions of all quizzes and tests as well as a model for administering the speaking portion of a proficiency test.

Teacher's Resource Materials

Teacher's Resource Materials provide a variety of copying masters, including:

- Proficiency practice situations—activities for use with each review unit—to help students improve communication skills
- Games to help develop fluency in German
- German songs for group singing activities
- Vocabulary lists with expansion and model exercises
- Realia—including authentic menus, transportation schedules, and invitations—with teaching suggestions and cross-references to textbook units
- Component correlation charts
- A glossary of grammatical terms with examples
- A pronunciation guide with suggestions for pronunciation practice

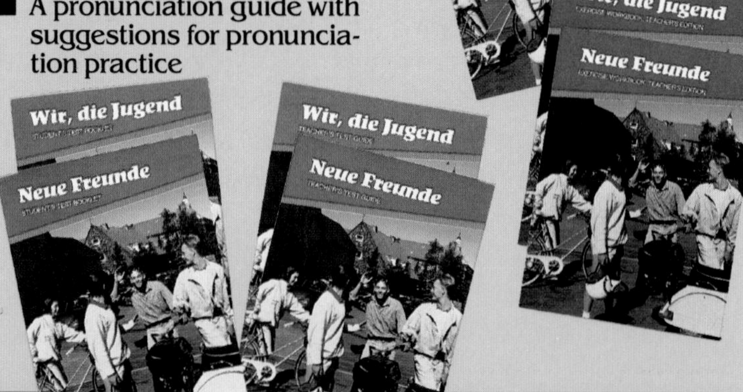

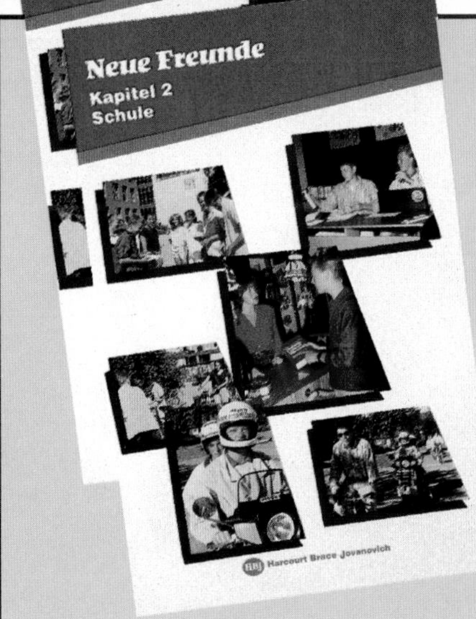

Wir, die Jugend
Kapitel 1
Ein neues Schuljahr beginnt
Neue Freunde
Kapitel 2
Schule
Harcourt Brace Jovanovich

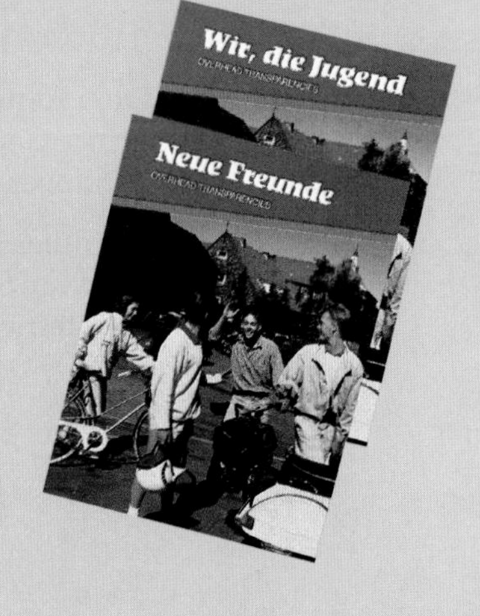

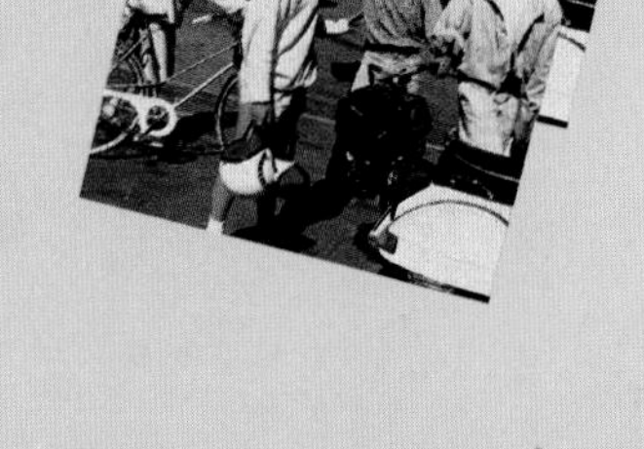

Unit Cassettes

Cassettes for instructional and review units include basic material, selected activities, listening comprehension and pronunciation exercises, and reading selections—all recorded by native speakers with pauses for student repetition and response, where appropriate. They also provide German songs.

Unit Cassette Guide

The *Unit Cassette Guide* includes an index to the *Unit Cassettes,* recording scripts for all *Unit Cassettes,* and copying masters for the listening comprehension exercises in the textbook.

Overhead Transparencies

Overhead Transparencies, with copying masters, accompany each instructional and review unit. Full-color map transparencies include overlays with geographical names. In addition, a Planning Guide contains suggestions for classroom use.

Unit Theme Posters

Colorful posters feature captivating photographs to enhance each unit in the textbook.

Videocassettes

Dramatic episodes, filmed on location and based on textbook themes, let students see and hear German young people in authentic settings. Interactive segments elicit student response.

Teacher's Edition Writers

Dora Kennedy
Prince George's County Public Schools
Landover, MD

Dorothea Bruschke
Parkway School District
Chesterfield, MO

Neue Freunde

Teacher's Edition

HBJ HARCOURT BRACE JOVANOVICH, PUBLISHERS
Orlando San Diego Chicago Dallas

Printed in the United States of America
ISBN 0-15-383501-X

We do not include a Teacher's Edition automatically with each shipment of a classroom set of textbooks. We prefer to send a Teacher's Edition only when it is part of a purchase order or when it is requested by the teacher or administrator concerned or by one of our representatives. A Teacher's Edition can be easily mislaid when it arrives as part of a shipment delivered to a school stockroom, and, since it contains answer materials, we would like to be sure it is sent directly to the person who will use it, or to someone concerned with the use or selection of textbooks.

If your class assignment changes and you no longer are using or examining this Teacher's Edition, you may wish to pass it on to a teacher who may have use for it.

CONTENTS

TO THE TEACHER

SCOPE AND SEQUENCE CHARTS AND TEACHER'S NOTES

TO THE TEACHER

In creating the new Harcourt Brace Jovanovich German Program, we have incorporated suggestions from foreign language teachers in all parts of the country. We are grateful to you for talking and writing to us. We feel that, based on your suggestions and on what we have observed about general trends in foreign language teaching, we have produced a program that you and your students will profit from and enjoy.

Philosophy and Goals

The primary goal of the Harcourt Brace Jovanovich German Program is to help students develop proficiency in the four basic skills: listening, speaking, reading, and writing. At the same time, it aims to increase the students' knowledge and appreciation of the diverse cultures of the countries whose language they are learning.

In order to become proficient in a foreign language, students must not only learn the vocabulary and structures of the language, but also apply what they have learned. Thus, students learn and practice the material in each unit; they also have many opportunities to apply their skills. Given ample opportunity for creative expression, students are on their way to developing proficiency.

The emphasis is on communication. The approach is based on the communicative purposes of young people at this level—to invite, inform, inquire, exclaim, agree, disagree, compliment, express emotions and opinions, and so on. These communicative purposes, or functions, in turn determine the selection and the amount of vocabulary and grammar that students need to learn. The communicative functions, grammar, and vocabulary are presented in culturally authentic situations that appeal to young people. They are followed by a variety of activities that promote both learning and application of the language, ultimately leading students to function with increasing proficiency in many new situations. The question to be asked constantly in measuring students' success is, "What can they do with the language they are learning, and how well?"

Description of the HBJ German Program

We have designed the materials of this program to be highly adaptable. You will be able to offer a variety of experiences in learning and using the foreign language, choosing materials that correspond to the learning needs of each student. The various parts of the program are:

Components of the program

- Pupil's Edition
- Teacher's Edition
- Activity Workbook
- Activity Workbook, Teacher's Edition
- Exercise Workbook
- Exercise Workbook, Teacher's Edition
- Overhead Transparencies
- Unit Theme Posters
- Testing Program
  - Student's Test Booklet
  - Teacher's Test Guide
  - Test Cassettes
- Audio Program
  - Unit Cassettes
  - Unit Cassette Guide
- Teacher's Resource Materials
- Videocassettes

Pupil's Edition

The student textbook is the core of the program. The opening pages, entitled "Getting to Know Your Textbook," take students on a guided, illustrated "walk-through" of the book. The introductory photo essay, "German and You," familiarizes students with the countries where German is spoken, provides information on the origin of the language and its influence on English, explores the application of a foreign language in careers, and gives students hints on how to study a foreign language.

Organization of the textbook

The book contains twelve units, grouped into three Parts. Each Part consists of three instructional units *(Kapitel)*, one review unit *(Wiederholungskapitel)*, and one photo essay *(Landeskunde)*. The book ends with a reference section. Here students will find summaries of the communicative functions, grammar, and vocabulary. Culturally authentic photographs, art, and realia appear throughout the book.

Organization of Instructional Units

Each instructional unit starts with two pages of photographs that illustrate the theme of the unit. Also appearing on these pages are a brief introduction and an outline of the unit that lists, section by section, the performance objectives, or communicative functions, that the students should expect to achieve.

Communicative functions

The instructional portion of each unit is divided into three (in four units, four) sections—Section A, Section B, and Section C. The communicative functions are repeated at the beginning of the section, followed by a brief introduction to the theme of the section. Each section includes basic material, presented in the form of a dialog, narrative, or letter; a grouping of the words and phrases necessary to the communicative function *(Wie sagt man das?)*; grammar *(Erklärung)*; a cultural note *(Ein wenig Landeskunde)*; usually, a listening comprehension exercise *(Hör gut zu!)*; and numerous activities *(Übungen)*, both oral and written. The activities range from those that help students acquire new skills and knowledge through practice to those that provide opportunities for them to apply their newly acquired skills in simulated real-life situations. Personalized questions encourage students to relate the material to their own experiences. Many of the activities recommend that students work in pairs or groups.

Color coding

All headings are color-coded. Blue signifies new material, communicative functions, and grammar. Orange signals activities. Green calls attention to the cultural notes.

Application

Following Section C is another section called Try Your Skills. The activities in this section are generally open-ended. They create situations in which students can apply what they have learned, bringing together the communicative functions, grammar, and vocabulary presented in the preceding sections. The Try Your Skills section is essential to the development of proficiency. At the end of the Try Your Skills section there are pronunciation, letter-sound correspondence, and dictation exercises that help students isolate and practice the sounds and spelling of German.

Self-check

A one-page self-check *(Was kannst du schon?)* follows the Try Your Skills section. Here a few key questions and check-up exercises help students assess their achievement of the objectives listed on the opening pages of the unit. You may use the self-check after completing Sections A, B, and C and Try Your Skills, or you may choose to use the appropriate part of the self-check after completing the corresponding section of the unit.

Vocabulary

On the page opposite the self-check is a list of active vocabulary words *(Wortschatz)* and their English equivalents, grouped by section. Below the list, a word-study exercise *(Wortschatzübungen)* focuses attention on the vocabulary list; it gives students practice in developing word-attack skills while expanding their German vocabulary.

Reading

The unit closes with one or more short reading selections *(Zum Lesen)* linked to the theme of the unit. The selections may be in the form of a poem, short story, article, or cartoon. The activities accompanying the reading selections seek to develop reading skills in the foreign language and to encourage critical thinking through open-ended questions.

The basic material, some of the activities, the listening comprehension and pronunciation exercises, and the reading selections of each unit are recorded on the Unit Cassettes.

Organization of Review Units

The three review units *(Wiederholungskapitel)*—Units 4, 8, and 12—are considerably shorter than the nine instructional units. A review unit presents familiar material in a different context. No new vocabulary, grammar, or communicative functions are presented. Like the Try Your Skills section within an instructional unit, a review unit contains activities that encourage students to combine and apply the skills they acquired in the preceding instructional units. The situations presented in the review unit may differ from those the students encountered previously; using skills in new situations is crucial to developing proficiency. Selected material from the review units is also recorded on the Unit Cassettes.

Teacher's Edition

Annotations

The Teacher's Edition is designed to be of maximum assistance to you. It includes the pages of the Pupil's Edition, fully annotated with background notes, answers to activities, teaching suggestions, and variations.

Teacher's Notes

In addition, special Teacher's Notes—pages tabbed in blue—accompany each unit. For your convenience the Teacher's Notes for each unit are placed immediately before the annotated pupil pages of that unit. The Teacher's Notes address not only each section of the unit but every item within the section. The teaching suggestions are cross-referenced to the corresponding material (A1, A2, etc.) in the pupil pages.

Scope and Sequence chart

The Teacher's Notes begin with a detailed Scope and Sequence chart for the unit that also contains suggestions for the consistent re-entry of previously learned material. Below the chart is a list of the relevant ancillary components of the program and suggested materials that you may wish to prepare or gather. The Teacher's Notes state objectives, provide cultural background, suggest motivating activities, and offer teaching suggestions for all basic material, for the functions, grammar, and culture notes, and for each activity. To help you adapt instruction to meet different learning styles, suggestions are given on how to accommodate slower-paced learning and how to provide a challenge. Also included are suggestions for using cooperative learning and TPR (Total Physical Response) techniques

(see page T7) and for combining the different language skills. The scripts of the listening comprehension exercises and the pronunciation exercises also appear in the Teacher's Notes.

Activity Workbook

The Activity Workbook *(Übungsheft)* offers additional activities, puzzles, and games that give students practice with communicative functions, vocabulary, and structure in a variety of entertaining and challenging ways. Culturally authentic photographs, art, and realia add an appealing visual dimension. All the exercises and activities are cross-referenced to those in the textbook.

The Teacher's Edition of the Activity Workbook provides you with the answers to the activities, printed in place.

Exercise Workbook

The Exercise Workbook *(Arbeitsheft)* contains exercises of a more structured nature, all of which are cross-referenced to the textbook. The grammar points taught in the textbook are restated in the Exercise Workbook, where they are followed by extensive practice.

The Teacher's Edition of the Exercise Workbook, like that of the Activity Workbook, contains the answers to the exercises, printed in place.

Testing Program

Student's Test Booklet

Section quizzes

Unit tests

Proficiency-based tests

The Student's Test Booklet has three parts. The first part contains quizzes based on every section of the nine instructional units in the textbook. The second part includes a unit test for each instructional unit, three review tests covering the three Parts of the textbook, a midterm test, and a final exam. Listening comprehension is an integral part of each quiz and test. The third part of the Student's Test Booklet contains three proficiency-based tests that are designed to assess students' levels of proficiency in all four language skills. You may wish to use the first two tests for practice during the second half of the school year and the third proficiency-based test at the end of the year. Although related to the content of the textbook, the proficiency-based tests do not measure students' mastery of specific material. Rather, they present a variety of situations in which students are expected to demonstrate their ability to function in German.

Teacher's Test Guide

The Teacher's Test Guide consists of several parts. The introduction describes the testing program and offers suggestions on how you may administer and score the quizzes and tests.

Following the introduction are the recording scripts of the listening parts of the quizzes, tests, and proficiency-based tests.

Speaking tests

The next section of the Teacher's Test Guide presents speaking tests for each unit in the textbook. Although these tests are optional, you are urged to administer them at the appropriate times. Suggestions for administering and scoring the speaking tests are given in the introduction to the Teacher's Test Guide.

The answer key to the entire testing program forms the final part of the Teacher's Test Guide.

Test Cassettes

The listening parts of the quizzes, tests, and proficiency-based tests are recorded on cassettes. Included is a recording of an examiner administering the speaking portion of a proficiency-based test to a student; it is intended to serve as a model if you are not familiar with proficiency testing.

Audio Program

Unit Cassettes

For each unit the recordings include the new or basic material, some of the activities, the listening and pronunciation exercises, and the reading selections. The texts of the three photo essays are also recorded. Where appropriate, pauses are provided for student repetition or response. In the textbook, items that are recorded are designated by means of a cassette symbol . The scripts of the recordings are provided in the Unit Cassette Guide. One of the Unit Cassettes contains several songs; the lyrics are provided in the Teacher's Resource Materials.

Unit Cassette Guide

The Unit Cassette Guide includes the reference index to the Unit Cassettes, the scripts of the Unit Cassettes, and student answer forms for the listening exercises in each unit.

Overhead Transparencies

Copying masters

A set of overhead transparencies with copying-master duplicates supplements the textbook. The set includes one transparency for each section of the nine instructional units, one for each of the three review units, and three maps. Each transparency depicts a situation that is closely related to the one in the corresponding section of the unit. The transparencies are accompanied by a Planning Guide booklet that offers suggestions on how to use them effectively.

Teaching suggestions

The transparencies are a valuable teaching aid. Students may be asked to describe what they see and then to imagine themselves in the situation and converse appropriately. Used in this manner, the transparencies serve to involve students in interactive communication. You may wish to use the transparencies in your presentation of basic material. As students learn new vocabulary and communicative functions, transparencies from previous units may be reintroduced to provide additional situations for the practice of the new material. When students view a new transparency, they may be encouraged to re-enter previously learned communicative functions and vocabulary. The copying masters enable you to distribute copies of the transparencies for use in cooperative learning groups, for individual or group writing assignments, and for homework.

Unit Theme Posters

Twelve full-color posters are available. Each poster displays one or more photographs relevant to the theme of the corresponding unit in the textbook. An accompanying guide suggests ways in which you might use the posters. Aside from creating a cultural ambiance in the classroom, they can be an effective teaching aid when you present and review a unit.

Teacher's Resource Materials

Proficiency practice

The Teacher's Resource Materials booklet contains numerous teaching aids. One section discusses learning and teaching strategies, such as Total Physical Response (TPR), group learning, study hints, and suggestions for planning total immersion experiences. Another provides copying masters for role-playing situations to be used with each review unit. You may reproduce and distribute them to the students to stimulate extemporaneous communication, oral or written.

Vocabulary exercises

Also included in the Teacher's Resource Materials are the vocabulary lists of the nine instructional units with the words regrouped according to their parts of speech. Supplementary vocabulary exercises complement each list. Enrichment vocabulary and useful classroom expressions complete the vocabulary section.

Realia

Games/songs

The booklet contains several pages of realia, authentic documents that you may reproduce for classroom use. In addition, there are suggestions for classroom games and the lyrics of favorite songs. The music has been recorded on one of the Unit Cassettes. Also included are a pronunciation guide, a glossary of grammar terms, a guide for teaching the use of the ess-tzet with exercises for each unit, and a listing of additional sources of instructional materials (magazines, films, software, etc.).

Videocassettes

The videocassettes show a series of dramatic episodes that closely parallel the themes of the units in the textbook. Filmed on location, the programs are authentic representations of the foreign culture. Students see and hear German young people doing and saying things that they themselves have simulated in the classroom. Special interactive segments involve the students. Activity sheets elicit student reaction to the episodes in a variety of ways. A guide suggests ways to use the videocassettes in the classroom.

Using the HBJ German Program

The following procedures and techniques are suggested to meet diverse learning styles and classroom circumstances and to help students achieve communicative competence.

Developing Proficiency in the Four Skills

Listening

From the beginning, students are eager to say things in the foreign language, but they should also hear authentic language, even if they do not grasp the meaning of every word. You will wish to provide an abundance of listening activities.

Authentic input

For this purpose, the textbook is a primary source. The basic material and selected activities in each unit are recorded so that students may hear authentic language spoken by a variety of native speakers. In addition, each section generally contains a listening exercise. When playing the recordings in class, consider that students need time to listen to the new material before you ask them to repeat it or apply it.

Listening strategies

Listening requires active mental participation. You may want to share these listening strategies with your students: (1) they should listen for key words that tell what the situation is about; (2) they should not feel that they must understand every word; (3) they should make guesses and verify their hunches by repeated listening.

TPR (Total Physical Response)

The TPR (Total Physical Response) technique is an effective means of developing proficiency in listening. TPR is a physical response to an oral stimulus. Students listen to instructions or commands and give nonverbal responses according to their comprehension of the message. These responses may include moving about the classroom, interacting silently with classmates, drawing, or arranging pictures in sequence. Some activities in the student textbook call for TPR responses. Suggestions for applying the TPR technique to other activities are given in the Teacher's Edition.

By minimizing the use of English in the classroom from the beginning, you provide more opportunity for students to hear the foreign language. You may want to make a practice of relating personal experiences and local or world happenings to the students in the foreign language. Students will pick up a great deal of this "incidental" language.

Speaking

Students want most to be able to speak the foreign language they are studying. Keep in mind that the speaking skill is the most fragile; it takes careful nurturing and encouraging, uninhibited by rigid standards. It is more important to encourage fluency first; accuracy will follow.

Interactive communication

Each of the units in the textbook focuses on the speaking skill. The majority of the activities are designed to lead to interaction and communication among students. Managed properly, these activities will provide the optimum speaking experiences for the students. The use of various grouping techniques will facilitate this procedure (see page T13).

Developing speaking proficiency

The development of the speaking skill follows this pattern: (1) repeating after adequate listening; (2) responding, using words and expressions of the lesson (up to this point no degree of proficiency should be expected); (3) manipulating learned material and recombining parts; (4) using what was previously learned in a new context.

When students use a previously learned expression spontaneously in a simulated situation as a natural thing to say at that time, they are truly beginning to speak the language. Students must be engaged in the application phase in order to develop proficiency beyond the novice level. Application activities are found particularly in the Try Your Skills section of each unit and in each review unit.

Reading

It is appropriate for students to read material they have been practicing, but they should also develop their reading skills using unfamiliar material. Require students to skim, scan, draw inferences, determine the main idea, and so forth. They should begin their reading by extracting the general ideas before they approach the details of a reading selection. The aim should be global comprehension in reading just as in listening.

Developing reading skills

You may help students approach reading selections through prereading strategies. Key words or expressions that might cause difficulty may be clarified, preferably in the foreign language. Students may be encouraged to examine the title and illustrations of a reading selection in search of clues to its meaning. You may elicit students' background knowledge of the subject of the reading through preliminary discussion; comprehension is definitely influenced by the prior information that students bring to a reading selection.

Also consider conducting directed reading lessons, requiring students to read selected passages silently with a purpose: to find answers to questions; to find reasons for actions and events; to find descriptions of characters. Students may be asked to write down all they recall of the content of a passage they have just read silently. In the follow-up lesson, you will wish not only to inquire about the who, what, and where of the content, but also to encourage critical thinking by asking why.

Critical thinking

The TPR technique may be used to develop reading proficiency as well as listening proficiency. In the case of reading, students are expected to respond nonverbally to directions they have read.

Writing

The development of the writing skill is analogous to that of the speaking skill. Although the first stage may consist of copying, learning to spell, filling in the blanks, and writing from dictation, this training does not constitute writing. Writing is transferring thoughts to paper. Hence, students should progress from directed writing to more creative expression. To this end, a variety of controlled and open-ended writing activities appear in the textbook. The Teacher's Notes identify other activities suitable for writing practice and suggest additional writing activities.

Writing activities

Communicative Functions

When people communicate with each other—either orally or in writing—they use language for a specific purpose: to describe, persuade, argue, express emotions and opinions, praise, complain, agree, and so on. The term "communicative functions," or simply "functions," is used to refer to these purposes for which people communicate.

In the HBJ German Program, the objectives of each instructional unit are phrased as communicative functions. They are clearly stated on the unit opener and are repeated on the section openers so that students can readily see the purpose for learning the language. Within the sections, the communicative functions are presented in new, or basic, material in a culturally authentic situation of interest to young people.

New (Basic) Material

Each section of an instructional unit opens with the presentation of basic material. In some sections there may be more than one piece of new material. The basic material may take different forms; it may be a dialog, an interview, a monolog, or a narrative. Its purpose is to introduce the expressions, grammar, and vocabulary necessary to the communicative function(s) to be learned in the section. Previously learned functions may reappear in the basic material where appropriate. Also, in any basic material there will necessarily appear new functions besides those to be practiced in the section. Another purpose of the basic material is to provide cultural information, either directly or indirectly.

Before introducing any basic material, consult the list of communicative functions in the Scope and Sequence chart in the Teacher's Notes for that unit. The new material should be presented in ways that emphasize these communicative functions.

Students should approach basic material with these questions in mind, "What is the communicative purpose of the native speakers in the particular situation, and how are they using their language to accomplish it?" Students should not be required to memorize the basic material. The dialog and narratives in the textbook are only samples of what a particular speaker of German might say in a given situation; they should not be taught as fixed and rigid sentences. The aim should be to transfer the communicative functions from the basic material to other situations. Students should use the language functions to communicate naturally and spontaneously in real situations.

To help students, the communicative function is restated and the expressions necessary to achieve it are grouped together under the heading *Wie sagt man das?* As the title suggests, this is how you say it, how you accomplish the communicative purpose or function. The expressions listed are primarily those introduced in the basic material. There may also be expressions from previous units that are appropriate to the communicative function; expressions that are learned to carry out one function may also be applied to carry out others. *Wie sagt man das?* then, is a statement of a communicative function and the expressions to accomplish it.

After students have read the basic material and done the related activities, direct their attention to the expressions in *Wie sagt man das?* You might make some statements in German and have students choose appropriate responses from the expressions listed. Or, you might have students suggest ways to use German to elicit the expressions from classmates.

The activities that follow *Wie sagt man das?* give students opportunities to carry out the intended communicative function by applying the expressions in real-life situations.

You will find detailed suggestions on how to present basic material and *Wie sagt man das?* in the Teacher's Notes preceding each unit. All basic material is recorded on the Unit Cassettes.

Activities

Practice/application

The heading *Übung* identifies the exercises in the textbook. There are two basic types of activities: (1) those that reinforce learning of the new material through practice and (2) those that require students to apply what they have learned.

The activities that follow the basic material are arranged in a planned progression from practice to application of the communicative functions, grammar, and vocabulary. Try Your Skills sections and review units contain only activities of the application type. Many application activities are designed to have the students converse in pairs or groups in order to foster communication and encourage creative expression.

The activities in the textbook may take many different forms. Those that relate to the basic material include questionnaires, sentence completions, true/false statements, identifications, and the sequencing of events. Personalized questions encourage students to relate the basic material to their own experiences. (Be careful to respect the privacy of individuals.) Grammar explanations are followed by practice exercises. Then, since the grammar is meant to support the communicative function(s), additional activities lead students to use the grammar in communicative situations.

Writing

Writing activities of two kinds appear throughout the textbook. Controlled exercises provide practice in writing the forms and structures of the language. Others provide opportunities for creative written expression. For further writing practice, many of the oral activities may be assigned to be written.

Listening

One or more listening comprehension activities, identified by the heading *Hör gut zu!*, appear in each instructional section of a unit. These listening exercises are recorded on the Unit Cassettes, and student answer forms for them are located in both the Unit Cassette Guide and the Teacher's Resource Materials booklet. The scripts of the listening exercises are reproduced in the Teacher's Notes preceding each unit in the Teacher's Edition, as well as in the Unit Cassette Guide.

Optional activities

A few activities have been identified in the Teacher's Notes as optional. Usually found at the end of a section, these activities are intended to enrich vocabulary. You may choose to use them or not, as time permits.

Pronunciation

In each instructional unit, at the end of the Try Your Skills section, you will find a pronunciation exercise. This exercise, called *Aussprache-, Lese- und Schreibübungen* is designed to teach the most difficult sounds of German. The sounds are presented first in a listening-speaking exercise that gives the students practice in saying them. Then a letter-sound correspondence exercise provides practice in reading the symbols that represent the sounds. Finally, sentences to be written from dictation afford practice in transcribing the sounds. These exercises are recorded on the Unit Cassettes; the scripts are located in the Teacher's Notes preceding each unit in the Teacher's Edition and in the Unit Cassette Guide.

Recordings

This cassette symbol signals the activities that are recorded on the Unit Cassettes. Frequently, activities have been modified to adapt them for recording. You will find that a communicative activity in the textbook may be more structured when recorded. For this reason, you will want to consult the scripts in the Unit Cassette Guide before you play the cassettes. In certain circumstances, you may wish to play the recorded version of an activity first and then have the students perform the activity as it was intended for the classroom.

Answers to all activities are indicated (in blue) in the annotated pupil pages of the Teacher's Edition.

Grammar

In each section of every unit except the review units, the main grammar points relating to the functional objectives of the unit are summarized.

Grammar may be approached inductively or deductively, depending on the nature of the item and on student learning styles. Younger students, in general, respond favorably to an inductive approach that leads them to draw conclusions about the forms they have been practicing and applying.

On the other hand, because of the relative complexity of some structures, there may be a need to explain them before the students practice and apply them. In this case, the deductive approach may be more effective. You will want to determine which approach is more suitable.

Grammar and proficiency

Regardless of the approach, it is important to remember that in the development of proficiency, grammar is a means and not an end. Only the grammar that is relevant to the communicative function is necessary.

Vocabulary

Vocabulary and proficiency

As in the case of grammar, consider the extent to which the amount and type of vocabulary presented serves the communicative purpose at hand. The introduction of excessive or irrelevant vocabulary, however interesting, may only complicate the task. The goal is to use vocabulary to communicate. Like grammar, vocabulary is a means, not an end.

Vocabulary is presented in context and listed at the end of each unit. A word-study activity following the list helps students understand and remember the vocabulary by pointing out word families, relationships, derivations, and so on.

You may use word games, puzzles, and mnemonic aids to teach vocabulary. An effective motivational practice is to have students devise their own games, puzzles, illustrative posters, and picture dictionaries to be used by their classmates.

Culture

Cultural expression

We hope to instill cultural awareness by exposing students to different kinds of cultural expression—authentic written and spoken language, a rich collection of photographs showing a cross-section of people and places, an abundance of realia, and special culture notes in English. We want students to get to know what German-speaking young people are like and to develop a feel for the everyday life in the foreign culture.

Throughout this Teacher's Edition we have noted additional cultural points that may interest you and your students or that clarify situations depicted in the units. The Teacher's Notes preceding each unit provide additional background information on the unit themes. You may want to consult these pages as you prepare to introduce each unit. Include in your teaching as much of this information as you find helpful.

Photo essays

Sources for cultural awareness are present on almost every page of the textbook. They are especially concentrated, however, in the photo essays that follow every review unit. To help you in presenting the photo essays, we have included background information on the various topics and some details about specific photographs in the Teacher's Notes preceding the review units.

Projects

Encourage your students to personalize the German-speaking cultures as they study and practice the themes and vocabulary of the units. Suggestions for projects are given in the units and in the Teacher's Notes; assign as many projects as possible. In doing projects, students not only practice their skills, but they also share in an experience that helps them learn about the particular country's culture in a direct and personal way.

You can enhance students' cultural awareness and appreciation by utilizing community resources and, if possible, by taking school trips to regions or countries where the foreign language is spoken.

Review

Quizzes

Frequent feedback is essential to assess your students' progress toward proficiency and their need for review. The quizzes based on each section of a unit are one means of assessment. They are short and are best checked immediately during the same class period.

The textbook itself is structured to ensure adequate review. The self-check *(Was kannst du schon?)* and the Try Your Skills section at the end of each unit, as well as the three review units, provide opportunities for students to review and recombine previously presented material.

Re-entry

In addition, you will want to make a practice of systematically re-entering material from previous units, especially during warm-up activities at the beginning of a class period. You will find suggestions for the re-entry of previously learned material in the Scope and Sequence chart in the Teacher's Notes preceding each instructional unit.

Testing and Evaluation

Evaluation is an ongoing process. Informal assessment should take place in the classroom on an almost daily basis, whether by observing students during their group work or by engaging individuals or groups briefly in conversation. The section quizzes and the unit tests in the Student's Test Booklet provide a formal check on progress in the areas of listening, reading, and writing. You may wish to administer a short speaking test after each unit. To save you preparation time, speaking tests are supplied in the Teacher's Test Guide.

Unlike achievement, which is the realization of the immediate objectives of a lesson, proficiency develops slowly. Therefore, assessments of proficiency should be made less frequently. Proficiency-based tests are a vital part of this program. There are two practice tests and a final test. Meant to be given during the second half of the year, they require students to demonstrate their abilities in all four language skills in situations beyond—but not completely unrelated to—the textbook.

Suggestions for Classroom Management

Classroom Climate

As you know, students are more enthusiastic and responsive in a friendly, nonthreatening atmosphere of mutual respect that fosters self-confidence. A tense atmosphere may inhibit the spontaneous use of the foreign language which is so necessary to the development of proficiency.

You may wish to consider the importance of organization and keeping students on task. Ground rules for classroom procedures will help you create an effective environment for learning. These procedures should include an explanation of how English is to be used and the distribution of a list of classroom expressions in German that students will gradually begin to use with confidence.

Another—but not the least—consideration is the positive effect of a classroom decorated with posters, maps, pictures, realia, and students' papers and projects.

English in the Classroom

The use of the foreign language in the classroom is basic to helping students develop listening proficiency. Students should become accustomed to hearing classroom directions in the foreign language. You will find lists of classroom expressions in German on page 28 of the Pupil's Edition and in the vocabulary section of the Teacher's Resource Materials.

It is natural for students to ask for explanations and want to make comments in English. You may wish to set aside a short segment of time at the end of a class period for clarifications in English.

Classroom Strategies

Two fundamental approaches to classroom instruction can be described as teacher-centered and student-centered. Both have a place in the foreign language classroom. In either approach the student is the primary focus.

A teacher-centered approach is most effective in the learning phase. You may wish to use this approach for directed teaching activities, such as presenting new material and conducting drills and question/answer sessions. Consider using various student-centered activities, such as simulated social situations and conversations, in the application phase to develop the independence that eventually leads to proficiency beyond the novice stage.

Grouping

Grouping maximizes opportunities for interaction among students in lifelike situations. It is an especially useful strategy in classes that have combined levels of students with varied learning styles and abilities.

Cooperative learning

Cooperative learning is one way in which students and teachers can achieve learning goals. In cooperative learning, small groups of students collaborate to achieve a common goal. There are four basic benefits of a cooperative learning group: (1) positive interdependence; (2) face-to-face interaction; (3) individual accountability; (4) appropriate use of interpersonal skills. Following are some suggestions for structuring cooperative learning activities.

Forming cooperative learning groups

1. Be sure the task is clear to everyone.
2. Set a time limit. Completion of the task and reporting to the class should take place during the class period.
3. Circulate among the students and assist them as needed.
4. Assign specific tasks to each group member.
5. Clarify any limitations of movement during the activity.
6. Select the group size most suited to the activity. Pairs are appropriate for many activities.

7. Assign students to groups. Heterogeneous groups are more desirable. Groups should not be permanent.
8. Evaluate the group's task when completed and discuss with the group the interaction of the members.

Many activities in the textbook lend themselves to cooperative learning.

Providing for Different Learning Styles

Different students learn best in different ways. Some learn new material most easily when they are allowed to listen to it and repeat it. Others do best when they see it in writing. Still others respond best to visual experiences—photographs, drawings, overhead transparencies. And some students need to be involved physically or emotionally with the material they are learning and to respond concretely and personally. Moreover, all students need variety in the learning experience; the same student may respond differently on different days.

Slower-paced learning

Slower-paced learning requires that you present and adapt materials differently than you do when a greater challenge is called for. The Teacher's Notes that precede each unit contain numerous suggestions for teaching strategies to be used in a slower-paced learning environment and in a challenge situation.

Challenge

In general, you may wish to consider strategies for slower-paced learning that involve breaking down an activity into smaller tasks and then rebuilding it gradually. Accept short answers and elicit passive, nonlinguistic responses more often. On the other hand, when you deal with students who need a greater challenge, consider expanding activities and adding new twists that require critical thinking and creativity.

Forming heterogeneous cooperative learning groups and pairing students of different abilities can be effective means of assisting all students, both academically and socially.

Homework

Differentiated assignments

Homework that reinforces and enriches class work should be an integral part of instruction. You may want to consider giving differentiated homework assignments to suit the varied needs of students instead of issuing identical assignments to all. For this purpose, the Activity Workbook and the Exercise Workbook provide numerous exercises of various types that are designed to meet different learning styles.

Homework should be collected and checked; otherwise students will not respect the practice. You may devise a system for students to check their own homework, but you must take care to avoid spending an entire class period checking homework. Long-term homework projects as well as short-term assignments are effective.

Use of Audio-Visual Materials

Audio-visual components

Students need to hear a variety of voices speaking German. The Unit Cassettes provide an auditory program to develop listening proficiency.

Students also need to see authentic representations of the foreign culture. The photographs in the textbook—in each unit and in the photo essays—can be used to motivate students before they launch into new material and also to increase cultural awareness. In addition, the unit theme posters and the transparencies related to each section of a unit depict culturally authentic situations.

Additional materials

You may want to use an overhead projector with a transparency instead of writing on the board to focus students' attention more directly. Where the facilities exist, students may create their own skits based on the units and record them on a videocassette for classroom viewing. Showing rented films, displaying posters, and sharing realia are other means you may consider to add a visual dimension to classroom instruction.

Planning

Pacing

Controlling the pace

It is helpful to devise a schedule of instruction for the year. Planning ahead is essential to setting the pace most appropriate for your classroom. The textbook is designed to be completed in one school year. Where needed, you can control the time spent on each unit by including or omitting optional exercises, by reading all or only one of the reading selections at the end of the unit, by doing some or all of the activities in the review unit, by insisting on total mastery of material before progressing or relying on the cumulative acquisition of the language.

Unit planning

Your schedule will vary according to the grade and ability level of your students and the number of interruptions in your school program. In general, an instructional unit can be taught in three weeks; in some cases an additional day may be needed for the unit test. A review unit will take one week, including the review test. Sufficient time should remain for discussing the cultural notes and photo essays, administering midterm, final tests, and proficiency-based tests, and conducting optional enrichment activities.

Lesson Plans

You will probably want to prepare a daily lesson plan that incorporates various language skills. Plans may vary, but the basic lesson should include the following to some degree, at least over a span of two days.

Planning sequence

- A warm-up activity, usually involving review
- A quiz or test when appropriate
- The presentation of new material preceded by a motivating activity and a statement of objectives
- Developmental activities and guided practice
- Application by the students of what they have learned
- Summarizing statements, preferably elicited from the students
- Closure (review with students what they have learned)
- Assignment, planning ahead, or previewing the next lesson
- Periodic long-range planning with the students

Unit Planning Guide

The following plan suggests how the material in Unit 2 may be distributed over fifteen days. You may wish to prepare similar lesson plans, adjusting them to suit the needs and interests of your students. For a faster pace, the exercises in parentheses might be assigned as homework or omitted.

	Daily Plans	Unit Resources
Day 1	Objective: To tell how you get to school Unit opener: discussion Section A: motivating activity Basic material A1 Wie sagt man das? A3 Erklärung A5 Übungen A2, A4, A6 Assign Übung A7	Unit 2 Poster Overhead Transparency 9 Unit 2 Cassette Activity Workbook Exercise Workbook
Day 2	Objective: To ask about prices of school supplies Quiz on Section A Section B: motivating activity Basic material B1 Übungen B2, B3, B4	Quiz 5 Overhead Transparency 10 Unit 2 Cassette Activity Workbook Exercise Workbook
Day 3	Objective: To ask about prices of school supplies Erklärung B6 Wie sagt man das? B8 Übungen B5, B7, B9, B10 Assign Übung B11	Unit 2 Cassette Activity Workbook Exercise Workbook
Day 4	Objective: To talk about prices Basic material B12 Erklärung B14 Übungen B17, B18 Assign Übung B19	Unit 2 Cassette Activity Workbook Exercise Workbook
Day 5	Objective: To talk about school supplies Basic material B20 Erklärung B22 Übungen B21, B23, B24	Unit 2 Cassette Activity Workbook Exercise Workbook
Day 6	Objective: To get someone's attention Wie sagt man das? B25 Übungen B26, B27 Assign Übung B28	Unit 2 Cassette Activity Workbook Exercise Workbook

	Daily Plans	Unit Resources
Day 7	Objective: To talk about school subjects Quiz on Section B Section C: motivating activity Basic material C1, C6 Übungen C3, C4, C5	Quiz 6 Overhead Transparency 11 Unit 2 Cassette Activity Workbook
Day 8	Objective: To tell time Basic material C7 Übungen C8, C9, Skills 10 (part 1)	Unit 2 Cassette Activity Workbook Exercise Workbook
Day 9	Objective: To talk about school subjects Basic material C10 Erklärung C12 Übungen C11, C13, C14, C15, C16 Assign Übung C17	Unit 2 Cassette Activity Workbook Exercise Workbook
Day 10	Objective: To talk about homework and grades Quiz on Section C Section D: motivating activity Basic material D1 Wie sagt man das? D5 Übungen D2, D3, D4, D6	Quiz 7 Unit 2 Cassette Activity Workbook Exercise Workbook
Day 11	Objective: To talk about school subjects and grades Basic material D7 Übungen D8, D9, D10, (D12) Assign Übung D11	Unit 2 Cassette Activity Workbook Exercise Workbook
Day 12	Objective: To use what you've learned Quiz on Section D Basic material Try Your Skills 1 Übungen 2, 3, 4, 6 Assign Übungen 5, 7	Quiz 8 Unit 2 Cassette Activity Workbook
Day 13	Objective: To use what you've learned; to prepare for Unit 2 Test Übungen 8, 9, 10 (parts 2 and 3) Was kannst du schon? Assign Wortschatz, Wortschatz-übungen	Unit 2 Cassette Activity Workbook Exercise Workbook Overhead Transparencies 9, 10, 11 Unit 2 Poster
Day 14	Objective: To assess progress Unit 2 Test	Unit 2 Test
Day 15	Objective: To read for practice and pleasure Zum Lesen: Hausaufgabenlied, (Der Traum) Übung page 88 (Übung page 89)	Unit 2 Cassette

Beyond the Classroom

In School

A vibrant foreign language program extends outside the classroom to other disciplines, the entire school, the community, and beyond.

Relating to other disciplines

By its very nature, the study of foreign languages is interdisciplinary. You may wish to consider cooperating with social studies teachers to promote global education. Since you deal with the art, music, and literature of the foreign culture, you complement the work of the art, music, and English teachers. Foreign language study raises students' level of general linguistic awareness, thereby reinforcing their work in English language arts. Learning about sports in other countries may increase the enthusiasm for sports among your students.

Foreign language classes should have an impact on the total school environment. You may have the students label areas of the building and prepare public address announcements in the foreign language. Staging assemblies, participating in school fairs, and celebrating foreign festivals schoolwide are other ways to provide students with opportunities to use their knowledge and skills outside the classroom, particularly during National Foreign Language Week in March.

Outside School

Your efforts to heighten enthusiasm for foreign language study might reach out into the community through field trips to ethnic restaurants, museums, embassies, and local areas where the foreign language is spoken. Encourage your students to present special foreign language programs in nursing homes and hospitals. If you receive radio and television programs in German, or if foreign movies are shown in your region, you will want your students to take advantage of them to improve their language skills as well as their cultural awareness.

The ultimate extension of foreign language study is a trip to or a stay in a country where the language is spoken. Working with school authorities, you may be able to arrange trips abroad for your students.

Total immersion

However, a total foreign language experience need not require travel outside the area. For a day, a weekend, or a longer period during a school vacation, the foreign culture can be recreated at the school, at a camp, or at a university to provide a total immersion experience. This activity requires detailed planning and preparation. Suggestions for planning total immersion experiences are presented in the Teacher's Resource Materials.

Whatever the nature of the endeavor to extend foreign language study beyond the classroom, you will need to develop guidelines with the students in addition to any school rules governing such activities. Adherence to an organized plan results in a more productive experience.

Career Awareness

For many students, foreign language study will form the basis of their life's work or enhance it.

Career awareness activities can be a strong motivating force to learn a foreign language. Students should be made aware of the types of professions and occupations prevailing in the foreign culture and those in their own culture that either depend on foreign language skills or are enhanced by such skills. The Introduction to the Pupil's Edition is a good place to start. It contains segments and activities dealing with career awareness.

You may want to collaborate with guidance counselors in your school to provide up-to-date information concerning career opportunities related to foreign languages. Many schools have career fairs in which you might consider participating.

Conclusion

Many teachers have found the following guidelines practical in planning their foreign language courses. You, too, may find them useful.

- Establish a positive climate.
- Have a classroom decor that reflects the foreign culture.
- Establish a fair-but-firm policy for classroom management.
- Take student interests into consideration when planning.
- Have a written plan.
- Discuss objectives with the students.
- Provide for varied learning styles and rates.
- Avoid lecturing.
- Maximize student involvement.
- Provide positive verbal and nonverbal feedback.
- Evaluate class procedures and outcomes with the students.

The aim of proficiency-oriented instruction is not that students learn language lessons. Rather, the goal is to encourage and guide students to use what they have learned in new situations. Without this application phase in the instructional procedure, proficiency will not be achieved. Therein lies the challenge to the foreign language teacher. We wish you much success in this exciting undertaking.

Specific suggestions for teaching each unit appear in the blue-tabbed pages preceding the unit. Additional suggestions and answers to activities are provided in the annotated pupil pages.

Neue Freunde

HBJ

Foreign Language Programs

GERMAN

- **Neue Freunde**
  Level 1
- **Wir, die Jugend**
  Level 2
- **Unsere Welt**
  Level 3

Neue Freunde

HBJ

HARCOURT BRACE JOVANOVICH, PUBLISHERS
Orlando San Diego Chicago Dallas

Printed in the United States of America
ISBN 0-15-383500-1

PHOTO CREDITS: All photos by George Winkler/Harbrace except: **1:** Horst Munzig/Anne Hamann; **2:** (tr circle)Hans Madej/Bilderberg; (c)Ossi Baumeister/Anne Hamann; (br)Hans Madej/Bilderberg; **3:** (insert)Ossi Baumeister/Anne Hamann; **4:** (c)Ossi Baumeister/Anne Hamann; (b)Walter Schmitz/Bilderberg;(insert)J. Messerschmidt/Stock Market; **5:** (t)R. Betzler/Anne Hamann; (bl)Margot Granitsas/Photo Researchers;(br)Guido Mangold/Anne Hamann; **6:** (t–insert)Andrej Reiser/Bilderberg; (c)Milan Horacek/Bilderberg; (b)Andrej Reiser/Bilderberg; (insert)Andrej Reiser/Bilderberg; **7:** (tl)Ossi Baumeister/Anne Hamann; (br)Alexas Urba/Stock Market; **8:** (t)Luis Villota/Stock Market; (t–insert)Guido Mangold/Anne Hamann; (b)Werner Müller/Peter Arnold; (b–insert)Werner Müller/Peter Arnold; **9:** (tl)Steve Vidler/Leo de Wys; (tr)G. Davies/Leo de Wys; (bl)Dagmar Fabricius/Stock Boston; (br)Steve Vidler/Leo de Wys; **10:** (tr)Ossi Baumeister/Anne Hamann; (br—2nd from bottom)Bob Krist/Leo de Wys; **11:** (tl)Culver; (tr)Bettmann Archive; (cl)Scala/Art Resource; (cr)Giraudon/Art Resource; (bl)Bettmann Archive; (bc)Ken Hawkins/Sygma; (br)Marburg/Art Resource; **12:** (tl)Culver; (tr)Bettmann Archive; (cl)Culver; (cr)Bettmann Archive; (bl)German Information Center; (br)Bettmann Archive; **13:** (tl insert)H. Newton/Sygma; (t)J.L. Atlan/Sygma; (bl)Sygma; (bc)H. Newton/Sygma; (br)Culver; **14:** (b)Adam Woolfitt/Woodfin Camp;

continued on page 391

Writer
George Winkler

Contributing Writer
Margrit Meinel Diehl

Editorial Advisors

Robert L. Baker
Middlebury College
Middlebury, VT

Pat Barr-Harrison
Prince George's County Schools
Landover, MD

Ellen N. Benson
Northwestern High School
Hyattsville, MD

Ann Beusch
Hood College
Frederick, MD

Guy Capelle
Université de Paris VIII
Paris, France

Inge D. Halpert
Columbia University
New York, NY

Charles R. Hancock
Ohio State University
Columbus, OH

William Jassey
Norwalk Board of Education
Norwalk, CT

Dora Kennedy
Prince George's County Schools
Landover, MD

Claire J. Kramsch
Massachusetts Institute of Technology
Cambridge, MA

Ilonka Schmidt Mackey
Université Laval
Québec, Canada

William F. Mackey
Université Laval
Québec, Canada

Consultants and Reviewers

Wolfgang M. Baur
Loyola High School
Los Angeles, CA

Dorothea Bruschke
Parkway School District
Chesterfield, MO

Edeltraut Ehrlich
Markgräfler Gymnasium
Müllheim, FRG

Eileen Johannsen
Nicolet High School
Glendale, WI

Gisela Schwab
Ramapo High School
Franklin Lakes, NJ

Field-Test Teachers

Cecilia Brisentine,
Baltimore, MD

Dieter Dose
Accompsett Intermediate School
Smithtown, NY

Maureen Helinski
Andover Senior High School
Baltimore, MD

Barbara Hoess
Springfield High School
Erdenheim, PA

Carol Paezold Kochefko
Staples High School
Westport, CT

Robert K. Krebs
Smithtown High School West
Smithtown, NY

Rita Leonardi
Brian McMahon High School
South Norwalk, CT

Lynn Preston
Haddon Township High School
Westmont, NJ

Renate Wilson
Frederick High School
Frederick, MD

ACKNOWLEDGMENTS

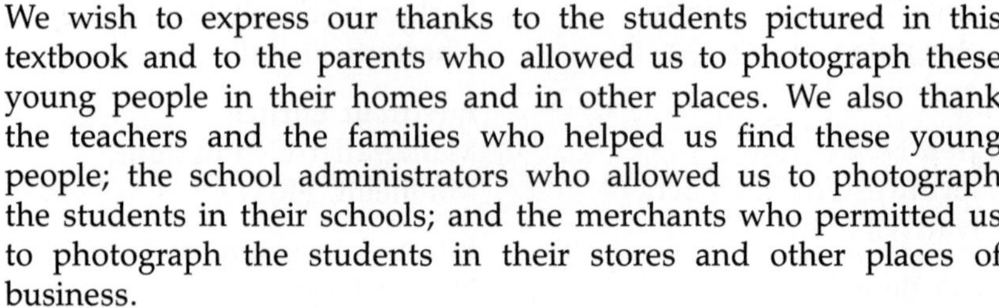

We wish to express our thanks to the students pictured in this textbook and to the parents who allowed us to photograph these young people in their homes and in other places. We also thank the teachers and the families who helped us find these young people; the school administrators who allowed us to photograph the students in their schools; and the merchants who permitted us to photograph the students in their stores and other places of business.

YOUNG PEOPLE
Christof Augenstein, Nadja Balawi, Jens Balcke, Anja Bayertz, Jutta Bolanz, Michael Böse, Bernhard Braun, Matthias Braun, Daniela Broghammer, Christine Cochius, Margit Dastl, Josef Eisenhofer, Hans-Georg Esser, Natalie Fiedler, Jörg Flechtner, Michael Gipp, Nicolas Golubvic, Olaf Günter, Anja Hauswirth, Herman Holst, Marina Hrusha, Mona Johannsen, Daniele Käser, Daniel Kehl, Katja Keiling, Josef Kerscher, Stefan Kiefer, Katja Kramer, Birte Kreuzer, Matthias Kroll, Eva Leonhardt, Michaela Mayer, Jörg Mast, Giuseppe Matano, Philipp Nedel, Wiebke Nedel, Meike Nimmermann, Sven Nipken, Gupse Özkan, Kathrin Pahulycz, Michael Pertsch, Christian Risch, Bruno Schmidlin, Ulrike Schwemmer, Tobias Steinhoff, Claudia Stromberger, Friederike Thyssen, Hendrik Wermier, Rita Werner, Christian Wild

TEACHERS AND FAMILIES
Fritz and Marianne Brunner, Dornbirn; Burkhardt and Edeltraut Ehrlich, Müllheim; Ernst and Christine Hofer, Wien; Hartmut and Sabine Nedel, Neuss; Karl-Uwe and Renate Sperling; Niebüll; Marianne Sperling, München

CONTENTS

INTRODUCTION German and You 1

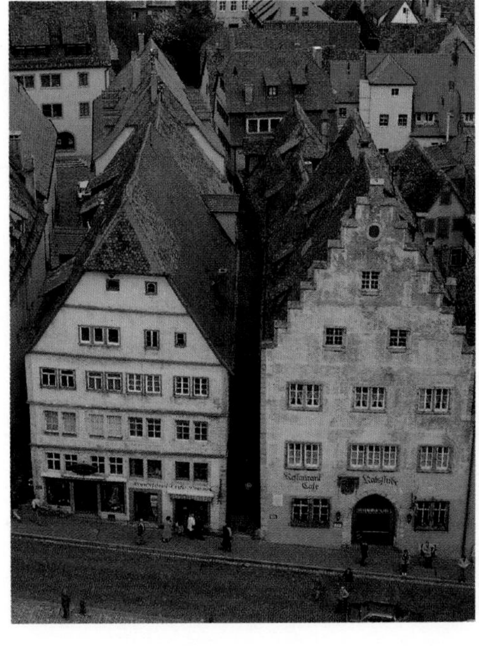

ERSTER TEIL

BASIC MATERIAL

KAPITEL 1
Neue Freunde 30

COMMUNICATIVE FUNCTIONS	GRAMMAR	CULTURE
Socializing • Saying hello and goodbye • Greeting adults		Popular first names of boys and girls Meeting and greeting people
Exchanging information • Asking and giving names • Asking who someone is	The definite articles **der, die, das**	German family names and German names in the United States
Exchanging information • Asking someone's age and telling your age **Counting** • Learning the numbers from 0 to 20	The personal pronouns and the verb **sein**	How numerals are written and how they are signaled by hand
Exchanging information • Asking where someone else is from and telling where you're from **Socializing** • Saying you don't understand and asking for clarification	Asking and answering questions	A map of the German-speaking countries showing where our friends live Using the **Sie**-form
Recombining communicative functions, grammar, and vocabulary		Writing a letter in German to a pen pal
Reading for practice and pleasure		Geography of German-speaking countries Greetings on postcards

BASIC MATERIAL

KAPITEL 2
Schule 60

COMMUNICATIVE FUNCTIONS	GRAMMAR	CULTURE
Exchanging information • Telling how you get to school	The verb **kommen**	How students get to school
Exchanging information • Asking about prices of school supplies **Socializing** • Saying please, thank you, and you're welcome • Getting someone's attention	The definite articles **der, die, das** Noun plurals **Was kostet—was kosten** The pronouns **er, sie, es,** and **sie** (plural)	German currency and how to read prices The concept of grammatical gender
Exchanging information • Giving information about your class schedule • Telling time	The verb **haben**	System of scheduling classes Subjects taught in German schools
Exchanging information • Talking about homework and grades **Expressing feelings and emotions** • Responding to good news and to bad news		System of grading
Recombining communicative functions, grammar, and vocabulary		A German exchange student talks about himself
Reading for practice and pleasure		

BASIC MATERIAL

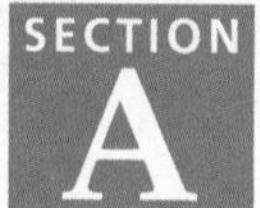

COMMUNICATIVE FUNCTIONS	GRAMMAR	CULTURE
Exchanging information • Asking someone about his or her interests	Using the **du**-form Using the **ihr**-form The present tense	Popular sports and hobbies Three ways of saying *you* in German
Exchanging information • Talking about when and how often you do your various sports and activities	Word order: verb in second place	How young people spend their free time
Expressing attitudes and opinions • Asking for an opinion; expressing enthusiasm or the lack of it • Expressing surprise, agreement, and disagreement **Expressing feelings and emotions** • Expressing likes, dislikes, and preferences	**gern, lieber, am liebsten, nicht gern**	Student survey: preferred sports activities
Recombining communicative functions, grammar, and vocabulary		Olympic sports symbols Pen-pal section from a magazine for young people
Reading for practice and pleasure		What young people read A computer hobbyist
Reviewing communicative functions, grammar, and vocabulary		Excerpts from a school newspaper

ZWEITER TEIL

KAPITEL 5
Auf nach Köln! 134

BASIC MATERIAL

COMMUNICATIVE FUNCTIONS	GRAMMAR	CULTURE
Exchanging information • Saying what you need to take on a trip	The definite article, nominative and accusative case	Map of Germany, showing cities with airports Welcome aboard—information for air travelers
Exchanging information • Asking for information and giving directions • Giving distances from one city to another using a map	The **möchte-**forms	Arriving at a German airport—international signs and symbols The German post office and phone company Measuring distances in kilometers
Socializing • Exchanging money • Making a phone call **Exchanging information** • Reading a flight monitor • Expressing flight numbers, departure times, and gate numbers		German money; exchanging money The 24-hour system of telling time The German telephone system
Recombining communicative functions, grammar, and vocabulary		At the airport information counter; plane and train schedules
Reading for practice and pleasure		Landmarks of the city of Cologne

COMMUNICATIVE FUNCTIONS	GRAMMAR	CULTURE
Socializing • Introducing someone, introducing yourself, and responding to an introduction	**ein** and **mein,** nominative case forms	Family members and close relatives
Exchanging information • Talking about your home **Socializing** • Complimenting someone and responding to a compliment • Saying thank you and you're welcome	Indefinite articles, accusative case The preposition **für**	Inside a German home How Germans respond to a compliment
Exchanging information • Talking about appearance and personal characteristics **Expressing attitudes and opinions** • Agreeing, disagreeing, and expressing surprise	The verb **aussehen** Third person pronouns, accusative case	
Recombining communicative functions, grammar, and vocabulary		Germany through the eyes of an American exchange student
Reading for practice and pleasure		Tradition of folklore

BASIC MATERIAL

COMMUNICATIVE FUNCTIONS	GRAMMAR	CULTURE
Exchanging information • Telling where you live and what kind of place it is • Pointing out landmarks • Asking for directions	The verb **wissen**	Some standard greetings States in the Federal Republic of Germany Landmarks of Munich
Exchanging information • Talking about shopping **Persuading** • Suggesting where to shop • Making requests	The verb **sollen**	Shopping for groceries Units of weight and liquid measure
Expressing feelings • Expressing annoyance **Expressing attitudes** • Asking and telling how something tastes **Socializing** • Saying you want or don't want more • Talking about the weather	The verb **essen** **noch ein,** another Making suggestions using command forms	Reading a menu with local specialties
Recombining communicative functions, grammar, and vocabulary		Conversations at the market
Reading for practice and pleasure		The city of Munich, culture and character
Reviewing communicative functions, grammar, and vocabulary		A train schedule A map of a train station Menu from a snack bar

DRITTER TEIL

BASIC MATERIAL

KAPITEL 9
Eine Party 238

COMMUNICATIVE FUNCTIONS	GRAMMAR	CULTURE
Socializing • Inviting someone to a party; accepting or declining an invitation	First and second person pronouns, accusative case The verbs **anrufen, einladen,** and **vorhaben**	Planning a party and inviting your friends
Exchanging information • Telling what there is to eat and drink		Some party foods and beverages
Socializing • Offering something to eat or drink; accepting or declining what is being offered **Exchanging information** • Making negative statements	**kein,** nominative and accusative case The verb **nehmen**	Accepting or declining something at a party
Persuading • Talking about things to do at a party; making suggestions and responding to ideas **Socializing** • Complimenting people and complimenting someone on food	Possessives, nominative and accusative case	What young people do at a party Polite small talk Responding to a compliment
Recombining communicative functions, grammar, and vocabulary		A party invitation
Reading for practice and pleasure		An American teenager in Germany comments on cultural differences A German recipe

BASIC MATERIAL

KAPITEL 10
Gehen wir aus! 268

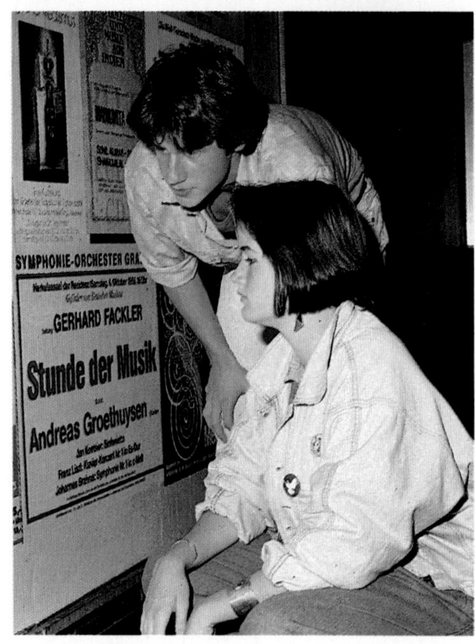

COMMUNICATIVE FUNCTIONS	GRAMMAR	CULTURE
Exchanging information • Talking about what you do in your spare time **Socializing** • Asking and responding to "How are you?" **Persuading** • Making suggestions	The verbs **können** and **wollen** The verbs **fahren, radfahren,** and **ausgehen**	Young people going out
Expressing attitudes • Making choices about where to go • Discussing types of movies **Expressing feelings** • Expressing preference or indifference **Exchanging information** • Asking for information	The verb **anfangen** **welcher, welche, welches,** nominative and accusative case **was für ein?** nominative and accusative case	Concerts and movies in Germany Going to the movies in Germany
Expressing feelings and emotions • Liking or disliking someone or something	The verb **mögen**	Movie and concert ads
Exchanging information • Talking about what you did	The conversational past tense	
Recombining communicative functions, grammar, and vocabulary		A young German writes to his American pen pal, who is coming to visit
Reading for practice and pleasure		Young people comment on their favorite stars and groups

BASIC MATERIAL

COMMUNICATIVE FUNCTIONS	GRAMMAR	CULTURE
Expressing attitudes and opinions • Wondering what to give as a present; asking for advice on what to give	Indirect objects; dative case forms of possessives The verb **geben**	Buying presents
Socializing • Getting someone's attention **Exchanging information** • Conversing with a salesperson; talking about colors	**dieser, jeder,** nominative and accusative case **der, die, das** used as demonstrative pronouns	Types of stores and store hours
Exchanging information • Saying the seasons and months • Giving the date **Socializing** • Expressing good wishes	Third person pronouns, dative case More past participles	Occasions for giving gifts; gifts to give a host or hostess
Recombining communicative functions, grammar, and vocabulary		Birthday cards and a thank-you note Birthday calendars
Reading for practice and pleasure		A man is talked into buying a pair of shoes
Reviewing communicative functions, grammar, and vocabulary		Vacation activities in Austria Travel brochure Menu from an Austrian café

FOR REFERENCE

MAPS

GETTING TO KNOW YOUR TEXTBOOK

WILLKOMMEN

Some of us are fortunate enough to be able to learn a new language by living in another country, but most of us are not. We begin learning the language and getting acquainted with the foreign culture in a classroom with the help of a teacher and a textbook. Your textbook can be a reliable guide if you know how to use it effectively. The following pages will help you get to know this book, **Neue Freunde** *(New Friends)*, and its various features.

INTRODUCTION

Who speaks German? Where is German spoken? Where did the language come from? Why should I learn it? How can I learn it well? You'll find the answers to these questions in English, illustrated with colorful photographs, in the Introduction, which begins on page 1.

INTRODUCTION

German and You

Welcome to the German-speaking world! During the coming year you will learn to understand, speak, read, and write German in a variety of situations. You will also learn more about the German-speaking world outside your classroom: daily life, customs, traditions, music, art, science, and history. As you begin your travels through the German-speaking world, here's wishing you . . .

Viel Glück!
Good luck!

In this introduction you will learn about:

Germany: a pictorial view

the German-speaking countries

German in the United States

German, English, and other languages

German and your future career

suggestions for studying German

1

ERSTER TEIL

29

PART OPENER

There are twelve units in Neue Freunde, **grouped in three Parts. Each Part contains three units and a review unit based on them. At the beginning of each Part, you'll see an illustrated table of contents like the one shown here. It will tell you the number, title, and opening page of each unit** (Kapitel) **and give you a brief preview, in English, of each unit's theme and content.**

UNIT OPENER

Nine units in your textbook present new material. Each of these units opens the same way. Before you begin a unit, examine its two opening pages. First scan the photos—they'll give you an idea of what the unit is about. Next read the introductory paragraph—it sets the theme and provides information about the life and customs of German-speaking people. Finally, look at the outline of the unit. Read the objectives of each section carefully. They'll tell you specifically what you'll be learning to communicate.

KAPITEL 1

Neue Freunde

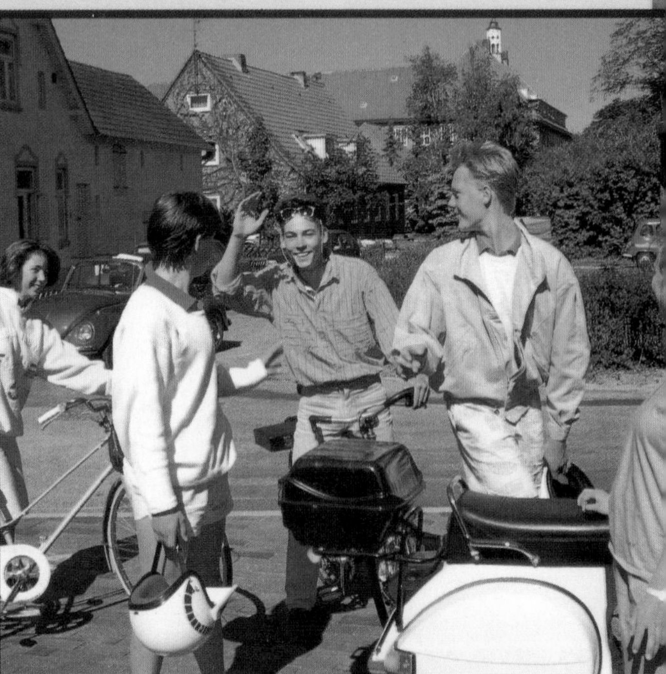

REVIEW UNIT OPENER

Review is essential to learning a second language. It's good to stop now and then to ask yourself what you've learned and, more importantly, to practice your new skills in different situations. That's just what each review unit (Wiederholungskapitel) will help you do. There is one review unit at the end of each Part—three in the book. In the review unit you'll be introduced to a new theme and

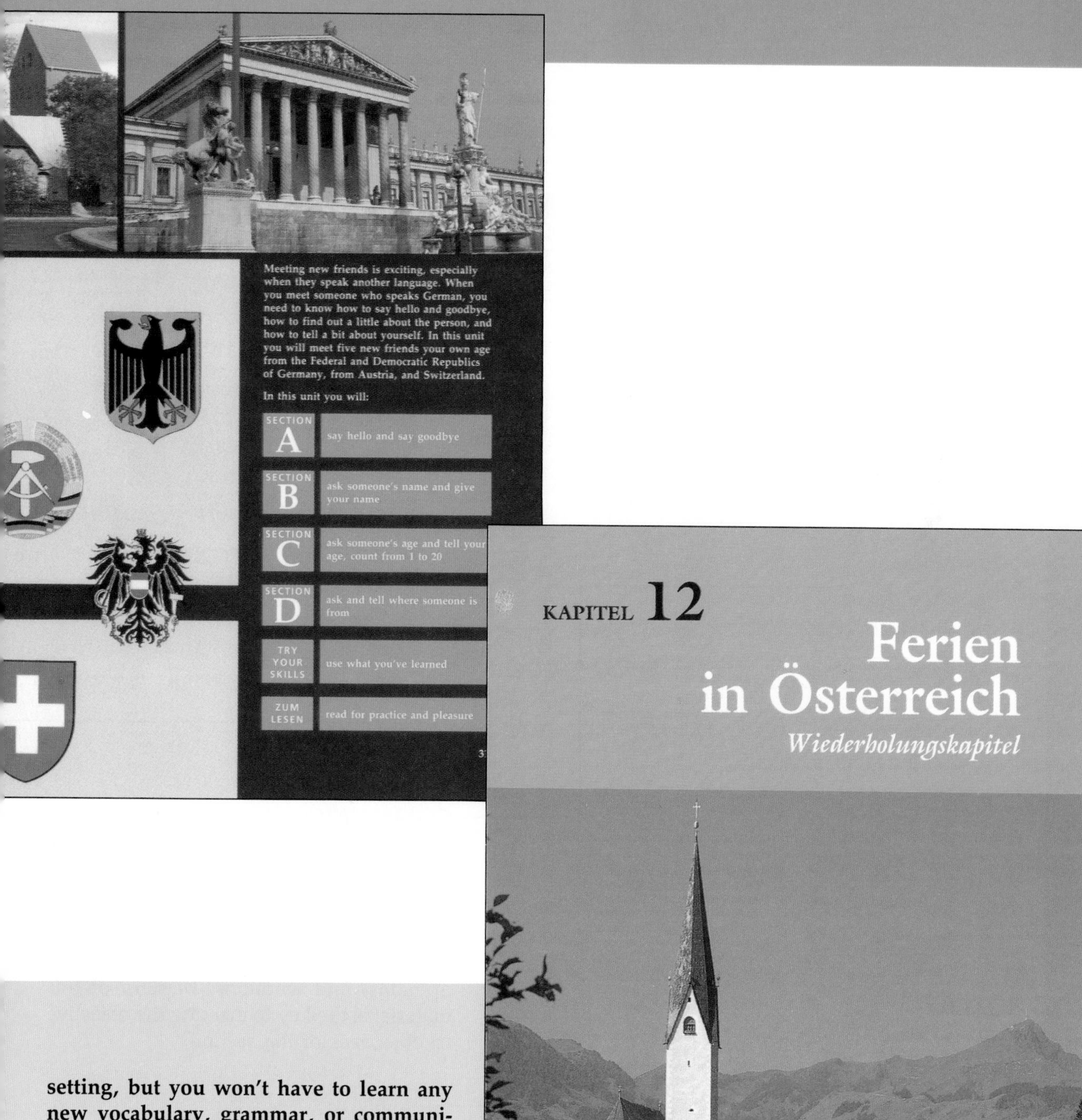
Meeting new friends is exciting, especially when they speak another language. When you meet someone who speaks German, you need to know how to say hello and goodbye, how to find out a little about the person, and how to tell a bit about yourself. In this unit you will meet five new friends your own age from the Federal and Democratic Republics of Germany, from Austria, and Switzerland.
In this unit you will:
SECTION A say hello and say goodbye
SECTION B ask someone's name and give your name
SECTION C ask someone's age and tell your age, count from 1 to 20
SECTION D ask and tell where someone is from
TRY YOUR SKILLS use what you've learned
ZUM LESEN read for practice and pleasure
KAPITEL 12
Ferien in Österreich
Wiederholungskapitel

setting, but you won't have to learn any new vocabulary, grammar, or communicative functions (language uses). Just concentrate on using what you've already studied in new and interesting ways.

SECTIONS

With the exception of the three review units, each unit is made up of three or four sections. The beginning of each section will remind you of your objective and introduce you briefly, in English, to the theme of the section. Read these introductions carefully—they'll give you pieces of information about German-speaking people and their way of life.

SECTION **D** asking and telling where you are from

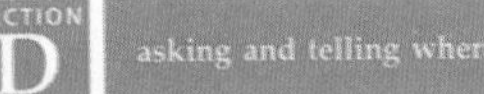

Now you will meet some young people from the German-speaking countries.

D1 Woher bist du?

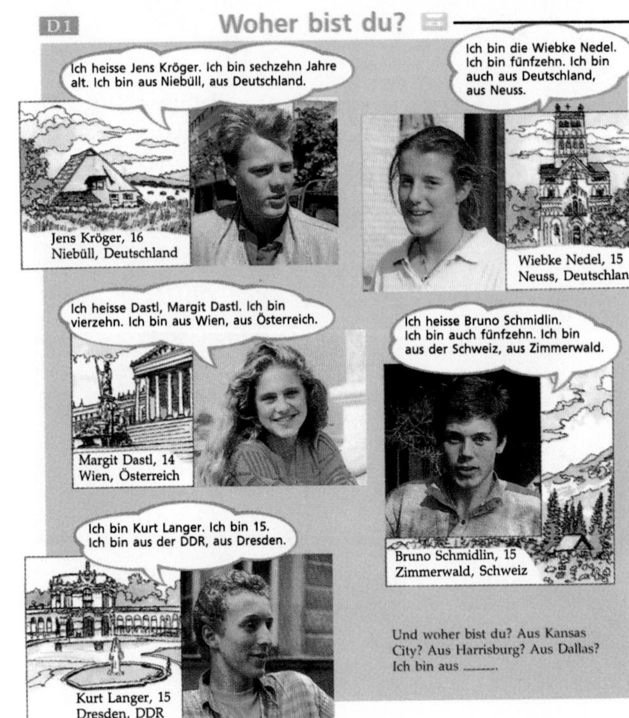

Ich heisse Jens Kröger. Ich bin sechzehn Jahre alt. Ich bin aus Niebüll, aus Deutschland.
Jens Kröger, 16
Niebüll, Deutschland
Ich bin die Wiebke Nedel. Ich bin fünfzehn. Ich bin auch aus Deutschland, aus Neuss.
Wiebke Nedel, 15
Neuss, Deutschland
Ich heisse Dastl, Margit Dastl. Ich bin vierzehn. Ich bin aus Wien, aus Österreich.
Margit Dastl, 14
Wien, Österreich
Ich heisse Bruno Schmidlin. Ich bin auch fünfzehn. Ich bin aus der Schweiz, aus Zimmerwald.
Bruno Schmidlin, 15
Zimmerwald, Schweiz
Ich bin Kurt Langer. Ich bin 15. Ich bin aus der DDR, aus Dresden.
Kurt Langer, 15
Dresden, DDR

Und woher bist du? Aus Kansas City? Aus Harrisburg? Aus Dallas? Ich bin aus ______.

Neue Freunde 45

C7 WIE SAGT MAN DAS?
Asking someone's age and telling yours

QUESTION	ANSWER
Wie alt bist du? How old are you?	**Ich bin dreizehn Jahre alt.** I'm thirteen years old.
Wie alt ist der Stefan? How old is Stefan?	**Er ist fünfzehn.** He is fifteen.
Wie alt ist die Sabine? How old is Sabine?	**Sie ist fünfzehn Jahre alt.** She's fifteen years old.
Wie alt sind Ulrike und Jochen? How old are Ulrike and Jochen?	**Sie sind auch fünfzehn.** They are also fifteen.

C8 ERKLÄRUNG *Explanation*
Personal Pronouns and the Verb sein

The phrases **ich bin, du bist, er ist, sie ist,** and **sie sind** each contain a subject pronoun corresponding to the English *I, you, he, she,* and *they,* plus a form of the verb **sein,** *to be: I am, you are, he/she/it is, they are.* **Sein** is one of the most frequently used verbs in German. The chart shows the plural forms **wir,** *we,* and **ihr,** *you* (plural), but you do not need to use them yet.

Singular			*Plural*		
Ich	**bin**	15 Jahre alt.	Wir	**sind**	15 Jahre alt.
Du	**bist**		Ihr	**seid**	
Der Stefan / Er	**ist**		Stefan and Sabine / Sie	**sind**	
Die Sabine / Sie	**ist**				

C9 Übung • Wie alt sind die Schüler? —Vierzehn.

Everyone in this group is 14 years old.

A: Wie alt ist der Fritz?
B: Er ist vierzehn.

1. Wie alt ist der Hans?
2. Wie alt ist die Monika?
3. Wie alt sind Hans und Monika?
4. Wie alt ist der Günter?
5. Wie alt ist die Ulrike?
6. Wie alt sind Günter and Ulrike?

Neue Freunde 43

COMMUNICATIVE FUNCTIONS

The material labeled **Wie sagt man das?** *(How do you say that?)* summarizes the sentences, phrases, and expressions you'll need in order to accomplish your purpose—that is, to express and react to requests, opinions, and emotions. Mastery of this material is the key to meeting the objective or objectives of the section.

GRAMMAR

In order to communicate effectively, you'll need to understand and use some grammatical forms. Look for these forms in the boxes with the heading **Erklärung** *(Explanation)*. Once again, the color blue is a cue that the material in the box is to be mastered.

BASIC MATERIAL

The material in each section is numbered in sequence together with the letter of the section: A1, A2, A3, and so on. The first presentation is always new or basic material, signaled by a number and title in blue. In some sections new material may be introduced in two or three other places. Whenever you see a heading in blue, you'll know that there's something new to learn. The new material is a model of what to say in a situation. Its authentic language and pictures will acquaint you with the way German-speaking people live, think, and feel and familiarize you with the various settings in which German is spoken.

CULTURE NOTES

The head **Ein wenig Landeskunde** *(A little culture)* printed in green invites you to find out more about the life of German-speaking people. These culture notes in English provide additional information about the theme of the section to help you increase your cultural awareness.

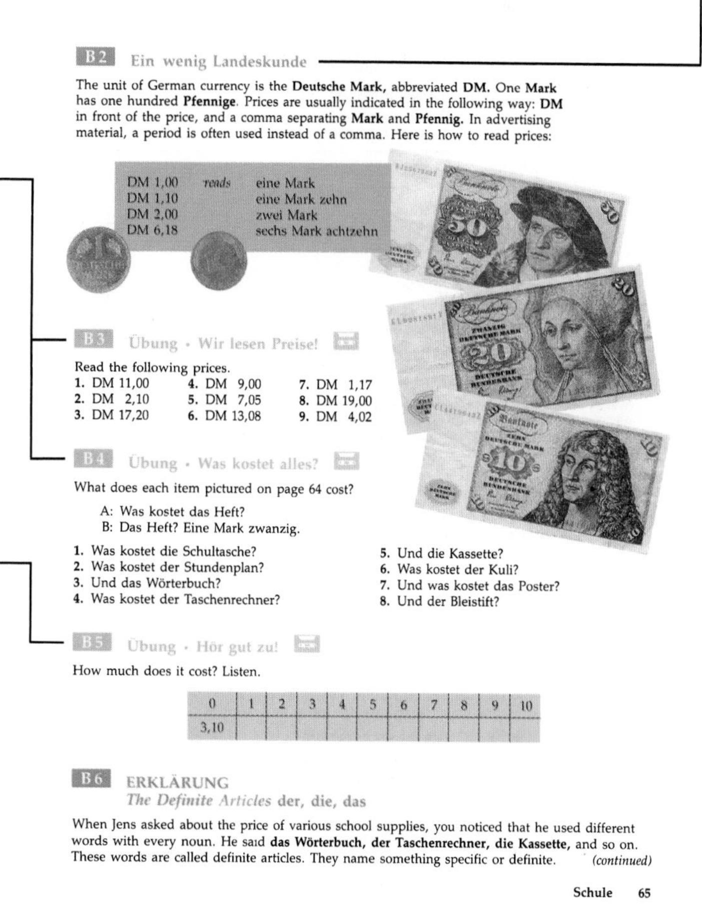

B2 Ein wenig Landeskunde

The unit of German currency is the **Deutsche Mark,** abbreviated **DM.** One **Mark** has one hundred **Pfennige**. Prices are usually indicated in the following way: **DM** in front of the price, and a comma separating **Mark** and **Pfennig.** In advertising material, a period is often used instead of a comma. Here is how to read prices:

DM 1,00	*reads*	eine Mark
DM 1,10		eine Mark zehn
DM 2,00		zwei Mark
DM 6,18		sechs Mark achtzehn

B3 Übung · Wir lesen Preise!

Read the following prices.

1. DM 11,00
2. DM 2,10
3. DM 17,20
4. DM 9,00
5. DM 7,05
6. DM 13,08
7. DM 1,17
8. DM 19,00
9. DM 4,02

B4 Übung · Was kostet alles?

What does each item pictured on page 64 cost?

A: Was kostet das Heft?
B: Das Heft? Eine Mark zwanzig.

1. Was kostet die Schultasche?
2. Was kostet der Stundenplan?
3. Und das Wörterbuch?
4. Was kostet der Taschenrechner?
5. Und die Kassette?
6. Was kostet der Kuli?
7. Und was kostet das Poster?
8. Und der Bleistift?

B5 Übung · Hör gut zu!

How much does it cost? Listen.

0	1	2	3	4	5	6	7	8	9	10
3,10										

B6 ERKLÄRUNG
The Definite Articles **der, die, das**

When Jens asked about the price of various school supplies, you noticed that he used different words with every noun. He said **das Wörterbuch, der Taschenrechner, die Kassette,** and so on. These words are called definite articles. They name something specific or definite. *(continued)*

Schule 65

ACTIVITIES

The headings of all the activities in the section begin with the word **Übung** in orange. This signals an opportunity to practice and work with new material—and sometimes old material—either orally or in writing. Many of the activities are designed so that you may work together with your classmates in pairs or in small groups.

LISTENING

Listening is an essential skill that requires practice to develop. Whenever you see this cassette symbol ▣ after a heading, you'll know that the material is recorded, with pauses provided for your repetition or responses. A special listening comprehension activity in each section is headed **Hör gut zu!** *(Listen carefully)*. In order to respond, you will need to listen as your teacher plays the cassette or reads the German to you.

TRY YOUR SKILLS

This section will let you experiment with the skills and knowledge you've gathered in the previous sections of the unit. Its variety of activities will give you many opportunities to practice communicating with others.

TRY YOUR SKILLS — using what you've learned

1 Gerd Ecker in den USA

Gerd Ecker, a student from Germany, introduces himself to your class.

Guten Tag! Ich heisse Gerd Ecker. Ich bin 16 Jahre alt. Ich bin aus Paderborn. Paderborn ist in der Bundesrepublik Deutschland. Ich gehe aufs Goerdeler Gymnasium. Ich komme mit dem Rad in die Schule, und die Klassenkameraden—ja, sie kommem mit dem Bus, mit dem Moped, mit dem Auto und auch zu Fuss.

Wir haben von Montag bis Freitag Schule. Wir haben Sonnabend frei. Die Schule beginnt um Viertel vor acht, und sie ist um ein Uhr aus.

Welche Fächer ich habe? Nun, ich habe Deutsch, Mathe, Englisch, Geschichte, Geographie, Sport und Kunst. Ich bin gut in Englisch und in Deutsch. Ich habe eine Eins in Englisch und eine Zwei in Deutsch. Englisch und Deutsch sind leicht. Ich bin nicht so gut in Mathe. Mathe ist schwer. Ich habe nur eine Vier.

2 Übung • Rollenspiel

A classmate plays the role of Gerd. You missed some of his presentation, so you ask him questions about himself. Then you take the role of Gerd, and your classmate asks you.

A: Wie heisst du?
B: Ich heisse. . .

3 Übung • Erzähl mal, was Gerd gesagt hat!

A friend of yours missed Gerd's presentation. You tell him or her what Gerd said.

Der Schüler aus Deutschland heisst. . .

4 Übung • Vortrag *Presentation*

You are visiting a class in Germany. Tell the class something about yourself and your school day.

82 Kapitel 2

SELF-CHECK

Each of the nine basic units ends with a one-page self-check called **Was kannst du schon?** *(What have you learned?)*. It includes a series of questions in English for you to ask yourself. Following the questions are short activities that will check your knowledge and skills. The questions and activities are grouped by section, so if you can't answer yes to a question or if the exercise shows that you need to review, you'll know which section to turn to.

WAS KANNST DU SCHON?

Let's review some important points that you have learned in this unit.

SECTION A

Can you greet young people and adults in German?
Say hello to the following people:

1. Katrin
2. Stefan
3. Mr. Sperling
4. Miss Seifert
5. Mrs. Meier
6. your teacher

Can you say goodbye in German?
Say goodbye to the same people.

SECTION B

Can you introduce yourself in German?

1. Say hello.
2. Give your name.
3. Ask a classmate his or her name.

Can you find out who someone is?

1. Ask a boy's name, then tell it to someone else.
2. Ask a girl's name, then tell it to someone else.
3. Ask who someone is and give the answer.

SECTION C

Can you ask someone's age and tell yours?
Write a question and answer about age for each of the following pronouns: ich, du, er, sie, sie (plural).

Do you know the numbers from 0 to 20?
Write out in German the numbers from 0 to 20.

Do you know the forms of the verb *sein*?
Complete the following sentences.

1. Das Mädchen ___ 15.
2. Ich ___ 13.
3. Der Junge ___ 16.
4. Frl. Seifert ___ aus Wien.
5. ___ du aus Deutschland?
6. Wer ___ das?
7. Jens und Wiebke ___ aus Deutschland.
8. Er ___ aus Österreich.

SECTION D

Can you say where you are from? Can you ask where others are from?
Say where you are from. Ask one of your classmates where he or she is from.

Can you ask questions anticipating a yes or no answer?
Make up three questions anticipating a yes or no answer.

Can you ask for information to be repeated?
What do you say if you don't understand part or all of the following statements?

1. Ich bin aus Deutschland.
2. Er heisst Jens Kröger.
3. Das Mädchen ist 15 Jahre alt.
4. Der Deutschlehrer heisst Sperling.

Can you address adults using the *Sie*-form?
Ask your teacher his or her name and where he or she is from.

54 Kapitel 1

WORTSCHATZ

SECTION A
armer Peter! *poor Peter!*
bei den Nedels *at the Nedels'*
der **Bruder, ¨** *brother*
da: wir sind da *we're here*
das sind *these are*
dass *that*
die **Freundin, -nen** *girl friend*
die **Geschwister** (pl) *brothers and sisters*
die **Grosseltern** (pl) *grandparents*
der **Hund, -e** *dog*
kennenlernen: du lernst viele Leute kennen *you're going to meet a lot of people*
die **Klassenkameradin, -nen** *classmate* (f)
die **Kusine, -n** *cousin* (f)
die **Leute** (pl) *people*
mein, meine *my*
die **Oma, -s** *grandma*
der **Onkel, -** *uncle*
der **Opa, -s** *grandpa*
schlimm *bad*
schön *nice;* schön, dass du da bist *nice that you're here*
die **Schwester, -n** *sister*
so *so, well then*
die **Tante, -n** *aunt*
der **Vetter, -n** *cousin* (m)
viele *many*
von *of;* ein Freund von Wiebke *a friend of Wiebke's*
Willkommen in Neuss! *welcome to Neuss!*

SECTION B
der **Audi, -s** *Audi* (a German-made automobile)
auf *on*
auspacken: er packt den Rucksack aus *he unpacks his backpack*
aussehen *to look (like), appear,* (see p 179)
das **Auto, -s** *car*
das **Bad, ¨er** *bathroom*
bekommen *to get, receive*
bitte schön *you're welcome*
das **Buch, ¨er** *book*
Dank: vielen Dank! *thanks a lot!* tausend Dank! *thanks a million!*
danken *to thank;* nichts zu danken *don't mention it*
dein, deine *your*
das **Esszimmer, -** *dining room*
finden: findest du? *do you think so?*
die **Garage, -n** *garage*
der **Garten, ¨** *garden*
das **Gästezimmer, -** *guest room*
gemütlich *cozy, comfortable*
gern: ja, gern *yes, I'd like that*
gross *big*
die **Halskette, -n** *necklace*
das **Haus, ¨er** *house*
hell *light*
der **Keller, -** *basement, cellar*
klein *small*
komm! *come on!*
die **Küche, -n** *kitchen*
mehr *more*
Mensch! *boy! wow!*
modern *modern*
oben *upstairs*
die **Party, -s** *party*
der **Rucksack, ¨e** *knapsack, backpack*
das **Schlafzimmer, -** *bedroom*
schön *pretty, beautiful*
sehen *to see*
sehr *very*
stehen: da steht noch mehr auf Peters Zettel *there's still more on Peter's slip*
tausend *thousand;* tausend Dank! *thanks a million!*
die **Toilette, -n** *toilet*
unten *downstairs*
wieviel? *how many?*
das **Wohnzimmer, -** *living room*
zeigen *to show;* ich zeig es dir *I'll show it to you*
der **Zettel, -** *note, slip of paper*
das **Zimmer, -** *room*

SECTION C
arrogant *arrogant*
attraktiv *attractive*
aussehen: gut aussehen *to look good; to be handsome, pretty, attractive*
blond *blond*
die **Brille, -n** *glasses*
brünett *brunette*
dunkel *dark*
dunkelblond *dark blond*
freundlich *friendly*
Geschmackssache: das ist Geschmackssache *that's a matter of taste*
gross *tall*
hübsch *pretty*
kennen *to know*
klein *short, small*
lustig *merry, funny*
meinen: meinst du? *do you think so?* meinst du nicht? *don't you think so?*
nett *nice*
nicht? *don't you thi*
recht haben *to be r*
schlank *slim*
sympathisch *likeabl*
unsympathisch *un*
not nice
vollschlank *heavyse*

WORTSCHATZÜBUNGEN

1. Look at the Wortschatz and make a list of all singular nouns with their definite articles. Then write the nouns again with their indefinite articles.
2. Pick out all the adjectives and write them down. How many pairs of opposites can you find? Write them next to each other.

Bei den Ned

VOCABULARY

The German-English vocabulary list **(Wortschatz)** after the self-check contains the unit words and phrases you'll need to know. They're grouped according to the sections of the unit. A word-study exercise, **Wortschatzübung,** below the list will focus your attention on various aspects of the vocabulary and provide helpful ways to work with and learn the new words and phrases.

ZUM LESEN

Ein Gewohnheitsmensch

Herr Neuschuh ist ein netter Mann. Er ist höflich°, pünktlich, immer korrekt. Er ist auch immer gut angezogen°: er kauft seine Sachen in den besten Geschäften°. Aber er macht sich wenig aus der Mode°. „Die Mode", so sagt er, „ist nur für die Jugend." Herr Neuschuh liebt den klassischen Stil. Seine Anzüge° kommen aus England, seine Krawatten kommen aus Frankreich und seine Schuhe aus Italien. Jeden Morgen, bevor Herr Neuschuh zur Arbeit geht, bürstet er seinen Anzug und putzt° seine Schuhe. Er ist ein schicker Herr°.

Nun, eines Tages möchte Herr Neuschuh ein Paar neue Schuhe. Er geht in das Schuhgeschäft, wo er immer seine Schuhe kauft. Dort kennt er alle Verkäufer.

„Guten Tag, Herr Neuschuh! Was darf es heute sein?"

„Ist Frl. Seidel nicht da?"

„Frl. Seidel ist gestern in Urlaub gegangen°."

„Ach, so was! —Nun, das macht nichts°. Ich möchte ein Paar Schuhe."

„Welche Marke°?"

„Diese hier."

ein Gewohnheitsmensch *a creature of habit;* **höflich** *polite;* **gut angezogen** *well-dressed;* **das Geschäft** *store;* **er macht sich wenig aus der Mode** *he doesn't pay much attention to fashion, to what's in style;* **der Anzug** *suit;* **putzen** *to clean, polish;* **ein schicker Herr** *a smartly-dressed gentleman;* **in Urlaub gehen** *to go on vacation;* **das macht nichts** *it doesn't matter;* **die Marke** *make*

324 Kapitel 11

READING

A reading section, **Zum Lesen** *(To Read),* concludes the unit. Here you'll find one or more reading selections related to the unit's theme. They include comic strips, postcards, interviews, opinion polls of German teenagers, factual selections, and stories. Most reading selections are followed by questions and activities designed to help you practice and develop your reading skills.

PHOTO ESSAYS

Following each of the three review units in the textbook, you'll find a cultural photo essay called **Landeskunde.** The three essays tell you more about the lives of the German-speaking people and the places where they live.

LANDESKUNDE 1

A Glimpse of the Federal Republic of Germany

Germany lies in the center of Europe. It is about six hundred miles long, bounded by the North Sea to the north and the Alps to the south. From east to west the country is narrow, seldom more than two hundred miles wide. Contained in this area is a surprising variety of landscapes. There are coastal regions and flatlands in northern Germany and gently rolling hills in the central and southwestern part of the country. South of the river Danube is a high plateau that reaches to the majestic Alpine range. It is surprising that in such a highly industrialized country more than half the area is farmland and another third is forest land.

❶ Promenadenkonzert auf der Nordseeinsel Sylt

❷ Kurort Badenweiler im Schwarzwald

❸ Die Zugspitze, Deutschlands höchster Berg, 2 963 m

125

LANDESKUNDE 2

Other German-speaking Countries and Regions

The German Democratic Republic

The German Democratic Republic (GDR) is located in Central Europe, with the Federal Republic to the west, Poland to the east, and Czechoslovakia to the south. The GDR is a socialist state, formed in 1949 from the Soviet-occupied zone of Germany, six months after the formation of the Federal Republic. In the GDR all decision making is in the hands of the communist party, officially known as the Socialist Unity Party (SED). Geographically, the northern and central parts of the GDR are a low-lying plain intersected by gentle ranges of hills. The southern part of the country is highland. Some of the chief cities are (East) Berlin, the capital; Leipzig, a center of printing and book trade and the site of trade fairs since 1100; Dresden, a baroque art city that has been carefully restored; and the port of Rostock on the Baltic Sea.

Die Deutsche Demokratische Republik feiert ihren 35. Geburtstag

LANDESKUNDE 3

Festivals and Holidays

It is said that in Germany festivals are as numerous as the days of the year. This is no exaggeration! Wherever you go, there is always something going on—a popular festival, a religious feast, a folk-dance, a historical or costume parade, or simply some occasion for public merry-making. The calendar of festivities begins with carnival, a season that starts on the seventh of January and lasts until Lent, 40 days before Easter. It is celebrated mostly in the Catholic areas. The Rhenish carnival turns Cologne, Düsseldorf, and Mainz upside down. During the famous "Fasching," its Bavarian counterpart, Munich celebrates. The Swabian "Fasnet" conjures up the ghosts and demons of old in the strange dance of bell-jingling masks.

❶ Fastnacht in Rottweil, Schwaben

❷ Lustige Maske

❸ Rosenmontag in Köln; keiner arbeitet, alle feiern Karneval auf der Strasse

❹ Kinderfasching

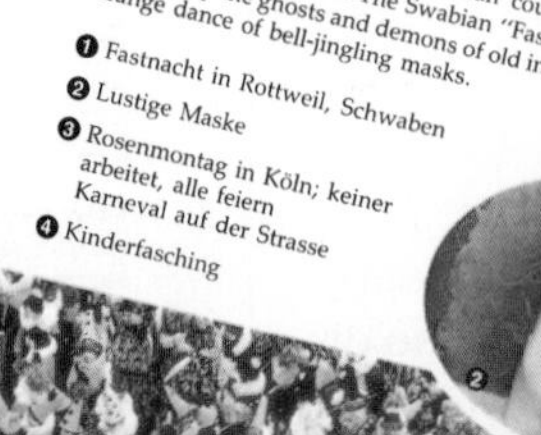

333

FOR REFERENCE

The reference section at the end of the textbook provides you with valuable aids. It is grouped into the following parts: Summary of Functions, Grammar Summary, Pronunciation, Numbers, English Equivalents, German-English Vocabulary, English-German Vocabulary, and Grammar Index.

SUMMARY OF FUNCTIONS

The Summary of Functions sums up the communicative functions you have learned and practiced in a variety of situations throughout this textbook. If you want to ask for directions, invite someone to a party, pay a compliment, or respond to a friend's good fortune, for example, you will find the appropriate phrases and sentences listed here, as well as the unit in which the particular function was introduced.

GRAMMAR SUMMARY

The grammar points that have been presented in the textbook are organized in tables for easy reference and review in the Grammar Summary.

GERMAN-ENGLISH VOCABULARY

The German-English Vocabulary includes almost all the words you will come across in this textbook. The numbers after each entry tell you in which unit the word first appeared. If the number is in heavy type, you are expected to know that word or phrase and be able to use it. In this Vocabulary, you can look up the English meanings of words and phrases, and you can check the gender of nouns as well as the plural forms.

SUMMARY OF FUNCTIONS

The term *functions* can be defined as what you do with language—what your purpose is in speaking. As you use this textbook, you will find yourself in a number of situations—in a store, in a restaurant, at a party, at the airport, in a new city. How do you "function" in these situations? How do you ask about prices in a store, order a meal in a restaurant, compliment your host at a party, greet arriving friends at an airport, or ask for directions in an unfamiliar city? You need to know certain basic functional expressions.

Here is a list of functions accompanied by the expressions you have learned to communicate them. The number of the unit in which the expressions were introduced is followed by the section letter and number in parentheses.

SOCIALIZING

Saying hello
1 (A3) Guten Morgen!
Guten Tag!
short forms: Morgen!
Tag!
informal: Hallo!
regional: Grüss dich!
7 (A1) Grüss Gott!
Gruetzi!

Saying goodbye
1 (A3) Auf Wiedersehen!
short form: Wiedersehen!
informal: Tschüs!
Tschau!
Bis dann!
5 (C6) Bis gleich!

Addressing people
1 (A1) *first name*
1 (A7) Herr + *last name*
Frau + *last name*

Responding to an introduction
6 (A3) Guten Tag, + *name*
Hallo, + *first name*
Grüss dich, + *first name.* Wie geht's?

Asking "How are you?"
10 (A9) Wie geht's?
Wie geht's denn?

Responding to "How are you?"
10 (A9) Ach, prima!
Danke, gut!
Nicht schlecht.
So lala.
Schlecht.
Miserabel.

Welcoming people
6 (A1) Willkommen in . . .!
Schön, dass du hier bist!

Getting someone's attention
2 (B25) Du, (Jens), . . .
Schau!
Schau, (Jens)!

GRAMMAR SUMMARY

DETERMINERS

In German, nouns can be grouped into three classes or genders: masculine, feminine, and neuter. There are words that tell you the gender of a noun. One of these is called the definite article. In English there is one definite article: *the.* In German there are three, one for each gender: **der, die,** and **das.**

Gender:	MASCULINE	FEMININE	NEUTER
Noun Phrase:	**der Junge** *the boy* **der Ball** *the ball*	**die Mutter** *the mother* **die Kassette** *the cassette*	**das Mädchen** *the girl* **das Haus** *the house*

Other words can be used with a noun instead of the definite article. Examples of these words in English are *a, this, that, my,* and *every.* These words and the definite article are called determiners. They help to make clear, or determine, which person or thing you mean—for example, whether you are talking about *this book, my book,* or just any book. A determiner plus a noun is called a noun phrase.

GERMAN-ENGLISH VOCABULARY

This vocabulary includes almost all words in this textbook, both active and passive. Active words and phrases are those introduced in basic material and listed in the **Wortschatz** sections of the units. You are expected to know and be able to use active vocabulary. All other words—those appearing in the Introduction, in exercises, in optional and visual material, in the Try Your Skills and **Zum Lesen** sections, in the review units, and in the pictorial **Landeskunde** sections—are considered passive. Passive vocabulary is for recognition only. The meaning of passive words and phrases can usually be understood from context or may be looked up in this vocabulary.

With some exceptions, the following are not included: most proper nouns, forms of verbs other than the infinitive, and forms of determiners other than the nominative.

Nouns are listed with definite article and plural form, when applicable. The numbers in the entries refer to the unit where the word or phrase first appears. A number in black, heavy type indicates that the word or phrase has been actively introduced in that unit. Passive vocabulary is followed by numerals in light type.

The following abbreviations are used in this vocabulary: adj (adjective), pl (plural), pp (past participle), sep (separable prefix), sing (singular), and s. th. (something).

A

ab *from, starting at,* **4;** *leaves,*

BITTE SCHÖN!

There it is, a special textbook that will help you enlarge your view of the world and enable you to contribute to better understanding and communication among people. Now you're ready to begin an exciting, rewarding experience—learning another language and meeting new friends, **Neue Freunde.**

German and You

What is Germany like? Where do German-speaking people live? How is German related to English? Why should I learn German? How should I go about it? The Introduction has been designed with such questions in mind. It provides information about German-speaking countries, the German language, and careers that require a knowledge of German, as well as hints on how to learn a second language. You may present the Introduction before or along with Unit 1 to motivate students. A list of materials that you may need while teaching the Introduction appears on page T4.

Page 1

OBJECTIVE To develop an understanding of the importance of German language and culture and to motivate students to learn German

1 GERMANY: A PICTORIAL VIEW

Pages 2–13

This photo essay is a visual description of Germany and the other German-speaking countries. Discuss the photos with the students and encourage them to begin looking for similarities and differences between the German-speaking countries and the United States.

When you fly over Germany, you will notice that much of the area of the country is covered with forest and fields—64 percent, in fact. **Niedersachsen, Bayern, Baden-Württemberg,** and parts of **Nordrhein-Westfalen** have large agricultural areas. The **Soester Börde** in **Nordrhein-Westfalen** is the most fertile area in West Germany. Point these areas out on a map. If possible, get a product map of the German-speaking countries or have the students make one as a project.

Page 2 Even in small mountain villages, potatoes are grown. It is harder to harvest them in the mountains. The girl pictured is loading potatoes onto a wheelbarrow that will be pulled home to the village. In the lower right-hand corner of the page, women are harvesting cabbages, an important product in **Baden-Württemberg.**

Page 3 The top photo shows the **Zugspitze,** the highest mountain in West Germany. In the background are the Austrian mountains. The center photo is of Grossefehn in northern Germany. The canal used to be the only means of transportation. People built their houses along the canal and used it to get their produce to market. Now, of course, there are roads; you can see them running alongside the canal. In the bottom photo, you see the **Schwarzwald.** The photo was taken in the spa of Badenweiler looking toward the town of Müllheim.

Page 4 At the top of the page, you see the **Wappen von Hamburg,** a large excursion boat that takes tourists to the North Sea island of **Helgoland.** The inset shows a barge on the Rhine passing the **Pfalz** near **Kaub.** The **Pfalz** used to be a toll station on the river.

Page 5 People are very proud of their regional costumes **(Trachten),** and in many areas they are worn on special occasions and holidays and for festivals. In some areas, especially in Bavaria and in Austria, there are people who wear regional costume all the time—**Dirndl, Lederhosen, Lodenmäntel,** and, as pictured on this page, **Tiroler Hüte.** The cities of Düsseldorf, Berlin, Munich, and Hamburg are centers of fashion.

Page 6 Industry is spread throughout the Federal Republic, but the states **Nordrhein-Westfalen, Baden-Württemberg, Hamburg,** and **Bremen** are the most heavily industrialized places. The top photo on this page shows a location in the **Ruhrgebiet,** the center of heavy industry in West Germany. Many handicrafts still flourish in the German-speaking countries. Swiss watchmakers are famed for their precision timepieces. East and West Germany, Austria, and Switzerland are known for the manufacture of fine musical instruments.

Page 7 The bakery pictured on this page is located in the town of Aurich in **Friesland.** Over a hundred different kinds of bread are baked and sold here. On the right is a photo of the **Auer Dult,** an open-air market in Munich. It is held three times a year for a week at a time. Here you can buy pottery, dishes, and handcrafted articles and browse through the popular flea market. Many people associate West Germany with fine luxury automobiles made by such firms as Mercedes-Benz, BMW, and Porsche.

Page 8 Great works of art are located in the many museums and galleries throughout the German-speaking countries. Pictured on this page are the **Alte Pinakothek** in Munich and the **Staatsgalerie** in Stuttgart. The **Staatsgalerie** recently opened a modern new wing, acclaimed for its architecture, which is shown here with a sculpture by Henry Moore in the foreground.

Page 9 Visiting Europe is like taking a walk through history. Many centuries-old structures are still standing; they are even put to use, not always for the purposes for which they were originally intended. The photos on this page, clockwise from top left, show the **Porta Nigra** in Trier, Germany's oldest city, founded by the Romans in the year 15 B.C.; Dinkelsbühl, a medieval town that stands today looking just as it did in the Middle Ages; the fortress **Marienberg** in Würzburg, dating back to A.D. 1201, with the **Mainbrücke,** a centuries-old stone bridge over the Main River; and the city of Frankfurt with the **Paulskirche** in the foreground.

Page 10 The German-speaking countries offer a wide variety of restaurants. Many chefs from these countries specialize in the most modern, elegant cuisine, and they travel around the world. Quite a few work in the United States and have opened restaurants here. In Germany you can eat everything from German "nouvelle cuisine" to the most simple regional fare. The **Gasthaus zum Hirschen,** pictured here, is in Staufen near Freiburg. Also pictured is a little **Weinstube** in Badenweiler near Freiburg. Street artists and musicians, as well as organ grinders, are a common sight in the cities of Germany, Austria, and Switzerland.

Pages 11, 12, and 13 Have the students look at the famous people pictured on these pages. Which ones do they recognize? What can they tell you about each one? As an assignment, you might have students find out the names of other important people from the German-speaking countries. List them on the board or on an overhead transparency. Then have the students choose one or two famous people to write reports about. You might make a bulletin board display or a scrapbook.

Pages 14–15

2 THE GERMAN–SPEAKING COUNTRIES

After the students have read the text, have them repeat the German names of the countries. Have volunteers point out the countries on a map of Europe, naming them in German. You might want to have the students work in cooperative learning groups, researching and writing reports on each of the countries. One group might report on other areas of the world where German is spoken, for example Alsace-Lorraine **(Elsass)** and the **Südtirol.**

3 GERMAN IN THE UNITED STATES

GERMAN AND YOU

Pages 16–18

Read this section aloud with the students or have them read the section silently. Ask if anyone is of German ancestry. What other nationalities are represented in the class?

Activities

In addition to the activities suggested, you may want to have the students find out more about some of the facts mentioned in this section. For example, why did German settlers come to the United States? What areas of the United States did they tend to settle in? What were some of the reasons for considering German as the language for the new country? Ask the students which German-born Americans they have learned about in their history, English, science, art, and music classes. Have them (1) make lists of famous German-born Americans who have distinguished themselves in the areas mentioned; (2) look in newspapers and magazines to find more examples of German words that have become part of our everyday language; and (3) talk about German customs they have observed in their own families or German customs that exist in the community.

4 GERMAN, ENGLISH, AND OTHER LANGUAGES

Pages 19–21

The students should find this section especially interesting. Here they can see the relationship of German and English to each other as well as to other languages. Ask if anyone in the class speaks one or more of the languages on the diagram or if they know anyone who does. Where does that person come from? Have the student locate that place on a map of the world. As a project, have the students work in cooperative learning groups to find out where the languages on the diagram are spoken. Each group should report to the class and point out the countries on the map of the world.

If possible, bring in German magazines and newspapers and have the students pick out examples of English words that have been incorporated into German.

When you read the alphabet with the students, point out that the German (Gothic) letters were once used in all German books and newspapers. Bring in an older edition of a book to show them. After the students have finished reading the text, use flashcards to teach them the alphabet in German. Practice five or six letters at a time; then go on to the next five or six letters. Continue in this way until the class is able to identify most of the letters.

For listening practice, distribute to the students a "secret message," in German, similar to the following one:

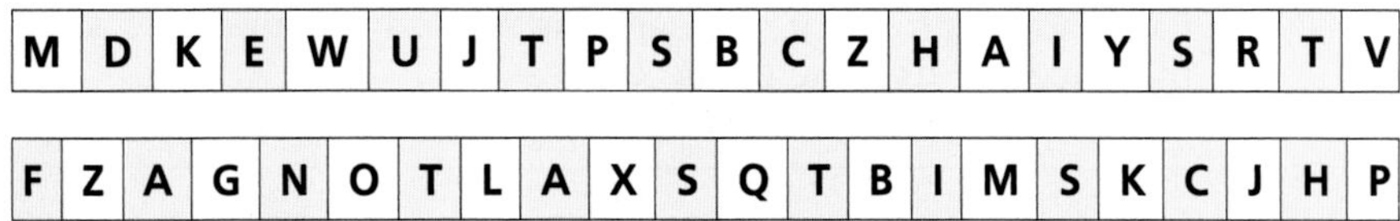

M	D	K	E	W	U	J	T	P	S	B	C	Z	H	A	I	Y	S	R	T	V
F	Z	A	G	N	O	T	L	A	X	S	Q	T	B	I	M	S	K	C	J	H	P

The students should cross out the letters they hear you say in order to find the message. When you have finished, have volunteers say in German which letters remain. Their answers should reveal the message: **Deutsch ist fantastisch.**

Activities

1. On the board or on an overhead transparency, write at random what the abbreviations stand for. Have the class match the abbreviations to the appropriate expressions. (**BMW** = Bayrische Motorenwerke; **VW** = Volkswagen; **dtv** = Deutscher Taschenbuchverlag; **ADAC** = Allgemeiner Deutscher Automobil Club; **BRD** = Bundesrepublik Deutschland; **DDR** = Deutsche Demokratische Republik; **USA** = United States of America; **GmbH** = Gesellschaft mit beschränkter Haftung)
2. Bring to class the items listed or pictures of them. Have the students look at the list and repeat the words after you. Then show them the items or pictures and have the students say the German words for them.

Pages 22–26

5 GERMAN AND YOUR FUTURE CAREER

Before the students read the text, have them think of careers for which German would be useful. List these on the board or on an overhead transparency. Have the students compare the list to what they have learned from reading the text.

Bring in back issues of newspapers from large metropolitan areas. Have the students look through the ads to find jobs that require a knowledge of German. They can then report their findings to the rest of the class.

Activities

Before beginning the second activity, ask several students what careers they are interested in. Their classmates should use their imaginations to suggest how German might be useful for those individuals. Then have the students complete the activity in groups, as instructed.

Pages 27–28

6 SUGGESTIONS FOR STUDYING GERMAN

Ask several students to prepare signs of the words that summarize how to study German. Display the signs in the classroom and refer to them periodically to remind the students of the techniques that can help them learn German.

Some Classroom Phrases

You might construct a language "ladder" in the classroom. Cut out strips of colored paper to make the vertical bars of the ladder and attach them to a wall or bulletin board in the classroom. Write each expression on a narrow strip of colored paper. As you say and act out the expression, show this "rung" to the class; then attach the "rung" to the vertical bars. As the language ladder grows, it will serve as a handy reminder to students when they need to use one of the expressions.

TEACHER–PREPARED MATERIALS

Introduction Maps of Europe, the United States, and the world, product map of German-speaking countries, German magazines and newspapers, letter flashcards, cognate vocabulary objects or pictures mentioned on page 21 (Activity 2), book printed in Gothic type, classified sections of metropolitan newspapers, language ladder

INTRODUCTION

German and You

Welcome to the German-speaking world! During the coming year you will learn to understand, speak, read, and write German in a variety of situations. You will also learn more about the German-speaking world outside your classroom: daily life, customs, traditions, music, art, science, and history. As you begin your travels through the German-speaking world, here's wishing you . . .

Viel Glück!
Good luck!

In this introduction you will learn about:

1 Germany: a pictorial view

2 the German-speaking countries

3 German in the United States

4 German, English, and other languages

5 German and your future career

6 suggestions for studying German

1 GERMANY: A PICTORIAL VIEW

What comes to mind when you think of Germany? Majestic castles along the Rhine? Quaint medieval villages? Fairy tales? The Black Forest? The Alps? Bavarian folk costume? Fast, elegant cars? Scientists? Modern technology? Beethoven? Goethe? Einstein?

Germany is all of these things—some of them just as you imagined, others quite different. But Germany is also images you may not have pictured. The following pages take you on an armchair tour of Germany. It's not the same as being there, of course, but see how these glimpses compare with your image of Germany.

Germany is a land of abundance . . .

and a land of contrasts—mountains and flatlands,

forests and farmlands,

seaports and overland routes.

The country is strongly regional

and busily cosmopolitan,

highly industrialized

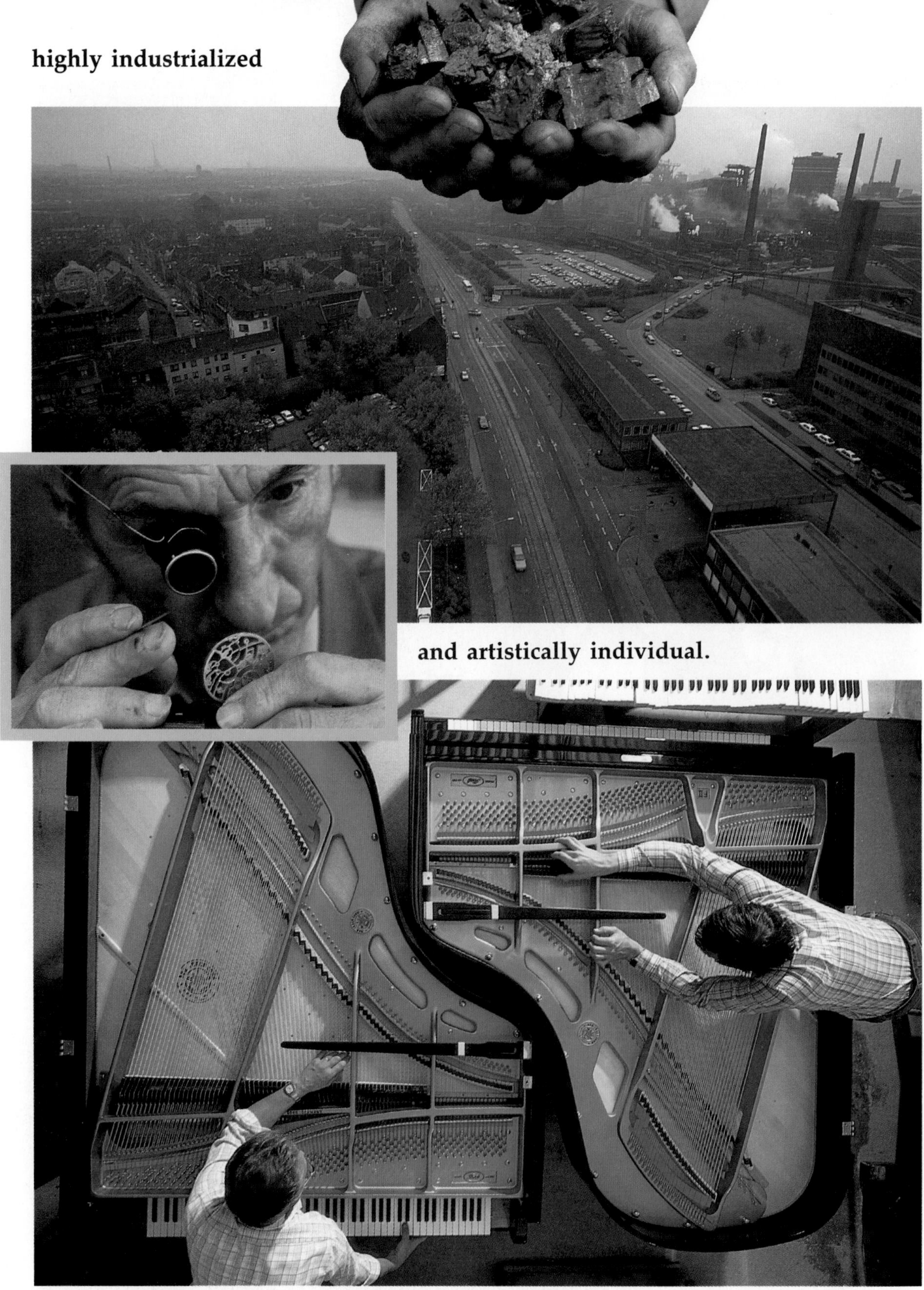

and artistically individual.

There are ordinary stores for everyday things

and elegant stores for luxuries.

Germany is rich in tradition . . .

and rich in innovation.

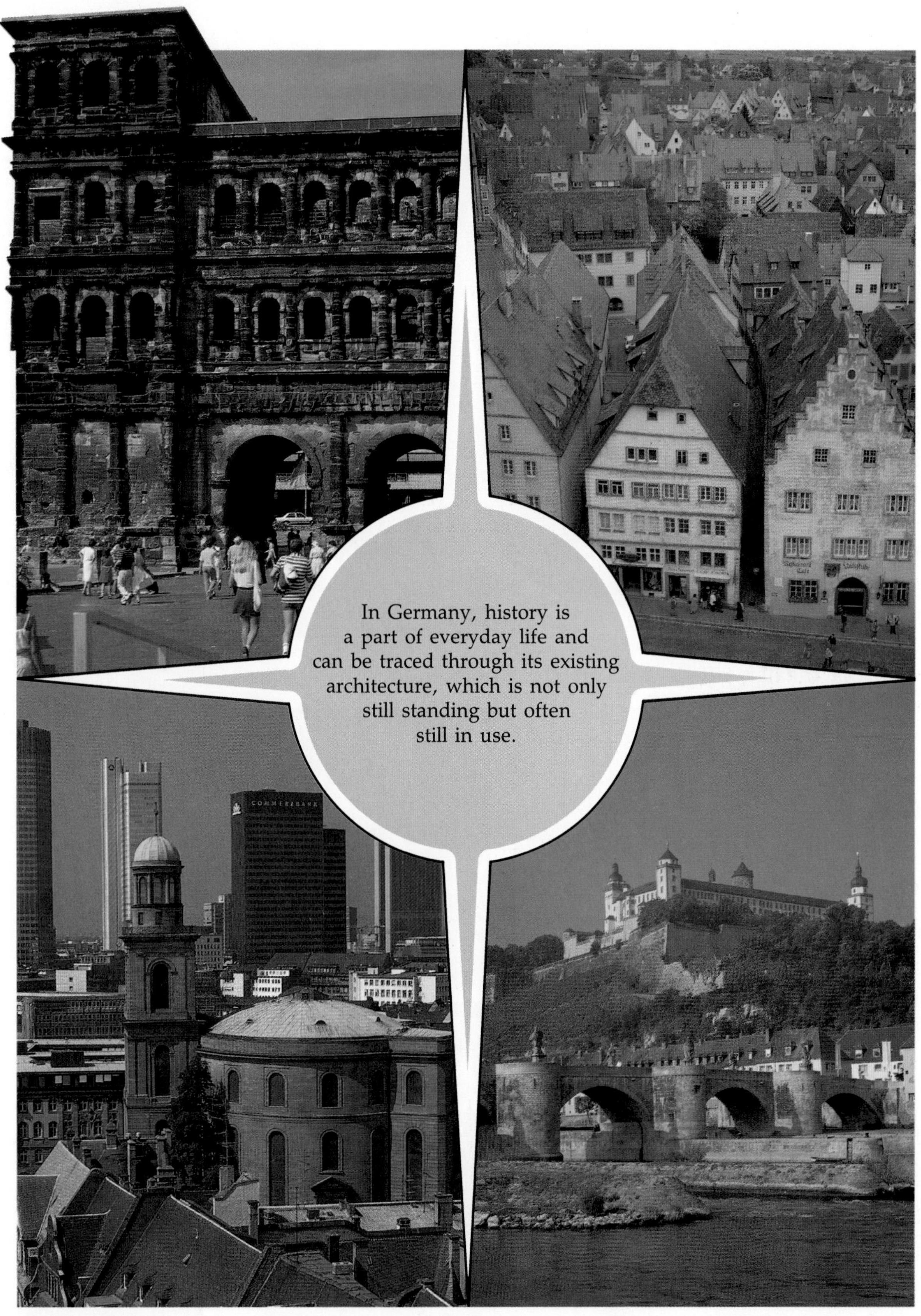

In Germany, history is a part of everyday life and can be traced through its existing architecture, which is not only still standing but often still in use.

Germany has elegant restaurants . . .

and cozy inns;

exciting theater, music, and art . . . both indoors

and outdoors.

And from Germany have come great composers,

J. S. Bach (1685–1750)

Beethoven (1770–1827)

great artists,

Kokoschka (1886–1980)

Dürer (1471–1528)

great poets and writers,

Hesse (1877–1963)

Grass (1927–)

Goethe (1749–1832)

great philosophers,

Kant (1724–1804)

Nietzsche (1844–1900)

great inventors,

Daimler (1834–1900)

Gutenberg (before 1400–1468)

great scientists,

Mössbauer (1929)

Einstein (1879–1955)

great filmmakers

von Trotta

Herzog

as well as great stars.

Brandauer

Dietrich

Schygulla

2 THE GERMAN-SPEAKING COUNTRIES

German is the native language of more than 100 million people in Austria, East and West Germany, Liechtenstein, Switzerland, and parts of France and Italy. It is used as a second language by many others in Central Europe.

For a map of the German-speaking countries turn to page 57.

Bundesrepublik Deutschland

Area: 96,010 sq. mi.
Population: 60.7 million
Monetary unit:
Deutsche Mark
Capital: Bonn

The area of Central Europe historically regarded as Germany was split into two zones of occupation after World War II. The western part of Germany was occupied by Britain, France, and the United States and is known today as the Federal Republic of Germany.

Deutsche Demokratische Republik

Area: 41,767 sq. mi.
Population: 16.7 million
Monetary unit:
Mark of the Deutsche Demokratische Republik
Capital: Berlin (Ost)

The eastern part of Germany was occupied by the Soviet Union after World War II and is known today as the German Democratic Republic. The prewar capital of Germany—Berlin—was also divided into occupation zones after the war. East Berlin is now the capital of the German Democratic Republic; West Berlin is a part of the Federal Republic.

Österreich

Area: 32,375 sq. mi.
Population: 7.6 million
Monetary unit:
Schilling
Capital: Vienna

Austria is just a little larger than the state of South Carolina. Its beautiful mountain scenery, art, and music attract millions of tourists each year. One fifth of the population of Austria lives in the capital city of Vienna.

Schweiz / Suisse / Svizzera

Area: 15,941 sq. mi.
Population: 6.5 million
Monetary unit:
Swiss franc
Capital: Bern

Switzerland is the land of the Alps, famous for its spectacular scenery, luxurious ski resorts, and, of course, Swiss cheese. Switzerland has three official languages: French, Italian, and German. Seventy percent of the population speaks Swiss German or **Schwyzerdütsch.** A fourth language, spoken by about 1 percent of the total population, is called Romansh. It is closely related to Latin and is spoken only in the canton of Graubünden.

Liechtenstein

Area: 61 sq. mi.
Population: 28,000
Monetary unit:
Swiss franc
Capital: Vaduz

Liechtenstein is one of the smallest countries in the world. Its area is less than that of Washington, D.C. Nestled between Germany, Austria, and Switzerland, the principality of Liechtenstein has close ties with Switzerland. The two countries share similar customs. Swiss currency is used in Liechtenstein, and Switzerland operates Liechtenstein's postal, telegraph, and telephone systems. Switzerland also represents Liechtenstein in diplomatic and trade relations.

3 GERMAN IN THE UNITED STATES

ew Yorker

eitung und Herold

art!

DDR: 15 Milliarden für die Volksarmee

Pasteur-Institut testet Aids-Impfstoffe

Can you guess how many Americans trace all or part of their ethnic background to the countries of Germany, Austria, or Switzerland?—5 million? 15 million? 25 million? 50 million? If you guessed 50 million, you are right! According to a recent survey published by the U.S. Census Bureau, 52 million people or 28.8 percent of the total population reported that they were at least partly of German ancestry.

Germans were among the earliest settlers in the United States. On October 6, 1683, a group arrived from Krefeld, Germany, on the *Concord*, a ship that has since been nicknamed the "German Mayflower." They settled in Pennsylvania and founded Germantown. These early settlers quickly established their own schools, print shops, and newspapers. It was a small German newspaper that gave the first report of the Declaration of Independence on July 5, 1776. In fact, German almost became the official language of the United States. The Continental Congress at one point thought of having a new language for this country, and German was considered a good choice for a number of reasons. When it came to a vote, however, English was chosen instead of German by the slim majority of one vote!

Since 1683 more than seven million immigrants from German-speaking regions of Europe have come to the shores of North America. These immigrants influenced the history and development of this country and over the years have made many contributions.

In many parts of the country there are reminders of the role Germans have played in the development of the United States. You can find names of towns and cities such as Hanover, Berlin, and Potsdam. Steubenville, Ohio, was named in honor of Friedrich Wilhelm von Steuben, the German officer who trained George Washington's army. The state where you live may have place names that are German in origin and would be interesting to research.

Baron von Steuben inspecting the squalid conditions at Valley Forge

The trial of John Peter Zenger in New York in 1735. The printer of the *New York Weekly Journal* was accused of criminal libel. He was acquitted, and this precedent established freedom of the press in this country.

German family names are also plentiful in the United States. There are last names such as Klein, Myer (or Meyer, Maier, Meier), and Schneider. Very often German family names indicate occupations (Bauer, *farmer*), places (Berlin or Berliner, *a citizen of Berlin*), or physical descriptions (Kraft, *strong*). If you are interested in tracing the origins of German family names, keep in mind that there may have been changes—for example, Schmidt may have become Smith; Mueller may have turned into Miller.

Many words and phrases contributed by the German immigrants have become part of our everyday language—pumpernickel, noodle, hausfrau, lager beer and bock beer, wienerwurst (often shortened to wiener or wienie), sauerbraten, schnitzel, dachshund, zwieback, delicatessen, kindergarten, and katzenjammer. And don't forget those "typically American" foods such as hamburgers, pretzels, liverwurst, and frankfurters with sauerkraut—all introduced by the Germans.

The Germans who came to the United States brought customs that have become part of our way of life. They introduced the Christmas tree (as well as many Christmas carols), the Easter bunny and Easter egg hunts, county fairs, and more recently, the folk march or Volksmarsch, which has made its appearance in many communities.

And there is a long list of individual Germans who have made invaluable contributions to this country in art and music, science and

Peter Lorre

John Jacob Astor

Levi Strauss

industry, education and politics. From John Peter Zenger to Levi Strauss, from Albert Einstein to Marlene Dietrich, German names appear throughout our history.

Activities

1. See how many German names you and your classmates can find in your local telephone book.
2. Get a map of your state and circle any German place names.
3. Visit your local historical society. Find out about any Germans who may have settled in your area. Historical societies often have documents, correspondence, and sometimes even pictures and memoirs of early settlers.
4. Choose a famous German-American to research in the library and give a short report to the class. As a class project, make a bulletin board display of famous German-Americans. Here are a few suggestions: John Peter Zenger, Friedrich Wilhelm von Steuben, John Jacob Astor, Carl Schurz, Levi Strauss, Leopold Damrosch, Maximilian Berlitz, Charles Steinmetz, Albert Einstein, Mies van der Rohe, Hannah Arendt, Wernher von Braun, Henry Kissinger.
5. As you study German this year, be aware of news about German-speaking countries. You may hear of visits by well-known Germans to the United States. Also, news about sports events, athletes, films, or new German cars may interest you. Keep track of current events in German-speaking countries. Keep a scrapbook with articles and information you find.

4 GERMAN, ENGLISH, AND OTHER LANGUAGES

Kristin ist 14 Jahre alt.

As you look at this German sentence, you may be able to guess its meaning because some words remind you of English. If you guessed "Kristin is fourteen years old," you are right. The verb *ist* is close to the English *is.* If you pronounce *Jahre,* it sounds something like the English *year,* and the German *alt* seems to be related to *old* in some way or other. The explanation for these similarities is that German and English belong to the same family tree. They are both Germanic languages, tracing their roots back to Germanic languages that began to appear in written form as early as the first century B.C.

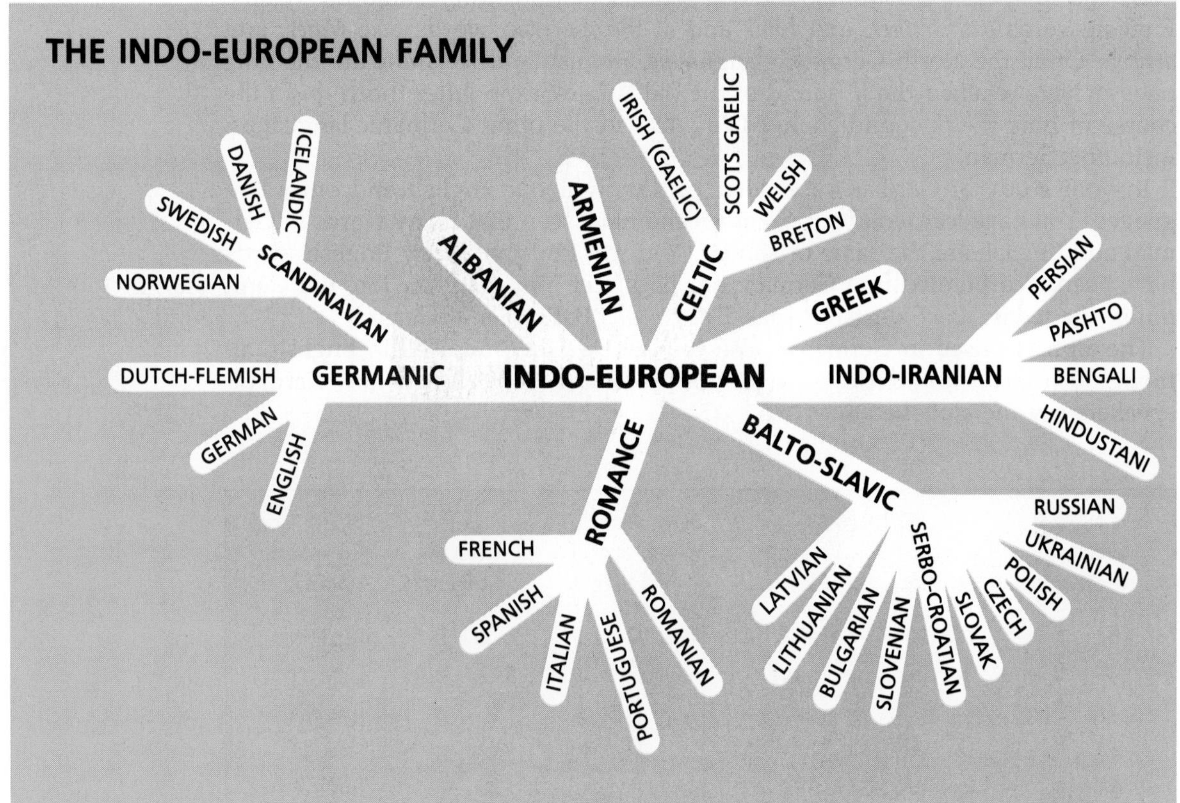

The Indo-European language family is divided into several groups, such as Germanic, Romance, and Balto-Slavic. About half of the people in the world speak a language belonging to this family.

About half the words in English are Germanic in origin. They are basic words in such categories as family, food, farming, parts of the body, and everyday living. See if you can guess the meaning of these German words: Vater, Mutter, Bruder, Milch, Apfel, Finger, Fuss, Hand. Easy! These look-alikes are called *cognates* and may help you particularly when you read German. But be careful of false cognates—words that look like English words but have totally different meanings. A **Teller** in German is a plate and not someone who works in a bank. **Gift** means poison in German, not a present!

German and English are also related to Dutch and to the Dutch-related languages of Flemish and Afrikaans, and also to Danish and the related languages of Norwegian and Swedish. They are all Germanic languages and have many words in common. Compare the following examples:

English	German	Dutch	Danish
bath	Bad	bad	bad
blind	blind	blind	blind
book	Buch	boek	bog
father	Vater	vader	fader
think	denken	denken	taenke

As you compare these words, you will notice something interesting. Look at the English words *bath, father,* and *think* and at the German words *Bad, Vater,* and *denken.* Of all the North Germanic languages, English and Icelandic are the only ones to have retained the *th* sound of the old Anglo-Saxon letter thorn, þ. In the course of time the *th* sound changed to *d* or *t* in the other Germanic languages, including German.

In your study of German, use what you know about English and other languages. You have learned about cognates and have seen that many words in German and English are the same or similar. You will find that many English words have been incorporated into German: der Boss, der Manager, der Job, der Computer, die Jeans, das Sweatshirt, das T-shirt, das Baby, der Teenager.

The alphabet used in German is also the same as the one used in English, although the names of the letters are pronounced differently. Here is how German-speakers say the alphabet:

German Letters	Roman Letters	German Name	German Letters	Roman Letters	German Name
𝕬 𝖆	A a	[ah]	𝕹 𝖓	N n	[en]
𝕭 𝖇	B b	[bay]	𝕺 𝖔	O o	[oh]
𝕮 𝖈	C c	[tsay]	𝕻 𝖕	P p	[pay]
𝕯 𝖉	D d	[day]	𝕼 𝖖	Q q	[koo]
𝕰 𝖊	E e	[ay]	𝕽 𝖗	R r	[air]
𝕱 𝖋	F f	[ef]	𝕾 𝖘	S s	[ess]
𝕲 𝖌	G g	[gay]	𝕿 𝖙	T t	[tay]
𝕳 𝖍	H h	[hah]	𝖀 𝖚	U u	[oo]
𝕴 𝖎	I i	[ee]	𝖁 𝖛	V v	[fow]
𝕵 𝖏	J j	[yot]	𝖂 𝖜	W w	[vay]
𝕶 𝖐	K k	[kah]	𝖃 𝖝	X x	[iks]
𝕷 𝖑	L l	[el]	𝖄 𝖞	Y y	[ipsilon]
𝕸 𝖒	M m	[em]	𝖅 𝖟	Z z	[tset]

As in English, German words can be grouped into word families. Look at the example below. Knowing the key word **Zimmer,** *room,* helps you to remember or to figure out the meaning of other words in the family.

Zimmer *room*	Badezimmer *bathroom*
Wohnzimmer *living room*	im Nebenzimmer *in the next room*
Schlafzimmer *bedroom*	Zimmerpflanze *house plant*
Arbeitszimmer *workroom*	

You will find other similarities between German and English, and you will also find differences. You have probably noticed that all nouns in German are capitalized. You will discover that there are many more endings to verbs, articles, and adjectives in German than there are in English. And word order in German sentences can be quite different. If you try to render a German sentence word for word in English, the results would be quite amusing! As you learn more German, you will become aware of other differences. Comparing these differences with English will help you to understand how both languages operate.

Activities

1. Can you spell aloud—in German—these common acronyms and abbreviations that are used in Germany?

1. BMW	3. dtv	5. BRD	7. USA
2. VW	4. ADAC	6. DDR	8. GmbH

2. Here is a list, in German, of items you can find at home or at school. See how many you can identify just by guessing. You can check your answers in the German-English Vocabulary at the back of this textbook.

1. die Lampe	6. die Tomate	11. die Schokolade
2. das Poster	7. der Joghurt	12. die Milch
3. das Sofa	8. das Telefon	13. die Waschmaschine
4. die Banane	9. das Mathematikbuch	14. der Fotoapparat
5. die Butter	10. das Papier	15. der Kassetten-Recorder

3. Pennsylvania Dutch (Dutch = Deutsch, *German*) is still spoken in the state of Pennsylvania. How it got there in the first place is an interesting story. Track down the history of this German dialect and give a report to the class.

5 GERMAN AND YOUR FUTURE CAREER

Have you ever wondered what you will be doing ten, fifteen, or even twenty years from now? Where you will be living and working? What kind of job you will have? For many jobs it is very helpful to know a foreign language such as German, and for some it is essential. Teachers of German must be fluent in the language and also know a great deal about the culture of German-speaking countries. They travel and study abroad or sometimes teach for a year in schools in Germany, Austria, or Switzerland to expand their knowledge. In addition, they must keep up with advances in educational technology such as microcomputers.

Interpreters of German, Spanish, and French translate speeches at the United Nations and at large international conferences. Interpreters must be able to think quickly in two languages.

Translators have to know not only the German language, but also the culture. Translators of literature need to study the author's background and style. Translators are also needed to prepare the subtitles or dubbing in English for German films shown in the United States.

Translators and interpreters at the United Nations are required to know at least two foreign languages.

These students are learning German in a language lab.

Most libraries have a foreign language section, and the knowledge of a foreign language can be most useful for a librarian.

Librarians find it very useful to know more than one language. And in the field of publishing, writers and editors use foreign language skills to produce teaching materials and textbooks like this one.

A knowledge of German can be an asset in many occupations and professions. Interested in a career in business? Over 25,000 companies in the United States are engaged in the export business and hire managers, shipping clerks, and specialists in export traffic. In addition, there are more than 500 large American companies based abroad: large manufacturing firms, major petroleum companies, banks, and engineering firms. These businesses employ more than 100,000 Americans overseas. German is particularly useful in technological fields. Many high-tech companies name German as the language they would prefer prospective employees to have studied.

Many German companies now have branches in the United States. They hire managers and other employees who speak German. Many American firms deal with companies in the German-speaking countries and need personnel who know German.

Buyers for large department stores and small specialty shops travel abroad to select merchandise—from clothing to fine china, from sports equipment to toys. German is needed not only to do business in the foreign country, but also to read catalogues, correspondence, and other documents.

People who work in the food industry often have to travel to foreign countries, where they sample and buy local products and are in close contact with local merchants. Chefs may train abroad. Food and travel writers visit restaurants and collect recipes.

Many highly skilled professionals find foreign languages an asset. Economists sometimes deal with foreign countries. Financial experts may work in the international commodity and money markets. Lawyers and paralegals who specialize in international law or handle cases or conduct negotiations with companies in German-speaking countries must know German. Legal translators are also very much in demand.

Reporters, including sportswriters and sportscasters, can do a much better job if they can speak the language of the country where they are working and can also understand its culture.

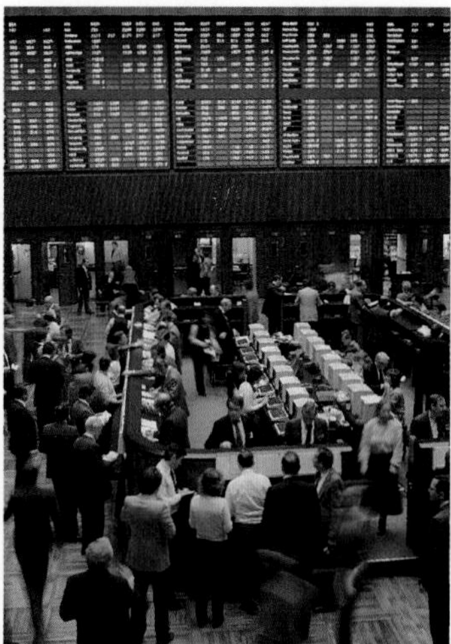

Knowledge of a foreign language can be of great advantage on the stock exchange.

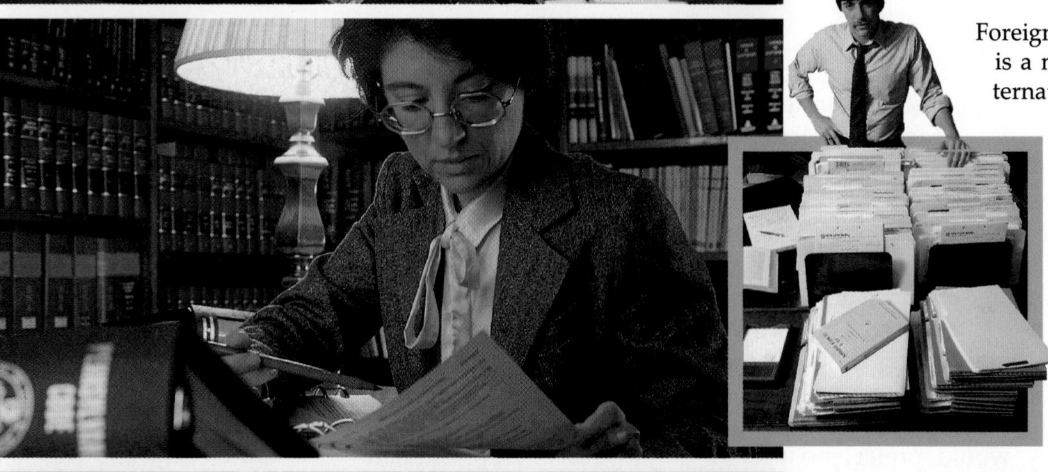

Foreign language is a must in international law.

Foreign correspondents need to know a foreign language to have first-hand knowledge about events.

Germany has many regional orchestras and opera companies, and young musicians often get experience playing and singing with them. A thorough knowledge of German and excellent pronunciation skills are essential for an opera singer who will sing roles in German.

A career with the U.S. government in the foreign service, with the diplomatic corps, or with the U.S. information services in foreign countries is an interesting way to use your foreign language ability.

Tourists from all over the world visit the United States. Travel agents, flight attendants, tour guides, salespeople in stores, desk clerks in hotels, waiters and waitresses in restaurants—anyone who deals with foreign travelers—should know more than one language.

To work in a foreign country you need to know the native language.

Opera singers sing roles in many languages.

Two foreign languages are required for international flight attendants.

Activities

1. Before you make your career choice, it is wise to talk to as many people as you can about their jobs—what they actually do, and what they like and don't like about their work. Find some people in your family, school, or neighborhood who use German in their work. Interview them, asking them to describe their jobs and to answer the following questions and others you might think of.

1. What do you like best about your job? What do you like least about it?
2. How do you use German in your work?
3. How did you prepare for your job? What types of German courses did you take?
4. Do you travel as part of your job?

Write up the interview or record it to share with the class.

2. Who are the people listed below and why are they speaking German? Work in a group of two or three students. Think of as many reasons as you can why German would be useful in the jobs listed. Take notes on your ideas and report to the class. Write up your notes to post on the bulletin board. Write an imaginary interview with one of these people.

salesperson in a bookstore	museum director
soccer coach	radio announcer
auto mechanic	travel agent
pilot	waiter or waitress
aerospace engineer	librarian
research scientist	reporter

3. Choose an occupation that you might be interested in. Write a paragraph telling why you are interested in this particular occupation and how German might be of help to you in that field. Attach a picture of someone in that field if you can find one in a newspaper or magazine.

Help Wanted 2600
BILINGUAL FEE PAID

Interlangue

GERMAN

MUSIC To $35,000
Ability to work independently & attention to detail nec as exec secy for int'l div Pres. Skills in Engl. Benefits.

FINANCE $30-35
Office administrator for int'l ment concern. Skills in English. organizational abilities nec. Ben

CULTURAL $30
Asst SR exec at mjr int'l corp both, ability to prioritize. Proje

LEGAL To
Midtown/downtown locatior for legal secretavy. Skills in ly. Fantastic benefits, bonus

JOURNALISM $
Bureau chief of major co cy. Diverse duties. Great involved in all aspects. Ex

INT'L BANK $
No steno necessary. To dept of major Europ train WP. Excellent ber

4 DAY WK
Export co sks admin V.P. Skills in Engl only

GERMAN-ENGL GUY-GAL
for smaller newspaper, full or time, W 72 St area. Call between 1 PM, 212-873-7400.

GERMAN/ENGL Fee Paid to $3
See our ad under "BILINGUAL
CALL 687-6335
William Harris Assoc 17 E 45 St. NY

German/Eng Secy $425
PRESTIGIOUS CO
PILOT, 198 Bway, rm 300 962-1430

BILINGUAL

GERMAN/ENGLISH RECEPTIONIST
To $18,000
Prestigious bank, located in midtn. needs to hire an expd recpt. Lite typing; excell benefits. For appt, please call / 212-682-5530.

GERMAN

Exec secy.CEO int'l co	to $35,000
Personal private secy	$30,000
Secy.Charming corp atty	$28,600
Secy.US corp+ 13% bonus	$27,000

Flight Attendants

SPRECHEN SIE DEUTSCH

Parlez-vous Français?

¿HABLA USTED ESPAÑOL?

日本語ができる。*

*"Do you speak German, French, Spanish or Japanese" or do you know someone who speaks German, French, Spanish or Japanese?

American Airlines offers you the opportunity to be someone special while working for a company where excellence is the standard. If ensuring customer satisfaction and working varied schedules appeal to you, we have what you're looking for. We presently have Flight Attendant positions available. Listed below are our minimum qualifications.

American Airlines, Inc.
Flight Service Recruitment, Dept. NYT-0287
P.O. Box 619410, Mail Drop 908
Dallas/Fort Worth Airport, TX 75261-9410

AmericanAirlines
An Equal Opportunity Employer

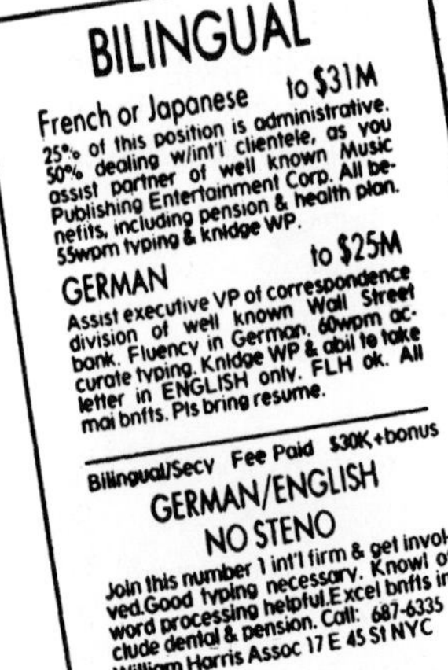

BILINGUAL

French or Japanese to $31M
25% of this position is administrative. 50% dealing w/int'l clientele, as you assist partner of well known Music Publishing Entertainment Corp. All benefits, including pension & health plan. 55wpm typing & knldge WP.

GERMAN to $25M
Assist executive VP of correspondence division of well known Wall Street bank. Fluency in German. 60wpm accurate typing. Knldge WP & abil to take letter in ENGLISH only. FLH ok. All mai bnfts. Pls bring resume.

Bilingual/Secy Fee Paid $30K+bonus
GERMAN/ENGLISH
NO STENO
Join this number 1 int'l firm & get involved. Good typing necessary. Knowl of word processing helpful. Excel bnfts include dental & pension. Call: 687-6335
William Harris Assoc 17 E 45 St NYC

ASSOCIATE SALES MANAGER

International Sales

Prominent periodical distribution organization offers a promising, challenging growth opportunity to an energetic, career-motivated sales achiever. Initial assignment will emphasize sales administration functions. The successful candidate will get involved in the planning, development and implementation of export distribution programs, preparation of new business proposals and travel to meet with our overseas wholesalers. We seek a candidate with proven sales ability, strong writing skills, and the desire to move ahead. Marketing degree preferred, knowledge of French or German an asset. Salary $21-$25,000 plus comprehensive company paid benefits package. Send resume including salary history in confidence to **T 7213 TIMES 10108.**

6 SUGGESTIONS FOR STUDYING GERMAN

LISTEN

Listening is particularly important at the beginning because you have to get used to a whole new set of sounds. Sometimes you will need to listen very carefully to understand what is being said to you, so that you can answer in German.

PRACTICE

Learning German—or any foreign language—is like learning to play a musical instrument. You have to practice speaking, listening, reading, and writing in order to make progress. You already have these skills in English. Now you have to apply them to a new language. Practice a little every day. Several short periods are more effective than one long, last-minute cramming session.

VISUALIZE

Remembering German vocabulary is easier if you visualize what a sentence, phrase, or word means as you're studying or practicing it, orally or in writing. For example, if you're practicing a sentence like *Die Kinder schwimmen,* try to picture children swimming as you say the sentence to yourself several times.

CONNECT

Make use of your English connections. Find cognates or near-cognates (schwimmen, *to swim;* Garten, *garden;* Wasser, *water*) to help you understand the meaning of a sentence or paragraph that you are reading. Also, group German words into families to help you remember—for example, Freund, *friend;* Freundschaft, *friendship;* freundlich, *friendly.*

ORGANIZE

Use memory devices. Look for ways to organize the material you have to learn. Invent a system to help you remember a word or concept. Group vocabulary in meaningful segments. Put words in context and learn phrases rather than isolated words. Your teacher will help you to recognize patterns and devices that will make learning easier.

EXPAND

Use German outside class. Speak German—perhaps on the phone—with friends who are also studying the language. Find people in your family or in the neighborhood who know some German and practice with them. Talk into your cassette recorder in German. If you have a shortwave radio, try to pick up German-language broadcasts. Look at German magazines, newspapers, and books—you may not understand much at first, but it will get easier.

ENJOY

You may want to choose a new name in German. Join the German Club and make new friends. If there are any German-speaking exchange students in the area, make a point of meeting them and making them feel welcome. Above all, don't be afraid to make mistakes in German! Concentrate on getting your message across and have fun doing it.

SOME CLASSROOM PHRASES

Your teacher will be using German to give routine directions in the classroom. Here are a few phrases that you should recognize.

Hör(t) zu, bitte!	*Please listen.*
Sprich (sprecht) nach!	*Repeat after me.*
Noch mal!	*Again! Say it again!*
Antworte(t), bitte!	*Please answer.*
Steh(t) auf!	*Get up.*
Setz dich! (to one person) Setzt euch! (to more than one person)	*Sit down.*
Nimm (nehmt) ein Blatt Papier!	*Take out a piece of paper.*
Ruhe, bitte!	*Quiet, please.*
Pass(t) auf!	*Pay attention.*
Das ist richtig.	*That's right.*
Gut! Prima!	*Good.*

ERSTER TEIL

As school begins, young people greet one another and then say goodbye as they go off to their classes. You are introduced to five students from German-speaking countries: Jens Kröger and Wiebke Nedel from the Federal Republic of Germany, Kurt Langer from the German Democratic Republic, Bruno Schmidlin from Switzerland, and Margit Dastl from Austria.

Your new friends from Unit 1 tell how they get to school. Two friends go shopping for school supplies. Jens Kröger shows you his class schedule and tells what subjects he has—on what day and at what time. Students discuss grades, commenting on how they have done. You also get a look at a German report card and find out about the grading system in German schools.

What are your favorite sports and hobbies? Your new friends discuss what they like and what they don't like. They tell what sports they take part in and how often, for each season of the year. A survey sheet filled out by a German student lists his favorite sports and activities as well as those he likes less or doesn't like at all.

Many German schools have a school newspaper. You will read an excerpt from one of them. There is a feature article about a class in which many students have English-speaking pen pals. The excerpt includes jokes, cartoons, and ads.

KAPITEL 1

KAPITEL 1 Neue Freunde

Scope and Sequence

	BASIC MATERIAL	COMMUNICATIVE FUNCTIONS
SECTION A	**Guten Tag! Auf Wiedersehen! (A1)** **Herr, Frau, Fräulein (A5)**	**Socializing** • Saying hello and goodbye • Greeting adults
SECTION B	**Wie heisst du? (B1)** **Wie heisst der Junge? Wie heisst das Mädchen? (B3)** **Wer ist das? (B8)**	**Exchanging information** • Asking and giving names • Asking who someone is
SECTION C	**Wie alt bist du? (C1)** **Die Zahlen von 0 bis 20 (C3)**	**Exchanging information** • Asking someone's age and telling yours **Counting** • Learning the numbers from 0 to 20
SECTION D	**Woher bist du? (D1)** **Ja oder nein? (D7)** **Wie bitte? (D13)** **Wie heissen Sie? Woher sind Sie? (D16)**	**Exchanging information** • Asking where someone else is from and telling where you're from • Saying you don't understand and asking for clarification
TRY YOUR SKILLS	Pronunciation **ich-**sound, **ach-**sound, /l/ Letter-sound correspondences **ch, l, w, z** Dictation	
ZUM LESEN	**Wo ist Deutschland?** (a description of Germany's location in Europe) **Postkarten** (postcards from German-speaking countries)	

WRITING A variety of controlled and open-ended writing activities appear in the Pupil's Edition. The Teacher's Notes identify other activities suitable for writing practice and suggest additional writing activities.

COOPERATIVE LEARNING Many of the activities in the Pupil's Edition lend themselves to cooperative learning. The Teacher's Notes explain some of the many instances where this teaching strategy can be particularly effective. For guidelines on how to use cooperative learning, see page T13.

GRAMMAR	CULTURE	RE–ENTRY
	Popular first names of boys and girls Meeting and greeting people	
The definite articles **der, die, das** (B11)	German family names and German names in the United States	First names of boys and girls
The personal pronouns and the verb **sein** (C8)	How numerals are written and how they are signaled by hand	Telling your name and age
Asking and answering questions (D8)	A map of the German-speaking countries showing where our friends live Using the **Sie**-form	Asking and telling someone's name
Recombining communicative functions, grammar, and vocabulary		
Reading for practice and pleasure		

TEACHER–PREPARED MATERIALS

Section A Flashcards with greetings and farewells
Section B Pictures of well-known people; phone book pages with German names
Section C Wall map of German-speaking countries
Zum Lesen Wall map of Western Europe; postcards from German-speaking countries

UNIT RESOURCES

Übungsheft, Unit 1
Arbeitsheft, Unit 1
Unit 1 Cassettes
Transparencies 1–4
Quizzes 1–4
Unit 1 Test

A1–2

OBJECTIVES **To socialize:** say hello and say goodbye; greet adults

CULTURAL BACKGROUND Germans insist on a greater degree of formality than Americans do. In the United States, adults may be on a first-name basis immediately. In Germany, adults who have known one another for 30 years may still be on **Sie**-terms. Come back to this point when you cover **Sie.**

The emblems shown on page 31 are those of the four German-speaking countries: the Federal Republic of Germany, the German Democratic Republic, Austria, and Switzerland.

MOTIVATING ACTIVITY Before starting on Section A, have the students list all the ways we greet one another in English and the ways we take leave of one another. Remind them to think of formal and informal expressions, of long forms and of short forms. See how many expressions they can think of. Put all suggestions on an overhead transparency or on the blackboard. Ask the students to come up with contexts for the various expressions: where might an informal expression be appropriate? A formal one?

Tell students that in German, too, there are many different ways of greeting people and of saying goodbye. They will learn the most common expressions—those that teenagers use with one another and the more formal expressions they would use with adults.

A1

Guten Tag! Auf Wiedersehen! 

Play the cassette once through or read the text aloud to introduce the three exchanges of greetings. At this point, students should just listen with their books closed. Repeat. Then, with books open, have the students listen to the cassette or to your reading of the text once more. Say the greetings in the first of the exchanges **(Steffi** and **Andreas).** Have the students repeat each phrase after you. When they can say each phrase reasonably well, turn the exchange into a dialog: you take one part and the students take the other. Repeat; then reverse roles. Follow the same procedure for the second and third sets of greetings.

Follow the same procedure for the leave-taking expressions. You may want to present the leave-taking expressions on another day, unless the students are still highly motivated.

CHALLENGE Have the students use greetings taken from one set with responses taken from another set: for example, one student might say **Tag!** and the other answer with **Hallo!** They should use their own names for this, unless they have already chosen a German name for the classroom.

SLOWER–PACED LEARNING For these students, you might put off one of the sets of greetings until the next day. You might also consider introducing *one* set of greetings coupled with *one* set of farewells at a time. However, do not leave the students with the impression that any one set of farewells must always be used with the same set of greetings.

A2

Übung

If you are planning to use German first names in the classroom, either A2 or A4 is a good place to introduce the idea. You might want to have a longer list of names on hand than the one provided in A4, especially if you have a large class. Currently popular names should predominate on your list, but include a few more traditional ones. Some other currently popular names are **Christian, Katharina,** and—surprise!—**Jennifer** and **Patrick.**

There are several advantages to having the students assume German names: names have cultural immediacy, and the German-speaking world will become real to your students from the outset. It's fun for students to assume a new identity—one that they have chosen themselves. Also, they won't have to break the flow of German sounds when speaking to one another. Finally, they can learn the German sound system in an effortless way. Stress names containing sounds that don't exist in English or that students find difficult for some other reason: /ü/, **Jürgen;** /x/, **Jochen;** /ʃt/, **Steffi.**

A3 WIE SAGT MAN DAS?

Remind the students of the motivating activity, in which they talked about kinds of greetings and farewells. Ask them to suggest appropriate situations for each of the greetings on the chart: in which situation would it be appropriate to say **Tag?** Which greeting or farewell might you use to an older person who is not a family member?

A4 Ein wenig Landeskunde

Ask the students to contrast the German first names with their English equivalents, where appropriate. This will give them a good introduction to German letter-sound correspondences. Ask them to put the names into three categories:

1. *Names that have equivalents or near-equivalents in English.* Have the students pronounce them, concentrating on the differences in sound and stress. Ask also what differences in spelling they notice. (Examples: **Stefan**/Steven, **Markus**/Marcus)
2. *Names that have no equivalent in English.* These are often easier for students to pronounce, because there is no interference from English. (Examples: **Antje, Silke**)
3. *Names that are of French origin.* These are written the same way and pronounced more or less the same way in German as in English. (Example: **Nicole**)

Students may need help from you on some of the names. They will not always recognize which names are of French origin; and the English equivalent of **Ulrike**—Ulrica—is comparatively rare. If any of your students are also taking French, call on them to help.

CHALLENGE Ask the students to find the full names of at least five famous German or Austrian composers. Put them on an overhead transparency or on the board. Have the class pronounce the names. Some examples are: **Johann Sebastian Bach, Georg Friedrich Händel, Wolfgang Amadeus Mozart,** and **Richard Wagner.**

As a variation, ask for the names of five famous German scientists or inventors.

A5 HERR, FRAU, FRÄULEIN

Follow the procedures suggested in A1 for using the cassette. Work especially on the pronunciation of **Fräulein.** Since only three words are new, the application should be almost immediate. Ask the students to identify the phrases used by the young people to greet adults (formal). Ask what the adults use (informal).

Have each student adopt a German last name from the list given below unless the student's last name is already German. Have the students print

A6–9

"their" German names on a card and hold it up. Go around the class modeling each name with its title. Have the students repeat after you: **Fräulein Müller, Herr Schmidt,** etc. Some common German last names follow:

Arendt	Erhardt	Huber	Lempke	Radler	Tillman
Bollman	Fiedler	Jost	Meier	Schmidt	Weiland
Braun	Grossmann	Krämer	Müller	Schulz	Zimmerman

Greet several students, using their titles: **Guten Tag, Herr/Fräulein . . .** The students should respond using your title and name. Then have the students pair off and greet each other formally using their names and the title of **Herr** or **Fräulein.** They should also say goodbye. They then choose a new partner and start all over. Repeat this several times.

A6 Übung • Jetzt bist du dran

As a variation, the students can role-play the people pictured. You might have them work in groups of three to five. Remind them to use the more formal greetings or farewells when addressing an "adult" and the less formal wordings when they are addressing a student.

A7 WIE SAGT MAN DAS?

Call attention to **Tag, Frau Meier!** Emphasize that you must be on comparatively familiar terms with an adult to use this informal form in conjunction with the title **Herr, Frau,** etc.

A8 Ein wenig Landeskunde

Have the students form groups of five. Tell them they are at a party in Germany. It is evening. One of them plays the host, one plays a new friend of the host, and the others play old friends. The host introduces the new friend to the others, saying **Das ist . . . und das ist . . .** Have them greet each other and shake hands. Have the students switch roles so that each one in turn gets to be host and newcomer. Ask them to vary their greetings and include **Guten Abend!** and **Abend!**

Then tell them the party is over. Practice **Danke für die Party!** and **Danke schön** with them. One of the students in each group should play the mother or father of the host. Have each student thank the host and the host's mother or father, say goodbye, and politely shake hands.

A9 Übung • Hör gut zu!

Play the cassette or read the following listening comprehension activity aloud.

You will hear nine hellos or goodbyes. Listen carefully and decide whether each hello or goodbye you hear addresses a male teacher, a female teacher, or a student. For each statement you hear, place your check mark in the appropriate column. For example, you hear: **Guten Morgen, Fräulein Braun!** You place your check mark in the column labeled *a female teacher*. Let's begin. **Fangen wir an!**

1. Grüss dich! *a student*
2. Auf Wiedersehen, Herr Kaiser! *a male teacher*
3. Guten Morgen, Herr Meier! *a male teacher*
4. Hallo, Karin! *a student*

5. Guten Tag, Frau Müller! *a female teacher*
6. Tschau, Silke! *a student*
7. Tschüs, Michael! *a student*
8. Wiedersehen, Herr Walden! *a male teacher*
9. Morgen, Fräulein Hofer! *a female teacher*

Now check your answers. *Read each item again and give the correct answer.*

A 10 Übung • Jetzt bist du dran

As a variation, call out names and have the students, individually or as a class, respond with an appropriate greeting. The names can be invented: **Herr Brückmann, Renate, Fräulein Müller, Walter.**

A 11 Schreibübung

For additional writing practice, play the spelling game Wheel of Fortune. Its purpose is to help the students learn the spelling of German words through visualizing the letters. Since the students are just beginning the language, at least two clues per word should be provided unless the words are short.

Divide the class into two teams. Their books should be closed. Have the incomplete words on an overhead transparency or a chart. Uncover one word at a time. Team A takes a guess at the first word. If right, team A can then take a guess at the second word. If wrong, team B gets a chance to guess the first word. If team B is also wrong, you provide an additional clue. Some sample words follow:

_s___u   __a_   t____s   __g
__r__n   _u_ _i_d___e__n   _r_s_   _e__

OBJECTIVE **To exchange information:** ask and give names; ask who someone is

CULTURAL BACKGROUND When adults introduce themselves to one another in German, they are usually quite formal. They may, in fact, just give the last name **(„Meier“ — „Balcke“),** accompanied by a handshake and a quick nod of the head.

MOTIVATING ACTIVITY Ask the students to list the different ways they introduce themselves in English to someone of their own age and ask for that person's name. They will probably come up with these possibilities:

Hi, my name is ____. What's yours?
Hi, I'm ____. Who are you?

Tell students that the most common way in German for young people to introduce themselves and ask for someone else's name is the first one. However, the German phrases used are not directly equivalent to the English. Remind students that they should give equivalents rather than translate. They should always ask themselves, "What do German-speaking people say in this situation?"

B 1 Wie heisst du?

When introducing new material to the class, it is a good idea to play the cassette several times with books closed so that the students can concentrate on

B2–7

listening to the new language patterns as they are spoken in natural exchanges. The language on the cassette has just the right pronunciation, intonation, and inflection for the particular situation depicted. If the cassettes are not available to you, you should model the new patterns yourself, playing both roles. After the students have heard the new material several times, explain the new vocabulary as necessary.

B2 Übung • Jetzt bist du dran

If you are using German names in the classroom, the students should use those names for this and subsequent activities. Expand on this activity by asking the students to respond to anything you say with an appropriate phrase, statement, or question. Rejoinders of this kind work well as warm-ups at the beginning of class or as a change of pace during class. You can also use them for oral or written quizzes or for homework. Try these:

1. Tschüs!
2. Wie heisst du?
3. Das ist Michael.
4. Guten Abend!
5. Wiedersehen, Klasse!

SLOWER–PACED LEARNING Prepare a longer list of items similar to those above, to be done as written homework. Ask for one answer to each item.

CHALLENGE Prepare the same list as above, but ask for two or more rejoinders to each stimulus. This also may be done as written homework.
Example: *Das ist Michael.* Guten Tag, Michael.
Wie heisst er?

B3 WIE HEISST DER JUNGE? DAS MÄDCHEN? 

Follow the steps previously suggested for the presentation of new material. In particular, work on reproducing the dialog without books. You take one role and the class takes the other.

B4 Übung • Wie heisst er? Wie heisst sie? 

After you have played the cassette or modeled the questions and answers several times, have the students work in groups of three. Each student represents one of the characters shown. "Ulrike" asks "Lars," referring to "Natalie," **Wie heisst sie?** "Lars" replies, **Sie heisst Natalie,** and so on.

B5 WIE SAGT MAN DAS?

As an informal drill, go around the classroom asking students for their own names or for that of a classmate. Increase your speed; see how quickly the students can come up with the proper response. Students usually enjoy these rapid-fire drills.

B6 Übung • Partnerarbeit

CHALLENGE The students may vary their responses, answering either with **Er heisst Jochen** or **Das ist der Jochen.**

B7 Schreibübung • Wie heissen deine Mitschüler?

As a variation, put the following scrambled dialog on the board or on an overhead transparency and have the students rewrite it in a logical order. Variations are possible. This may be assigned as written homework.

Und wie heisst er?	Guten Tag!	Er heisst Peter.	Ich heisse Andreas.
Ich heisse Mark.	Und sie?	Wie heisst du?	Sie heisst Natalie.

B8 WER IST DAS?

Introduce the new material in the same manner as previously. Then put several names on an overhead transparency or on the board: **Sabine, Stefan, Michael, Silke, Kirsten,** and **Monika.** Tell the students that they are going to role-play bringing their mothers to an activity at school. Each mother will meet some of the friends she has heard about. Have each student point out friends to his or her mother. Then have them point out the German teacher.

Now your students introduce their mothers to each one of the friends and to the German teacher:

STUDENT Mutti, das ist die Sabine.
MUTTER Tag, Sabine!

B9 WIE SAGT MAN DAS?

Point out that **der** or **die** in front of a name is an informal usage. Also point out to the students that the translation given for **Das ist die Sabine,** for example, is simply *That's Sabine.*

B10 Übung • Jetzt bist du dran

This can be done first as an exercise involving the whole class and then in pairs or small groups. Use the students' German classroom names.

B11 ERKLÄRUNG

The students will probably be surprised that the word for *girl* is neuter. Explain that this is because of the ending, **-chen,** and that they will learn more about it in future lessons.

CHALLENGE See if the students can guess what these people do for a living. All the professions have something to do with school.

der Lehrer	der Rektor	der Hausmeister
der Schüler	der Sekretär	der Busfahrer

Then have them look at the pattern in B11 and see if they can make these masculine nouns feminine.

B12 Schreibübung

You can expand this activity by having the students write answers for the questions and questions for the statements: **Die Lehrerin heisst Meier. — Wie heisst die Lehrerin?** Point out that this usage—last name only—is not disrespectful in the context.

B13 Übung • Ein Spiel

Even in high school, students love games—especially those with a competitive element! If you are going to use the students' German names for this, and you will probably want to, they should have become sufficiently well established that the students will have a fair chance.

B14 Übung • Hör gut zu!

Play the cassette or read the text aloud.

KAPITEL 1

B15–16

You will hear the question **Wer ist das?** and an answer that may refer to a boy or a man or to a girl or a woman. For example, you will hear, **Wer ist das?** and the answer, **Das ist Herr Meier.** Place your check mark in the column labeled *refers to a boy or a man,* because the answer you heard refers to a man. Let's begin. **Fangen wir an!**

1. Wer ist das? — Das ist die Katrin. *refers to a girl*
2. Wer ist das? — Das ist die Lehrerin. *refers to a woman*
3. Wer ist das? — Das ist Herr Seifert. *refers to a man*
4. Wer ist das? — Das ist Fräulein Müller. *refers to a woman*
5. Wer ist das? — Das ist der Junge. *refers to a boy*
6. Wer ist das? — Das ist der Lehrer. *refers to a man*
7. Wer ist das? — Das ist das Mädchen, die Silke. *refers to a girl*
8. Wer ist das? — Das ist der Deutschlehrer, Herr Stefan. *refers to a man*

Now check your answers. *Read each item again and give the correct answer.*

B 15 Übung • Ratespiel: Wer ist das?

As the students will probably not yet recognize many prominent German personalities of past or present, this will inevitably involve switching to English in mid-sentence. However, you might prepare them a day or so ahead by introducing some of the personalities in the Introduction (pages 11–13) with their full names—**Günter Grass** and **Hanna Schygulla,** for example—and making sure that they can pronounce the names of such well-known personalities as **Marlene Dietrich, Albert Einstein,** and **Johann Sebastian Bach** in German.

B 16 Ein wenig Landeskunde

CHALLENGE Have the students find out how these common German last names originated. Ask them to give a brief possible explanation in English for each one.

1. Klein
2. Grossmann
3. Schneider
4. Müller
5. Schmidt
6. Zimmermann
7. Meier
8. Freund
9. Sperling
10. Seifert
11. Kurtz
12. Jäger

SECTION C

OBJECTIVES **To exchange information:** ask someone's age and tell your age; **to count:** learn the numbers from 0 to 20

CULTURAL BACKGROUND In Germany, as in other European countries, dates are given in the order day/month/year. This causes endless confusion for Germans and other Europeans filling out forms in the United States—most people don't look to see if a blank specifies *day* or *month,* so they will automatically write a birthdate as 22-9-70 rather than 9-22-70.

MOTIVATING ACTIVITY Show your students some samples of German dating style. You might prepare a fragment of a typical "official" form on hand—an airplane landing card would do. You could also show them samples of the dateline on correspondence, using actual letters, if you have them (otherwise prepare some). Show the variations: 8-9-88; Hamburg, den 8. 9. 1988. Ask them which is the month.

C1

Wie alt bist du? 

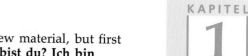

Follow the steps previously suggested for introducing new material, but first do the first set of questions and answers only. **(Wie alt bist du? Ich bin dreizehn Jahre alt.)** Teach the numbers from 0 to 20. Work especially with the numbers 13–16, so that the students will be able to give their own ages. Teach the numbers as part of the phrase **Ich bin ______. Then add the question Wie alt bist du?** Allow the students to answer with the short form or the long form: **Ich bin vierzehn (Jahre alt).**

Then introduce the second and third sets of questions and answers in C1, asking the ages of other students. Apply the new phrases to individual students. Ask them, **Wie alt bist du?** After a student answers, immediately ask the class, **Wie alt ist er (sie)?**

C2

Übung • Wie alt sind die Jungen und Mädchen?

The students may need extra work on the plural form. Ask, **Wie alt ist der Jochen? Wie alt ist die Ulrike? Wie alt sind Jochen and Ulrike?** Have sets of pictures of other young people ready. Ask the same type of question. Point to students of the same age and ask questions about each one of them and about both of them. As you model, slip in the word **auch** in such a manner that it will become clear from context. Have the students respond with **auch.**

> Stefan ist vierzehn. Und Michael? —Er ist auch vierzehn.
> Gisela ist fünfzehn. Und du?

C3

DIE ZAHLEN VON 0 BIS 20

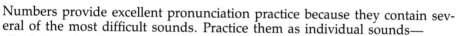

Numbers provide excellent pronunciation practice because they contain several of the most difficult sounds. Practice them as individual sounds—

> /ts/ zwei, zehn, zwölf — /ç/ sechzehn — /ks/ sechs
> /ai/ eins, zwei, drei — /l/ elf, zwölf, null
> /x/ acht, achtzehn — /ü/ fünf, fünfzehn

—and as pairs:

> zwei und zwölf — sechs und sechzehn
> vier und vierzehn — sieben und siebzehn

C4

Ein wenig Landeskunde

Have the students practice writing numbers in the German style. You might have them write numbers this way on all papers for your class. They could also date their papers in the German manner: 17 September or 17. September instead of September 17. However, caution them not to carry these practices over into any other classes.

You might also have them practice the number signals, using the thumb for one and so forth.

C5

Übung • Wir üben mit Zahlen

CHALLENGE Have the students plan a second-grade math class. Several students should take turns at playing the teacher and give simple arithmetic problems to the class. You should first teach the phrases **Wieviel sind ______ und ______?** and **Was ist ______ weniger ______?** If the class is doing really well, you can add **Gut! Sehr gut!** and **Ausgezeichnet!**

C6 Übung • Zahlenlotto

Have the students cross out each square as they hear the corresponding number. To give them additional practice with numbers and to give more students a chance to be the winner, you might play several rounds of the game or have them do a second round in which the winner is the first one to fill in a *vertical* line.

C7 WIE SAGT MAN DAS?

If you did not do so when presenting C1, call attention to the absence of the definite article before the names in the sentence **Wie alt sind Ulrike und Jochen?** Point out that the use of **die** and **der** is not obligatory but that it can be used even in this situation.

C8 ERKLÄRUNG

If your students still need help internalizing the forms of **sein,** put **sein, bist, ist,** and **sind** on an overhead transparency or on the board in random order. Repeat them at least four times in different patterns. Ask the students to quickly say which of the pronouns they think of when they see that form of the verb or what sounds right to them. Then have them give the entire pronoun-verb phrase. Do this chorally and individually.

C9 Übung • Wie alt sind die Schüler? — Vierzehn.

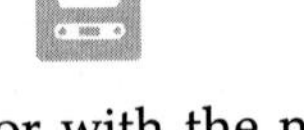

If you feel the students need more practice with the forms or with the numbers, vary the age: **fünfzehn, neun,** and so on. They could also pair off after the first round.

C10 Übung • Und wie alt sind diese Schüler?

Call attention to the variations: **Dieter und Petra sind 16 / Die Karin und der Bernd sind 13.** Remind them that you can use or not use the definite article in this instance.

CHALLENGE If your students have mastered the material and you feel they will not be confused by additional vocabulary, you can introduce **Sie sind beide fünfzehn** and **Sie sind auch beide fünfzehn.**

C11 Übung • Hör gut zu!

You will hear eight statements that refer to either a boy or a girl. For example, you hear, **Der Stefan ist fünfzehn.** You place your check mark in the row labeled *Junge,* because the statement you heard refers to a boy. Let's begin. **Fangen wir an!**

1. Der Michael ist auch 14 Jahre alt. *Junge*
2. Wie alt ist die Silke? *Mädchen*
3. Sie ist auch fünfzehn. *Mädchen*
4. Der Andreas ist vierzehn. *Junge*
5. Wie alt ist der Michael? *Junge*
6. Die Katrin ist sechzehn Jahre alt. *Mädchen*
7. Wie alt ist die Sabine? *Mädchen*
8. Er ist auch fünfzehn. *Junge*

Now check your answers. *Read each item again and give the correct answer.*

C12

Übung • Jetzt bist du dran

When the students can successfully combine the elements of this dialog, put the following dialog on an overhead transparency or on the board. Have the students work in pairs. Ask them to complete the dialog, putting a lot of expression into it. Then have them switch roles.

A: Guten Tag!
B: Guten Tag!
A: Wie heisst du?
B: ______. Und du?
A: ______.
B: Wie alt bist du?
A: ______. Und du?
B: ______ auch ______.

C13

Schreibübung

Students might be interested to learn that in Germany the number of digits in a telephone number varies according to the town or city. A typical arrangement for a larger town or city is **000/00 00 00,** where the first three-digit number is a **Vorwahlnummer,** or area code. Postal code numbers **(Postleitzahlen)** have four digits and precede the name of the city. In international correspondence, they are preceded by **D** for **Deutschland** *(Germany):* **D-1000 Berlin; D-2000 Hamburg; D-8000 München.**

OBJECTIVES **To exchange information:** ask where someone else is from and tell where you're from; **to socialize:** say you don't understand and ask for clarification

CULTURAL BACKGROUND The five students featured here all speak German, but if you listen to them, they sound very different. Most of them use local dialects but know standard German from television and school.

MOTIVATING ACTIVITY Prepare a map of Central Europe with the borders of the German-speaking countries given and the locations of the capitals marked; the actual names should be left out, but the names of surrounding countries may be included for reference. Your map should have a compass rose with the points marked **Norden, Osten, Süden,** and **Westen.** Introduce these terms. Then have the students fill in the map with the following items:

Bonn	Bundesrepublik Deutschland (BRD)
Berlin (Ost)	Deutsche Demokratische Republik (DDR)
Wien	Österreich
Bern	die Schweiz

You could give mnemonic devices to aid the students in memorizing some of the names or locations: **Österreich** and **Berlin (Ost)** both contain **Ost-** *(East),* so they must be to the east. **Wiener** sausages come from **Wien,** *Vienna.* Have them keep these maps in their folders—you may want to use them again.

D1

Woher bist du?

Follow the steps outlined in A1. Introduce Jens Kröger. First ask basic questions about him, such as **Wie heisst der Junge? Wie alt ist er?** Then expand, first modeling any additional vocabulary and the type of answer you expect.

Ist Jens fünfzehn? — Nein.
Ist Jens aus Niebüll? — Ja.

Have the students locate Niebüll on the map on page 18 and write it on their own maps. Go on to Wiebke Nedel, proceeding as with Jens. Then use Jens or Wiebke as lead-ins to ask personalized questions such as these:

Jens ist sechzehn. Wie alt bist du?
Wiebke ist aus Neuss. Und woher bist du?

Continue with the other three characters. Before introducing Kurt and Bruno, practice individual phrases that tell where people are from:

aus Deutschland	aus Amerika	aus <u>der</u> DDR
aus Österreich	aus <u>den</u> USA	aus <u>der</u> Schweiz
aus Niebüll		

SLOWER–PACED LEARNING Do not attempt to cover all the material the first day with these students. Furthermore, they may not be ready to handle any questions involving new vocabulary till a later day, if at all.

CHALLENGE Vary your questioning a little. Introduce the necessary new vocabulary—**wer, oder**—and demonstrate the type of answer you expect. This should be short-answer: **Wiebke, im Norden, aus der Schweiz.** Start with questions that ask the students to combine information about Jens, Wiebke, and so forth. Then have the students refer to their maps and interpret information.

Woher ist Bruno, aus der Schweiz oder aus Österreich?
Wer ist fünfzehn, Jens oder Wiebke?
Wer ist aus Niebüll, Jens oder Wiebke?
Ist Niebüll im Norden oder im Süden?
Ist Niebüll in der BRD oder der DDR?

D2 Übung • Woher sind unsere Freunde?

As a variation, try the following: introduce **Wo ist . . . ?** (for comprehension purposes only). Referring to the maps on pages 18 and 46, ask such questions as **Ist Neuss in der DDR oder in der BRD? Wo ist Wien, in Österreich oder in der Schweiz?** As a game, have the students complete these sentences according to the pattern.

Er ist aus Wien.	Er ist Wiener.
Er ist aus Berlin.	Er ist Berliner.
Hamburg.	Er ist ____.
Frankfurt.	Er ist ____.

D3 Übung • Schau auf die Karte! Woher ist . . . ?

Before having the students pair off, model the variations **(Woher ist Margit? — Sie ist aus Österreich/Margit ist aus Österreich.)** Then ask several students the questions. Finally, have them ask one another several of the questions.

D4 WIE SAGT MAN DAS?

You might discuss the emergence of the two Germanies and call the students' attention to the fact that, on page 45, Wiebke and Jens both said **Ich bin aus Deutschland,** while Kurt said **Ich bin aus der DDR.**

D5 Übung • Jetzt bist du dran

CHALLENGE Tell the students to imagine that they have a group of German, Swiss, or Austrian exchange students visiting their school. These students do not come from the same city or town. An American student—each of your students in turn—invites three exchange students to his or her home and introduces them to his or her mother or father, giving their name, home town, and country. Have the students work in groups of five, one playing a parent, one the American student, and the others the exchange students. Put **Mutti (Vati), das ist ______.** on the board as a prompt.

D6 Schreibübung • Etwas über deine Freunde, etwas über dich

If you had your students do the challenge activity for D5, they could use the exchange students they invented for it. In that case, prepare them by jotting "notes" on the board: **Heinz, 16, aus Österreich,** for example. Since this is a written activity, it can be used as well with students who did not do the challenge activity: supply a few names and appropriate data.

D7 JA ODER NEIN?

You have very likely been using **ja** and **nein** informally before, so the students should have no difficulty with these. However, do not ask them to produce a sentence with **nicht.** After a **nein** response, they should correct the speaker and give a sentence in the positive, which is a much more natural way to respond. **Heisst er Nedel? — Nein, (er heisst) Kröger.** Furthermore, asking the students to respond with a negative forces them to think and to come up with an alternate on their own rather than repeat all or part of the first speaker's sentence.

D8 ERKLÄRUNG

You can draw parallels to the English language here. Ask the students what letter most of our question words start with. Then ask them what letter most of the German question words start with. Remind them that English and German belong to the same family. Ask them to come up with a few questions in English using question words. What kind of answer would they expect? Then ask for a few questions without question words, also in English. What kind of answer do they expect?

D9 Übung • Jetzt bist du dran

SLOWER–PACED LEARNING Have the students work in pairs. One asks questions and the other answers, but with the absolute minimum of a reply, since he or she is **mundfaul**— a lazy talker.

> Bist du fünfzehn? — Ja.
> Bist du sechzehn? — Nein, fünfzehn.
> Heisst du Michael? — Ja.
> Heisst er Markus? — Nein, Michael.

D10 Übung • Wer ist dein Partner?

SLOWER–PACED LEARNING Limit the choice of city to the ones shown in the text. You will have a much higher probability of repeats. Have the students write out the questions in advance: **Woher bist du? Wie alt bist du?**

D11–14

D11 Übung • Hör gut zu!

You will hear five questions. In your text are five answers. As you hear each question, write the number of the question in the box next to the appropriate answer. For example, you hear, **Woher ist sie?** The answer is, of course, **Sie ist aus Deutschland.** Let's begin. **Fangen wir an!**

1. Wie heisst er? *Er heisst Michael. (number 2)*
2. Woher bist du? *Ich bin aus der Schweiz. (number 5)*
3. Wie alt bist du? *Ich bin vierzehn. (number 1)*
4. Wie alt ist sie? *Sie ist fünfzehn. (number 3)*
5. Wer ist das? *Das ist Jens Kröger. (number 4)*

Now check your answers. *Read each item again and give the correct answer.*

D12 Schreibübung • Was sagt er? Was sagt sie?

These partial dialogs, with either the stimulus or the response left open to be filled in by the students in cloze-exercise fashion, are excellent for promoting higher-level thinking in general and thinking in the target language in particular. You can put one dialog on an overhead transparency or on the board and have the class supply the missing lines. Then have the students work in pairs. They should complete the second dialog and then read it to each other. If you prefer, they can work in small groups.

CHALLENGE Students, in pairs or in small groups, complete the second dialog. Then they continue it on their own, adding two lines or so.

SLOWER–PACED LEARNING For students who need additional help in doing cloze-type dialogs, supply some suggestions for completion or give English cues; for example, **Jens/Niebüll** or *give a greeting / ask who that is / ask where she is from.*

D13 WIE BITTE?

See if the students understand what is happening here. Ask them to concentrate on the girl's replies, listening to *how* she answers. What type of sentences does she use? Why is she doing this? What is this type of language use called? If the students do not understand the function of the girl's questions, demonstrate the use of **nachfragen** yourself. Have students ask you questions, any questions, and act as if you don't quite understand all or part of it. Act out your puzzlement.

Have additional questions and statements ready for the students to react to. Put them on an overhead transparency or on the board.

D14 WIE SAGT MAN DAS?

Demonstrate to the class the variety of questions that one statement can lead to. For example, **Der Stefan ist aus Oberpfaffenhofen** could be the basis for **Wie bitte?** as shown or **Wer?** (it is unlikely that the students are ready for **Wer ist aus Oberpfaffenhofen?**) or **Woher ist der Stefan?**

CHALLENGE Make up some really long statements similar to the ones that follow. See if the class gets enough of the gist of each statement to ask you about it. This should be treated as fun; they are not put on the spot, because they can always respond with **Wie bitte?**

Ich bin aus Oberammergau in den Alpen.
Berlin ist siebenhundertfünfzig Jahre alt.
Die Frau heisst Luise Mathilde Anna Gerstenhofer.

D 15 Übung • Jetzt bist du dran

SLOWER–PACED LEARNING These students may need additional preparation. Have them make up four statements, one for each of the following question categories (put the categories on an overhead transparency or a handout).

1. Wie heisst—? **2.** Wie alt—? **3.** Woher—? **4.** Wer—?

Working as a class, call on individuals to address one of their statements to another student. The other student replies with a question on all or part of the statement. When you are satisfied that they have it, have them pair off.

D 16 WIE HEISSEN SIE? WOHER SIND SIE?

Ask the students to concentrate on the questions the girl asks. What is different about them? To whom is she talking? Briefly discuss the use of **Sie** and point to the verb forms **sind** and **heissen.**

Then go to D16 in the book. Have the students ask you the questions given in the book, but answer them with statements about yourself. Repeat this. Have individual students ask you different questions. Put the following on an overhead transparency and have the students copy it:

Wer sind Sie?
Wie alt sind Sie? Sind Sie _______ ?
Woher sind Sie?
Wie heissen Sie? Heissen Sie _______ ?

D 17 Übung • Frag deinen Lehrer!

To expand this activity, supply data on teachers or other adults you have yourself invented: for example, **Fräulein Beel / Musiklehrerin / aus Köln.** Put these on the board or on handouts. Then have students play the parts of those teachers, while other students question them.

D 18 Übung • Guten Tag! Ich heisse . . .

For this activity, you might supply a fairly extensive list of German family names and tell the students which ones are typical of a particular area. If a student has chosen a town in Bavaria as a home town, he or she might like to choose a distinctly Bavarian family name to go with it. Invite the students to ask you about the meanings of the names once they have chosen one.

TRY YOUR SKILLS

OBJECTIVE To recombine communicative functions, grammar, and vocabulary

CULTURAL BACKGROUND Young Germans travel a great deal. As a result, they are interested in foreign languages; and because of the geography of Europe, they have ample opportunity to practice them. They are also quite likely to have a pen pal in another country.

SKILLS 1–5

1 Zwei Briefe 

CHALLENGE Prepare a handout of a "torn letter" like the one shown. Have the students complete the part that was torn off so that the letter reads well and makes sense.

Lieber And
Ich heisse
bin aus Fran
in Deutschland
Du? Aus New York
Ich bin sechz
bin sportlich. Un
Bitte schreib mir.
Viele Gr

2 Übung • Woher ist das Mädchen? Wer ist der Junge?

You can use the pictures from D5 on page 47 of the text as prompts for the answers or have magazine cutouts of teenagers ready and let the students invent backgrounds for them. Another possibility is to put the students into "committees"—groups of 3–5 students each—and have them invent backgrounds for one of the young people pictured. Then put two groups together. Students from one group should take turns asking questions about the teenager on the other group's picture; students from the other group reply. Then the groups switch roles.

3 Übung • Brieffreunde

Find out whether any of your students already have pen pals. Ask them whether they would be interested in corresponding with German teenagers, and try to arrange for it.

4 Übung • Du triffst neue Freunde. Was sagst du?

Tell the students something about youth hostels: that there is an international organization with national affiliates all over the world; that your American Youth Hostels Association membership card entitles you to use hostels in any other member country; and that hostels are good places to meet other young people, pick up travel tips, and share interests and experiences. Consider writing away for information to share with your class.

5 Schreibübung • Unsere Freunde

If you used magazine cutouts for the last activity, the students could write their paragraphs based on the new characters and information. Have several of the paragraphs put on the board.

6 Aussprache-, Lese- und Schreibübungen 

1. At first, some German sounds may seem hard to pronounce. German has some sounds that do not exist in English. Other sounds may seem easy but when you listen closely you may realize that they are pronounced somewhat differently from similar sounds in English. You must practice all German sounds to develop a pronunciation that a native speaker can understand. Let's work on some of the sounds in German words.

/ç/ Listen carefully to the **ich**-sound in these words: **ich, dich, Michael, Mädchen, Österreich.** The **ich**-sound does not exist in English. It is called the **ich**-sound because it occurs in the word **ich** *(I).* To produce the **ich**-sound, put the tip of your tongue in position to form the sound at the beginning of the English word *yes.* Now pretend that you are trying very hard to say *yes* but can't quite get started. Don't say the English sound, but exhale through the tongue position, and you will say the **ich**-sound. Now repeat each of the following words: **ich, dich, Michael, Mädchen, Österreich.** Now repeat the following sentences: **Grüss dich! Ich bin der Michael. Das Mädchen ist aus Österreich.**

/x/ Listen carefully to the **ach**-sound in these words: **acht, achtzehn, auch.** The **ach**-sound does not exist in English either. It is called the **ach**-sound because it occurs in the word **ach** (*Oh!* or *Ah!*) The **ach**-sound is produced at the back of the mouth. Say the English word *look* and hold on to the position you take for the /k/ sound in *look* as if you could not let go. In this position, the back of your tongue is locked against the back part of your mouth. Now slowly relax your hold on the position until you can force air through between your tongue and the roof of your mouth. The sound of the friction you hear is the **ach**-sound. Now repeat each of the following words: **acht, achtzehn, auch.** Now repeat the following sentences:

Er ist acht. Bist du auch achtzehn?

/l/ Listen carefully to the /l/ sound in these words: **alt, elf, alles, hallo, null, wieviel, Lehrer.** Most Americans pronounce one kind of /l/ sound in words such as *bill* and *mill* and a different kind in words such as *million* and *billion.* The /l/ sound most Americans use in *million* is very much like the German sound /l/. Now repeat each of the following words:

alt, elf, zwölf, Zahlen, Schüler, Fräulein, alles, Deutschland, Hallo, wieviel, null, Basel, Lehrer

Now repeat the following sentences or phrases: **Hallo, Schüler! Die Zahlen elf und zwölf.**

2. In this second section you will practice reading the words printed in your textbook on page 53. Now listen and then read each of the printed words in the pause provided.

ch 1. The letters **ch** (*tse-ha* in German) represent both the **ich**-sound and the **ach**-sound: **ich, acht, dich, auch.**

l 2. The letter **l** represents the /l/ sound most Americans use when pronouncing the word *million:* **alt, elf, null.**

w 3. The letter **w** (*veh* in German) represents a /v/ sound, as in the word *violin:* **wie, wer, Wien, wir, wo, woher, Wiedersehen.**

z 4. The letter **z** (*tsett* in German) represents the /ts/ sound in the word *hits:* **Zahl, zwei, zehn, Schweiz.**

3. Now close your textbook and write the sentences you hear.

1. Wo ist Wien?
2. Wie alt ist Michael?
3. Zehn und zwei ist zwölf.
4. Ich bin auch elf.

WAS KANNST DU SCHON?

Review the various greetings that have been used in the text so far. Ask the students which are less formal. Which are more formal? Which would be appropriate to use in greeting your teacher? A friend of your own age? Your mother? Then proceed with numbers 1–6. Follow the same procedure for saying goodbye.

Remind the students that they are introducing themselves to another teenager. The greetings should be informal. Which form do they use, the **du**-form or the **Sie**-form?

You may skip the pair **Wie alt bin ich? — Ich bin dreizehn,** as this is not likely to occur often and they will in any case be giving an **ich**-answer to the **du**-question. Ask the students to give both short- and long-answer forms: **Ich bin vierzehn / Ich bin vierzehn Jahre alt.** Practice the forms of **sein** in context before the students do the fill-ins: throw out a few subjects—mix pronouns and nouns—and have them give you the correct form of **sein** in each case.

Review the question words before doing Section D. Take one or two sample sentences, such as **Jens Kröger ist aus Niebüll** or **Silke ist 13 Jahre alt,** and ask the students how many questions they can come up with for those statements.

WORTSCHATZ

Ask for sentences using the vocabulary items; for example, **Wien: Er ist aus Wien** or **Bist du aus Wien?** Call the students' attention to the note that follows the **Wortschatz.**

WORTSCHATZÜBUNGEN

The students should have a **Wortschatz** section in their notebooks to keep information from the **Wortschatzübungen** and other vocabulary notes.

Review the concept of *noun* with the students. Some of them may still be unsure of what a noun is. Tell them that in German they will never have to worry about what is a common noun and what is a proper noun.

Discuss orthography. Point out that German is a *phonetic* language: the same combination of letters will almost always be pronounced the same way. Furthermore, in many cases they will be able to spell a word just by hearing it. There are exceptions: **z/tz; k/ck; i/ie.**

ZUM LESEN

OBJECTIVE To read for practice and pleasure

WO IST DEUTSCHLAND? 

Before beginning the reading selection, you may want to bring in a world map or a map of Europe to show the students the location of Germany in Europe. Then have the students look at the map on page 57. Ask them to name Germany's neighbors. What countries border Germany on the north, the south, the east, and the west? After the students have named the countries in English, point out the countries, saying their names in German. Now have the students read the text silently. As they read each sentence, tell them to check what the sentence says on the map.

Übung • Beantworte die Fragen!

Read the questions aloud as the students skim the text. Ask for oral answers first; these may be in short-answer format. Then have the students complete the activity as a written assignment, either in class or for homework.

CHALLENGE Have the students copy five statements from the reading but change one item in each sentence to make the information incorrect. Make enough copies of the "quizzes" to have one for each student. The students must find the errors, correct them, and give each corrected statement orally.

Übung • Stimmt oder stimmt nicht?

Repeat each of the statements at least twice, with a pause before each repetition. If one student correctly identifies a statement as incorrect but is unable to correct it, call on another student and then ask the first student if the statement is now correct as stands: **Stimmt?**

Übung • Klassenprojekt

To stimulate interest in the cookbook project, mention some typical German, Swiss, or Austrian dishes, including regional specialities such as **Königsberger Klops** or **Palatschinken.** You might also mention the strong Hungarian influence on Austrian cooking and the French influence on the Swiss cuisine. If students have German-speaking neighbors or relatives, encourage them to go to these sources for recipes; if not, make this a library project.

POSTKARTEN 

After you have played the cassette or read the text of the postcards aloud, have the students read them aloud. They can use these as models for their own postcards.

Übung • Jetzt bist du dran

If some of the students want to say things on their postcards for which they don't yet have the vocabulary, help them. If any students have postcards that their parents or friends have received from German-speaking countries, have them bring those postcards to class and say where they are from: **Diese Karte ist aus ______**. They can make a visual display of these, drawing an oversized map of the four countries and placing the cards at the appropriate location on the map.

KAPITEL 1

Neue Freunde

Meeting new friends is exciting, especially when they speak another language. When you meet someone who speaks German, you need to know how to say hello and goodbye, how to find out a little about the person, and how to tell a bit about yourself. In this unit you will meet five new friends your own age from the Federal and Democratic Republics of Germany and from Austria and Switzerland.

In this unit you will:

SECTION A	say hello and say goodbye
SECTION B	ask someone's name and give your name
SECTION C	ask someone's age and tell your age; count from 1 to 20
SECTION D	ask and tell where someone is from
TRY YOUR SKILLS	use what you've learned
ZUM LESEN	read for practice and pleasure

For teaching suggestions, see the Teacher's Notes preceding this unit, pp. T24–T43.

saying hello and saying goodbye

School begins. Students meet and greet one another on their way to class. Let's hear what they're saying.

A1 Guten Tag! Auf Wiedersehen!

Tag, Steffi!

Grüss dich, Andreas!

Grüss dich, Stefan!

Hallo, Michael.

Morgen, Natalie!

Guten Morgen!

See below.

Tschüs!

Bis dann!

Wiedersehen! Tschau![1]

Auf Wiedersehen!

[1]**Tschau!** is the German spelling of the Italian **ciao.**

When taking leave of someone in the evening, German-speakers say "Guten Abend!" or just "Abend!" They usually say "Gute Nacht!" only before actually going to sleep.

Photo p. 30: Niebüll, hinter dem Marktplatz
Photo p. 31, right: Parlament in Wien mit Brunnensäule der Pallas Athene (Göttin der Weisheit)

A2 Übung • *Exercise*

The longer forms "Guten Morgen!," "Guten Tag!," "Auf Wiedersehen!" are more formal than the shorter forms "Morgen!," "Tag!," "Wiedersehen!" Tell the students they would use the longer forms with adults they do not know too well, such as the school principal.

Make a name tag for yourself, with your own name or one chosen from those shown in A4. Practice saying hello and goodbye to your classmates, using the names on the tags. Use different expressions.

A3 WIE SAGT MAN DAS? *How do you say that?*

Saying hello and goodbye

Here are some ways of saying hello and goodbye. **Guten Morgen!, Guten Tag!,** and **Auf Wiedersehen!** are standard. They can be used in almost any situation. You can also use the abbreviated forms **Morgen!, Tag!,** and **Wiedersehen!** The phrases **Hallo!, Grüss dich!, Tschüs!, Tschau!,** and **Bis dann!** are more casual.

SAYING HELLO		SAYING GOODBYE	
Guten Morgen! Morgen! Guten Tag! Tag!	Good morning! Morning. Hello! Hi!	Auf Wiedersehen! Wiedersehen!	Goodbye! Bye!
Grüss dich! Hallo!	Hi!	Tschüs! Tschau! Bis dann!	Bye! So long! See you later.

A4 Ein wenig Landeskunde *A little culture*

These are popular first names of German boys and girls today.

Vornamen für Jungen	Vornamen für Mädchen
Frank, Markus, Jörg, Mark, Stefan, Sven, Dirk, Christof, Holger, Andreas, Michael, Matthias	Antje, Ulrike, Monika, Katja, Daniele, Claudia, Natalie, Marina, Kirsten, Nicole, Silke, Michaela

German words have no single c, only combinations with ch or sch, unless the word is of Romance origin—Nicole is French, Claudia is Latin. Notice that in German all syllables are pronounced: Mi-cha-el, Mi-cha-e-la, Da-ni-e-le, Clau-di-a. Certain foreign words are exceptions, however—the names Natalie and Nicole, for example.

A5 HERR, FRAU, FRÄULEIN 

All but very young-looking women are politely addressed as "Frau."

As the students enter their classrooms, they greet their teachers.

Guten Morgen, Herr Sperling!
Tag, Antje!

Guten Tag, Frau Meier!
Grüss dich, Michael!

Wiedersehen, Fräulein Seifert!
Auf Wiedersehen!

A6 Übung • Jetzt bist du dran *Now it's your turn* 

Project pictures on overhead, model and have students repeat: Guten Morgen, Fräulein Müller! Grüss dich, Jörg! Auf Wiedersehen, Frl. Müller! Tschüs, Uschi!

Greet each of the people pictured below. Then say goodbye to each one.

Lars

Uschi

Frl.[1] Müller

Herr Braun

Frau Binder

(Guten) Morgen/(Guten) Tag, . . . !
(Auf) Wiedersehen!

Hallo/Grüss dich, . . . !
Tschüs!/Tschau!/Bis dann!

[1] **Frl.** is the abbreviation of **Fräulein.**

A7 WIE SAGT MAN DAS? *How do you say that?*
Greeting adults

In German, you use **Herr** for *Mister (Mr.)*, **Frau** for *Mrs.*, and **Fräulein** for *Miss.*

Guten Tag, Herr Sperling!	Hello, Mr. Sperling.
Tag, Frau Meier!	Hi, Mrs. Meier.
Guten Morgen, Fräulein Seifert!	Good morning, Miss Seifert.

A8 Ein wenig Landeskunde *A little culture*

When you greet someone, you shake hands and make eye contact. When you greet adults, it's polite to also nod your head slightly.

A9 Übung • Hör gut zu! *Listen carefully*

For script and answers, see p. T28.

Do you say this to a teacher or to a student? Listen.

	0	1	2	3	4	5	6	7	8	9
a male teacher			✓	✓					✓	
a female teacher	✓					✓				✓
a student		✓			✓		✓	✓		

A10 Übung • Jetzt bist du dran *Now it's your turn*

1. Greet your teacher. Guten Morgen/Guten Tag, Herr/Frau . . . !
2. Tell the class how you greet each of your teachers.

A11 Schreibübung *Writing practice*

Write how you would greet and say goodbye to the following people:

1. your friend Peter
2. your German teacher
3. your principal

1. Grüss dich/Tschüs, Peter! 2. Guten Morgen/Auf Wiedersehen, Herr/Frau/Fräulein . . . !
3. Guten Tag/Auf Wiedersehen, Herr/Frau/Fräulein . . . !

SECTION B

introducing yourself

Now that you know how to say hello, let's find out how you introduce yourself.

B1 Wie heisst du?

Grüss dich! Ich heisse Andreas. Und wie heisst du?
Ich heisse Natalie.
Und wie heisst du?
Ich heisse ____ .

B2 Übung • Jetzt bist du dran

1. With a classmate, practice reading this short dialog aloud, filling in your own names. Then try saying the dialog without looking at the printed words.

   A: Hallo! Ich heisse ____ . Und wie heisst du?
   B: Ich heisse ____ .

2. Now practice with other classmates.

Activity: Go around class asking students for their own names or those of classmate As they gain confidence, go faster and faster: Wie heisst du? Und du? Wie heisst e Und er? Und er? Wie heisst sie? Und sie? Und sie?

B3 WIE HEISST DER JUNGE? WIE HEISST DAS MÄDCHEN?

Because you still do not know many of the boys and girls in your class, you ask someone to tell you their names.

Wie heisst der Junge?
Er heisst Stefan.

Und das Mädchen? Wie heisst sie?
Sie heisst Sabine.

B4 Übung • Wie heisst er? Wie heisst sie? 

1. Ulrike
Sie heisst Ulrike.

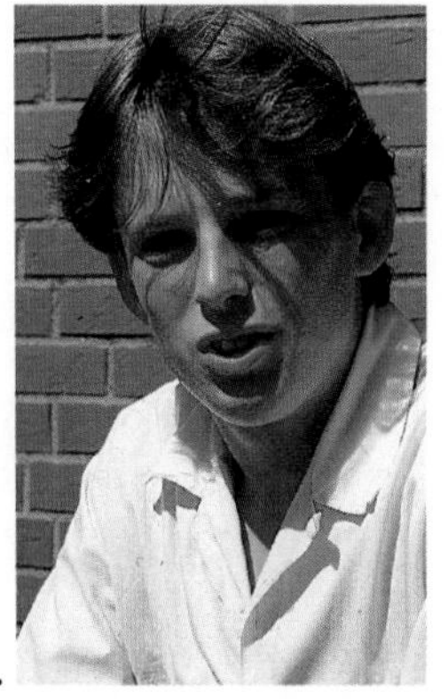

2. Lars
Er heisst Lars.

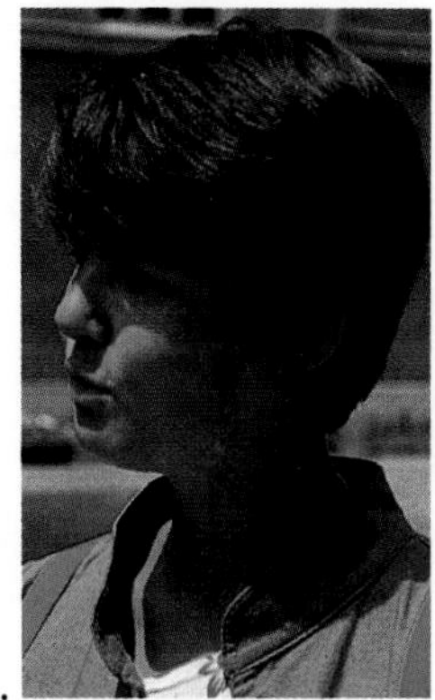

3. Natalie
Sie heisst Natalie.

4. Andreas
Er heisst Andreas.

B5 WIE SAGT MAN DAS?
Asking and giving names

QUESTION	ANSWER
Wie heisst du? What's your name?	Ich heisse Andreas. My name is Andreas.
Wie heisst der Junge? What's the boy's name?	Er heisst Stefan. His name is Stefan.
Wie heisst das Mädchen? What's the girl's name?	Sie heisst Sabine. Her name is Sabine.

B6 Übung • Partnerarbeit *Teamwork*

Team up with a classmate. Ask each other the names of several other students in your class.

Homework: Give students several greetings, statements, and questions to respond to. Basic: One response for each. Challenge: Two or more for each. Example: Das ist Michael. Guten Tag, Michael!/Wie heisst er?/Und das ist Markus./Nein, das ist Peter./Guten Tag. Ich heisse . . .

B7 Schreibübung • Wie heissen deine Mitschüler?

You are new in the class and want to find out the names of your new classmates. Rewrite each dialog, filling in the missing words.

A: Wie ____ du? heisst
B: ____ ____ Andreas. Ich heisse

A: ____ heisst der Junge? Wie
B: Er ____ Stefan. heisst

A: Und das Mädchen? Wie ____ sie? heisst
B: Sie ____ Ulrike. heisst

A: Wie heisst ____? du
B: Ich ____ ____. heisse . . .

B8 WER IST DAS?

Here is another way of finding out who someone is.

Ask students if they can see a pattern of usage for "der" and "die" before proper names.

Wer ist das?
Das ist der Stefan.
Und wer ist das?
Das ist Herr Sperling, der Lehrer.

Wer ist das?
Das ist die Sabine.
Und das ist Frau Meier, die Lehrerin.

Herr Sperling, der Deutschlehrer

Frau Meier, die Deutschlehrerin

B9 WIE SAGT MAN DAS?
Asking who someone is

QUESTION	ANSWER
Wer ist das? Who is that?	Das ist der Stefan. Das ist die Sabine. That's Stefan. That's Sabine.
	Das ist Herr Sperling, der Deutschlehrer. That's Mr. Sperling, the German teacher.
	Das ist Frau Meier, die Deutschlehrerin. That's Mrs. Meier, the German teacher.

In everyday speech, the articles **der** and **die** are often used together with proper names when referring to other people, especially if you know the people well. Also well-known people, celebrities, etc.

B10 Übung • Jetzt bist du dran

Activity: Schwerhörig (Hard of Hearing) Model the conversations first with 2 to 3 students, taking part A yourself. Students work in pairs, reverse roles:

A: Wer ist das?
B: Das ist ____ .
A: Wie heisst er/sie?
B: Er/sie heisst ____ .

Ask a classmate to identify various people in your class, including your teacher.

A: Wer ist das?
B: Das ist . . .

B11 ERKLÄRUNG *Explanation*
The Definite Articles der, die, das

German has three words for *the:* **der, die,** and **das,** called the definite articles. These words tell us which class (or gender) a German noun belongs to. For example, **der Junge,** *the boy,* belongs to a class called "masculine"; **die Lehrerin,** *the female teacher,* to a class called "feminine"; and **das Mädchen,** *the girl,* to a class called "neuter." You will learn more about this in Unit 2.

Masculine Nouns	*Feminine Nouns*	*Neuter Nouns*
der Junge		**das Mädchen**
der Lehrer	**die Lehrerin**	
der Deutschlehrer	**die Deutschlehrerin**	

B12 Schreibübung *Writing practice*

Rewrite the sentences, filling in the missing words.

1. Wie heisst __der__ Junge?
2. __Die__ Lehrerin heisst Meier.
3. Das ist __der__ Lehrer.
4. __Das__ Mädchen heisst Sabine.
5. Wie heisst __die__ Deutschlehrerin?
6. Und __der__ Deutschlehrer?

B13 Übung • Ein Spiel *A game* (optional)

Do you know everyone in your class? Divide the class into two teams. The first student on Team A identifies himself or herself, saying **Ich heisse . . .** and then points to a student on the same team, asking **Wer ist das?** The first student on Team B must give the correct name. If the answer is correct, the student stays in the game. If it is incorrect, the student is out. Continue in this way, alternating teams.

B14 Übung • Hör gut zu! *Listen carefully*

For script and answers, see p. T31.

Are you referring to a girl or a boy? To a woman or a man?

	0	1	2	3	4	5	6	7	8
refers to a girl or a woman		✓	✓		✓			✓	
refers to a boy or a man	✓			✓		✓	✓		✓

B 15 Übung • Ratespiel: Wer ist das? *Guessing game*

Bring in pictures of well-known people and ask the class to identify them.

A: Wer ist das? *or* A: Wie heisst er? Wie heisst sie?
B: Das ist . . . B: Er heisst . . . Sie heisst . . .

B 16 Ein wenig Landeskunde *A little culture*

In German, as in English, many family names reflect the occupation or characteristics of ancestors. Many family names were given to help identify people at a time when only first names were customary.

Wie heisst er? Er heisst

1. Fritz. . . Fischer

2. Herman. . . Bäcker

3. Hans. . . Schuhmacher

4. Gerhard. . . Gärtner

5. Paul. . . Müller

Do you know someone with a German name? The United States' census of 1980 revealed that 27.4 percent of the population of the United States can claim German ancestry. It is therefore not surprising to find German family names in all parts of the United States, and there may be a number of students with a German name in your class. What German names do you know? In Germany today, the most common last name is **Müller.** See also the Introduction: German and You, pp. 16–17.

SECTION C

asking someone's age and telling your age

How old are your friends? How old are you?

C1 Wie alt bist du?

Wie alt bist du?
Ich bin dreizehn Jahre alt.
Wie alt ist die Sabine?
Die Sabine ist fünfzehn.
Und wie alt ist der Stefan?
Der Stefan ist auch fünfzehn.
Wie alt sind Ulrike und Jochen?
Sie sind auch fünfzehn Jahre alt.
Jochen
Ulrike
Und wie alt bist du?
Ich bin ____ .

C2 Übung • Wie alt sind die Jungen und Mädchen?

1. Wie alt ist der Stefan?
2. Wie alt ist die Sabine?
3. Wie alt ist der Jochen?
4. Und die Ulrike?
5. Wie alt sind Stefan und Jochen?
6. Und wie alt bist du?

1. Der Stefan ist fünfzehn.
2. Die Sabine ist (auch) fünfzehn.
3. Der Jochen ist (auch) fünfzehn.
4. Die Ulrike ist (auch) fünfzehn
5. Sie sind (auch) fünfzehn.
6. Ich bin . . . .

C3 DIE ZAHLEN VON NULL BIS ZWANZIG

0	1	2	3	4	5	6	7	8	9	10
null	eins	zwei	drei	vier	fünf	sechs	sieben	acht	neun	zehn

11	12	13	14	15	16	17	18	19	20
elf	zwölf	dreizehn	vierzehn	fünfzehn	sechzehn	siebzehn	achtzehn	neunzehn	zwanzig

C4 Ein wenig Landeskunde

Notice in C3 how the numerals are written in German. Pay particular attention to the numerals 1 and 7.

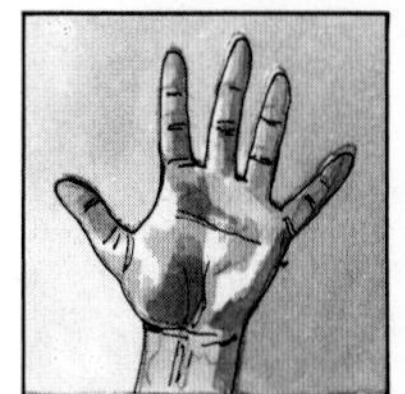

When using hand signals to indicate numbers, you use the thumb to indicate one, the thumb and the index finger to indicate two, and so on.

C5 Übung • Wir üben mit Zahlen

1. Count off in sequence: first student, **eins,** second student, **zwei,** etc.
2. Choose one student to count aloud all the boys and all the girls.
3. Complete each sequence of numbers. Say the numbers aloud in German.

   3, 4, 5, __6__ drei, vier, fünf, sechs

   1. 9, 10, 11, __12__
   2. 16, 17, 18, __19__
   3. 1, 2, 3, __4__
   4. 11, 12, 13, __14__
   5. 2, 4, 6, __8__
   6. 12, 14, 16, __18__
   7. 6, 8, 10, __12__
   8. 14, 16, 18, __20__
   9. 5, 4, 3, __2__
   10. 10, 9, 8, __7__
   11. 20, 19, 18, __17__
   12. 6, 5, 4, __3__

4. Tell the class your phone number in German. Your classmates should write it down as you say it.

   Meine Telefonnummer ist . . .

Activities:
1. Have students make up similar patterns in 3.
2. Teacher or student gives a number, another student or whole class supplies next 3. Count forwards or backwards: 6 (7, 8, 9) Or 6 (5, 4, 3)

Challenge Activity: Have students come up with other patterns for the class to figure out:
4:8 = 10: ____ (vier ist zu acht wie zehn zu ____)
2:6 = 3: ____
16:4 = 20: ____

C6 Übung • Zahlenlotto *Number Lotto*

Draw a rectangle and divide it into twenty squares as shown. Number the squares from 1 to 20 in any order you choose. Use each number only once. One student calls numbers from 1 to 20 in random order. As you hear each number, mark the corresponding square. The winner is the first one to fill in a horizontal line.

8	2	5	13	14
7	1	6	4	15
9	10	3	19	17
18	11	16	12	20

C7 WIE SAGT MAN DAS?
Asking someone's age and telling yours

QUESTION	ANSWER
Wie alt bist du? How old are you?	Ich bin dreizehn Jahre alt. I'm thirteen years old.
Wie alt ist der Stefan? How old is Stefan?	Er ist fünfzehn. He is fifteen.
Wie alt ist die Sabine? How old is Sabine?	Sie ist fünfzehn Jahre alt. She's fifteen years old.
Wie alt sind Ulrike und Jochen? How old are Ulrike and Jochen?	Sie sind auch fünfzehn. They are also fifteen.

C8 ERKLÄRUNG *Explanation*
Personal Pronouns and the Verb sein

The phrases **ich bin, du bist, er ist, sie ist,** and **sie sind** each contain a subject pronoun corresponding to the English *I, you, he, she,* and *they,* plus a form of the verb **sein,** *to be: I am, you are, he/she/it is, they are.* **Sein** is one of the most frequently used verbs in German. The chart shows the plural forms **wir,** *we,* and **ihr,** *you* (plural), but you do not need to use them yet.

Singular			*Plural*		
Ich	**bin**	15 Jahre alt.	Wir	**sind**	15 Jahre alt.
Du	**bist**		Ihr	**seid**	
Der Stefan / Er	**ist**		Stefan and Sabine / Sie	**sind**	
Die Sabine / Sie	**ist**				

C9 Übung • Wie alt sind die Schüler? —Vierzehn.

Everyone in this group is 14 years old.

A: Wie alt ist der Fritz?
B: Er ist vierzehn.

1. Wie alt ist der Hans?
2. Wie alt ist die Monika?
3. Wie alt sind Hans und Monika?

1. Er ist (auch) vierzehn.
2. Sie ist (auch) vierzehn.
3. Sie sind (auch) vierzehn.

4. Wie alt ist der Günter?
5. Wie alt ist die Ulrike?
6. Wie alt sind Günter and Ulrike?

4. Er ist (auch) vierzehn.
5. Sie ist (auch) vierzehn.
6. Sie sind (auch) vierzehn.

C10 Übung • Und wie alt sind diese Schüler?

The young people in each pair are the same age.

A: Der Jochen ist fünfzehn. Und die Ulrike?
B: Sie ist auch fünfzehn.

1. Die Sabine ist 15. Und der Stefan?
2. Der Andreas ist 11. Und die Erika?
3. Dieter and Petra sind 16. Und Peter und Monika?
4. Die Katrin ist 15. Und der Kurt?
5. Der Michael ist 17. Und die Helga?
6. Die Karin und der Bernd sind 13. Und der Hans und die Sabine?

1. Er ist auch fünfzehn. 2. Sie ist auch elf. 3. Sie sind auch sechzehn. 4. Er ist auch fünfzehn. 5. Sie ist auch siebzehn. 6. Sie sind auch dreizehn.

C11 Übung • Hör gut zu!

For script and answers, see p. T34.

Which sentences refer to a girl and which to a boy? Listen.

	0	1	2	3	4	5	6	7	8
Junge	✓	✓			✓	✓			✓
Mädchen			✓	✓			✓	✓	

C12 Übung • Jetzt bist du dran

Your teacher has asked you to introduce three students to the class, giving their names and ages. First ask each of the three students, and then introduce them to the class.

A: Wie heisst du? Wie alt bist du?
B: Ich heisse . . . Ich bin . . .
A: Das ist . . . Er ist . . . Sie ist . . .

Activity: Ask the students to bring pictures of friends or sisters and brothers. Students, in pairs, tell their partners about the people in the photos, giving name and age.

C13 Schreibübung

1. Which verb form is missing?
   1. Wer ____ das? ist
   2. Das ____ Sabine. ist
   3. Sie ____ 14 Jahre alt. ist
   4. Wie alt ____ du? bist
   5. Peter und Ulrike ____ vierzehn. sind
   6. Ich ____ . . . bin
2. Write the numbers.
   1. Write your phone number, using German numerals.
   2. In German, dictate your phone number to a classmate. Have him or her write it down and read it back to you. Reverse roles.
   3. Now do the same thing with your ZIP code.

SECTION D asking and telling where you are from

Now you will meet some young people from the German-speaking countries.

D1 Woher bist du?

Ich heisse Jens Kröger. Ich bin sechzehn Jahre alt. Ich bin aus Niebüll, aus Deutschland.

Jens Kröger, 16
Niebüll, Deutschland

Ich bin die Wiebke Nedel. Ich bin fünfzehn. Ich bin auch aus Deutschland, aus Neuss.

Wiebke Nedel, 15
Neuss, Deutschland

Ich heisse Dastl, Margit Dastl. Ich bin vierzehn. Ich bin aus Wien, aus Österreich.

Margit Dastl, 14
Wien, Österreich

Ich heisse Bruno Schmidlin. Ich bin auch fünfzehn. Ich bin aus der Schweiz, aus Zimmerwald.

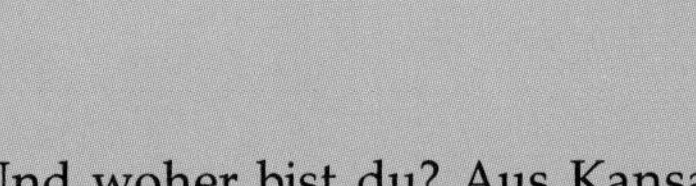

Bruno Schmidlin, 15
Zimmerwald, Schweiz

Ich bin Kurt Langer. Ich bin 15. Ich bin aus der DDR, aus Dresden.

Kurt Langer, 15
Dresden, DDR

Und woher bist du? Aus Kansas City? Aus Harrisburg? Aus Dallas? Ich bin aus ____.

When students are familiar with the map, ask overall questions such as:
1. Wie heissen die vier Länder?
2. Wo ist Wien, in Österreich oder in der Schweiz?
3. Woher kommt Kurt Langer, aus Österreich?

D2 Übung • Woher sind unsere Freunde?

Take a look at the map, and locate where our friends live. Say where each one is from.

D3 Übung • Schau auf die Karte! Woher ist . . .?

Look at the map and pictures on the preceding page and ask a classmate where the different young people are from.

A: Woher ist Jens?
B: Er ist aus Niebüll.

A: Wer ist aus Wien?
B: Margit Dastl ist aus Wien.

D4 WIE SAGT MAN DAS?
Talking about where you are from

QUESTION	ANSWER
Jens, woher bist du? Jens, where are you from?	Ich bin aus Deutschland. Aus Niebüll. I'm from Germany. From Niebüll.
Woher ist Wiebke?	Sie ist aus Deutschland.
Woher ist Margit?	Margit ist aus Österreich.
Woher ist Bruno?	Er ist aus der Schweiz.
Woher ist Kurt?	Er ist aus der DDR.

D5 Übung • Jetzt bist du dran

1. Say hello to a classmate you haven't met yet. Ask his or her name and age and where he or she is from.
2. Introduce your new friend to the class. Give his or her name and age, and tell where he or she is from.
3. Talk about the girl or boy in each picture, telling the name and age and where she or he is from.

Kurt Langer/15

1. Dresden, DDR

Margit Dastl/14

2. Wien, Österreich

Bruno Schmidlin/15

3. Zimmerwald, Schweiz

Wiebke Nedel/15

4. Neuss, Deutschland

Jens Kröger/16
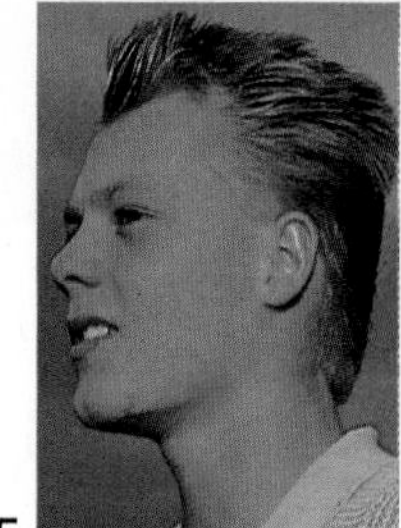
5. Niebüll, Deutschland

4. Now introduce yourself, giving your name and age and where you are from.

D6 Schreibübung • Etwas über deine Freunde, etwas über dich

1. Pick two of the new friends you met in D1 and write a few sentences about each one, telling the name and age and where he or she is from.
2. Write a few sentences about yourself.

   Ich heisse . . .

D7 JA ODER NEIN?

Let's listen to how our friends answer the following questions.

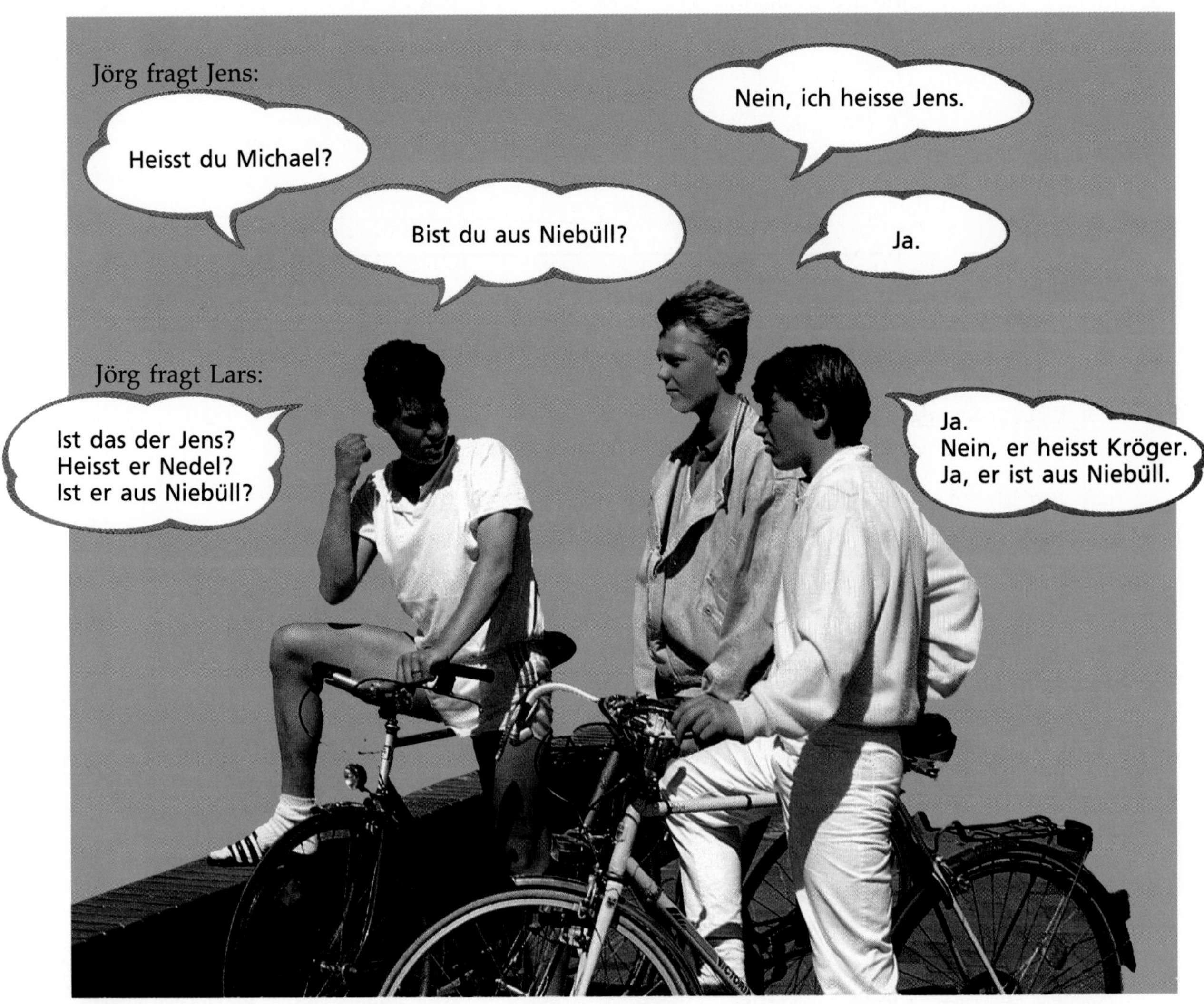

D8 ERKLÄRUNG
Asking and Answering Questions

1. There are questions that begin with a question word like **wer?**, *who?*, **wie?**, *how?*, and **woher?**, *from where?*

Questions beginning with a question word	*Answers*
Wer ist das?	Das ist Jens.
Wie alt ist er?	Er ist sechzehn.
Woher ist er?	Er ist aus Deutschland.

2. There are also questions that begin with verbs. Such questions anticipate answers that start with **ja,** *yes,* or **nein,** *no.*

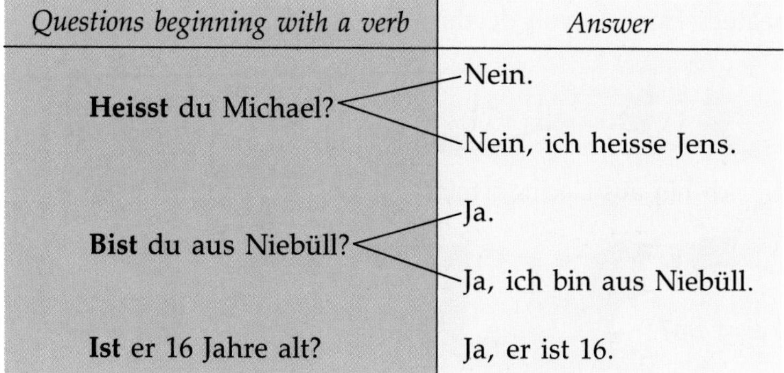

Questions beginning with a verb	*Answer*
Heisst du Michael?	Nein.
	Nein, ich heisse Jens.
Bist du aus Niebüll?	Ja.
	Ja, ich bin aus Niebüll.
Ist er 16 Jahre alt?	Ja, er ist 16.

D9 Übung • Jetzt bist du dran

Ask different classmates questions about themselves, anticipating *yes* or *no* answers.

Heisst du . . .? Bist du fünfzehn? Bist du aus . . .?

D10 Übung • Wer ist dein Partner?

Write an age from 13 to 15 and the name of one of the cities in a German-speaking country on an index card and put the card in your pocket. Mingle with your classmates and try to find a partner whose card has information that matches your own. Be sure to ask and answer in German.

D11 Übung • Hör gut zu!

Questions and answers. Which ones go together? Listen. For script and answers, see p. T38.

	Ex.	Sie ist aus Deutschland.	3	4	Sie ist fünfzehn.
1	3	Ich bin vierzehn.	4	5	Das ist Jens Kröger.
2	1	Er heisst Michael.	5	2	Ich bin aus der Schweiz.

D12 Schreibübung • Was sagt er? Was sagt sie?

Rewrite each dialog, supplying appropriate lines.

SCHÜLER 1 Guten Morgen!
SCHÜLER 2 Guten Morgen!
SCHÜLER 1 Wer ist das?
SCHÜLER 2 Das ist der Jens Kröger.
SCHÜLER 1 Woher ist er/sie?
SCHÜLER 2 Er ist aus Niebüll.

FRAU MEIER Tag, Jochen!
SCHÜLER Guten Tag, Frau Meier!
FRAU MEIER Wer ist das?
SCHÜLER Das ist die Wiebke Nedel.
FRAU MEIER Woher ist sie?
SCHÜLER Sie ist aus Neuss.

D13 WIE BITTE?

Sometimes you do not quite hear or understand what someone has said and need the information repeated. How do you do this?

D14 WIE SAGT MAN DAS?
What to say if you don't understand

If you have not heard or understood what someone has said, you ask for the information to be repeated. In German, this is generally done with **Wie bitte?** or more specifically, with a word such as **wer?,** *who?* or **woher?,** *from where?,* or by repeating the key word. Make sure to raise the tone of your voice.

You did not understand what was said and ask for the entire statement to be repeated.	Der Stefan ist aus Oberpfaffenhofen.	Wie bitte?	I beg your pardon?
You did not understand part of what was said and ask only for a part to be repeated.	Er ist aus Wien. Das ist der Lehrer. Wie alt ist der Stefan? Wie heisst du?	Woher? Wer ist das? Der Stefan? Ich?	From where? Who is that? Stefan? Me?

D 15 Übung • Jetzt bist du dran

A classmate makes a statement or asks a question, and you ask that person to repeat the information that you did not understand. Your classmate then gives an appropriate response.

A: Sabine ist 15 Jahre alt.
B: Wer? *or* Wie alt? *or* Wie bitte?
A: Sabine. *or* Fünfzehn. *or* Sabine ist 15 Jahre alt.

D 16 WIE HEISSEN SIE? WOHER SIND SIE? 

How do you ask your teacher some of the questions you have been asking your classmates? When you talk to your teacher and to most other adults outside your family, you use the **Sie**-form.

D 17 Übung • Frag deinen Lehrer! *Ask your teacher!*

1. Wie heissen Sie?
2. Woher sind Sie? Sind Sie aus Deutschland?

Homework: Tell students to imagine that they see a really good-looking young teacher in school whom they do not know. They ask the teacher who she is and where she is from. She tells them that she is a math teacher from Germany. She even tells them her age. The assignment is to write a short conversation between the nosy student and the young teacher.

D 18 Übung • Guten Tag! Ich heisse . . .

Pick a German first and last name for yourself. Then select a city in one of the German-speaking countries as your home town. Tell the class who you are now.

TRY YOUR SKILLS

using what you've learned

Now you know how to greet people, to talk a little about yourself, and to ask others about themselves. Here are some more opportunities to use what you have learned.

1 Zwei Briefe

It is fun to have a pen pal. As you continue your study of German, perhaps you, too, will have a pen pal. Imagine that these letters are for you.

Lieber Eric!

Ich heisse Petra Schmitt. Ich bin aus Salzburg. Das ist in Österreich. Ich bin 15 Jahre alt.

Woher bist Du? Wie alt bist Du? Bitte schreib mir!

Viele Grüsse
Petra

Liebe Mary!

Ich heisse Günter Weiss. Ich bin aus Frankfurt. Frankfurt ist in Deutschland. Ich bin 14 Jahre alt.

Woher bist Du? Wie alt bist Du?

Viele Grüsse
Günter

Look at these letters. How do they start? Why do you think the greetings are spelled differently? How is the word **Du** spelled?

2 Übung • Woher ist das Mädchen? Wer ist der Junge?

1. Wie heisst das Mädchen?
2. Woher ist sie?
3. Wie alt ist sie?
4. Wie heisst der Junge?
5. Woher ist er?
6. Wie alt ist er?

1. Sie heisst Petra Schmitt. 2. Sie ist aus Salzburg, aus Österreich. 3. Sie ist fünfzehn Jahre alt. 4. Er heisst Günter Weiss. 5. Er ist aus Deutschland, aus Frankfurt. 6. Er ist vierzehn Jahre alt.

3 Übung • Brieffreunde *Pen Pals*

You choose a pen pal and a pen pal chooses you!

1. Write a letter like one of the sample letters, introducing yourself in German to a pen pal in a German-speaking country.
2. Write a letter that one of our friends from abroad (p. 45) might have written to you.

4 Übung • Du triffst neue Freunde. Was sagst du? *You meet new friends. What do you say?*

Imagine that you are staying at a youth hostel in Germany. A youth hostel is an inexpensive hotel for young people. While there, you meet several of our young German-speaking friends pictured on page 45. Exchange greetings and tell one another something about yourselves—for example, your name and age and where you are from.

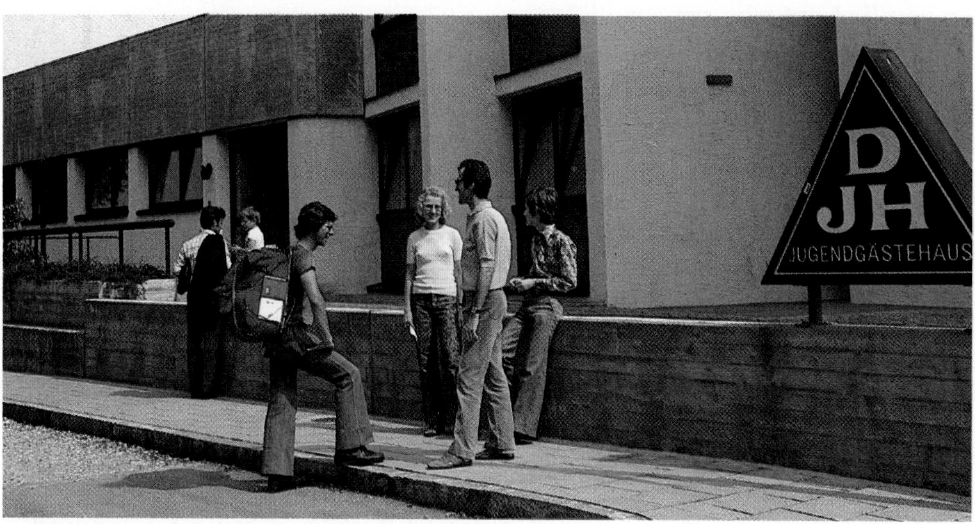

5 Schreibübung • Unsere Freunde

Write a brief paragraph about the five friends from abroad. Write their names and ages and where they are from.

6 Aussprache-, Lese- und Schreibübungen *Pronunciation, Reading, and Writing Exercises*

For script, see p. T41.

1. Listen carefully and repeat what you hear.
2. Listen, then read aloud.
   ich, acht, dich, auch; alt, elf, null; wie, wer, Wien, wir,
   wo, woher, Wiedersehen; Zahl, zwei, zehn, Schweiz
3. Copy the following sentences to prepare yourself to write them from dictation.
   1. Wo ist Wien?
   2. Wie alt ist Michael?
   3. Zehn und zwei ist zwölf.
   4. Ich bin auch elf.

WAS KANNST DU SCHON?

Let's review some important points that you have learned in this unit.

Can you greet young people and adults in German?

Say hello to the following people: 1., 2. Hallo/Grüss dich, . . . ! 3.–6. (Guten) Morgen/(Guten) Tag, . . . !

1. Katrin
2. Stefan
3. Mr. Sperling
4. Miss Seifert
5. Mrs. Meier
6. your teacher

Can you say goodbye in German?

Say goodbye to the same people. 1., 2. Tschüs!/Tschau!/Bis dann! 3.–6. (Auf) Wiedersehen!

Can you introduce yourself in German?

1. Say hello. Hallo / Guten Tag
2. Give your name. Ich heisse . . .
3. Ask a classmate his or her name. Wie heisst du?

Can you find out who someone is?

1. Ask a boy's name, then tell it to someone else. Wie heisst der Junge? Er heisst . . .
2. Ask a girl's name, then tell it to someone else. Wie heisst das Mädchen? Sie heisst . . .
3. Ask who someone is and give the answer. Wer ist das? Das ist der/die . . .

Can you ask someone's age and tell yours?

Write a question and answer about age for each of the following pronouns: ich, du, er, sie, sie (plural). Possible answers: Wie alt bin ich? Ich bin fünfzehn Jahre alt./Wie alt bist du? Ich bin vierzehn./Wie alt ist er? Er ist auch vierzehn./ Wie alt ist sie? Sie ist . . . Wie alt sind sie? Sie sind . . .

Do you know the numbers from 0 to 20?

Write out in German the numbers from 0 to 20. null, eins, zwei, drei, vier, fünf, sechs, sieben, acht, neun, zehn, elf, zwölf, dreizehn, vierzehn, fünfzehn, sechzehn, siebzehn, achtzehn, neunzehn, zwanzig

Do you know the forms of the verb *sein*?

Complete the following sentences.

1. Das Mädchen _ist_ 15.
2. Ich _bin_ 13.
3. Der Junge _ist_ 16.
4. Frl. Seifert _ist_ aus Wien.
5. _Bist_ du aus Deutschland?
6. Wer _ist_ das?
7. Jens und Wiebke _sind_ aus Deutschland.
8. Er _ist_ aus Österreich.

Can you say where you are from? Can you ask where others are from?

Say where you are from. Ask one of your classmates where he or she is from. Ich bin aus . . . Woher bist du?

Can you ask questions anticipating a yes or no answer?

Make up three questions anticipating a yes or no answer.
Possible answers: Heisst du Peter?/Bist du aus New York?/Ist er sechzehn?

Can you ask for information to be repeated?

What do you say if you don't understand part or all of the following statements? Wie bitte?

1. Ich bin aus Deutschland. Woher?
2. Er heisst Jens Kröger. Wie heisst er?
3. Das Mädchen ist 15 Jahre alt. Wie alt ist sie?
4. Der Deutschlehrer heisst Sperling. Wie heisst er?

Can you address adults using the *Sie*-form?

Ask your teacher his or her name and where he or she is from.

Wie heissen Sie? Woher sind Sie?

WORTSCHATZ *Vocabulary*

SECTION A

auf Wiedersehen! *goodbye!*
bis dann! *see you later!*
Frau *Mrs.*
Fräulein *Miss*
Frl. = Fräulein *Miss*
grüss dich! *hi!*
guten Morgen! *good morning!*
guten Tag! *hello!*
hallo! *hello! hi!*
Herr *Mr.*
Morgen! *morning!*
Tag! *hello! hi!*
tschau! *bye! so long!*
tschüs! *bye, so long!*
Wiedersehen! *bye!*

SECTION B

das *the; that*
das ist . . . *that's . . .*
der *the*
der **Deutschlehrer** *the German teacher* (m)
die **Deutschlehrerin** *the German teacher* (f)
die *the*
er heisst *his name is*
ich heisse *my name is*
der **Junge** *the boy*
der **Lehrer** *the teacher* (m)
die **Lehrerin** *the teacher* (f)
das **Mädchen** *the girl*
sie heisst *her name is*
und *and*
wer? *who?*
wer ist das? *who's that?*
wie heisst das Mädchen? *what's the girl's name?*
wie heisst der Junge? *what's the boy's name?*
wie heisst du? *what's your name?*
wie heisst er? *what's his name?*
wie heisst sie? *what's her name?*

SECTION C

alt *old*
auch *also*
du bist *you are*
er ist *he is*
ich bin *I am*
ich bin dreizehn. *I am thirteen.*
ich bin sechzehn Jahre alt. *I am sixteen years old.*
sie ist *she is*
sie sind *they are*
wie? *how?*
wie alt bist du? *how old are you?*
die **Zahlen** *the numbers*
die **Zahlen von null bis zwanzig** *the numbers from zero to twenty,* see page 42

SECTION D

aus *from*
aus der Schweiz *from Switzerland*
DDR = Deutsche Demokratische Republik *German Democratic Republic*[1]
Deutschland *Germany*
fragt *asks*
heissen Sie Müller? *is your name Müller?*
heisst du Michael? *is your name Michael?*
ich? *me?*
ich bin aus *I'm from*
ja *yes*
der **Mathematiklehrer** *the math teacher*
München *Munich*
nein *no*
oder *or*
Österreich *Austria*
Schweiz *Switzerland*
wie bitte? *I beg your pardon?*
wie heissen Sie? *what's your name?*
Wien *Vienna*
woher? *from where?*
woher bist du? *where are you from?*
woher sind . . .? *where are . . . from?*
woher sind Sie? *where are you from?*

---

[1]German words are usually stressed on the first syllable. When this is not the case, it will be indicated on the vocabulary list so you will know how to pronounce the word. The stress will be marked by an underscore or a dot. In addition to stress, the underscore will signify a long vowel; the dot will signify a short vowel.

1. Frau, Fräulein, Herr, Morgen, Tag, Wiedersehen, Deutschlehrer, Deutschlehrerin, Junge, Lehrer, Lehrerin, Mädchen, Zahlen, DDR, Deutschland, Mathematiklehrer, München, Österreich, Schweiz, Wien
2. Fräulein, grüss dich!, tschüs!, Mädchen, Müller, München, Österreich

WORTSCHATZÜBUNGEN *Vocabulary Activities*

1. All German nouns begin with a capital letter. Look at the **Wortschatz** and pick out all the nouns.

2. German has several letters that do not exist in English: **ä, ö, ü,** and **äu.** The marking ¨ is called an umlaut. Look at the **Wortschatz** above. Pick out all the words that have an umlaut, write them down, and say them.

Note that cognates and some unfamiliar words have not been glossed at the bottom of the pages. Encourage students to concentrate on understanding the general meaning of what they are reading rather than on translating each word.

ZUM LESEN

Wo ist Deutschland?

Deutschland ist in Europa. Deutschland: das sind zwei Länder°, die Bundesrepublik Deutschland (BRD) und die Deutsche Demokratische Republik (DDR).

Die Bundesrepublik Deutschland hat° neun Nachbarn°: die Deutsche Demokratische Republik, die Tschechoslowakei, Österreich, die Schweiz, Frankreich, Luxemburg, Belgien, die Niederlande und Dänemark.

Wo ist Dänemark?—Dänemark ist nördlich von° Deutschland. Die Deutsche Demokratische Republik und die Tschechoslowakei sind östlich°, Österreich und die Schweiz sind südlich°, und Frankreich, Luxemburg, Belgien und die Niederlande sind westlich von° Deutschland.

Margit Dastl ist aus Wien. Wien ist die Hauptstadt° von Österreich. Die Hauptstadt der Bundesrepublik Deutschland ist Bonn. Berlin (Ost) ist die Hauptstadt der Deutschen Demokratischen Republik, und Bern ist die Hauptstadt der Schweiz.

Man spricht Deutsch° in Deutschland: in der Bundesrepublik und in der Deutschen Demokratischen Republik. Man spricht Deutsch auch in Österreich, in der Schweiz, in Liechtenstein (zwischen° Österreich und der Schweiz), auch in einem Teil von° Luxemburg und in Norditalien (in Südtirol).

Think about what you have read. What information could you give to someone who asked you "Where is Germany?" What else could you tell him or her?

Übung • Beantworte die Fragen! *Answer the questions.*

1. Wo ist Deutschland?
2. Wie heissen die Nachbarn?
3. Wo ist Österreich? Und Frankreich?
4. Welche° Nachbarn sind westlich der Bundesrepublik? Und östlich? Südlich?
5. Was ist Wien? Berlin (Ost)? Bern? Bonn?
6. Wo spricht man Deutsch?
7. Wo spricht man Deutsch in den Vereinigten Staaten°?
8. Wie heissen unsere Nachbarn?
9. Und wie heisst unsere Hauptstadt?

1. Deutschland ist in Europa. 2. Deutschlands Nachbarn heissen: die Deutsche Demokratische Republik, die Tschechoslowakei, Österreich, die Schweiz, Frankreich, Luxemburg, Belgien, die Niederlande und Dänemark. 3. Österreich ist südlich von Deutschland. Frankreich ist westlich von Deutschland. 4. Frankreich, Luxemburg, Belgien und die Niederlande sind westlich von Deutschland. Die Deutsche Demokratische Republik und die Tschechoslowakei sind östlich von Deutschland. Österreich und die Schweiz sind südlich von Deutschland. 5. Wien ist die Hauptstadt von Österreich. Berlin (Ost) ist die Hauptstadt der Deutschen Demokratischen Republik. Bern ist die Hauptstadt der Schweiz. Bonn ist die Hauptstadt der Bundesrepublik Deutschland. (Continued on page 58)

---

wo *where;* **Länder** *countries;* **hat** *has;* **Nachbarn** *neighbors;* **nördlich von** *north of;* **östlich** *east (of);* **südlich** *south (of);* **westlich von** *west of;* **die Hauptstadt** *the capital;* **man spricht Deutsch** *German is spoken;* **zwischen** *between;* **in einem Teil von** *in a part of;* **welche** *which;* **in den Vereinigten Staaten** *in the United States*

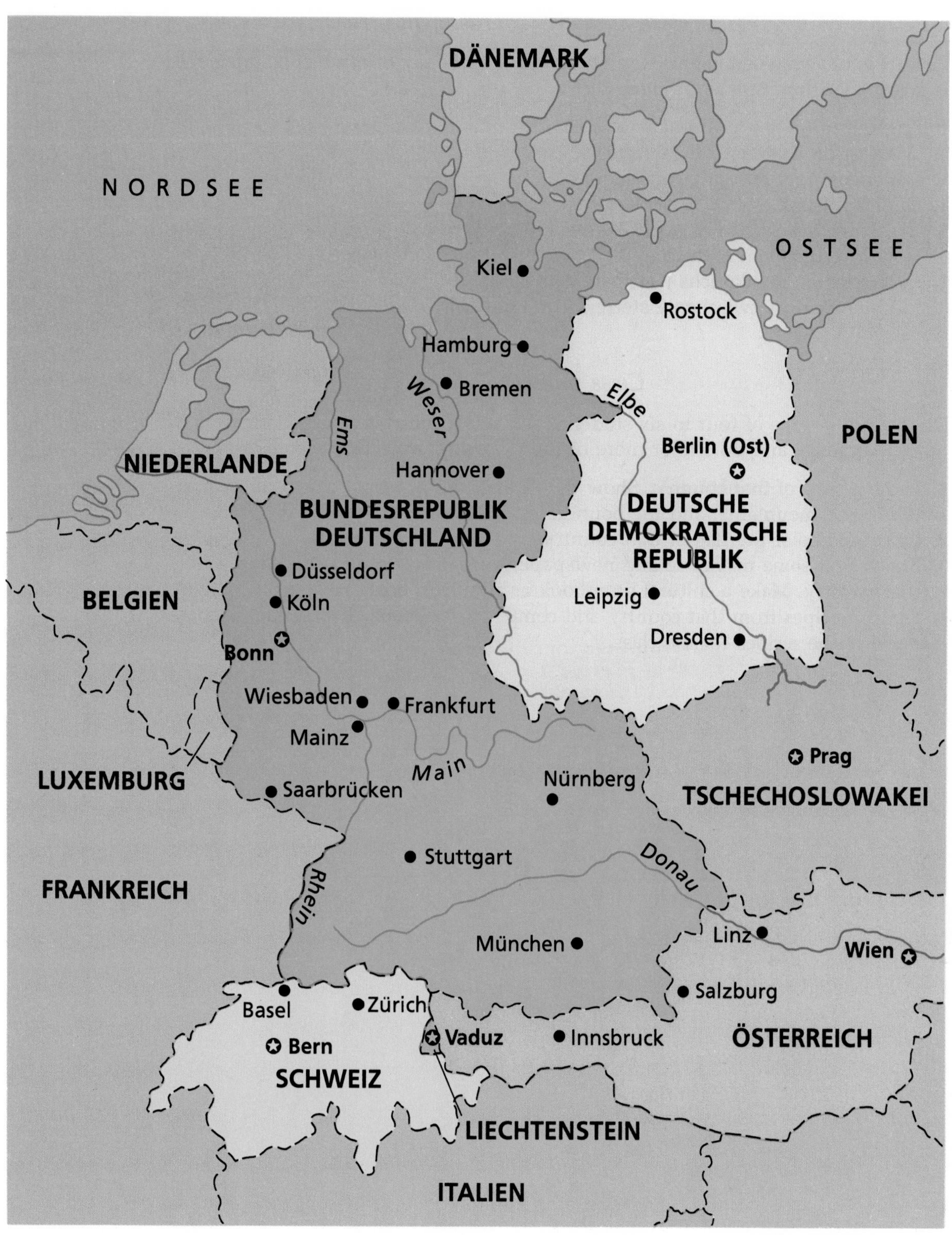

DÄNEMARK
NORDSEE
OSTSEE
Kiel
Rostock
Hamburg
Bremen
Weser
Elbe
Ems
POLEN
NIEDERLANDE
Hannover
Berlin (Ost)
BUNDESREPUBLIK DEUTSCHLAND
DEUTSCHE DEMOKRATISCHE REPUBLIK
Düsseldorf
Köln
BELGIEN
Leipzig
Dresden
Bonn
Wiesbaden
Frankfurt
Mainz
Prag
LUXEMBURG
Main
Nürnberg
Saarbrücken
TSCHECHOSLOWAKEI
Stuttgart
Donau
FRANKREICH
Rhein
München
Linz
Wien
Basel
Zürich
Salzburg
Bern
Vaduz
Innsbruck
ÖSTERREICH
SCHWEIZ
LIECHTENSTEIN
ITALIEN

Übung • Stimmt oder stimmt nicht? *True or not true?*

Read the following statements. If a statement is true, say **Stimmt!** If a statement is false, say **Stimmt nicht!** Then correct it.

1. England ist mitten in Europa. Stimmt nicht!
2. Wien ist die Hauptstadt Österreichs. Stimmt!
3. Dänemark liegt nördlich von Deutschland. Stimmt!
4. Die Hauptstadt der DDR ist Bern. Stimmt nicht!
5. Die Schweiz liegt östlich von Österreich. Stimmt nicht!
6. In der DDR spricht man Deutsch. Stimmt!
7. Österreich ist Frankreichs Nachbar. Stimmt nicht!
8. Liechtenstein ist zwischen Österreich und der Schweiz. Stimmt!

Übung • Klassenprojekt *Class project*

Divide into groups of four to six students. Choose a country where German is the official language and do one or more of the following projects:

1. Draw a map of that country. Show the capital, the principal cities, the major rivers and mountains, and the boundaries.
2. Draw and color the flag of that country.
3. Try to find some magazine and newspaper articles and photos pertaining to that country. Make a cultural scrapbook or a bulletin board.
4. Collect recipes from that country and compile a cookbook. If possible, prepare some of the recipes for the class.

(Continued from page 56)

6. Man spricht Deutsch in Deutschland, in der Bundesrepublik und in der Deutschen Demokratischen Republik. Man spricht Deutsch auch in Österreich, in der Schweiz, in Liechtenstein, in einem Teil von Luxemburg und in Norditalien (Südtirol).
7. Man spricht Deutsch in Pennsylvanien, Minnesota, Wisconsin, Texas und Alabama.
8. Unsere Nachbarn heissen Kanada und Mexiko.
9. Unsere Hauptstadt heisst Washington.

Postkarten

Our new friends are traveling. Here are some postcards they sent to their friends.

Schweiz . Suisse . Svizzera
Bern - Hauptstadt der Schweiz

Herzliche Grüsse
aus der Schweiz.
Ich bin in
Bern.
Wiebke

Frl. Katja Hauser
Haupt... 17
7840 ...

Wien . Vienna
Parlament

Grüss dich!
Ich bin in
Österreich,
in Wien!
Tschüs, Bruno

Herrn Michael Pertsch
Bahnhofstrasse 38
4790 Paderborn

Übung • Jetzt bist du dran!

Now write in German a postcard to a friend back home from one or all of the following places: Wien, Dresden, Hamburg, Innsbruck.

KAPITEL 2

KAPITEL 2 Schule

Scope and Sequence

	BASIC MATERIAL	COMMUNICATIVE FUNCTIONS
SECTION A	**Wie kommst du in die Schule? (A1)**	**Exchanging information** • Telling how you get to school
SECTION B	**Schulsachen (B1)** **Was kosten die Schulsachen? (B12)** **Du, wo ist das Wörterbuch? (B20)**	**Exchanging information** • Asking about prices of school supplies **Socializing** • Saying please, thank you, and you're welcome • Getting someone's attention
SECTION C	**Welche Fächer hast du heute? (C1)** **Zahlen** *(from 5 to 60 counting by fives)* **(C6)** **Wann hat Jens Mathe? (C7)** **Was habt ihr jetzt? (C10)**	**Exchanging information** • Giving information about your class schedule • Telling time
SECTION D	**Hausaufgaben und Noten (D1)** **Ist Bio schwer? (D7)**	**Exchanging information** • Talking about homework and grades **Expressing feelings and emotions** • Responding to good and to bad news
TRY YOUR SKILLS	Pronunciation /a:/, /e:/, /i:/, /o:/, /u:/, /ɔ/, /ü/, /ö/ Letter-sound correspondences long **a, e, i, o, u; ah, ie, ü, ö,** final **d, g, -ig** Dictation	
ZUM LESEN	**Hausaufgabenlied** (a student's reaction to homework in verse) **Der Traum** (cartoon: a frightening dream)	

WRITING A variety of controlled and open-ended writing activities appear in the Pupil's Edition. The Teacher's Notes identify other activities suitable for writing practice and suggest additional writing activities.

COOPERATIVE LEARNING Many of the activities in the Pupil's Edition lend themselves to cooperative learning. The Teacher's Notes explain some of the many instances where this teaching strategy can be particularly effective. For guidelines on how to use cooperative learning, see page T13.

GRAMMAR	CULTURE	RE–ENTRY
The verb **kommen** (A5)	How students get to school	Personal pronouns Asking questions
The definite articles **der, die, das** (B6) Noun plurals (B14) **Was kostet—was kosten** (B16) The pronouns **er, sie, es,** and **sie** (plural) (B22)	German currency and how to read prices The concept of grammatical gender	Definite articles Numbers from 0 to 20
The verb **haben** (C12)	System of scheduling classes Subjects taught in German schools	Numbers Personal pronouns
	System of grading	Numbers School subjects School supplies
Recombining communicative functions, grammar, and vocabulary		
Reading for practice and pleasure		

TEACHER–PREPARED MATERIALS

Section A Pictures of vehicles; flashcards of subjects, **kommen,** means of transportation
Section B School supplies; money; price tags; cards of nouns listed in B6
Section C Class schedule; clock; flashcards: school subjects, days of the week
Section D Flashcards with expressions responding to good news and bad news

UNIT RESOURCES

Übungsheft, Unit 2
Arbeitsheft, Unit 2
Unit 2 Cassettes
Transparencies 5–7
Quizzes 5–8
Unit 2 Test

KAPITEL

2

A1–5

OBJECTIVE **To exchange information:** tell how you get to school

CULTURAL BACKGROUND In German-speaking countries, getting to school is not just a matter of walking or taking the bus or driving. There are no school buses, and teenagers are not allowed to drive till age 18. Also, students may have to go to another part of the city or even another town to get to school. Therefore, students frequently use subways, public buses, or streetcars and sometimes even trains. If they live fairly near school, they may go by bicycle or motorized bike **(Moped).** Long rows of bicycle stands are a common sight in schoolyards.

MOTIVATING ACTIVITY Before starting on Section A, have the students think about what would happen if school were several miles from their homes and there were no school buses. How would they get to school? Could they use any public transportation? Discuss the students' findings with them.

A1 Wie kommst du in die Schule?

Play the cassette or read the text aloud as the students listen with their books closed. Stop after the initial dialog and personalize it: **Kommst du mit dem Bus oder zu Fuss? Ich komme mit dem Auto. Wie kommst du in die Schule?** Continue with the presentation of the other segments, proceeding in the usual manner. Call the students' attention to the key phrases **mit dem Moped, mit dem Rad,** and so forth. Can they discover a pattern? Which phrases are different and do not fit the pattern? **(Mit *der* Strassenbahn, zu Fuss)** Put the phrases on an overhead transparency or on the board.

A2 Übung • Beantworte die Fragen!

SLOWER–PACED LEARNING Require short-answer responses only: **mit dem Moped, zu Fuss, Jens.** Later, after these students have become more familiar with the new material, you might come back to this activity and ask for complete sentences.

A3 WIE SAGT MAN DAS?

This is a good place to point out to the students that they should not look for exact equivalents in other languages. There is a word for *go* as well as a word for *come* in German; but you wouldn't use it in this context.

A4 Übung • Und du? Wie steht's mit dir?

As a variation, put the following mini-dialog on an overhead transparency or make copies. Have the students work in pairs to complete the conversation. Check their work. Use the mini-dialog for reading practice.

A: Wie kommst du in die Schule?
B: ______. Und du?
A: ______.
B: Mit dem Auto?
A: Ja, ______ achtzehn.

A5 ERKLÄRUNG

To keep up the students' interest while practicing the forms of **kommen,** vary the prepositional phrase. Say, for example, **zu Fuss.** The students reply, **Ich komme zu Fuss, Du kommst zu Fuss,** and so on.

A6 Übung • Jetzt bist du dran

As a variation, have the students ask one another questions requiring a **ja** or a **nein** answer: **Wie kommst du in die Schule? Mit dem Moped? —Nein, mit dem Rad.** Model one or two of these first, so that they can see what kind of response you expect.

CHALLENGE Have the students do the above variation, but ask them to reply in complete sentences: **Nein, ich komme mit dem Rad** or **Ja, ich komme mit dem Moped.**

A7 Übung • Wie kommen alle in die Schule?

As a variation, tell the students to imagine themselves attending school in **Düsseldorf.** The city has an elaborate system of streetcars and buses, but no subway. Some students live far away from school, others live not so far away, and a few live quite close to school. What would the results of a poll taken in a class of that school look like? Have each student pick a means of getting to school. Two students should play the pollsters and ask each student how he or she gets to school.

OBJECTIVES **To exchange information:** ask about prices of school supplies; **to socialize:** say please, thank you, and you're welcome; get someone's attention

CULTURAL BACKGROUND Although in Germany textbooks are generally free, in some areas students have to buy their books as well as their school supplies—that is, the parents pay for the textbooks. Textbooks are available in large bookstores.

German students carry all their school supplies in a sturdy briefcase, often very colorful, made of leather or heavy plastic.

MOTIVATING ACTIVITY Ask the students to list all the common school supplies that they buy, especially in fall or at the start of the school year. They should keep this list for later reference and discussion.

B1 Schulsachen

Follow the general procedures suggested in A1 of Unit 1. Break the dialog into manageable segments. After playing the first segment or reading it aloud several times, ask the students how much they understood. Discuss how one listens for the gist of a conversation:

1. Listen for key words that give the situation away. For example, in this case, the word **kostet** and the numbers with the word **Mark** after them signal a talk about prices.
2. Relax. Do not feel that you must understand every word.
3. Make guesses and inferences. Verify your hunches by repeated listening.

Introduce the new vocabulary, dramatizing words the students cannot guess. For example, for **Entschuldigung,** walk up to a student and ask for help: **Entschuldigung, ist das Peter Schmidt?** or bump into a student's table and say: **Entschuldigung.** Or, for **Taschenrechner,** make some math calculations on the board. Get them wrong. Redo them. Say: **Ich rechne und rechne . . . Wo ist mein Taschenrechner? Das geht schneller,** and so forth.

Note: The input given by the teacher can and should be slightly above the level of the students' active knowledge. Students will pick up a great deal of the incidental language and retain it well because of the vividness of the situation and personal involvement.

Have the students repeat difficult words in the dialog several times: **Entschuldigung, Wörterbuch, Taschenrechner.** Concentrate on the **sch-** combinations, the **ö,** and the **ach-**sound.

Now make a game of it. Give a sound. Ask the students to find the words that contain that particular sound.

/ʃt/ Bleistift, Stundenplan
/ʃ/ Taschenrechner, Schulsachen, Schultasche
/x/ Wörterbuch
/R/ Taschenrechner
/u:/ Kuli, Schulsachen

You may include some of the words from A1 in your search: /ʃt/, **Strassenbahn;** /R/, **Rad;** /u:/, **Fuss.**

Ask the students to take out the list of school supplies they made up for the motivating activity and compare it to the German school supplies listed here.

B2 Ein wenig Landeskunde

Have each student make up a pattern using numbers up to 20. The other students must guess the pattern and complete it up to 20; for example:

zwei, vier, sechs . . .
drei, sechs, neun . . .
fünf, zehn, fünfzehn . . .
eins, drei, fünf

B3 Übung • Wir lesen Preise!

For extra practice, dictate some more prices. Then have each student prepare five prices. They should then pair off and practice dictating their five sets of prices to one another.

ANSWERS

1. elf Mark
2. zwei Mark zehn
3. siebzehn Mark zwanzig
4. neun Mark
5. sieben Mark fünf
6. dreizehn Mark acht
7. eine Mark siebzehn
8. neunzehn Mark
9. vier Mark zwei

B4 Übung • Was kostet alles?

The students can give long or short answers: **Was kostet das Wörterbuch? — (Das Wörterbuch kostet) dreizehn Mark.**

B5 Übung • Hör gut zu!

You will hear the prices for ten school items. Listen to the price of each item and then write it down. For example, you hear: **Das Buch kostet DM 3,10.** You write down: *3 comma 10,* the price of the book. Let's begin. **Fangen wir an!**

1. Die Kassette kostet DM 8,20. *eight twenty*
2. Das Poster kostet DM 5,00. *five*
3. Der Taschenrechner kostet DM 13,00. *thirteen*
4. Der Stundenplan kostet DM 1,00. *one*
5. Der Kuli kostet DM 1,15. *one fifteen*
6. Das Wörterbuch kostet DM 12,00. *twelve*
7. Die Schultasche kostet DM 18,00. *eighteen*
8. Das Heft kostet DM 1,10. *one ten*
9. Der Taschenrechner kostet DM 19,20. *nineteen twenty*
10. Das Buch kostet DM 11,00. *eleven*

Now check your answers. *Read each item again and give the correct answer.*

B6

ERKLÄRUNG

Generally, refer to **der**-words, **die**-words, and **das**-words in preference to masculine, feminine, and so on. To make the task of learning genders a little easier for the students, simplify the list as follows:

1. Ask the students to list those nouns that have natural gender—that is, are inherently feminine or masculine.
2. Tell students to look for patterns among the **die**-words. They should come up with the endings **-in** (always feminine) and **-e** (usually feminine). Tell them that there are others, which they will learn in time.
3. Try giving the students mnemonic devices, such as the following: **Kuli** and **Bleistift** are both writing instruments and are both **der**-words. **Heft, Poster,** and **Buch** are all made out of paper and are all **das**-words. *Make it clear to the students that these* are *mnemonic devices*—do not leave them with the impression that all paper goods are **das**-words in German or that all writing instruments are **der**-words.
4. This leaves **Taschenrechner**—and instruments ending in **-er** are always **der**-words—**Stundenplan, Zahl,** and **Wörterbuch.** The last three are straight memorization.

B7

Übung • Was kostet . . . ?

CHALLENGE The students pair off. The first student asks and gives the price he or she thinks is right: **Was kostet das Heft? Eine Mark?** The second student answers with the correct price: **Nein, eine Mark zwanzig.**

B8

WIE SAGT MAN DAS?

To demonstrate the dual use of **bitte,** go around the classroom asking students for various classroom objects, preferably using active vocabulary. If they don't know the German word for an object, just point to it as you say the word. Thank them, and model the reply **Bitte!** They should quickly get the idea.

B9

Übung • Rollenspiel

Teach the name and gender of a few additional school-supply items that American students commonly use and have with them. Include these in the role-play: **das Papier, der Hefter** *(binder),* **der Filzstift** *(felt-tip pen, marker),* **der Radiergummi.**

You can expand the activity by having the salesperson unsure he or she correctly understands the customer:

A: Was kostet der Kuli, bitte?
B: Der Kuli?
A: Ja.
B: Der Kuli kostet fünf Mark.
A: Danke.
B: Bitte.

B 10 Übung • Hör gut zu!

You will hear ten questions. Each one contains a noun. Listen to each question and determine whether the noun you hear is masculine, feminine, or neuter. For example, you hear: **Was kostet die Schultasche, bitte?** You place a check mark in the row labeled *feminine*, because the question you heard contains a feminine noun. Let's begin. **Fangen wir an!**

1. Was kostet der Taschenrechner, bitte? *masculine*
2. Woher ist die Verkäuferin? *feminine*
3. Wer ist die Lehrerin? *feminine*
4. Was kostet der Kuli, bitte? *masculine*
5. Wer ist das Mädchen? *neuter*
6. Was kostet das Wörterbuch, bitte? *neuter*
7. Wer ist der Lehrer? *masculine*
8. Wie heisst die Zahl? *feminine*
9. Was kostet der Bleistift, bitte? *masculine*
10. Woher ist der Deutschlehrer, bitte? *masculine*

Now check your answers. *Read each item again and give the correct answer.*

B 11 Schreibübung • Im Laden

You may also use this as an oral activity. Ask the students to respond to anything you say with an appropriate phrase, statement, or question. Use these as stimuli:

Das Wörterbuch, bitte.
Was kostet das?
Das kostet nur achtzehn Mark?
Kostet das zehn Mark oder mehr?

B 12 WAS KOSTEN DIE SCHULSACHEN?

In this case, you might have the students look at the picture before you play the cassette or read the text aloud. Ask them to look at the photo and the drawings with words and prices. Tell them that *all* the words are in the plural. Which have changed? How?

After you have played the cassette or read the text aloud, have them repeat the plurals after you. Concentrate on the form and pronunciation of **Bücher.** Point out that the **ach**-sound of **Buch** changes to an **ich**-sound in the plural **(Bücher).**

B 13 Übung • Was kostet alles?

First do this activity as question/answer practice with the entire class. Then have the students pair off and ask each other the questions, alternating roles each time.

B14 ERKLÄRUNG

Have the students look at the chart and read the noun plurals after you. Ask them if they see any patterns in the formation of plurals. If not, help them find the patterns.

—Nouns ending in **-e** usually take the plural ending **-en.**
—Nouns ending in **-in** always take the plural ending **-nen.**
—Nouns ending in **-er** and **-en** do not add an ending.

This reduces the list of plurals to be learned by rote to six: **Bleistifte, Hefte, Stundenpläne, Zahlen, Bücher,** and **Kulis.**

Explain that the last part of a compound noun determines the gender of the compound noun and also its plural. By learning **Stundenpläne** and **Bleistifte,** students really learn that in the plural any **Plan** becomes **Pläne** and any **Stift** becomes **Stifte.**

B15 Übung • Singular and Plural

Run through the list at least three times, calling on different students each time. Ask the students which nouns are ambiguous—that is, could be either singular or plural without the gender marker.

B16 ERKLÄRUNG

Practice **was kostet?** and **was kosten?** with several appropriate nouns from B15. Call for each noun in both singular and plural. This will prepare the students for the following activity.

B17 Übung • Jetzt bist du dran

To introduce this activity, hold up one item or two items of the same kind. The items should be school-supply items or objects listed in B14. Have the students ask for the price. Then have them pair off, one student playing the customer and the other playing the salesperson.

B18 Übung • Hör gut zu!

You will hear ten questions, each containing a noun. Some of the nouns are singular and some are plural. Listen carefully to each sentence and determine whether the noun is singular or plural. For example, you hear, **Was kostet die Schultasche?** You place your check mark in the row labeled *singular.* Let's begin. **Fangen wir an!**

1. Was kosten die Kulis? *plural*
2. Was kosten die Poster? *plural*
3. Was kostet der Taschenrechner? *singular*
4. Was kostet die Kassette? *singular*
5. Was kostet das Heft? *singular*
6. Was kosten die Bücher? *plural*
7. Was kosten die Bleistifte? *plural*
8. Was kostet das Wörterbuch? *singular*
9. Was kostet der Stundenplan? *singular*
10. Was kosten die Kassetten? *plural*

Now check your answers. *Read each item again and give the correct answer.*

B 19 Schreibübung

To expand this activity, put some mini-dialogs on an overhead transparency or a handout and have the students complete them. A sample mini-dialog follows:

A:	______?	A:	______.
B:	Wie bitte?	B:	Sechzehn Mark.

B 20 DU, WO IST DAS WÖRTERBUCH?

Introduce the material one exchange at a time. Play the cassette or read the exchange aloud as the students listen with their books closed. Repeat every exchange at least once. Act out such words or expressions as **dort drüben, dort,** and **Schau!** When you repeat the tape or read the exchange through again, ask, **Wo ist das Wörterbuch?** The students should answer, **Es ist dort drüben.** Say, **Das Wörterbuch, es ist dort drüben.** Proceed similarly with the other exchanges, modeling new vocabulary and asking appropriate questions.

On an overhead transparency or on the board, put **das Wörterbuch, der Taschenrechner,** and **die Kassette.** Ask the students to give you the right pronouns. After you introduce the exchange between Jens and Frau Meier, put the following on an overhead transparency or on the board: **die Poster, die Taschenrechner,** and **die Kassetten.** Have the students give you the corresponding pronoun.

B 21 Übung • Wo ist . . . ?

If you have practiced similar structures thoroughly in presenting the basic material, you might proceed directly to working in pairs.

B 22 ERKLÄRUNG

Help students remember the noun-pronoun relationship by stressing the similarities in sound: **der —er, die —sie, das —es.** See if they fully understand by giving them unknown words, along with their definite articles, from their immediate environment. Hold up the item and point to it as you ask for the pronoun.

Wo ist die Kreide?	die Schere?	der Tesafilm?
der Tafelwischer?	der Spitzer?	der Papierkorb?

Students are to answer with **Er (sie, es) ist dort drüben.**

B 23 Übung • So eine Unordnung!

The students work in pairs. One student "looks" for an item, while the other one "finds" it. They reverse roles after each item.

B 24 Übung • Die Schule beginnt. Wo ist . . . ?

Have the students do the question/answer practice in pairs. As a variation or as a warm-up, you could play the new teacher who doesn't know his or her students too well yet. Use the students' real names.

LEHRER Wo ist Peter Smith? (Susi Johnson)?
KLASSE Er (sie) ist da.
LEHRER Ach ja, danke.

B 25 WIE SAGT MAN DAS?

Point out that the attention getters **du, schau,** and **schau mal** should only be used with young people, close friends, and family members, not with teachers or other unrelated adults. You can consolidate many of the expressions the students have learned by playing **Scharaden** with them. They guess which phrase you are illustrating. For example, to illustrate **Entschuldigung!**, you might brush against someone and look embarrassed. For **Schau mal!**, you could wave to someone to come and look. Shrug your shoulders for **Ich weiss nicht.** Look inquisitive for **Wie bitte?** and so on.

B 26 Übung • Partnerarbeit

Before having the students work in pairs or small groups—these dialogs are adaptable for more than two participants—demonstrate a few for the class as a whole. Here is a sample adaptation for three speakers:

A: Du, ______, wo ist der Taschenrechner?
B: Ich weiss nicht.
C: Schau mal! Er ist dort drüben!

B 27 Übung • Hör gut zu!

You will hear twelve questions, each containing a noun. Each question is followed by another question that is incomplete. Listen carefully to the questions and determine which word you would use in the second question to refer to the noun in the first question. For example, you hear, **Wo ist die Schultasche? —Du, wo ist ______?** You place a check mark in the row labeled ***sie*** because the word **sie** refers to **die Schultasche** in the first question. Let's begin. **Fangen wir an!**

1. Wo ist der Kuli? — Du, wo ist ______? *er*
2. Wo sind die Bleistifte? — Du, wo sind ______? *sie*
3. Wo ist das Heft? — Du, wo ist ______? *es*
4. Wo ist die Sabine? — Du, wo ist ______? *sie*
5. Wo ist der Lehrer? — Du, wo ist ______? *er*
6. Wo ist das Poster? — Du, wo ist ______? *es*
7. Wo ist der Taschenrechner? — Du, wo ist ______? *er*
8. Wo sind die Mädchen? — Du, wo sind ______? *sie*
9. Wo ist die Schultasche? — Du, wo ist ______? *sie*
10. Wo ist der Bleistift? — Du, wo ist ______? *er*
11. Wo ist die Kassette? — Du, wo ist ______? *sie*
12. Wo ist die Lehrerin? — Du, wo ist ______? *sie*

Now check your answers. *Read each item again and give the correct answer.*

B 28 Schreibübung • Entschuldigung! Was kostet . . . ?

To expand this activity, tell the students to imagine an office supply store in Germany having a big sale. All items are advertised as being **„nur . . . Mark." (Tesafilm — nur DM 1,00! Kulis — nur DM 4,20!)** Have them make up a page of sales items as it might appear in a newspaper. They may print the names of the items or use both pictures (cutouts or drawings) and print.

KAPITEL 2

C1–3

SECTION C

OBJECTIVE **To exchange information:** give information about your class schedule; tell time

CULTURAL BACKGROUND The students may have been wondering why students in Europe need to buy a special form to fill in their schedules. In Section C, this will become clear.

MOTIVATING ACTIVITY Have the students make out their own schedules on 3 × 5 cards. Make an enlarged copy of Jens' schedule and put it on an overhead transparency. Ask the students what they notice about the number of subjects Jens has as compared to their own. The length of class periods? The number and length of breaks? When does Jens' school day start and end?

C1 Welche Fächer hast du heute? 

Play the cassette or read the dialog aloud as the students listen with their books closed. Repeat this at least once. Ask some questions (accept minimal answers): **Wer fragt: „Welche Fächer hast du heute?" Was ist heute? Was hat Jens heute?** Then go through the conversation again as the students listen, this time with their books open.

Take the role of Frau Kröger and have the students take the role of Jens. Work on difficult words and phrases. Use backward build-up for the long question by Frau Kröger: **heute. hast du heute? Welche Fächer hast du heute?**

Ask detailed questions about the dialog. Use Jens' **Stundenplan** to teach the days of the week. Add **Sonntag.** Ask questions on the days of the week: **Was ist heute? Morgen?**

Play hard of hearing: have one student read a sentence. Stop the student. Ask a question as if you didn't understand. The student has to give you the needed information.

> Jens geht auf die Oberschule in Niebüll.
> Wer geht auf die Oberschule? —Jens.
> Wo? —In Niebüll.

C2 Ein wenig Landeskunde

This theme of school is ideal for really leading students into the target culture on a deeper than surface level, for the American student brings to it a great deal of knowledge and personal interest. In the United States, life for most students revolves around school. They will be eager to find out what it's like to go to school in German-speaking countries. Through learning linguistic and cultural items related to school, students will find cultural significance in information that seems unimportant at first encounter. For example, a **Stundenplan** is simply a schedule. The cultural implications of that word, however, are significant and need to be understood by students.

C3 Übung • Stimmt oder stimmt nicht? 

CHALLENGE Have some students prepare their own statements about Jens' schedule, following the pattern set in the book. Some of those should be factually right and some wrong. Next day, have the students read their statements to the class and have the class respond.

C4 Übung • Jens' Stundenplan

You could assign this as a written exercise, to be done in class or for homework. If you use it as a written exercise, ask the students to give all answers in full.

C5 Übung • Und du? Wie steht's mit dir?

Since your students probably have the same subjects every day, you may ask them to pretend that they are German students—perhaps using the classroom personalities you have established along with their German names. In that case, you might provide them with an expanded list of possible subjects.

C6 ZAHLEN

Practice counting by fives and by tens (starting on 5 or on 10). Then, using the items from B1, have the students tell which of those items they have many of: **(Kassetten) Ich habe 15 Kassetten.**

C7 WANN HAT JENS MATHE?

After you have introduced this section, have the students practice telling time in pairs. Each student should make a simple clock out of a paper plate, manila paper, and a metal fastener. Students first have to come up with one answer to **Wie spät ist es?** In a second round, they should state the time in two different ways, where possible.

CHALLENGE Set the clock to different times. Have the students respond, but have them purposely make an error in the hour. Question the time they give. The students should then correct themselves.

LEHRER Wie spät ist es?
SCHÜLER Es ist halb elf.
LEHRER Halb elf?
SCHÜLER Oh, nein, es ist halb zwölf.

C8 Übung • Wie spät ist es?

SLOWER–PACED LEARNING You might prepare extra clock faces for additional practice. Group them 3:20, 4:20, 5:20; 11:15, 12:15, 1:15; and so on. Initially require only one way to express the times. The next day, do the exercise again, this time having the students give two ways.

C9 Übung • Rollenspiel

This dialog can be adapted for groups of three or more. There is, of course, no need to stick to Jens' actual schedule; but the subjects should be subjects that would actually be taught at a German high school. A sample dialog follows:

WOLFGANG Was hast du am Montag um halb elf?
JENS Um halb elf? Moment mal! — Ich habe Biologie um halb elf. Und du?
WOLFGANG Ich habe Mathematik. Und du, Christa?
CHRISTA Ich? Ich habe Latein.

C10–15

C10 WAS HABT IHR JETZT?

Introduce the concept of **ihr** and reintroduce the concept of **wir** verbally and through gestures. Pointing to various students, say **Was hast du jetzt? Und was hast du jetzt?** Then, emphasizing the **ihr,** say **Was habt ihr jetzt?** Then say, **Ich habe jetzt Biologie.** Point to someone else: **Und Susi hat auch Biologie.** Then, emphasizing the **wir,** say **Wir haben jetzt Biologie.**

Play the cassette or read the conversation aloud as the students listen with their books closed. Then have them follow in their books as you read it again. Go on to the picture captions. Practice such difficult words as **Klassenkameraden** and **Parallelklasse.**

C11 Übung • Beantworte die Fragen!

As a warm-up for this exercise, give students sentences for completion. These should be taken from the conversation and the picture captions, either verbatim or slightly changed.

Jörg und Kristin haben ______.
Sie sind ______.
Mona und Lars sind ______.
Sie gehen in die ______.
Die 9a und 9b sind ______.
Ein Klassenarbeit? Na, dann ______.

C12 ERKLÄRUNG

Ask the students to suggest more subjects or other items to interpolate as you practice the forms: **Ich habe Biologie, wir haben eine Klassenarbeit,** and so on.

C13 Übung • Wer hat heute Deutsch?

As a variation, you can have the students answer in the negative: **Haben Jörg und Kristin heute Deutsch? — Nein, sie haben heute Mathe.**

C14 Übung • Was haben die Schüler heute?

SLOWER–PACED LEARNING Have the names of school subjects on the board or on an overhead transparency. Give several subjects requiring **hat-**answers first: **Mona/das Mädchen/er/Lars;** then several requiring **haben: Jörg und Kristin/wir/sie.**

C15 Übung • Hör gut zu!

You will hear ten sentences, each telling a time of day. Write the number of each sentence you hear in the appropriate box. For example, you hear **1. Es ist 7 Uhr 20.** You place the number 1, for sentence 1, in the box showing 7.20. Let's begin. **Fangen wir an!**

1. Es ist 7 Uhr 20. *seven-twenty*
2. Es ist 10 Uhr 40. *ten-forty*
3. Es ist 9 Uhr 35. *nine thirty-five*
4. Es ist Viertel nach vier. *four-fifteen*

5. Es ist halb eins. *twelve-thirty*
6. Es ist 2 Uhr 25. *two twenty-five*
7. Es ist 1 Uhr 10. *one-ten*
8. Es ist Viertel vor zwölf. *eleven forty-five*
9. Es ist 8 Uhr 45. *eight forty-five*
10. Es ist 6 Uhr 50. *six-fifty*

Now check your answers. *Read each item again and give the correct answer.*

C16

Übung • Partnerarbeit

CHALLENGE For the second of the two activities, have the students work in groups of three to five and produce dialogs that they can later present in front of the class as a whole.

C17

Schreibübung

For the third activity, have on hand a list of German terms for subjects that haven't appeared in the textbook so far. You may put these, along with the additional subjects suggested in C16, on the board or on an overhead transparency.

SECTION D

OBJECTIVES **To exchange information:** talk about homework and grades; **to express feelings and emotions:** respond to good and to bad news

CULTURAL BACKGROUND German high school students get quite a bit of homework in every subject. They take their studies seriously and strive for good grades. If students are held back more than once, they are expelled from school. It is not possible to repeat a particular course if you have failed it. The result of failing two major subjects is having to repeat that grade—with *all* its subjects!

MOTIVATING ACTIVITY Ask the students to think about the grading system used in American schools. Have them list the grades and then express each grade verbally; for example, A = very good, B = good, and so on. Next have them look at the grade record of a German student, given on page 78. What do they think the German grading system is? What is best? What is the poorest grade this student has?

D1

Hausaufgaben und Noten 

Introduce the narrative on Jens in the usual manner. Ask a few comprehension questions. Then introduce the dialog between Kristin and Jens. Ask such questions as *What are Kristin and Jens talking about? How does Kristin react? What does she say?*

Work with long sentences. Use backward build-up for longer sentences: **in Mathe. eine Vier in Mathe. Aber ich habe nur eine Vier in Mathe.** When you have the students read the dialog, have them work in pairs and ask them to use a lot of expression. Then have the students react, either positively or negatively, to various statements you make.

Ich habe eine Eins in Englisch.
Meine Noten in Mathe sind sehr schlecht.
Ich habe 1 000 Dollar.
Die Kassetten kosten nur 3 D-Mark.

KAPITEL 2

D2–7

D2 Ein wenig Landeskunde

Present a chart that shows the approximate equivalents of grades:

1 = Honors, A+, (A)	4 = (C), C−, D+
2 = (A), A−, B+ (B)	5 = D, D−
3 = (B), B−, C+ (C)	6 = F

Ask, **Was ist ungenügend?** The answer should be **eine Sechs.** Then ask, **Und was ist das in Amerika?** The answer should be **ein F.**

Work with the behavioral or social grades. Which of these behaviors are not graded in American schools? What does the fact that these behaviors *are* graded in Germany say about German culture?

CHALLENGE Have the students, working in cooperative learning groups, find the adjective equivalents for **Fleiss, Aufmerksamkeit,** and **Ordnung.** Then have them write compliments or reprimands of the kind a teacher or parent might give to one of their friends, brothers, or sisters: **Peter, du bist sehr fleissig!** or **Karin, du bist nicht ordentlich!**

D3 Übung • Beantworte die Fragen!

SLOWER–PACED LEARNING You might initially have the students answer the questions in short-answer form. Then they could write out the complete answers for homework.

CHALLENGE Have the students make up two or three additional questions about Jens and prepare the answers. They can then pair off and ask one another the questions.

D4 Übung • Und du? Wie steht's mit dir?

Have the students respond with the German equivalents of grades, i.e., the way an American grade would translate into the German system as in the chart you presented in D2.

D5 WIE SAGT MAN DAS?

Include **sehr gut** and **sehr schlecht** in the responses. **Sehr** is one of the most common qualifiers used with predicate adjectives and adverbs.

D6 Übung • Jetzt bist du dran

As a variation, have the students, working in pairs, talk about grades and react to one another. Call the students' attention to the cartoon; why does the boy need a fishing pole?

A: Bist du gut in ______?
B: ______.
A: Was hast du?
B: Eine ______.
A: Das ist ______!

D7 IST BIO SCHWER?

Introduce the concepts of **leicht** and **schwer.** Demonstrate them by means of math problems on the board, easy and hard words, and so on. Then have the students repeat sentences with these adjectives:

A: Bio ist schwer, sehr schwer.
B: Nein, Bio ist nicht schwer. Es ist leicht, sehr leicht!

As you play the cassette of the first exchange or read it aloud, ask simple comprehension questions: **Was hat das Mädchen in Bio? Wie ist Bio für sie?** Proceed similarly for the second exchange.

D 8 Übung • Jetzt bist du dran

Have the students ask each other for advice on subjects they might take next semester or year.

A: Du hast ______ ?
B: Ja.
A: Ist ______ schwer?
B: Ja, sehr ______ . *[or]* Nein, nicht ______ . Es ist ______ .

To expand this activity, have each student make a 10-point scale on paper (construction paper is best) going from **sehr leicht** on the left to **sehr schwer** on the right. They are to label the scale **Skala leicht bis schwer.** Have the students put all the subjects they presently have or have had in the past on that line:

sehr leicht									sehr schwer
1	2	3	4	5	6	7	8	9	10
Kunst		Englisch		Deutsch		Mathe		Physik Chemie	

Display all the scales.

D 9 Übung • Gut oder schlecht?

Illustrate the way you would like your students to dramatize their responses. Respond with exaggerated horror, for example, to **Ich habe eine Sechs in Algebra.**

D 10 Übung • Hör gut zu!

You will hear ten statements that express either good news or bad news. For each sentence you hear, determine which category it belongs in and place your check mark in the appropriate column. For example, you hear, **Ich habe eine Vier in Algebra. Das ist blöd.** You place a check mark in the row labeled *bad news.* Let's begin. **Fangen wir an!**

1. Du hast eine Eins in Geschichte. Das ist prima! *good news*
2. Phantastisch! Ich habe eine Eins in Deutsch. *good news*
3. In Mathe habe ich eine Vier. Das ist schade! *bad news*
4. Sie hat eine Vier in Französisch. Das ist nicht so gut. *bad news*
5. Prima! Du hast eine Zwei in Englisch. *good news*
6. Biologie ist toll! Ich habe eine Eins. *good news*
7. Mathe ist schwer. Ich habe eine Fünf. *bad news*
8. Du, das ist Spitze! Eine Zwei in Physik! *good news*
9. Ach, Deutsch ist prima! Ich habe eine Zwei. *good news*
10. Nur eine Vier in Englisch. Das ist schade! *bad news*

Now check your answers. *Read each item again and give the correct answer.*

D11 **Schreibübung • Was meinst du?**

To expand this activity, have the students give their opinion or react to these statements orally or in writing:

Physik ist schwer.	Wir haben jetzt Bio.
Mathe ist leicht.	Ich habe Englisch und Latein.
Ich habe eine Vier in Geschichte.	Wir haben eine Klassenarbeit.

ANSWERS (to 1.)
1. **A:** Was hast du in Deutsch? **B:** Ich habe eine Eins. **A:** Das ist toll!
2. **A:** Was hat Barbara in English? **B:** Sie hat eine Fünf. **A:** Das ist schlecht.
3. **A:** Was hat Peter in Erdkunde? **B:** Er hat eine Sechs. **A:** Schade!
4. **A:** Was haben Jens und Kristin in Latein? **B:** Sie haben eine zwei. **A:** Das ist gut!

D12 **Übung • Wer hat gute Augen?**

SLOWER–PACED LEARNING Briefly review the names of school supplies in German. Then do this as a group activity, using the blackboard.

TRY YOUR SKILLS

OBJECTIVE To recombine communicative functions, grammar, and vocabulary

CULTURAL BACKGROUND There are many student exchange programs sponsored by various German and American organizations. If you are interested in getting more information about exchange programs, contact the national office of the AATG (American Association of Teachers of German) in Cherry Hill, New Jersey.

1 **Gerd Ecker in den USA** 

Play the cassette or read the text aloud several times. Then have the students follow in their books as you read the text or play the cassette again.

SLOWER–PACED LEARNING Announce a **Diktat** *(dictation).* Take one or more of the paragraphs and dictate it to the students.

CHALLENGE Take one or more of the paragraphs and use it for a spot dictation—that is, leave out one or more strategic words for each sentence. Indicate the gaps by a lengthy pause. The students then have to fill in the gaps.

2 **Übung • Rollenspiel**

As a warm-up for this activity, lead the class in developing possible questions to ask Gerd. They may need help in transforming the statements into questions.

ANSWERS
A: Wie alt bist du? **B:** 16 Jahre alt. / **A:** Woher bist du? **B:** Aus Paderborn. / **A:** Wo ist Paderborn? **B:** In der Bundesrepublik Deutschland. / **A:** Auf welche Schule gehst du? **B:** Aufs Goerdeler Gymnasium. / **A:** Wie kommst du in die Schule? **B:** Mit dem Rad. / **A:** Wie kommen

die Klassenkameraden in die Schule? **B:** Mit dem Bus, mit dem Moped, mit dem Auto und auch zu Fuss. / **A:** Wann habt ihr Schule? **B:** Von Montag bis Freitag. Wir haben Sonnabend frei. / **A:** Wann beginnt die Schule? **B:** Um Viertel vor acht. / **A:** Wann ist die Schule aus? **B:** Um ein Uhr. / **A:** Welche Fächer hast du? **B:** Deutsch, Mathe, Englisch, Geschichte, Geographie, Sport and Kunst. / **A:** Welche Noten hast du? **B:** Ich habe eine Eins in Englisch und eine Zwei in Deutsch. Ich habe nur eine Vier in Mathe.

3 Übung • Erzähl mal, was Gerd gesagt hat!

As a variation, have one student make a presentation in front of the class while the rest verify the information.

CHALLENGE One student presents the material as before, but slips in a number of deliberate misstatements. The other students confirm or deny each statement with **Stimmt!** or **Stimmt nicht!** If the statement is incorrect, they should restate it correctly.

ANSWERS

Der Schüler aus Deutschland heisst Gerd Ecker. Er ist 16 Jahre alt. Er ist aus Paderborn in der Bundesrepublik Deutschland. Er geht aufs Goerdeler Gymnasium, und er kommt mit dem Rad in die Schule. Die Klassenkameraden kommen mit dem Bus, mit dem Moped, mit dem Auto und zu Fuss. Gerd hat von Montag bis Freitag Schule. Er hat Sonnabend frei. Die Schule beginnt um Viertel vor acht, und sie ist um ein Uhr aus. Er hat die Fächer Deutsch, Mathe, Englisch, Geschichte, Geographie, Sport und Kunst. Er ist gut in Englisch und in Deutsch. Er hat eine Eins in Englisch und eine Zwei in Deutsch. Er ist nicht so gut in Mathe. Er hat nur eine Vier.

4 Übung • Vortrag

As a preparation for this activity, choose one student as a model. Have that student answer questions while the rest of the class takes notes.

5 Schreibübung • Ein Artikel für die Schülerzeitung

Your class could actually start a class newspaper. If you have more than one section of German 1, they could all contribute. Have the students choose the best pieces to go in the newspaper.

6 Übung • Immer diese Schule!

CHALLENGE Have the students work in groups of three to five. Make a competition of it—who can keep going the longest? Time the conversations.

7 Schreibübung • Was passt zusammen?

After the students have done the written activity, have them cover up the right-hand side and give original oral responses to the questions or statements.

8 Übung • Was sagen sie?

After you have gone over several possible responses with the class, using the suggestion box for inspiration, have the students act the situations out.

SKILLS 9–10

9 **Übung • Reklame in der Zeitung**

Discuss the special terms used in the ads, but give the students a chance to guess at the meanings. In particular, have them look for cognates. Then have them scan the ads for information. Do not hold them responsible for the additional vocabulary.

10 **Aussprache-, Lese- und Schreibübungen** 

1. Listen carefully to the long vowel sounds /a:/, /e:/, /i:/, /o:/, and /u:/ in these words:

/a:/ /e:/ /i:/ /o:/ /u:/

da, sag, Rad; zehn, dem; vier, sieben, hier, prima; wo, Moped, Montag; du, Schule, Kuli, Fuss, gut

Did you listen carefully? What did you notice about the vowel sounds, especially in the words **dem, wo,** and **du?** The vowels **e, o,** and **u** have a "pure" quality. They do not glide from one vowel to another: not *dame,* but **dem;** not *vo-* as in English *vote,* but **wo;** not *doo-* as in English *doom,* but **du.** This changing or gliding quality of English vowels is one of the most prominent features of an American accent in German. Now repeat each of the following words with /a:/ sounds: **da, sag, Rad, Tag, Zahl, haben, nach, schade, Basel.** Repeat each of the following words with /e:/ sounds: **dem, zehn, geht, gehen.** Repeat each of the following words with /i:/ sounds: **sie, sieben, vier, wir, hier, viel, prima, Wien.** Repeat each of the following words with /o:/ sounds: **so, wo, Note, Moped, Montag.** And repeat each of the words with /u:/ sounds: **du, gut, Schule, nur, Fuss, Uhr.**

/ɔ/ Of the short vowel sounds, only the /ɔ/ sound (as in doch) needs attention. Depending on where you are from, your own speech may contain one or more English vowel sounds similar to /ɔ/ . For many speakers of American English, this German vowel sound is somewhat like the first vowel sound in the English word *awful.* However, the German /ɔ/ is much shorter and is produced with the lips in a more rounded position.

Listen to the sound /ɔ/ in these words: **kosten, toll, von, Sport, Mittwoch, Donnerstag, Sonnabend.** Repeat each of the following words with the /ɔ/ sound: **kosten, toll, von, Sport, Mittwoch, Donnerstag, Sonnabend.**

/ü/ Listen carefully to the /ü/ sounds in these words: **für, grüss, drüben; fünf, München, Niebüll, Glück, Tschüs.** The /ü/ sound does not exist in English. To make it, round your lips as if you were going to whistle. Without moving your lips from their position, try to say the vowel sound in the English word *bee.* You will say /ü:/. Now repeat each of the following words: (long /ü:/ sound) **für, grüss, drüben;** (short /ü/ sound) **fünf, München, Niebüll, Glück, Tschüs.**

/ö/ Listen carefully to the /ö/ sounds in these words: **blöd, Kröger, Österreich, Wörterbuch.** The /ö/ sound does not exist in English either. To make it, round your lips as if you were going to whistle. Without moving your lips from this position, try to say the vowel sound in the English word *bay.* You will say /ö:/. Now repeat each of the following words: (long /ö:/ sound) **blöd, Kröger, Österreich;** (short /ö/ sound) **Wörterbuch.**

2. In this section, you will practice reading the words printed in your textbook on page 85. Pay attention to the following:
   1. The vowels **a, e, i, o,** and **u** can represent long or short vowel

a e i o u sounds. They are long in the following words: **da, dem, wir, wo, du.** A vowel plus **h** is always long: **zehn, Zahl, Uhr.** The vowel combination **ie** is always long: **sie, wie, hier, sieben, vier, Wien.** Now listen and then read each of the printed words in the pause provided: **da, sag, Rad, Tag, schade, Zahl; dem, zehn; wir, prima, sie, wie, vier, sieben, hier, Wien; wo, Montag, Moped; du, Schule, Kuli, Fuss, gut, nur, Uhr.**

ü, ö
2. The letter **u** with two dots over it, which is the indication for an umlaut, represents the /ü/ sound. The letter **o** with an umlaut represents the /ö/ sound. Now listen and then read each of the printed words in the pause provided: **für, grüss, drüben; fünf, München, Niebüll, Glück, Tschüs; blöd, Kröger, Österreich, Wörterbuch.**

final d
3. The letter **d** at the end of a word or syllable is always pronounced /t/. Now listen and then read each of the printed words in the pause provided: **und, sind, Rad, blöd, Deutschland, Sonnabend, Klassenkamerad.**

final g
4. The letter **g** at the end of a word or syllable is pronounced /k/. Now listen and then read each of the printed words in the pause provided: **sag, Tag, Montag, Dienstag, Donnerstag, Freitag, Samstag, Sonntag, weg.**

final ig
5. The letter sequence **-ig** at the end of words is pronounced /iç/, as in the word **ich.** Now listen and then read each of the printed words in the pause provided: **zwanzig, dreissig, vierzig, fünzig, sechzig.**

3. Now close your textbook and write the sentences you hear.

1. Die Zahl sieben.
2. Um vier Uhr.
3. Sie sind in Wien.
4. Mit dem Rad.

WAS KANNST DU SCHON?

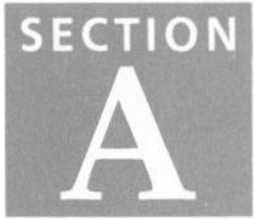

You might have the students put their sentences on the board or on an overhead transparency and correct them as a class. If you have not yet had them do so, you might now have them start keeping a **Was kannst du schon?** section in their notebooks. This is a convenient way for them to review.

You might call out words, for example **Kuli**—and the students answer **der Kuli, die Kulis—er.** Then repeat the correct answer, in case some of them didn't get it right.

ANSWERS

Was kostet der Kuli, bitte? — Der Kuli kostet vier Mark. / Danke! — Bitte!
Was kostet das Heft, bitte? — Das Heft kostet eine Mark zwanzig. / Danke! — Bitte!
Was kostet die Schultasche, bitte? — Sie kostet zwanzig Mark. / Danke! — Bitte!
Was kosten die Kassetten? — Sie kosten sechs Mark. / Danke! — Bitte!

Hold up a clock—this can be of the cardboard type typically used for classroom practice—and set the arms to the position desired, as the students call out the answers. You might also have the students fill in actual class schedules.

See if somebody can give another response. The students can practice the second item in pairs, with the second student reacting to the first and perhaps giving a further response.

WORTSCHATZ

Ask the students to form compound nouns by following the pattern established.

die Schule + die Tasche = die Schultasche

+ die Klasse	+ der Tag	+ der Kamerad
+ die Woche	+ der Bus	+ die Sachen

die Klasse + die Arbeit = die Klassenarbeit

+ der Kamerad + der Lehrer

Ask the students to demonstrate their understanding of the "little" words in each sentence by using each of them in an original sentence.

Ich habe nur eine Drei.
Wir haben Bio, dann Mathe.
Kommst du am Freitag um vier Uhr?
Es ist Viertel nach elf.
Er ist gut in Deutsch, aber schlecht in Mathe.

Ask the students for the words that they find hard to remember or say. Put a list on an overhead transparency or on the board. Ask the students whether they can share ways of remembering difficult words.

WORTSCHATZÜBUNGEN

Read out the cognates to be sure that the students have caught them all. Have the students put the cognates into the **Wortschatz** section of their notebooks. This is an activity you can do for the **Wortschatz** section of every unit.

ZUM LESEN

HAUSAUFGABENLIED 

After students have read the homework song and you are satisfied that they understand the meaning of the individual lines, ask them to write the lines that reflect what they think about school and homework.

Übung • Beantworte die Fragen!

This activity may also be used as a written exercise, to be done in class or for homework. If you do use it as a written exercise, ask for answers in the form of complete sentences.

DER TRAUM 

Have the students identify the speaker of each line in Paul's dream. Then have them read the mini-play in groups of four, one student playing the role of Paul and the other students those of his mother, classmate, and teacher.

Übung • Stimmt oder stimmt nicht?

Ask the students to correct the false statements by providing additional information. They might correct number 1, for example, by saying, **Es ist Sonntag.**

KAPITEL **2**

Schule

In this unit you will meet some high school students from German-speaking countries. About 35 percent of the young people between the ages of 10 and 19 attend academic high schools, and many, though not all, will continue to a university or to another school of higher learning.

In this unit you will:

SECTION A	tell how you get to school
SECTION B	talk about school supplies and how much they cost
SECTION C	talk about your class schedule, tell time
SECTION D	talk about homework and grades
TRY YOUR SKILLS	use what you've learned
ZUM LESEN	read for practice and pleasure

For teaching suggestions, see the Teacher's Notes preceding this unit, pp. T44–65.

telling how you get to school

These are the ways some of our friends from abroad get to school. Let's see if they are different from the way you get to school.

Streetcars are common in larger cities. Like buses, they are an inexpensive means of public transportation.

Mopeds are popular. You need a license and can get one at 16. You may also mention the term *Mofa* (short for Motorfahrrad).

A1 Wie kommst du in die Schule?

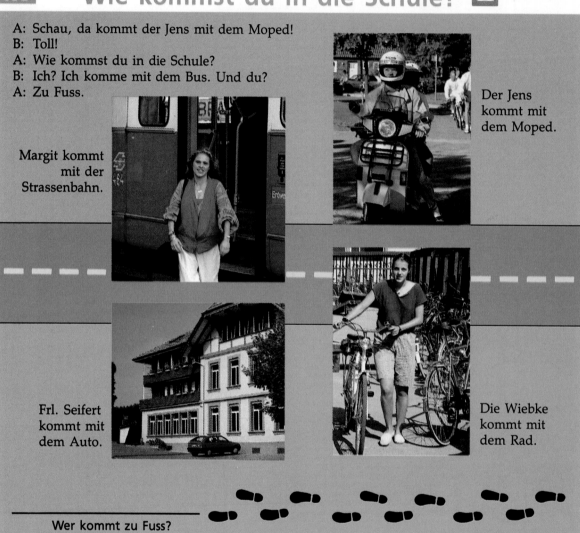

A: Schau, da kommt der Jens mit dem Moped!
B: Toll!
A: Wie kommst du in die Schule?
B: Ich? Ich komme mit dem Bus. Und du?
A: Zu Fuss.

Margit kommt mit der Strassenbahn.

Der Jens kommt mit dem Moped.

Frl. Seifert kommt mit dem Auto.

Die Wiebke kommt mit dem Rad.

Wer kommt zu Fuss?

A2 Übung • Beantworte die Fragen! *Answer the questions.*

1. Wie kommt Jens in die Schule?
2. Wie kommt Margit in die Schule?
3. Und Wiebke?
4. Wie kommt Frl. Seifert in die Schule?
5. Wer kommt mit dem Moped?

1. Mit dem Moped. / Jens kommt mit dem Moped. / Er kommt . . .
2. Mit der Strassenbahn. / Margit kommt mit der Strassenbahn. / Sie . . .
3. Mit dem Rad. / Wiebke kommt mit dem Rad. / Sie . . .
4. Mit dem Auto. / Frl. Seifert kommt mit dem Auto. / Sie . . .
5. Jens. / Jens kommt mit dem Moped.

A3 WIE SAGT MAN DAS?
Saying how you get to school

The verb **kommen** can have different meanings.

Schau, da kommt der Jens mit dem Moped.	Look, here comes Jens on his moped.
Wie kommt Margit in die Schule?	How does Margit get to school?
Margit kommt mit der Strassenbahn.	Margit comes by streetcar.
Wer kommt zu Fuss?	Who walks?

A4 Übung • Und du? Wie steht's mit dir? *And what about you?*

1. Wie kommst du in die Schule?
2. Wer kommt mit dem Rad?
3. Wer kommt mit dem Bus?
4. Wer kommt zu Fuss?

A5 ERKLÄRUNG
The Verb kommen

The verb **kommen** has the following forms. You do not have to use **wir,** *we,* and **ihr,** *you* (plural) yet.

Singular			*Plural*		
Ich	**komme**	mit dem Rad.	Wir	**kommen**	mit dem Rad.
Du	**kommst**		Ihr	**kommt**	
Jens (er) Karin (sie)	**kommt** **kommt**		Jens und Karin (sie)	**kommen**	

A6 Übung • Jetzt bist du dran

The "ihr-" and "wir-" forms are passive here. They will be introduced actively in Unit 3. Teach and practice only the other forms at this point.

1. You are conducting a survey for your teacher. Go around the class and find out how everyone gets to school.

   A: Wie kommst du in die Schule?
   B: Ich komme . . .

2. Now tell your teacher how everybody gets to school.

   Der Peter kommt . . . Die Barbara kommt . . .
   Der Paul, der Martin, die Mary und die Heidi kommen . . .

A7 Übung • Wie kommen alle in die Schule?

Mit dem Bus:	10
Mit . . .	

1. Pick four classmates and one of your teachers and write sentences telling how each one gets to school.
2. Make a chart showing how your classmates get to school. Report your findings to the class.

Photo p. 60, bottom: Theodor Schwann Gymnasium in Neuss
Photo p. 61, top: Im Innenhof des Realgymnasiums in Niebüll

SECTION B

asking about prices of school supplies

At the beginning of the school year, everyone has to buy school supplies. Jens goes to a store where school supplies are displayed in the window. He goes inside and asks about prices. What supplies do you need for school?

"Kuli" is short for "Kugelschreiber."

B1 Schulsachen 

Wörterbuch
DM 13,00

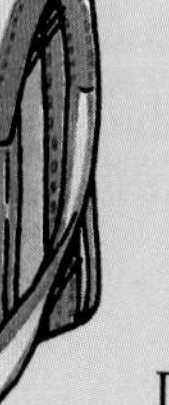

Schultasche
DM 20,00

Bleistift
DM 1,00

Kuli
DM 4,00

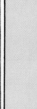

Kassette
DM 6,00

Stundenplan
DM 1,10

Heft
DM 1,20

Taschenrechner
DM 18,00

Poster
DM 5,00

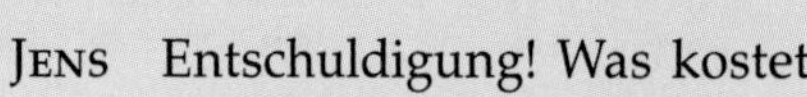

JENS Entschuldigung! Was kostet das Wörterbuch, bitte?
VERKÄUFERIN Das Wörterbuch? —Dreizehn Mark.
JENS Und was kostet der Taschenrechner?
VERKÄUFERIN Achtzehn Mark.
JENS Wie bitte?
VERKÄUFERIN Achtzehn Mark.
JENS Prima, nur achtzehn Mark! Und was kostet die Kassette?
VERKÄUFERIN Sechs Mark.
JENS Danke!
VERKÄUFERIN Bitte!

Stundenplan: Since the class schedule varies each day, students need to fill out a weekly schedule. They usually have two copies, one at home over their desk, and one in their school bag.

B2 Ein wenig Landeskunde

The German unit of currency is the **Deutsche Mark,** abbreviated **DM.** One **Mark** has one hundred **Pfennige.** Prices are usually indicated in the following way: **DM** in front of the price, and a comma separating **Mark** and **Pfennig.** In advertising material, a period is often used instead of a comma. Here is how to read prices:

DM 1,00	*reads*	eine Mark
DM 1,10		eine Mark zehn
DM 2,00		zwei Mark
DM 6,18		sechs Mark achtzehn

B3 Übung • Wir lesen Preise!

Read the following prices. For answers, see p. T48.

1. DM 11,00
2. DM 2,10
3. DM 17,20
4. DM 9,00
5. DM 7,05
6. DM 13,08
7. DM 1,17
8. DM 19,00
9. DM 4,02

B4 Übung • Was kostet alles?

What does each item pictured on page 64 cost?

A: Was kostet das Heft?
B: Das Heft? Eine Mark zwanzig.

1. Was kostet die Schultasche? zwanzig Mark
2. Was kostet der Stundenplan? eine Mark zehn
3. Und das Wörterbuch? dreizehn Mark
4. Was kostet der Taschenrechner? achtzehn Mark
5. Und die Kassette? sechs Mark
6. Was kostet der Kuli? vier Mark
7. Und was kostet das Poster? fünf Mark
8. Und der Bleistift? eine Mark

B5 Übung • Hör gut zu!

For script and answers, see p. T49.

How much does it cost? Listen.

0	1	2	3	4	5	6	7	8	9	10
3,10	8,20	5,00	13,00	1,00	1,15	12,00	18,00	1,10	19,20	11,00

B6 ERKLÄRUNG
The Definite Articles der, die, das

When Jens asked about the price of various school supplies, you noticed that he used different words with every noun. He said **das Wörterbuch, der Taschenrechner, die Kassette,** and so on. These words are called definite articles. They name something specific or definite. *(continued)*

There are three genders of German nouns: masculine, feminine, and neuter. The definite articles **der, die,** and **das** tell you the gender—they are gender markers. The gender marker **der** tells you **der Bleistift,** *the pencil,* is masculine; **die** tells you **die Schultasche,** *the schoolbag,* is feminine; **das** tells you **das Heft,** *the notebook,* is neuter. Since usually there is no other way of telling the gender of a noun, you must remember each noun with its gender marker, the definite article.

Nouns for people are generally masculine for males **(der Junge)** and feminine for females **(die Lehrerin).** There are a few exceptions, such as **das Mädchen,** *the girl,* which is neuter because of its ending, **-chen.** All nouns with the ending **-chen** are neuter.

Here is a list of the nouns that you have learned so far. Study them with their gender markers.

Masculine	*Feminine*	*Neuter*
der Lehrer	**die Frau**	**das Mädchen**
der Junge	**die Lehrerin**	**das Heft**
der Kuli	**die Verkäuferin**	**das Poster**
der Bleistift	**die Zahl**	**das Wörterbuch**
der Stundenplan	**die Schule**	
der Taschenrechner	**die Schultasche**	
	die Kassette	

B7 Übung • Was kostet . . .?

Your friend wants to know what each item costs. Tell him or her.

1. Das Heft kostet DM 1,20. **2.** Der Taschenrechner . . .

1. DM 1,20

2. DM 18,00

3. DM 20,00

4. DM 4,00

5. DM 13,00

6. DM 5,00

7. DM 1,00

8. DM 6,00

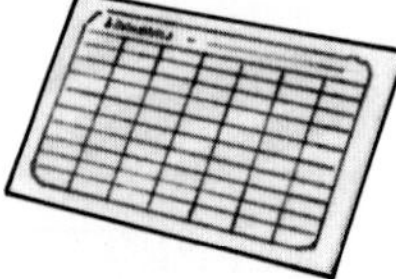

9. DM 1,10

1. Das Heft/eine Mark zwanzig
2. Der Taschenrechner/achtzehn Mark
3. Die Schultasche/zwanzig Mark
4. Der Kuli/vier Mark
5. Das Wörterbuch/dreizehn Mark
6. Das Poster/fünf Mark
7. Der Bleistift/eine Mark
8. Die Kassette/sechs Mark
9. Der Stundenplan/eine Mark zehn

B8 WIE SAGT MAN DAS?
Saying please, thank you, and you're welcome

The word **bitte** means both *please* and *you're welcome.*

Das Poster, bitte!	The poster, please.
Danke!	Thank you.
Bitte!	You're welcome.

B9 Übung • Rollenspiel *Role playing*

Lay out various school supplies (a pen, a notebook, and so on) on a table. Make a price tag for each item and turn it face down. Take turns with classmates playing salesperson and customer. Practice polite exchanges: the customer asks the price of an item, the salesperson looks it up and answers. Don't forget to say please, thank you, and you're welcome. Remind students not to use numbers over 20.

A: Was kostet das Poster, bitte?
B: Das Poster kostet sieben Mark.
A: Danke!
B: Bitte!

B10 Übung • Hör gut zu!  For script and answers, see p. T50.

Is the noun masculine, feminine, or neuter? Listen.

	0	1	2	3	4	5	6	7	8	9	10
masculine		✓			✓			✓		✓	✓
feminine	✓		✓	✓					✓		
neuter						✓	✓				

B11 Schreibübung • Im Laden *In the store*

You want to buy a dictionary, a schoolbag, and a pocket calculator. You are asking the salesperson for prices. Write out your conversation. Be polite!

B12 WAS KOSTEN DIE SCHULSACHEN? 

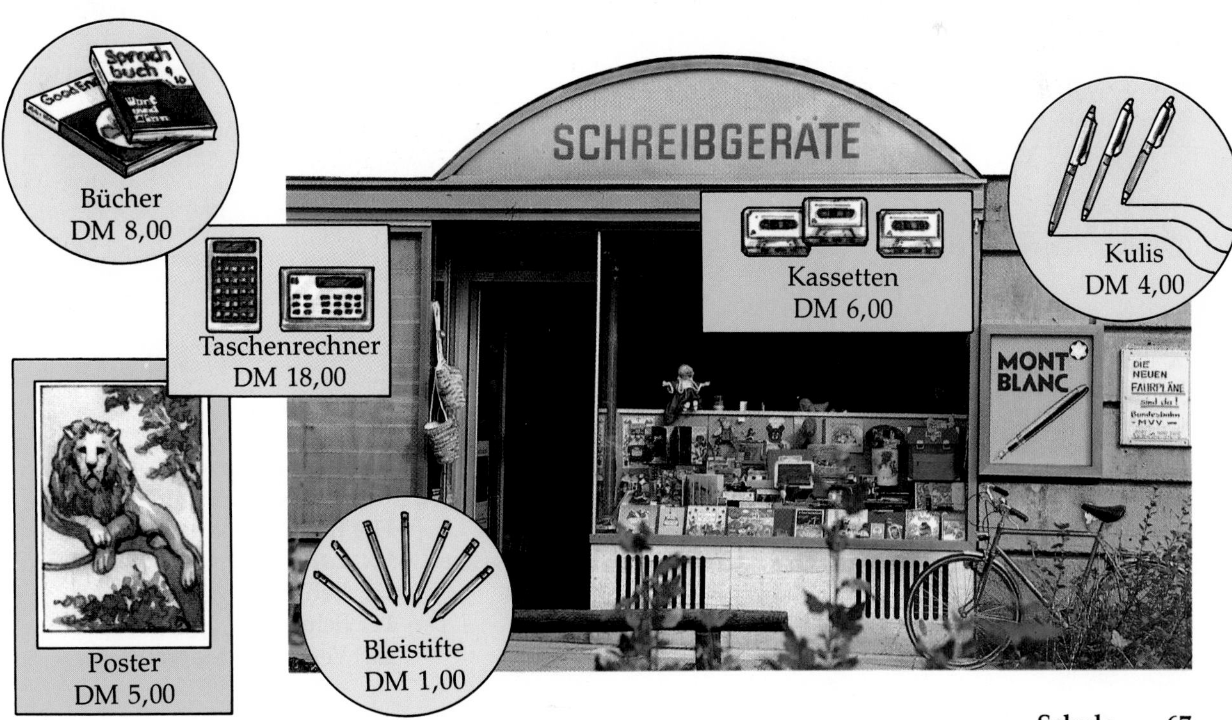

B13 Übung • Was kostet alles?

1. Was kosten die Kassetten? sechs Mark
2. Was kosten die Poster? fünf Mark
3. Und die Bücher? acht Mark
4. Was kosten die Taschenrechner? achtzehn Mark
5. Was kosten die Bleistifte? eine Mark
6. Und was kosten die Kulis? vier Mark

B14 ERKLÄRUNG
Noun Plurals

1. There is no gender distinction in the plural. The definite article used with all plural nouns is **die.**

Singular	*Plural*
der Kuli	Kulis
die Kassette → **die**	– Kassetten
das Poster	Poster

2. The plural form of most German nouns is not predictable from the singular form and must be learned for each noun. The following list shows you the plural forms of the German nouns that you have learned so far. Each noun is listed with its definite article and its plural form.

Singular	*Plural*		*Singular*	*Plural*	
der Bleistift das Heft	die Bleistifte die Hefte	**-e** **-e**	das Buch das Wörterbuch	die Bücher die Wörterbücher	**¨er** **¨er**
der Stundenplan	die Stundenpläne	**¨e**	der Kuli	die Kulis	**-s**
der Junge die Kassette die Schule die Schultasche	die Jungen die Kassetten die Schulen die Schultaschen	**-n** **-n** **-n** **-n**	der Lehrer das Mädchen das Poster der Taschenrechner	die Lehrer die Mädchen die Poster die Taschenrechner	**-** **-** **-** **-**
die Zahl die Lehrerin die Verkäuferin	die Zahlen die Lehrerinnen die Verkäuferinnen	**-en** **-nen** **-nen**			

B15 Übung • Singular und Plural

Say the article and the plural form for each of the following nouns.

A: Heft
B: das Heft, die Hefte

1. Bleistift der, Bleistifte
2. Lehrerin die, Lehrerinnen
3. Poster das, Poster
4. Wörterbuch das, Wörterbücher
5. Kuli der, Kulis
6. Mädchen das, Mädchen
7. Schultasche die, Schultaschen
8. Junge der, Jungen
9. Buch das, Bücher
10. Kassette die, Kassetten
11. Taschenrechner der, Taschenrechner
12. Zahl die, Zahlen
13. Lehrer der, Lehrer
14. Schule die, Schulen
15. Verkäuferin die, Verkäuferinnen

B 16 ERKLÄRUNG
Was kostet—was kosten

asking for one item	Was **kostet** die Kassette?	*How much is the cassette?*
asking for more than one item	Was **kosten** die Bleistifte?	*How much are the pencils?*

B 17 Übung • Jetzt bist du dran

You are in the store and are asking about prices.

das Poster Was kostet das Poster?
die Bleistifte Was kosten die Bleistifte?

1. die Schultasche kostet
2. der Taschenrechner kostet
3. die Kassetten kosten
4. das Buch kostet
5. die Bleistifte kosten
6. das Wörterbuch kostet
7. der Kuli kostet
8. das Heft kostet

B 18 Übung • Hör gut zu! 

Singular or plural? Listen. For script and answers, see p. T51.

	0	1	2	3	4	5	6	7	8	9	10
singular	✓			✓	✓	✓			✓	✓	
plural		✓	✓				✓	✓			✓

B 19 Schreibübung

1. Write the plural form of each of the following nouns.

der Junge die Jungen

1. das Mädchen die Mädchen
2. das Poster die Poster
3. das Wörterbuch die Wörterbücher
4. der Kuli die Kulis
5. die Verkäuferin die Verkäuferinnen
6. der Bleistift die Bleistifte
7. der Stundenplan die Stundenpläne
8. der Taschenrechner die Taschenrechner

2. Write each of the following questions in the plural.

Was kostet das Poster? Was kosten die Poster?

1. Was kostet das Heft?
2. Was kostet die Schultasche?
3. Was kostet das Buch?
4. Was kostet die Kassette?
5. Was kostet der Bleistift?
6. Was kostet der Taschenrechner?
7. Was kostet das Wörterbuch?
8. Was kostet der Stundenplan?

3. Write a dialogue that takes place in a **Schreibwarengeschäft.**

Get the salesperson's attention and ask for the prices of the following items: pens, pencils, posters, cassettes, notebooks, calculators, schoolbags, and dictionaries.

1. Was kosten die Hefte? 2. die Schultaschen? 3. die Bücher? 4. die Kassetten? 5. die Bleistifte? 6. die Taschenrechner? 7. die Wörterbücher? 8. die Stundenpläne?

B 20 DU, WO IST DAS WÖRTERBUCH? 

Du, Jens, wo ist das Wörterbuch?

Es ist dort drüben. Schau, Kristin, dort!

Du, Kristin, der Taschenrechner ist weg.

Unsinn! Er ist da.

Jens, wo ist die Kassette?

Ist sie nicht da?—Schau mal, Kristin! Hier ist sie.

Entschuldigung, Frau Meier! Wo sind die Poster, bitte?

Ich weiss nicht. Sind sie nicht da?

Nein, sie sind weg.

Weg? Schau mal, sie sind da drüben!

B 21 Übung • Wo ist . . .?

First practice as shown, then have student take role of teacher.

You are looking for the following items. Ask your teacher.

SCHÜLER Wo ist die Schultasche?
LEHRER Schau, sie ist hier. *or* Sie ist da. *or* Sie ist dort drüben.

Possible answers:

1. Wo ist das Wörterbuch? Es ist hier.
2. Wo sind die Poster? Schau, sie sind da.
3. Wo ist der Kuli? Er ist dort drüben.
4. Wo ist die Kassette? Schau, sie ist hier.
5. Wo ist der Jens? Er ist dort drüben.
6. Wo ist die Kristin? Sie ist da.

B 22 ERKLÄRUNG
The Pronouns er, sie, es, *and* sie *(plural)*

You can refer to noun phrases such as **der Taschenrechner, die Kassette, das Wörterbuch, die Poster,** using the words **er, sie,** and **es.** These words are called pronouns. The pronoun **er** refers to a masculine noun; **sie** refers to a feminine noun or a plural noun, and **es** refers to a neuter noun. Notice that **er, sie,** and **es**—when referring to things in the singular—all mean *it.*

		Noun Phrase	*Pronoun*	
Singular	*Masculine*	Wo ist **der Taschenrechner?**	**Er** ist dort drüben.	*It is . . .*
	Feminine	Wo ist **die Kassette?**	**Sie** ist dort drüben.	
	Neuter	Wo ist **das Wörterbuch?**	**Es** ist dort drüben.	
Plural	*(no gender)*	Wo sind **die Poster?**	**Sie** sind dort drüben.	*They are . . .*

B 23 Übung • So eine Unordnung!

What a mess! You and your friend can't find anything. Help each other out.

A: Die Schultasche ist weg!
B: Unsinn! Sie ist hier!

1. Der Stundenplan ist weg! Er
2. Die Bleistifte sind weg! Sie
3. Das Wörterbuch ist weg! Es
4. Die Kassette ist weg! Sie
5. Die Hefte sind weg! Sie
6. Der Kuli ist weg! Er
7. Das Poster ist weg! Es
8. Der Taschenrechner ist weg! Er

B 24 Übung • Die Schule beginnt. Wo ist . . .?

When you get to school, you ask a friend where the following people are.

A: Wo ist Herr Sperling?
B: Ist er nicht da?

1. Wo ist der Jens? Ist er
2. Wo sind Jens und Kristin? Sind sie
3. Wo ist Frl. Seifert? Ist sie
4. Wo ist der Deutschlehrer? Ist er
5. Wo ist das Mädchen[1]? Ist sie
6. Wo ist der Junge? Ist er

[1] The pronoun **sie** is used to refer to **das Mädchen.**

B 25 WIE SAGT MAN DAS?
Getting someone's attention

Here are some expressions you can use to get someone's attention.

Entschuldigung!	Excuse me.
Du, Jens, . . .	Hey, Jens, . . .
Schau!	Look!
Schau, Jens!	Look, Jens!
Schau mal!	Take a look!
Schau mal, Kristin!	Take a look, Kristin!

B 26 Übung • Partnerarbeit

1.

Wörterbuch
Kassetten
Taschenrechner
Bleistifte
Kuli
Schultasche
Heft

Here is a list of school supplies that have been misplaced. A classmate is asking you about each of these items. You tell where they are, or you may say that you don't know. Vary your answers, using the words and phrases given on the right.

A: Du, Paul, wo ist das Wörterbuch?
B: Schau mal! Es ist hier.
A: Prima!

Wo sind die Kassetten? Sie sind/Wo ist der Taschenrechner? Er ist/Wo sind die Bleistifte? Sie sind/Wo ist der Kuli? Er ist/Wo ist die Schultasche? Sie ist/Wo ist das Heft? Es ist

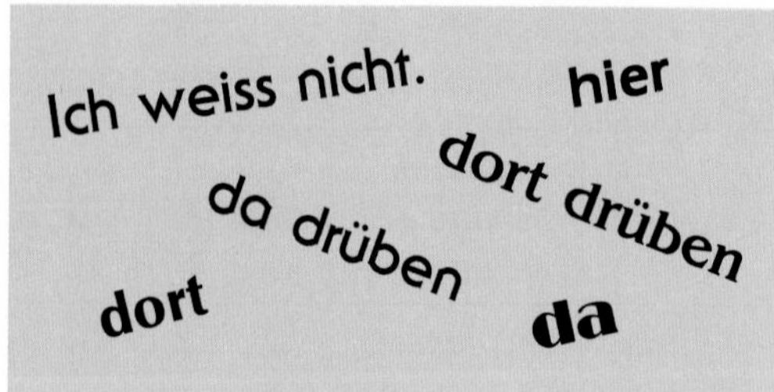

Ich weiss nicht.
hier
dort drüben
da drüben
dort
da

2. You are looking at school supplies with a friend. Practice the following dialog, substituting the words given on the right. Give a price or say you don't know.

A: Schau mal, Jens! Der Taschenrechner ist prima!
B: Du, was kostet er?
A: . . .

das Wörterbuch ist, was kostet es?/die Kassette ist, was kostet sie?/die Hefte sind, was kosten sie/der Kuli ist, was kostet er?/das Poster ist, was kostet es?

3. You are asking for someone's name. Practice the following dialog, substituting a person listed on the right. Make up a name for each person.

A: Entschuldigung! Wie heisst der Deutschlehrer?
B: Er heisst Sperling.
A: Ach ja, Sperling.

die Verkäuferin, sie/der Junge, er/die Deutschlehrerin, sie/der Lehrer, er/das Mädchen, sie

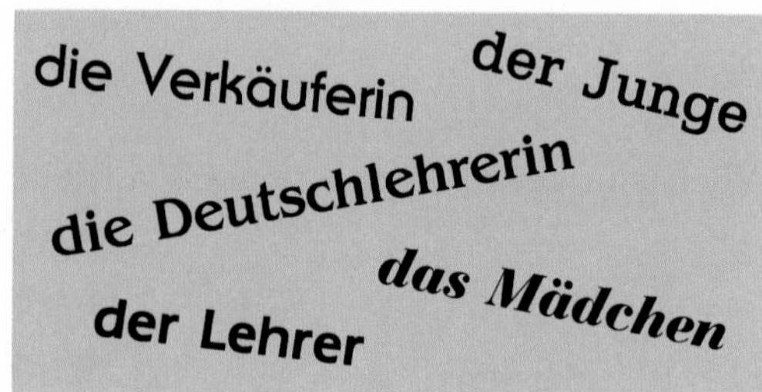

B 27 Übung • Hör gut zu!

For script and answers, see p. T53.

Er, sie, or **es?** Listen.

	0	1	2	3	4	5	6	7	8	9	10	11	12
er		✓				✓		✓			✓		
sie	✓		✓		✓				✓	✓		✓	✓
es				✓			✓						

B 28 Schreibübung • Entschuldigung! Was kostet . . .?

Write a dialog that takes place in a store. The customer gets the salesperson's attention and asks about the price of various school supplies. The salesperson tells the prices, using pronouns to refer to the items. The customer thanks the salesperson and he or she responds. Practice your dialog with a classmate.

SECTION C giving information about your class schedule

German high school students in the upper grades must take a number of core subjects, and they are limited in their choice of minor subjects. Take a look at Jens' schedule, a typical ninth grade schedule, and compare it with your own.

C1 Welche Fächer hast du heute?

FRAU KRÖGER Welche Fächer hast du heute?
JENS Ich habe Mathe, Geschichte, Moment mal! Schau, hier ist der Stundenplan. Heute ist Dienstag?
FRAU KRÖGER Ja.
JENS Ich habe um acht Uhr Deutsch, um Viertel vor neun Mathe. Ich habe dann Englisch und Geschichte.

Wann hast du Physik?
Am Freitag.

Jens geht auf die Oberschule in Niebüll. Er hat von Montag bis Freitag Schule. Jens hat sonnabends frei. Die Schule beginnt um acht Uhr, und sie ist um ein Uhr aus.

Welche Fächer hat er? Hier ist Jens' Stundenplan.

Stundenplan für Jens Kröger 9a

Zeit	Montag	Dienstag	Mittwoch	Donnerstag	Freitag	Samstag
8.00-8.40	Deutsch	Deutsch	Mathe	—	Physik	frei
8.45-9.30	Deutsch	Mathe	Deutsch	Physik	Mathe	
9.30-9.45	—	—	Pause	—	—	
9.45-10.30	Religion	Englisch	Englisch	Biologie	Deutsch	
10.30-11.15	Biologie	Englisch	Latein	Englisch	Latein	
11.15-11.30	—	—	Pause	—		
11.30-12.15	Latein	Geschichte	Sport	Geschichte	Kunst	
12.15-13.00	Musik	—	Sport	Geographie		

C2 Ein wenig Landeskunde

Jens is in a high school that emphasizes science subjects: mathematics, physics, biology, and chemistry, a subject that Jens will start in the tenth grade. At the same time, Jens is required to take two foreign languages, English and Latin. As you can see, his class schedule varies from day to day, and he takes more subjects than you do. He does not have the same subject at the same time every day, nor does he always have the same subjects every day. Jens and his classmates stay together for all their classes, and for the most part, they stay in the same classroom, unless they go to the science lab, the art room, or the gym. In German schools, the teachers move from room to room. German students generally spend less time in school than American students. There are no study halls or lunch periods. After school there are few school-sponsored sports, clubs, or social activities.

C3 Übung • Stimmt oder stimmt nicht? 

Check each of the following statements against Jens' class schedule. If a statement is true, say **Stimmt;** if it is not true, say **Stimmt nicht!**

1. Jens hat am Montag Latein. Stimmt!
2. Er hat am Dienstag Geographie. Stimmt nicht!
3. Jens hat am Donnerstag Deutsch. Stimmt nicht!
4. Er hat sonnabends frei. Stimmt!
5. Er hat am Dienstag um acht Uhr Deutsch, dann Latein und Sport. Stimmt nicht!

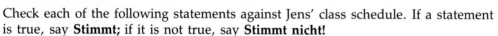

1. auf die Oberschule in Niebüll. 2. von Montag bis Freitag 3. Deutsch, Religion, Biologie, Latein und Musik 4. Deutsch, Mathe, Englisch und Geschichte

C4 Übung • Jens' Stundenplan

1. Auf welche Schule geht Jens?
2. Wann hat Jens Schule?
3. Welche Fächer hat er am Montag?
4. Was hat er am Dienstag?
5. Welche Fächer hat er am Mittwoch?
6. Was hat er am Donnerstag?
7. Welche Fächer hat er am Freitag?
8. Was hat er sonnabends?
9. Wann beginnt die Schule?
10. Wann ist sie aus?

5. Mathe, Deutsch, Englisch, Latein, Sport 6. Physik, Biologie, Englisch, Geschichte, Geographie 7. Physik, Mathe, Deutsch, Latein, Kunst 8. Er hat frei. 9. Um acht Uhr. 10. Um ein Uhr.

C5 Übung • Und du? Wie steht's mit dir?

1. Auf welche Schule gehst du?
2. Welche Fächer hast du?
3. Welche Fächer hast du am Montag?
4. Was hast du am Dienstag?
5. Wann hast du Deutsch?
6. Wann hast du frei?
7. Wann beginnt die Schule?
8. Wann ist sie aus?

C6 ZAHLEN 

Let's count by fives.

5	10	15	20	25	30
fünf	zehn	fünfzehn	zwanzig	fünfundzwanzig	dreissig
35	**40**	**45**	**50**	**55**	**60**
fünfunddreissig	vierzig	fünfundvierzig	fünfzig	fünfundfünfzig	sechzig

C7 WANN HAT JENS MATHE? 

um ein Uhr
um eins

um zwei Uhr
um zwei

Wie spät ist es? Es ist . . .

neun Uhr

neun Uhr fünf
fünf nach neun

neun Uhr zehn
zehn nach neun

neun Uhr fünfzehn
Viertel nach neun

neun Uhr zwanzig
zwanzig nach neun

neun Uhr fünfundzwanzig
fünfundzwanzig nach neun

neun Uhr dreissig
halb zehn

neun Uhr fünf-unddreissig

neun Uhr vierzig

neun Uhr fünfundvierzig
Viertel vor zehn

neun Uhr fünfzig
zehn vor zehn

neun Uhr fünf-undfünfzig
fünf vor zehn

C8 Übung • Wie spät ist es? 

See if you can express the following times in two different ways.

Es ist . . . oder . . .

1.

2.

3.

4.

5.

6.

1. drei Uhr zwanzig/zwanzig nach drei 2. elf Uhr fünfzehn/Viertel nach elf 3. zwei Uhr fünfunddreissig 4. fünf Uhr fünfundvierzig/Viertel vor sechs 5. acht Uhr fünf/fünf nach acht 6. vier Uhr dreissig/halb fünf

C9 Übung • Rollenspiel

Pretend you are Jens. Practice the following dialog with a classmate.

Montag um 10.30? MITSCHÜLER Was hast du am Montag um halb elf?
JENS Um halb elf? Moment mal! —Ich habe Biologie um halb elf.

1. Dienstag um 8.45? Mathe
2. Um 11.15? Pause
3. Mittwoch um 11.30? Sport
4. Montag um 11.45? Latein
5. Freitag um 9.45? Deutsch
6. Montag um 8.00? Deutsch

C10 WAS HABT IHR JETZT?

Was habt ihr jetzt?
Mathe. Wir haben eine Klassenarbeit.
Wir haben jetzt Bio. Und ihr?
Na, dann viel Glück!

Jörg und Kristin sind Klassenkameraden. Sie gehen in die neunte Klasse, die 9a.

Mona und Lars sind auch Klassenkameraden. Sie gehen auch in die neunte Klasse, in die Parallelklasse, die 9b.

C11 Übung • Beantworte die Fragen!

1. Wer sind Lars und Mona? Klassenkameraden
2. In welche Klasse gehen sie? in die neunte Klasse, die 9b
3. Welches Fach haben sie jetzt? Bio
4. Und Jörg und Kristin? Was haben sie jetzt? Mathe

C12 ERKLÄRUNG
The Verb haben

The verb **haben,** *to have,* has the following forms.

Ich	**habe**	Deutsch.	Wir	**haben**	Deutsch.
Du	**hast**		Ihr	**habt**	
Jens (er)	**hat**		Jens und Kristin (sie)	**haben**	
Kristin (sie)	**hat**				

C13 Übung • Wer hat heute Deutsch?

Do all these students have German today? They do!

Jens? Ja, er hat heute Deutsch.

1. Kristin? sie hat
2. Jörg und Kristin? sie haben
3. Du? ich habe
4. Der Junge? er hat
5. Ihr? wir haben
6. Ich? du hast
7. Das Mädchen? sie hat
8. Wir? ihr habt

C14 Übung • Was haben die Schüler heute?

What courses do the students have? Use a different course in each answer.

Jörg? Er hat Geschichte.

1. Ich? du hast
2. Das Mädchen? sie hat
3. Der Junge? er hat
4. Wir? ihr habt
5. Lars und Mona? sie haben
6. Kristin? sie hat

C15 Übung • Hör gut zu!  For script and answers, see p. T56.

What time is it?

10	5	3	7	2	8	4	1	6	9
6.50	12.30	9.35	1.10	10.40	11.45	4.15	7.20	2.25	8.45

C16 Übung • Partnerarbeit

Practice the following activities with a classmate.

1. Ask what time it is, and after he or she responds, say thank you. Begin by saying:
   Wie spät ist es?
2. Tell what subjects you have and when you have them. Here are some additional subjects that you might have. Not all of them are taught in German high schools: Chemie, Sozialkunde *(social studies)*, Naturwissenschaft *(science)*, Algebra, Geometrie, Französisch, Spanisch, Zeichnen *(drawing)*, Hauswirtschaftskunde *(home economics)*, Werken *(industrial arts)*, Musik, Schulorchester, Schulkapelle *(band)*, Schulchor, Fahrunterricht *(driver's education)*, Schreibmaschineschreiben *(typing)*.

C17 Schreibübung

1. Rewrite each sentence, filling in the correct form of **haben.**

   1. Ich _habe_ heute Deutsch.
   2. Was _hast_ du heute?
   3. Der Jens _hat_ jetzt Mathe.
   4. Wir _haben_ jetzt auch Mathe.
   5. Was _habt_ ihr dann?
   6. Jens und Kristin _haben_ Biologie.

2. Write out what time it is. 1. Es ist zwei Uhr dreissig (halb drei). 2. drei Uhr fünfundvierzig (Viertel vor vier) 3. sieben Uhr zehn (zehn nach sieben) 4. sechs Uhr fünfzehn (Viertel nach sechs) 5. neun Uhr dreissig (halb zehn) 6. acht Uhr fünfzig (zehn vor neun)

   5.10 Es ist fünf Uhr zehn (zehn nach fünf).

   1. 2.30 2. 3.45 3. 7.10 4. 6.15 5. 9.30 6. 8.50

3. Write out your own class schedule, using German words for your subjects. How well do you know your schedule? Exchange schedules with a classmate and ask each other questions.
   Wann hast du Geschichte? Was hast du am Dienstag um . . .?

talking about homework and grades

Homework takes up a large part of a student's afternoon. There is homework in many subjects, and students have to work hard to get good grades to stay in school.

D1 Hausaufgaben und Noten

Jens macht Hausaufgaben. Er macht Mathe. In Mathe ist Jens nicht so gut. Welche Noten hat er in Mathe? Eine Vier, eine Drei, eine Vier.

Zensuren-spiegel

Fächer	Noten			Halbj.-zeugn.	Noten			Jahres-zeugn.
Deutsch	2	2	1					
	2							
Englisch	1	1	2					
	1	1						
Mathematik	4	3	4					
~~Franz.~~ Latein	3	1	2					
	2							
Physik	3	2	2					
	1							
Chemie								
Biologie	1	2	2					
Erdkunde	3	3						
Geschichte	4	1	2					
Musik	1	1						
Kunst	2	1						
Religion	1	2						

Hier sind Jens' Noten.

Was hast du?
Eine Eins!
Toll!
Prima!
Schade!
Blöd!

KRISTIN Du, Jens, was hast du in Deutsch?
JENS Eine Zwei.
KRISTIN Das ist prima! Eine Zwei in Deutsch. Phantastisch!
JENS Ja, das ist gut. Aber ich habe nur eine Vier in Mathe. Blöd!
KRISTIN Ja, das ist schlecht. Schade!

The record of grades above is used to keep track of grades. It is not a Zeugnis, or report card. The first-semester report card (Halbjahreszeugnis) has not been issued yet. On the right side there is room for recording the second-semester grades.

D2 Ein wenig Landeskunde

Note that these equivalents are only approximate. It is much harder to receive a "1" than an A. A "2" is a very good grade.

In German schools, grades range from 1 to 6: 1 (sehr gut, *excellent*), 2 (gut, *good*), 3 (befriedigend, *satisfactory*), 4 (ausreichend, *just passing*), 5 (mangelhaft, *almost failing*), and 6 (ungenügend, *failing*)—corresponding to A, B, C, D, and F in American schools. On report cards, German students also receive grades in Betragen, *conduct,* Fleiss, *diligence,* Aufmerksamkeit, *attentiveness,* and Ordnung, *neatness.* Behavioral grades are very important. They include more than just conduct.

D3 Übung • Beantworte die Fragen!

1. Was macht Jens? Hausaufgaben
2. Ist er gut in Mathe? Nein
3. Welche Noten hat er in Mathe? 4, 3, 4
4. Welche Noten hat er in Latein? 3, 1, 2, 2

D4 Übung • Und du? Wie steht's mit dir?

1. Bist du gut in Mathe?
2. Was hast du in Mathe?
3. Welche Noten hast du in Deutsch?
4. Was hast du in Englisch?

D5 WIE SAGT MAN DAS?

Some ways of responding to good news and to bad news

good news	Gut!	Good!
	Prima!	Terrific!
	Phantastisch!	Fantastic!
	Toll!	Great!
bad news	Blöd!	Too dumb!
	Das ist nicht so gut.	That's not so good.
	Das ist schlecht.	That's bad!
	Schade!	Too bad!

D6 Übung • Jetzt bist du dran

Now ask your classmates what their grades are in different subjects and react to the good news or bad news. Then have a classmate ask you the same questions.

A: Was hast du in Biologie?
B: Ich habe eine. . .
A: . . . *or* . . .

D7 IST BIO SCHWER?

D8 Übung • Jetzt bist du dran

A: Wie ist Bio? Schwer? Leicht?

B: Bio ist nicht schwer. Bio ist . . .

Geschichte Bio Physik

Deutsch Latein Geographie

Englisch Mathe Musik

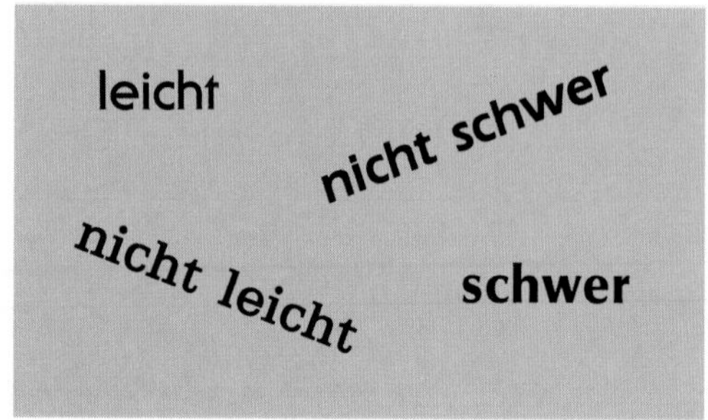

D9 Übung • Gut oder schlecht?

Choose a partner. React to each of the following statements made by your partner. Use different expressions as you respond to good news or bad news.

A: Ich habe eine Zwei in Deutsch.
B: Das ist prima!

Possible answers:

1. Ich habe eine Fünf in Physik. Schade!
2. Ich habe eine Drei in Mathe. Das ist gut!
3. Ich habe eine Eins in Biologie. Phantastisch!
4. Ich habe eine Vier in Geschichte. Das ist nicht so gut.
5. Ich habe eine Sechs in Algebra. Das ist schlecht.
6. Ich habe eine Zwei in Erdkunde. Das ist toll!

D10 Übung • Hör gut zu!

For script and answers, see p. T59.

Is it good news or bad news? Listen.

	0	1	2	3	4	5	6	7	8	9	10
good news		✓	✓			✓	✓		✓	✓	
bad news	✓			✓	✓			✓			✓

D11 Schreibübung • Was meinst du? *What do you think?*

For answers, see p. T60.

1. Write four short dialogs, asking friends about their grades and reacting to the good or bad news.

Peter, Geschichte, Vier
A: Was hat Peter in Geschichte?
B: Er hat eine Vier.
A: Das ist schade!

1. du, Deutsch, Eins
2. Barbara, Englisch, Fünf
3. Peter, Erdkunde, Sechs
4. Jens und Kristin, Latein, Zwei

2. Write sentences agreeing or disagreeing with each of the following statements.

A: Algebra ist schwer.
B: Ja, Algebra ist schwer. *or* Nein, Algebra ist nicht schwer.
or Nein, Algebra ist leicht.

1. Biologie ist leicht.
2. Kunst ist nicht leicht.
3. Deutsch ist toll.
4. Englisch ist schwer.
5. Geschichte ist nicht schwer.
6. Die Hausaufgaben sind schwer.

D12 Übung • Wer hat gute Augen? *Who has good eyes?*

Was ist alles auf diesem Bild?

das Poster, die Schultasche, die Kassette, der Taschenrechner, das Heft, der Stundenplan, der Kuli, die Bleistifte, die Bücher

Und was fehlt hier?

das Poster, die Bücher, der Kuli, der Stundenplan, die Kassette, der Taschenrechner

TRY YOUR SKILLS

using what you've learned

1 Gerd Ecker in den USA

Gerd Ecker, a student from Germany, introduces himself to your class.

Guten Tag! Ich heisse Gerd Ecker. Ich bin 16 Jahre alt. Ich bin aus Paderborn. Paderborn ist in der Bundesrepublik Deutschland. Ich gehe aufs Goerdeler Gymnasium. Ich komme mit dem Rad in die Schule, und die Klassenkameraden—ja, sie kommen mit dem Bus, mit dem Moped, mit dem Auto und auch zu Fuss.

Wir haben von Montag bis Freitag Schule. Wir haben Sonnabend frei. Die Schule beginnt um Viertel vor acht, und sie ist um ein Uhr aus.

Welche Fächer ich habe? Nun, ich habe Deutsch, Mathe, Englisch, Geschichte, Geographie, Sport und Kunst. Ich bin gut in Englisch und in Deutsch. Ich habe eine Eins in Englisch und eine Zwei in Deutsch. Englisch und Deutsch sind leicht. Ich bin nicht so gut in Mathe. Mathe ist schwer. Ich habe nur eine Vier.

2 Übung • Rollenspiel For answers, see p. T60.

A classmate plays the role of Gerd. You missed some of his presentation, so you ask him questions about himself. Then you take the role of Gerd, and your classmate asks you.

A: Wie heisst du?
B: Ich heisse. . .

3 Übung • Erzähl mal, was Gerd gesagt hat! For answers, see p. T61.

A friend of yours missed Gerd's presentation. You tell him or her what Gerd said.

Der Schüler aus Deutschland heisst. . .

4 Übung • Vortrag *Presentation*

You are visiting a class in Germany. Tell the class something about yourself and your school day.

5 Schreibübung • Ein Artikel für die Schülerzeitung

The school newspaper in the German school you are visiting would like to write an article about you. Write up the presentation you gave to the class for the school newspaper. Include a picture of yourself.

6 Übung • Immer diese Schule! *School, school, school!*

Practice the following dialogs with a classmate. Try to come up with as many variations as possible and see how long you can keep each conversation going.

1. You talk about how to get to school.
A: Wie kommst du in die Schule?
B: Ich komme mit. . .

2. You are in a store and want to know what different school items cost.
A: Entschuldigung! Was kostet der Kuli?
B: Er kostet vier Mark.
A: Danke!
B: Bitte!

3. You ask your classmate what subjects he or she has on certain days.
A: Was hast du am Montag?
B: Ich habe. . .

4. You ask your classmate when he or she has certain subjects.
A: Wann hast du Deutsch?
B: Um Viertel vor zehn.

5. You ask your classmates what their grades are in different subjects.
A: Du, was hast du in Bio?
B: Ich habe eine Zwei.
A: Das ist prima!

6. You talk about how easy or difficult certain subjects are.
A: Mathe ist schwer.
B: Nein. Mathe ist leicht.

7 Schreibübung • Was passt zusammen? *What goes together?*

Write the pairs.

1. Auf welche Schule gehst du? j
2. Wo ist sie? i
3. Wie kommst du in die Schule? d
4. Was kostet das Wörterbuch? f
5. Wie spät ist es? h
6. Ich habe um neun Uhr Deutsch. a
7. Wann hast du Mathe? g
8. Ich habe eine Zwei in Mathe. b
9. Du hast eine Eins in Geschichte? c
10. Entschuldigung, ist das Herr Meier? e

a. Und wann hast du Englisch?
b. Ich habe nur eine Drei.
c. Ja, was hast du?
d. Mit dem Rad.
e. Ja, das ist er.
f. Zwölf Mark sechzig.
g. Um zehn Uhr zwanzig.
h. Es ist acht Uhr.
i. In Westbury.
j. Ich gehe auf die Kennedy-Schule.

8 Übung • Was sagen sie?

Explain that the letter ess-tzet in *Rosenstrasse 8* (lower left of ad) is an alternate form of ss. The students do not have to learn to write it, but they should be able to recognize it when they see it. For more information on the ess-tzet, see the section on Teacher's Resource Materials, p. T6.

9 Übung • Reklame in der Zeitung *Ads in the paper*

Look at the following ad and write out what each of the items costs.

Die Bleistifte kosten. . . 8,40 DM.

ACHTUNG! SCHULANFANG

jetzt kaufen – in Ruhe auswählen:

Unser Schul–Spezial–Angebot mit reduzierten Preisen

Bleistifte, 12 Stück	bisher DM 9,60	jetzt	8,40 DM
Hefte	bisher DM 1,60	jetzt	1,20 DM
Kulis, alle Farben	bisher DM 3,20	jetzt	2,50 DM
Jeans-Taschen	bisher DM 20,50	jetzt	17,50 DM
Taschenrechner	bisher DM 19,50	jetzt	16,20 DM
Stundenpläne	bisher DM 1,60	jetzt	1,30 DM
Kassetten, 3 Stück	bisher DM 18,00	jetzt	15,00 DM
Wörterbücher	bisher DM 16,40	jetzt	14,90 DM

Wo? Im Schul-Shop

KAUT-BULLINGER&CO GMBH & CO KG

Rosenstraße 8

8000 München 2

Telefon: 62 26 - 0

Die Hefte kosten 1,20 DM.
Die Kulis kosten 2,50 DM.
Die Jeans-Taschen kosten 17,50 DM.
Die Taschenrechner kosten 16,20 DM.
Die Stundenpläne kosten 1,30 DM.
Die Kassetten kosten 15,00 DM.
Die Wörterbücher kosten 14,90 DM.

10 Aussprache-, Lese- und Schreibübungen  For script, see p. T62.

1. Listen carefully and repeat what you hear.

2. Listen, then read aloud.

1. da, sag, Rad, Tag, schade, Zahl; dem, zehn; wir, prima, sie, wie, vier, sieben, hier, Wien; wo, Montag, Moped; du, Schule, Kuli, Fuss, gut, nur, Uhr
2. für, grüss, drüben; fünf, München, Niebüll, Glück, Tschüs; blöd, Kröger, Österreich, Wörterbuch *Tschüs* can have either a long or a short /ü/ sound.
3. und, sind, Rad, blöd, Deutschland, Sonnabend, Klassenkamerad
4. sag, Tag, Montag, Dienstag, Donnerstag, Freitag, Samstag, Sonntag, weg
5. zwanzig, dreissig, vierzig, fünfzig, sechzig

3. Copy the following sentences to prepare yourself to write them from dictation.

1. Die Zahl sieben.
2. Um vier Uhr.
3. Sie sind in Wien.
4. Mit dem Rad.

WAS KANNST DU SCHON?

Let's review some important points that you have learned in this unit.

Can you say how to get to school?
Using the verb **kommen,** make complete sentences saying how each person comes to school. Vary the means of transportation.

1. Kristin 2. er 3. du 4. Peter und Barbara 5. ich

1. Kristin kommt . . . 2. Er kommt . . . 3. Du kommst . . . 4. Peter und Barbara kommen . . . 5. Ich komme . . .

Can you name some school supplies?
Say the definite article and the plural form of:

Heft, Wörterbuch, Kuli, Bleistift, Schultasche, Taschenrechner, Kassette, Stundenplan

Can you buy things in a store, asking for prices and saying thank you and you're welcome?
Ask how much these items cost and give an answer. Say thank you and you're welcome.

Kuli, Heft, Schultasche, Kassetten

Can you use the right pronoun for people and things?
For each of these nouns, use the pronoun that correctly refers to it:

Schultasche, Lehrer, Mädchen, Taschenrechner, Karin, Bleistifte, Frl. Seifert, Jens, Wörterbuch, Heft

Can you talk about your class schedule?
Say what subjects you have on each day of the week.

Say the names of the days of the week.

Do you know the forms of the verb *haben?*
Write the forms of **haben** that go with these subjects:

1. ich 2. er 3. Sabine und Peter 4. Sabine 5. du
6. Peter 7. sie 8. wir 9. ihr

Can you tell time?
Say what time it is: 7.30; 9.45; 12.50; 1.30; 5.20; 8.15

sieben Uhr dreissig/halb acht; neun Uhr fünfundvierzig/Viertel vor zehn; zwölf Uhr fünfzig/zehn vor eins; ein Uhr dreissig/halb zwei; fünf Uhr zwanzig/zwanzig nach fünf; acht Uhr fünfzehn/Viertel nach acht

SECTION D

Can you talk about grades?
What would you say if you got an A? an F?

Can you say whether or not a subject is easy or difficult?
Respond to the following questions:

Du hast eine Eins in Bio? Eine Fünf in Mathe?

1. Schulen, Bleistifte, Hefte, Kassetten, Kulis, Mark, Poster, Schultaschen, Stundenpläne, Taschenrechner, Wörterbücher, Fächer, Klassen, Klassenarbeiten, Klassenkameraden, Namen, Oberschulen, Parallelklassen, Pausen, Noten

WORTSCHATZ

SECTION A

da *there; here*
kommen *to come*
mit dem Auto *by car*
mit dem Bus *by bus*
mit dem Moped *by moped*
mit dem Rad *by bicycle*
mit der Strassenbahn *by streetcar*
schau! *look!*
die **Schule, -n** *school*
toll! *great!*
wie kommst du in die Schule? *how do you get to school?*
zu Fuss *on foot*

SECTION B

bitte *please; you're welcome*
der **Bleistift, -e** *pencil*
da drüben *over there*
danke *thank you, thanks*
DM = Deutsche Mark *German mark*
dort *there*
dort drüben *over there*
du, . . . *hey, . . .*
Entschuldigung! *excuse me!*
er *he; it*
es *it; she*
das **Heft, -e** *notebook*
hier *here*
die **Kassette, -n** *cassette*
der **Kuli, -s** *ballpoint pen*
die **Mark, -** *mark* (German monetary unit); eine Mark *one mark*
nicht *not*
nur *only*
das **Poster, -** *poster*
prima! *great!*
schau mal! *look!*
die **Schulsachen** (pl) *school supplies*
die **Schultasche, -n** *schoolbag*
sie *she; it; they*
der **Stundenplan, ¨e** *class schedule*
der **Taschenrechner, -** *pocket calculator*
Unsinn! *nonsense!*
die **Verkäuferin** *salesperson*
was? *what?*
was kosten? *how much are?*
was kostet? *how much is?*
weg *gone*
weiss: ich weiss nicht *I don't know*
wo? *where?*
das **Wörterbuch, ¨er** *dictionary*

SECTION C

am Freitag *on Friday*
aus *out, over*
beginnt *begins*
Bio *short for* Biologie
Biologie *biology*
dann *then*
Deutsch *German*
der **Dienstag** *Tuesday*
der **Donnerstag** *Thursday*
ein, eine *a, an*
Englisch *English*
das **Fach, ¨er** *subject*
frei *off;* er hat frei *he has off, he has no school*
der **Freitag** *Friday*
gehen: sie gehen in die neunte Klasse *they're in the ninth grade*
Geographie *geography*
Geschichte *history*
haben *to have*
halb: halb zehn *nine thirty*
heute *today*
ihr *you* (pl)
in *in*
jetzt *now*
die **Klasse, -n** *class; grade*
die **Klassenarbeit, -en** *test*
der **Klassenkamerad, -en** *classmate*
Kunst *art*
Latein *Latin*
Mathe *math*
der **Mittwoch** *Wednesday*
Moment mal! *wait a minute!*
der **Montag** *Monday*
Musik *music*
na *well*
nach *after, past*
der **Name, -n** *name*
die **Oberschule, -n** *high school;* er geht auf die Oberschule *he goes to high school*
die **Parallelklasse, -n** *class of the same grade*
die **Pause, -n** *break, recess*
Physik *physics*
Religion *religion*
der **Sonnabend** *Saturday*
sonnabends *(on) Saturdays*
spät: wie spät ist es? *what time is it?* (see page 75)
um *at;* um acht Uhr *at eight o'clock;* um eins *at one*
viel Glück! *good luck!*
Viertel nach neun *a quarter after nine*
vor *before, of*
wann? *when?*
welche? *which, what?*
wir *we*
die **Zahlen von 5 bis 60** *the numbers from 5 to 60* (p. 74)
die **Zeit** *time*

SECTION D

aber *but*
Algebra *algebra*
blöd *stupid, dumb*
eine **Eins** *a one* (see page 79)
gut *good*
die **Hausaufgaben** (pl) *homework*
leicht *easy*
macht: er macht Mathe *he's doing math*
die **Note, -n** *grade, mark*
phantastisch *fantastic, great*
schade! *too bad!*
schlecht *bad*
schwer *difficult*
so *so*

WORTSCHATZÜBUNGEN

1. Look at the nouns in the **Wortschatz** above and note how the plural forms are indicated. Then write out each noun in the plural.
2. Make a list of all the words that are similar to English, writing both the German and the English. Compare the spelling and meaning of the words in each pair.

2. kommen (come), Auto (car), Bus (bus), Moped (moped), hier (here), Kassette (cassette), Poster (poster), kosten (cost), beginnt (begins), Biologie (biology), Englisch (English), Klasse (class, grade), Geographie (geography), in (in), Latein (Latin), Mathe (math), Musik (music), Name (name), Pause (break), Physik (physics), Religion (religion), Algebra (algebra), Note (grade), phantastisch (fantastic), so (so)

ZUM LESEN

Hausaufgabenlied

Endlich° ist die Schule aus,
und ich gehe jetzt nach Haus',
pack' alles aus der Tasche aus.

Bleistift, Kuli und Papier,
Hefte, Bücher—zwei, drei, vier.
Taschenrechner? Ja, alles hier.

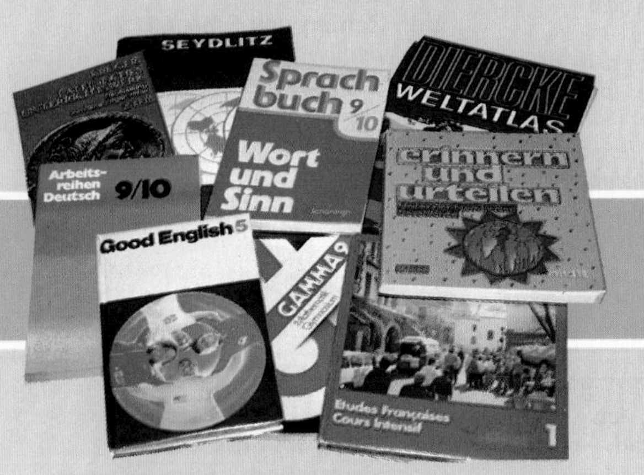

Mathe, Deutsch, Biologie,
Englisch, Kunst, Geographie,
Latein, Geschichte und Chemie.

Hausaufgaben muss ich machen°,
Hausaufgaben, nichts zu lachen°!
Hausaufgaben—viel° zu schwer!
Hausaufgaben—danke sehr°!

Übung • Beantworte die Fragen!

1. Was ist aus? die Schule
2. Wohin geht der Schüler? nach Haus'
3. Was macht er? Er packt alles aus der Tasche aus.
4. Was packt er aus der Tasche? Bleistift, Kuli, Papier, Hefte, Bücher, Taschenrechner
5. Welche Fächer hat er? Mathe, Deutsch, Biologie, Englisch, Kunst, Geographie, Latein, Geschichte, Chemie
6. Was macht er jetzt? Hausaufgaben
7. Sind die Hausaufgaben leicht? Nein, sie sind schwer.

Hausaufgabenlied *homework song* **endlich** *finally* **muss ich machen** *I have to do* **nichts zu lachen** *no laughing matter* **viel** *much* **danke sehr** *thank you very much—you can have them*

Der Traum

Schnell°, Paul! Es ist Montag, und es ist acht Uhr!
Was?!

‚Schnell, schnell! Ich komme zu spät°!'

Moment mal! Warten°!

Ah, da ist der Paul!
Endlich°, die Schule!

So, Paul, wo hast du die Hausaufgaben?
Die Hausaufgaben? —Zu Hause°!

Gott sei Dank°! Es ist Sonntag°!

Übung • Stimmt oder stimmt nicht?

According to Paul's dream, are these statements true or not true?

1. Es ist Montag. Stimmt!
2. Paul kommt zu spät in die Schule. Stimmt!
3. Paul kommt mit dem Bus in die Schule. Stimmt nicht!
4. Pauls Freunde kommen auch zu spät. Stimmt nicht!
5. Paul hat die Hausaufgaben. Stimmt nicht!
6. Was?! Es ist Sonnabend. Stimmt nicht!

---

der Traum *dream* **schnell!** *hurry up!* **ich komme zu spät** *I'll be late* **warten!** *wait!* **endlich** *finally* **zu Hause** *at home* **Gott sei Dank!** *Thank heavens!* **Sonntag** *Sunday*

KAPITEL 3

KAPITEL 3 Freizeit
Scope and Sequence

	BASIC MATERIAL	COMMUNICATIVE FUNCTIONS
SECTION A	**Freizeit: Sport und Hobbys (A1)** **Und was macht ihr? (A11)**	**Exchanging information** • Asking someone about his or her interests
SECTION B	**Wann machst du Sport? (B1)** **Wie oft macht ihr Sport? (B3)**	**Exchanging information** • Talking about when and how often you do your various sports and activities
SECTION C	**Fussball ist Klasse! (C1)** **Stimmt! Stimmt nicht! (C6)** **Was machst du gern? (C10)**	**Expressing attitudes and opinions** • Asking for an opinion; expressing enthusiasm or the lack of it • Expressing surprise, agreement, and disagreement **Expressing feelings and emotions** • Expressing likes, dislikes, and preferences
TRY YOUR SKILLS	Pronunciation /R/, /ʌ/, /ai/, /au/, /ɔi/, /ʃ/ Letter-sound correspondences **r, -er, ei, au, eu/äu, sch, sp, st** Dictation	
ZUM LESEN	**Keine Freizeitmuffel** (interviews with students about their reading habits) **Wie findet ihr Comics?** (students' reactions to comics)	

WRITING A variety of controlled and open-ended writing activities appear in the Pupil's Edition. The Teacher's Notes identify other activities suitable for writing practice and suggest additional writing activities.

COOPERATIVE LEARNING Many of the activities in the Pupil's Edition lend themselves to cooperative learning. The Teacher's Notes explain some of the many instances where this teaching strategy can be particularly effective. For guidelines on how to use cooperative learning, see page T13.

GRAMMAR	CULTURE	RE–ENTRY
Using the **du**-form (A4) Using the **ihr**-form (A15) The present tense (A19)	Popular sports and hobbies Three ways of saying *you* in German	Asking questions Personal pronouns
Word order: verb in second place (B6)	How young people spend their free time	Sports and activities Days of the week
gern, lieber, am liebsten, nicht gern (C11)	Student survey: preferred sports activities	Sports and activities Seasons, words answering the question **wie oft?**
Recombining communicative functions, grammar, and vocabulary		
Reading for practice and pleasure		

TEACHER–PREPARED MATERIALS

Section A Pictures of sports and activities; flashcards of personal pronouns, verb infinitives

Section B Calendar; flashcards of seasons, expressions of frequency, conjugated verb forms

Section C Pictures of new sports and activities; flashcards of **gern, lieber, am liebsten**

UNIT RESOURCES

Übungsheft, Unit 3
Arbeitsheft, Unit 3
Unit 3 Cassettes
Transparencies 8–10
Quizzes 9–11
Unit 3 Test

A1–3

OBJECTIVE **To exchange information:** ask someone about his or her interests

CULTURAL BACKGROUND German teenagers like to spend their spare time doing many of the same things American teenagers like to do. However, in the United States, school is the focus of students' extracurricular activities; in German-speaking countries, school is in the main simply a place for learning. Sports teams are privately sponsored; there are no cheerleading squads and consequently little of the kind of school spirit associated with American schools.

MOTIVATING ACTIVITY Ask your students to list the things they do in their spare time: sports, hobbies, clubs, and interests. Have them keep their lists for discussion later on in the unit, when they learn how German teenagers spend their spare time.

A1

Freizeit: Sport und Hobbys 

Play the cassette or read the interview aloud as the students listen with their books closed. Take the interview one segment at a time. Introduce the new vocabulary through modeling it and acting it out. For example, to illustrate **Freizeit,** you might say, **Ich habe Freizeit. Am Samstag habe ich frei. Ich habe keine Schule.**

Play or read the section of the interview again. This time ask questions about the conversation.

—Wer sind die Sprecher?
—Der Interviewer fragt Jens: ,,Was machst du in deiner Freizeit?" Was antwortet Jens?

Follow the same procedure for the next four sections of the interview. Then read or play the interview again as the students follow in their books. Finally, read the interview aloud with the class, the students taking the role of Jens. Ask for good intonation, proper pauses **(Tja . . .),** expression **(Na klar!),** and pronunciation. Practice difficult sounds in new words, first in individual words and then in sentences.

/fr/ frei, Freund Ich habe frei. Ich habe Freunde.

Continue with /ts/ **(Freizeit),** /x/ **(besuchen, machen),** /ʃp/ **(spielen, Sport),** and /ʃv/ **(schwimmen).** Call attention to the cognates **Instrument** and **Gitarre.** Emphasize the stress of **Instrumẹnt.**

A2

Übung • Mix-Match: Was macht Jens?

As a variation, ask the students to come up with additional utterances, such as **Und was spielt er noch? (Er spielt auch Fussball.)** or **Spielt er auch Schach? (Ja, er spielt auch Schach.)**

A3

Übung • Bilder-Quiz: Was macht Jens? Er . . . 

Expand this activity by using the pictures to stimulate questions and answers. Have the students work in pairs. Start them off by demonstrating some **was-**questions and answers **(Was spielst du? Ich spiele Fussball.)** and some questions expressing surprise, with appropriate responses **(Du spielst Fussball? Ja, ich spiele Fussball.)**

A4 ERKLÄRUNG

Keep your explanation extremely simple: refer to the **du-**form and the **ich-**form in preference to "second person singular," and do not bring up the **Sie-**form at this point. Some students from German-speaking households may bring it up themselves; say that the subject will be covered later on.

Give the students additional questions to see if they can answer properly. The words in parentheses are prompts.

1. Auf welche Schule gehst du? (auf die . . .)
2. Wie kommst du in die Schule? (Bus)
3. Wann beginnst du? (um acht Uhr)
4. Was hast du in Deutsch? (eine Zwei)
5. Machst du Sport? (ja)
6. Was für Hausaufgaben machst du? (Mathe)

A5 Übung • Jetzt bist du dran

As a variation, play **Scharaden** *(charades)*. Have one student act out one of the activities in 1–6 and let the others tell what he or she is doing: **Du spielst Gitarre.**

A6 Übung • Frag deinen Mitschüler!

A variation of this exercise is to have the students, still working in pairs, "compete" with Jens. One says all the things that Jens does; the other one says that he or she does it too: **Jens schwimmt. — Ich schwimme auch!**

A7 WIE SAGT MAN DAS?

Point out that the German **Was machst du?** does double duty for both *What do you do?* and *What are you doing?*

Model a brief conversation based on the expressions given; then have the students pair off for conversations of their own.

SLOWER–PACED LEARNING Rather than having the students pair off, call out questions. The students can respond in short-answer form. For example, the answer to **Machst du Sport?** might be **Na klar!** or **Ja, Fussball.**

A8 Übung • Partnerarbeit

Give the students additional vocabulary so that they can express what they do in their spare time. Let them suggest many of the additional vocabulary items. Write these on the board.

Sport	Musik	Hobbys
ich spiele	ich spiele	ich sehe
Volleyball	Klavier	fern
Basketball	Violine	Videos
Football	Flöte	ich lese
Baseball		Bücher
ich mache		Zeitschriften
Gymnastik		ich arbeite am Computer
ich jogge		

KAPITEL

3

A9–11

Encourage the students to respond to each question with more than one sentence.

—Machst du Sport?
—Ja, ich schwimme und spiele Tennis. Ich spiele auch Basketball. Im Herbst spiele ich Fussball. Und du?

SLOWER–PACED LEARNING These students may respond enthusiastically to the opportunity to talk about themselves. They may surprise you by coming up with considerably more complex sentences than usual, given the vocabulary. Don't discourage them, but do work with the class as a whole before going on to **Partnerarbeit.**

A 9 Neu im Sport

Encourage a discussion of the sports represented; some will be unfamiliar to your students. Perhaps one or more of your students engage in one of the sports and can tell the class more. Also, if any of your students have visited Germany or another German-speaking country, they might like to tell the class which sports they found popular there.

A 10 Übung • Und du? Wie steht's mit dir?

You may wish to provide your students with a list of other sports and hobbies you think they are likely to be involved in. Go over the list with them prior to doing the activity.

SLOWER–PACED LEARNING Provide the students with the following list of responses and have them supply the corresponding questions from A10.

1. Ja, Tennis und Handball.
2. Na klar! Ich sammle Videokassetten. Ich spiele auch Trivial Pursuit.
3. Oh, ich sehe fern; ich höre Musik; ich lese; ich . . .
4. Nein, aber ich spiele Volleyball.
5. Ich spiele Videospiele mit dem Computer; ich spiele Gitarre; ich besuche Freunde.

A 11 UND WAS MACHT IHR?

Review the concept of **ihr,** first introduced in Section C of Unit 2, using both questions and statements in addressing students. Point to them as you talk.

Du spielst Basketball und du spielst Basketball.
Ihr spielt Basketball.
Hast du Hobbys? Und du? Hast du Hobbys?
Habt ihr Hobbys?

Introduce the new material in the usual manner. Stop after each segment to read the interview with the class and to ask questions. Use the photo to explain the meaning of **Münzen** (or use real coins). Before starting on the last segment **(Mau-Mau),** demonstrate the meaning of **mogeln** and **verlieren** so that the passage can be understood.

Concentrate on all the **ihr-**questions. Ask the students to identify the people addressed with **ihr.**

—Der Interviewer sagt: „Und was macht ihr? Macht ihr auch Sport?" Wen fragt er?
—Kristin sagt: „Aber ihr mogelt." Wen meint sie?

A 12 Übung • Mix-Match: Was machen die Jungen und Mädchen?

As a variation, use this as a completion activity. Have the students cover up the right-hand side of the page and give *any* plausible answer.

A 13 Übung • Bilder-Quiz: Was machen die Jungen und Mädchen?

To expand this activity, use the same pictures to have the students tell what *they* are doing, using **wir.** Then ask them to imagine that they are addressing a group of friends: **ihr segelt, ihr spielt Hockey,** and so on.

A 14 Übung • Der Sport- und Hobbymuffel

Vary this by having one student initiate the exchange with the statement, for example, **Ich segle nicht.** The other student expresses astonishment: **Was? Du segelst nicht?**

ANSWERS
Spielst du Hockey? — Nein, ich spiele nicht Hockey.
Spielst du Basketball? — Nein, ich spiele nicht Basketball.
Spielst du Karten? — Nein, ich spiele nicht Karten.
Spielst du Tennis, — Nein, ich spiele nicht Tennis.
Spielst du Gitarre? — Nein, ich spiele nicht Gitarre.
Sammelst du Münzen? — Nein, ich sammle nicht Münzen.
Hörst du Musikkassetten? — Nein, ich höre nicht Musikkassetten.

A 15 ERKLÄRUNG

After you have explained the **ihr-**form, practice the question/answer pairs aloud with the class. Give the students additional questions such as the following to see if they can apply what they have learned. The suggestions in parentheses are prompts.

Auf welche Schule geht ihr? (auf die . . .)
Wie kommt ihr in die Schule? (zu Fuss)
In welche Klasse geht ihr? (in die . . .te)
Was habt ihr in Mathe? (eine Drei)
Habt ihr auch Kunst? (ja)

A 16 Übung • Interview

After you have done the activity, demonstrate other possible answers, of a more informal kind. Ask the students to imagine that you are also a student (otherwise they would have to address you with **Sie**). Have them address the questions to you and another student. (You answer for both.)

Spielt ihr Schach? — Na klar!
Verliert ihr? — Ja, immer!

A 17 Übung • Was macht ihr?

CHALLENGE Call for a second response of student A. The response must fit the situation. A sample dialog follows.

A: Wir sind sauer.
B: Wirklich? Ihr seid sauer?
A: Ja, ihr mogelt.

A 18 Übung • Lücken-Dialog

Once you have done the activity, you might have the students create their own **Lücken-Dialoge** and put several of these on the board. The rest of the class has to fill them in.

A 19 ERKLÄRUNG

Ask the students to look for patterns in the verb endings. Draw their attention to **sie** and **Sie** in particular. Point out that **Sie** meaning "you" is capitalized. Have them practice the **Sie**-form by asking *you* questions. If you have them pair off and practice with one another, ask them to assume adult roles. Do not encourage them to get into the habit of addressing their contemporaries with **Sie.**

To bring home the point that the German **Präsens** does double duty for *to do* and *to be doing,* ask them **Segelt ihr?** and elicit, by prompting, **Ja, wir segeln.** Then ask, **Segelt ihr heute?** and elicit a **nein-**answer.

A 20 Übung • Bilder-Quiz: Was machen die Schüler?

As a variation, have the students create new sentences by moving each subject one slot to the right. This should produce, for example, **Wir spielen Tennis,** and so on.

SLOWER–PACED LEARNING Use only one picture at a time and have the students form a sentence for each subject given. Alternatively, go through all the pictures using only one subject.

A 21 Übung • Frag mal deinen Lehrer!

To give the students additional practice, have them go back to the interview in A1 and conduct the interview with an adult (played by you or by another student). Give them help with the one question that is difficult: **Was machen Sie in Ihrer Freizeit?** Remind them to omit questions one would not ask an adult **(Wie alt sind Sie?).**

A 22 Übung • Versteckte Sätze

CHALLENGE Have the students make up similar "hidden sentences" for the next day and put them on a transparency. The class has to find them.

A 23 Übung • Hör gut zu!

You will hear ten questions. Listen carefully to each one and decide whether it addresses one student, several students, or an adult. For example, you hear, **Was macht ihr in der Freizeit?** You place your check mark in the row labeled *addressing several students.* Let's begin. **Fangen wir an!**

1. Spielt ihr Karten oder Schach? *several students*
2. Hören Sie Musikkassetten? *an adult*
3. Was machst du? *one student*
4. Verlierst du das Spiel? *one student*
5. Sammeln Sie Briefmarken? *an adult*
6. Besucht ihr Freunde? *several students*
7. Gewinnt ihr das Spiel? *several students*

8. Mogelst du? *one student*
9. Was machen Sie? *an adult*
10. Segelt ihr heute? *several students*

Now check your answers. *Read each item again and give the correct answer.*

A 24 **Schreibübung**

The second of these activities in particular could equally well serve as an oral activity, either in addition to or instead of its use as a written activity. Students can give their questions one at a time, with other students responding.

SECTION B

OBJECTIVES **To exchange information:** talk about when and how often you do your various sports and activities

CULTURAL BACKGROUND **Fussball**—that is, soccer, not American football—is the most popular sport in Germany. Children learn it at a young age.

Entire classes may go on trips for winter sports during the **Winterferien,** usually staying in youth hostels. Students may be given an entire week off to go skiing.

MOTIVATING ACTIVITY On a piece of paper, have the students make a big circle and divide it into quadrants. They should put **das Jahr** in the middle and one of the seasons on the outside of each quadrant: **Frühling, Sommer, Herbst,** and **Winter.** (Note that **Frühling** is more common than **Frühjahr** when giving all four seasons in enumeration and that it will in any case be easier for the students to remember all four seasons with the same definite article.) Have them put the sports they participate in into the quadrants.

B 1 **Wann machst du Sport?**

Play the cassette or read the text aloud as the students listen with their books closed. Ask them to listen for any differences in the word order. Have them note it, but don't say anything yet. When they have listened to the material a second time, ask them what they noticed about the word order. If they do not notice the inversion, point it out. Then proceed in the usual manner.

Demonstrate the verb in second place by doing the following visualization exercise. Write the sentence elements of several sentences that contain adverbs of time on large cards or pieces of paper. The writing should be legible in the last row of the class. Pass out the elements of one of these sentences to several students, who come to the front of the room and stand in line so as to form a sentence, for example:

| Ich | spiele | Tennis | im Sommer. |

Then ask the person with **im Sommer** to come to the front of the line and show what happens to the **ich.** It gets kicked out of its place before the verb and must go to the place after the verb! Do this with several more sentences. This right-brain demonstration of word order is very effective. It will stick in students' minds much longer than any long verbal explanation.

B2 Übung • Und du? Wie steht's mit dir?

You can expand and personalize this activity by bringing in pictures of additional sports and activities or by having the students bring in drawings or magazine cutouts of their favorite sports and activities, based on the wheel of the seasons they did for the Motivating Activity.

B3 WIE OFT MACHT IHR SPORT?

Introduce the first section by playing the cassette or reading the material aloud as the students follow in their texts and look at the graph. Use this small paragraph for reading practice, first verbatim **(Was sagt Petra?)** and then in the third person **(Was weisst du über Petra?).** Ask questions: **Wie oft spielt Petra Tennis? Wann? Was macht sie im Winter?** Introduce the second section the same way.

B4 Übung • Was sagt Michael? Was sagt Petra? Erzähl mal!

This activity may also be used as a written exercise, to be done in class or for homework. For further practice with adverbial expressions of time, ask the students questions designed to elicit such answers as **Dreimal in der Woche, Nie,** and so on. (Model them if you aren't getting the right kind of answers.) Some sample questions follow:

1. Wie oft hast du Deutsch?
2. Wie oft hast du eine Eins?
3. Wie oft kommst du mit dem Moped?
4. Wie oft bekommst du ein Zeugnis?
5. Wie oft besuchst du Freunde?
6. Wie oft hörst du Kassetten?
7. Wie oft spielst du Gitarre?

Using the pictures from B2 or magazine cutouts, ask the students how often they do the activities.

einmal im Jahr
viermal am Tag
dreimal in der Woche
einmal im Monat
sechsmal im Jahr
am Wochenende

B5 Ein wenig Landeskunde

Before starting the reading and discussion, have the students take out the list of their own spare-time activities they prepared for the motivating activity for Section A. Have them read the cultural note with attention to similarities and differences in the amount of spare time that young people have here and abroad and on the use they make of it. Discussion will probably center on the pros and cons of school sports teams, musical ensembles, and clubs, as well as on the pros and cons of part-time jobs.

B6 ERKLÄRUNG

Remind the students of the demonstration with the cards they did for B1. Rather than speak of inverted word order, ask them what happened to the verb when the adverbial element (use the exact wording—**im Sommer,** if that was the case) changed places with the subject. (Nothing. It stayed where it was.) Then go over the sentences in B6 with them, giving more examples if necessary.

Practice word order by giving the students sentences in normal word order. The students then have to invert them.

B7 Übung • Frag deine Mitschüler! Frag deinen Lehrer!

For questions addressed to **ihr,** one student should answer for the group. Ask for three or four responses for each dialog.

B8 Übung • Hör gut zu!

You will hear ten statements, each one containing a phrase that answers either a question with **wann?** or a question with **wie oft?** Now assume that you did not understand the phrase answering this question. Which question word would you use, **wann?** or **wie oft?,** to get information? For example, you hear, **Ich spiele einmal in der Woche Fussball.** If you didn't understand the time phrase **einmal in der Woche,** you would ask, **Wie oft?** Let's begin. **Fangen wir an!**

1. Ich segle am Wochenende. *wann?*
2. Im Winter laufe ich Schi. *wann?*
3. Er spielt dreimal in der Woche Basketball. *wie oft?*
4. Am Sonntag faulenze ich. *wann?*
5. Einmal im Monat besuche ich Freunde. *wie oft?*
6. Ich höre selten Musikkassetten. *wie oft?*
7. Im Herbst spielen wir immer Tennis. *wann?*
8. Ich schwimme zweimal in der Woche. *wie oft?*
9. Am Wochenende spielen wir Fussball. *wann?*
10. Einmal im Jahr laufe ich Schi. *wie oft?*

Now check your answers. *Read each item again and give the correct answer.*

B9 Schreibübung • Sport ist prima!

As a variation, you could have the students write a paragraph about their own activities, again using inverted word order.

ANSWERS

Sport ist prima! Am Dienstag und am Freitag spiele ich Tennis. Am Samstag spiele ich Fussball. Im Sommer spiele ich auch Fussball. Fussball ist toll! Wir sind gut. Meistens gewinnen wir; wir verlieren selten. Im Winter laufe ich Schi, und ich spiele Hockey. Einmal in der Woche habe ich Musik. Ich spiele Gitarre. Oft besuche ich Freunde, und wir hören Kassetten. Das ist auch toll!

C1–3

OBJECTIVES **To express attitudes and opinions:** ask for an opinion and express enthusiasm or the lack of it; express surprise, agreement, and disagreement; **to express feelings and emotions:** express likes, dislikes, and preferences

CULTURAL BACKGROUND Germans are enthusiastic about fresh air—they love to go out for walks—and physical fitness. All German students have to meet minimum standards for physical fitness. Many belong to a **Turnverein,** a club where they get together to do gymnastics, or to another sports club. These clubs frequently meet for competitions.

MOTIVATING ACTIVITY Ask the students to give you the most common ways we express likes and dislikes in English. Put the answers on an overhead transparency. Most probably you will get *I like it!, It's fun!, It's great!* for likes, and *I don't like it, It's boring, It's dumb* for dislikes. Tell the students to listen closely for the way German teenagers express their opinions.

C1

Fussball ist Klasse! 

Play the cassette or read the text aloud as the students listen with their books open, but with only the pictures exposed. Take the material one interview at a time. Stop and introduce new vocabulary each time. In this case, a lot of the vocabulary will be clear from context—the sports are illustrated. But you can illustrate the expressions of like or dislike: a look of extreme boredom for **langweilig** and an enthusiastic tone for **Prima!** will do it.

Have the students listen to the first interview again. This time ask questions. Go from simple recall questions—**Was macht Margit?**—to comprehension questions: **Warum macht Margit Gymnastik?** Structure your questions in such a way as to avoid a response that requires **kein.** Proceed in the same way with the other interviews. In the later interviews, ask questions that include vocabulary and phrases introduced in previous interviews: for example, **Was macht Wiebke Spass, Lesen oder Gymnastik?** In this particular interview, call the students' attention to **Fantasy-Bücher** and compare it to the word **phantastisch,** which they have had in another context. Explain that the latter is a recent loan word borrowed directly from English, which accounts for the discrepancy in the spelling.

Before you go on to reading the interviews with the class, work on the pronunciation of difficult words. Students may, for example, stumble over **Margit** because of its resemblance to the English; at least, they will try to slip in an extra **r. Jörg** presents difficulties because of the /ö/ and the final **g; Gymnastik,** the hard **g; Spass** and **Spitze,** the /ʃp/; **langweilig,** /ai/, /l/, and final /iç/; **Wiebke,** the **w** and the **-bk-.** They will probably also be tempted to accent **Romane** on the wrong syllable. Call attention to the cognate **interessant.**

C2

Übung • Mix-Match: Was machen die drei Schüler?

As a variation, have the students cover up the right-hand side—the completions column—and come up with their own completions.

C3

WIE SAGT MAN DAS?

After having the students read the summary and the German examples in the chart, have them replace **Fussball** with other sports or activities. One student starts out by asking for an opinion. Several other students express their enthusiasm or lack of enthusiasm for the activity.

C4 Übung • Was meint dein Freund?

To give the students more practice and to re-enter old vocabulary, you can have them substitute the names of the school subjects taught in C1 and D1 of Unit 2 for the sports.

C5 Übung • Jetzt bist du dran

To expand this activity, have the students ask a classmate about more than one of the activities listed. They must vary their responses and use **auch** if they like both subjects. A sample dialog follows:

A: Wie findest du Gymnastik?
B: Gymnastik ist Klasse!
A: Und Tennis?
B: Tennis ist auch interessant. *[or]* Tennis ist blöd.

C6 STIMMT! STIMMT NICHT! 

Play the cassette or read the dialogs aloud. Proceed in the usual manner, taking the dialogs one at a time. In repetition and practice, ask for lots of expression to show surprise, agreement, or disagreement. Stop after each of the mini-dialogs and ask for other things or activities to agree or disagree about. This is an excellent opportunity for re-entering vocabulary. Have these stimuli ready on overhead transparencies or large cards.

for	*re-enter*
1. ______ ist Klasse.	(sports and activities)
2. Wie findest du ______?	das Buch/das Poster/die Comics
3. Du sammelst ______?	Münzen/Poster/Kassetten/Videos
4. ______ ist (auch) langweilig.	Hausaufgaben machen/ Romane lesen/Gitarrespielen/ Münzensammeln/Autofahren/ das Wochenende

C7 WIE SAGT MAN DAS?

CHALLENGE After you have covered the material with the class, have the students give a different response for the last line of each dialog in C6. For example, if the response was **Was! Das finde ich nicht,** the student might substitute **Das finde ich auch.**

C8 Übung • Partnerarbeit

Expand this activity by taking an informal poll of the class. Which sports and activities are the most popular? The least popular? Have each student report what his or her partner said.

C9 Übung • Und du? Wie steht's mit dir?

CHALLENGE After the students agree or disagree with the statements given in the book, have them make up additional ones on their own.

C10–13

C10 WAS MACHST DU GERN?

Introduce the phrases **gern, lieber,** and **am liebsten** by demonstrating things you like to do. Make your demonstration as vivid as possible. As the students listen and watch, they try to figure out what the new words mean. If necessary, use one, two, and three plus signs on the board as you talk:

Ich gehe gern zu Fuss. (+)
Ich fahre lieber mit dem Rad. (++)
Ich fahre am liebsten mit dem Auto. (+++)

When you think that the students have grasped the concepts, give them the new terms in a mixed-up order:

gern — nicht gern — am liebsten — lieber

Ask them to rearrange these words and phrases according to a scale of negative (−) to very positive (+++).

Now introduce the boy and his preference scale by playing the cassette or reading the text aloud. Have the students read along silently. Introduce the verb **faulenzen.** Students will love to use the adjective, the verb, and the noun applied to a lazy person.

Er macht nichts.
Er ist faul.
Er faulenzt.
Er ist ein Faulenzer.
Er faulenzt am liebsten.

C11 WIE SAGT MAN DAS?

Avoid the terms *positive, comparative,* and *superlative,* and don't vary the position of **gern** within the sentence. At this stage, it is apt to confuse your students.

C12 Übung • Und du? Wie steht's mit dir?

To lead into this activity, tell the students that you have a hunch as to what they like and dislike. They confirm your hunches and give you a reason for their choice of activity. For example, you say, **Du spielst gern Karten, nicht?** and the student replies, **Ja, Kartenspielen macht Spass.** To elicit a negative answer, you say, **Du liest nicht gern, nicht?** and the student replies, **Nein, Lesen ist langweilig.** Some sample sentences follow:

1. Du spielst nicht gern Schach, nicht?
2. Du schwimmst gern, nicht?
3. Du faulenzt gern, nicht?
4. Du verlierst nicht gern, nicht?
5. Du liest gern Comics, nicht?

C13 Übung • Der Sport- und Hobbyfreund: Was macht er denn alles?

When you have done the activity, ask the students, singling them out, **Bist du auch ein Sport- und Hobbyfreund? Was machst du denn alles?** They reply, either using the picture as a guide or giving their actual sports and hobbies. Leave this up to them.

C14 Übung • Hör gut zu!

You will hear ten statements. Listen carefully to each one and determine if it expresses what someone likes, does not like, prefers, or likes most of all. For example, you hear, **Ich höre lieber Musikkassetten.** You place your check mark in the row labeled *prefers,* because the sentence **Ich höre lieber Musikkassetten** expresses what the person prefers. Let's begin. **Fangen wir an!**

1. Ich lese am liebsten Comics. *likes most of all*
2. Der Michael spielt gern Tennis. *likes*
3. Wir sammeln lieber Münzen. *prefers*
4. Die Wiebke segelt nicht gern. *does not like*
5. Die Margit macht am liebsten Gymnastik. *likes most of all*
6. Der Jens findet Segeln langweilig. *does not like*
7. Der Jörg hat Sport am liebsten. *likes most of all*
8. Der Kurt liest gern Romane. *likes*
9. Ich lese lieber Hobbybücher. *prefers*
10. Der Jens findet Tennis prima; er spielt gern. *likes*

Now check your answers. *Read each item again and give the correct answer.*

C15 Schreibübung • Was machen die Schüler gern? Und du?

As a variation, instead of doing the second of the two activities, have each student pick a partner, ask questions, and fill in a chart on that partner. The partner does likewise. They then write sentences based on the charts. This can be done a second time with another partner.

ANSWERS

1. 1. Paul macht gern Gymnastik. Er schwimmt am liebsten. Er spielt Basketball nicht gern.
2. Sabine spielt Karten gern. Sie spielt Mau-Mau am liebsten. Sie spielt Schach nicht gern.
3. Monika und Anke hören Kassetten gern. Sie machen Sport am liebsten. Sie sammeln nicht gern.

C16 Übung • Umfrage: Was machst du in deiner Freizeit?

SLOWER–PACED LEARNING Have the students give only one statement about each line, moving vertically; for example, **Er spielt am liebsten Fussball. Er spielt Basketball im Frühjahr,** and so on.

CHALLENGE After doing the activity orally, have the students write a paragraph about Markus' likes and dislikes.

C17 Übung • Klassenprojekt

For this, have a blank survey sheet on the overhead or on the board and do it as a **Gruppenarbeit,** *group project.* One student can elicit information from the group while another tabulates the results.

TRY YOUR SKILLS

OBJECTIVE To recombine communicative functions, grammar, and vocabulary

CULTURAL BACKGROUND Students in Germany are apt to get together in the afternoon at one another's homes to socialize and relax for a while before they go off to their several activities. This is rather a ritual with Jens, Jörg, and Lars; Jens is always the one who prepares coffee for the group.

1

Stimmt nicht! Du bist nur sauer! 

After you have covered the material with the students, have them pair off and read the conversation with each other. They should show real interest in the other person and put a lot of expression into phrases that express an opinion.

As a variant, you can have the conversation take place between two adults who have met at a spa and are trying to find out each other's interests. One of the adults likes **Schach;** the other **Kartenspielen.** Tell the students to leave out the last sentence, since it would be impolite to say **und Sie sind sauer.**

2

Übung • Deine Meinung — meine Meinung

Do the mini-dialogs as suggested. If necessary, give cues to encourage more varied exchanges: **lesen/Sportbücher; hören/Countrymusik; machen/Mathe; sammeln/Münzen;** and so on.

3

Übung • Stimmt! — Stimmt nicht!

CHALLENGE Have the students react to opinions about things other than sports and activities. Do this as a class first and then have the students work in pairs or small groups. Ask for sample reactions from each group.

1. Geschichte ist langweilig!
2. Eine Drei in Englisch ist prima!
3. Musikkassetten sind billig, nur DM 6!
4. Videokassetten sind teuer, DM 20!
5. Die Schweiz ist wunderbar!

4

Übung • Sport und Spiel

Expand the activity by having the students respond to these questions on preferences orally or in writing:

1. Was spielst du lieber, Karten oder Monopoly?
2. Was liest du lieber, Biographien oder Romane?
3. Was hörst du lieber, Country-Western oder Rock?
4. Was findest du schwerer, Deutsch oder Mathe?
5. Was sagst du lieber, „Guten Tag" oder „Grüss Gott"?
6. Wann kommst du lieber in die Schule, um acht oder um neun?
7. Wie kommst du lieber, mit dem Bus oder mit dem Rad?

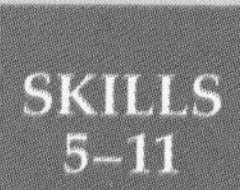

5 **Übung • Wann spielen sie was?**

As a variation, change the writing in the center boxes from seasons to other time expressions, such as **dreimal in der Woche, am Wochenende, sehr oft,** and **am Mittwoch und Samstag.**

6 **Übung • Hallo! Wer schreibt uns?**

Model some of the structures you want the students to use: **Ich wohne in Ulm, Schulstrasse 17. Meine Interessen sind . . .**

ANSWERS
Die Schülerin heisst Bettina Schilling. Sie ist vierzehn Jahre alt. Ihre Adresse ist Schulstrasse 17, D-7900 Ulm. Ihre Hobbys und Interessen sind Schwimmen, Segeln und Basketballspielen.
Der Schüler heisst Markus Wallner. Er ist fünfzehn Jahre alt. Seine Adresse ist Hebbelstrasse 8, D-6100 Darmstadt. Seine Hobbys und Interessen sind Fussball, Gymnastik und Briefmarkensammeln.

7 **Schreibübung • Interview und Anzeige**

As a variation, have the interviewer get the information from a young adult who is studying German and who would also like to have a pen pal. They must, of course, use the **Sie**-form.

8 **Übung • Ein Brief an Markus Wallner**

After you have read the letter with the class—help them with deciphering the form of the capital **I** and the lower-case **r**—have them write out an ad like the ones in Try Your Skills 6, based on the information in Martin's letter to Markus. What might an **Anzeige** of Martin's look like? Point out the capitalization of **du** and **dein** in the letter. Remind the students that this extends to forms of **ihr.**

9 **Schreibübung • Jetzt bist du dran**

CHALLENGE Choose one of the students' letters and use it for a dictation. Remind the students to capitalize **du,** if applicable.

SLOWER–PACED LEARNING Have two of the students read their letters aloud while the others take notes. Compare the notes afterwards.

10 **Schreibübung • Klassenprojekt**

This project can be carried out as a tandem project with a class in Germany, Austria, or Switzerland. (Ask the AATG or the Austrian Institute for help in establishing contacts.) It could also be carried out as a partner project with a German class in the United States, preferably in another part of the country, so that the letter exchange is real.

11 **Übung • Dialog-Mischmasch**

As a homework assignment, you could have the students make up scrambled dialogs of their own. Put some of them on the board or on an overhead the next day and have the rest of the class unscramble them.

SKILLS 12

12 Aussprache-, Lese- und Schreibübungen

1. Different native speakers of German may use somewhat different ver- /R/ sions of the sound /R/. Some Germans use a /R/ sound that is trilled with the top of the tongue; but the majority of native speakers of German, especially those living in cities, use a sound that is produced at the back of the throat and is called *uvular r*. This is the sound that you will learn to use. This /R/ sound can be produced by saying the **ach-**sound with a simultaneous vibration of the vocal cords. A vibration of the vocal cords can be observed by holding your hand to your throat as you say a /s/ sound and then change it to a /z/ sound *(sssszzzz)*; or when you say a /f/ sound and then change to a /v/ sound *(ffffvvvv)*. You feel the vibration after you switch to the second sound in each case. Now do the same with the **ach-**sound, and you will produce a /R/ sound *(chchchchrrr)*. **Hör zu und wiederhole!** Now listen and repeat each of the following words:

   frei, Freizeit, Freund, Frau, Briefmarke, drei, dreimal, prima, hören, verlieren, Morgen, Karte, Rad, Roman

   /ʌ/ Now listen to the final sound in these words:

   vier, ihr, hier, wir, er, der

   You know that these words are spelled with an **r** at the end. Did you hear the sound /R/? No, you did not. What you heard was a sound somewhat like a vowel. When you produce this sound, hold your tongue fairly flat, the tip touching your lower front teeth. **Hör zu und wiederhole!** Now listen and repeat each of the following words:

   ihr, vier, hier, wir, er, der, schwer

   Now listen to the final sound in these words:

   aber, lieber, immer, oder, Sommer

   The final sound in these words is a /ʌ/ sound. **Hör zu und wiederhole!** Now listen and repeat each of the following words:

   aber, oder, lieber, immer, Sommer, Winter, sauer, Schüler, Lehrer, super

   Among the vowel sounds of both German and English are blends or glides, called diphthongs, as in the words *mice, house,* and *boy*. In German, the first element of these glided sounds is shorter than it is in English. **Hör zu und wiederhole!** Now listen and repeat each of the following words:

   /ai/ /ai/ ein, eine, eins, einmal, dreimal, heisse, Freizeit, Latein, Bleistift

   /au/ /au/ Mau-Mau, faulenzen, sauer, Hausaufgabe, schau, aus, auch, Tschau

   /ɔi/ /ɔi/ neun, heute, Freund, Freundin, neunzehn; Fräulein, Verkäuferin

   /ʃ/ The sound /ʃ/ is pronounced like the English *sh* in *shine* and *shiver*, but in German the lips are a little more protruded while saying /ʃ/. **Hör zu und wiederhole!** Listen and repeat each of the following words:

   Schule, Schi, schwer, schlecht; spielen, Sport, spät; Stundenplan, Bleistift

2. In this section you will practice reading the words printed in your textbook on page 113. Pay attention to the following:

r 1. The letter **r** represents the /R/ sound you hear in these words:
frei, Frau, Freund, drei, dreimal, prima, hören, Karte, Roman, Rad

2. The letter **r** at the end of these words represents a vowel-like sound:
ihr, vier, hier, wir, er, der, schwer

-er 3. The letters **er** at the end of these words represent the /ʌ/ sound:
aber, oder, lieber, immer, Sommer, Winter, sauer, Schüler, Lehrer, super

ei 4. The letter combination **ei** represents the diphthong /ai/:
ein, eine, eins, einmal, heisse, Latein

au 5. The letter combination **au** represents the sound /au/:
Mau-Mau, sauer, schau, aus, auch

eu/äu 6. The letter combination **eu** represents the diphthong /ɔi/. So does the letter combination **äu.**
neun, heute, Freund, neunzehn; Fräulein, Verkäuferin

sch 7. The letters **sch** represent the sound /ʃ/:
Schule, Schi, schwer, schlecht

sp, st 8. The letter **s** represents the sound /ʃ/ before the letters **p** or **t:**
spielen, Sport, Spitze, spät; Stundenplan, Bleistift

3. Now close your textbook and write the sentences you hear.

1. Wir haben immer frei.
2. Fräulein Meier spielt heute.
3. Meine Freundin heisst Winter.
4. Die Schule ist schwer.

WAS KANNST DU SCHON?

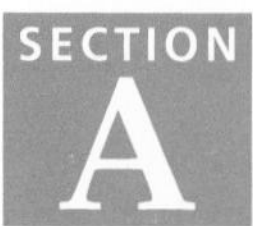

Supply verb cards for **machen, spielen,** and so on. Have the students address questions to you, to individual classmates, and to groups of classmates. Have them pair off for some of the work.

Play the game Accordion Sentences. Put the students into groups of three or more. Three would be ideal, since the students are not yet up to sentences with too many elements. One student writes a subject and verb—for example, **Ich spiele**—and folds the paper over. The second student knows only that the first student has supplied a subject and verb; he or she supplies an activity or sport and folds the paper. The third student supplies a time expression. Then the sheet of paper is unfolded. Make sure that you give the students fairly specific instructions: you do not want to have them come up with ungrammatical sentences, as might happen if one student contributed the subject and the other the verb. The fun comes from the unexpected and amusing combinations sometimes produced.

Put the class into two concentric circles, of which the outer one remains stationary. The inner one moves in a clockwise direction, each student in turn asking questions of his or her neighbor in the outer circle.

WORTSCHATZ

The students may be wondering why **Spitze** and **Klasse** are capitalized, since they appear to be adjectives. Explain that they are actually nouns.

WORTSCHATZÜBUNGEN

When you have the students pick out the gerunds, don't use the term *gerunds* or even *verbal nouns;* just speak of "**-en** words that describe activities, like *sailing, swimming,* and so on." Point out that **segeln** in Section A means "to sail" and **Segeln** in Section C means "sailing."

ZUM LESEN

OBJECTIVE To read for practice and pleasure

KEINE FREIZEITMUFFEL! 

This section should be of great appeal to American students learning German for several reasons. First of all, the students should feel proud of having "arrived." This is real reading, presenting new information. The language is simple, yet very natural and varied in style, because of the many different people who get to report on their reading habits. Secondly, the students should be interested in the topic itself. They, too, are often asked how much they read, what they read, and what their preferences are. In the United States, one also worries that television is taking people away from reading. Thirdly, the students should find it challenging to encounter new words and phrases and to guess their meaning from a context that is largely familiar.

Besides enjoyment, the goals of these readings are building self-esteem, getting new information, and making cultural comparisons of similarities and differences.

Have the students read the introductory paragraph silently as you play the cassette or read the paragraph aloud. On the second reading, ask comprehension questions, all in German: **Stimmt das auch für die USA? Gehen Jungen und Mädchen in Amerika auch ins Kino?** Point out cognates such as **Konzert, diskutieren,** and **philosophieren.** When you get to the table, ask comprehension questions, for example:

> Sehen die deutschen Jungen und Mädchen viel fern?
> Wie oft lesen die Jugendlichen in Büchern?
> Von 1968—1980: lesen sie mehr Bücher oder weniger Bücher?
> Wie weisst du das?

As you continue, have the students read, decipher, and guess the titles of **Zeitschriften** and **Zeitungen.** When you have finished the interview, ask some personalized questions on reading habits. Allow responses in short-answer format.

Welche Zeitung liest deine Familie?
Liest du täglich die Zeitung?
Welche Zeitschrift liest du gern?
Wie oft kommt sie?
Wie oft liest du sie?

Übung • Sprechen wir darüber!

CHALLENGE Have the students write a very brief report about their reading habits, similar to those given by the three young people. Have them put their reports in "bubble form" next to pictures or drawings of themselves. Display these in class.

WIE FINDET IHR COMICS? 

As an additional individual or class project, ask the students to look for and bring in books or comics showing the characters illustrated—there are, for example, German editions of **Astérix.**

Übung • Und du? Wie steht's mit dir?

In addition to or in preparation for these questions, you can ask some general comprehension questions. Allow very brief answers. Demonstrate the unfamiliar vocabulary as necessary.

1. Gibt es amerikanische Comics nur auf Englisch oder auch auf Deutsch?
2. Sind deutsche Comics sehr populär?
3. Welche Zeichner sind populär?
4. Was sind „Superhelden-Comics"?
5. Was meinst du, sind Comics Kunst oder Kitsch *(bad art)?*
6. Wie sind die Frauen in den meisten Comics: altmodisch oder emanzipiert?

Neue Hobbys 

Ask the students about their favorite computer games. Does anybody play computer chess?

KAPITEL 3
Freizeit

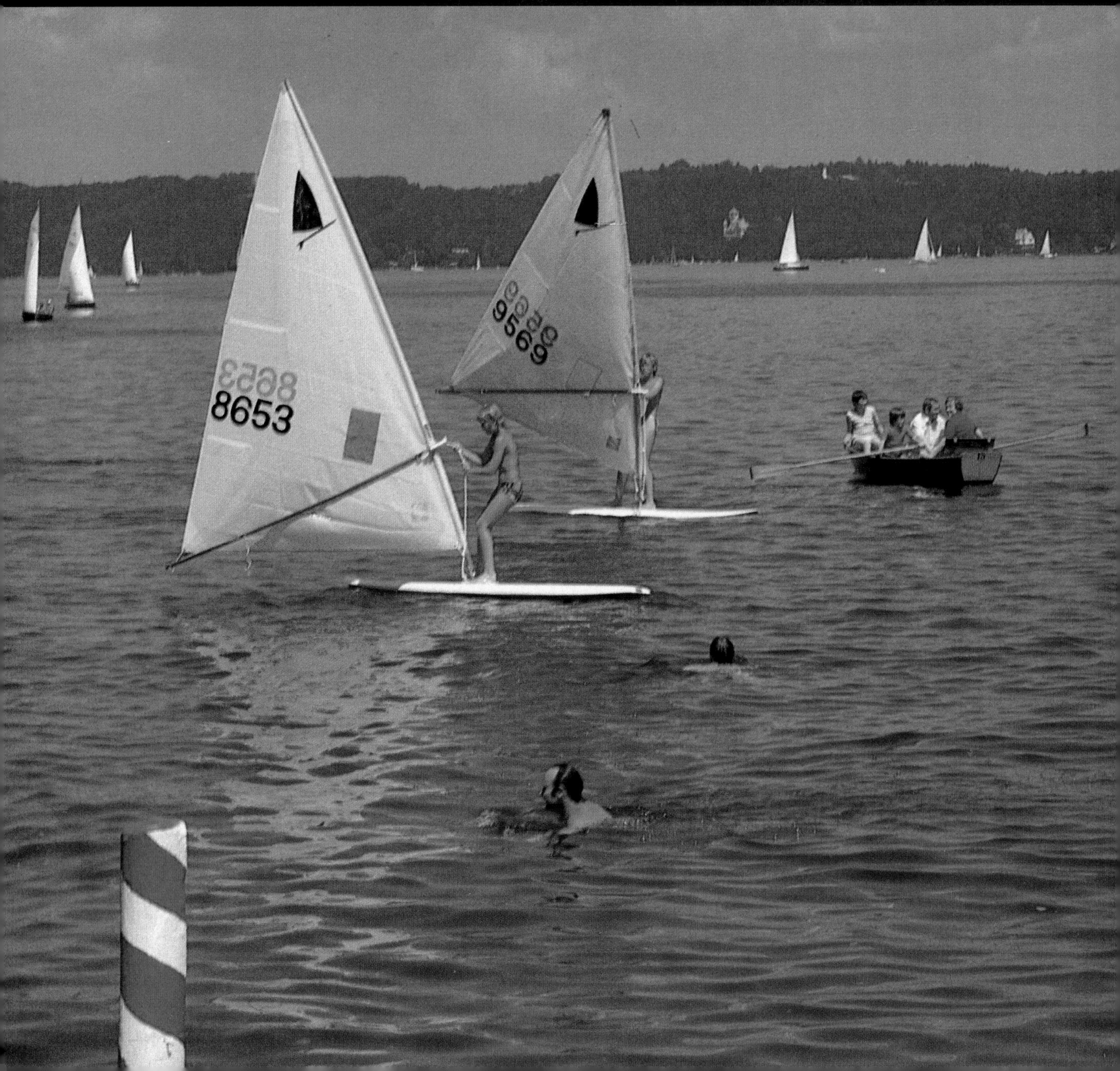

Young people in German-speaking countries like to do many of the same things you do in your free time. Their free time, however, is often limited. Many teenagers are in apprenticeship programs. They work full-time most of the week and attend trade school one or two days. Young people who attend high school are required to put a great deal of time into their studies.

In this unit you will:

SECTION A	talk about your favorite sports and activities
SECTION B	say when and how often you do these activities
SECTION C	express an opinion, agree or disagree, and say what you like, dislike, or prefer
TRY YOUR SKILLS	use what you've learned
ZUM LESEN	read for practice and pleasure

For teaching suggestions, see the Teacher's Notes preceding this unit, pp. T66–85.

SECTION A asking someone about his or her interests

What do young Germans do in their free time? They participate in sports, play games, and have hobbies. They enjoy music and like to get together with their friends. How do you spend your free time?

Point out that English words taken over into German form the plurals with *-s* only, even if they end in *-y* in the singular.

A1 Freizeit: Sport und Hobbys

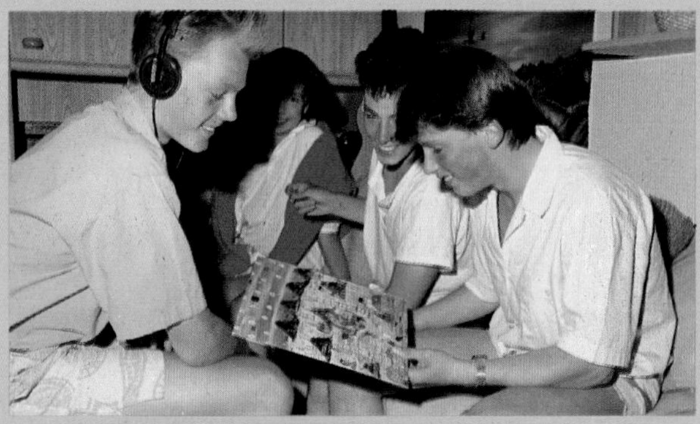

Jens besucht Freunde. Sie hören Musikkassetten.

INTERVIEWER Wie heisst du?
JENS Ich heisse Jens.
INTERVIEWER Wie alt bist du?
JENS Sechzehn.
INTERVIEWER Was machst du in deiner Freizeit?
JENS Tja, ich besuche Freunde, ich höre Musikkassetten, ich. . .

Jens schwimmt, und er spielt Tennis.

INTERVIEWER Machst du Sport?
JENS Ja. Ich schwimme, und ich spiele Tennis.

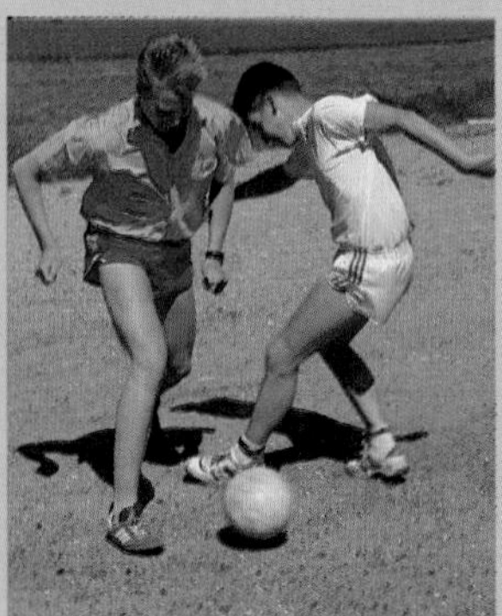

Jens spielt auch Fussball.

INTERVIEWER Spielst du auch Fussball?
JENS Na klar!

INTERVIEWER Spielst du ein Instrument?
JENS Ja, ich spiele Gitarre.

Er spielt Gitarre.

Jens sammelt Briefmarken.

INTERVIEWER Hast du auch Hobbys?
JENS Ich sammle Briefmarken, und ich spiele Schach.

Note the parallel construction in German for playing games and instruments: Er spielt Fussball. Er spielt Gitarre. There is no definite article.

A2 Übung • Mix-Match: Was macht Jens?

1. Jens besucht . . . Freunde	Briefmarken.
2. Er hört . . . Musikkassetten	Freunde.
3. Jens spielt auch . . . Tennis	Musikkassetten.
4. Und er . . . schwimmt	schwimmt.
5. Er sammelt . . . Briefmarken	Tennis.

A3 Übung • Bilder-Quiz: Was macht Jens? Er . . . 

1. spielt Fussball

2. spielt Tennis

3. spielt Gitarre

4. sammelt Briefmarken

5. spielt Schach

A4 ERKLÄRUNG
Addressing Someone Using the du-*form*

When you talk to a friend in German, use **du** with the verb form ending in **-st: du bist, du hast, du spielst.** When someone addresses you, respond using **ich** with the verb form ending in **-e: ich habe, ich spiele.** The form **ich bin** is an exception.

du-*form*	ich-*form*
Wie **heisst du?**	**Ich heisse** Jens.
Wie alt **bist du?**	**Ich bin** fünfzehn.
Hast du Hobbys?	Ja, **ich habe** auch Hobbys.
Spielst du Tennis?	Nein, **ich spiele** Fussball.
Sammelst du Briefmarken?	Ja, **ich sammle** Briefmarken.

A5 Übung • Jetzt bist du dran 

The interviewer asks and you answer yes to all the questions.

A: Machst du Sport?
B: Ja, ich mache Sport.

1. Spielst du Gitarre? ich spiele
2. Hast du Hobbys? ich habe
3. Sammelst du Briefmarken? ich sammle
4. Besuchst du Freunde? ich besuche
5. Hörst du Musikkassetten? ich höre
6. Schwimmst du auch? ich schwimme

A6 Übung • Frag deinen Mitschüler! 

Ask your classmate if he or she has the same interests as Jens does.

A: Jens spielt Schach.
B: Spielst du auch Schach?

1. Jens besucht Freunde.
2. Jens hat Musikkassetten.
3. Jens sammelt Briefmarken.
4. Jens spielt Fussball.
5. Jens schwimmt.
6. Jens spielt Gitarre.

1. Besuchst du auch Freunde? 2. Hast du auch Musikkassetten? 3. Sammelst du auch Briefmarken? 4. Spielst du auch Fussball? 5. Schwimmst du auch? 6. Spielst du auch Gitarre?

Photo p. 90, bottom: Am Starnberger See in Oberbayern

A7 WIE SAGT MAN DAS?
Asking about someone's interests

Here are some phrases that you can use to ask a friend about his or her interests.

Was machst du?	What are you doing?
Was machst du in deiner Freizeit?	What do you do in your spare time?
Machst du Sport?	Do you participate in sports?
Spielst du Fussball?	Do you play soccer?
Hast du Hobbys?	Do you have hobbies?

A8 Übung • Partnerarbeit 

Now ask your classmates what they do in their spare time.
Then have a classmate ask you.

A: Was machst du in deiner Freizeit?
B: Ich . . .

1.  höre Musikkassetten
2.  sammle Briefmarken
3.  besuche Freunde
4.  spiele Schach
5.  spiele Fussball
6.  schwimme
7.  spiele Gitarre
8.  spiele Tennis

A9 Neu im Sport

Drachenfliegen, Eistanzen, Gymnastik, Aerobics und Windsurfen sind heute sehr populär.

1. 2. 3. 4. 5.

A10 Übung • Und du? Wie steht's mit dir?

1. Was machst du in deiner Freizeit?
2. Machst du Sport?
3. Spielst du auch Tennis?
4. Hast du Hobbys?

A 11 UND WAS MACHT IHR?

INTERVIEWER	Und was macht ihr? Macht ihr auch Sport?
GÜNTER	Wir spielen Basketball.

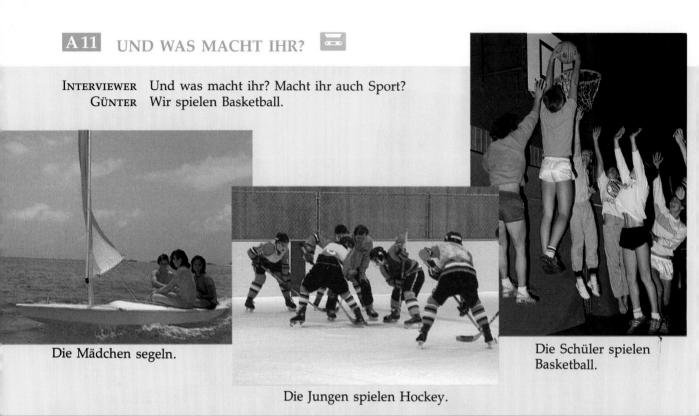

Die Mädchen segeln.

Die Jungen spielen Hockey.

Die Schüler spielen Basketball.

Günter und Kurt sammeln Münzen.

INTERVIEWER	Habt ihr Hobbys?
GÜNTER	Ja, ich sammle Münzen.
INTERVIEWER	Und du, Kurt?
KURT	Ich auch.

Die vier Klassenkameraden spielen Karten. Das Spiel heisst Mau-Mau.

INTERVIEWER	Was spielt ihr?
KRISTIN	Mau-Mau[1].
INTERVIEWER	Wirklich? Wer gewinnt?
KRISTIN	Der Jens und der Jörg.
JENS	Wie immer.
KRISTIN	Aber ihr mogelt. Wie immer.
JENS	Was?! Wir mogeln nicht. Ihr verliert, und ihr seid sauer. Haha!

[1] **Mau-Mau** is a card game similar to crazy eights.

A 12 Übung • Mix-Match: Was machen die Jungen und Mädchen?

1. Günter und Kurt . . . spielen Basketball.
2. Sie sammeln auch . . . Münzen.
3. Die Mädchen . . . segeln.
4. Die Jungen . . . spielen Hockey.
5. Die vier Klassenkameraden . . . spielen Karten.
6. Das Spiel heisst . . . Mau-Mau.
7. Wer gewinnt . . . das Spiel?
8. Jens und Jörg . . . gewinnen.
9. Mogeln . . . die Jungen?
10. Nein, sie mogeln . . . nicht.

das Spiel?
die Jungen?
gewinnen.
Mau-Mau.
Münzen.
nicht.
segeln.
spielen Basketball.
spielen Hockey.
spielen Karten.

A 13 Übung • Bilder-Quiz: Was machen die Jungen und Mädchen?

Sie segeln. Sie . . .

1. segeln
2. spielen Hockey
3. spielen Basketball
4. spielen Karten
5. spielen Tennis
6. spielen Gitarre
7. sammeln Münzen
8. hören Musikkassetten

A 14 Übung • Der Sport- und Hobbymuffel!

For answers, see p. T71.

This boy doesn't do anything! When you ask him if he does the activities pictured in A13, he always answers no!

Segelst du? Nein, ich segle nicht.
Spielst du . . .?

A 15 ERKLÄRUNG
Addressing People Using the ihr-*form*

When you talk to two friends in German, use **ihr** with the verb form ending in **-t: ihr macht, ihr spielt, ihr habt.** When you answer for yourself and somebody else, use **wir** and the verb form ending in **-en** or only in **-n.** The forms **ihr seid** and **wir sind** are exceptions.

ihr-*form*	**wir**-*form*
Was **macht ihr?**	**Wir machen** Sport.
Habt ihr Hobbys?	Ja, **wir haben** Hobbys.
Spielt ihr Tennis?	**Wir spielen** Fussball.
Segelt ihr?	Ja, **wir segeln.**
Seid ihr sauer?	Ja, **wir sind** sauer.

A 16 Übung • Interview 

The interviewer is asking you and your friends what you do. You speak for everyone and answer yes. 1. Wir spielen Basketball. 2. Wir segeln. 3. Wir sammeln Münzen. 4. Wir spielen Schach. 5. Wir verlieren. 6. Wir sind sauer.

A: Macht ihr Sport?
B: Ja, wir machen Sport.

1. Spielt ihr Basketball?
2. Segelt ihr?
3. Sammelt ihr Münzen?
4. Spielt ihr Schach?
5. Verliert ihr?
6. Seid ihr sauer?

A 17 Übung • Was macht ihr? 

The interviewer is surprised at your answers. What does he say?

A: Wir spielen Karten.
B: Wirklich? Ihr spielt Karten?

1. Wir spielen Basketball. ihr spielt
2. Wir spielen Gitarre. ihr spielt
3. Wir sammeln Münzen. ihr sammelt
4. Wir spielen Mau-Mau. ihr spielt
5. Wir gewinnen. ihr gewinnt
6. Wir sind sauer. ihr seid

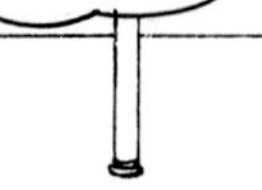

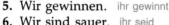

A 18 Übung • Lücken-Dialog

Practice the following dialog with a classmate, supplying the missing words.

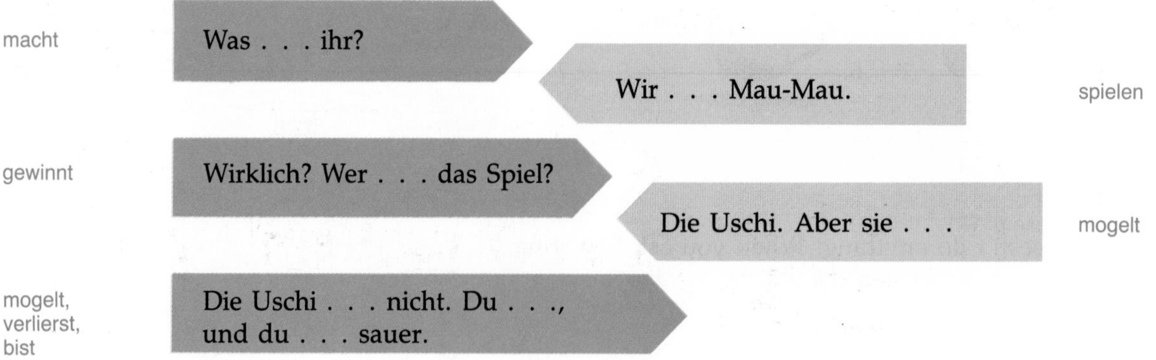

macht
Was . . . ihr?
Wir . . . Mau-Mau.
spielen
gewinnt
Wirklich? Wer . . . das Spiel?
Die Uschi. Aber sie . . .
mogelt
mogelt, verlierst, bist
Die Uschi . . . nicht. Du . . ., und du . . . sauer.

A 19 ERKLÄRUNG
The Present Tense

1. The statements and questions that you have been practicing all refer to present time. Therefore, the verbs in these statements and questions are in the present tense.

   Was **machst** du? Ich **spiele** Tennis.

2. Present tense verb forms have endings. The ending you use depends upon the noun **(Jens, Ursel, Jens und Ursel)** or the pronoun **(ich, du, er, sie, es, wir, ihr, sie)** used with the verb.

3. The following chart summarizes the different verb forms, using **spielen** as a model.

Singular			*Plural*		
Ich	spiel**e**	Tennis.	Wir	spiel**en**	Tennis.
Du	spiel**st**		Ihr	spiel**t**	
Jens (er)	spiel**t**		Jens und Ursel (sie)	spiel**en**	
Ursel (sie)	spiel**t**				

4. When speaking to adults such as your teacher, salespeople, or any adults who are not family members or relatives, you must use the formal form of address: **Sie. Sie** is used with the verb form ending in **-en,** the same verb form used with **wir** and **sie** (plural).

Point out that there are three words for "you" in German: du, ihr, and Sie.

   Wie **heissen Sie?** Was **machen Sie?**
   Woher **sind Sie,** Herr Huber? **Spielen Sie** Tennis?

5. All verbs have a base form, the form appearing in your word list **(Wortschatz)** or in a dictionary. This form is called the infinitive. The infinitive of most German verbs has the ending **-en,** as in **spielen,** *to play*. Some verbs end in **-n,** such as **segeln,** *to sail*, **mogeln,** *to cheat*, **sammeln,** *to collect*. The **ich**-form of these verbs is: **ich segle, ich mogle, ich sammle.**

A 20 Übung • Bilder-Quiz: Was machen die Schüler? 

Say what everyone does, using the words and pictures as cues.

Wir . . .
segeln.

Jens . . .
spielt Tennis.

Ihr . . .
sammelt Briefmarken.

Ich . . .
spiele Fussball.

Die Mädchen . . .
hören Musikkassetten.

Du . . .
spielst Gitarre.

Die Jungen . . .
schwimmen.

Wir . . .
spielen Karten.

Er . . .
spielt Schach.

Du . . .?
spielst Hockey?

A 21 Übung • Frag mal deinen Lehrer!

Was spielen Sie? Segeln Sie? Spielen Sie Tennis? Sammeln Sie Briefmarken? Spielen Sie Fussball? Hören Sie Musikkassetten? Spielen Sie Gitarre? Schwimmen Sie? Spielen Sie Karten? Spielen Sie Schach? Spielen Sie Hockey?

Now ask your teacher about his or her sports and hobbies. Use the following questions and the pictures in A20 as a guide.

1. Was . . . Sie? **2.** Spiel- . . .?

A 22 Übung • Versteckte Sätze *Hidden sentences*

Look for sentences. How many can you make?

Ich spiele Karten.

ich	besuchen	das Spiel
du	hört	Freunde
Jens	ist	immer
wir	mogelt	Karten
ihr	sammelst	Münzen
die Jungen	spiele	Musik
Ursel	verlieren	sauer

Possible answers: Du sammelst Münzen. Jens hört Musik. Wir besuchen Freunde. Ihr mogelt. Die Jungen verlieren das Spiel. Ursel ist sauer.

A 23 Übung • Hör gut zu!

For script and answers, see p. T72.

Are you talking to one friend, several friends, or an adult? Listen.

	0	1	2	3	4	5	6	7	8	9	10
addressing one student				✓	✓				✓		
addressing several students	✓	✓					✓	✓			✓
addressing an adult			✓			✓				✓	

A 24 Schreibübung

1. Rewrite the following questions and statements, supplying the appropriate verb endings.

1. Was mach_st_ du? Ich spiel_e_ Karten.
2. Was mach_t_ Jens? Er spiel_t_ Tennis.
3. Die Jungen spiel_en_ Mau-Mau. Mogel_t_ der Jens?
4. Mach_t_ ihr Sport? Ja, wir schwimm_en_.
5. Spiel_en_ Sie Schach, Herr Huber?

2. You have met two young people and would like to know more about them. What questions would you ask? Think of at least eight questions and write them down. Remember to use the **ihr**-form. Possible answers: Wie heisst ihr? Wie alt seid ihr? Woher seid ihr? Wie kommt ihr in die Schule? Was macht ihr? Was spielt ihr? Macht ihr Sport? Spielt ihr Fussball? Sammelt ihr Briefmarken? Welche Fächer habt ihr?

SECTION B

talking about when and how often you do your various sports and activities

Young people pursue sports and activities after school and on the weekend. They take tennis and music lessons, and they belong to sports and computer clubs. When do you have your activities? Do you take any lessons? Do you belong to a club?

Note that Frühling and Frühjahr are used interchangeably.

B1 Wann machst du Sport? 

Was macht ihr im Sommer? Im Herbst? Im Winter? Im Frühjahr?

Ursel
Im Sommer spiele ich Tennis, und ich schwimme.

Peter
Im Herbst spiele ich Fussball.

Hans
Im Winter spiele ich Eishockey, und ich laufe Schi.

Karin
Im Frühjahr spiele ich Basketball.

Jörg, was machst du am Wochenende?

Am Wochenende spiele ich Fussball.

JULI 7 SONNTAG

JULI 13 SONNAB./SAMST.

JULI 14 SONNTAG

am Sonntag

am Wochenende

"Fussball," called soccer in English, is the national sport for European countries. It is as popular and important as football and baseball in the U.S.

B2 Übung • Und du? Wie steht's mit dir?

1. Was machst du im Sommer?
   Ich . . .
2. Was machst du im Winter?
   Ich . . .
3. Was machst du im Frühjahr?
   Ich . . .
4. Was machst du im Herbst?
   Ich . . .

B3 WIE OFT MACHT IHR SPORT?

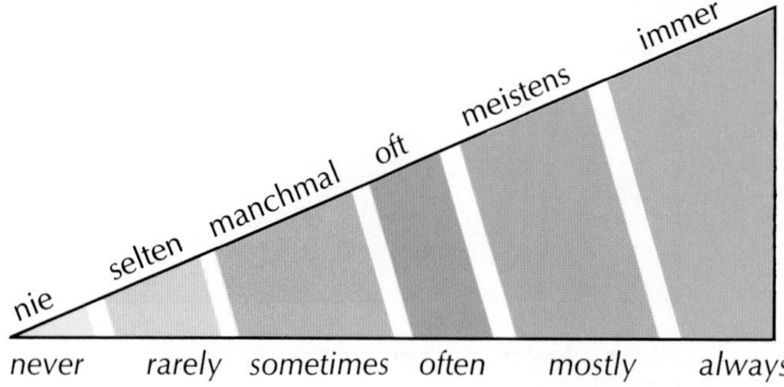

PETRA:
„Ich spiele selten Tennis. Ja, manchmal im Sommer. Im Winter spiele ich oft Basketball."

Do not talk about inversion of subject and verb. Have students discover it. See suggestions for introducing B1.

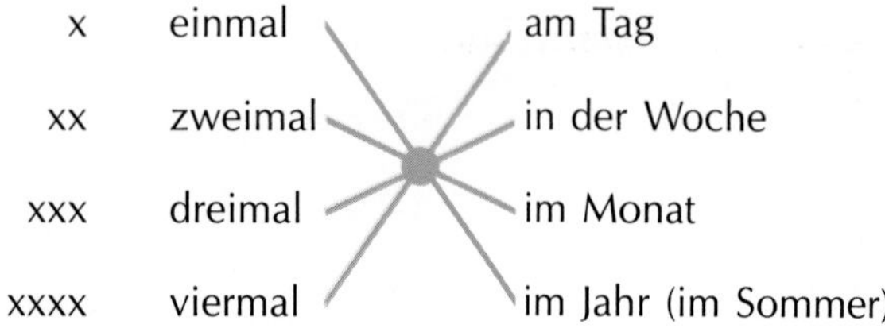

MICHAEL:
„Ich mache Sport viermal in der Woche. Einmal, meistens am Mittwoch, spiele ich Tennis. Am Wochenende spiele ich Fussball, und ich schwimme zweimal in der Woche."

B4 Übung • Was sagt Michael? Was sagt Petra? Erzähl mal!

Report what these students have just told you about how often they have their activities.

1. Michael sagt, er macht . . . Sport viermal in der Woche. Einmal, meistens am Mittwoch, spielt er Tennis. Am Wochenende spielt er Fussball, und er schwimmt zweimal in der Woche.
2. Petra sagt, sie spielt . . . selten Tennis. Ja, manchmal im Sommer. Im Winter spielt sie oft Basketball.

B5 Ein wenig Landeskunde

How much free time do young Germans actually have? Many teenagers are learning a trade and are required to be at work all day. They may have one day a week of classes at a **Berufsschule,** *vocational school.* Their free time is limited to evenings and weekends.

Teenagers who attend high schools have more free time. The school day is over by 1:00 P.M., and though some states in Germany have school on Saturday twice a month, most do not. Many students belong to **Sportvereine,** *sport clubs,* outside of school. Students have **Sport,** *gym,* as part of the curriculum, but there are few intramural sports and school teams. Musical activities are usually not part of school. There are many orchestras, choirs, and music clubs as well as other types of clubs for people of all ages in the community.

High school students usually do not have part-time jobs, though some may do things like distributing flyers for a local store or babysitting.

B6 ERKLÄRUNG
Word Order: Verb in Second Place

If you listen to what these students are saying, you will notice that most of the statements do not begin with **ich,** but with some other phrase, such as **im Sommer, am Wochenende,** etc. The verb, however, always remains in second place.

	Verb in second place		
Ich	**spiele**	am Wochenende	Fussball.
Am Wochenende	**spiele**	ich	Fussball.
Ich	**spiele**	im Winter	Basketball.
Im Winter	**spiele**	ich	Basketball.

B7 Übung • Frag deine Mitschüler! Frag deinen Lehrer!

Ask your classmates what they do in various seasons of the year and on various days of the week. Ask them how often they do their sports and hobbies. First ask one classmate, then ask a few at once, and then ask your teacher.

A: Was machst du im Winter?
B: Im Winter . . .

A: Was machst du am Wochenende?
B: Am Wochenende . . .

A: Wie oft machst du Sport?
B: Zweimal in der Woche . . .

A: Wie oft spielst du Tennis?
B: Tennis . . .

B8 Übung • Hör gut zu!

For script and answers, see p. T75.

When or how often? Listen.

	0	1	2	3	4	5	6	7	8	9	10
wann		✓	✓		✓			✓		✓	
wie oft?	✓			✓		✓	✓		✓		✓

B9 Schreibübung • Sport ist prima!

For answers, see p. T75.

Rewrite the following paragraph, varying word order.

Sport ist prima! Ich spiele am Dienstag und am Freitag Tennis. Ich spiele am Samstag Fussball. Ich spiele auch Fussball im Sommer. Fussball ist toll! Wir sind gut. Wir gewinnen meistens; wir verlieren selten. Ich laufe im Winter Schi, und ich spiele Hockey. Ich habe einmal in der Woche Musik. Ich spiele Gitarre. Ich besuche oft Freunde, und wir hören Kassetten. Das ist auch toll!

SECTION C

asking about someone's likes, dislikes, and preferences and expressing your own

Young people like to sit around and discuss their opinions and talk about their interests. What do you like to do? What are your favorite activities?

C1 Fussball ist Klasse!

INTERVIEWER Was machst du, Margit? Machst du Sport?
MARGIT Ich mache Gymnastik.
INTERVIEWER Wirklich?
MARGIT Ja, Gymnastik macht Spass!

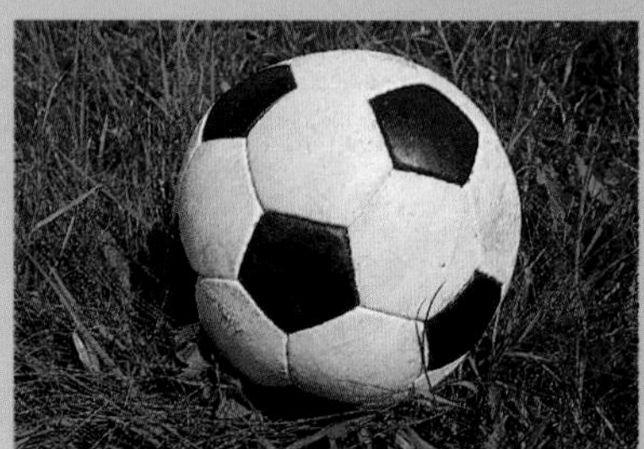

INTERVIEWER Jörg, du spielst Fussball?
JÖRG Ja, Fussball ist Klasse.
INTERVIEWER Spielst du auch Tennis?
JÖRG Nein. Ich finde Tennis langweilig.

INTERVIEWER Wiebke, was machst du in deiner Freizeit?
WIEBKE Ich lese viel.
INTERVIEWER Das ist interessant. Was liest du?
WIEBKE Romane, Sportbücher, Fantasy-Bücher . . . sie sind Spitze!
INTERVIEWER Wie findest du Comics?
WIEBKE Blöd!

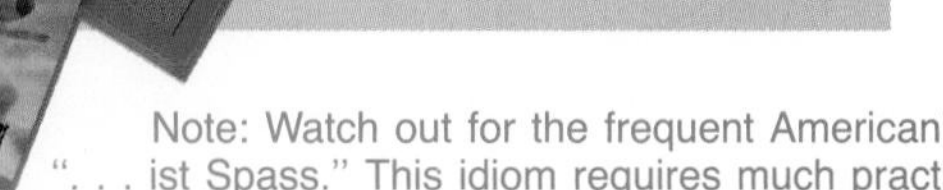

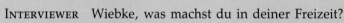

Note: Watch out for the frequent Americanism ". . . ist Spass." This idiom requires much practice, especially since other common expressions using nouns have the "ist"construction: . . . ist Klasse! . . . ist Spitze!

C2 Übung • Mix-Match: Was machen die drei Schüler?

1. Die Margit macht . . . Gymnastik
2. Das macht . . . Spass
3. Der Jörg sagt, Fussball . . . ist Klasse
4. Er spielt nicht . . . Tennis
5. Er findet Tennis . . . langweilig
6. Wiebke sagt: Ich . . . lese viel
7. Ich lese . . . Romane
8. Die Comics . . . sind blöd

Romane.
Gymnastik.
ist Klasse.
langweilig.
lese viel.
sind blöd.
Spass.
Tennis.

C3 WIE SAGT MAN DAS?

Asking for an opinion, expressing enthusiasm or lack of it

You already know some expressions for good news **(Das ist gut, prima, phantastisch, toll!)** and for bad news **(Das ist blöd!).** You can also use them to express your opinion about activities you like and dislike. Here are some more words and expressions.

asking for an opinion	Wie findest du Fussball?	What do you think of soccer?
expressing enthusiasm	Ich finde Fussball interessant! Fussball ist Klasse! Das ist Spitze! Fussball macht Spass!	I think soccer is interesting! Soccer is terrific! That's great! Soccer is fun!
lack of enthusiasm	Ich finde Fussball blöd. Fussball ist langweilig.	I think soccer is dumb. Soccer is boring.

C4 Übung • Was meint dein Freund? *What does your friend think?* 

You tell your friend what you think and he or she agrees.

A: Hockey ist toll!
B: Ich finde Hockey auch toll!

1. Fussball ist Spitze. — Ich finde Fussball auch Spitze!
2. Tennis ist Klasse. — Ich finde Tennis auch Klasse!
3. Sammeln ist interessant. — Ich finde Sammeln auch interessant!
4. Kartenspielen ist blöd. — Ich finde Kartenspielen auch blöd!
5. Mau-Mau ist langweilig. — Ich finde Mau-Mau auch langweilig!
6. Gymnastik ist prima. — Ich finde Gymnastik auch prima!

C5 Übung • Jetzt bist du dran

Ask your classmates how they like the sports and activities shown below.

A: Wie findest du . . . *or* Wie findet ihr . . . ?
B: Ich finde Fussball . . . *or* Fussball ist . . .

Mau-Mau **Fussball** *Hockey* Tennis Segeln
Lesen Briefmarkensammeln **Sport** Schach *Musik*
Basketball Gymnastik Kartenspielen Schwimmen

Spitze!
super!
Klasse!
toll!
prima!
phantastisch!
interessant!
macht Spass!

langweilig!
blöd!

C6 STIMMT! STIMMT NICHT! 

A: Fussball ist Klasse!
B: Stimmt!

A: Wie findest du die Kassette?
B: Super! Sie ist Spitze!
A: Wirklich? Ich finde sie blöd.

A: Du sammelst Briefmarken?
B: Ja. Sammeln macht Spass.
A: Was? Das finde ich nicht.

A: Kartenspielen ist langweilig.
B: Das finde ich auch.

A: Segeln ist auch langweilig.
B: Stimmt nicht! Segeln ist prima!

C7 WIE SAGT MAN DAS?
Expressing surprise, agreement, disagreement

surprise	Was? Wirklich?	What? Really?
agreement	Stimmt! Das finde ich auch.	True! That's right! I think so, too.
disagreement	Stimmt nicht! Das finde ich nicht.	Not true! That's not so. I don't think so.

C8 Übung • Partnerarbeit 

Team up with a classmate. Express an opinion about some sport or activity. Your classmate should agree with your opinion or express surprise and disagree. Then reverse roles.

A: Kartenspielen ist langweilig.
B: Stimmt! *or* Das finde ich auch.

A: Ich finde Hockey prima.
B: Wirklich? Das finde ich nicht.

C9 Übung • Und du? Wie steht's mit dir?

See C7 for expressions of agreement and disagreement.

Agree or disagree with the following statements.

1. Segeln ist Klasse!
2. Kartenspielen ist langweilig.
3. Deutsch ist interessant.
4. Eine Zwei in Deutsch ist prima.
5. Wir haben am Samstag Schule.
6. Die Hausaufgaben sind leicht.
7. Briefmarkensammeln ist blöd!
8. Comics sind Spitze!

C10 WAS MACHST DU GERN?

Ich faulenze am liebsten.
am liebsten
Ich spiele lieber Fussball.
lieber
Ich mache gern Gymnastik.
gern
Ich segle nicht gern.
nicht gern

C11 WIE SAGT MAN DAS?
Expressing likes, dislikes, and preferences

Use the word **gern** together with a verb to express the idea of liking something and **nicht gern** to express disliking something.

liking	Ich spiele **gern** Karten.	I like to play cards.
disliking	Ich spiele **nicht gern** Karten.	I don't like to play cards.

Use the word **lieber** together with a verb to express preference. Use **am liebsten** to express what you like best of all.

preference	Ich spiele **lieber** Fussball.	I prefer playing soccer.
strong preference	Ich spiele **am liebsten** Tennis.	I like tennis best of all.

C12 Übung • Und du? Wie steht's mit dir? 

1. Tell which of the following you like and which you don't like.

   Ich spiele gern Tennis.
   Ich . . . gern . . .

   Ich spiele nicht gern Schach.
   Ich . . . nicht gern . . .

2. Tell what you prefer.

   Ich lese nicht gern Comics. Ich lese lieber . . .

3. Now tell what you like to do best of all.

   Ich mache am liebsten . . .

4. Ask your classmates what they like and what they don't like to do. Ask them what they prefer and what they like most of all.

C13 Übung • Der Sport- und Hobbyfreund: Was macht er denn alles?

Er spielt Tennis, Fussball und Hockey. Er hört Kassetten. Er läuft Schi. Er spielt Gitarre. Er liest Bücher.

C14 Übung • Hör gut zu!

For script and answers, see p. T79.

Do you like this activity or don't you? What do you prefer? What do you like best of all? Listen.

	0	1	2	3	4	5	6	7	8	9	10
likes			✓						✓		✓
does not like					✓		✓				
prefers	✓			✓						✓	
likes most of all		✓				✓		✓			

C15 Schreibübung • Was machen die Schüler gern? Und du?

For answers, see p. T79.

1. Write what each student likes and doesn't like to do. Use the following cues.

	gern	am liebsten	nicht gern
1. Paul:	Gymnastik	schwimmen	Basketball
2. Sabine:	Karten	Mau-Mau	Schach
3. Monika und Anke:	Kassetten	Sport	sammeln

1. Paul macht gern Gymnastik. Er . . .　　2. Sabine . . .

2. Write a paragraph about what you like and don't like to do.

C16 Übung • Umfrage: Was machst du in deiner Freizeit?

The survey sheet below was given to a German 9th-grade class. The students were asked to rank their sports activities, putting their favorite sport at the top of the list. Read the survey sheet and discuss it in class. Tell what this student likes and dislikes, what he prefers, and when and how often he does the various activities listed.

Name: *Markus Walden*

	Was?	Wann?					Wie oft?								
		im Frühjahr	im Sommer	im Herbst	im Winter	am Wochenende	nie	selten	manchmal	oft	immer	am Tag	in der Woche	im Monat	im Jahr
am liebsten	*Fussball*		✓	✓		✓				✓			2X		
	Basketball	✓			✓						✓		1X		
lieber	*Windsurfen*		✓			✓			✓					4X	
	Segeln		✓	✓					✓					1X	
gern	*Volleyball*	✓								✓			1X		
	Gymnastik				✓					✓			3X		
nicht gern	*Handball*				✓			✓						1X	
	Golf			✓				✓							1X

C17 Übung • Klassenprojekt

Do a similar survey in your class and discuss the results.

TRY YOUR SKILLS

using what you've learned

Friends do not always have the same opinion about sports and activities.

---

1 Stimmt nicht! Du bist nur sauer!

HELMUT Hast du ein Hobby?
JENS Ja, Schach.
HELMUT Was? Schach ist so langweilig.
JENS Das finde ich nicht. Schach ist interessant. Es macht Spass! Spielst du auch Schach?
HELMUT Ja, aber nicht oft.
JENS Bist du gut? Gewinnst du oft?
HELMUT Nein, ich verliere meistens.
JENS Ach so! Du verlierst immer, und du bist sauer.

Aber Lars, Jörg und Jens spielen gern Schach.

2 Übung • Deine Meinung—meine Meinung *Your opinion—my opinion*

Ask a classmate to tell you five things that he or she likes to do. After each response, give your own opinion. If you like the same thing, say why. If you don't like it, say that you prefer something else. Your conversation might go like this:

A: Was machst du gern?
B: Ich spiele gern Hockey.
A: Ich auch. Hockey ist toll! *or* Ich nicht. Ich laufe lieber Schi.

3 Übung • Stimmt!—Stimmt nicht!

Some of your classmates have definite opinions when it comes to certain sports and activities. Listen to what they say and agree or disagree. One classmate might begin by saying:

A: Ach, Hockey ist so langweilig!
B: Das finde ich nicht. *or* Stimmt!

4 Übung • Sport und Spiel

The following are pictorial symbols you can see in stadiums where sports events take place.

1. Identify each symbol:
   1. Fussball
   2. . . . Gymnastik
   3. Tennis
   4. Segeln
   5. Basketball
   6. Hockey
   7. Schwimmen
   8. Schilaufen

1. 
2. 
3. 
4. 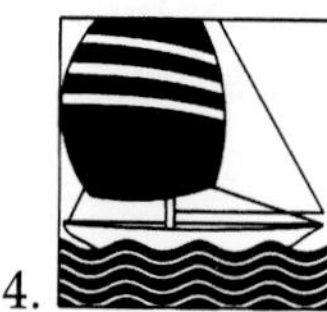
5. 
6. 
7. 
8. 

2. Look at the activities depicted and answer these questions.
   Was machst du gern?
   Was machst du nicht gern?
   Was machst du am liebsten?

3. Now give an opinion on each of the activities shown.
   Ich finde . . .

5 Übung • Wann spielen sie was?

These German friends participate in different sports during different seasons. According to the diagram, who does what, and when?

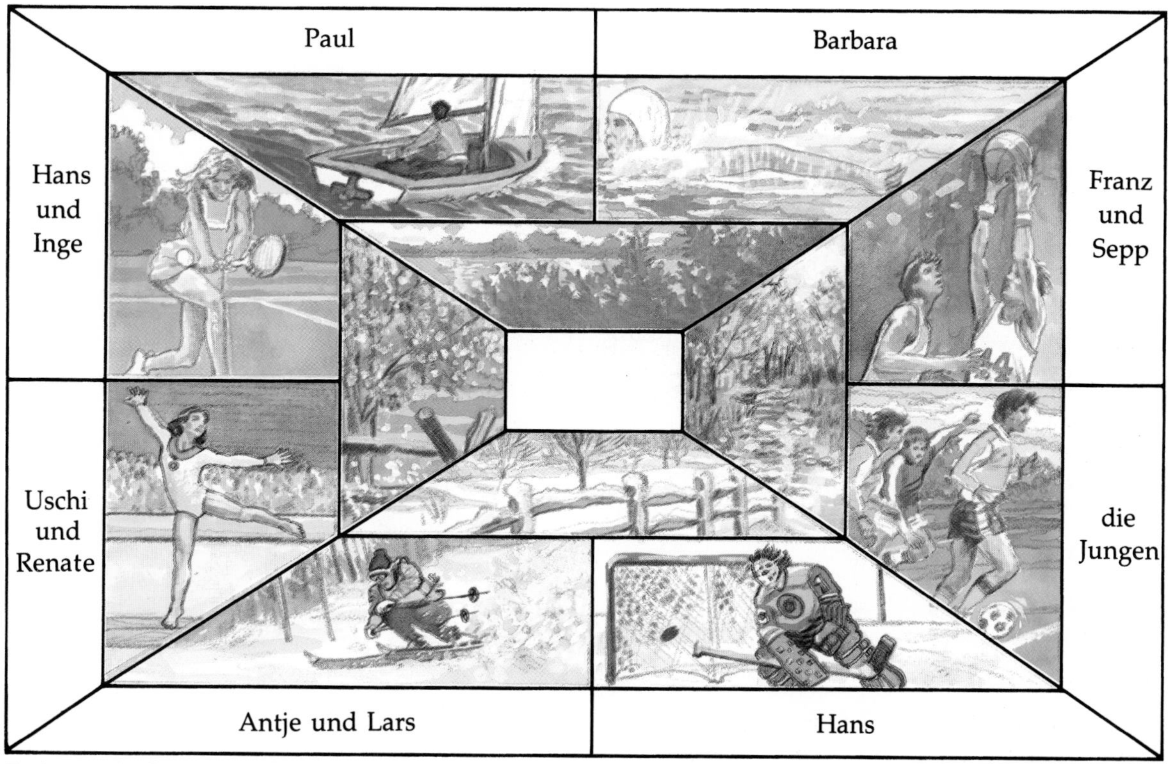

Paul segelt im Sommer. Im Sommer schwimmt Barbara. Franz und Sepp spielen im Herbst Basketball. Die Jungen spielen im Herbst Fussball. Im Winter spielt Hans Eishockey. Antje und Lars laufen im Winter Schi. Uschi und Renate machen im Frühjahr Gymnastik. Im Frühjahr spielen Hans und Inge Tennis.

6 Übung • Hallo! Wer schreibt uns? For answers, see p. T81.

The following excerpts are from a special report, „Hallo! Wer schreibt uns? Wir antworten!", which appeared in a magazine for young people. Report to a classmate or to your teacher what these two ads say. Use complete sentences.

Vorname: Bettina
Nachname: Schilling
Alter: 14
Strasse: Schulstrasse 17
Stadt: D - 7900 Ulm
Hobbys/Interessen: schwimmen, segeln, Basketball spielen

Vorname: Markus
Nachname: Wallner
Alter: 15
Strasse: Hebbelstrasse 8
Stadt: D - 6100 Darmstadt
Hobbys/Interessen: Fussball, Gymnastik, Briefmarken sammeln

7 Schreibübung • Interview und Anzeige

1. Pretend that you would like to place a similar ad in this magazine in order to find a pen pal, and you are giving information about yourself over the phone.

INTERVIEWER Wie heisst du? Wie alt bist du? Was ist deine Adresse? Was sind deine Hobbys und Interessen?
DU . . .

2. Write down the phone conversation you had with a person from this magazine.
3. Write how your ad would appear in the column.

8 Übung • Ein Brief an Markus Wallner

Here is a letter that was written in response to Markus Wallner's ad. Read the letter.

Lieber Markus!

Ich heisse Martin Obermeyer. Ich bin 14 Jahre alt und wohne in Regensburg (D-8400) Bahnhofstasse 17. Meine Interessen sind Musik und Sport. Ich höre gern Musikgruppen aus England. Ich schwimme gern, ich spiele Squash, und am liebsten spiele ich Fussball.

Was machst Du? Bitte schreib mir!

Dein
Martin

Ask the students if they can find a spelling mistake in Martin's letter. (Line 2: Bahnhofstrasse)

9 Schreibübung • Jetzt bist du dran

Now write a letter of your own, similar to the one on the preceding page. Answer either Markus Wallner's ad or Bettina Schilling's.

10 Schreibübung • Klassenprojekt

After your class has written ads to appear in the pen-pal column „Hallo! Wer schreibt uns?", exchange ads with another German class. Pick a pen pal and write a letter in response to the ad.

11 Übung • Dialog-Mischmasch

With the help of a classmate, unscramble the following dialog. Start with 1. Write down your dialog and read it aloud together.

5 Bist du gut? Gewinnst du oft?

7 Ach, ich verliere oft.

2 Na klar! Ich spiele Tennis.

1. Machst du Sport?

6 Ich gewinne meistens. Und du?

3 Tennis? Ich finde Tennis langweilig.

8 Soso. Du bist nur sauer.

4 Wirklich? Ich spiele gern, und ich finde Tennis Spitze.

12 Aussprache-, Lese- und Schreibübungen

For script, see p. T82.

1. Listen carefully and repeat what you hear.

2. Listen, then read aloud.

1. frei, Frau, Freund, drei, dreimal, prima, hören, Karte, Roman, Rad
2. ihr, vier, hier, wir, er, der, schwer
3. aber, oder, lieber, immer, Sommer, Winter, sauer, Schüler, Lehrer, super
4. ein, eine, eins, einmal, heisse, Latein
5. Mau-Mau, sauer, schau, aus, auch
6. neun, heute, Freund, neunzehn; Fräulein, Verkäuferin
7. Schule, Schi, schwer, schlecht
8. spielen, Sport, Spitze, spät; Stundenplan, Bleistift

3. Copy the following sentences to prepare yourself to write them from dictation.

1. Wir haben immer frei.
2. Fräulein Meier spielt heute.
3. Meine Freundin heisst Winter.
4. Die Schule ist schwer.

WAS KANNST DU SCHON?

Let's review some important points that you have learned in this unit.

Can you address a person using the *du*-form?
Ask a friend questions about his or her interests using the following verbs:
machen, spielen, sammeln, schwimmen, besuchen
Machst du . . . ?/Spielst du/Sammelst du/Schwimmst du/Besuchst du
Give a reply for each question.
Ich mache/spiele/sammle/schwimme/besuche . . .

Can you address a group of people using the *ihr*-form?
Approach a group of people and ask them what they are doing. Give an appropriate response. Was macht ihr? Wir . . .

Do you know how to address adults?
Ask your teacher about his or her activities.
Was machen Sie? Haben Sie Hobbys? Spielen Sie . . . ?

Can you say when and how often you do various sports and activities?
Mention four activities. Tell when you do them (in what season or on what day) and how often. Im . . . spiele ich/mache ich . . . (ein)mal in der Woche.

Mention activities that you rarely or never do, as well as ones you do sometimes, often, and always. Ich mache . . . selten/nie/manchmal/oft/immer.

Can you ask about someone's interests?
Ask a friend what he or she thinks of the following: Wie findest du . . . ?
Tennis, Fussball, Gymnastik, Kartenspielen, Briefmarkensammeln

Do you know how to express enthusiasm or lack of enthusiasm?
Give your opinion about five different sports and activities. Possible answers: Ich finde Fussball langweilig/Kartenspielen toll/Gymnastik super!/Mau-Mau ist blöd./Tennis macht Spass!

Can you express surprise and also say that you agree or disagree with something?
Respond to each of the following statements, expressing surprise, agreement or disagreement. Possible answers:

1. Deutsch ist leicht. Stimmt!
2. Schach ist interessant. Wirklich?
3. Comics sind super. Stimmt nicht!
4. Tennis ist schwer. Das finde ich auch.
5. Briefmarkensammeln ist blöd. Was? Das finde ich nicht.

Can you talk about your likes, dislikes, and preferences?
Tell what you like to do, what you prefer to do, and what you like to do most of all. Tell what you don't like to do. Ich (segle) gern. Ich . . . lieber. Ich . . . am liebsten. Ich . . . nicht gern.
Now ask a friend about his or her likes and dislikes.
Was machst du gern? Was machst du lieber? Was machst du am liebsten? Was machst du nicht gern?

WORTSCHATZ

SECTION A

auch: ich auch *me too*
Basketball *basketball*
besuchen *to visit*
die **Briefmarke, -n** *stamp*
ein *a, an*
die **Freizeit** *free time;* in deiner Freizeit *in your free time*
der **Freund, -e** *friend*
Fussball *soccer*
gewinnen *to win*
die **Gitarre, -n** *guitar*
haha! *ha ha!*
das **Hobby, -s** *hobby*
Hockey *hockey*
hören *to listen (to)*
das **Instrument, -e** *instrument*
der **Interviewer, -** *interviewer*
die **Karten** (pl) *cards*
machen *to do;* was machst du? *what are you doing? what do you do?*
Mau-Mau (card game similar to crazy eights)
mogeln *to cheat*
die **Münze, -n** *coin*
die **Musikkassette, -n** *music cassette*
na klar! *of course!*
sammeln *to collect*
sauer *sore*
Schach *chess*
der **Schüler, -** *student, pupil*
schwimmen *to swim*
segeln *to sail*
Sie *you* (formal)
das **Spiel, -e** *game*
spielen *to play*
der **Sport** *sport; sports;* Sport machen *to participate in a sport, to do sports*
Tennis *tennis*
tja *hm*
verlieren *to lose*
was!? *what!?*
wie immer *as always*
wirklich? *really?*

SECTION B

am Sonntag *on Sunday*
am Tag *(times) a day*
am Wochenende *on the weekend*
dreimal *three times*
einmal *once*
Eishockey *ice hockey*
im Frühjahr *in the spring*
im Herbst *in the fall*
im Jahr *(times) a year*
im Monat *(times) a month*
im Sommer *in the summer*
im Winter *in the winter*
immer *always*
in der Woche *(times) a week*
manchmal *sometimes*
meistens *mostly*
nie *never*
oft *often*
Samstag *Saturday*
Schi: ich laufe Schi *I go skiing*
selten *seldom*
Sonntag *Sunday*
viermal *four times*
wie oft? *how often?*
zweimal *twice*

SECTION C

am liebsten (machen) *to like (to do) most of all*
Comics (pl) *comics*
das **Fantasy-Buch, ⸚er** *fantasy book*
faulenzen *to lie around, be lazy*
finden *to find, think (have the opinion about something);* das finde ich nicht *I don't think so;* wie findest du . . .? *how do you like . . .? what do you think of . . .?*
gern (machen) *to like (to do)*
Gymnastik *gymnastics;* Gymnastik machen *to do gymnastics*
interessant *interesting*
Kartenspielen *playing cards*
Klasse! *great!*
langweilig *boring*
lesen *to read*
lieber (machen) *to prefer (to do);* ich spiele lieber Fussball *I'd rather play soccer*
liest: was liest du? *what do you read?*
nicht gern (machen) *to not like (to do)*
der **Roman, -e** *novel*
Sammeln *collecting*
Segeln *sailing*
Spass *fun;* Gymnastik macht Spass *gymnastics are fun*
Spitze! *terrific!*
das **Sportbuch, ⸚er** *book about sports*
stimmt! *that's right! true!*
stimmt nicht! *not true! that's not so!*
super! *super! terrific!*
viel *much, a lot*

1. besuch/en, gewinn/en, hör/en, mach/en, mogel/n, sammel/n, segel/n, spiel/en, verlier/en, faulenz/en, find/en, les/en. Most verbs end in *en*.

WORTSCHATZÜBUNGEN

1. Look at the **Wortschatz** and make a list of all the verbs. What do most verbs end in? (Look at the last two or three letters.) Now put a slash between the verb infinitive stem and the ending.
2. Pick out the words that are listed twice. What is the difference in spelling? What is the difference in meaning? 2. sammeln/Sammeln segeln/Segeln The nouns are capitalized; the verbs are lowercased.
3. Make a list of all the words that are similar to English, writing them both in German and English. Compare the spelling and the meaning of each pair of words.

3. Basketball (basketball), Freund (friend), Fussball (soccer), Gitarre (guitar), Hobby (hobby), Hockey (hockey), Instrument (instrument), Interviewer (interviewer), Karten (cards), Musikkassette (music cassette), sauer (sour, sore), schwimmen (swim), Sport (sport, sports), Tennis (tennis), Eishockey (ice hockey), Sommer (summer), Winter (winter), oft (often), Schi (skiing), selten (seldom), Comics (comics), finden (find), Gymnastik (gymnastics), interessant (interesting), super (super)

ZUM LESEN

Keine Freizeitmuffel!

Was machen Jungen und Mädchen in der Freizeit?—Sie machen Sport, sie gehen ins Kino, ins Konzert, zu Sportveranstaltungen. Sie hören Musik, diskutieren und philosophieren. Was machen sie noch? Fragen wir sie mal!

Lest ihr gern, oder seht ihr nur fern°?

Frage an Jungen und Mädchen: Wie oft lest ihr in Büchern?	**1968**	**1986**
—täglich°:	10%	12%
—2–3 mal in der Woche:	19%	21%
—einmal in der Woche:	13%	11%
—gar nicht:	32%	28%

Was lest ihr? Lest ihr auch Bücher, oder seid ihr Büchermuffel?

„Ich lese viel. Ich lese Zeitschriften°, Hobbybücher—am liebsten lese ich Comics."

Zeitschriften

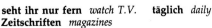

seht ihr nur fern *watch T.V.* **täglich** *daily* **Zeitschriften** *magazines*

deutsche Zeitungen

Thomas Mann (1875–1955)

Heinrich Böll (1917–1985)

moderne Autoren der deutschen Sprache

Günter Grass (1927)

Übung • Sprechen wir darüber! *Let's talk about it!*

6. Bravo, Bunte, Tier, abc Journal
7. Die Zeit, Handelsblatt, Kitzinger Zeitung, Main Post, Nürnberger Nachrichten

1. Was machst du in der Freizeit?
2. Was liest du?
3. Wie oft liest du Bücher? Oder bist du ein Büchermuffel?
4. Was liest du gern? Am liebsten?
5. Welche Autoren liest du?
6. Wie heissen einige deutsche Zeitschriften?
7. Wie heissen einige deutsche Zeitungen?
8. Wie heissen einige Autoren?
9. Die *Buddenbrooks* sind von . . .?
10. Und *Der Butt?*

8. Thomas Mann, Heinrich Böll, Günter Grass
9. Thomas Mann
10. Günter Grass

Wie findet ihr Comics?

„Ich lese schon lange° Comics. Am liebsten lese ich amerikanische Superhelden°-Comics. Manchmal lese ich sie im Original."

„Es gibt auch deutsche Comics. Sie sind nicht so gut. Ich finde Matthias Schultheiss und amerikanische Comics toll."

„Viele° Comics sind blöd. Nur Moebius lese ich gern. Ich finde die Frauen° in den meisten° Comics nicht gut. Sie sind immer blöd und hilflos°."

Andrea

Michael

Kristin

Natalie

Kurt

„Ich liebe° Comics, und ich sammle Comics-Hefte. Die Zeichner° Mercier und Moebius finde ich sehr gut."

„Ich lese Comics selten. Mein Interesse ist Kunst. Aber für mich sind Comics auch Kunst. Am liebsten lese ich MAD."

---

lange *for a long time* **der Superheld** *super hero* **viele** *many* **die Frau** *woman* **die meisten** *most* **hilflos** *helpless*
lieben *to love* **der Zeichner** *artist*

Welche° Figuren kennen° die deutschen Jungen und Mädchen?

Übung • Und du? Wie steht's mit dir?

1. Welche Comics kennst du?
2. Welche Zeichner findest du gut?
3. Welche Comics gibt es?
4. Welche Figuren kennst du?
5. Sammelst du Comics-Hefte?

Neue Hobbys 

„Mein Hobby ist der Homecomputer. Ich mache Computerspiele , ich spiele ‚Hangman', und jetzt lerne ich Schach. Schach mit dem Computer! Das ist toll, das macht Spass!"

---

welche *which* **kennen** *to know*

KAPITEL 4

1

KAPITEL 4 Aus einer Schülerzeitung

Wiederholungskapitel

TEACHER–PREPARED MATERIALS	UNIT RESOURCES
Overhead transparency: Steckbrief—Name, Alter, Hobby, Lieblingsfächer, Schulweg	**Übungsheft,** Unit 4 **Arbeitsheft,** Unit 4 Unit 4 Cassette Review Test 1 Transparency 11 (also 1–10)

Unit 4 contains functions, grammar, and vocabulary that the students have studied in Units 1–3. This unit provides communicative and writing practice in different situations; some of its activities lend themselves to cooperative learning. If your students require further practice, you will find additional review exercises in Unit 4 of the **Übungsheft** and the **Arbeitsheft.** On the other hand, if your students know how to use the material in Units 1–3, you may wish to omit parts of Unit 4.

OBJECTIVE To review communicative functions, grammar, and vocabulary from Units 1–3

CULTURAL BACKGROUND Most German schools have school newspapers. These are encouraged by the State Office of Education, which even sponsors **Bundeskonferenzen,** conferences on the national level, for editors of and contributors to school newspapers.

These newspapers are somewhat more mature and serious in character than American school newspapers (although they are decidedly not without humor!). There are political cartoons and articles, for example. The papers are sold in school at a nominal cost—typically DM 1,00 per copy. They are supported by the income from advertising from local businesses.

MOTIVATING ACTIVITY Have the students look closely at the group portrait on page 120 and ask them what they notice that they think might be typically German in the setting and the way the young people are positioned. Give the students time to really look for cultural differences. They will probably notice these things:

—the hooked arms of the two girls in the second row (a typical sign of friendship and familiarity; used with family members and friends, not just between a boy and a girl or a man and a woman)
—one boy's arm around another boy's shoulder; again, a typical sign of friendship not limited to use between a boy and a girl
—the clothing

1

Schüler aus der 9c 

Use two of the students pictured in row 2 or 3 to introduce the idea of a **Steckbrief—**basically, a police "mug shot." On an overhead transparency or on the board, put the five areas of information about each student: **Name, Alter, Hobby, Lieblingsfächer,** and **Schulweg.** Then elicit information from the class, not necessarily in that order:

1. Wie alt ist der Junge/das Mädchen in Steckbrief Nummer ______?
2. Was für Hobbys hat er/sie?
3. Was sind seine/ihre Lieblingsfächer?

Play the cassette or read the first three **Steckbriefe** aloud as the students listen with their books closed. Stop after each one to elicit the information from the students. Work especially with **seine Hobbys/seine Lieblingsfächer** and **ihre Hobbys/ihre Lieblingsfächer,** so that the students have these phrases available to them for reporting. Ask the students to report on one of the students in **Steckbrief** 1, 2, or 3 with their books open, summarizing the information given. Put a sample summary on an overhead transparency or on the board.

Go on to **Steckbriefe** 4–6. Ask the students to cover up the picture captions, leaving only the photo and the names visible. Play the cassette or read the information for **Steckbrief** 4 twice through to see how much information the students can recall from listening alone. Ask questions similar to the previous ones. Continue with **Steckbriefe** 5 and 6 in the same manner. Then have the students uncover the text and ask them questions that include all three students, for example: **Wer ist musikalisch? —Warum meinst du das?** or **Wer wohnt weit von der Schule? —Wie weisst du das?** By the time you get to **Steckbriefe** 7–9, students should be quite familiar with the pattern and be able to recall most of the information just from hearing it.

2 Übung • Beantworte die Fragen!

Expand this activity by asking questions that will require the students to scan *all* the **Steckbriefe** for the needed information:

Welches Fach ist am populärsten? Warum ist das so?
Was meint ihr, wer ist gut in Mathe? In Chemie? In Bio?
Was sind populäre Hobbys? Wer von den Schülern hat diese Hobbys?
Wer wohnt weit von der Schule?
Wer wohnt nicht weit? Wie kommen diese Schüler in die Schule?

ANSWERS (to activity)

1. in die 9c
2. die List Realschule
3. Sie korrespondieren mit englischen und amerikanischen Schülern.
4. Natalie Fiedler, Nicolas Kraindl, Steffi Huber, Michael Strasser, Monika Schönfeld, Andreas Reichel, Marina Welzel, Stefan Knötzinger und Matthias Blick
6. Schülerin 1 heisst Natalie Fiedler. Sie ist 15 Jahre alt. Ihre Hobbys sind Gymnastik, Tanzen, Windsurfen und Schwimmen. Ihre Lieblingsfächer sind Erdkunde, Musik and Englisch. Sie kommt mit dem Rad in die Schule. Schüler 2 heisst Nicolas Kraindl. Er . . .
7. Natalie, Nicolas, Steffi, Stefan und Matthias sind fünfzehn Jahre alt. Michael, Monika, Andreas and Marina sind sechzehn.
8. Natalie, Monika und Matthias kommen mit dem Rad in die Schule.
9. Nicolas kommt mit der Strassenbahn in die Schule. Steffi und Michael kommen mit der U-Bahn.
10. Monika kommt manchmal zu Fuss in die Schule. Marina kommt zu Fuss. Andreas kommt mit dem Moped, und Stefan kommt mit dem Bus.

3 Übung • Jetzt bist du dran

You might instead have each student pick out three other students and do a **Steckbrief** on each one. The best ones can go in your German class newspaper.

CHALLENGE Have the students go back to Unit 3 and write a **Steckbrief** for Jens based on the information in Al and in Try Your Skills of that unit.

4 Schreibübung • Partnerarbeit

Put the best of the students' questions on an overhead transparency. Then have the students ask their partners those questions and take notes on the answers.

ANSWERS (probable)
Wie heisst du? Wie alt bist du? Woher bist du? Bist du aus Deutschland? Wie heissen deine Freunde? Wie heissen deine Lehrer? Wie kommst du in die Schule? Wie heisst deine Schule? Welche Fächer hast du? Was hast du in Mathe? Bist du gut in Englisch? Was machst du in deiner Freizeit? Machst du Sport? Spielst du ein Instrument? Sammelst du gern? Was sammelst du? Wie findest du Tennis? Was machst du gern? Was machst du am liebsten? Was machst du nicht gern? Liest du gern? Was liest du?

5 Schreibübung • Interview

SLOWER–PACED LEARNING As before, the students work in pairs. One plays "the reluctant interviewee," who is not eager to talk and gives only the most minimal of answers.

CHALLENGE As before, the students work in pairs. One plays "the overeager interviewee," who is a great talker and is only too ready to give all the information asked and then some.

6 Schreibübung • Ein Freund aus der List-Schule

An alternative is to take one of the interviews the students wrote for 5 and use it as a dictation. You could also wait till they have written up their interviews in article form and dictate one of those.

7 Übung • Klassenprojekt

Have the students make up a lot of visuals (magazine cutouts, line drawings, colorful background shapes, and so on) for the bulletin board display of the newspaper articles. Some of these can actually illustrate the articles—ask the students to make them colorful.

8 Leseübung • Ruth Maier hat alles für die Schule!

Have the students read the advertisement aloud—model the pronunciation where necessary—and invite them to guess at the meanings of unfamiliar words and abbreviations. You can illustrate some of these: pick up a German-English/English-German dictionary, for example, to illustrate **Wörterbuch D/E—E/D;** or ten pencils, to illustrate **10 St.**

9 Übung • Beantworte die Fragen!

You can make this a role-playing exercise. Tell the students to imagine that they failed to see the ad and are asking a friend about the prices. Again, tell them to disregard the word **ab.**

10 Schreibübung • In der Buchhandlung

You might have groups of students get together and perform a combined version of their dialogs. In that case, encourage them *not* to write out the whole dialog but only keep notes to guide them along as they talk and react to one another. For true communication to take place, students must learn to work with language and manipulate it freely.

11 Übung • Aus dem List-Käfer

Read through the captions for **Montag, Dienstag, Mittwoch,** and **Donnerstag.** Model the phrases with a great deal of expression and then have the students repeat them after you. Let them guess the meaning of each phrase. They should be able to guess all of them except for the caption for **Donnerstag.** Ask them to make up captions for **Freitag, Samstag,** and **Sonntag.** Some suggestions follow:

Hurrah, morgen ist Samstag!
Freitag, das ist Musik für mich!
Hurrah, hurrah, keine Schule!
Sonntag ist prima!

LANDES-KUNDE 1

Page 125

LANDESKUNDE 1

A Glimpse of the Federal Republic of Germany

OBJECTIVE To read for cultural awareness

MOTIVATING ACTIVITY Ask the students what they know about the Germans who live in the Federal Republic of Germany (FRG) and what they know about the FRG itself. List their impressions on the board or on an overhead transparency. Compare these later to the impressions they develop after reading the photo essay.

CULTURAL BACKGROUND The FRG is a small country, from north to south 50 minutes by plane, 12 hours by train, or 10 hours or less by car. About 62 million people live in this country, but seen from the air, it is amazing how rural the landscape appears. Of all the area in the FRG,

55 percent is agricultural land
30 percent is covered with forests
3 percent is used up by water or by barren land
12 percent is made up by cities, towns, villages, highways, and so on.

Background to the Photos

1. The island of Sylt, like all North Sea islands, is a popular vacation center. Sylt is connected to the mainland by a dam, the **Hindenburgdamm,** on which a car train, originating in Niebüll, carries automobiles and passengers across.
2. Badenweiler is a peaceful and elegant spa built on a hillside within sight of the Rhine Plain and the Vosges Mountains across the border in France. In this spa, respiratory and circulatory ailments are treated by the thermal springs that the Romans used nearly two thousand years ago. In the **Kurpark** are the ruins of a Roman bath, as well as the ruins of a castle built around A.D. 800 that provides a magnificent view of the valley.
3. The Zugspitze, towering over Garmisch-Partenkirchen in Bavaria, is Germany's highest mountain. It is part of the Alpine Range, which marks the border between the FRG and Austria. The peak can be reached by train and cable car.

Pages 126–27

THE NORTH

CULTURAL BACKGROUND The North is distinctly different from the South. It is said that the line of demarcation is the Main River (in jest called the **Weisswurstäquator**). The landscape is different: the farther north you travel, the flatter the country becomes. The architecture is different; there is more red brick, especially in small towns and in the country. And the people are different—less jovial and outgoing and more proper and reserved than the people in the South.

Background to the Photos

1. The island of Helgoland in the North Sea, eighty miles off the coast, is probably the most popular and touristed island. It is located outside the German customs area. Tourists go there to buy their legal limit of duty-free merchandise. The difference in price can be enough to offset the fare of the five-hour boat ride from the mainland.

   The village, with its submarine harbor, was completely destroyed during World War II. The island was used as a practice bombing target until 1952, when it was again turned over to the FRG.
2. This house is typical of many in Nordfriesland. Its thatched roof has been restored nicely; however, the owner seems to be worried that tourists may take too many straws from his roof. Thatched-roof houses can be found in many areas of both Nordfriesland and Ostfriesland, but due to larger fire insurance premiums, they are becoming rare.
3. A traditional costume worn by a native of Föhr, an island south of Sylt. Many people, especially in rural areas, wear their local costume on Sundays and on special days—and not only for the tourists.
4. Bensersiel is a charming fishing village in Ostfriesland, the home port of pleasure boats that go to the island of Langeoog, about six miles from the mainland. Like every fishing village along the coast, Bensersiel offers tourists an inexpensive vacation: good swimming and boating and supervised walks across the mud flats **(Wattwanderungen)** to Langeoog—but only when the tide is low.
5. Bremen, on the Weser River, is the oldest German maritime city and, after Hamburg, the second-largest commercial port. One of Bremen's most famous sights is the **Rathaus,** built in the Weser Renaissance style. A huge statue of Roland is in front of the **Rathaus,** facing the cathedral and symbolizing the freedom and independence of the city of Bremen.
6. Lübeck, sometimes called "the Gate to the North," is an important port on the Baltic Sea, especially for commerce with the Scandinavian countries. Among many things, Lübeck is famous for its **Marzipan** and for Thomas Mann, who was born here in 1875. His novel ***Buddenbrooks,*** for which he was awarded the Nobel Prize for Literature in 1929, uses his home town for much of the background. The **Holstentor,** shown in the picture, used to be part of Lübeck's fortifications.
8. The Lüneburger Heide is a large area south of Hamburg, best known for the spectacular bloom of the heather **(Heidekraut)** in August and September. The most attractive part of the Heide is a national park today, off limits to motorized traffic. Tourists stay in charming villages from which they can hike, ride horseback, and make excursions into the Heide in horse-drawn carriages. A shepherd with his flock of **Heidschnucken** and his dog is a famous sight of the Heide.
9. Hamburg on the Elbe River is the largest city in West Germany proper (1.8 million) and is West Germany's largest industrial city and busiest port. Hamburg ranks among the largest and busiest ports in the world. Due to its international commerce, Hamburg is a city of intense diplomatic and cultural activity.
10. Berlin is the largest city of the FRG (2.1 million) and is one of the social and intellectual centers of the Federal Republic. It is unique as a symbol of the world's division. Completely isolated in the DDR and divided by the infamous wall, since 1945 no longer the capital, badly destroyed in World War II, it is nonetheless a vibrant, vigorous, and exciting modern city.

LANDES-
KUNDE
1

Pages
128–29

CENTRAL GERMANY

CULTURAL BACKGROUND The central part of the Federal Republic consists of such a variety of regions with so much diversity that it is difficult to make any general assumptions characterizing the entire area. In earlier times this area was made up of many different principalities, dukedoms, bishoprics, and free cities, each developing its own traditions and religion (after the Reformation). These areas, along with the other areas of pre-war Germany, joined to become a nation in 1871.

Background to the Photos

1. Paderborn, situated at the eastern end of Germany's most fertile agricultural area **(Soester Börde),** is an old Imperial city. The present cathedral dates from the thirteenth century and is located where five earlier churches stood since A.D. 806. The old part of the city has many beautiful half-timbered houses **(Fachwerkhäuser).**
2. The cathedral of Worms is one of the most important examples of late Romanesque architecture. It was in the city of Worms that Martin Luther engaged in his famous debate with the emperor in 1521.
3. Bacharach is one of the leading wine-producing towns along the Rhine. It has an ancient and romantic castle that today is a famous youth hostel.
4. According to legend, Trier was founded 2050 B.C., making it older than any other German city. Trier was the northern capital of the Roman Empire. The well-preserved Roman-built **Porta Nigra** is Trier's most famous monument.
5. Germany is an industrial nation. Every effort is made to conserve and rehabilitate that part of the environment that has been marred by industrial activity. Areas affected by strip mining are carefully restored to their original beauty. Villages are resettled and artificial lakes are created for beauty and recreation.
7. In the industrial area, the **Ruhrgebiet,** the Rhine is no longer a romantic river, but an important commercial artery. It is heavily polluted, but efforts are being made to restore the river to a healthy state.
8. Frankfurt is a prosperous and cosmopolitan city. This magnificent medieval city was destroyed during World World II and not rebuilt. A few old buildings remain and some others (such as the **Römer**) have been lovingly restored, so Frankfurt is a mixture of old and new. Frankfurt has been a trade center since Roman times and is the printing center of Europe. Its annual Book Fair **(Buchmesse)** is the largest of its kind in the world. Johann Wolfgang von Goethe was born in Frankfurt in 1749.

Pages
130–31

THE SOUTH

CULTURAL BACKGROUND Most German vacationers as well as most foreign visitors spend their vacation time in the south of Germany. The weather is warmer and often sunnier than in the North. The mountains and the lakes are an added attraction, as well as the famous southern **Gemütlichkeit.**

Background to the Photos

1. Freiburg, lying at the foot of the mountains and surrounded by vineyards, is the chief city in the Black Forest area. Its Gothic cathedral **(Freiburger Münster),** built between the twelfth and the sixteenth

centuries, is the symbol of Freiburg. The cathedral is surrounded by an open-air market and medieval buildings, such as the **Kornhaus,** a place where grain was once stored.

4. The university city Heidelberg on the Neckar was made famous in the United States by Sigmund Romberg's operetta *The Student Prince,* which is set there. The famous castle, parts of which date to 1398, stands on a hill overlooking the town and the river.

6. Tübingen is another beautiful university town on the Neckar River. The poets Möricke, Uhland, and Hölderlin were educated here, as well as the philosophers Hegel and Schelling and the astronomer Kepler.

7. Würzburg is a beautiful Baroque city on the river Main. It has one of the largest and grandest Baroque palaces in Germany. The ceiling above the staircase in the palace was painted by Tiepolo in 1753. It is the world's largest painting of this kind.

8. Ulm, on the Danube, boasts of having a Gothic cathedral **(Ulmer Münster)** whose spire tops the tallest church steeple in the world (nearly 500 feet). The church, begun in 1377, has a capacity for 29,000 people. Another famous medieval building is the **Rathaus** (1370), which was decorated in 1540 with colorful frescos. The astronomical clock on the east façade was built in 1520 and is still running.

9. Landshut is a beautifully preserved medieval town northeast of Munich, on the Isar River. The town has a colorful history. Every four years Landshut's greatest historical event is recreated by the townspeople with great authenticity. The **Landshuter Hochzeit** recreates the wedding between the son of Duke Georg der Reiche of Bavaria and Jadwiga, daughter of the King of Poland, in 1475. This colorful event takes place on four weekends in August and attracts thousands of visitors from all over the world.

Page 132

1. Mainau is a small, privately owned island in Lake Constance. The island is known for its tropical fauna. Because of the mild climate, even palm trees and lemon trees can thrive in this part of Germany. The island has been turned into a public park by its owner, Count Bernadotte of Sweden.

2. Mittenwald is a small, picturesque Bavarian town surrounded by high mountains, close to the Austrian border. The town is best known for its excellent skiing conditions and for violin making.

3. Augsburg is the third-largest city in Bavaria, after Munich and Nuremberg. The city was founded by the Romans and is much older than Munich. One of Augsburg's attractions is the **Fuggerei.** It is a small town of 250 houses within the city. The Fuggers, who were wealthy merchants and moneylenders to kings and emperors, founded this small town for the poor people of Augsburg. Only poor families and natives of Augsburg can live in the **Fuggerei,** and the monthly rent is still the equivalent of one Rhenish guilder—less than two marks today.

4. The Tegernsee is one of the many lakes in Bavaria. On its shores are the towns of Tegernsee, Bad Wiessee, and Rottach, where many of Bavaria's affluent citizens have their second homes. The area around the lake is popular for hiking and skiing.

5. **Lüftlmalerei,** painting house façades on wet stucco, is a popular form of decorating the outside of one's home. Many villages and small towns in southern Bavaria have houses decorated in this fashion, as in Oberammergau, where **Lüftlmalerei** is a centuries-old tradition. Oberammergau is otherwise famous for its woodcarvings and especially for its Passion Play, which has been performed every ten years since 1634.

KAPITEL 4

Aus einer Schülerzeitung

Wiederholungskapitel

For teaching suggestions, see the Teacher's Notes preceding this unit, pp. T86–T89.

1 Schüler aus der 9c

Wir sind Schüler aus der 9c in der List Realschule in München. Wir sind diesen Monat in unserer Schülerzeitung, im List-Käfer. Warum? Wir korrespondieren mit englischen und amerikanischen Schülern.

Das sind unsere „Steckbriefe."

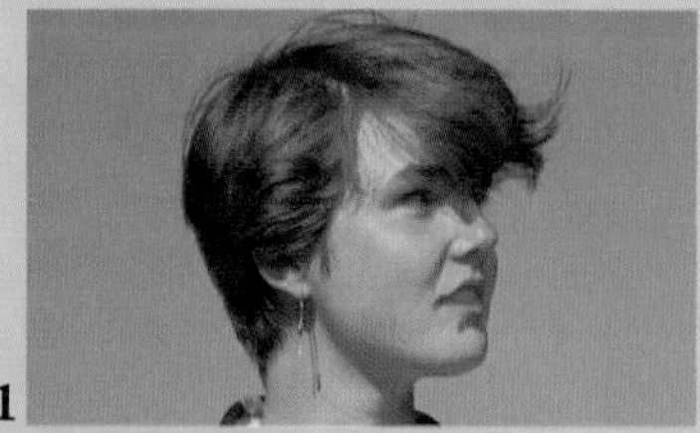

1
Name: Natalie Fiedler
Alter: 15 J.
Hobby: Gymnastik, Tanzen, Windsurfen, Schwimmen
Lieblingsfächer: Ek[1], Mu, E
Schulweg: Rad

2
Name: Nicolas Kraindl
Alter: 15 J.
Hobby: Squash, Musik (Gitarre spielen)
Lieblingsfächer: Mu, E
Schulweg: Strassenbahn

3
Name: Steffi Huber
Alter: 15 J.
Hobby: Gymnastik, Volleyball, Schi laufen
Lieblingsfächer: M, G
Schulweg: U-Bahn

4
Name: Michael Strasser
Alter: 16 J.
Hobby: Hockey, Judo, Schach
Lieblingsfächer: Ku, Ch
Schulweg: U-Bahn

5
Name: Monika Schönfeld
Alter: 16 J.
Hobby: Klavier, Schwimmen, Windsurfen, Tennis
Lieblingsfächer: Mu, E, D
Schulweg: Rad/zu Fuss

6
Name: Andreas Reichel
Alter: 16 J.
Hobby: Tennis, Fussball, Briefmarken
Lieblingsfächer: D, Bio
Schulweg: Moped

7
Name: Marina Welzel
Alter: 16 J.
Hobby: Musik (Klavier), Segeln, Schi laufen
Lieblingsfächer: Mu, E, D
Schulweg: zu Fuss

8
Name: Stefan Knötzinger
Alter: 15 J.
Hobby: Schach, Tennis, Basketball
Lieblingsfächer: M, E, Ek
Schulweg: Bus

9
Name: Matthias Blick
Alter: 15 J.
Hobby: Fussball, Schwimmen, Schi laufen, Münzen
Lieblingsfächer: D, E
Schulweg: Rad

[1]Abkürzungen: Ek = Erdkunde; Mu = Musik; E = Englisch; M = Mathematik; G = Geographie; Ku = Kunst; Ch = Chemie; D = Deutsch; Bio = Biologie; **Schi laufen: sie läuft Schi** *she skis;* **U-Bahn: mit der U-Bahn** *by subway;* **Klavier** *piano*

Photo p. 120: Hinter der List Schule (Wirtschafts-Realschule) in München

2 Übung • Beantworte die Fragen!

For answers, see p. T87.

1. In welche Klasse gehen die Schüler?
2. Wie heisst ihre Schule?
3. Warum sind sie in der Schülerzeitung?
4. Wie heissen die Schüler?
5. Lies die neun Steckbriefe!
6. Identifiziere die Schüler! (Sag, wie sie heissen, wie alt sie sind, was für Hobbys sie haben, was ihre Lieblingsfächer sind und wie sie in die Schule kommen!)
7. Wer ist 15 Jahre alt? Wer ist 16?
8. Wer kommt mit dem Rad in die Schule?
9. Wer kommt mit der Strassenbahn? Und mit der U-Bahn?
10. Wie kommen die andern in die Schule?

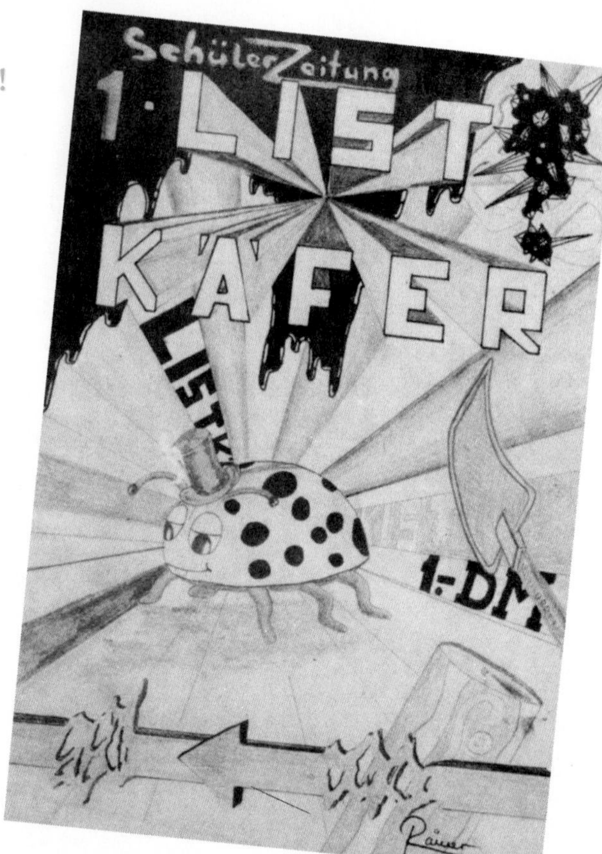

3 Übung • Jetzt bist du dran

Your German class is going to be featured in the **List-Käfer.** Interview your classmates and write a **Steckbrief** for each one.

4 Schreibübung • Partnerarbeit For answers, see p. T88.

You and your partner are going to interview one of the students shown on page 121. Look back through Units 1, 2, and 3 and make a list of questions you could ask the student.

5 Schreibübung • Interview

Pretend that you are interviewing one of the students on page 121. Write out your interview. Then you and your partner take the roles of the interviewer and the student and present it to the class. Your classmates may have other questions to ask.

6 Schreibübung • Ein Freund aus der List-Schule

Now you and your partner take the interview you have written and rewrite it as a newspaper article.

7 Übung • Klassenprojekt

Collect the articles written by your classmates and make a scrapbook or a bulletin board titled **Unsere Freunde aus der List-Schule.**

Ruth Maier BUCHHANDLUNG AM RATHAUS

STARNBERG • HAUPTSTRASSE 14 • TELEFON 7341

Bücher, Schallplatten, Schreibwaren & Posters

Bücher—und alles für die Schule
Ruth Maier hat's!

WELTATLAS

Schulsachen

Schultaschen	DM 15,00
Taschenrechner	22,00
Kulis	2,10
Hefte	1,20

Wörterbücher

Wörterbuch D/E—E/D nur DM 12,00!

Bleistifte (10 St.) DM 3,50

Poster ab DM 4,00

Musik

Platten	ab DM	7,00
Kassetten	ab	6,80
Video-Kassetten	ab	12,00

Spiele

Computerspiele DM 23,00

Bücher ab DM 6,00

9 Übung • Beantworte die Fragen!

1. Was hat die Buchhandlung am Rathaus alles?
2. Was kostet alles? Was kostet . . .? Was kosten . . .?

10 Schreibübung • In der Buchhandlung

You go into Ruth Maier's bookstore and want to know the prices of four items. Write out a dialog and practice it with a classmate. Don't forget to be polite.

11 Übung • Aus dem List-Käfer

So sehen die Schüler der List-Schule ihre Schulwoche—Und du? Wie steht's mit dir? Wie siehst du deine Schulwoche?

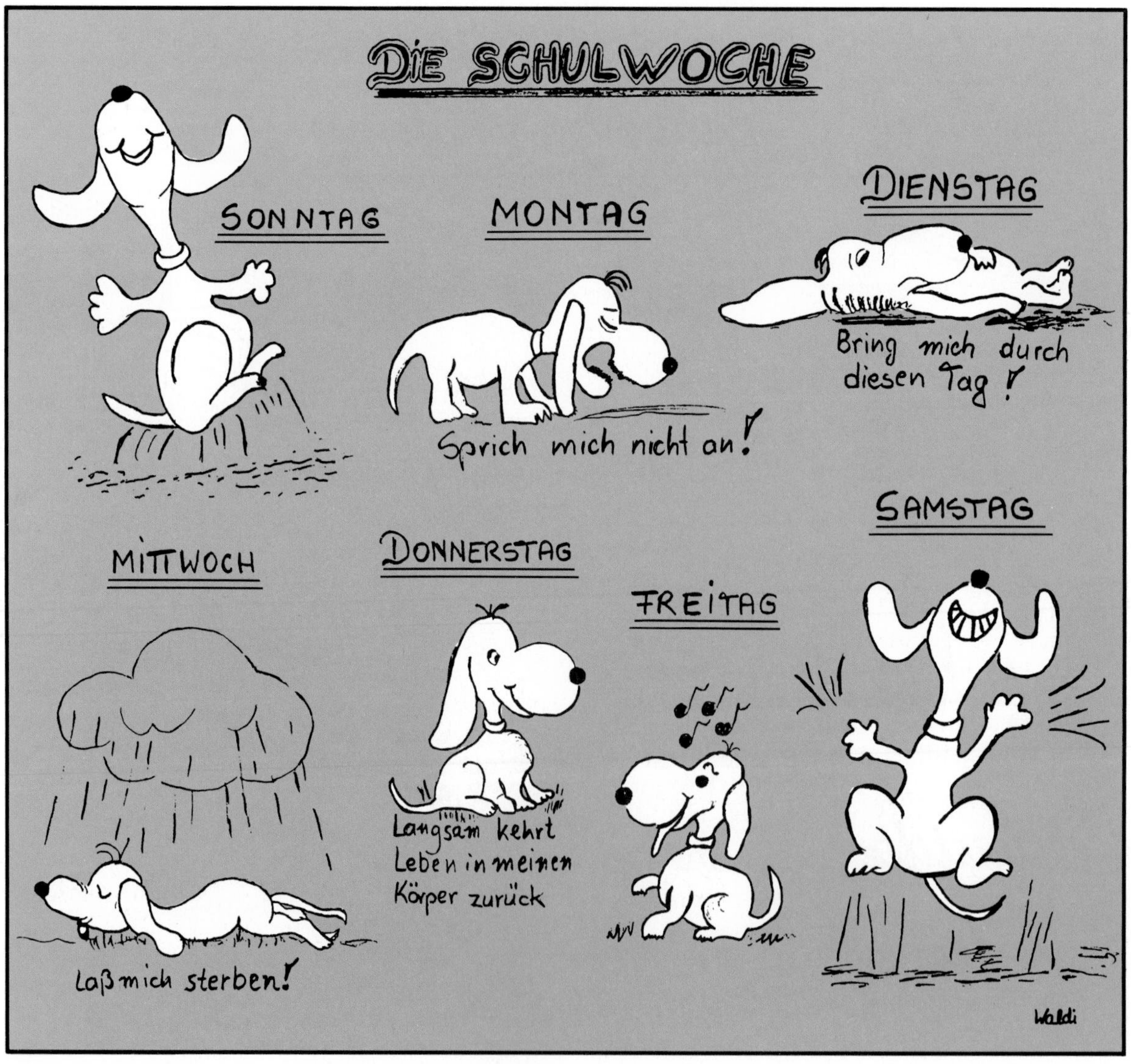

LANDESKUNDE 1

A Glimpse of the Federal Republic of Germany

Germany lies in the center of Europe. It is about six hundred miles long, bounded by the North Sea to the north and the Alps to the south. From east to west the country is narrow, seldom more than two hundred miles wide. Contained in this area is a surprising variety of landscapes. There are coastal regions and flatlands in northern Germany and gently rolling hills in the central and southwestern part of the country. South of the river Danube is a high plateau that reaches to the majestic Alpine range. It is surprising that in such a highly industrialized country more than half the area is farmland and another third is forest land.

❶ Promenadenkonzert auf der Nordseeinsel Sylt

❷ Kurort Badenweiler im Schwarzwald

❸ Die Zugspitze, Deutschlands höchster Berg, 2 963 m

The North

The North abounds in architectural and artistic treasures and is the area of Germany most influenced by the sea. There are several historic Hanseatic cities, including the great port cities of Hamburg, Bremen, Kiel, and Lübeck. The coasts of the Baltic Sea and the North Sea are dotted with fishing villages. Many have become popular summer resorts, but fishing is still an important industry. Inland is a rich agricultural area that supports a thriving dairy industry. There are many towns with red brick buildings that are characteristic of the north, and villages that still have windmills and thatched-roof houses.

Lieber Gast!
Bitte keine Halme (Reet) rausziehen. Wenn jeder einen Halm nehmen würde, hätte ich bald kein Dach mehr über dem Kopf.
Der Eigentümer

❶ Ausflugsschiffe vor der Insel Helgoland

❷ Nordfriesenhaus mit Reetdach auf der Insel Föhr

❸ Tracht auf der Insel Föhr

❹ Fischerhafen Bensersiel in Ostfriesland

❺ Das Rathaus von Bremen

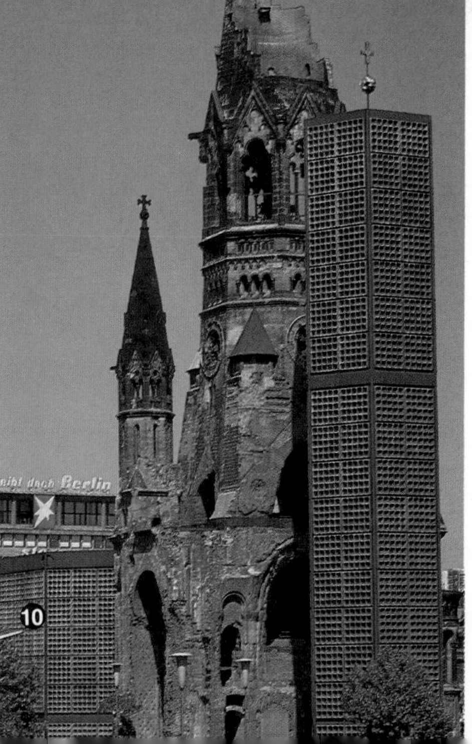

❻ Lübeck mit Blick auf das Holstentor (1477)

❼ Schaffner vor dem Lübecker Rathaus

❽ Lüneburger Heide: Schäfer mit Hund und Heidschnucken

❾ Hamburg, grösste Stadt der Bundesrepublik

❿ Berlin: Ruine und Neubau der Kaiser-Wilhelm Gedächtniskirche

Central Germany

The central part of Germany is highly diversified in both geography and character. The busy Moselle River flows through Trier, the oldest city in Germany. The famous Rhine River cuts a scenic path through terraced vineyards, past romantic castles and the rock upon which the fabled Lorelei sat, through the great cities of Cologne, Düsseldorf, and Bonn, the capital of the Federal Republic of Germany. The state of North Rhine–Westphalia, its rolling hills sprinkled with old castles, is called the forge of Germany because of its highly industrialized Ruhr area with such cities as Essen and Dortmund. The second largest industrialized area of the Rhine-Main region is Hessia, but it is also known as the land of healing springs because of its many spas. Located in Hessia is the city of Frankfurt, the business and banking capital of the Federal Republic.

❶ Fachwerkhäuser in Paderborn, Westfalen

❷ Der Wormser Dom aus dem 11. und 12. Jahrhundert

❸ Weinberge in Bacharach am Rhein

❹ Trier, die älteste Stadt, mit der Porta Nigra aus der Zeit der Römer

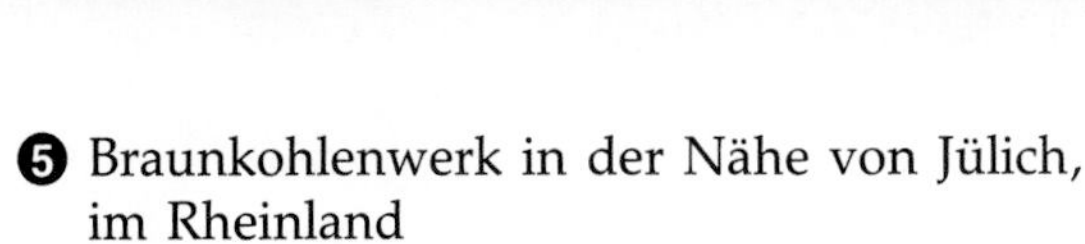

❺ Braunkohlenwerk in der Nähe von Jülich, im Rheinland

❻ Arbeiter im Ruhrgebiet

❼ Der Rhein in der Nähe von Duisburg

❽ Frankfurt am Main, Finanzzentrum der Bundesrepublik

The South

The South, a beautiful and historic region, begins at the River Main and stretches all the way to Switzerland, Lake Constance, and the Alps. In this area are found the old university cities of Heidelberg, Tübingen, and Freiburg; historic art cities such as Würzburg, Nürnberg, and Bamberg; perfectly preserved medieval towns such as Rothenburg, Dinkelsbühl, and Nördlingen; wine-growing regions in the southwest; and spas that pre-date Roman times. Munich, the capital of Bavaria, is in the southeast, a center of art and culture, and the city in which sixty-nine percent of all Germans would like to live. The area around Munich offers both natural and man-made wonders, baroque churches, monasteries, and King Ludwig's castles. The Alps themselves offer magnificent scenery, dotted with lakes, forests, flower-filled meadows, and charming Alpine villages that are year-round resorts.

❶ Blumenfrau auf dem Marktplatz in Freiburg

❷ Gasthaus zur Sonne

❸ Schwarzwälder Schinken und Bauernbrot

❹ Heidelberg am Neckar, Universitätsstadt seit 1386

❺ Rathausfassade von Staufen an der Badener Weinstrasse

❻ Tübingen am Neckar, Universitätsstadt seit 1477

❼ Treppenhaus in der Würzburger Residenz mit dem in der Welt grössten Deckenfresko von Tiepolo

❽ Das Rathaus von Ulm mit Fresken von 1540

❾ Landshut an der Isar, mit Giebelhäusern aus dem 15. und 16. Jahrhundert

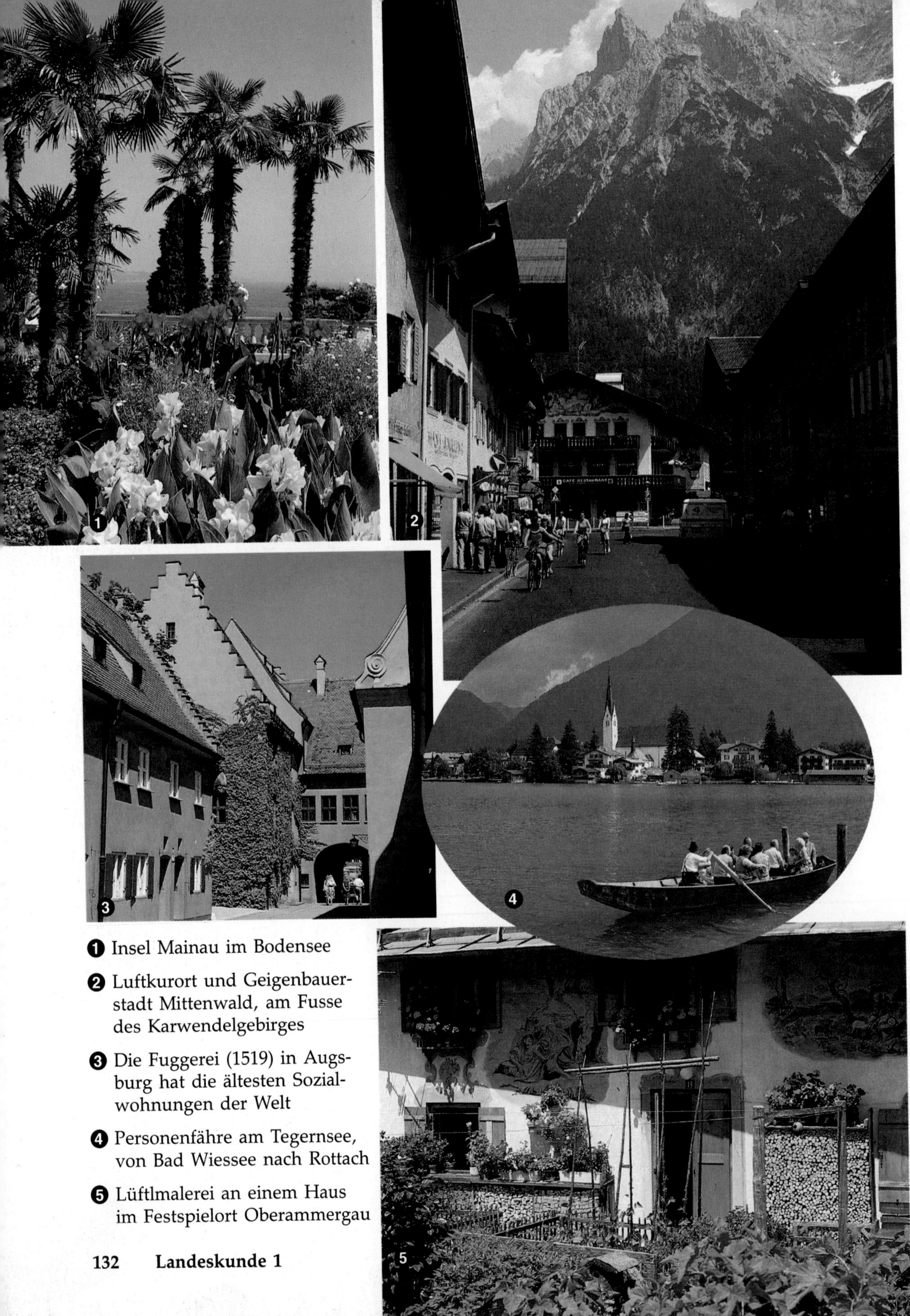

❶ Insel Mainau im Bodensee

❷ Luftkurort und Geigenbauerstadt Mittenwald, am Fusse des Karwendelgebirges

❸ Die Fuggerei (1519) in Augsburg hat die ältesten Sozialwohnungen der Welt

❹ Personenfähre am Tegernsee, von Bad Wiessee nach Rottach

❺ Lüftlmalerei an einem Haus im Festspielort Oberammergau

KAPITEL 5

KAPITEL 5 Auf nach Köln!

Scope and Sequence

	BASIC MATERIAL	COMMUNICATIVE FUNCTIONS
SECTION A	**Auf nach Deutschland! (A1)** **Was braucht Peter für die Reise? (A7)** **Was suchst du? Wen fragst du? (A10)**	**Exchanging information** • Saying what you need to take on a trip
SECTION B	**Peter in Frankfurt (B1)** **Was sagen die Reisenden? (B8)** **Wie kommt Peter nach Neuss? (B15)** **Die Zahlen von 20 bis 1 000 (B17)**	**Exchanging information** • Asking for information and giving directions • Giving distances from one city to another using a map
SECTION C	**Peter wechselt Geld (C1)** **Das deutsche Geld (C2)** **Telefonieren ist nicht schwer (C6)** **Wann geht der Flug nach Köln? (C13)**	**Socializing** • Exchanging money • Making a phone call **Exchanging information** • Reading a flight monitor • Expressing flight numbers, departure times, and gate numbers
TRY YOUR SKILLS	Pronunciation /l/, **ach**-sound, /ü/, /ö/ Letter-sound correspondences **ch, ng, j, s, ss, v** Dictation	
ZUM LESEN	**Köln am Rhein** (a pictorial tour of one of Germany's most famous cities) **Ein kleines Missverständnis** (a short story about a mix-up in an airport)	

WRITING A variety of controlled and open-ended writing activities appear in the Pupil's Edition. The Teacher's Notes identify other activities suitable for writing practice and suggest additional writing activities.

COOPERATIVE LEARNING Many of the activities in the Pupil's Edition lend themselves to cooperative learning. The Teacher's Notes explain some of the many instances where this teaching strategy can be particularly effective. For guidelines on how to use cooperative learning, see page T13.

GRAMMAR	CULTURE	RE–ENTRY
The definite article, nominative and accusative case (A12)	Map of Germany, showing cities with airports Welcome aboard—information for air travelers	Definite articles Interrogatives School supplies (or items you would take on a trip)
The **möchte**-forms, present tense (B11)	Signs and symbols The German post office and phone company Measuring in kilometers	Direction words Numbers, pronouns Means of transportation: "How do you get to . . . ?"
	German money; exchanging money The 24-hour system of telling time The German telephone system	**Möchte**-forms Numbers Saying please and thank you Expressing time
Recombining communicative functions, grammar, and vocabulary		
Reading for practice and pleasure		

TEACHER–PREPARED MATERIALS

Section A Pictures of items in A7; brochures of airlines of German-speaking countries; flashcards of people listed in A15 with definite article

Section B Pictures of signs in B1; flashcards of places and directions in B2

Section C German money; rate-of-exchange tables; toy phones; 24-hour digital clock that can be easily changed

UNIT RESOURCES

Übungsheft, Unit 5
Arbeitsheft, Unit 5
Unit 5 Cassettes
Transparencies 12–14
Quizzes 12–14
Unit 5 Test

A1–3

OBJECTIVES **To exchange information:** say what you need to take on a trip

CULTURAL BACKGROUND In recent years, air travel between continents has become less expensive, affording many more Americans the opportunity to travel abroad. Young people are able to take advantage of this opportunity because once they arrive, good public transportation within Europe makes it easy for them to travel.

MOTIVATING ACTIVITY Ask the students to list questions they would ask a friend who is leaving on a trip to Germany. They will probably come up with some or all of these: Where are you going? When are you leaving? What are you going to do there? How long are you staying? When are you coming back? How much will the trip cost? Whom are you visiting? Ask the students to keep this list until later on in the unit. They will be able to ask and answer questions like these in German.

A1

Auf nach Deutschland! 

Follow the usual procedure. After having the students listen to the introductory paragraph, model the new vocabulary; for example, to illustrate **besetzt,** you might say: **Die Klasse hat (dreissig) Plätze. (Zwei) Plätze sind frei. (Achtundzwanzig) Plätze sind besetzt.** Use a map of Germany (such as an enlargement of the map on page 136) on an overhead transparency to demonstrate vocabulary and show the locations of cities. Ask questions such as the following, accepting very short answers: **Wohin fliegt das Flugzeug? Wer ist im Flugzeug? Nur Deutsche? Warum fliegen Amerikaner nach Deutschland?** Proceed the same way with each exchange in turn.

Have the students open their books and listen to all of A1 again, reading silently. Then ask questions on the text, sentence by sentence.

Read the mini-dialogs with the class, first taking the role of the questioners, then the role of the respondents. Ask for good intonation. Practice difficult words and phrases first.

/x/ /ç/ nach München
Ich fliege nach München.
/i/ /ai/ fliege weiter
Nein, ich fliege weiter nach Wien.
/ü/ /ö/ München, Köln

CHALLENGE Ask the students to combine three of the exchanges into one, using either Paul or Peter as the key person, and to change the reason for going to Germany and the length of time they plan to stay there.

A2

Übung • Stimmt! Stimmt nicht!

CHALLENGE Ask the students to come up with five or more additional statements that are *not* true. Then ask them to come up with several that *could* be true, for example: **Peter besucht Freunde in Köln.**

A3

Übung • Wohin fliegen die Schüler?

Have pairs of students ask each other about the travel plans of the five young people. Have them use either of the following formats.

A: Wohin fliegt (Peter)?
B: (Er) fliegt nach Köln.

A: Wer fliegt nach Köln?
B: Peter.

A4 Übung • Wohin fliegst du?

As a variation, tell the students to imagine that they are young Germans flying to a city in the United States. Their German friends are impressed.

A: Wohin fliegst du?
B: Ich fliege nach Miami.
A: Miami? Das ist toll (prima, super)!

A5 Übung • Bleibst du hier oder fliegst du weiter?

Tell the students to imagine that they are flying to Frankfurt and from there to a city that is *not* in Germany. Have them select four of the following cities. Help them pronounce the names properly. The stress is indicated where it differs from English: **Paris, Brüssel, Athen, Luxemburg, Lissabon, Rom, Wien, Madrid, Genf, Kopenhagen, Stockholm, Amsterdam.**

A6 Übung • Und du? Wie steht's mit dir?

To expand this activity, have the students write a short paragraph answering the questions. If they have nothing to write for one or more questions, have them make up information about an imaginary pen pal.

A7 WAS BRAUCHT PETER FÜR DIE REISE?

Have the students listen to the conversation between Peter and his father with their books closed. Ask how much they understood: What is the topic of conversation? Who is talking? Introduce the new vocabulary through realia and demonstration. Then have the students listen to the conversation again. Ask questions, reinforcing the new form **den** (at this stage, for recognition only): **Peter braucht den Pass. Wer hat den Pass?** Then have the students listen and follow in their books. Finally, have the students take the part of Peter while you play a parent (**Vati** or **Mutti**).

Continue with the other items Peter needs. Help the students with the pronunciation and stress of new cognates: **das Adressbuch, die Kamera, der Film.** Ask questions, letting the students refer to their books. **Peter will Fotos machen. Was braucht er? Peter will besser Deutsch lernen. Was braucht er?**

Have the students listen to the first paragraph at the bottom of the page. Work with the pronunciation of **Amerikaner** and **Kalifornien.** Ask questions about Peter: **Ist Peter Deutscher oder Amerikaner? Wie alt ist er? Wo wohnt er? Woher ist der Vater? Woher ist die Mutter?** Then reverse roles and have the students make up questions and ask you. Continue with the second paragraph. Have the students write a caption for Peter's photo.

A8 Übung • Peter plant seine Reise

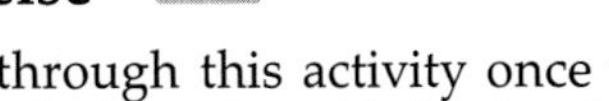

SLOWER–PACED LEARNING Run through this activity once with books open. Then, for additional practice, do it again with books closed.

A9 Übung • Etwas über Peter Seber

As an expansion, have the students write down more questions they would want to ask Peter about himself. They may refer to the bottom of page 138.

A10 WAS SUCHST DU? WEN FRAGST DU?

Have the students listen to the conversation between Peter and his sister,

following in their books. Ask questions: **Was fragt Peters Schwester? Was sucht Peter? Weiss Peters Schwester, wer den Pass hat? Wen fragt sie?** Explain that **mal** is a conversational filler. The word carries no meaning but makes a sentence more pleasant and natural.

> Mach mal die Hausaufgaben! *(Why don't you do your homework?)*
> Besuchst du uns mal? *(Are you going to visit us?)*

Have the students practice the exchange with each other, using their own names. Have them reverse roles. As a variation, have student B look for a different item from A8.

A 11 Übung • Wer hat was?

Model a question and answer and then have the students work in pairs. Have them look at the people on the right. What do they notice about all males except **die Jungen?** Make a list of the male persons on an overhead transparency or on the board. Ask what function these phrases must have in the sentence (object of a verb). Which ones change: nouns for males, for females, or for people in the plural? Ask the students to recall that articles are used with names of people they are on familiar terms with. Point out that this is also true when using the accusative.

As an expansion, put the students in groups of three. Student B actually asks the other person, who has the item. The students can switch roles.

> A: Wer hat (den Walkman)?
> B: Ich nicht. Ich frage mal (den Michael). Du, Michael, hast du (den Walkman von . . .)?
> C: Ja, hier ist (er).

As a variation, have the students write out a dialog in which the person asked is an adult **(Entschuldigung, Herr . . . ! Haben Sie das Wörterbuch?).**

A 12 ERKLÄRUNG

Work especially with **Herr, Junge,** and **Klassenkamerad.** Tell the students that normally German nouns do not take endings in the singular; they will just have to learn which ones take an **n** in the accusative. There will be more such nouns for you to point out to them later.

A 13 Übung

Use the picture cues to vary the item sought. As an expansion, add the function of **nachfragen** to the activity.

> A: Was suchst du?
> B: Den Pass.
> A: Den Pass?
> B: Ja, er ist weg!
> A: Unsinn, hier ist er.

> A: Ich brauche den Reiseführer.
> B: Den Reiseführer?
> A: Ja. Wo ist er?
> B: Hier ist er.
> A: Danke.

For additional practice, recycle the school supplies from Unit 2. Use pictures and words as cues.

A 14 Übung • Wo hast du deine Sachen?

Do the mini-dialogs as shown in the examples, but add the function of **nachfragen.** This function is used not only to re-question, but also to stall the other speaker and gain time to think and react.

A15 Übung • Wen suchst du?

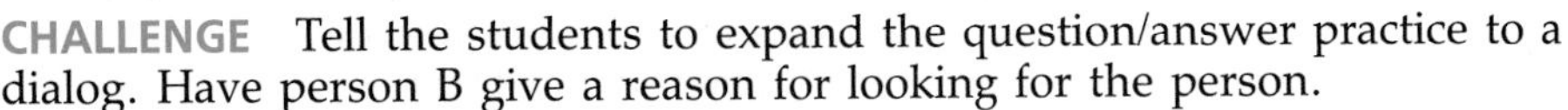

CHALLENGE Tell the students to expand the question/answer practice to a dialog. Have person B give a reason for looking for the person.

A: Wen suchst du?
B: Ich suche Herrn Hausmann.
A: Warum?
B: Er hat die Reiseschecks.

A16 Übung • Wen? oder Was?

CHALLENGE Have the students make up more items eliciting **wen?** or **was?** questions. As a variation, change the pattern: **Wen suchst du? Den Jörg? — Nein, den Jens.**

A17 Übung • Merkspiel

As an expansion, supply the students with additional vocabulary. (They tell you in English what they would pack; you supply the German.)

A18 Übung • Beim Packen

Have the students list all the things Peter packs in each bag. As in A17, have them start with **In den Rucksack packt er . . .** Each student adds one item from those given.

As an expansion, tell the students to imagine that they are helping a friend pack for a trip abroad. They hold up each item and the traveler tells them where to put it: **Die Reiseschecks? — In die Reisetasche.** On the board or on an overhead transparency, put the names of some other items to go into the **Rucksack.**

der Pullover	die Shorts	die Tennisschuhe
das T-Shirt	die Jeans	die Socken

A19 Übung • Hör gut zu!

You will hear ten statements. Each one contains a noun phrase that is either the subject or the direct object of the sentence. Listen carefully and determine which one it is. For example, you hear, **Ich suche das Flugticket.** You place your check mark in the row labeled *direct object*, because the noun phrase **das Flugticket** is a direct object. Let's begin. **Fangen wir an!**

1. Ich brauche heute die Kamera. *direct object*
2. Der Peter fliegt nach Köln. *subject*
3. Er fragt den Vater. *direct object*
4. Die Schüler spielen am Samstag. *subject*
5. Ich verliere wieder das Spiel. *direct object*
6. Er findet die Musikkassette nicht. *direct object*
7. Die Lehrer bleiben in Deutschland. *subject*
8. Der Peter fliegt im August wieder zurück. *subject*
9. Ich habe den Pass und die Reiseschecks. *direct object*
10. Wir suchen den Reiseführer. *direct object*

Now check your answers. *Read each item again and give the correct answer.*

A 20 Übung • Im Flughafen

CHALLENGE Have the students work in pairs to write out the entire conversation with the student. (Have them include responses to the questions.)

A 21 Schreibübung • Gespräch im Flugzeug

As a variation, have the students write the dialog asking the questions of an older person. (They will address this person with **Sie.**)

A 22 Information für junge Reisende

Explain that these cards are distributed by Lufthansa to their younger passengers. The card at the upper left gives the English and German vocabulary for various flight terms.

SECTION B

OBJECTIVES **To exchange information:** ask for information and give directions; give distances from one city to another using a map

CULTURAL BACKGROUND Frankfurt's airport, the **Rhein-Main-Flughafen,** is the third largest in Europe. It is a modern facility, equipped with conveniences such as "people movers."

MOTIVATING ACTIVITY Ask the students to think of signs and pictorial symbols that they might have seen at an airport. Have them describe some signs briefly. Perhaps somebody in class knows where to find such pictorial symbols in the school library—check the book out and compare the symbols with the ones used in this unit.

B 1 Peter in Frankfurt 

Follow the usual procedure. Divide the presentation into five parts. As you go through the first segment the second time, stop to work on the pronunciation of new words: **Reisenden, Passkontrolle, Gepäck,** and /ts/ **Zoll.** Do scanning and sentence completion, for example: **Das Flugzeug landet** ______. **Die Reisenden gehen** ______.

After presenting the second segment, take the role of the customs official. Have the students answer. Then ask comprehension questions: **Was fragt der Beamte? Was wünscht er? Sagt er „Sie" oder „du" zu Peter?** Tell the students briefly that it is **ein Beamter** but **der Beamte.** (Do not discuss adjective endings. Just treat it as a vocabulary item at this time.) Finally, have the students read the dialog in pairs. After presenting the third segment, work with new phrases and demonstrate new vocabulary:

> Die Reisetasche fehlt. Sie ist nicht da!
> Ich habe Kaffee und Zigaretten. Ich habe etwas zu verzollen. Ich gehe bei Rot durch.

Put the students into cooperative learning groups of three. Have them put statements about Peter's trip into the correct sequence: **Er geht zur Gepäckausgabe. Er landet in Frankfurt.** Have them take turns telling what comes next. Before you cover the pictogram section, introduce the names of all the places shown. Since some are cognates, they are difficult to say because of interference from English, in both pronunciation and stress.

> die Post die Toilette (Toi-let-te) die Bank das Telefon
> das Restaurant (similar to French pronunciation: between /ã/ and /ŋ/)

Practice the words first individually and then in the pictogram sequence.

B2 Übung • Partnerarbeit

Review adverbs of place and directions from Unit 2 (in the right-hand box) and practice the three new ones: **links, rechts, geradeaus.** Then have the students stand up. Give them directions. They must indicate the direction with hand signals and motions. (Have them show **da (dort)** as a short distance away from themselves and **da (dort) drüben** as farther away.) Then combine two directional phrases: **Da drüben, links. Geradeaus, dann rechts.**

B3 WIE SAGT MAN DAS?

Give the students some sentences such as **Wo ist der Ausgang? Was kostet die Reisetasche?** and have them add **bitte** to everything you say, putting it at the end *or* in the middle. Then have them practice putting **bitte** at the beginning or end of typical requests made by officials: **Den Pass! An Bord gehen! Weitergehen! Warten! Anschnallen!**

B4 Übung • Wo ist . . . ?

For additional practice, do the activity a second time. This time, ask where classroom objects are (using vocabulary from Unit 2).

B5 Übung • Was bedeuten die Piktogramme?

SLOWER–PACED LEARNING Do the activity with questions and answers in incomplete sentences, e.g., **Nummer acht? Die Schliessfächer.** A correction by person A would be, for example, **Nein, die Post.**

B6 Übung • Was suchst du?

To expand the dialog, have the students imagine that they see an adult at the airport who looks lost. They themselves are not sure of directions and need time to think.

A: Was suchen Sie?
B: Ich suche die Bank.
A: Die Bank? Moment mal. — Oh, die Bank ist da drüben, links.
B: Danke!

B7 Übung • Rollenspiel

To expand the airport situation, have the students mingle and talk. They can ask each other for directions, introduce themselves, and hold conversations.

B8 WAS SAGEN DIE REISENDEN? 

CHALLENGE Have the students play the part of the traveler who would like to take care of various needs, while you play an official in the information booth who helps them. Put key phrases that the students can use on an overhead transparency or a handout. Give ample practice to all phrases. Add greetings and thank-you's to the exchange.

REISENDER Ich möchte mir die Hände waschen.
AUSKUNFT Die Toiletten sind da drüben, links.
REISENDER Danke.
AUSKUNFT Bitte.

das Gepäck holen/abgeben
Frankfurt sehen

Have the students practice the same exchanges with each other.

B 9 Ein wenig Landeskunde

The German post office also performs some banking functions. Many Germans keep a postal savings account, which is convenient for travelers because it can be drawn on in different European countries.

B 10 Übung • Was suchst du?

As an expansion, add to the dialog the idea that the person who asks wants to join the other person. He or she wants to do the same activity.

A: Was suchst du?
B: Die Post. Ich möchte telefonieren.
A: Oh gut! Ich möchte auch telefonieren. Dort drüben ist die Post.

B 11 ERKLÄRUNG

Concentrate on the position of **möchten** in a sentence. The students have already practiced **ich möchte** with various verbs. Now make **du möchtest** and **Möchtest du . . . ?** active using the following role-play. Tell the students to imagine that they are spending a month with a German family who try hard to make them welcome and ask about their wishes. What would the family ask? Put the students in groups of three to four, one playing the American, the others the German father and/or mother and sister or brother. Have each family member make up three questions typical for that role.

VATER Möchtest du nach Amerika telephonieren?
MUTTER Möchtest du etwas essen?
SOHN Möchtest du Fussball sehen?
TOCHTER Möchtest du einkaufen gehen?

Have the American guest answer briefly: **Ja, gern. Nein, danke. Später.**

B 12 Übung • Was möchten diese Leute machen?

As a variation, have the students form questions instead of statements, using the subjects and pictograms given.

SLOWER–PACED LEARNING Have the students go through all the forms with one pictogram at a time before they move on to the next action.

B 13 Übung • Hör gut zu!

Part A. You are going to identify pictorial symbols found in an airport. For example, you hear, **1. Wo ist das Telefon?** You write the number 1 in row A under the symbol for telephone. Let's begin. **Fangen wir an!**

2. Wo ist der Ausgang?
3. Wo sind die Schliessfächer?
4. Wo ist die Bank?
5. Wo ist der Geschenkladen?
6. Wo ist die Auskunft?
7. Wo ist das Restaurant?
8. Wo ist die Post?

Now check your answers. The sequence of numbers in row A from left to right should be: *4, 8, 3, 7, 6, 1, 5, 2.*

Part B. In this section you will hear a question and an incomplete answer telling you where you can find what you are looking for. For example, you hear, **1. Ich möchte telefonieren. —Dort drüben ist das ______.** You write the number 1 in row B under the symbol for telephone. Let's begin. **Fangen wir an!**

2. Ich möchte etwas essen und trinken. —Dort drüben ist das ______. *Restaurant*
3. Ich möchte mit dem Bus nach Köln. —Dort drüben ist der ______. *Ausgang*
4. Entschuldigung! Ich möchte etwas fragen. —Dort drüben ist die ______. *Auskunft*
5. Ich sammle Briefmarken, und ich möchte gern deutsche Briefmarken haben. —Dort drüben ist die ______. *Post*
6. Ich möchte ein Geschenk kaufen. —Dort drüben ist der ______. *Geschenkladen*
7. Ich fliege in acht Stunden weiter. Ich möchte mit dem Bus nach Köln, aber ich habe so viel Gepäck. —Dort drüben sind die ______. *Schliessfächer*
8. Ich brauche jetzt deutsches Geld. Wo kann ich Dollar in D-Mark wechseln? —Dort drüben ist die ______. *Bank*

Now check your answers. The sequence of numbers in row B from left to right should be: 8, 5, 7, 2, 4, 1, 6, 3. *Now read each item again with the complete answer.*

B 14 Schreibübung • Wo ist die Post?

SLOWER–PACED LEARNING Help the students write variations of the dialog by giving them cues. Include some people so they can also use **wen.**

die Bank — Geld wechseln/Reiseschecks kaufen
der Lehrer — etwas fragen/etwas holen

B 15 WIE KOMMT PETER NACH NEUSS?

Have the students listen to the conversation with their books closed and see if they understand most of it, particularly if the map is shown on an overhead transparency. Ask questions such as **Wie kommt Peter von Frankfurt nach Köln? Wie weit ist das? Wie messen die Deutschen, in Kilometern oder in Meilen?** Repeat the conversation. As you work with the two new expressions, **mit dem Flugzeug** and **mit der Bahn,** review all the means of transportation from Unit 2. Ask the students questions such as **Wie kommst du in die Schule? Wie kommst du von hier nach New York?**

B 16 Ein wenig Landeskunde

Ask the students if they have seen measurements in kilometers, and where (speed-limit signs in some areas, speedometers of some cars). Explain that in the German-speaking countries, other measurements, such as height and weight, are also indicated in the metric system. You might have the students measure or weigh some objects using a dual-system tape measure or scale.

B 17 DIE ZAHLEN VON 20 BIS 1 000

Teach 20–100, counting aloud every number for at least two sets of tens.

Then stagger the numbers, writing numerals on the board as you say the numbers. Work especially with sound and spelling changes and with compound numbers.

zwei — zwölf — zwanzig
elf — zwölf
vierzehn — vierzig
sechs — sechzehn — sechzig
sieben — siebzehn — siebzig
zweiundzwanzig

Teach the hundreds in sequence. Work with 100 (= **einhundert** or **hundert;** pronounced **hundert** as opposed to *hundred* in English).

B18 Übung • Lies die Zahlen!

Practice until the students can say these numbers well. Then have them add the next number or the next two numbers: 22, 23 or 22, 23, 24.

B19 Übung • Jetzt bist du dran

SLOWER–PACED LEARNING Do one part of the activities at a time. (Have the students say how to get there and then find how far it is.)

OBJECTIVES **To socialize:** exchange money; make a phone call; **to exchange information:** read a flight monitor; express flight numbers, departure times, and gate numbers

CULTURAL BACKGROUND It is frequently necessary to exchange money in Europe because borders are so close. Many people who travel often carry different currencies to avoid having to exchange money for a short trip.

MOTIVATING ACTIVITY Monetary units and the exchange rate hold great interest for students. Using foreign coins and bills is an exciting cultural experience. The following materials will be useful in introducing Section C:

1. A collection of real D-Mark bills and coins for showing around
2. If possible, a real German coin purse and a German billfold
3. Toy money for use in activities
4. Copies of exchange rate listings from newspapers

C1 Peter wechselt Geld 

Have the students listen to the whole conversation. This dialog is ideal for listening practice since it has several give-aways: **Dollar, D-Mark,** and a familiar introductory sentence. Ask some easy comprehension questions: **Geht Peter zur Bank oder zur Post? Was braucht er, D-Mark oder Dollar? Warum?**

Read the dialog with the class, taking the role first of the bank clerk, then of Peter. First explain the term **Kurs:**

Ich habe einen Dollar. Das sind ______ D-Mark.
Der Kurs ist heute ______ DM.
Die Wechselkurse für D-Mark, Schilling und Schweizer Franken stehen in der Zeitung. Was ist heute der Kurs? Mal sehen! (Read some rates, for example: **1 Dollar = ______ Franken)**

Have pairs of students read the dialog. Ask questions about the photo: **Wie heisst die Bank? Was für Geldsorten verkauft die Bank? Was macht der Mann im Foto? Warum?**

CHALLENGE Have the students read the dialog, altering the currency and looking on the chart for the appropriate exchange rate. (See the teacher's notes to Try Your Skills 3 for the names of currencies.) They could also add a few additional lines, such as **Guten Tag. Sie möchten, bitte? Was ist der Kurs? Wieviel D-Mark sind das?**

C2 DAS DEUTSCHE GELD

If you have real German money, you might want to use it to teach the coins and bills. Have the students listen to the material and follow in their books. Have them say these difficult phrases aloud. Ask questions such as **Wie viele deutsche Geldscheine gibt es? Welchen Geldschein findest du schön? Was sind die Mark-Münzen? Haben wir Dollar-Münzen?**

Have the students make change with toy money. Have one student count out the bills and coins, the other one verify.

A: Ich möchte 20 DM wechseln. Ich brauche Kleingeld.
B: Also, hier sind zehn Mark.
A: Zehn Mark.
B: Und ein fünf-Mark-Stück.
A: Fünfzehn Mark.
B: Und vier ein-Mark-Stücke.
A: Neunzehn Mark.
B: Und zwei fünfzig-Pfennig-Stücke.
A: Das sind zwanzig Mark. Danke.
B: Bitte.

As a variation, students use a short version: **fünfmal eine Mark.**

C3 Ein wenig Landeskunde

Have the students bring in a newspaper clipping with the current exchange rate for U.S. dollars. Compare the listings with those in the text. **Ist der Kurs heute besser oder schlechter? Was bekomme ich heute für einen Dollar? Für wen ist der Kurs gut, für die Deutschen oder die Amerikaner?**

C4 Übung • Rollenspiel

As preparation for the exercise, have the students referring to C2, decide how to make change and write it out for each sum given.

SLOWER–PACED LEARNING Have the students, following the example, identify the coins and bills in change that has already been made.

ANSWERS

1. Das sind ein 50-Mark-Schein, ein 20-Mark-Schein, ein 5-Mark-Stück, ein 2-Mark-Stück, ein Markstück, ein 50-Pfennig-Stück, ein 10-Pfennig-Stück.
2. Das sind ein 100-Mark-Schein, ein 20-Mark-Schein, ein 10-Mark-Schein, ein 5-Mark-Stück, ein Markstück, ein 50-Pfennig-Stück, zwei 10-Pfennig-Stücke, ein 5-Pfennig-Stück.
3. Das sind zwei 100-Mark-Scheine, ein 50-Mark-Schein, ein 20-Mark-Schein, ein 10-Mark-Schein, ein 5-Mark-Stück, ein Markstück, ein 50-Pfennig-Stück, vier 10-Pfennig-Stücke, vier Pfennig.
4. Das sind drei 100-Mark-Scheine, ein 50-Mark-Schein, ein 10-Mark-Schein, ein 5-Mark-Stück, vier 10-Pfennig-Stücke, ein 5-Pfennig-Stück, zwei Pfennig.

C5–6

C5 Schreibübung • In der Bank

To expand the activity, have the students write out dialogs for amounts of money other than one hundred dollars.

C6 TELEFONIEREN IST NICHT SCHWER

First introduce the paragraph on page 152 using a wall telephone (real or drawn on cardboard): **Telefonieren ist nicht schwer. Das ist der Hörer. Ich hebe den Hörer ab,** and so forth. Repeat this once or twice. Have the students repeat the key parts of the procedure and act them out. Next have the students listen to the paragraph with their books closed. Ask easy questions such as **Ist Telefonieren schwer? Was nimmst du ab?** Have pairs of students refer to their books as one plays a nervous foreign student, the other a German.

A: Ich möchte telefonieren, aber . . .
B: Telefonieren ist wirklich nicht schwer.
A: Nein? Was mache ich?
B: Du hebst den Hörer ab, steckst Münzen in den Apparat und wählst die Nummer.
A: Das ist alles? Danke!

Introduce the section at the top of page 153 through actions and drawings.

Das Telefon klingelt. Rrrrrr! Es ist nicht besetzt.
Das Telefon macht tüt-tüt-tüt-tüt-tüt. Es ist besetzt.
Hier sind viele Telefonzellen.
Alle sind besetzt. (Draw on board.)
(Erase one person.) Hier, diese Telefonzelle ist frei!
Oh, der Apparat geht nicht. Er ist kaputt. Schade!

Repeat several times, having the students repeat key phrases. Then have the students react to your cues for ringing, busy signal, and out of order. Ask questions about the pictures and captions. Ask the students to tell about Peter's experience. **(Peter Seber kommt in Frankfurt an. Er möchte telefonieren. Aber . . .)**

Have the students listen to the telephone conversation in the third part and read along. Repeat the conversation. Demonstrate new vocabulary with examples such as the following: **Peter kommt um 13 Uhr 10 in Frankfurt an. Nedels sind um 13 Uhr 10 da. Sie sind pünktlich da.** Read the dialog with the class, taking the part of Frau (Herr) Nedel. Ask questions, taking the exchange out of sequence, and see if the students can respond: **Seid ihr pünktlich da? Wo bist du denn?**

Have the students write their name and a German telephone number on a piece of paper and exchange it with a partner. Tell them to call each other, identify themselves, and ask where the other person is.

A: (dials number, says it aloud)
B: Hier (last name).
A: Ja, hier ist ______ .
B: Ach, du bist's, ______! Wo bist du denn?
A: In ______. Im Flughafen.
B: Oh, gut!

C7 Übung • Stimmt! Stimmt nicht!

As a variation, have the students make up some questions to ask one another. These also should be answerable with **Stimmt!** or **Stimmt nicht!**

C8 Ein wenig Landeskunde

Ask the students if they know any other environment in which 24-hour time is used. Some may know that this system is used by the U.S. military services.

C9 Übung • Wann fliegst du?

Before the students start on the mini-dialog, review telling time.

zehn vor, zehn nach	halb (zehn)
Viertel vor, Viertel nach	(zehn) Uhr

SLOWER–PACED LEARNING Use a clock face or digital 24-hour clock to practice telling time. Be sure you can manipulate it easily.

C10 Ein wenig Landeskunde

Tell the students to imagine that they are calling home from Germany. A German friend helps them make the connection, but when they have dialed all the numbers, the line is busy. Have the students act this out in pairs.

A: Ich möchte nach den USA telefonieren.
B: Ja, gut. Die Nummer für die USA is 001. Hast du die Telefonnummer in den USA, auch die Vorwahlnummer?
A: Ja. Also, 001, dann die Vorwahlnummer —___— und dann ___-____.
B: Klingelt es?
A: Nein, es macht tüt-tüt-tüt.
B: Das Telefon ist besetzt. Versuch es später noch einmal!

Have the students keep a record of the information about how to call the U.S. from abroad.

C11 WIE SAGT MAN DAS?

Point out the differences in identifying oneself on the phone between Americans and German speakers.

U.S.	German-speaking countries
Hello?	Schmitt.
The Smith residence.	Hier Schmitt.
Andrew Smith.	Andreas Schmitt.

C12 Übung • Am Telefon

As a variation, have the students add questions **(Wie? Wann? Wie bitte?)** and repetitions because the connection is very bad.

CHALLENGE As a writing assignment, have the students compose a telephone call that includes all the common behaviors and responses plus some misunderstandings due to a poor connection. They should include such phrases as **(wir sind) pünktlich da** and **Bis bald!**

KAPITEL 5

C13–SKILLS 1

C13 WANN GEHT DER FLUG NACH KÖLN?

Review the letters of the alphabet used in the flight numbers. Have the students look closely at the monitor. Ask questions such as **Wer fliegt nach Bristol? Was meint ihr, wie spät ist es hier am Flughafen? Ist Peters Flug noch auf dem Monitor?**

C14 Übung • Rollenspiel

As an expansion, have the student who is receiving the information jot down the time and the gate number of the departing flight.

C15 Übung • Hör gut zu!

You will hear six flight announcements for planes going at different times to different destinations. Listen carefully to each announcement and write the departure gate for each flight announcement in the appropriate box—that is, next to the city announced under the correct departure time. For example, you hear, **1. Der Lufthansa-Flug LH 404 nach New York, Abflug um 17 Uhr 10 von Ausgang A17.** You write *A17* in the row beside *New York* below *17:10*. **Fangen wir an!**

2. Flug IA 72 der Iberia Airlines nach Madrid, planmässiger Abflug um 16:45, Ausgang B53. *B53: beside **Madrid,** below **16:45***
3. Pan-Am Flug PA 827 nach Tel Aviv, Abflug jetzt um 18:30, Ausgang A68. *A68: beside **Tel Aviv,** below **18:30***
4. Der Lufthansa Flug LH 1268 nach Hamburg, planmässiger Abflug um 16:05, Ausgang B48. *B48: beside **Hamburg,*** below ***16:05***
5. Die Maschine der Air–France, Flugnummer AF 431 nach Paris, fliegt jetzt um 15:15 von Ausgang B35 ab. *B35: beside **Paris,** below **15:15***
6. Flug SA 30 der Sabena Airlines nach Brüssel fliegt um 17:45 von Ausgang A22 ab. *A22: beside **Brüssel,** below **17:45***

Now check your answers. *Read each announcement again and give the correct answer.*

TRY YOUR SKILLS

OBJECTIVE To recombine communicative functions, grammar, and vocabulary

CULTURAL BACKGROUND Usually, employees at information centers in Europe must have a working knowledge of several languages. This is also true for many store employees. Stores often post signs stating which languages are spoken.

1 An der Auskunft

Have the students listen to the paragraph and read along. Do scanning, taking sentences out of sequence and making slight changes, for example:

Ich spreche ______.
Ich arbeite von ______.
Ich bin manchmal auch ______.
Manchmal sind die Fragen ______.

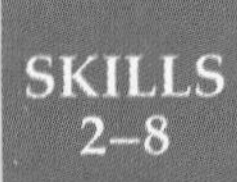

Ask **Welche Fragen sind normal? Welche Fragen sind sehr blöd?** Have the students imagine that they have Silvia's job and answer the questions, using information from previous parts of the unit where needed.

2 Übung • Rollenspiel

Have the students do the role-play as suggested, but have the information booth attendant repeat the pertinent information.

A: Wie weit ist es nach Hamburg?
B: Nach Hamburg? Moment mal. Das sind 495 km.

3 Übung • Geld wechseln

Before the students do the role-play, teach the terms for the foreign currencies they are to exchange for D-Mark.

Währungen

österreichische Schilling (öS)
schwedische Kronen (skr)
Schweizer Franken (sfrs)
US Dollar (US $)
spanische Peseten (Ptas.)

Be sure that the mathematics does not get in the way in this exercise; use 100 each time as the amount to be exchanged.

4 Übung • Am Telefon

SLOWER–PACED LEARNING As a preparation for the dialog, use the chart to ask the students specific directed questions about two cities: **Du fährst von ______ bis ______. Wann geht der Zug? Wann bist du in ______?**

5 Schreibübung • An Bord

CHALLENGE To expand the activity, have the students bring in topics other than destination. They could, for example, discuss hobbies and school.

6 Übung • Ach du Schreck!

To expand the activity, bring in vocabulary from other units, such as names of school supplies that might be needed on a trip.

7 Übung • Was passt zusammen?

CHALLENGE First have the students match the items. Then have them make up a different response to each item in the left column.

8 Übung • Hör gut zu!

You will hear five brief conversations. Listen carefully and decide where each conversation takes place. For example, you hear:

A: Bleibst du lange in Deutschland?
B: Fünf Wochen. Und du?
A: Ich bleibe acht Wochen, zwei Monate.
B: Prima! —Du, sag, wann sind wir in Frankfurt?
A: Um 7 Uhr 40. Warum?
B: Ich möchte um 9 Uhr 10 den Zug nach Kassel nehmen.

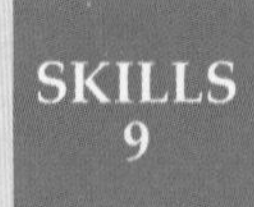

You place your check mark in the row labeled ***im Flugzeug,*** because this conversation probably took place in an airplane. Let's begin. **Fangen wir an!**

1. A: Hier Weiss!
B: Tag, Ursel! Hier ist die Renate!
A: Was? Renate, ja wo bist du? Kommst du her?
B: Du, ich bin im Flughafen, und ich möchte nur schnell guten Tag sagen. Ich fliege in zwanzig Minuten weiter.
A: Was, du kommst nicht? Du besuchst uns aber bald einmal.
B: Du, in zwei Wochen fliege ich zurück, und da möchte ich zwei Tage zu euch kommen!
A: Du, das ist prima!
B: Du, Ursel, ich muss gehen, mein Flug wartet nicht. Tschüs! Bis bald!
A: Tschüs! Guten Flug! *am Telefon*

2. A: Ja, bitte?
B: Ich brauche ein Buch.
A: Tja, was möchten Sie?
B: Ein Hobbybuch für einen Freund. Er sammelt gern.
A: Dort drüben haben wir Hobbybücher.
B: Danke!
A: Bitte! *im Geschenkladen*

3. A: Ich möchte weiter nach München fliegen. Wann geht der nächste Flug, bitte?
B: Moment, bitte! Nach München, da ist ein Lufthansa-Flug um 13 Uhr 40, Flug Nummer LH 783.
A: Und wann bin ich in München?
B: Um 14 Uhr 30.
A: Danke!
B: Bitte! *an der Auskunft*

4. A: Den Pass, bitte! Wie lange bleiben Sie in Deutschland?
B: Fünf Wochen.
A: Was machen Sie hier?
B: Ich mache Ferien, und ich besuche Freunde.
A: Gut! Na, dann schöne Ferien!
B: Danke! *an der Passkontrolle*

5. A: Ich brauche deutsches Geld.
B: Ja, wieviel möchten Sie denn wechseln?
A: 50 Dollar, bitte.
B: Gut! 50 Dollar, das sind . . . 107 Mark. *in der Bank*

Now check your answers. *Read each dialog again and give the correct answer.*

9 Schreibübung • Ich möchte . . .

As a variation, make cards with the pictograms on them and use them for a speed drill with cues as shown and with questions. To expand, have the students respond using a pronoun: **Wo ist die Toilette? — Sie ist da drüben, rechts.**

SLOWER–PACED LEARNING Hold up the cards and have the students name the object. Be sure they include the article each time.

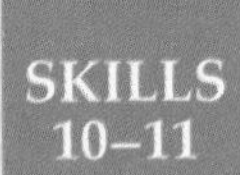

10 Schreibübung • Was fragen die Leute?

As a variation, have the students give as many questions as possible for a given answer. This requires the use of many different verbs.

Example: *Um 16 Uhr.* Wann fliegst du ab?
kommst du an?
bist du in . . . ?
geht der Flug?
rufst du an?

1. *Dort drüben, links.*
2. *Ich besuche Verwandte.*
3. *100 D-Mark.*

11 Aussprache-, Lese- und Schreibübungen

1. Remember to use /l/ as in *million* when producing the German sound
/l/ /l/. Listen and repeat:
Geld, Film, Köln, voll, mal, Zoll, fliegen, bleiben, planen, holen, fehlen, Meile, Kilometer, telefonieren, landen, alles, Dollar
/x/ The following words review the **ach**-sound. Listen and repeat:
Woche, nach, Schliessfach, Schach, Buch, machen, machst, besuchen, besucht, besuchst, Wochenende, Schulsachen, Fach, Mittwoch
/ü/ /ö/ The following words review /ü/ and /ö/. Listen and repeat.
Bücher, Frühjahr, Schüler, Reiseführer; Münze, Mütter, zurück, fünfzig; schöne Ferien, hören; möchte, Köln

2. In this section you will practice reading the words printed in your textbook on page 159. Pay attention to the following:
ch 1. In the following group of words, both the **ich**-sound and the **ach**-sound are used. Can you discover a rule as to when to use the **ich**-sound and when to use the **ach**-sound? Listen and repeat: **schlecht, Fach, nichts, Woche, durch, Buch, manchmal, leicht, auch, möchte, nach.**
ng 2. The letter combination **ng** in words like **Junge** represents a single sound, similar to the sound at the end of the English word *bring*. Listen and repeat: **Junge, lange, Ausgang, Inge.**
j 3. The letter **j** always represents a /y/ sound as at the beginning of the English word *yes*. Listen and repeat: **ja, Jahr, Jens, jetzt, Junge.**
s, ss 4. The letter **s** can be a /s/ sound as in the English word *post*. The letters **ss** always represent this sound. Listen and repeat: **aus, Ausgang, Post, alles, nichts, etwas; Pass, essen, Schliessfach.**
s 5. The letter **s** can also represent a /z/ sound as in the English word *zebra*. It has this sound if it begins a word and is followed by a vowel, or if it stands within a word at the beginning of a syllable. Listen and repeat: **sagen, suchen, seine, sieben, segeln, selten; Reise, besetzt, besuchen, lesen.**
v 6. The letter **v** represents a /f/ sound as in the English word *for*. Listen and repeat: **vier, vor, von, viel, voll, Vati, Vater, Verwandte, verlieren.**

3. Now close your textbook and write the sentences you hear.
1. Der Junge ist sieben Jahre.
2. Ich besuche sie jetzt.
3. Jens und Inge lesen selten.
4. Suchst du auch den Ausgang?

WAS KANNST DU SCHON?

Have the students write on a card the three items of information called for in the first part, in note form (not complete sentences), to remind themselves of what their answer is. Have them circulate and ask three others the questions.

In the first part, use the pictogram cards in the variation for Try Your Skills 9. Form two groups of students. When you hold up a card, one group should ask the question and the other give an answer.

Use a clock you can manipulate easily to elicit time answers. Use the monitor in C13 to elicit information about flights.

WORTSCHATZ

Have the students pick out of the list all the cognates, the words whose meanings they would guess even if they had no knowledge of German.

WORTSCHATZÜBUNGEN

Have the students write the compound nouns on the list in the following pattern: **der Flug + das Ticket = das Flugticket.**

Ask the students to demonstrate their understanding of the little words that they have learned **(zurück, weiter, noch, nach, mal, von, durch, usw.)** by using each word in a sentence of their own.

Have the students come up with sentences illustrating the difference between words that are easily confused, for example: **Alle gehen durch die Passkontrolle. Peter hat alles für die Reise.**

nach — noch wen — wann wo — wohin
da ist/sind — es gibt

ZUM LESEN

OBJECTIVE To read for practice and pleasure

KÖLN AM RHEIN 

Köln *(Cologne)* was one of the northern outposts of the Roman empire. Its name is of Roman (Latin) origin: *colonia,* or "colony." To this day the city has structures left from that time. This is true for many cities, but **Köln** holds the greatest collection of artifacts from the Roman empire in its famous **Römisch-Germanisches Museum,** built on a former Roman site. During the

relatively recent building of the museum, a large mosaic of Dionysos, the Greek god of wine, was discovered on what was formerly the floor of a Roman house. Another great cultural attraction of **Köln** is the magnificent cathedral, the **Kölner Dom.**

Have the students read the captions and look at the pictures. Ask questions on both the text and the photos, such as **An welchem Fluss liegt Köln? Warum heisst das Schiff „Köln-Düsseldorfer"?**

Tell the students to imagine that they are Peter and are writing a postcard to their parents from **Köln.** What would Peter write? Have them refer to the photos.

EIN KLEINES MISSVERSTÄNDNIS 

This reading selection lends itself well to silent reading by the whole class, since the content is largely familiar and the story line not too difficult. Have the students read the whole story for global meaning, then go on to the comprehension questions in English.

Have the students read the selection in groups, taking the roles of narrator, Gabi, Bärbel, and Bill. Ask them to use lots of expression.

Übung • Hast du die Geschichte verstanden?

Have the students cite the first evidence they see that the young American might not be Will Baden. Ask how the mix-up could have occured on the part of both parties.

Übung • Stimmt! Stimmt nicht!

CHALLENGE Have the students make up some more statements. Then have the class react to these with **Stimmt!** or **Stimmt nicht!**

Übung • Wer ist wer?

As a variation, have the students tell about each character in the first person. Have them take the role of one person and tell about their part in the story.

KAPITEL **5**

Auf nach Köln!

It is interesting and fun to travel to a foreign country, especially if you have been learning the language of that country. In Europe, traveling is easy because the countries are so close together. Young Europeans often spend their vacations with families in different countries. There are also many student exchanges between the United States and European countries. Young people participate in exchanges between schools, and they travel privately or with groups, sometimes with their families, visiting friends and relatives abroad.

In this unit you will:

SECTION A	talk about going to Germany and what you need to take
SECTION B	ask for information and give directions
SECTION C	exchange money, make a phone call, tell official time
TRY YOUR SKILLS	use what you've learned
ZUM LESEN	read for practice and pleasure

For teaching suggestions, see the Teacher's Notes preceding this unit, pp. T94–T113.

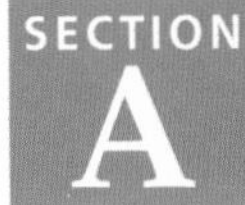

talking about going to Germany; what to take on the trip

Many young people, Americans and Germans alike, travel abroad, especially in the summer. They may be in an exchange program, or they may be visiting friends and relatives abroad. Where do they go? What do they take on the trip?

A1 Auf nach Deutschland!

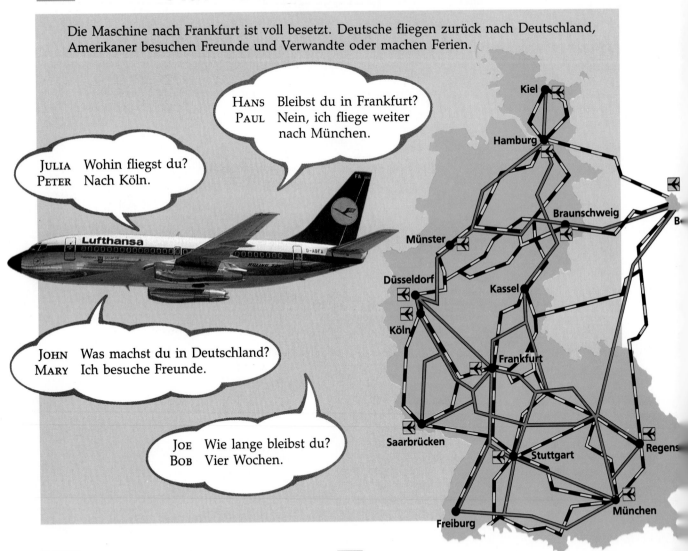

Die Maschine nach Frankfurt ist voll besetzt. Deutsche fliegen zurück nach Deutschland, Amerikaner besuchen Freunde und Verwandte oder machen Ferien.

HANS Bleibst du in Frankfurt?
PAUL Nein, ich fliege weiter nach München.

JULIA Wohin fliegst du?
PETER Nach Köln.

JOHN Was machst du in Deutschland?
MARY Ich besuche Freunde.

JOE Wie lange bleibst du?
BOB Vier Wochen.

A2 Übung • Stimmt! Stimmt nicht!

1. Die Maschine fliegt nach Köln. Stimmt nicht!
2. Die Maschine ist voll besetzt. Stimmt!
3. Deutsche fliegen zurück nach Amerika. Stimmt nicht!
4. Amerikaner machen Ferien. Stimmt!
5. Mary fliegt weiter nach Köln. Stimmt nicht!
6. Paul besucht Freunde. Stimmt nicht!
7. Bob bleibt fünf Wochen. Stimmt nicht!
8. Peter fliegt nach Köln. Stimmt!

Photo p. 135, top left: Köln: Ausflugsdampfer an der Deutzer Brücke

A3 Übung • Wohin fliegen die Schüler? 

Köln Kölner Dom

Peter . . . fliegt nach Köln.

München Dom und Rathaus

Paul . . . fliegt nach München.

Berlin Kongresshalle

Julia . . . fliegt nach Berlin.

Hamburg Die Maxim Gorki

Mary . . . fliegt nach Hamburg.

Wien Naturhistorisches Museum

Joe . . . fliegt nach Wien.

A4 Übung • Wohin fliegst du?

Schau auf die Karte auf Seite 136. Welche Städte möchtest du sehen und welche nicht?

A: Wohin fliegst du?
B: Ich fliege nach . . .
A: Prima! . . . ist toll!

A: Fliegst du auch nach Hamburg?
B: Nein, ich fliege nicht nach Hamburg.
A: Schade.

A5 Übung • Bleibst du hier oder fliegst du weiter? 

A: Wohin fliegst du?
B: Ich fliege nach Frankfurt.
A: Bleibst du in Frankfurt?
B: Nein, ich fliege weiter nach München.

Frankfurt / München
1. Frankfurt / Berlin
2. München / Wien
3. Köln / Hamburg

A6 Übung • Und du? Wie steht's mit dir?

1. Hast du Freunde oder Verwandte in Deutschland?
2. Wo in Deutschland?
3. Besuchst du deine Freunde manchmal?
4. Wie oft besuchst du sie?
5. Wie lange bleibst du?
6. Wohin fliegst du manchmal?
7. Was machst du dort?

A7 WAS BRAUCHT PETER FÜR DIE REISE? 

Peter Seber, a young American, is getting everything ready for his trip to Germany. What are some of the things he needs? What do you need when you take a trip?

Vati, wo ist das Flugticket? Und der Reiseführer?
Peter, hier hab' ich den Pass, das Flugticket und den Reiseführer.
Prima! Danke, Vati! Und wo sind die Reiseschecks? Ich brauche auch Geld.
Stimmt. Hier sind die Reiseschecks. Hast du jetzt alles? Was brauchst du noch?

Ich brauche . . .
WÖRTERBUCH ENGLISCH
Deutsch-Englisch
Englisch-Deutsch
Pawlak
AGFA COLOR

das Wörterbuch

den Walkman

die Musikkassetten

das Adressbuch

die Kamera

den Film

und die Spielkarten!

Wer ist Peter?

Peter Seber ist Amerikaner. Er ist 15 Jahre alt und wohnt in New York. Peters Vater ist aus Österreich, die Mutter aus Kalifornien.

Die Sebers haben Freunde in Deutschland, die Familie Nedel in Neuss. Peter besucht die Nedels. Er fliegt morgen nach Frankfurt und von dort weiter nach Köln.

A 8 Übung • Peter plant seine Reise 

Peters Vater fragt:
Wo ist (sind) . . .?

Peter schaut nach, ob er alles hat:
Ich habe . . .

ist der Pass
ist das Flugticket
sind die Reiseschecks
sind die Spielkarten
ist die Kamera
sind die Musikkassetten
ist der Walkman
ist das Wörterbuch
ist der Film
ist der Reiseführer
ist das Adressbuch

die Kamera
den Walkman
den Pass
das Flugticket
den Film
die Spielkarten
das Wörterbuch
den Reiseführer
die Musikkassetten
das Adressbuch
die Reiseschecks

A 9 Übung • Etwas über Peter Seber

1. Wohin fliegt Peter Seber? Nach Deutschland.
2. Was macht er in Deutschland? Er besucht Freunde.
3. Woher sind Peters Vater und Mutter? Peters Vater ist aus Österreich, die Mutter aus Kalifornien.

A 10 WAS SUCHST DU? WEN FRAGST DU?

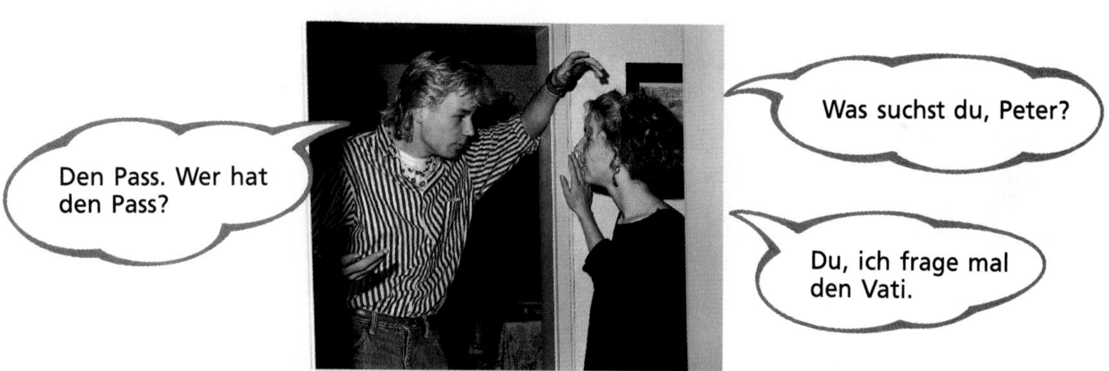

Was suchst du, Peter?
Den Pass. Wer hat den Pass?
Du, ich frage mal den Vati.

A 11 Übung • Wer hat was?

A: Wer hat . . .?

B: Du, ich frage mal . . .

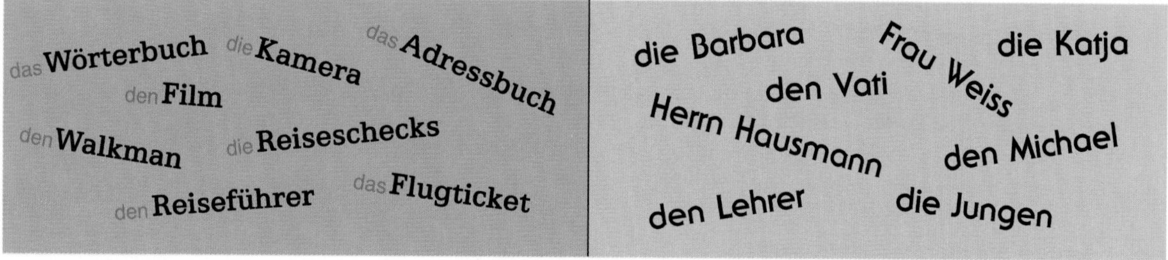

das Wörterbuch
die Kamera
das Adressbuch
den Film
den Walkman
die Reiseschecks
den Reiseführer
das Flugticket
die Barbara
Frau Weiss
die Katja
den Vati
Herrn Hausmann
den Michael
den Lehrer
die Jungen

A 12 ERKLÄRUNG

The Definite Article, Nominative and Accusative Case

1. Peter asks his father **Wo ist das Flugticket? Und der Reiseführer?** The noun phrases **das Flugticket** and **der Reiseführer** function as subjects and are in the nominative case.
2. Peter's father responds **Hier hab' ich den Pass, das Flugticket und den Reiseführer.** In this sentence, the noun phrases function as direct objects and are in the accusative case.

	Noun Phrase as Subject (Nominative Case)			*Noun Phrase as Direct Object (Accusative Case)*		
Masculine *Feminine* *Neuter*	Wo ist	**der** **die** **das**	Pass? Kamera? Flugticket?	Ich brauche	**den** **die** **das**	Pass. Kamera. Flugticket.
Plural	Wo sind	**die**	Reiseschecks?	Ich brauche	**die**	Reiseschecks.

3. From this chart you can see that subject and direct object are clearly signaled only when the noun is masculine. The noun phrases that contain a feminine, a neuter, or a plural noun are identical when they function as subject or direct object.
4. There are a few masculine nouns that add the ending **-n** or **-en** when used in the accusative case. You have learned **der Herr, der Junge, der Klassenkamerad.**

   Ich frage Herr**n** Sperling. Er fragt den Junge**n.** Sie fragt den Klassenkamerad**en.**

5. There are many verbs that can take a direct object in the accusative case. You have learned the following: **besuchen, brauchen, finden, fragen, gewinnen, haben, hören, machen, sammeln, spielen, suchen, verlieren.**
6. You have been using the interrogative **wer?** and **was?** The accusative forms are **wen?** and **was?**

	Referring to people (one or many)	*Referring to things (one or many)*
Nominative	**wer?** *who?*	**was?** *what?*
Accusative	**wen?** *whom?*	**was?** *what?*

Peter fragt **den Vati.** **Wen** fragt er?
Peter sucht **den Pass.** **Was** sucht er?

A 13 Übung 

Frag mal einen Mitschüler!

A: Was suchst du?
B: Den Pass.
A: Ach so!

A: Ich brauche den Pass.
B: Hier ist er.
A: Danke!

die Reiseschecks/ Hier sind sie.
den Reiseführer/ Hier ist er.
den Walkman/ Hier ist er.

die Kamera/ Hier ist sie.
die Flugtickets/ Hier sind sie. or: das Flugticket/ Hier ist es.
den Pass/ Hier ist er.

A 14 Übung • Wo hast du deine Sachen? 

Frag mal eine Mitschülerin!

A: Wo hast du den Reiseführer?
B: Schau, er ist da!
A: Gut!

A: Du, wie findest du den Reiseführer?
B: Er ist prima.
A: Das finde ich auch.

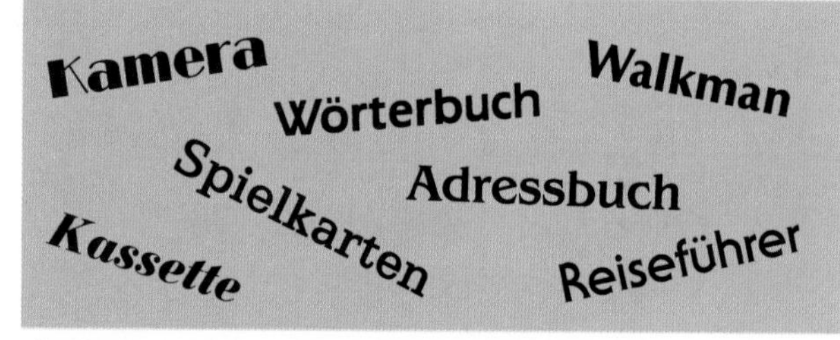

die Kamera, sie/das Wörterbuch, es/den Walkman, ihn/die Spielkarten, sie sind/das Adressbuch, es/die Kassette, sie/den Reiseführer, ihn

A 15 Übung • Wen suchst du? 

A: Wen suchst du?
B: Ich suche Herrn Hausmann.

1. Herr Seber (Herrn Seber)   **2.** Frau Meier (die Frau Meier)   **3.** Jens (den Jens)   **4.** Kristin (die Kristin)   5. der Junge (den Jungen)

A 16 Übung • Wen? oder Was?

A: Peter fragt die Inge.
B: Wie bitte? Wen fragt er?

A: Peter sucht den Pass.
B: Wie bitte? Was sucht er?

1. Peter sucht den Vater. Wen sucht er?
2. Peter sucht das Wörterbuch. Was sucht er?
3. Peter braucht den Film. Was braucht er?
4. Peter braucht den Lehrer. Wen braucht er?
5. Peter hat die Kamera. Was hat er?
6. Peter besucht die Nedels. Wen besucht er?
7. Peter fragt Frau Meier. Wen fragt er?
8. Peter sucht den Walkman. Was sucht er?

A 17 Übung • Merkspiel *Memory Game*

Das Merkspiel heisst: Reisetasche packen

PETER In die Reisetasche packe ich: das Wörterbuch.
INGE In die Reisetasche packe ich: das Wörterbuch und den Reiseführer.
KATJA In die Reisetasche packe ich: das Wörterbuch, den Reiseführer und den Pass.
DU . . .

Have the students put the items in either the backpack or the travel bag. den Film, das Flugticket, den Walkman, das Adressbuch, den Taschenrechner, den Reiseführer, die D-Mark, die Spielkarten, die Kassetten, die Reiseschecks, die Kamera, den Kuli, das Wörterbuch

A 18 Übung • Beim Packen

Peter packt den Rucksack und die Reisetasche.

Was packt er in den Rucksack?

Was packt er in die Reisetasche?

Film
Adressbuch
Reiseführer
Spielkarten
Kamera
Walkman
Kassetten
Kuli
Flugticket
Taschenrechner
D-Mark
Reiseschecks
Wörterbuch

A 19 Übung • Hör gut zu!

For script and answers, see p. T99.

Is it the subject or the direct object? Listen.

	0	1	2	3	4	5	6	7	8	9	10
subject			✓		✓			✓	✓		
direct object	✓	✓		✓		✓	✓			✓	✓

A 20 Übung • Im Flughafen

Du sprichst mit einem deutschen Schüler. Frag ihn oder sie:

1. woher er/sie ist Woher bist du?
2. wohin er/sie fliegt Wohin fliegst du?
3. wann er/sie in . . . ist Wann bist du in . . . ?
4. was er/sie dort macht Was machst du dort/in . . . ?
5. wie lange er/sie dort bleibt Wie lange bleibst du dort?
6. wann er/sie zurück nach Deutschland fliegt Wann fliegst du zurück nach Deutschland?

A 21 Schreibübung • Gespräch im Flugzeug

Peter sitzt im Flugzeug. Er spricht mit einem deutschen Schüler. Was fragt der Schüler? Schreib den Dialog!

SCHÜLER . . .? Wohin fliegst du?
PETER Nach Frankfurt.
SCHÜLER . . .? Bleibst du in Frankfurt?
PETER Nein, ich fliege weiter nach Köln.
SCHÜLER . . .? Was machst du in Köln?
PETER Ich besuche Freunde in Neuss.
SCHÜLER . . .? Wie kommst du nach Neuss?
PETER Mit dem Auto.
SCHÜLER . . .? Wann sind wir in Frankfurt?
PETER Um neun Uhr sind wir in Frankfurt.

Information für junge Reisende

Hallo Junioren, das interessiert Euch bestimmt:
Hello Juniors, some interesting flight jargons:

Airway = Luftstraße
Approach = Anflug
Arrival = Ankunft
Autopilot = Automatische Steuerung
Boarding = Einsteigen
Cargo = Luftfracht
Climb = Steigflug
Duty free = Zollfrei
Exit = Ausgang
Purser = Chefsteward
Terminal = Abfertigungsgebäude

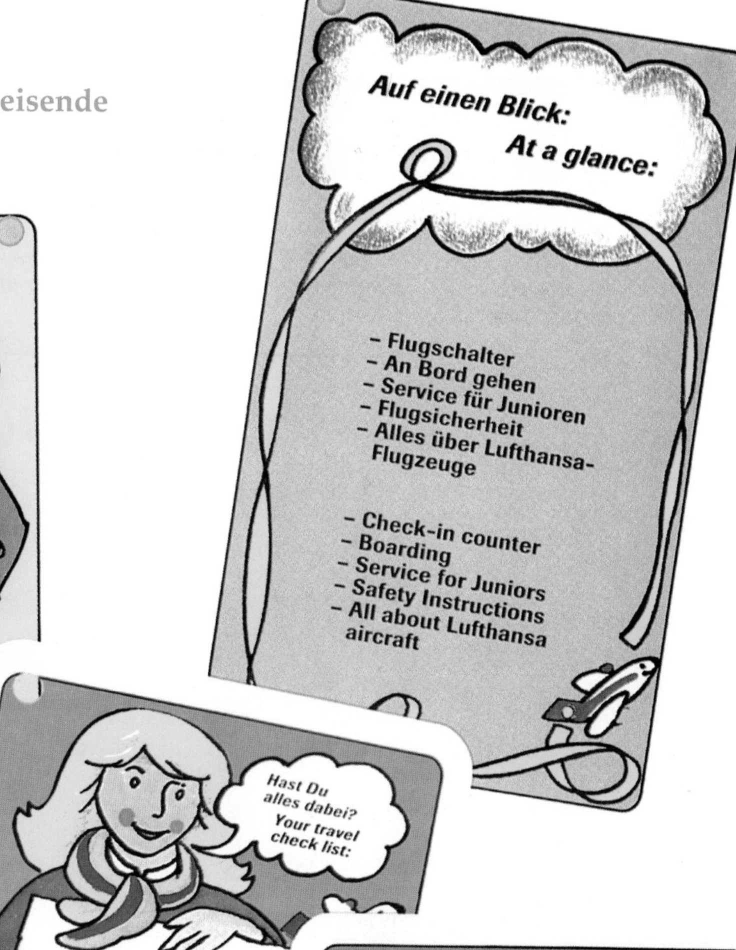

Auf einen Blick:
At a glance:
– Flugschalter
– An Bord gehen
– Service für Junioren
– Flugsicherheit
– Alles über Lufthansa-Flugzeuge
– Check-in counter
– Boarding
– Service for Juniors
– Safety Instructions
– All about Lufthansa aircraft

Hast Du alles dabei?
Your travel check list:

Paß, Flugticket, Gel
Kamera und Filme,
alles zum Anziehen,
Schuhe, Jacke, Mant
Sport-und Badesache

Passport, Ticket, Money, Camera and Films, Clothing, Shoes, Jacket, Coat and Sport and Swimming gear.

Sicherheit Safety

Bei Start und Landung gilt: „Anschnallen" und „Nicht Rauchen". During take-off and landing please fasten your seat-belt and observe the No-smoking sign.

Airport Frankfurt
Frankfurt Main
Lufthansa
Die Lufthansa-Crew wünscht Dir einen guten Flug.
Lufthansa crew wishes you an enjoyable flight.
18 Millionen Fluggäste und 220 000 Starts und Landungen jährlich
Größter deutscher Flughafen
18 Million passengers and 220,000 take-offs and arrivals yearly
Largest german airport.

asking for information, giving directions

When you arrive abroad, you'll have to go through passport control, get your luggage, and go through customs. But even at an airport as big as Frankfurt's, it is easy to get around. There are signs that help you find most airport facilities, and if you don't find what you are looking for—well, you simply ask.

B1 Peter in Frankfurt

Das Flugzeug landet in Frankfurt. Die Reisenden gehen durch die Passkontrolle, sie holen das Gepäck und gehen durch den Zoll.

Ankunft / Arrivals
Nur für Fluggäste / Passengers only
Gepäckausgabe / Baggage Claim

BEAMTER Den Pass, bitte!
PETER Bitte!
BEAMTER Wie lange bleiben Sie?
PETER Vier Wochen.
BEAMTER Gut. Und schöne Ferien!
PETER Danke!

JULIA Hast du alles?
PETER Die Reisetasche fehlt.
JULIA Schau, da ist sie!
PETER Gott sei Dank!

Anmeldefreie Waren
Nothing to declare

Anmeldepflichtige Waren
Goods to declare

Peter hat nichts zu verzollen. Er geht bei Grün durch.

1. der Ausgang 2. die Auskunft 3. der Geschenkladen 4. die Post 5. das Telefon 6. die Wartehalle 7. die Toiletten 8. die Schliessfächer 9. die Bank 10. das Restaurant

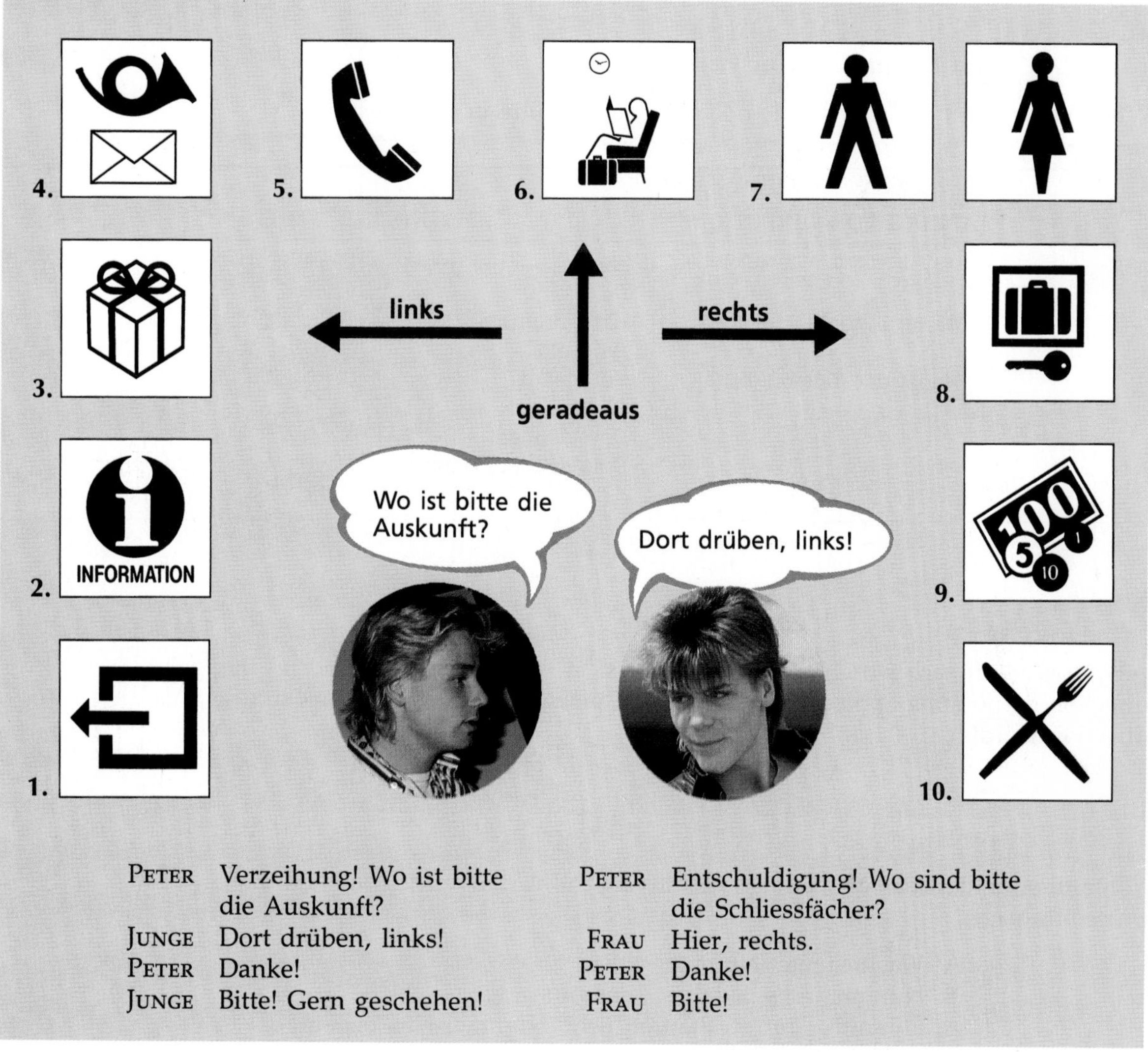

PETER	Verzeihung! Wo ist bitte die Auskunft?
JUNGE	Dort drüben, links!
PETER	Danke!
JUNGE	Bitte! Gern geschehen!

PETER	Entschuldigung! Wo sind bitte die Schliessfächer?
FRAU	Hier, rechts.
PETER	Danke!
FRAU	Bitte!

B2 Übung • Partnerarbeit

Team up with a classmate and practice asking and giving directions. Use the dialogs above and the words and phrases shown below.

Wo ist/sind bitte . . . ?

was?

die Auskunft
die Toilette
das Telefon
der Ausgang
die Schliessfächer (pl)
die Wartehalle
die Post
das Restaurant
der Geschenkladen
die Bank

wo?

Da drüben.
Links.
Hier, rechts.
Dort drüben, links.
Da.
Hier.
Geradeaus.

B3 WIE SAGT MAN DAS?
Asking for and giving directions

When you ask for directions, it is polite to include **bitte** in the question.

ASKING FOR DIRECTIONS	GIVING DIRECTIONS	
	Hier!	Here!
	Da.	There.
Wo ist bitte das Telefon?	Hier, rechts!	Here, on the right!
	Da, links.	There, to the left.
Wo ist das Telefon, bitte?	Geradeaus.	Straight ahead.
	Da drüben. / Dort drüben.	Over there.
	Dort drüben, rechts.	Over there, to the right.

B4 Übung • Wo ist . . .?

As you read off each word or phrase in the list in B3, a classmate indicates the direction by pointing appropriately. Then you point as your partner reads the direction word(s).

B5 Übung • Was bedeuten die Piktogramme?

You and your classmates take turns identifying the various pictograms on the preceding page.

A: Was bedeutet Nummer eins?
B: Nummer eins bedeutet „der Ausgang“.
A: Stimmt! *or* Stimmt nicht! Nummer eins bedeutet . . .

B6 Übung • Was suchst du?

Referring to the pictograms on the preceding page, practice the following dialog with a classmate. Vary the directions.

A: Was suchst du?
B: Ich suche den Ausgang. (die Auskunft/den Geschenkladen/die Post/das Telefon/die Wartehalle/die Toiletten/die Schliessfächer/die Bank/das Restaurant)
A: Dort drüben ist der Ausgang. (Hier/Da/Rechts/Links/Geradeaus/Da drüben)
B: Danke!

B7 Übung • Rollenspiel

Turn your classroom into an airport. Draw pictograms on poster paper. Several students stand in different parts of the classroom, each holding up a pictogram. One student stands behind the information counter. Other students are travelers coming into the airport and asking directions.

B8 WAS SAGEN DIE REISENDEN? 

Ich suche die Auskunft. Ich möchte etwas fragen.

Ich suche das Restaurant. Ich möchte etwas essen und trinken.

Ich suche die Post. Ich möchte telefonieren und Briefmarken kaufen.

Ich suche die Bank. Ich möchte Geld wechseln.

Ich suche den Geschenkladen. Ich möchte ein Geschenk kaufen.

B9 Ein wenig Landeskunde

In Germany, the post office is also the telephone company. For this reason, telephones are located in all post offices, both inside and outside. You will recognize a post office by a plaque with the word **Postamt** printed below either a black eagle or a black posthorn, with a yellow background. All mail boxes and postal vehicles are painted yellow, the postal color. In Germany, the postal service as well as the railroad are owned and operated by the federal government.

B10 Übung • Was suchst du? 

Using the following dialog as a model and the signs above as cues, ask different classmates what they are looking for.

A: Was suchst du?
B: Die Post. Ich möchte telefonieren.
A: Schau! Dort drüben ist die Post.

B 11 ERKLÄRUNG
The **möchte**-*forms*

1. The **möchte**-forms express a wish, conveying the idea of "would like (to)."
2. **Möchte** has the following forms:

ich **möchte** du **möchtest** er, sie, es **möchte**	wir **möchten** ihr **möchtet** sie, Sie **möchten**

3. The **möchte**-forms are often used with another verb. In such sentences there are two verbs:
   a. The inflected verb, that is the verb form whose ending changes to match the subject. The inflected verb is always in the second position.
   b. The infinitive, which is always in last position.

	2nd Position		*Last Position*
Subject	*Inflected Verb*		*Infinitive*
Peter	**möchte**	Geld	**wechseln.**
Du	**möchtest**	ein Geschenk	**kaufen?**

B 12 Übung • Was möchten diese Leute machen?

1. Wir . . .
möchten etwas essen.

2. Peter . . .
möchte telefonieren.

3. Die Jungen . . .
möchten etwas fragen.

4. Ich . . . möchte
ein Geschenk kaufen.

5. . . . du . . .?
Mochtest du Geld wechseln?

6. . . . ihr . . .?
Möchtet ihr ein Geschenk kaufen?

7. Kristin . . .
möchte Geld wechseln.

8. Ich . . .
möchte etwas essen.

9. Wir . . .
möchten telefonieren.

10. . . . Sie . . .?
Möchten Sie etwas fragen?

B 13 Übung • Hör gut zu!

What is each person looking for? Listen.

					INFORMATION			
A	4	8	3	7	6	1	5	2
B	8	5	7	2	4	1	6	3

B14 Schreibübung • Wo ist die Post?

Practice the following conversation with your classmates, varying the form of address according to the person or persons you are speaking to.

A: Peter! Was suchst du?
B: Ich suche die Post.
A: Möchtest du Briefmarken kaufen?
B: Nein, ich möchte telefonieren.

1. You are talking to Mrs. Meier. Was suchen Sie?/Möchten Sie . . .
2. Sabine and Antje are looking for the post office. Was sucht ihr?/Wir suchen/Möchtet ihr/wir möchten
3. You are talking to your friend Paul. Paul! Was suchst du?

Write dialogs modeled on the one above. First address your teacher; then address two friends of yours.

B15 WIE KOMMT PETER NACH NEUSS? 

Before working with the chart below, complete B16–B18; then see B19.

JULIA Wie kommst du nach Neuss, Peter?
PETER Von Frankfurt nach Köln mit dem Flugzeug und von Köln nach Neuss mit dem Auto.
JULIA Wie weit ist es von Frankfurt nach Köln?
PETER Moment mal! — Schau, 189 Kilometer! Das sind ungefähr 120 Meilen.

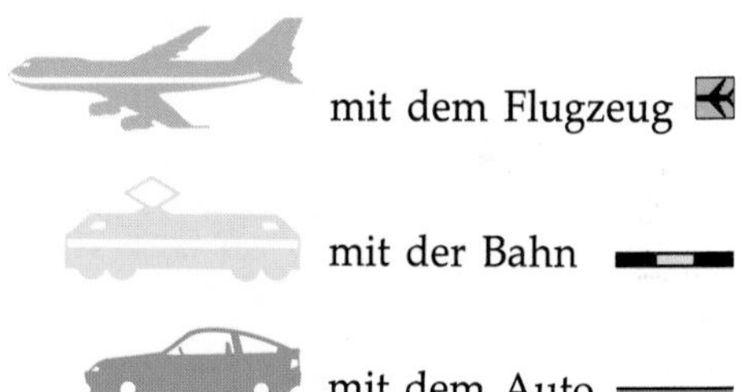

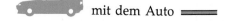

Berlin	Düsseldorf	Frankfurt/M.	Hamburg	Kiel	Köln	München	Münster	Regensburg	Saarbrücken	Stuttgart	Kilometer
	572	555	289	370	569	584	466	499	745	624	Berlin
572		232	427	520	47	621	135	558	332	419	Düsseldorf
555	232		495	588	189	395	326	332	202	217	Frankfurt/M.
289	427	495		93	422	782	271	719	685	700	Hamburg
370	520	588	93		515	875	364	812	778	793	Kiel
569	47	189	422	515		578	150	515	289	376	Köln
584	621	395	782	875	578		715	120	431	220	München
466	135	326	271	364	150	715		652	426	513	Münster
499	558	332	719	812	515	120	652		505	289	Regensburg
795	332	202	685	778	289	431	426	505		226	Saarbrücken
624	419	217	700	793	376	220	513	289	226		Stuttgart

Note that there are only three main routes that connect Berlin with West Germany.

B 16 Ein wenig Landeskunde

In German-speaking countries, the metric system is used to measure distances. One measure of distance is the kilometer. To convert kilometers to miles, you divide the number of kilometers by 1.6.

eine Meile = 1,6 Kilometer
ein Kilometer = 0,62 Meilen

B 17 DIE ZAHLEN VON 20 BIS 1 000

20	21	22	23	24
zwanzig	einundzwanzig	zweiundzwanzig	dreiundzwanzig	vierundzwanzig

30	31	40	50	60	70
dreissig	einundreissig	vierzig	fünfzig	sechzig	siebzig

80	90	100	101	102	103
achtzig	neunzig	hundert	hunderteins	hundertzwei	hundertdrei

200	201	300	400	1000
zweihundert	zweihunderteins	dreihundert	vierhundert	tausend

B 18 Übung • Lies die Zahlen!

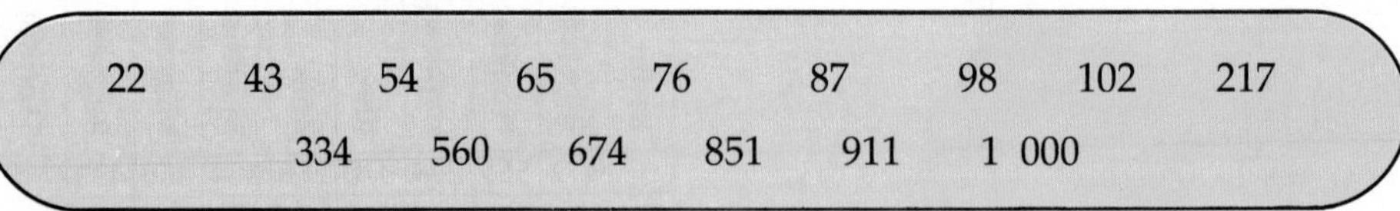

22 43 54 65 76 87 98 102 217
334 560 674 851 911 1 000

zweiundzwanzig, dreiundvierzig, vierundfünfzig, fünfundsechzig, sechsundsiebzig, siebenundachtzig, achtundneunzig, hundertzwei, zweihundertsiebzehn, dreihundertvierunddreissig, fünfhundertsechzig, sechshundertvierundsiebzig, achthunderteinundfünfzig, neunhundertelf, tausend

B 19 Übung • Jetzt bist du dran

1. Schau auf die Karte auf Seite 149! Wie kommst du zum Beispiel von Frankfurt nach Saarbrücken? Jetzt schau auf die Tabelle! Wie weit ist es von Frankfurt nach Saarbrücken? Mit der Bahn. Es sind 202 Kilometer.
2. Deine Klassenkameraden besuchen Freunde und Verwandte in anderen Städten. Wie kommen sie dorthin? Wie weit ist es? Frag sie mal!

exchanging money, making a phone call, and telling official time

Exchanging money, making a phone call—simple things can be a problem in a foreign country unless you know the procedures and have some knowledge of the language. Peter finds out what to do.

C1 Peter wechselt Geld

PETER Ich möchte 50 Dollar wechseln.
BANKANGESTELLTER Wieviel, bitte?
PETER 50 Dollar.
BANKANGESTELLTER In D-Mark?
PETER Ja, bitte!
BANKANGESTELLTER Der Kurs ist heute DM 2,34.
PETER Nicht schlecht.
BANKANGESTELLTER Das sind 117 Mark.
PETER Danke!
BANKANGESTELLTER Bitte! Und schöne Ferien!
PETER Danke!

C2 DAS DEUTSCHE GELD 

Es gibt Scheine:

ein 10-Mark-Schein

ein 20-Mark-Schein

ein 50-Mark-Schein

ein 100-Mark-Schein

und es gibt Münzen:

ein Pfennig

zwei Pfennig

fünf Pfennig

zehn Pfennig

fünfzig Pfennig

ein Markstück

ein 2-Mark-Stück

ein 5-Mark-Stück

C3 Ein wenig Landeskunde

The German bank notes shown in C2 are the most common in circulation. There are also 500-Mark notes and 1000-Mark notes. The bills have different sizes and colors. When you exchange money, the amount of German marks you receive in exchange for your dollars depends on **der Kurs,** *the rate of exchange,* an amount that is fixed daily. For example, the exchange rate on a certain day may be DM 2,40—that means you will get 2 **Mark** and 40 **Pfennig** for each dollar you exchange. Before you exchange money, you can always check the exchange rate on boards posted at the entrance of every bank that has an exchange office. You can also check the rate of exchange in most newspapers.

USA

42-013/19 186

Devisenkurse

1,– US$ = DM 2,40 DM 1,– = 0,42 US$

US$	DM	US$	DM	DM	US$
0,05	0,12	30,–	72,–	0,10	0,04
0,10	0,24	40,–	96,–	0,20	0,08
0,15	0,36	45,–	108,–	0,50	0,21
0,25	0,60	80,–	192,–	1,–	0,42
0,50	1,20	95,–	228,–	2,–	0,83
1,–	2,40	120,–	288,–	5,–	2,08
1,50	3,60	150,–	360,–	10,–	4,17
2,–	4,80	180,–	432,–	20,–	8,33
2,50	6,–	200,–	480,–	50,–	20,84
3,–	7,20	230,–	552,–	100,–	41,67
4,–	9,60	400,–	960,–	150,–	62,51
5,–	12,–	450,–	1.080,–	200,–	83,34
7,50	18,–	800,–	1.920,–	250,–	104,18
10,–	24,–	1.000,–	2.400,–	300,–	125,01
20,–	48,–	5.000,–	12.000,–	400,–	166,68

Bitte berücksichtigen Sie, daß sich die Kurse kurzfristig ändern können.

Deutsche Bank

C4 Übung • Rollenspiel  For answers, see p. T105.

You are the teller at the exchange window. Count out the money as you give it to each customer.

DM 132,00 Das sind zwei 50-Mark-Scheine, ein 20-Mark-Schein, ein 10-Mark-Schein, ein 2-Mark-Stück.

1. DM 78,60
2. DM 136,75
3. DM 286,94
4. DM 365,47

C5 Schreibübung • In der Bank

You want to exchange $100. Write out your conversation with the bank teller.

C6 TELEFONIEREN IST NICHT SCHWER

Telefonieren in Deutschland ist wirklich nicht schwer! Du hebst den Hörer ab, steckst Münzen in den Apparat und wählst die Nummer. Das ist alles.

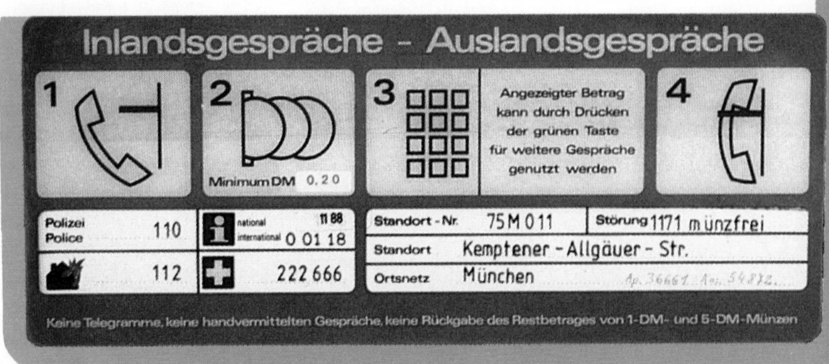

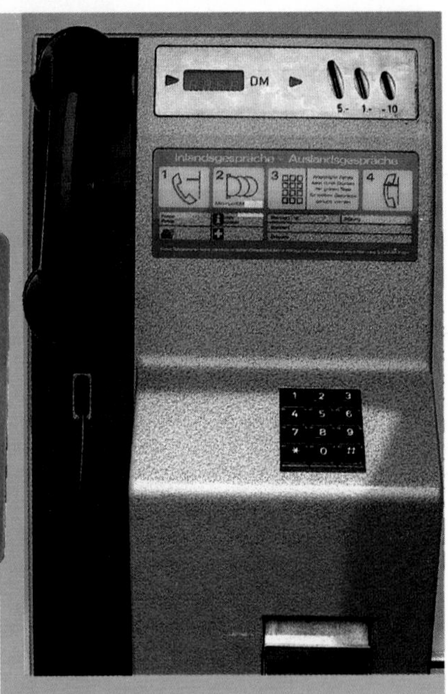

From a phone like this booth both national and international calls can be made. You must be sure to have enough coins to "feed" the phone, or else you'll be cut off! Point out the emergency numbers, information numbers, and Red Cross phone number.

Aber manchmal . . .
sind alle Telefonzellen besetzt . . .

oder der Apparat
geht nicht

Endlich! Aber . . .

Peter versucht es noch einmal. (tüt, tüt, tüt)

PETER	0 3 4 3 1 6 4 2 3
FRAU NEDEL	Hier Nedel.
PETER	Ja, hier Peter Seber.
FRAU NEDEL	Du bist's, Peter! Wo bist du denn?
PETER	In Frankfurt. Im Flughafen.
FRAU NEDEL	Ach so! Und du bist um 13 Uhr 10 in Köln?
PETER	Ja, wie verabredet. Ich habe den Flug LH 368.
FRAU NEDEL	Gut! Wir sind pünktlich da. Bis gleich! Tschüs!
PETER	Auf Wiedersehen!
FRAU NEDEL	Auf Wiederhören!

A typical mail box. Tell your students that the mail carrier never touches the mail when emptying a mail box—a mail bag is pulled out from its track and closed, and an empty bag is inserted.

C7 Übung • Stimmt! Stimmt nicht!

1. Peter ist in Köln. Stimmt nicht!
2. Er ist im Flughafen. Stimmt!
3. Er telefoniert mit Wiebke Nedel. Stimmt nicht!
4. Peter ist um zehn nach eins in Köln. Stimmt!

C8 Ein wenig Landeskunde

In German-speaking countries and in many other places in the world, the 24-hour system of telling time is used on official schedules. When you travel, it is important to know this system. The 24-hour system is based on 24 hours, starting with 1 A.M. One o'clock in the afternoon is **13 Uhr,** 2 P.M. is **14 Uhr,** 12 P.M. (midnight) is **24 Uhr.** For example, a plane departing at 19.30 **(neunzehn Uhr dreissig)** leaves at 7:30 P.M.

C9 Übung • Wann fliegst du?

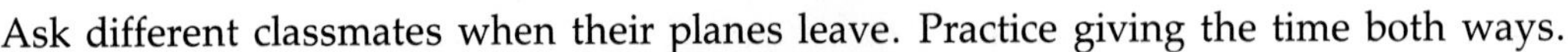

Ask different classmates when their planes leave. Practice giving the time both ways.

A: Wann fliegst du?
B: Um halb sieben. *or*
Um achtzehn Uhr dreissig.

18:30

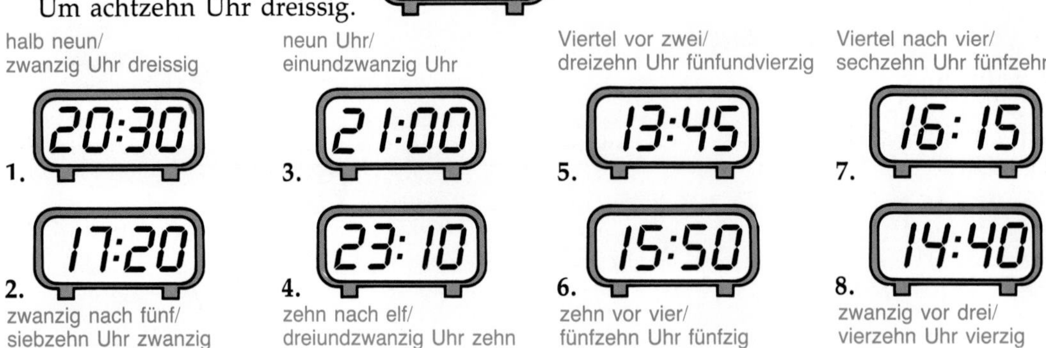

1. halb neun/ zwanzig Uhr dreissig
2. zwanzig nach fünf/ siebzehn Uhr zwanzig
3. neun Uhr/ einundzwanzig Uhr
4. zehn nach elf/ dreiundzwanzig Uhr zehn
5. Viertel vor zwei/ dreizehn Uhr fünfundvierzig
6. zehn vor vier/ fünfzehn Uhr fünfzig
7. Viertel nach vier/ sechzehn Uhr fünfzehn
8. zwanzig vor drei/ vierzehn Uhr vierzig

C10 Ein wenig Landeskunde

The German telephone system is fully automated, and it is very easy to make a telephone call from any public booth. Most public booths carry the sign **Inland/ Ausland,** *National/International,* and from here you can call all over the world. All you need is your access code for a particular country, the area code, and the phone number—and lots of coins, because you have to "feed" the telephone. When calling within Germany, you need **die Vorwahlnummer,** *the area code,* of the city or area you are calling. Here are some area codes for big cities:

Berlin	030	Frankfurt	069	Köln	0221
Düsseldorf	0211	Hamburg	040	München	089

If you want to call the United States from Germany, you must dial the access code for the United States, your area code, and your phone number. The access code for the United States is 001.

C11 WIE SAGT MAN DAS?
Making a phone call

Here are some ways of beginning and ending a phone conversation:

the person who answers says	Nedel. Hier Nedel.
the person who is calling responds with	Hier Peter Seber. Hier ist Peter.
the conversation may end with	Auf Wiederhören! Tschüs! Bis gleich!

C12 Übung • Am Telefon 

Ein Freund ruft an und sagt, wann er kommt.
Du hebst den Hörer ab und sagst:

A: Hier . . .
B: Ja, hier ist . . .
A: Du bist's, . . . ! Wann bist du in Chicago?
B: Um 14 Uhr 10.
A: Prima! Bis gleich! Tschüs!
B: Tschüs!

Du wohnst
1. in Chicago — 14:10
2. in St. Louis — 18:30
um achtzehn Uhr dreissig
3. in Los Angeles — 19:45
um neunzehn Uhr fünfundvierzig

C13 WANN GEHT DER FLUG NACH KÖLN? 

Das ist der Monitor.

FLUG FLIGHT	NACH TO	ÜBER VIA	PLANM. SCHED.	ERW. EXP.	AUSG. GATE	SCHALTER COUNTER
LH 784	HAMBURG		12 00		A72	89-107
SK 626	KOPENHAGEN		12 15		B51	59-72
OA 182	ATHEN	THESSALONIKI	12 20		B64	73-84
LH 174	BARCELONA		12 35		A75	89-107
LT3146	ALICANTE		12 40			1-58
LH 316	ATHEN	MUENCHEN	12 50			89-107
LH1364	BRISTOL		12 50		A85	89-107
LH1005	FRANKFURT	AIRPORTEX.	12 55			
LT 114	LAS PALMAS		12 55			1-58
AF 765	PARIS		13 00			89-107
LH 408	NEW YORK		13 15			89-107
LL 338	BASTIA		13 25			1-58
HF 411	MALAGA		13 35			1-58
LH 052	LONDON	HEATHROW	13 45			89-107

Abflüge werden nicht ausgerufen! Departures will not be announced!

PETER: Wann geht der Flug nach Köln? Ich habe Flugnummer LH 368.
AUSKUNFT: Flug LH 368 nach Köln um 12 Uhr 40. Ausgang B10.
PETER: Danke!
AUSKUNFT: Bitte sehr! Guten Flug!

C14 Übung • Rollenspiel 

You are a traveler. A classmate works at the information booth. Pick a destination and a flight off the monitor. You ask about your flight, and your classmate tells you the time and the gate number.

C15 Übung • Hör gut zu! 

For script and answers, see p. T108.

Which gate do you go to? Listen.

	17.10	18.30	15.15	16.45	16.05	17.45
Hamburg					B48	
New York	A17					
Madrid				B53		
Brüssel						A22
Paris			B35			
Tel Aviv		A68				

TRY YOUR SKILLS using what you've learned

1 An der Auskunft

Ich heisse Silvia Friedrich. Ich bin hier in der Flughafen-Auskunft von Montag bis Freitag, von acht bis siebzehn Uhr. Manchmal bin ich auch am Wochenende da; dann habe ich ein oder zwei Tage in der Woche frei. Ich spreche Englisch und Französisch—ja, und ich beantworte viele Fragen. Manchmal sind die Fragen auch langweilig und blöd! Aber ich finde meine Arbeit gut.

Information
Ist heute Montag oder Dienstag?
Bin ich hier in Frankfurt oder in Stuttgart?
Ich heisse Meier. Und Sie?
Wie weit ist es von Frankfurt nach Stuttgart?
Ich brauche ein Taxi!
Wann geht der Flug nach Hamburg?

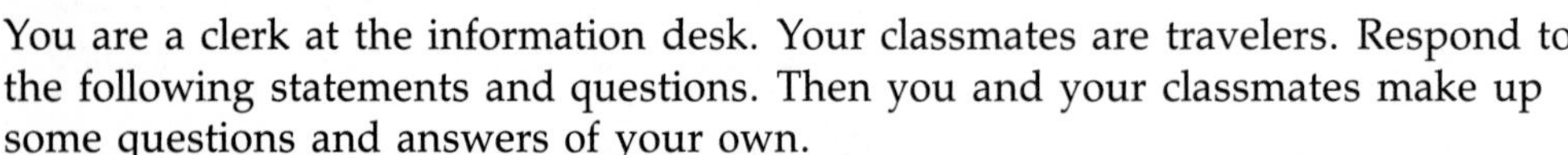

2 Übung • Rollenspiel

You are a clerk at the information desk. Your classmates are travelers. Respond to the following statements and questions. Then you and your classmates make up some questions and answers of your own.

Possible answers:

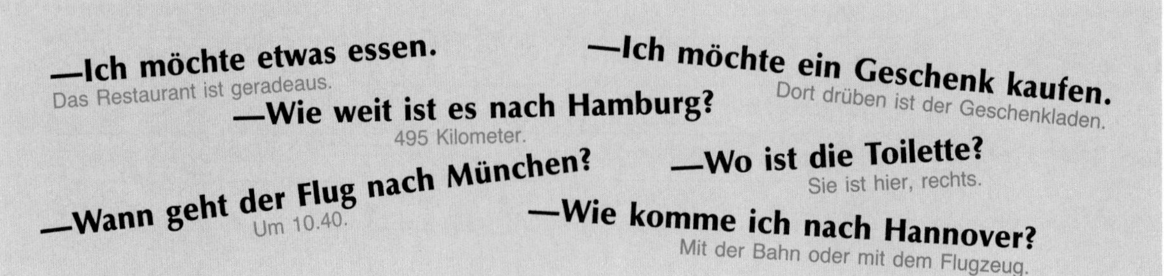

—Ich möchte etwas essen.
Das Restaurant ist geradeaus.
—Ich möchte ein Geschenk kaufen.
Dort drüben ist der Geschenkladen.
—Wie weit ist es nach Hamburg?
495 Kilometer.
—Wann geht der Flug nach München?
Um 10.40.
—Wo ist die Toilette?
Sie ist hier, rechts.
—Wie komme ich nach Hannover?
Mit der Bahn oder mit dem Flugzeug.

3 Übung • Geld wechseln

Ankauf: 14,15; 30,20; 120,25; 1,53; 2,20
Verkauf: 14,33; 31,90; 122,25; 1,64; 2,28
Note the different rates for buying and selling (*Ankauf* and *Verkauf*).

You are a clerk at the currency exchange window at the airport. Your classmates are tourists. Armed with a calculator and referring to the conversion table, you change money for them. The tourists are from different countries, so they will have different kinds of currency.

Land	Währung	Ankauf	Verkauf
Österreich	100 öS		
Schweden	100 skr		
Schweiz	100 sfrs		
Spanien	100 Ptas.		
USA	1 US $		
Krügerrand			

ANGESTELLTER Wieviel Geld möchten Sie wechseln?
TOURIST Hundert Dollar, bitte!
ANGESTELLTER Hundert Dollar . . . das sind . . . Mark.

4 Übung • Am Telefon 

You arrive in Frankfurt and are going on to a different city. Check the train and plane schedules and call your friends to tell them how and when you will arrive.

A: Hier . . .
B: Hier ist . . .! Guten Tag!
A: Du bist's, . . .! Grüss dich! Wo bist du?
B: In Frankfurt.
A: Prima! Wann bist du in Stuttgart?
B: Ich komme mit dem Zug um . . . *or* Der Flug geht um . . . Uhr.
Ich bin um . . . in Stuttgart. Ich bin um . . . Uhr in Stuttgart.

Explain *ab* and *an* ("departing" and "arriving") to the students before beginning the activity.

Fahrplan 

von Frankfurt

nach	Hamburg	München	Stuttgart
ab an	10.24 14.56	10.21 14.03	10.45 12.51
ab an	11.24 15.56	10.50 15.10	11.03 13.27
ab an	12.24 16.56	11.21 15.24	11.45 13.51
ab an	12.41 17.46	12.21 16.03	12.45 14.51

Flugplan

nach Hamburg

10.15–11.20	LH 764	727	Nonstop
10.40–11.40	PA 314	737	Nonstop
11.15–12.20	LH 763	727	Nonstop

nach München

10.40–11.35	LH 312	727	Nonstop
11.05–12.05	TW 164	737	Nonstop
11.40–12.35	LH 451	AB	Nonstop

nach Stuttgart

11.50–12.30	PA 328	727	Nonstop
12.40–13.25	LH 906	737	Nonstop
13.20–14.00	LH 455	AB	Nonstop

5 Schreibübung • An Bord

With a classmate, make up a conversation between two travelers on a flight to Germany. Then write down your dialog and act it out in front of the class.

6 Übung • Ach du Schreck!

den Walkman, er
das Wörterbuch, es
den Pass, er
den Taschenrechner, er
die Kassetten, sie

While waiting for your connecting flight, you suddenly panic. Do you have everything? You had better check!

Du Wo hab' ich die Kamera?
Gut, hier ist sie.

7 Übung • Was passt zusammen?

1. Hast du alles? g
2. Wann bist du in Köln? h
3. Ich möchte Briefmarken kaufen. d
4. Hier Schmidt. f
5. Guten Flug! b
6. Wann geht der Flug nach Köln? i
7. Ich möchte Geld wechseln. c
8. Bis gleich! a
9. Wo bist du? e

a. Auf Wiedersehen!
b. Danke!
c. Der Kurs ist heute gut.
d. Dort drüben ist die Post.
e. Im Flughafen.
f. Ja, hier Karin Braun.
g. Du, wo ist der Pass?
h. Morgen um 9.
i. Schau, da ist der Monitor!

8 Übung • Hör gut zu!

For script and answers, see p. T109.

Where is each conversation taking place? Listen.

	0	1	2	3	4	5
im Flugzeug	✓					
an der Passkontrolle					✓	
am Telefon		✓				
an der Auskunft				✓		
in der Bank						✓
im Geschenkladen			✓			

Briefmarken kaufen/die Post; etwas essen/das Restaurant; etwas fragen/die Auskunft; Geld wechseln/die Bank; ein Geschenk kaufen/der Geschenkladen

9 Schreibübung • Ich möchte . . .

For each pictogram, write an exchange modeled on the one below.

10 Schreibübung • Was fragen die Leute?

You overheard the following responses. Now write an appropriate question for each one.

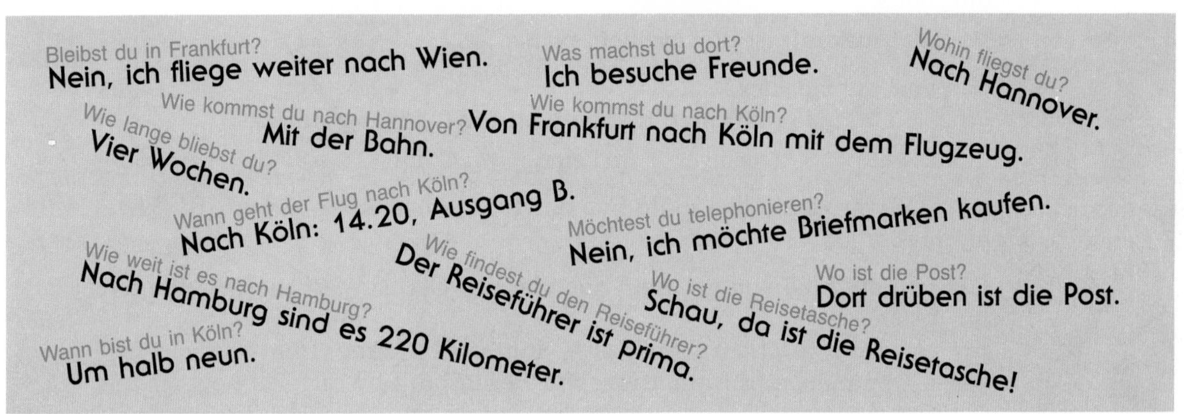

Bleibst du in Frankfurt?
Nein, ich fliege weiter nach Wien.
Was machst du dort?
Ich besuche Freunde.
Wohin fliegst du?
Nach Hannover.
Wie kommst du nach Hannover?
Mit der Bahn.
Wie kommst du nach Köln?
Von Frankfurt nach Köln mit dem Flugzeug.
Wie lange bliebst du?
Vier Wochen.
Wann geht der Flug nach Köln?
Nach Köln: 14.20, Ausgang B.
Möchtest du telephonieren?
Nein, ich möchte Briefmarken kaufen.
Wie weit ist es nach Hamburg?
Nach Hamburg sind es 220 Kilometer.
Wie findest du den Reiseführer?
Der Reiseführer ist prima.
Wo ist die Reisetasche?
Schau, da ist die Reisetasche!
Wo ist die Post?
Dort drüben ist die Post.
Wann bist du in Köln?
Um halb neun.

11 Aussprache-, Lese- und Schreibübungen

For script, see p. T111.

1. Listen carefully and repeat what you hear.

2. Listen, then read aloud.
1. schlecht, Fach, nichts, Woche, durch, Buch, manchmal, leicht, auch, möchte, nach
2. Junge, lange, Ausgang, Inge
3. ja, Jahr, Jens, jetzt, Junge
4. aus, Ausgang, Post, alles, nichts, etwas; Pass, essen, Schliessfach
5. sagen, suchen, seine, sieben, segeln, selten; Reise, besetzt, besuchen, lesen
6. vier, vor, von, viel, voll, Vati, Vater, Verwandte, verlieren

3. Copy the following sentences to prepare yourself to write them from dictation.
1. Der Junge ist sieben Jahre.
2. Ich besuche sie jetzt.
3. Jens und Inge lesen selten.
4. Suchst du auch den Ausgang?

WAS KANNST DU SCHON?

Let's review some important points you have learned in this unit.

Can you give some information about your travel plans?
You are planning a trip. Tell where you are going, how long you are staying, and what you are going to do there. Ich fliege nach . . . Ich bleibe . . . Ich . . .

Name at least ten items you need for your trip. Ich brauche . . . das Flugticket/Wörterbuch/Adressbuch; den Pass/Walkman/ Film/Reiseführer/Kuli/Taschenrechner; die Reiseschecks/Spielkarten/Kamera/Musikkassetten

You can't find any of these items. Ask the following people. Ich frage mal . . .

1. den Vati 2. die Mutter 3. den Lehrer 4. Herr*n* Schmidt 5. den Junge*n* 6. die Barbara

Can you identify pictograms in public places?
Ask directions to eight facilities in the airport.

Wo ist bitte die Auskunft? Wo ist . . . (sind) der Ausgang/der Geschenkladen/die Post/das Telefon/die Wartehalle/die Toiletten/die Schliessfächer/die Bank/das Restaurant

Now give directions for finding each facility you named. Use different directions.

Die Auskunft ist dort drüben, rechts. da drüben/links/da/hier/geradeaus

Can you use *möchten*?
Write the forms of **möchten** that go with the following subjects:

1. wir möchten 2. ich möchte 3. Peter möchte 4. ihr möchtet 5. du möchtest 6. Sie möchten

Say that you would like to do five different things at the airport. Use the **möchte-**forms. Ich möchte etwas fragen/telefonieren/Briefmarken kaufen/etwas essen/etwas trinken/Geld wechseln/ein Geschenk kaufen

Can you say how you get from one place in Germany to another and give the distance?
Say you are going from Frankfurt to Stuttgart by plane, from Stuttgart to Munich by train, and from Munich to Regensburg by car. Tell how far it is.
Ich komme von Frankfurt nach Stuttgart mit dem Flugzeug, von Stuttgart nach München mit dem Zug und von München nach Regensburg mit dem Auto. Das sind 557 Kilometer.

Can you identify German money and exchange your dollars? 10-/20-/50-/100-Mark
Name the German bills and coins: Es gibt . . . Scheine und Münzen: ein Pfennig, zwei Pfennig, fünf Pfennig, zehn Pfennig, Mark-Stück, 2-Mark-Stück, 5-Mark-Stück
Exchange $100. Write the conversation at the exchange window.

Can you answer the phone and say goodbye on the phone?
What do you say when you answer the phone? How do you say goodbye at the end of a phone conversation? (Hier) . . .
Auf Wiederhören!/Tschüs!/Bis gleich!

Do you know the two ways of expressing time?
Say what time it is in two ways: 1. halb zehn/einundzwanzig Uhr dreissig 2. Viertel nach elf/dreiundzwanzig Uhr fünfzehn 3. Viertel vor sechs/siebzehn Uhr fünfundvierzig

1. 21.30 2. 23.15 3. 17.45 4. 16.05 5. 14.50

4. fünf nach vier/sechzehn Uhr fünf 5. zehn vor drei/vierzehn Uhr fünfzig

Do you know how to ask for flight information?
You are on flight number LH 348 to Cologne. Ask when it leaves.
Wann geht der Flug LH 348 nach Köln?

WORTSCHATZ

SECTION A

das **Adressbuch, ¨-er** *address book*
alles *everything*
der **Amerikaner, -** *American* (person); er ist Amerikaner *he's an American*
auf nach . . . *off to . . .*
besetzt *occupied*
bleiben *to stay*
brauchen *to need*
der **Deutsche, -n** *German* (person)
die **Familie, -n** *family*
die **Ferien** (pl) *vacation;* Ferien machen *to go on vacation*
der **Film, -e** *(camera) film*
fliegen *to fly*
das **Flugticket, -s** *plane ticket*
fragen *to ask*
für *for*
das **Geld** *money*
Kalifornien *California*
die **Kamera, -s** *camera*
Köln *Cologne*
mal: ich frag' mal den Vati *I'll just ask Dad*
die **Maschine, -n** *plane*
morgen *tomorrow*
die **Mutter, ¨** *mother*
nach *to*
noch *still*
ob *if, whether*
der **Pass, ¨-e** *passport*
planen *to plan*
die **Reise, -n** *trip*
der **Reiseführer, -** *travel guide*
der **Reisescheck, -s** *traveler's check*
schauen *to look;* Peter schaut nach *Peter checks*
seine *his*
die **Spielkarten** (pl) *cards*
suchen *to look for*
der **Vater, ¨** *father*
der **Vati, -s** *dad*
der **Verwandte, -n** *relative*
voll *full*
von *from*
der **Walkman** *Walkman*
weiter *further, on*
wen? *whom?*
wie lange? *how long?*
die **Woche, -n** *week*
wohin? *to where?*
wohnen *to live*
zurück *back*

SECTION B

der **Ausgang, ¨-e** *exit*
die **Auskunft** *information*
die **Bahn: mit der Bahn** *by train*
die **Bank** *bank*
der **Beamte, -n** *official*
bei Grün *by the green symbol*
bitte! *here you are!*
das sind *that comes to*
durch *through*
essen *to eat*
etwas *something*
fehlen *to be missing*
das **Flugzeug, -e** *airplane*
gehen *to go*
das **Gepäck** *baggage*
geradeaus *straight ahead*
gern geschehen! *my pleasure!*
das **Geschenk, -e** *present*
der **Geschenkladen, ¨** *gift shop*
Gott sei Dank! *thank God!*
gut *ok, good*
holen *to get, pick up*
kaufen *to buy*
der **Kilometer, -** *kilometer*
kommen nach *to get to*
landen *to land*
links *left, on the left*
die **Meile, -n** *mile*
möchten *would like to*
nichts *nothing*
die **Passkontrolle** *passport check*
die **Post** *post office*
rechts *right, on the right*
der **Reisende, -n** *traveler*
die **Reisetasche, -n** *travel bag*
das **Restaurant, -s** *restaurant*
sagen *to say*
das **Schliessfach, ¨-er** *locker*
schöne Ferien! *have a nice vacation!*
das **Telefon, -e** *telephone*
telefonieren *to telephone*
die **Toilette, -n** *restroom*
trinken *to drink*
ungefähr *approximately*
Verzeihung! *excuse me!*
verzollen *to declare at customs*
die **Wartehalle, -n** *waiting room*
wechseln *to exchange*
weit *far*
die **Zahlen von 20 bis 1000** see p 150
der **Zoll** *customs*
zu *to*

SECTION C

ach so! *oh, I see!*
alle *all*
alles *all*
der **Apparat, -e** *phone*
auf Wiederhören! *goodbye*
der **Bankangestellte, -n** *bank teller*
besetzt *busy* (a phone)
bis gleich *see you soon*
bitte sehr! *you're welcome!*
da: wir sind da *we'll be there*
die **D-Mark = Deutsche Mark** German monetary unit
denn: wo bist du denn? *where are you?*
das **deutsche Geld** *German money*
der **Dollar, -** *dollar*
du bist's *it's you*
endlich *finally*
es gibt *there is, there are*
der **Flug, ¨-e** *flight;* guten Flug! *have a good flight!*
der **Flughafen, ¨** *airport*
gehen: der Apparat geht nicht *the phone is out of order*
heben: du hebst den Hörer ab *you lift the receiver*
hier Nedel *Nedel speaking*
der **Hörer, -** *telephone receiver*
im = in dem *in the*
in *into*
der **Kurs** *rate of exchange*
noch einmal *again, once more*
der **Pfennig, -(e)** *penny*
pünktlich *on time, punctual*
der **Schein, -e** *bill* (money)
stecken *to stick, put*
das **Stück: ein 5-Mark-Stück** *a five-mark piece*
das **Telefonieren** *telephoning*
die **Telefonzelle, -n** *phone booth*
verabredet: wie verabredet *as planned*
versuchen *to try*
wählen *to dial*
wie *as, like*
wieviel? *how much?*
wirklich *really*

ZUM LESEN

Köln am Rhein

Nedels holen den Peter am Flughafen in Köln ab°. „Jetzt fahren wir über den Rhein, Peter! Siehst du die Schiffe da unten°?"

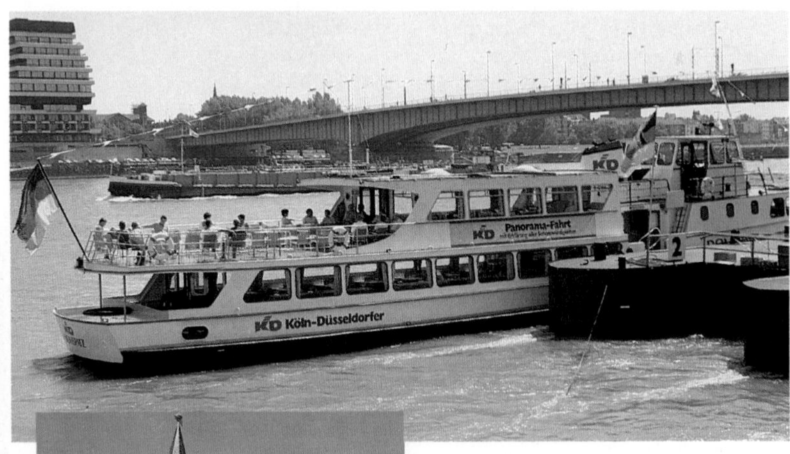

„Was ist das?"

„Das ist Gross St. Martin, eine Kirche; sehr alt, um 1172."

„Und das ist unser Dom, der berühmte° Kölner Dom. Man hat lange an diesem Dom gebaut, etwa sechshundert Jahre!"

This cathedral is the largest Gothic cathedral in Germany. It was begun in 1248, but not finished until 1880.

---

holen ab *pick up* **da unten** *down there* **berühmt** *famous*

„Siehst du das alte Tor dort drüben? Das haben die Römer gebaut, schon um 50 nach Christo°!"

DAS RÖMISCHE NORDTOR
ERBAUT BEI GRÜNDUNG
DER COLONIE
50 nach CHR.
Der mittlere Torbogen trug
auf der Feldseite den Stadtnamen
C. C. A. A.
Colonia Claudia Ara Agrippinensium
Von den Seitenbögen ist einer 1971
hier wieder über den sichtbar
erhaltenen Resten von Tor und Mauer
aufgebaut worden.

„Und dort rechts ist das Römisch-Germanische Museum! Da gehen wir mal hin!"

„Und hier ist die Hohe Strasse—die Geschäftsstrasse° Kölns."

„Ja, Peter, Köln ist eine alte Stadt, zweitausend Jahre alt. Köln hat heute fast° eine Million Einwohner°—es ist die viertgrösste° Stadt in der Bundesrepublik, und es ist die grösste Stadt am Rhein."

---

nach Christo *A.D.* **Geschäftsstrasse** *shopping street* **fast** *almost* **Einwohner** *inhabitant* **viertgrösste** *fourth largest*

Ein kleines Missverständnis

Gabi Sauer is going to the airport to meet an American exchange student. Look at the title of the story. What do you think happens? Here is a clue: the word **Verständnis** comes from **verstehen,** *to understand.* The prefix **Miss-** is the same as *mis-* in English. Read the story and see how much you understand.

Heute nachmittag wollen Bärbel Wegener und Gabi Sauer zum Flughafen fahren. Die Wegeners erwarten einen jungen Amerikaner, einen Brieffreund von Bärbels Bruder Werner. Aber um halb eins klingelt bei Gabi das Telefon.

„Gabi, hier ist die Bärbel. Grüss dich!"

„Grüss dich, Bärbel! Was gibt's?"

„Du, Gabi, kannst du allein zum Flugplatz fahren? Ich kann nicht, ich bin krank."

„Was? Ich?—Der Amerikaner kommt zu euch! Und ich weiss nicht, wie der junge Mann aussieht."

„Du, das ist einfach: er ist gross, er hat schwarzes Haar. Er schreibt, er kommt mit einem roten Rucksack."

„O.K. Und wie heisst er?"

„Will Baden. Er ist aus Denver. Du, und die Maschine ist um 14.30 in München."

„Na, gut, Bärbel. Ich finde deinen Amerikaner schon. Tschüs!"

„Ja, bis später!"

Gabi ist im Flugplatz. Es ist Viertel nach zwei. Sie wartet dort, wo die Reisenden durch den Zoll kommen.—Ah! Da ist er. Ein grosser Junge, der Will Baden. Ja, das ist er—der grosse, rote Rucksack!

„Will Baden?"

„Ja. Guten Tag!"

„Grüss dich! Ich bin die Gabi. Ich bin Bärbels Freundin. Die Bärbel kann nicht kommen, und der Werner ist auch nicht da."

„Das ist schade. Aber prima, dass du da bist!—Du, ich möchte Geld wechseln. Ich brauche D-Mark."

„Komm, ich habe Geld. Dein Geld kannst du später wechseln. Dort drüben ist ein Taxi!"

Die beiden sitzen im Taxi. Der junge Amerikaner ist sehr nett, denkt Gabi.

„Denver ist eine schöne Stadt.“
„Denver? Ja, ich weiss nicht.“
„Du kommst doch aus Denver, ja?“
„Ich? Nein, ich komme aus Chicago.“
„Chicago? Aber die Bärbel sagt, du kommst aus Denver.“
„Wer ist Bärbel?“
„Die Bärbel Wegener. Du besuchst doch die Familie Wegener.“
„Ich weiss nicht, wer die Familie Wegener ist.“
„Ja, sag, bist du denn der Will Baden?“
„Nein. Ich heisse Bill Barton. Und ich komme aus Chicago und besuche die Familie Krause hier in München.“
„Ach, du meine Güte!—Fahren Sie bitte zurück zum Flugplatz!“

In der Wartehalle steht ein grosser Junge: schwarze Haare, Brille—und da ist ein grosser, roter Rucksack! Der Junge hat ein Schild in der Hand: Will Baden. Im selben Augenblick hört man über den Lautsprecher: „Bill Barton bitte zur Auskunft kommen. Ein Fräulein Krause wartet hier auf Sie!“

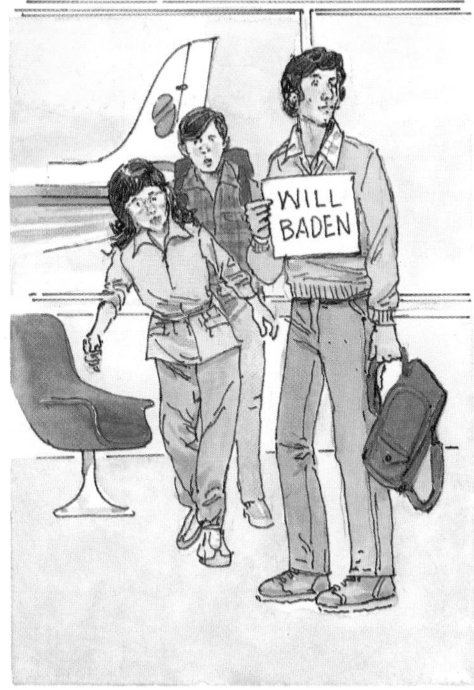

Ende gut, alles gut!

Übung • Hast du die Geschichte verstanden?

1. Whom is Gabi supposed to meet? Will Baden or Bill Barton? Will Baden.
2. What is the point of this story—Gabi goes to the wrong airport or Gabi thinks that Bill Barton is Will Baden? Gabi thinks Bill Barton is Will Baden.
3. Why is the last line „Ende gut, alles gut“? Is it because Gabi returns to the airport and finds her friend's real pen pal or because Bill Barton's pen pal is named Bärbel Wegener? Gabi returns to the airport and finds her friend's real pen pal.
4. Which passages in the story give you clues that there might be a misunderstanding?
   Bärbel can't go to the airport and Gabi doesn't know what Will looks like; Bärbel gives a very general description; Gabi sees someone fifteen minutes too early; Bill doesn't know Denver.

Übung • Stimmt! Stimmt nicht!

1. Die Deutschen sprechen Will Baden aus wie Bill Barton. Stimmt!
2. Die beiden Jungen sind gross und blond. Stimmt nicht!
3. Die zwei sind Amerikaner. Stimmt!
4. Die beiden kommen aus Denver. Stimmt nicht!
5. Sie besuchen deutsche Familien. Stimmt!

Übung • Wer ist wer?

Possible answers:
1. Gabi is Bärbel's friend who goes to the airport for her.
2. Bärbel is supposed to pick up her brother's American pen pal from the airport.

Who's who in this story? Identify these people and say a little about each one.

1. Gabi **2.** Bärbel **3.** Will Baden **4.** Bill Barton

3. Will is the American to be picked up by Bärbel and Gabi. He is tall, dark, and has glasses and a red backpack.
4. Bill is supposed to visit the Krauses and is mistakenly picked up by Gabi. He has a red backpack.

KAPITEL 6

KAPITEL 6 Bei den Nedels
Scope and Sequence

	BASIC MATERIAL	COMMUNICATIVE FUNCTIONS
SECTION A	**Freunde und Verwandte (A1)**	**Socializing** • Introducing someone, introducing yourself, and responding to an introduction
SECTION B	**Peter findet das Haus toll! (B1)** **Peter hat für alle Nedels ein Geschenk (B11)**	**Exchanging information** • Talking about your home **Socializing** • Complimenting someone and responding to a compliment • Saying thank you and you're welcome
SECTION C	**Kennst du Wiebkes Freunde? (C1)**	**Exchanging information** • Talking about appearance and personal characteristics **Expressing attitudes and opinions** • Agreeing, disagreeing, and expressing surprise
TRY YOUR SKILLS	Pronunciation long vowels, /R/, /ʌ/, /x/, /ä:/ (/e:/), medial /t/ Letter-sound correspondences **r, ä, -b; b, d, g** before **-st, -t** Dictation	
ZUM LESEN	**Märchen** (a survey of teenagers' feelings about fairy tales) **Die Brüder Grimm** (about the Brothers Grimm) **Kennt ihr diese Märchen?** (brief descriptions of eight fairy tales)	

WRITING A variety of controlled and open-ended writing activities appear in the Pupil's Edition. The Teacher's Notes identify other activities suitable for writing practice and suggest additional writing activities.

COOPERATIVE LEARNING Many of the activities in the Pupil's Edition lend themselves to cooperative learning. The Teacher's Notes explain some of the many instances where this teaching strategy can be particularly effective. For guidelines on how to use cooperative learning, see page T13.

GRAMMAR	CULTURE	RE–ENTRY
ein and **mein,** nominative case forms (A6)	Family members and close relatives	Greetings
Indefinite articles, accusative case (B6) The preposition **für** (B13)	Inside a German home How Germans respond to a compliment	Expressing opinions, enthusiasm Indefinite articles School supplies to give as presents Items to take on a trip Saying thank you
The verb **aussehen** (C5) Third-person pronouns, accusative case (C11)		Expressing opinions Expressing agreement, disagreement, surprise Family members Sports and activities
Recombining communicative functions, grammar, and vocabulary		
Reading for practice and pleasure		

TEACHER–PREPARED MATERIALS

Section A Family tree; flashcards of names of family members

Section B Pictures of German houses and apartments, different rooms, gift items

Section C Flashcards of adjectives; humorous pictures of people

UNIT RESOURCES

Übungsheft, Unit 6
Arbeitsheft, Unit 6
Unit 6 Cassettes
Transparencies 15–17
Quizzes 15–17
Unit 6 Test
Midterm Test
Proficiency Test 1

OBJECTIVES **To socialize:** introduce someone, introduce yourself, and respond to an introduction

CULTURAL BACKGROUND German young people are generally very interested in America and all things American. Many, like Wiebke, want to go to the United States themselves someday; so the arrival of the American visitor is a big event for which the whole family gathers.

MOTIVATING ACTIVITY Ask the students to imagine that an exchange student from a German-speaking country is going to stay with them. Who are all the people they would want to introduce the foreign student to? Ask them to think of their relatives and list them.

Tell the students to watch for all the cognate nouns that German has for family members. Learning these nouns will be very easy for them.

Ask the students to write down the English nouns denoting more than one relative (other than simply the plural of one noun, such as *sisters*). Tell the students that German will have an additional very common collective noun and tell them to watch for it.

A1 Freunde und Verwandte 

Introduce each section by having the students listen and follow in their books. When asking questions, include some to which the answer is not in the text but can be discerned from the photo or is implicit in the situation, such as **Wie kommt Peter vom Flugplatz zu Nedels?** Point to pictures of the people on page 132 as you present the new vocabulary (preferably on an overhead transparency):

> Das ist die Familie Nedel. In der Familie Nedel sind viele Leute:
> die Grosseltern, Onkel und Tante, . . .

Have the students summarize all the people Peter met on page 168 in a list arranged according to gender. (Review the concept of natural gender.) Then ask **Wen lernt er kennen?** (eliciting the accusative case forms **den Vater, die Mutter,** and so forth).

Work with the pronunciation of new phrases and words:

> Du lernst viele Leute kennen. Willkommen in Neuss!
> Ach, das ist nicht so schlimm. Schön, dass du da bist!
>
> /f/ Vater, Vetter /ʃv/ Geschwister, Schwester
> /u:/ Bruder, Kusine, Julian /R/ Grosseltern, Graf

Have the students, doubling up on some parts, do a dramatic reading of page 168 in groups of five. Have them switch roles and repeat.

Make the students aware of the many cognates that exist between German and English because both are Germanic languages. Cognates are easy to recognize but more difficult to pronounce. Have the students fill in equivalents for the list they prepared in the motivating activity. Point out differences in pronunciation and spelling.

Next introduce Wiebke's friends and classmates. Stop after each introduction and have the *students* come up with questions. Work with singular and plural forms that are easily confused (e.g., **der Freund, die Freunde, die Freundin**). Ask questions such as **Was ist Markus? Was ist Monika? Was sind beide?** Also work with the possessive used with names (e.g., **Wiebkes Freundin**).

A2 Übung • Wer ist wer?

To expand this activity, have the students come up with a different completion for items in the left column. (For some items, this will not be possible.)

> Philipp und Ulrike sind ______.
> Wiebkes Geschwister.
> die Geschwister von Wiebke.
> Bruder und Schwester.
> der Vetter und die Kusine von Julian und Ali.

Prepare a simple partial family tree for Wiebke. The students, in cooperative learning groups, must fill in the designation for each member of Wiebke's family as well as the person's name. Give some cues.

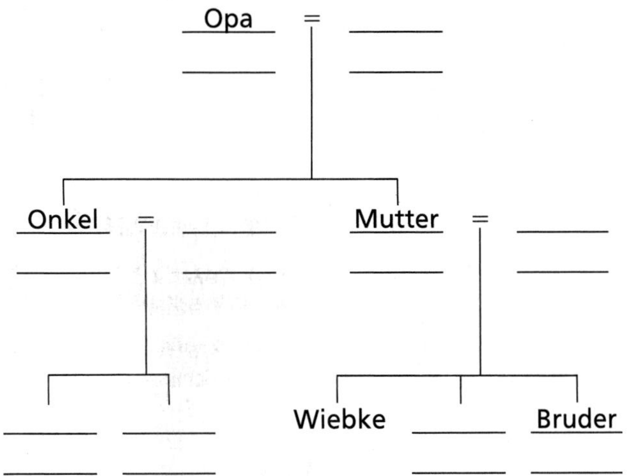

Using the family tree, have the students talk about Wiebke's family to each other: **Das sind Wiebkes Geschwister. Der Bruder heisst Philipp,** and so on.

A3 WIE SAGT MAN DAS?

Have the students go through all the introductions in A1, citing what Wiebke says when she introduces her relatives and what Wiebke's friends say when they introduce themselves. Next have the students read examples on the chart and then change the introduction to another person: **Peter, das ist meine Kusine Ali.**

A4 Übung • Wer ist das?

Have the students complete the tasks in 1 and 2. Then ask questions with **wen** about these people, eliciting accusative case forms.

> Wen lernt Peter Seber kennen?
> den Vater von Wiebke
> die Mutter von Wiebke
> die Verwandten

A5 Übung • Jetzt bist du dran

Before starting the mini-dialogs, work with the indefinite article and the possessive **mein.** See if the students can discover patterns in the reading for the indefinite articles and possessives. Then have them say groups such as the following very fast.

der Freund — ein Freund — mein Freund
die Tante — eine Tante — meine Tante

A6 ERKLÄRUNG

Have the students read through the explanation. Then practice application. Ask questions in the following pattern:

Ist das dein Bruder? — Nein, mein Vetter.
dein Vater?
dein Freund?
dein Vetter?
deine Oma?
deine Kusine?
deine Schwester?
deine Tante?

As an expansion, have the students use possessives with vocabulary from Unit 5. They get panicky as they can't find something. Fortunately, someone can help them.

A: Der Pass! Wo ist mein Pass?
B: Hier ist er!

Die Kamera! Das Geld! Die Reiseschecks!
Das Adressbuch! Die Reisetasche! Der Kuli!

A7 Übung • Kennst du Wiebkes Klassenkameraden?

As an expansion, personalize the activity. Ask questions about students in the class: **Wer ist . . . ? — Das ist ein Freund von . . .**

A8 Übung • Wiebke stellt ihre Familie und Freunde vor

After completing question/answer practice, have the students create mini-dialogs following this pattern. Wiebke is asked about her family and friends but the person who asks has all the relationships wrong.

A: Wer ist die Ali, deine Schwester?
B: Nein, meine Kusine.
A: Ah, deine Kusine!

Wer ist Frau Graf, deine Tante?
Wer ist Beppo, dein Freund?
Wer ist Herr Wolf, dein Lehrer?

A9 Übung • Deine Familie

Ask the students to bring in photos of their own family or friends and show them to their classmates. Put the students in cooperative learning groups of 3 or 4 students around a table. Have them take turns showing their photographs while the others ask questions: **Wer ist das? Und das? Ist das dein Bruder? Wie heisst sie? Das ist deine Schwester?** and so forth.

If you prefer, the students can make up an imaginary family of their own, which can be funny, using cutouts from magazines. The "family members" should have names, and relationships should be indicated. Display the pictures on a bulletin board.

A10 Schreibübung • Meine Klassenkameraden

As a variation, have the students pretend they are at a party and are introducing a friend around: **Das ist . . . Er/sie ist aus . . .** As an alternative, they could introduce themselves: **Guten Tag! Ich bin . . . Ich bin aus . . .**

SECTION B

OBJECTIVES **To exchange information:** talk about your home; **to socialize:** compliment someone and respond to a compliment; say thank you and you're welcome

CULTURAL BACKGROUND German homes are different from American homes in some ways because of physical and cultural differences between the countries. The students will discover some of these differences in the motivating activity.

MOTIVATING ACTIVITY Have the students look closely at the photos on pages 172–73 and 166–67 and note all the things they see that strike them as different. Ask them to order these observations under three headings:

1. the Nedels' house as seen from outside
2. the Nedels' house inside—the room layout and size (as much as they can see)
3. the furnishings and decor

To 1: The students should notice the fence, gate, and shrubs grown all around the property, an expression of the Europeans' desire for privacy. They should also note:

—the mailbox (to be emptied from inside the gate)
—the tiled roof (which lasts much longer than a composition roof; houses are built to last hundreds of years)
—the steepness of the roof (lets the rain and snow run off easily)
—the relatively small windows (keeps the house warm and dry, important in the wet and cool climate of the Rhineland)

To 2: The students will probably notice the smaller scale of the rooms, especially the bedrooms. In a two-story house, one or two of the children usually have the rooms under the roof **(Dachkammer).** Here they have their privacy, can play their own kind of music and do their own decorating.

To 3: The students should notice the mixing of modern furniture with some older, more ornate pieces. In general, furniture is on a smaller scale than in America because of the smaller-sized rooms. It is simple, well-constructed, and functional.

You might want to show additional slides, photos or magazine pictures of houses and apartments from German-speaking countries. This would put "the" German home seen here into a larger context and allow the students to make further comparisons.

B1 Peter findet das Haus toll! 

Follow the usual procedure. Break B1 into segments (as determined by the

KAPITEL 6

B2–4

photos and the dialogs) and use these conversations for guided oral practice, including question/answer activities.

The students may need help with the pronunciation of:

/ts/ Zimmer, sechs Zimmer, zeig   /ü/ Küche
/ç/ Küche   /ü:/ gemütlich

Watch for negative transfer from English in:

Garage (Ga-ra-ge)   hell
Auto   modern

To make the students conscious of the differences, have them say the word slowly in both languages. Repeat this several times if necessary.

After introducing all the segments, ask general questions: **Warum heisst der Dialog „Peter findet das Haus toll"? Was für Komplimente macht er? Wiebke zeigt Peter das Haus von unten bis oben. Was zeigt sie Peter noch?** and so on.

B2 Übung • Wie sieht Nedels Haus aus?

To check the students' comprehension of the material, ask summarizing questions: **Wieviel Zimmer hat das Haus? Was sind die Zimmer? Was für andere Räume hat das Haus?** Have the students tell what the house is like using this pattern: **Nedels haben ein Einfamilienhaus mit . . . und . . .**

Have the students tell what the function of each room is. Start them off by saying:

Wir sind viel im Wohnzimmer.
Wir wohnen im Wohnzimmer.
Was machen wir im Esszimmer?
Schlafzimmer?
Badezimmer?
Arbeitszimmer?

Ask the students how Peter describes the house. Have them make a list of the adjectives he uses during his tour.

B3 WIE SAGT MAN DAS?

When the students understand how compliments are made and received, ask for variations of the compliment phrases given. If possible, use picture cues from other sources as stimuli.

Wie schön das ist!
(Das Esszimmer) sieht so gemütlich aus!
Ich finde (den Garten) prima!
Das ist so gross und hell!
schön, gross, hell, modern, freundlich, klein, gemütlich
prima, super (cannot be qualified with so or wie)

B4 Ein wenig Landeskunde

Read parts of B1 aloud to the students again. Add some downplaying comments by Wiebke at appropriate places (after Peter's compliments).

CHALLENGE Have the students practice reacting to compliments. Have them use both the questions given and comments such as **Ja, aber es ist zu klein.**

B 5 Übung • Rollenspiel — Partnerarbeit

As a variation, have the students bring in magazine pictures of a house, a garden, and rooms to show their partner. You can allow them to include ridiculous pictures if you like.

B 6 ERKLÄRUNG

As an expansion, have the students find instances of indefinite articles in the accusative case in B1. Have them make their own chart similar to the one shown.

B 7 Übung • Und was habt ihr?

For additional practice with indefinite articles in the accusative case, recycle school supplies vocabulary. One student offers another something, but the second student already has one: **Hier ist der Taschenrechner. Ich habe auch einen Taschenrechner.**

B 8 Übung • Schüler erzählen

Give the students the word **Wohnung** so that those with apartments can use it as they explain. You may also need to give them the following vocabulary frequently used by American students to describe their homes:

> die Terrasse *(patio)*
> die Veranda *(porch)*
> die Wohnküche *("live-in" or eat-in kitchen)*

Tell the students that there is no real equivalent for the American "family room." It simply doesn't exist since space is at a premium. One would need to describe it as something like a second living room; **ein zweites Wohnzimmer, nicht so formell, zum Fernsehen und Ausruhen.** Words that come close to the meaning are **Fernsehraum** and **Hobbyraum.**

B 9 Übung • Und du? Wie steht's mit dir?

This activity should be done by matching items randomly, not as a drill using each item in order. Be careful to keep to the construction in two sentences as shown to avoid bringing in adjective endings **(Wir haben eine moderne Küche).**

B 10 Schreibübung

Have the students start their description with **Ich wohne in . . . Das ist in . . .** Encourage the students to bring some variation into their description through the use of adjectives, for example: **(es) ist sehr gross und modern; ich finde das/die/den . . . schön; das . . . ist prima.** Again, be sure that they do not try to place the adjectives *before* nouns.

B 11 PETER HAT FÜR ALLE NEDELS EIN GESCHENK

Start the presentation of B11 by demonstrating new vocabulary.

> Peter Seber ist Gast bei Nedels.
> Er bring Gastgeschenke für alle.
> Alle Nedels <u>bekommen</u> ein Geschenk.

Er hat eine Halskette für die Wiebke.
Was bekommt der Philipp? Einen Taschenrechner.

Have the students listen to each segment. Have them listen especially for the way people say "Thank you" and "You're welcome." Ask simple comprehension questions. After oral practice with the new material, ask higher-level questions:

Warum bringt Peter so viele Geschenke mit?
Sind das die richtigen Geschenke für die Nedel Kinder? Was meint ihr?
Wer sind die drei im Foto rechts? Wer bekommt ein Geschenk?
Was meint ihr, was ist das für ein Buch? Was ist der Titel?
Ist Peter jetzt fertig oder hat er noch mehr Geschenke?
Was meint ihr, für wen in der Nedel Familie hat der Peter Geschenke?
Für den . . .
Für die . . .

B12 Übung • Mix-Match

CHALLENGE Have the students write some Mix-Match items of their own, referring to B11. Then have the class complete the new activity.

B13 ERKLÄRUNG

After going over the explanation, practice the forms. Have the students use the names of all the people who appeared in A1 in sentences.

B14 Übung • Peter hat noch mehr Geschenke

As a variation, have the students role-play Wiebke helping Peter distribute the gifts he brought. She has to ask him which present is for which person.

A: Für wen sind die Spielkarten?
B: Für den Philipp.

B15 Schreibübung • Was sagt Peters Mutter?

To expand the activity, have the students add to the list of presents. (Each person is receiving more than one gift.)

B16 WIE SAGT MAN DAS?

Reinforce these expressions by taking many opportunities to use them. For instance, ask the students to use them while conducting class business (such as passing out papers: **Danke!**).

B17 Übung • Für wen sind die Geschenke?

As a variation, tell the students to imagine that they have just completed their shopping for gifts for all the members of their family and for friends. They are now at home and are checking that they have at least one gift for everyone.

Also, für den Vater habe ich . . .
Und für die Mutter . . .

You may wish to supply additional vocabulary if the students need it, such as **Stiefvater** and **Patenonkel.**

B 18 Übung • Hör gut zu!

You will hear six fragments of conversations. Some refer to Wiebke showing Peter the house; others refer to Peter distributing gifts. Decide which one it is you hear and place your check mark in the appropriate row. For example, you hear, **Hier hab' ich ein Geschenk für den Opa. Briefmarken. Mein Vater sagt, der Opa sammelt Briefmarken.** You place your check mark in the row labeled *Peter distributing gifts.* Let's begin. **Fangen wir an!**

1. Nichts zu danken! Es ist nur ein Buch. Aber Mutti sagt, du liest gern. *Peter distributing gifts*
2. Ist unser Wohnzimmer nicht phantastisch für eine Party? Es ist so gross und so hell! *Wiebke showing Peter the house*
3. Und das ist mein Zimmer. Nicht gross, aber sehr gemütlich. *Wiebke showing Peter the house*
4. Hier ist etwas für die Wiebke. Eine Halskette von Mutti. Ist sie nicht schön, die Kette? *Peter distributing gifts*
5. Und was habe ich für den Philipp? Wo ist denn . . . ? Jetzt pack' ich mal die Reisetasche aus. Ja, hier ist er, der Taschenrechner für den Philipp. *Peter distributing gifts*
6. Komm, jetzt zeig' ich dir dein Zimmer. Es ist unser Gästezimmer. *Wiebke showing Peter the house*

Now check your answers. *Read each item again and give the correct answer.*

OBJECTIVES **To exchange information:** talk about appearance and personal characteristics; **to express attitudes and opinions:** agree, disagree, and express surprise

CULTURAL BACKGROUND As is evident from the pictures in C1, many Germans do not fit the blond, blue-eyed stereotype. This complexion is found commonly in northern Germany, but the inhabitants of southern Germany tend to have darker coloring.

Germans in general do not hesitate to describe each other's physical and personality characteristics matter-of-factly, without the extremely sensitive attitude of some Americans.

MOTIVATING ACTIVITY Ask the students to think about the most common ways to *briefly* describe a classmate or friend to another person. What would they say about their classmate's appearance? How would they briefly convey their opinion about his or her personality? Ask the students to list these characteristics, and collect their responses on an overhead transparency or on the board. They will probably come up with a list like this:

Looks	*Personality*
tall—small	nice, pleasant, friendly, likeable
slim—heavy (fat)	interesting—boring
attractive, pretty, good-looking	funny
dark-haired—blond	

Tell the students to keep this chart for later reference. They will learn to express most of these concepts in German.

KAPITEL

C1–5

C1

Kennst du Wiebkes Freunde? 

Follow the usual procedure. Treat the material exchange by exchange, looking at the pictures. The students will need a lot of help with pronunciation and stress, since so many words are cognates.

blond		arrogant
attraktiv		sympathisch
brünett	/ʃ/	Geschmack, Geschmackssache

Work with **sympathisch** and **unsympathisch.**

Ich finde ihn/sie sympathisch.
unsympathisch.

This is the most common way to say that one likes or does not like a person. It is noncommittal, similar to **Ich finde ihn/sie (nicht) nett.** Be sure that the students do not misinterpret **sympathisch** as meaning "sympathetic."

After all the segments have been presented and practiced, ask the students about their opinion of Wiebke and her friends.

Wen findest du attraktiv?
Wer sieht sehr sportlich aus?
Wer sieht intelligent aus?
Wie findest du Wiebke? Findest du sie sympathisch? Wie sieht sie aus?
Und Peter Seber? Findest du ihn attraktiv? Sympathisch?

Then direct the students' attention to page 168 and ask their opinions about Wiebke's relatives.

Wen findest du attraktiv? Wer sieht gut aus?
Wer sieht sympathisch aus? Wer ist sehr nett? Was meinst du?
Sind die jungen Leute schlank oder vollschlank?
(Note: Introduce the nice German expression for "on the heavy side." **Vollschlank** can be indeed quite heavy!)
Peter ist sehr gross. Und Wiebkes Eltern? Sind sie gross oder mittelgross? Sind sie schlank oder vollschlank?

C2

Übung • Wer sind Wiebkes Freunde? Wie sehen sie aus?

To expand the activity, have the students use the new vocabulary to describe the characters they got acquainted with in Unit 1.

C3

WIE SAGT MAN DAS?

While talking about describing how people look, you may wish to discuss the distinction between fact and opinion with the students. You might use the examples **Er ist blond** as opposed to **Er sieht gut aus.**

C4

Übung • Und du?

For writing practice, have the students write out their answers. As a variation, have them bring in pictures of real or imaginary friends to tell about.

C5

ERKLÄRUNG

SLOWER–PACED LEARNING The students may need a lot of practice with this separable-prefix verb. Use different adjectives and pose questions for them to answer: **Sieht er nett aus? — Ja, er sieht nett aus.**

C6 Übung • Frag, wie alle aussehen! 

As an expansion, use the following activity, which adds the function of **nachfragen.** Have the students confirm which person they are being asked about before they give a description.

A: Kennst du die Wiebke?
B: Die Wiebke Nedel? Die Freundin von Monika?
A: Ja. Wie sieht sie aus?
B: Oh, sehr nett. Sie ist mittelgross, schlank, brünett . . .

C7 Übung • Wiebkes Familie sieht nett aus! 

For additional practice, have the students make up and answer questions about all the members of Wiebke's family not mentioned in the activity.

C8 Übung • Ratespiel: Wer ist das?

Be sure the students confine themselves to facts (no opinions). In the second game, make sure that the students ask only yes/no questions.

C9 WIE SAGT MAN DAS?

Before giving the students the summary of how to express agreement, disagreement, and surprise, have them come up with their own collection of phrases from C1 and B1. Ask them to list each phrase under one of these three headings. Then have the students compare their own chart with the one given. Did they miss any expressions?

Practice the expressions by asking the students to react to your statements by agreeing, disagreeing, or showing surprise. Remind them first that certain replies must be changed when they address you.

Sie haben recht!
Meinen Sie?

Recycle situations and vocabulary from previous units.

Mathematik ist leicht.
Eine Zwei ist eine gute Note.
Ich finde Tennis langweilig.
Hobbybücher sind leicht zu lesen.
Montag ist der beste Tag in der Woche.
Köln ist eine schöne Stadt.
Reisen macht Spass.
Telefonieren in Deutschland ist sehr schwer.

C10 Übung • Wie findest du Wiebkes Freunde?

The students may need help in coming up with opposites. Put the following list on an overhead transparency or on the board:

+	–
freundlich	unfreundlich
nett	nicht nett
interessant	langweilig
sympathisch	unsympathisch
attraktiv	nicht attraktiv
hübsch	nicht so hübsch

C11 ERKLÄRUNG

SLOWER–PACED LEARNING Practice the forms first by grouping questions by the gender of the nouns; then mix the genders. You might start with people, but be sure the students grasp the idea that the pronouns also refer to things.

C12 Übung • Wie findest du . . . ?

For additional practice, do the activity again, reversing the order of nominative and accusative case in the pattern: **Findest du den Thomas nett? — Ja, er ist nett.**

C13 Übung • Der Miesmacher

As an expansion, play the **Miesmacher** and make a statement; for example, **Ich finde den Markus nicht nett.** The students should either agree or express surprise and disagree.

C14 Übung • Hör gut zu!

You will hear ten statements. The statements may talk about a boy, a girl, a room in a house, or two classmates. You determine who or what is being talked about and place your check mark in the appropriate row. For example, you hear, **Sie ist hübsch, schlank, sehr attraktiv. Aber ich finde sie etwas arrogant.** You place your check mark in the row labeled ***ein Mädchen,*** because the statement refers to a girl. Let's begin. **Fangen wir an!**

1. Sie sind sehr sympathisch, sehr freundlich. Und sie sind immer so lustig. *zwei Schulfreunde*
2. Er ist gross, blond, aber furchtbar langweilig. *ein Junge*
3. Ich finde ihn sehr hübsch, sehr gemütlich, besonders für Partys. *das Haus*
4. Er sieht nicht besonders gut aus, aber ich finde ihn nett und sehr sympathisch. *ein Junge*
5. Ich finde sie auch sehr lustig und sehr attraktiv; sie ist klein und brünett, er gross, schlank, dunkel. *zwei Schulfreunde*
6. Sie ist sehr gross und hell; ich finde sie prima. Sehr gemütlich, und wir essen hier gern. *das Haus*
7. Sie hat eine Brille, aber ich finde sie sehr attraktiv. Und sie ist immer lustig. *ein Mädchen*
8. Er sieht nicht gut aus — schlank, zu schlank. Aber das ist Geschmackssache. *ein Junge*
9. Sie sind attraktiv, aber unsympathisch. Meinst du nicht? Ich finde sie auch arrogant. *zwei Schulfreunde*
10. Sie sieht prima aus. Findest du nicht auch? Und sie ist so sympathisch, immer nett und freundlich. *ein Mädchen*

Now check your answers. *Read each item again and give the correct answer.*

C15 Übung • Wie sind diese Leute?

To expand this activity, have the students bring in pictures of themselves. Have them write a description of each class member for a bulletin board display.

C16 **Übung • Hör gut zu!**

For this exercise, open your textbook to page 183 and look at the characters pictured in C16. You will hear five brief descriptions of people. Match each description you hear with the corresponding drawing. Let's begin. **Fangen wir an!**

1. Ich finde sie sehr nett, schlank, blond — und sie sieht so lustig aus. *Nummer 4, das Mädchen*
2. Er sieht gut aus, dunkel, Brille — aber ich finde ihn arrogant. *Nummer 5, der Junge*
3. Sie sieht so langweilig aus, aber sie ist sehr nett. Sie ist auch hübsch: brünett, sympathisch. Meinst du nicht? *Nummer 1, das Mädchen*
4. Er ist ja sehr unfreundlich und unsympathisch. Findest du nicht? *Nummer 3, der Junge*
5. Sieht er nicht prima aus? Gross und blond und sehr sympathisch. *Nummer 2, der Junge*

Now check your answers. *Read each item again and give the correct answer.*

C17 **Schreibübung • Kennst du . . . ?**

When the students have completed all the suggested activities, add this on for fun. Tell the students that rumor has it that they have a new boyfriend or girlfriend. Nobody has met him or her yet but they want to know how he or she looks, what he or she is like. The group asks, the one student answers.

Du hast einen Freund/eine Freundin? — Ja!
Wie sieht (er) aus?
Wie heisst (er)?
Wie alt ist (er)?
Ist (er) attraktiv?
Ist (er) sportlich?
Ist (er) intelligent?
Warum findest du (ihn) nett?

Have the students write this conversation up in paragraph form.

TRY YOUR SKILLS

OBJECTIVE To recombine communicative functions, grammar, and vocabulary

CULTURAL BACKGROUND Hamburg is the largest city in the Federal Republic of Germany. It is also Germany's largest port. Hamburg was first a castle built by Charlemagne, and the city was part of the medieval Hanseatic League, a German mercantile league. Despite the destruction of World War II, the rebuilt city of Hamburg is still a center of industry and culture.

1 **Ein Brief aus Deutschland**

Although the letter presents easy reading, the students may have trouble pulling all the information together. Take sentences from the letter. Start each one and have the students complete it. Follow the sequence of the letter.

Was schreibt Richard?
Kühnemanns Wohnung ______.
Ich habe das ______.
Herr Kühnemann ist ______.

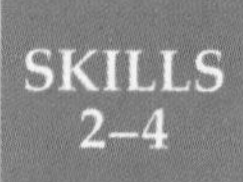

Then do another scanning activity, but stay with one topic and make slight variations:

> Die Familie Kühnemann, meine Gastfamilie, ______.
> Ich finde sie ______.
> Herr Kühnemann ist ______. Er ist ______.
> Frau Kühnemann ist ______.
> Heino, mein Gastbruder, ______.
> Heino hat zwei ______.
> Die Silke ist ______. Sie ist ______. Sie wohnt jetzt______.
> Die Kirstin ist ______. Sie hat ______.

Then ask the students comprehension questions:

> An wen schreibt Richard? Warum?
> Was meint ihr, ist Richard schon lange in Hamburg?
> Wie wohnen die Kühnemanns?
> Über welches Thema schreibt er sehr viel? Die Gastfamilie, die Schule, die Wohnung oder die Stadt?
> Was meint ihr, ist Richard gern in Hamburg bei Kühnemanns? Wen und was findet er alles gut und nett?
> Richard hat auch ein paar Probleme. Was sind die?

2 Übung • Was schreibt Richard?

CHALLENGE Have the students role-play Richard's family. They have received a similar letter and have all read it except for Dad, who is too tired to read the letter but wants to know all the news. Family members take turns telling Dad about Richard. Each "family" should have at least four persons.

ANSWERS
über seine Gastfamilie: die Gastfamilie ist sehr nett, er findet sie alle sehr sympathisch. Herr Kühnemann ist Bankangestellter. Er ist sehr lustig; er versucht immer, Englisch zu sprechen, aber sein Englisch ist furchtbar. Frau Kühnemann ist Lehrerin für Deutsch und Sport. Heino, der Gastbruder, ist nett und lustig, spielt auch Schach. Heino hat zwei Schwestern. Die Silke ist achtzehn, die Kirstin ist dreizehn. Silke ist Au-pair Mädchen in Frankreich. Kirstin und ihre Freundinnen sind Nina Hagen Fans.
über die Wohnung: die Wohnung ist sehr gross. Sie haben vier Schlafzimmer, ein Wohnzimmer, ein Esszimmer, eine Küche, ein Bad und zwei Toiletten. Er hat das Gästezimmer. Es ist nicht sehr gross, aber hell und gemütlich.
über die Schule: Er fährt mit dem Stadtbus in die Schule. Er hat jeden Tag fünf bis sechs Fächer. Mathe und Physik findet er leicht, aber Geschichte, Erdkunde und Biologie sind für ihn schwer. Die Lehrer sind sehr nett. Der Mathematiklehrer kennt St. Louis gut.

3 Schreibübung • Ein Brief von Peter aus Neuss

SLOWER–PACED LEARNING For cooperative learning, have the students work as a group to review the information needed. Put the information on the board. Then have them write their own letters.

4 Übung • Deine Meinung — meine Meinung 

CHALLENGE Have each student bring in a picture of a well-known person

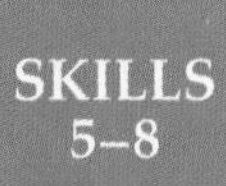

and have the class ask questions about the person such as **Wer ist das? Was macht er?** The student with the picture should find out enough about the person to answer basic questions.

5 Übung • Geschenke für die Nedels

To expand the activity, play a memory game, each student "outdoing" the preceding one by adding an item to the list of gifts for one person: **Für den Philipp habe ich . . . , . . . , . . .** Accept ridiculous answers as well as serious ones.

ANSWERS
für die Ulrike, für sie, eine Halskette; die Halskette, sie
für den Hartmut, für ihn, einen Taschenrechner; den Taschenrechner, ihn
für die Wiebke, für sie, ein Poster; das Poster, es
für den Opa, für ihn, Briefmarken; die Briefmarken, sie
für die Oma, für sie, ein Buch; das Buch, es

6 Übung • Danke! — Bitte schön!

As a variation, have the students hand each other personal or classroom items as "presents." The recipient should say thank you and the giver respond, following the example.

7 Schreibübung • Wie heisst die Frage?

CHALLENGE Have the students think up more answers like those in the box. Have others come up with a question to go with each one.

ANSWERS
1. Wie findest du den Markus?
2. Wie heissen Wiebkes Geschwister?
3. Wie sieht sie aus?
4. Kennst du Herrn Graf?
5. Wer bist du?
6. Wieviel Zimmer habt ihr?
7. Habt ihr ein Auto?

8 Übung • Ein Wohnungsplan

Tell the students to imagine that they are at the home of a friend whose family has recently moved. They hear one side of a telephone conversation about the new house. Have them supply the questions the caller might be asking.

A:
B: Es ist sehr schön, so gross und hell!
A:
B: Sechs Zimmer.
A:
B: Ja, zwei und eine Toilette.
A:
B: Mein Zimmer ist oben.
A:
B: Nicht sehr gross, aber sehr gemütlich.
A:
B: Ja, komm her. Ingrid ist auch da. Ich zeige euch das Haus.

9 Schreibübung • Wir wohnen in Wien

To expand the activity, have one student read his or her rewritten paragraph aloud as a dictation. You may want to give the dictation yourself, reading the paragraph with pronouns substituted where appropriate.

10 Übung • Hör gut zu!

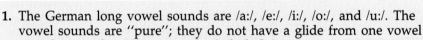

You will hear a number of statements or questions. Some express agreement, some disagreement; some express surprise; others express gratitude. Listen carefully to each statement, determine what it expresses, and place your check mark in the appropriate row. For example, you hear, **Die Karin sieht gut aus. — Das stimmt. Und du hast recht, sie ist auch sehr lustig.** You place your check mark in the row labeled *agreement*. Let's begin. **Fangen wir an!**

1. Du sagst, der Peter ist arrogant. Das finde ich nicht. Ich sage, er ist sehr nett. *disagreement*
2. Du meinst, die Renate sieht nicht gut aus. Das ist Geschmackssache. Ich finde, sie sieht sehr gut aus. *disagreement*
3. Ich finde die Karin auch sehr hübsch. *agreement*
4. Wirklich?! Du hast ein Geschenk für mich? *surprise*
5. Tausend Dank für das Geschenk! Ich finde es prima! *gratitude*
6. Der Kurt hat kein Hobby, er macht keinen Sport. — Ich finde auch, er ist sehr langweilig. *agreement*
7. Die Halskette sieht hübsch aus. Vielen Dank! *gratitude*
8. Du sagst, die Monika ist nicht sehr freundlich. Das finde ich nicht. Ich finde sie sehr lustig. *disagreement*
9. Was? Du findest den Jochen unsympathisch? Meinst du das wirklich? *surprise*
10. Die Karin sieht gut aus. — Das stimmt. Und du hast recht, sie ist auch sehr lustig. *agreement*

Now check your answers. *Read each item again and give the correct answer.*

11 Übung • Was sagen sie?

CHALLENGE Have the students write different captions for the pictures. Supply additional vocabulary as needed. The dialogs may be humorous.

12 Aussprache-, Lese- und Schreibübungen

1. The German long vowel sounds are /a:/, /e:/, /i:/, /o:/, and /u:/. The vowel sounds are "pure"; they do not have a glide from one vowel sound to another. **Hör zu und wiederhole!**

Wörter mit

/a:/ /a:/ Schlafzimmer, Bad, Vater, Bahn, planen
/e:/ /e:/ sehen, sehr, Peter, steht, gehen, fehlen
/i:/ /i:/ viele, wie, Spiel, spielen, verlieren
/o:/ /o:/ Oma, Opa, gross, Grosseltern, wohnen, Wohnzimmer
/u:/ /u:/ Bruder, Kusine, Buch, suchen, Flug

/R/ Remember that the letter **r** sounds like an **ach**-sound after /p/, /t/, /k/, and /f/. **Hör zu und wiederhole: Freund, Freundin, trinken.**

The letter **r** sounds like a voiced **ach-**sound at the beginning of a word or syllable and after /b/, /d/, and /g/. **Hör zu und wiederhole!**

rechts, Rucksack, Ferien, Garage, Bruder, Brille, brauchen, brünett, drei, dreissig, drüben, gross, grün

The letter **r** in final position after a long vowel sounds like a vowel similar to the vowel sound you hear at the end of the English word *sofa.* **Hör zu und wiederhole: mehr, sehr, dir, hier, Monitor.**

/ʌ/ The **r** in the letter combination **-er** represents a /ʌ/ sound, also similar to the vowel sound you hear at the end of the English word *sofa.* **Hör zu und wiederhole!**

Bruder, Schwester, Vater, Mutter, Vetter, Zimmer, Keller, Beamter, weiter

/ä:/ /e:/ The long /ä:/ sound, as in **Mädchen,** is similar to the long /e:/ sound in **geht.** The sounds are so similar that many native speakers of German do not make a distinction between them at all. However, some people do make this distinction. You may hear **das Mädchen** /ä:/ or **das Mädchen** /e:/; **spät** /ä:/ or **spät** /e:/. The difference between /e:/ and /ä:/ is that /ä:/ is produced with your mouth slightly more open than for /e:/ : /e:/ /ä:/. Let's practice the sound /ä:/ by opposing it with the sound /e:/ in the same word. **Hör zu und wiederhole!**

Mädchen /e:/ — Mädchen /ä:/ ; spät — spät; Väter — Väter; wählen — wählen; Bäder — Bäder; Flughäfen — Flughäfen

/t/ Make sure that the /t/ sound in the middle of words like **Mutter** remains a /t/ sound and does not become a /d/ sound. **Hör zu und wiederhole!**

Mutter, Vetter, bitte, Zettel, Halskette, Kassette, attraktiv, Tante

2. In this section you will practice reading the words printed in your textbook on page 187. Pay attention to the following:

r
1. The letter **r** represents a range of sound; it can be an **ach-**sound, a voiced **ach-**sound, or a vowel sound similar to the vowel sound you hear in the English word *sofa.* **Hör zu und wiederhole!**
   trinken, Brille, drei, Freund, mehr, Vater, gross, sehr, brauchen, Zimmer

ä
2. The letter **ä** can represent a long /ä:/ sound; when short, it sounds like a short /e/ sound. **Hör zu und wiederhole!**
   Väter, wählen, Bäder, Flughäfen, ungefähr; Pässe, Gepäck, Gästezimmer

final b
3. The letter **b** at the end of a word or syllable is always pronounced as /p/. **Hör zu und wiederhole: ob, halb, abheben, verabredet, Wiebke.**

b, d, g before st, t
4. Before **st** and **t,** the letters **b, d,** and **g** represent a /p/, /t/, and /k/ sound, respectively. This occurs very commonly in the **du-, er-,** and **ihr-**form of many verbs whose stems end in **b, d,** or **g. Hör zu und wiederhole!**
   geben: ich gebe; *but* du gibst, er gibt, ihr gebt
   bleiben: ich bleibe, du bleibst, er bleibt, ihr bleibt
   sagen: ich sage, du sagst, er sagt, ihr sagt
   fragen: ich frage, du fragst, er fragt, ihr fragt
5. Pay attention to the sound contrasts in the following word pairs: **Hör zu und wiederhole!**
   hab' — habe, bleib' — bleibe; Freund — Freunde, Hund — Hunde; frag' — frage

3. Now close your textbook and write the sentences you hear.
   1. Ich hab' einen Freund.
   2. Wie spät ist es, bitte?
   3. Bleib bitte hier.
   4. Die Flughäfen sind sehr gross.

WAS KANNST DU SCHON?

Have the students do a role-play. Have one student take a role listed and have another introduce him or her to a classmate.

For the second part, draw a floor plan on the board and have one student "show people around" while others make comments. Encourage the students to really play it up, gushing about each room.

For the second part, hold up pictures of people. Use the well-known people from Try Your Skills 4, or turn to pages in earlier units that have photos of people. Have the students make positive and negative comments.

WORTSCHATZ

Have the students find all the cognates in the list. Remind them about the misleading cognate **sympathisch;** they should note that it does not mean "sympathetic." Then have the students pick out all the compound words.

WORTSCHATZÜBUNGEN

As an additional activity, have the students find the three verbs in the vocabulary list that have separable prefixes.

ZUM LESEN

OBJECTIVE To read for practice and pleasure

SIND MÄRCHEN WIEDER „IN"? 

Read the paragraph on the first page with the students, helping them as necessary. Have them read the rest of the material on their own.

Übung • Was sagst du?

Refer the students to the next two pages before completing this activity. They will need to know the titles of the fairy tales to answer the second question.

Übung • Sprechen wir darüber!

Point out to the students that, generally, fairy tales were not created for children only. Many contain social commentary; characters represent real people or influences in society. The problems they deal with, though specific to a time and place in the past, often have universal application. For this reason, fairy tales are quoted or alluded to frequently, just as other works of literature are.

Übung • Klassenprojekte

Point out to the students that the Brothers Grimm also had other accomplishments. Among other things, they studied German grammar and the relationship among Germanic languages. You will need to direct the students in the last activity. You may need to supply additional vocabulary.

KENNT IHR DIESE MÄRCHEN? 

Point out the **Fraktur** in which the titles in the box are set. Tell the students that all German printed material used to be set in this kind of type. Help the students read the titles. Then have them read the summaries silently and write down which fairy tale each one describes.

KAPITEL 6

Bei den Nedels

The arrival of an exchange student from the United States is a big occasion. Germans are very interested in other countries and cultures and they love to travel. The United States has an especially great influence on Germany. It is most obvious in the language, dress, music, and television programs. Many people are critical of this influence. What influence has Germany had on the United States? What about the influence of other cultures on the United States?

In this unit you will:

SECTION A	introduce someone, introduce yourself and members of your family
SECTION B	talk about the rooms in your home
SECTION C	discuss appearance and personal characteristics
TRY YOUR SKILLS	use what you've learned
ZUM LESEN	read for practice and pleasure

For teaching suggestions, see the Teacher's Notes preceding this unit, pp. T114–T133.

SECTION A introducing someone, introducing yourself

When you visit new places, you also meet new people. How are you introduced and what do you say? How do you introduce yourself? When Peter arrives in Neuss, many of the Nedels' family and friends are waiting to meet him.

A1 Freunde und Verwandte

HERR NEDEL So, Peter, wir sind da. Jetzt lernst du viele Leute kennen. Armer Peter!
PETER Ach, das ist nicht so schlimm.

WIEBKE Peter, das sind meine Grosseltern—Herr und Frau Graf—mein Opa, meine Oma.
PETER Guten Tag, Frau Graf! Guten Tag, Herr Graf!
HERR GRAF Willkommen in Neuss!
PETER Danke!

WIEBKE Mein Onkel und meine Tante, Jürgen und Christa Wolf.
PETER Guten Tag!

WIEBKE Das sind meine Geschwister—mein Bruder Philipp und meine Schwester Ulrike.
PETER Hallo, Philipp! Wie geht's?
PHILIPP Schön, dass du da bist.

Und das ist mein Hund, der Beppo.

WIEBKE Das ist mein Vetter Julian.
PETER Tag, Julian!

WIEBKE Und meine Kusine Alice, die Ali.
PETER Guten Tag, Ali!

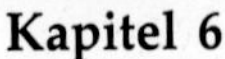

A2 Übung • Wer ist wer?

1. Jürgen Wolf ist	6	der Julian.
2. Herr und Frau Graf	4	der Hund.
3. Wiebkes Bruder	7	ein Klassenkamerad.
4. Beppo, so heisst	1	ein Onkel von Wiebke.
5. Philipp und Ulrike sind	10	eine Klassenkameradin.
6. Wiebkes Vetter ist	8	heisst Monika.
7. Jochen ist	3	heisst Philipp.
8. Wiebkes Freundin	2	sind die Grosseltern.
9. Markus ist ein Freund	9	von Wiebke.
10. Und die Antje ist	5	Wiebkes Geschwister.

A3 WIE SAGT MAN DAS?

Introducing someone, introducing yourself

These are some informal ways of introducing someone, and of introducing yourself. When being introduced, you respond by saying hello.

introducing someone	Peter, das ist mein Onkel, Herr Wolf.
introducing yourself	Ich heisse Markus. Ich bin ein Freund von Wiebke. Ich bin die Alice, Wiebkes Kusine.
responding to an introduction	Guten Tag, Frau Graf! Hallo, Philipp! Grüss dich, Antje! Wie geht's?

1. Frau Nedel ist Wiebkes Mutter. Alice ist die Kusine von Wiebke. Christa Wolf ist Wiebkes Tante. Julian ist Wiebkes Vetter. Herr und Frau Graf sind die Grosseltern von Wiebke. Jürgen Wolf ist Wiebkes Onkel. Philipp ist der Bruder von Wiebke. Ulrike ist Wiebkes Schwester.

A4 Übung • Wer ist das?

1. Tell who is who in Wiebke's family. Tell how each of the following people are related to Wiebke: Herr Nedel, Frau Nedel, Alice, Christa Wolf, Julian, Herr und Frau Graf, Jürgen Wolf, Philipp, Ulrike.

   Herr Nedel ist der Vater von Wiebke.
   Frau Nedel ist . . .

2. Introduce Wiebke's friends and mention if they are classmates, friends, or both.

   Das ist Jochen. Er ist . . . ein Klassenkamerad von Wiebke.
   Das ist der Markus. Er ist ein Freund von Wiebke.
   Das ist die Monika. Sie ist Wiebkes Freundin.
   Das ist die Antje. Sie ist eine Klassenkameradin von Wiebke.

A5 Übung • Jetzt bist du dran

1. Introduce yourself to some of your classmates. Say that you are a friend or a classmate of some other student.

   A: Ich heisse . . .; ich bin ein/eine . . . von . . .
   B: Tag, . . .! Wie geht's?

2. Introduce different classmates to each other and mention whose friend or classmate he or she is.

   A: Das ist . . ., ein Freund/eine Freundin von . . .
   B: Grüss dich, . . .!

A6 ERKLÄRUNG
ein *and* mein, *Nominative Case Forms*

1. The word **ein,** *a, an,* is called the indefinite article. The indefinite articles corresponding to **der, die,** and **das** are **ein, eine,** and **ein.** Before a masculine and a neuter noun, the form is **ein;** before a feminine noun, **eine.** There is no plural form of **ein.**

Masculine	Markus ist	der / ein	Freund von Wiebke.
Feminine	Antje ist	die / eine	Klassenkameradin.
Neuter	Monika ist	das / ein	Mädchen aus Köln.
Plural	Antje und Jochen sind	die / —	Klassenkameraden von Wiebke.

Mein should be the only possessive you hold the students responsible for at this point. You may wish to use *dein* in your presentation.

2. The words **mein** and **meine,** *my,* are called possessives. Their endings are the same as those of the indefinite articles. The possessives, however, have plural forms. You will learn other possessives later.

Masculine	**der**	**ein**	**mein**
Feminine	**die**	**eine**	**meine**
Neuter	**das**	**ein**	**mein**
Plural	**die**	**—**	**meine**

A7 Übung • Kennst du Wiebkes Klassenkameraden?

A: Wer ist der Jochen?
B: Der Jochen ist ein Klassenkamerad von Wiebke.

1. Wer ist die Antje? eine Klassenkameradin
2. Wer sind Antje und Jochen? Klassenkameraden
3. Wer ist der Jochen? ein Klassenkamerad
4. Wer ist die Monika? eine Freundin
5. Wer sind Monika und Markus? Freunde

A8 Übung • Wiebke stellt ihre Familie und Freunde vor

A: Wer ist Frau Nedel?
B: Das ist meine Mutter.

1. Wer ist Herr Nedel? mein Vater
2. Wer sind Herr und Frau Graf? meine Grosseltern
3. Wer ist Ali? meine Kusine
4. Wer ist Julian? mein Vetter
5. Wer ist Philipp? mein Bruder
6. Wer ist Jürgen Wolf? mein Onkel
7. Wer ist Ulrike? meine Schwester
8. Wer ist Christa Wolf? meine Tante

A9 Übung • Deine Familie

Draw a sketch depicting the members of your immediate family. Now introduce each family member to the class, pointing to the corresponding figure.

Das ist meine Mutter, Frau . . .; Das ist mein Bruder.
Er heisst . . . Er ist . . . Jahre alt.

A10 Schreibübung • Meine Klassenkameraden

Pick ten people in your class and write a sentence introducing each one:

Das ist . . ., ein Freund von . . .,
or ein Junge/ein Mädchen aus . . .

SECTION B

talking about your home

Wiebke shows Peter around the house. How does Peter like it? What does he say? How do you like the Nedels' home?

B1 Peter findet das Haus toll!

PETER Du, Wiebke, ich finde das Haus toll!
WIEBKE Ja, wirklich?
PETER Es ist gross, modern . . . Wieviel Zimmer habt ihr?
WIEBKE Möchtest du das Haus sehen?
PETER Ja, gern.
WIEBKE Komm! Ich zeig es dir.

WIEBKE Wir haben sechs Zimmer, eine Küche, . . .
PETER Wie modern sie ist!

WIEBKE Ein Wohnzimmer . . .
PETER Es sieht so gemütlich aus!
WIEBKE Findest du?
PETER Ja, sehr gemütlich!

WIEBKE Ein Esszimmer, . . .

WIEBKE Ein Bad und zwei Toiletten, eine unten und eine oben.
PETER So gross und hell!

Point out to the students the contrast between *Bad* (full bath) and *Toilette*.

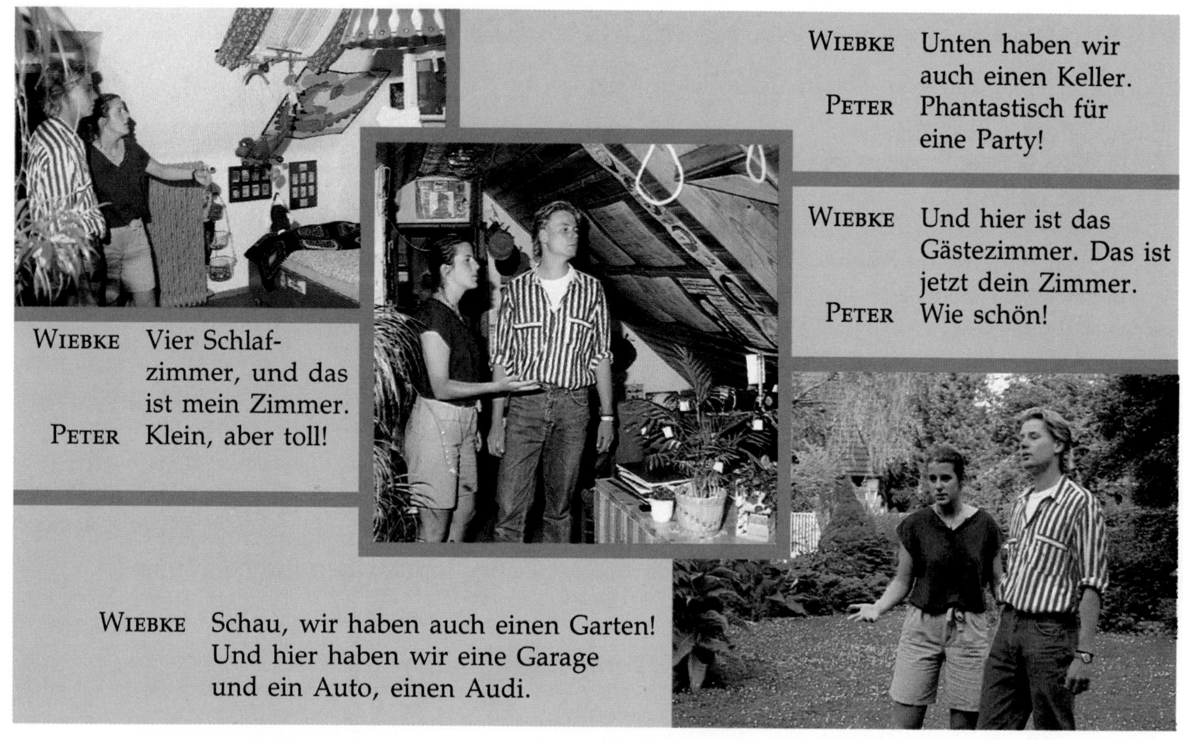

WIEBKE Unten haben wir auch einen Keller.
PETER Phantastisch für eine Party!
WIEBKE Und hier ist das Gästezimmer. Das ist jetzt dein Zimmer.
PETER Wie schön!
WIEBKE Vier Schlafzimmer, und das ist mein Zimmer.
PETER Klein, aber toll!
WIEBKE Schau, wir haben auch einen Garten! Und hier haben wir eine Garage und ein Auto, einen Audi.

B2 Übung • Wie sieht Nedels Haus aus?

Wieviel Zimmer hat das Haus? Was sagt Wiebke? Wir haben sechs Zimmer, eine Küche, ein Wohnzimmer, ein Esszimmer, ein Bad und zwei Toiletten, vier Schlafzimmer und einen Keller. Wir haben auch einen Garten und eine Garage.

B3 WIE SAGT MAN DAS?
Complimenting and responding to a compliment

complimenting	Ich finde das Haus toll! Das Wohnzimmer sieht gemütlich aus.	I think your house is great! The living room looks cozy!
responding to compliments	Ja, wirklich? Findest du?	Really? (You think so?) You think so?

How would you compliment someone in English? How would you respond to a compliment?

B4 Ein wenig Landeskunde

When somebody compliments you, you usually say thank you. In German-speaking countries the reaction to a compliment is quite different. German-speakers will either respond with another question—**Findest du?** or **Meinst du?**—or they will downplay the compliment. For example, a typical German response to the comment "I find this room very cozy" would be "Yes, but it really needs new wallpaper."

B5 Übung • Rollenspiel—Partnerarbeit

You are Wiebke and your classmate is Peter. Wiebke shows Peter around the house.

A: Hier ist die Küche.
B: Wie schön!
A: Ja, wirklich?

A: Wir haben eine Küche.
B: So gross und hell!
A: Findest du?

Wie modern! Klasse! *Wie schön (sie) ist!* Toll! So gemütlich. Phantastisch für eine Party. Prima! Wie gross (sie) ist! So gross und so hell.

B6 ERKLÄRUNG
Indefinite Articles, Accusative Case

On page 170 you learned the nominative forms of the indefinite article. You use nominative forms when the noun phrase functions as the subject of a sentence. Listed below are the accusative forms of the indefinite article. You use accusative forms when the noun phrase functions as the direct object of a sentence.

		Nominative		*Accusative*
Masculine *Feminine* *Neuter*	Da ist	**ein** Garten. **eine** Küche **ein** Bad.	Wir haben	**einen** Garten. **eine** Küche. **ein** Bad.
Plural	Da sind	vier Zimmer.	Wir haben	vier Zimmer.

B7 Übung • Und was habt ihr? 

A: Hier ist die Garage.
B: Wir haben auch eine Garage.

1. Hier ist der Garten.
2. Hier ist das Esszimmer.
3. Hier ist der Keller.
4. Hier ist die Garage.
5. Hier ist das Auto.
6. Hier ist der Audi.

einen Garten/ein Esszimmer/einen Keller/eine Garage/ein Auto/einen Audi

B8 Übung • Schüler erzählen

Draw a simple floor plan of your house or apartment, or make up a floor plan. With the help of your drawing, explain to a classmate what rooms you have. For example:

„Wir haben ein Haus. Es hat vier Zimmer. Wir haben ein Wohnzimmer, ein Esszimmer, eine Küche, zwei Schlafzimmer, ein Bad, eine Toilette, einen Keller und eine Garage. Das Wohnzimmer ist gross und gemütlich, die Schlafzimmer sind klein, die Küche ist hell und modern und . . .“

B9 Übung • Und du? Wie steht's mit dir?

Was habt ihr? Erzähl mal!

wir haben eine Wohnung ein Haus	Schlafzimmer Wohnzimmer Esszimmer Küche Bad Toilette Keller Garten Garage Auto	. . . ist schön gross, klein hell modern gemütlich nicht (gross) toll! prima! Klasse!

B10 Schreibübung

Write a paragraph describing where you live, or describing some other place you know. What kind of house or apartment is it? How many rooms are there? What are they? What are they like? You may refer to the list above and the narration in B8.

B11 PETER HAT FÜR ALLE NEDELS EIN GESCHENK 

Peter packt den Rucksack aus. Alle Nedels bekommen ein Geschenk.

PETER Hier ist eine Halskette für die Wiebke.
WIEBKE Toll! Vielen Dank, Peter!
PETER Nichts zu danken!

PETER Und hier hab' ich einen Taschenrechner für den Philipp.
PHILIPP Mensch, prima! Tausend Dank!

PETER Und da ist ein Buch für die Ulrike.
ULRIKE Danke, Peter!
PETER Bitte schön!

Da steht noch mehr auf Peters Zettel!

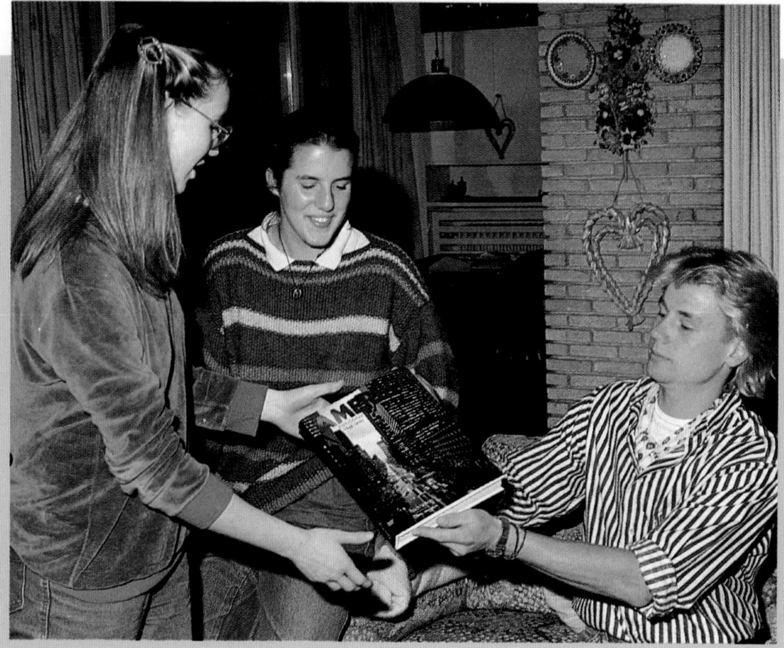

B12 Übung • Mix-Match

1. Peter packt	6	Dank!
2. Alle Nedels bekommen	1	den Rucksack aus.
3. Da ist eine Halskette	5	ein Buch.
4. Und für den Philipp	2	ein Geschenk.
5. Die Ulrike bekommt	4	ein Taschenrechner.
6. Peter, tausend	3	für die Wiebke.
7. Bitte	7	schön!
8. Nichts	8	zu danken.

B13 ERKLÄRUNG
The Preposition für

The preposition **für** is always followed by accusative case forms.

		Accusative	
Masculine *Feminine* *Neuter* *Plural*	Das Geschenk ist für	**den** Philipp. **die** Wiebke. **das** Mädchen. **die** Grosseltern.	
	Für	**wen**	ist das Geschenk?

B14 Übung • Peter hat noch mehr Geschenke

ein Buch für den Herrn Graf/eine Münze für die Ali/Briefmarken für den Hartmut/ein Kuli für die Wiebke/Spielkarten für den Philipp

Hier ist Peters Zettel. Wer bekommt was?

Kassette / Sabine
Buch / Herr Graf
Münze / Ali
Briefmarken / Hartmut
Kuli / Wiebke
Spielkarten / Philipp

Hier ist eine Kassette für die Sabine.
Hier ist . . .

B15 Schreibübung • Was sagt Peters Mutter?

Peter's mother gave him the note above to remind him who all the presents were for. Write what she said as she handed him the note.

Die Kassette ist für die . . . Sabine. Das Buch ist für den Herrn Graf. Die Münze ist für die Ali. Die Briefmarken sind für den Harmut. Der Kuli ist für die Wiebke. Die Spielkarten sind für den Philipp.

B16 WIE SAGT MAN DAS?
Saying thank you and you're welcome

You have learned to say thank you and you're welcome when shopping and when asking for information—for example, when asking for directions. Here are some more ways of expressing gratitude. These are appropriate to use when you receive a present.

saying thank you	Danke! Tausend Dank! Vielen Dank!	Thanks. Thanks a million. Thanks a lot.
responding to a thank you	Bitte schön! Nichts zu danken.	You're welcome. Don't mention it.

B17 Übung • Für wen sind die Geschenke?

Du hast auch Geschenke für die Nedels. Für wen sind sie?

A: Hier ist ein Buch für die Ulrike.
B: Vielen Dank!
A: Bitte schön!

or

A: Hier hab' ich eine Kassette für den Philipp.
B: Tausend Dank!
A: Nichts zu danken.

B18 Übung • Hör gut zu!

For script and answers, see p. T123.

Which conversation are you overhearing? Listen.

	0	1	2	3	4	5	6
Wiebke showing Peter the house			✓	✓			✓
Peter distributing gifts	✓	✓			✓	✓	

SECTION C talking about appearance and personal characteristics

At the gathering for Peter, Wiebke and her friends are talking. Do you agree with their opinions? What do you think?

C1 Kennst du Wiebkes Freunde?

Die Antje ist klein, blond, schlank. Sie ist sehr hübsch.

MARKUS Die Antje ist so attraktiv.
JOCHEN Das ist Geschmackssache. Ich finde sie nicht unsympathisch.
MARKUS Wirklich?

Das ist der Markus. Er ist gross, dunkel, er hat eine Brille.

ALI Der Markus sieht gut aus, nicht?
ANTJE Ja, das stimmt. Und er ist auch gar nicht arrogant.
ALI Meinst du?

Der Jochen ist dunkelblond.

ANTJE Mensch, ist der Jochen langweilig!
WIEBKE Was?! Das finde ich nicht. Ich finde ihn nett.
ANTJE Nett, ja—aber langweilig!
WIEBKE Das stimmt nicht!

Die Monika ist brünett.

PHILIPP Die Monika ist sehr freundlich, meinst du nicht?
JOCHEN Du hast recht. Sie ist lustig, und ich finde sie sehr sympathisch.
PHILIPP Ich auch.

C2 Übung • Wer sind Wiebkes Freunde? Wie sehen sie aus?

1. Wer ist Markus? Wie sieht er aus?
2. Wer ist Antje? Wie sieht sie aus?
3. Und wie sieht die Monika aus? brünett
4. Und der Jochen? dunkelblond

1. gross, dunkel, hat eine Brille 2. klein, blond, schlank, sehr hübsch

C3 WIE SAGT MAN DAS?
Talking about appearance

To describe how someone looks, you can use the verb **aussehen,** *to look, to look like.*

Wie sieht er aus?	What does he look like?
Er sieht gut aus.	He is good-looking.
Er ist gross und schlank.	He is tall and slim.

C4 Übung • Und du? For additional vocabulary, see p. 182 (C15).

1. Wie heissen deine Freunde?
2. Wie alt sind sie?
3. Wie sehen sie aus?

C5 ERKLÄRUNG
The Verb **aussehen**

The verb **aussehen,** *to look (like),* is a verb with a prefix. The prefix **aus-** is often separated from the verb and is placed at the end of the sentence. The verb **aussehen** also has a vowel change in the **du-** and **er/sie-**forms.

Singular				*Plural*			
Ich	**sehe**	gut	**aus.**	Wir	**sehen**	gut	**aus.**
Du	**siehst**			Ihr	**seht**		
Markus (er)	**sieht**			Die Geschwister (sie)	**sehen**		
Antje (sie)	**sieht**						
Sie	**sehen**			Sie	**sehen**		

C6 Übung • Frag, wie alle aussehen! 

A: Kennst du den Thomas?
B: Wie sieht er aus?

1. Kennst du die Wiebke? sieht sie aus?
2. Kennst du Jochen und Ursel? sehen sie aus?
3. Kennst du Wiebkes Eltern? sehen sie aus?
4. Kennst du Wiebkes Bruder? sieht er aus?
5. Kennst du Wiebkes Kusine? sieht sie aus?
6. Kennst du Wiebkes Grossvater? sieht er aus?

C7 Übung • Wiebkes Familie sieht nett aus! 

A: Wie sieht Wiebkes Vater aus?
B: Er sieht nett aus.

1. Wie sieht Philipp aus? Er sieht nett aus.
2. Wie sehen Wiebkes Grosseltern aus? Sie sehen nett aus.
3. Wie sieht Wiebkes Onkel aus? Er sieht nett aus.
4. Wie sieht die Alice aus? Sie sieht nett aus.

C8 Übung • Ratespiel: Wer ist das?

Play these guessing games with your classmates.

1. You think of someone and give a brief description of that person. Your classmates have to guess who it is. (Sie ist gross und schlank, blond, 16 Jahre alt. Sie spielt Tennis. Sie sammelt Briefmarken. Sie ist aus . . . —Wer ist das?)
2. You think of someone and your classmates ask questions to find out who it is. (Ist sie gross? Ist sie dunkel? Ist sie schon 16? Hat sie eine Schwester? etc.)

C9 WIE SAGT MAN DAS?
Agreeing, disagreeing, expressing surprise

You already know some phrases for expressing agreement, disagreement, and surprise. Some other expressions have been added to this list.

agreeing	Das stimmt. Du hast recht. Das finde ich auch. Ich auch.	That's right./That's true. You're right. I think so, too. Me, too.
disagreeing	Das stimmt nicht. Das finde ich nicht. Das ist Geschmackssache.	That's not so. I don't think so. That's a matter of taste.
expressing surprise	Wirklich? Was?! Meinst du?	Really? Do you think so? What?! Do you think so?

C10 Übung • Wie findest du Wiebkes Freunde?

Somebody expresses an opinion about one of Wiebke's friends or relatives. Agree with that opinion or express surprise and disagree.

A: Ich finde den Jochen lustig.
B: Ich auch. *or* Was? Ich finde den Jochen langweilig.

C11 ERKLÄRUNG
Third Person Pronouns, Accusative Case

In Unit 2, you learned the pronouns **er, sie, es,** and **sie.** These pronouns refer to both people and things. You use them to refer to noun phrases that are in the nominative case.

The pronouns **ihn, sie, es,** and **sie** also refer to both people and things, but you use them to refer to noun phrases that are in the accusative case. **Ihn** refers to a masculine noun phrase, **es** to a neuter noun phrase, and **sie** to a feminine or plural noun phrase.

		Accusative		*Accusative*	
Masculine *Feminine* *Neuter*	Wie findest du	**den Jungen? den Garten?** **die Oma? die Küche?** **das Mädchen? das Poster?**	Ich finde	**ihn** **sie** **es**	nett.
Plural		**die Kinder? die Zimmer?**		**sie**	

C12 Übung • Wie findest du . . .?

A: Ist der Thomas nett?
B: Ja, ich finde ihn nett.

1. Ist die Antje lustig? sie
2. Ist die Küche gemütlich? sie
3. Ist der Markus arrogant? ihn
4. Sind die Zimmer gross? sie
5. Ist der Audi toll? ihn
6. Sind die Kinder nett? sie
7. Ist die Ali sympathisch? sie
8. Ist der Jochen freundlich? ihn
9. Ist das Haus schön? es

C13 Übung • Der Miesmacher

Kennst du den Miesmacher? Er sagt nie etwas Nettes!

1. Findest du den Markus nett?
2. Findest du die Antje hübsch?
3. Findest du die Ali interessant?
4. Findest du den Jochen freundlich?
5. Findest du den Philipp sympathisch?

1. Ich finde ihn arrogant.
2. Ich finde sie nicht attraktiv.
3. Ich finde sie langweilig.
4. Ich finde ihn unfreundlich.
5. Ich finde ihn unsympathisch.

Nein, ich finde ihn . . .

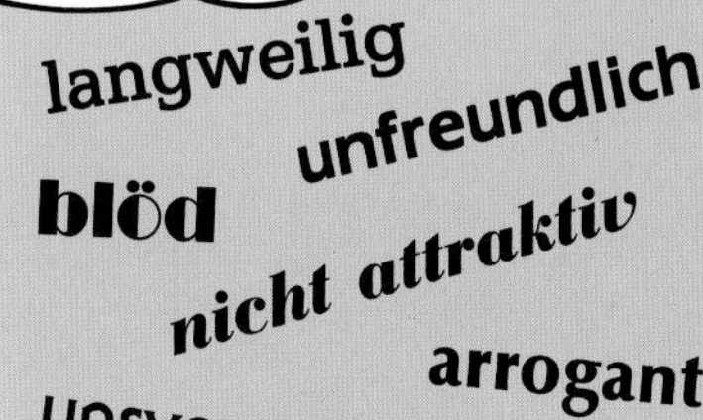

C14 Übung • Hör gut zu!

For script and answers, see p. T126.

Who or what is being talked about? Listen.

	0	1	2	3	4	5	6	7	8	9	10
ein Junge			✓		✓				✓		
ein Mädchen	✓							✓			✓
das Haus				✓			✓				
zwei Schulfreunde		✓				✓				✓	

C15 Übung • Wie sind diese Leute?

Wie sehen sie aus? Wie findest du sie?

Hans

Herr Krauss

Gerda

Frau Hagen

Fritz

These new adjectives are passive vocabulary.

er/sie ist	**gross, klein** **schlank, vollschlank** **hübsch, sehr hübsch** **dunkel, blond, dunkelblond, brünett** **nett** hat schwarze Haare, rote Haare
er/sie sieht . . . aus	**gut, nicht gut** **hübsch, sehr hübsch, nett** **toll, prima** **alt, interessant**
er/sie	**hat eine Brille**
ich finde ihn/sie	**(sehr) nett, attraktiv, freundlich, lustig, sympathisch, hübsch, unsympathisch, arrogant, unfreundlich, langweilig, blöd**

Was kannst du auch sagen?

Er/sie ist:	Er/sie sieht . . . aus.
intelligent	dumm
sportlich	ordentlich
musikalisch	schlampig

Du erzählst: Das ist Fritz. Er ist gross, vollschlank, blond. Er sieht nett und intelligent aus. Er hat eine Brille. Ich finde ihn sehr sympathisch.

C16 Übung • Hör gut zu!

For script and answers, see p. T127.

Who fits the description?

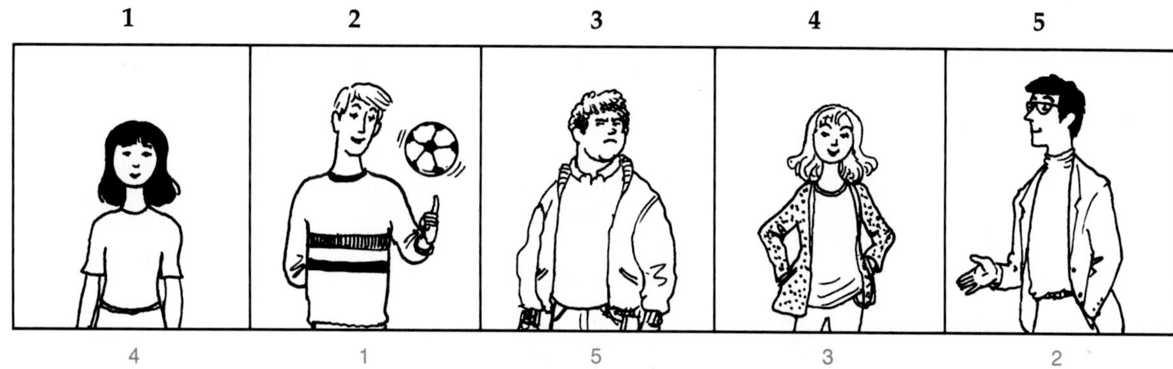

4 1 5 3 2

C17 Schreibübung • Kennst du . . . ?

1. Petra has just come to the gathering at the Nedels. She does not know many people, so Jochen is pointing out who some of them are. For each person Jochen notices, write the conversation he and Petra might have.

JOCHEN Kennst du den Frank, den Freund von Wiebke?
PETRA Nein, ich kenne ihn nicht. *or* Ja, ich kenne ihn.

1. Monika, eine Schwester von Thomas die, sie
2. Philipp, der Bruder von Wiebke den, ihn
3. Elke, eine Freundin von Monika die, sie
4. Ursel, eine Kusine aus Wien die, sie
5. Peter, ein Freund aus Amerika den, ihn

2. Write a logical answer to each question, using the word or words in parentheses.

Ist er gross? (klein) Nein, er ist klein.
Macht sie Sport? (Tennis) Ja, sie spielt Tennis.

1. Ist sie blond? (brünett) Nein, sie ist brünett.
2. Hat er einen Bruder? (eine Schwester) Nein, er hat eine Schwester.
3. Ist sie hübsch? (sehr hübsch) Ja, sie ist sehr hübsch.
4. Ist er 15 Jahre alt? (16) Nein, er ist 16.
5. Ist er blond? (dunkelblond) Ja, er ist dunkelblond.
6. Sieht er gut aus? (toll) Ja, er sieht toll aus!
7. Sieht sie nett aus? (sehr nett) Ja, sie sieht sehr nett aus.
8. Hat sie Geschwister? (drei Geschwister: einen Bruder und zwei Schwestern) Ja, sie hat drei Geschwister: einen Bruder und zwei Schwestern.

3. Pick three photos of relatives or friends, or find pictures in a magazine and write a description of each person pictured. You may want to start by describing the students pictured below.

TRY YOUR SKILLS using what you've learned

An American exchange student writes home to his German teacher.

1 Ein Brief aus Deutschland

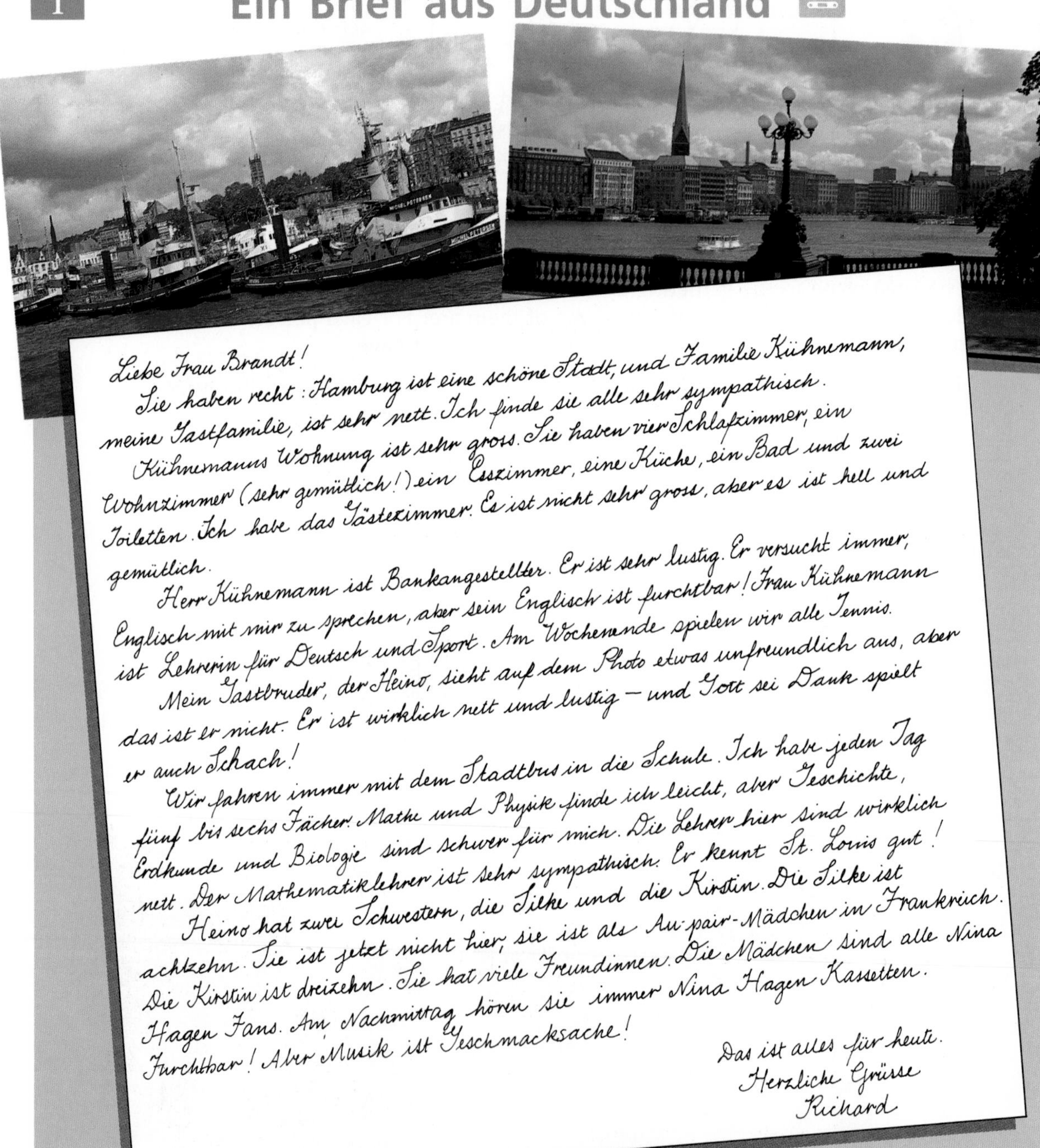

Liebe Frau Brandt!

Sie haben recht: Hamburg ist eine schöne Stadt, und Familie Kühnemann, meine Gastfamilie, ist sehr nett. Ich finde sie alle sehr sympathisch.

Kühnemanns Wohnung ist sehr gross. Sie haben vier Schlafzimmer, ein Wohnzimmer (sehr gemütlich!) ein Esszimmer, eine Küche, ein Bad und zwei Toiletten. Ich habe das Gästezimmer. Es ist nicht sehr gross, aber es ist hell und gemütlich.

Herr Kühnemann ist Bankangestellter. Er ist sehr lustig. Er versucht immer, Englisch mit mir zu sprechen, aber sein Englisch ist furchtbar! Frau Kühnemann ist Lehrerin für Deutsch und Sport. Am Wochenende spielen wir alle Tennis.

Mein Gastbruder, der Heino, sieht auf dem Photo etwas unfreundlich aus, aber das ist er nicht. Er ist wirklich nett und lustig — und Gott sei Dank spielt er auch Schach!

Wir fahren immer mit dem Stadtbus in die Schule. Ich habe jeden Tag fünf bis sechs Fächer. Mathe und Physik finde ich leicht, aber Geschichte, Erdkunde und Biologie sind schwer für mich. Die Lehrer hier sind wirklich nett. Der Mathematiklehrer ist sehr sympathisch. Er kennt St. Louis gut!

Heino hat zwei Schwestern, die Silke und die Kirstin. Die Silke ist achtzehn. Sie ist jetzt nicht hier; sie ist als Au-pair-Mädchen in Frankreich. Die Kirstin ist dreizehn. Sie hat viele Freundinnen. Die Mädchen sind alle Nina Hagen Fans. Am Nachmittag hören sie immer Nina Hagen Kassetten. Furchtbar! Aber Musik ist Geschmacksache!

Das ist alles für heute.
Herzliche Grüsse
Richard

2 Übung • Was schreibt Richard? For answers, see p. T128.

Was schreibt Richard über seine Gastfamilie? über die Wohnung? über die Schule?

3 Schreibübung • Ein Brief von Peter aus Neuss

Du bist jetzt Peter. Schreib einen Brief an deine Eltern. Beschreibe die Familie Nedel und Nedels Haus in Neuss!

> Liebe Eltern!
> Grüsse aus Neuss! Ich bin schon eine Woche hier, und es ist sehr schön. Die Nedels sind . . .

4 Übung • Deine Meinung—meine Meinung

Bring in pictures of well-known people and discuss each person with your classmates. Express your opinion and agree or disagree with the various comments.

A: Wie findest du . . .?

B: Ich finde sie arrogant.
A: Wirklich? Ich finde sie nett.

or

B: Ich finde sie sehr nett.
A: Meinst du? Ich finde sie unsympathisch.

5 Übung • Geschenke für die Nedels  For answers, see p. T129.

Peter kauft Geschenke für die Familie Nedel. Seine Mutter fragt, was er für jeden hat.

MUTTER Was hast du für den Philipp?
PETER Für ihn habe ich eine Musikkassette.
MUTTER Gut.
PETER Schau! Wie findest du die Kassette?
MUTTER Du, ich finde sie prima!

Philipp

Ulrike

Hartmut

Wiebke

Opa

Oma

6 Übung • Danke!—Bitte schön! 

für die Halskette, für den Taschenrechner, für das Poster, für die Briefmarken, für das Buch

Die Nedels danken Peter für die Geschenke.

PHILIPP Danke für die Musikkassette.
PETER Nichts zu danken!

Alternative responses: Bitte schön!
Gern geschehen!

ULRIKE . . .
PETER . . .

7 Schreibübung • Wie heisst die Frage? For answers, see p. T129.

Ich finde den Markus arrogant.

Wiebkes Geschwister heissen Philipp und Ulrike.

Sie ist gross, blond, schlank.

Nein, ich kenne Herrn Graf nicht.

Wir haben fünf Zimmer.

Ich bin ein Klassenkamerad von Markus.

Ja, einen Audi.

8 Übung • Ein Wohnungsplan

1. Beschreibe die Wohnung! Was ist rechts? Was ist links?
2. Jemand zeigt dir die Wohnung. Was sagst du?

A: Hier ist das Wohnzimmer.
B: Es ist sehr hell. Ich finde es sehr schön.

Die Wohnung hat rechts zwei Schlafzimmer, ein Bad und eine Toilette. Links hat die Wohnung eine Küche, ein Wohnzimmer, ein Esszimmer und einen Balkon. Sie hat auch einen Flur.

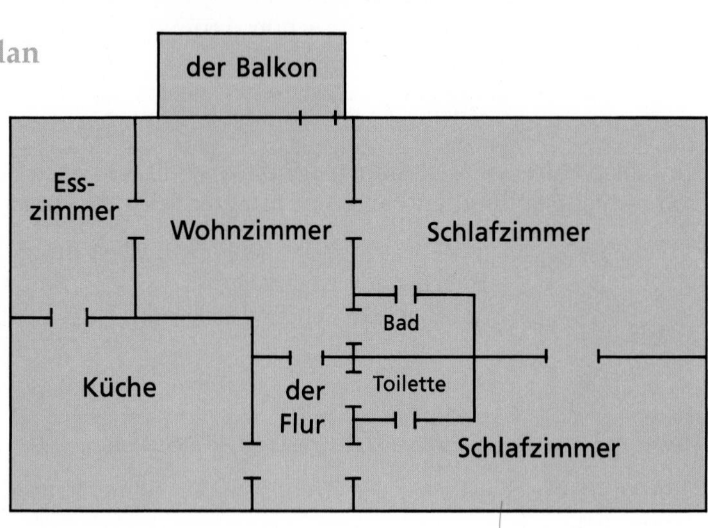

9 Schreibübung • Wir wohnen in Wien

Rewrite the following selection, replacing each underlined noun phrase with a pronoun.

Wir haben ein Haus in Wien. Wir finden <u>das Haus</u> toll! Wir haben einen Garten. <u>Der Garten</u> ist sehr gross und schön, und wir finden <u>den Garten</u> prima. Meine Grosseltern wohnen auch in Wien. Wir sehen <u>meine Grosseltern</u> oft. Sie haben eine Wohnung. <u>Die Wohnung</u> ist sehr gemütlich. Mein Grossvater und ich spielen immer Schach. Ich finde <u>das Spiel</u> interessant. Mein Bruder Fritz findet Schach langweilig. Ich finde <u>den Fritz</u> blöd.

es
er, ihn
sie
sie
es
ihn

10 Übung • Hör gut zu! For script and answers, see p. T130.

Does the statement express agreement, disagreement, surprise, or gratitude? Listen.

	0	1	2	3	4	5	6	7	8	9	10
agreement	✓			✓			✓				✓
disagreement		✓	✓						✓		
surprise					✓					✓	
gratitude						✓		✓			

1. Eine Halskette! Vielen Dank, Peter!/Nichts zu danken! 2. Hier ist das Wohnzimmer./Wie gemütlich! 3. Das ist mein Freund Kurt./Grüss dich! 4. Die Antje sieht toll aus!/Das ist Geschmackssache.

11 Übung • Was sagen sie?

Hier ist das Wohnzimmer.

Das ist mein Freund Kurt.

Nichts zu danken!

Die Antje sieht toll aus!

Eine Halskette! Vielen Dank, Peter!

Das ist Geschmackssache.

Wie gemütlich!

Grüss dich!

12 Aussprache-, Lese- und Schreibübungen

For script, see p. T130.

1. Listen carefully and repeat what you hear.

2. Listen, then read aloud.

1. trinken, Brille, drei, Freund, mehr, Vater, gross, sehr, brauchen, Zimmer
2. Väter, wählen, Bäder, Flughäfen, ungefähr; Pässe, Gepäck, Gästezimmer
3. ob, halb, abheben, verabredet, Wiebke
4. gebe, gibst, gebt; bleibe, bleibst, bleibt; sage, sagst, sagt; frage, fragst, fragt
5. hab'—habe, bleib'—bleibe, Freund—Freunde, Hund—Hunde, frag'—frage

3. Copy the following sentences to prepare yourself to write them from dictation.

1. Ich hab' einen Freund.
2. Wie spät ist es, bitte?
3. Bleib bitte hier!
4. Die Flughäfen sind sehr gross.

WAS KANNST DU SCHON?

Let's review some important points that you have learned in this unit.

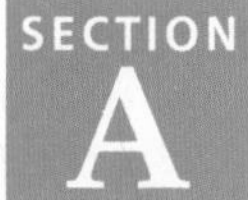

Can you introduce someone and introduce yourself?
Introduce the following people to a classmate: . . . , das ist (sind)

your father, your mother, a sister, a brother, an uncle, an aunt, your grandparents mein Vater/meine Mutter/meine Schwester . . ./mein Bruder . . ./mein Onkel, . . ./meine Tante, . . ./meine Grosseltern, Herr und Frau . . . /mein Opa, meine Oma

Introduce yourself to a classmate and say you are a friend of another classmate.

Ich heisse . . . Ich bin ein Freund/eine Freundin von . . .

Can you describe your home or an imaginary home?
Say how many rooms you have and what they are. Wir haben . . . Zimmer, Küche/Wohnzimmer/Esszimmer/Bad/Toilette/Keller/Gästezimmer/Schlafzimmer/Garten/Garage

Can you comment on someone else's home?
Someone is showing you his or her home. Make some appropriate comments. Wie modern/schön/gross/hell/gemütlich/toll!

Can you specify that something is for someone?
You have brought gifts to the Nedel family. Say that you have the following gifts for each person:

Poster / Wiebke Ich habe ein Poster für die Wiebke.

1. Kassette / Ulrike 2. Taschenrechner / Philipp 3. Buch / Oma
4. Briefmarken / Hartmut eine Kassette für die Ulrike/einen Taschenrechner für den Philipp/ein Buch für die Oma/Briefmarken für den Hartmut

Do you know how to say thank you when you receive a present?
You have just received a book as a present. Give three ways of saying thank you. Danke! Vielen Dank! Tausend Dank!

Say you're welcome. Bitte schön!/Nichts zu danken.

Do you know how to describe someone?
Describe three people in your class, using the verb **aussehen.** . . . sieht . . . aus.

Do you know how to express an opinion?
Describe someone you like and someone you don't like. Ich finde sie/ihn (sehr) nett/attraktiv/freundlich/lustig/sympathisch/hübsch [oder] unsympathisch/arrogant/blöd/langweilig

Do you know how to agree or disagree with someone else's opinion?
Respond to the following statements, first agreeing, then disagreeing.

1. Ich finde die Antje nett. (Das finde) ich auch. Das ist Geschmackssache.
2. Philipp ist lustig. Das stimmt. Das finde ich nicht.
3. Wiebke ist hübsch. Du hast recht. Das stimmt nicht.

WORTSCHATZ

SECTION A

armer Peter! *poor Peter!*
bei den Nedels *at the Nedels'*
der **Bruder, ¨** *brother*
da: wir sind da *we're here*
das sind *these are*
dass *that*
die **Freundin, -nen** *girl friend*
die **Geschwister** (pl) *brothers and sisters*
die **Grosseltern** (pl) *grandparents*
der **Hund, -e** *dog*
kennenlernen: du lernst viele Leute kennen *you're going to meet a lot of people*
die **Klassenkameradin, -nen** *classmate* (f)
die **Kusine, -n** *cousin* (f)
die **Leute** (pl) *people*
mein, meine *my*
die **Oma, -s** *grandma*
der **Onkel, -** *uncle*
der **Opa, -s** *grandpa*
schlimm *bad*
schön *nice;* schön, dass du da bist *nice that you're here*
die **Schwester, -n** *sister*
so *so, well then*
die **Tante, -n** *aunt*
der **Vetter, -n** *cousin* (m)
viele *many*
von *of;* ein Freund von Wiebke *a friend of Wiebke's*
Willkommen in Neuss! *welcome to Neuss!*

SECTION B

der **Audi, -s** *Audi* (a German-made automobile)
auf *on*
auspacken: er packt den Rucksack aus *he unpacks his backpack*
aussehen *to look (like), appear,* (see p 179)
das **Auto, -s** *car*
das **Bad, ¨er** *bathroom*
bekommen *to get, receive*
bitte schön *you're welcome*
das **Buch, ¨er** *book*
Dank: vielen Dank! *thanks a lot!* tausend Dank! *thanks a million!*
danken *to thank;* nichts zu danken *don't mention it*
dein, deine *your*
das **Esszimmer, -** *dining room*
finden: findest du? *do you think so?*
die **Garage, -n** *garage*
der **Garten, ¨** *garden*
das **Gästezimmer, -** *guest room*
gemütlich *cozy, comfortable*
gern: ja, gern *yes, I'd like that*
gross *big*
die **Halskette, -n** *necklace*
das **Haus, ¨er** *house*
hell *light*
der **Keller, -** *basement, cellar*
klein *small*
komm! *come on!*
die **Küche, -n** *kitchen*
mehr *more*
Mensch! *boy! wow!*
modern *modern*
oben *upstairs*
die **Party, -s** *party*
der **Rucksack, ¨e** *knapsack, backpack*
das **Schlafzimmer, -** *bedroom*
schön *pretty, beautiful*
sehen *to see*
sehr *very*
stehen: da steht noch mehr auf Peters Zettel *there's still more on Peter's list*
tausend *thousand;* tausend Dank! *thanks a million!*
die **Toilette, -n** *toilet*
unten *downstairs*
wieviel? *how many?*
das **Wohnzimmer, -** *living room*
zeigen *to show;* ich zeig es dir *I'll show it to you*
der **Zettel, -** *list, slip of paper*
das **Zimmer, -** *room*

SECTION C

arrogant *arrogant*
attraktiv *attractive*
aussehen: gut aussehen *to look good; to be handsome, pretty, attractive*
blond *blond*
die **Brille, -n** *glasses*
brünett *brunette*
dunkel *dark*
dunkelblond *dark blond*
freundlich *friendly*
Geschmackssache: das ist Geschmackssache *that's a matter of taste*
gross *tall*
hübsch *pretty*
kennen *to know*
klein *short, small*
lustig *merry, funny*
meinen: meinst du? *do you think so?* meinst du nicht? *don't you think so?*
nett *nice*
nicht? *don't you think so?*
recht haben *to be right*
schlank *slim*
sympathisch *likeable, nice*
unsympathisch *unpleasant, not nice*
vollschlank *heavyset*

WORTSCHATZÜBUNGEN

1. Look at the Wortschatz and make a list of all singular nouns with their definite articles. Then write the nouns again with their indefinite articles.
der/ein Bruder, die/eine Freundin, der/ein Hund, die/eine Klassenkameradin, die/eine Kusine, die/eine Oma,
2. Pick out all the adjectives and write them down. How many pairs of opposites can you find? Write them next to each other. schlimm/schön; gross/klein; arrogant, unsympathisch/sympathisch, freundlich, nett, lustig; schlank/vollschlank; blond/brünett, dunkel; hell/dunkel

1. (cont.) der/ein Onkel, der/ein Opa, die/eine Schwester, die/eine Tante, der/ein Vetter, der/ein Audi, das/ein Auto, das/ein Bad, das/ein Buch, das/ein Esszimmer, die/eine Garage, der/ein Garten, das/ein Gästezimmer, die/eine Halskette, das/ein Haus, der/ein Keller, die/eine Küche, die/eine Party, der/ein Rucksack, das/ein Schlafzimmer, das/ein Wohnzimmer, der/ein Zettel, das/ein Zimmer, die/eine Brille

ZUM LESEN

Märchen

Sind Märchen° wieder „in"? 

We're asking teenagers how they feel about fairy tales. What do they say?

Die klassischen Märchen wie „Schneewittchen", „Rotkäppchen", „Rumpelstilzchen" waren lange Zeit nicht mehr „in". Viele Eltern und Erzieher° sagten, die Märchen haben heute mit uns nichts zu tun°, sie sind unwahr°, sie zeigen den Kindern eine Welt° mit einem König° an der Spitze°, eine Welt, wo nur Männer regieren.

Heute erkennt man, dass° Märchen nicht nur für Kinder sind. Die Märchensymbole sind für jung und alt. Die Symbole sind stark°, klar, einfach°: Apfel und Gürtel° sind Symbole für Liebe°, Zepter und Krone sind Symbole für Macht°, Hexe, Wolf und Wald° sind Symbole für die bösen Mächte° in der Welt. Diese Symbole haben eine Beziehung° zu der Welt heute; sie haben eine Bedeutung° für uns. Vielleicht° sind deshalb° die Märchen auch heute noch bei Kindern und Erwachsenen° so beliebt°.

Märchen sind nicht nur für kleine Kinder; sie können uns viel über das Leben° heute sagen.

Ich lese zum Beispiel Märchen lieber als Comics. Ich finde Comics blöd: der Superman ist für mich sehr unrealistisch.

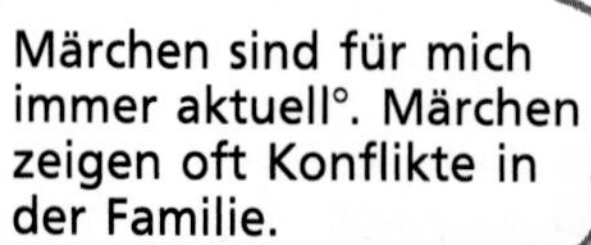

Märchen sind für mich immer aktuell°. Märchen zeigen oft Konflikte in der Familie.

Ich finde Märchen prima. Sie sind manchmal ein bisschen brutal, aber es gibt doch immer ein „Happy End".

Märchen *fairy tales;* **Erzieher** *educators;* **tun** *to do;* **unwahr** *untrue;* **eine Welt** *a world;* **der König** *king;* **an der Spitze** *at the top;* **heute erkennt man, dass** *today people recognize that;* **stark** *strong;* **einfach** *simple;* **der Gürtel** *belt;* **die Liebe** *love;* **die Macht** *power, force;* **der Wald** *forest;* **die bösen Mächte** *bad influences, evil forces;* **die Beziehung** *connection;* **die Bedeutung** *meaning;* **vielleicht** *maybe;* **deshalb** *therefore;* **Erwachsene** *adults;* **beliebt** *popular;* **das Leben** *life;* **aktuell** *current, up-to-date*

Kinder- und Hausmärchen

der

Brüder Grimm

Gesamtausgabe

mit 90 Holzschnitten

und 6 Tonbildern

von

Ludwig Richter

Die Brüder Grimm 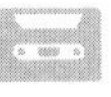

Diesen Namen kennt ihr von „Grimm's Fairy Tales". Die Brüder heissen Jakob und Wilhelm Grimm. Ihr zweihundertster Geburtstag war 1985/86. In der hessischen Stadt Kassel ist das Brüder-Grimm-Museum. Hier können Besucher die Bücher und Manuskripte der Brüder Grimm sehen.

Die Märchen der Brüder Grimm waren schon im 19. Jahrhundert ein grosser Erfolg°. Nur die Bibel wurde noch öfter gedruckt°. Und heute leben° die Märchen noch! Es gab noch nie so viele Märchenbücher, Märchenkassetten und Märchenfilme wie heute!

---

der Erfolg *success;* . . . **gedruckt** *only the Bible had more printings;* **leben** *to live*

Übung • Was sagst du?

1. Wie findest du Märchen?
2. Welche Märchen liest du am liebsten? Welche Märchen hast du nicht gern? Warum?

Übung • Sprechen wir darüber!

1. How do fairy tales reflect problems in our society today?
2. Discuss some of the symbols found in popular fairy tales. What could the symbols stand for in our contemporary world?

Übung • Klassenprojekte

1. Write a report on the Brothers Grimm and present it to the class.
2. Find illustrated editions of Grimms' "Kinder- und Hausmärchen" in German and in English. Compare the titles of various tales in both languages.
3. Choose one of the fairy tales and write a modern version in English. As a class project, write one of the stories in dialog form in German and act it out for the class.

Kennt ihr diese Märchen? 

Könnt ihr raten, wie die Märchen heissen?

Refer the students to the introduction (p. 20) for a chart showing Fraktur.

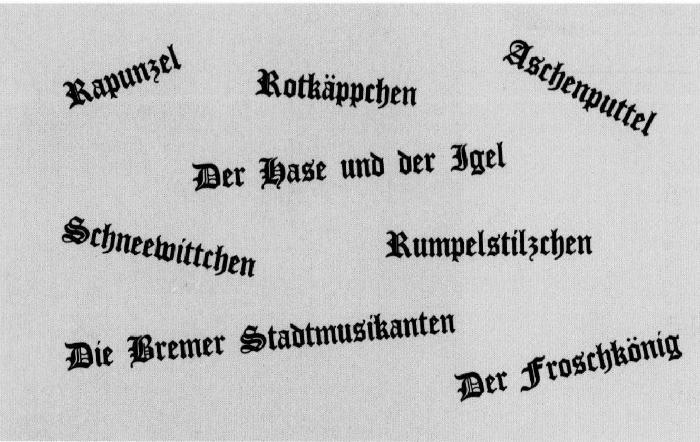

Rapunzel
Rotkäppchen
Aschenputtel
Der Hase und der Igel
Schneewittchen
Rumpelstilzchen
Die Bremer Stadtmusikanten
Der Froschkönig

Dieses Mädchen hat eine Stiefmutter und zwei böse Schwestern. Sie muss hart arbeiten. Sie geht auf einen Ball . . . Sie tanzt mit dem Prinzen, sie verliert einen Schuh . . .

Aschenputtel

Eine Königstochter spielt mit ihrem goldenen Ball. Der Ball fällt in den Brunnen. Hier wohnt der hässliche Frosch. Aber ist er wirklich ein Frosch? Muss die Königstochter ihn küssen?

Der Froschkönig

Herr Langohr ist arrogant. Der kleine Dicke ist intelligent. Sie machen eine Wette. Der kleine Dicke gewinnt die Wette . . . Wer ist jetzt der Dummkopf?

Der Hase und der Igel

Die Königstochter hat eine böse Stiefmutter. Die schaut immer in den Spiegel und fragt: „Spieglein, Spieglein an der Wand, wer ist die schönste im ganzen Land?" Die sieben Zwerge helfen der Königstochter . . .

Schneewittchen

Die vier Freunde wandern zu einer grossen Stadt in Norddeutschland. Sie wollen Musik machen. Im Wald wohnen Räuber in einem Haus. Die vier Freunde wollen in dem Haus schlafen . . .

Die Bremer Stadtmusikanten

Kennt ihr diesen kleinen Mann? Er spinnt Stroh zu Gold für die Müllerstochter. Dann will er ihr erstes Kind haben . . . Aber wie heisst er?

Rumpelstilzchen

Warum sitzt das schöne Mädchen ganz allein im Turm? Warum hängt ihr langes goldenes Haar herunter? Wer besucht sie in der Nacht? Wie kommt der Königssohn in den Turm?

Rapunzel

„Grossmutter, was hast du für grosse Augen!"
„Damit ich dich besser sehen kann!"

Rotkäppchen

KAPITEL 7

KAPITEL 7 Wo wohnen sie?

Scope and Sequence

	BASIC MATERIAL	COMMUNICATIVE FUNCTIONS
SECTION A	**Wo wohnen unsere Freunde? (A1)** **In München (A10)** **Entschuldigung, wo ist bitte . . . ? (A13)**	**Exchanging information** • Telling where you live and what kind of place it is • Pointing out landmarks • Asking for directions
SECTION B	**Steffi geht einkaufen (B1)**	**Exchanging information** • Talking about shopping **Persuading** • Making requests • Suggesting where to go shopping
SECTION C	**Schade, es regnet. (C1)** **Der Flori hat Hunger (C7)** **Wie schmeckt's? (C11)**	**Expressing feelings and emotions** • Expressing annoyance **Expressing attitudes and opinions** • Asking/telling how something tastes **Socializing** • Saying you want or don't want more • Talking about the weather
TRY YOUR SKILLS	Pronunciation diphthongs /ei/, /au/, /ɔi/; /ɔ/, /pf/, /ʃv/ Letter-sound correspondences **ei/ay, eu/äu; o, z, w** Dictation	
ZUM LESEN	**München** (a travel article about Munich)	

WRITING A variety of controlled and open-ended writing activities appear in the Pupil's Edition. The Teacher's Notes identify other activities suitable for writing practice and suggest additional writing activities.

COOPERATIVE LEARNING Many of the activities in the Pupil's Edition lend themselves to cooperative learning. The Teacher's Notes explain some of the many instances where this teaching strategy can be particularly effective. For guidelines on how to use cooperative learning, see page T13.

GRAMMAR	CULTURE	RE–ENTRY
The verb **wissen** (A16)	Greetings in different German-speaking areas States in the FRG Landmarks of Munich Map of the city of Munich	Getting someone's attention Asking directions Saying you don't know
The verb **sollen** (B6)	Shopping for groceries Units of weight and liquid measure	Numbers Asking what something costs
The verb **essen** (C9) **noch ein,** *another* (C14) Making suggestions using command forms (C18)	Reading a menu with local specialties	**möchte-**forms Foods Verbs
Recombining communicative functions, grammar, and vocabulary		
Reading for practice and pleasure		

TEACHER–PREPARED MATERIALS

Section A Map of the German-speaking world; pictures of Munich

Section B Pictures of food items; flash-cards of stores, quantities, and prices

Section C Weather map; pictures showing different kinds of weather; menu

UNIT RESOURCES

Übungsheft, Unit 7
Arbeitsheft, Unit 7
Unit 7 Cassettes
Transparencies 18–20
Quizzes 18–20
Unit 7 Test

KAPITEL 7

A1

SECTION A

OBJECTIVES **To exchange information:** tell where you live and what kind of place it is; point out landmarks; ask for directions and say you don't know

CULTURAL BACKGROUND Unlike many American cities where the downtown area "dies" with the close of business, German city centers house a number of residents as well. Because of the scarcity of open spaces, many people live in apartments above the downtown shops. Some areas, called **Fussgängerzonen,** are closed to automobiles and reserved for pedestrians.

MOTIVATING ACTIVITY First ask the students to think about the way they would tell someone where they live and then to give the population and location of their home town. Ask for several responses and see how much variation there is. Tell the students to also expect some variations in the way people express the same idea in German. Advancing in language learning means—among other things—having several ways of expressing oneself.

Next ask the students to think what the different places are that Americans live in (cities, towns, suburbs, villages). Tell the students to listen closely to the way their German-speaking friends talk about their home towns.

A1

Wo wohnen unsere Freunde? 

Follow the usual procedure. First review the names of the German-speaking countries and how location in those countries is expressed.

in Deutschland	in der Bundesrepublik, in der BRD
in Österreich	in der Deutschen Demokratischen Republik, in der DDR
	in der Schweiz

Then introduce each section by having the students listen and follow in their books. Use a map of Western Europe to show the locations. Practice the pronunciation of difficult words and phrases, such as **Schleswig-Holstein** and **ein Komma fünf Millionen Einwohner,** before asking students to use these actively in answers to questions or in reading aloud. Ask questions on each section, allowing short answers. Then ask questions covering all four young people, such as **Wer wohnt in einer Hauptstadt? Wer wohnt nicht in der Bundesrepublik? Wer wohnt in den Bergen?**

Have the students complete sentences:

Bern ist in ______ .
Wien ist in ______ .
München ist in ______ .
Niebüll ist eine Stadt in ______ .
1,3 Millionen Einwohner, das ist eine ______ .

Next work on the names of the people. Have the students write and say all the names. Also have them write all the greetings: **Margit sagt: „Grüss dich!"**, and so forth. Ask them, **Wo sagen die Leute „Grüss dich!" „Grüss Gott!" „Gruetzi!" — im Norden oder im Süden?** Refer to the culture note in A2.

Now go back to D1 of Unit 1 and have the students read each introduction but make these changes: use the verb **wohnen;** tell in which **Land** the city is located.

Ask questions opposing **aus (der)** with **in (der):**

Woher ist Jens Kröger? Aus ______ .
Wo wohnt er? In ______ .

A2 Ein wenig Landeskunde

You may wish to give these additional examples: **Moin! (Friesland); Servus! (Bayern, Tirol); Salü! (Schweiz).** Explain that dialects in Germany can differ from one another more greatly than regional accents in the U.S. do—in some cases, speakers from two different regions cannot understand each other's dialects.

A3 Übung • Mix-Match

As an expansion, have the students make similar statements about some other cities. Display a large map of Germany for them to refer to.

A4 Übung • Und du?

As an expansion, ask these additional questions: **Wo ist das? Wohnst du gern in . . . ?** You can rephrase question 1 as **Woher bist du?**

A5 Ein wenig Landeskunde

The German Democratic Republic is also organized in smaller divisions. The districts are: Berlin, Cottbus, Dresden, Erfurt, Frankfurt (Oder), Gera, Halle, Karl-Marx-Stadt, Leipzig, Magdeburg, Neubrandenburg, Potsdam, Rostock, Schwerin, Suhl.

A6 Übung • Die Bundesrepublik und ihre Länder

To expand the activity, divide the class into four groups and have each group draw a map of one of the German-speaking countries. Have them show the major divisions (Federal Republic, **Länder;** German Democratic Republic, **Bezirke;** Austria, **Bundesstaaten;** Switzerland, **Kantone**).

A7 Übung • Länderspiel

If the students have completed the expansion in A6, you can have the class play the game using Austria or Switzerland as the country.

A8 Übung • Rollenspiel

CHALLENGE To expand, change the monolog into a dialog. Have one partner ask questions to elicit the information from the foreign young person.

A9 Schreibübung • Unsere Freunde

As an expansion, have the students write about themselves, giving the information the characters give in A1. Have them keep this paragraph for a German notebook. Many forms filled out in Germany for various purposes include a space for **Wohnort.** If you can find an authentic form that does, have the students fill it out as part of the activity.

A10 IN MÜNCHEN

Have the students listen to the text for one photo at a time, following in their books. Start with the middle section. At most, introduce one page a day, and introduce some of the new vocabulary and place names for recognition only at this point. Introduce some of the common words for buildings

A11–14

and places that one would find in any big city, using drawings or picture cues to demonstrate meaning.

der: Platz, Dom, Turm *die:* Kirche
das: Rathaus, Museum, Theater, Schloss

In question/answer practice, ask some questions which have answers not stated in the text, such as **Die Leute nennen München die „heimliche Hauptstadt" Deutschlands. Was ist die richtige Hauptstadt Deutschlands? Was ist das offizielle Wappen Münchens? Wer ist der kleine Mann im Wappen?** Explain difficult words:

Sehenswürdigkeit (**sehen** + **würdig** [+ **s**], "worth seeing"—a thing worth seeing, a famous sight)
Wahrzeichen (**wahr** + **das Zeichen**—true sign, a symbol, a landmark)
Innenstadt (innen, in der Mitte; innen in der Stadt)

To review the buildings and places vocabulary, ask the students about their own city or town. List these terms on the board and have the students say which ones their hometown has and give the names.

Wahrzeichen	Oper	Flughafen	Kirche(n)
Bahnhof	Dom	Theater	Fussgängerzone
Rathaus	Museum	Schule(n)	Stadtpark

A 11 Übung • Mix-Match: Die Stadt München

Have the students work through the mix-match several times if necessary. Then have them cover up the left side and see how many sentences they can start with phrases given at the right.

A 12 Ein wenig Landeskunde

The students will probably be interested in learning more about the **Oktoberfest.** For more information, see the reading selection on pages 220–23.

A 13 ENTSCHULDIGUNG, WO IST BITTE . . . ?

Have the students listen to the mini-dialogs and read along. Stop after each section to work with the new material. Then practice the whole sequence.

Have the students, in groups of four, role-play Florian and passers-by. Have them switch roles. As an expansion, encourage the students to vary their questions and answers by freely recombining and using phrases that fit. If necessary, put the phrases on a chart or on the board for reference.

openers:	Entschuldigung! / Verzeihung! / Wo ist bitte . . . ? / Weisst du (Wissen Sie), wo . . . ist?
negative answers:	Nein, keine Ahnung. / Ich weiss (es) (leider) nicht. / Nein, ich bin nicht von hier (ich bin Amerikaner).
positive answers:	Ja, dort drüben. / Geradeaus, dann links. / In der _______ strasse. / Am _______ platz.
unsure:	Wie bitte? / Was? / Der (Die, Das) . . . ?
places:	der Dom / der Marktplatz / die Kirche / die Oper / das Rathaus / das Museum / das Theater / das Schloss

A 14 WIE SAGT MAN DAS?

To expand the information, add the familiar function of *giving* directions. Review the direction words from Unit 5 with the students.

A 15 Übung • Wo ist . . . ?

To expand the activity to include giving directions, have person A ask two people; the second person knows where the place is. Refer to A18.

A 16 ERKLÄRUNG

Practice the forms of **wissen** with short questions and answers or statements and responses.

> Weisst du, wo das Glockenspiel ist? — Ja, ich weiss es.
> Weiss Florian, . . . ?
> Wissen die Münchner, . . . ?
> Wisst ihr, . . . ?
>
> Das neue Rathaus ist am Marienplatz. — Ja, wir wissen das./Ich weiss.

A 17 Übung • Wer weiss es?

Have the students form sentences using the picture cue and the subject given. Repeat as necessary. Then move the subject one place to the right.

A 18 Übung • Wissen Sie, wo . . . ?

Have the students refer to the map for the streets these sights are located on. You may wish to supply the students with additional location words.

A 19 Übung • Hör gut zu!

For this exercise, open your textbook to page 204. Look at the photos. You will now hear eight statements, each one referring to one of the sights shown. Listen to the statement and match it with the photo. Let's begin. **Fangen wir an!**

1. Das offizielle Wahrzeichen Münchens ist das Münchner Kindl. *Foto 4*
2. Ein anderes Wahrzeichen ist die Peterskirche, für die Einwohner Münchens „Der Alte Peter". *Foto 7*
3. Und hier ist der Marienplatz mit dem Neuen Rathaus. Und dort oben ist das Glockenspiel. *Foto 1*
4. Und hier ist der Chinesische Turm im Englischen Garten. *Foto 5*
5. Die gotische Kirche mit den zwei Türmen ist der Dom. *Foto 2*
6. Möchtest du in die Oper gehen? Hier ist das Nationaltheater. *Foto 6*
7. Die Theatinerkirche ist eine schöne Barockkirche. Sie hat auch zwei Türme. *Foto 8*
8. Schloss Nymphenburg ist ein sehr schönes Schloss. *Foto 3*

Now check your answers. *Read each item again and give the correct answer.*

A 20 Lese- und Schreibübung • Florian schreibt nach Hause

For writing practice, have the students recopy the card, including the illegible words. Then have them refer to Flori's card as an example as they write their own cards.

B1

SECTION B

OBJECTIVES **To exchange information:** talk about shopping; **to persuade:** make requests; suggest where to go shopping

CULTURAL BACKGROUND Tell the students to look at the photo of Steffi preparing to go shopping. What do they notice? (the big shopping basket) What does that tell us about how shopping for groceries is done? (Shopping is done in the neighborhood stores, not too far away, and foods are carried back home.) Introduce the typical implements used for carrying grocery items. (Put drawings on an overhead transparency or show slides of people carrying one of the typical shopping bags.)

der Einkaufskorb   die Einkaufstasche   das Einkaufsnetz
die Plastiktüte (given away free or for a charge of 10 Pfennig, used as an advertising device by stores)

MOTIVATING ACTIVITY Prepare two typical shopping lists, one written by an American housewife, one by a German housewife. Have the same items appear on both lists, but on the German one, quantities are more defined. Put both on an overhead transparency or a handout and ask the students to compare the two lists and write down what they notice about the German list. They should notice:

—the smaller quantities (expressed in **g [Gramm], Pfd [Pfund], kg [Kilogramm],** also the smaller number of items to be bought)
—**Mineralwasser** (bought by Germans the way we purchase soda)
—**Eier** (bought in cartons of 10 or by the piece)

Ask the students to think about what the German list tells us about food storage and shopping habits.

—Germans shop for food more often
—refrigerators must be smaller
—Germans like fresh foods; meat, cold cuts, fruit, and vegetables are bought and used up right away

Tell the students they will learn more about German shopping habits as they listen to B1.

B1

Steffi geht einkaufen 

Follow the usual procedure. This long dialog will need to be broken into three sections: lines 1–5, 6–11, and 12–16. Use the pictures on pages 205 and 206 to explain new vocabulary. Ask questions such as **Sagt die Mutter, was sie alles braucht? Was gibt sie der Steffi?** Allow short answers. Work on the pronunciation of new words:

/au/	kaufen, einkaufen, pass auf, pass bitte auf
/ts/	der Zettel, einen Zettel für dich
/z/	der Supermarkt, die Semmeln
/ʃ/	das Fleisch, das Hackfleisch
/o:/, /ü:/	das Obst, das Gemüse, beim Gemüsehändler
/i:/	verlier, verlier das Geld nicht

After the students have been introduced to the whole dialog and have had a chance to practice it orally with you and with each other, ask them to look at *the way* Frau Huber is making her requests: **Was macht Frau Huber, *fragt* sie die Steffi oder *sagt* sie der Steffi, was sie machen soll?** Ask about each request: **Steffi soll einkaufen gehen. Was sagt die Mutter?** Ask questions about the pictures following the dialog, for example: **Was kauft Steffi beim Metzger? Wieviel? Essen wir viel Hackfleisch in den USA?**

You can use this situation to review counting out change: **Die Lebensmittel kosten 88,23 DM. Steffi bring 11,77 DM zurück. Sie zählt das Geld auf den Tisch. Was sagt sie zu ihrer Mutter?**

B2 Übung • Mix-Match: Steffi geht einkaufen

CHALLENGE To review word order, have the students cover up the left side and make sentences that start with phrases in the right-hand column.

B3 Übung • Und du?

As an expansion, ask the students additional personal questions:

Wer geht in deiner Familie einkaufen?
Wie oft gehst du mit?
Wie heisst ein Supermarkt, den ihr besucht?
Wie kommt ihr zum Supermarkt? Mit dem Auto? Zu Fuss?
Habt ihr einen grossen Einkaufskorb? Eine Einkaufstasche?

B4 WIE SAGT MAN DAS?

After reading the summary, have the students work with the little words.

bitte—makes requests polite
doch—adds emphasis, similar to "why don't you" or "please *do*"
mal—short for **einmal** = "once, for once"; used in introductory requests only: **Geh doch mal zum Bäcker und kauf . . .**

Practice the little words, recycling vocabulary from previous units:

Kauf Brot und Semmeln! (doch . . . bitte)
Fahr mit dem Bus! (doch mal)
Spiel Tennis! (mal)
Pass auf! (doch)
Steck eine Münze in den Apparat! (bitte)
Versuch es später noch mal! (doch)
Sei pünktlich da! (doch bitte)

Have the students add one word at a time to a request, making it longer and more colloquial.

Kauf Aufschnitt!
Kauf doch Aufschnitt!
Kauf doch bitte Aufschnitt!
Kauf doch bitte mal Aufschnitt!

Frag den Lehrer!
Pack den Rucksack aus!
Ruf deinen Brieffreund an!
Warte auf mich!
Hol die Fotos!
Lies den Brief von Peter!

B5 Übung • Wo soll ich alles kaufen? 

As a variation, have the students prepare a shopping list with several items from each column. As they ask their partner for advice on where to shop, they read items off their list. Have them reverse roles. Ask students to use both **holen** and **kaufen.**

SLOWER–PACED LEARNING Play a memory game with the food items listed to reinforce new vocabulary. Have each person add one item to buy.

ANSWERS

den Aufschnitt beim Metzger, den Salat beim Gemüsehändler, den Käse im Supermarkt, den Kaffee im Supermarkt, den Zucker im Supermarkt, den Joghurt im Supermarkt; die Wurst beim Metzger, die Semmeln beim Bäcker, die Gurken beim Gemüsehändler, die Tomaten beim Gemüsehändler, die Kirschen beim Gemüsehändler, die Milch im Supermarkt, die Butter im Supermarkt; das Hackfleisch beim Metzger, das Brot beim Bäcker, die Eier im Supermarkt, das Mineralwasser im Supermarkt, das Obst beim Gemüsehändler

B6 ERKLÄRUNG

CHALLENGE For cooperative learning, ask the students to think of all the things they are supposed to do each day in school and write them down (for example, **Wir sollen aufpassen. Wir sollen nicht laut sein**). The group with the longest and most original list wins.

B7 Übung • Was soll ich kaufen?

CHALLENGE Use the picture cues, but add other items to each statement, for example: **Ich soll das Brot und die Semmeln beim Bäcker kaufen.**

B8 Ein wenig Landeskunde

Ask the students to look for any objects at home on which the weight is given in metric units, such as canned items or bags of flour. Have them make a list of the items and the weights.

B9 Leseübung • Wie schwer ist ein Pfund?

To illustrate the difference between German and American pounds, bring in a dual scale and weigh typical classroom objects on it.

B10 Übung • Geh mal für mich einkaufen!

Have the students read the lists aloud to practice verbalizing the measures of weight. You might also use the lists for a dictation exercise, asking the students to use the abbreviations.

B11 Übung • Preisinformation

You might have groups of students make advertising posters that include items and prices. Have them use food vocabulary not used in B10.

B12 Übung • Was hat die Steffi alles im Netz? Rate mal!

Bring in some food containers and label them with German prices. Have one student role-play a cashier and name the item and read off the price. (See the lists in B10 for prices of the items pictured.)

B13 Übung • Hör gut zu!

You will hear ten statements Steffi makes as she shops in different stores: at the baker's, **beim Bäcker,** at the butcher's, **beim Metzger,** at the greengrocer's, **beim Gemüsehändler,** and in the supermarket, **im Supermarkt.** As you hear each statement, determine where Steffi is and place your check mark in the appropriate row. For example, you hear, **Ja, wo ist jetzt der Zucker?** You place your check mark in the row labeled **im Supermarkt,** the place Steffi would buy sugar. Let's begin. **Fangen wir an!**

1. Und jetzt brauche ich noch ein halbes Pfund Aufschnitt. *beim Metzger*
2. Sind die Semmeln frisch? Dann möchte ich vier. *beim Bäcker*
3. So, jetzt hole ich noch einen Liter Milch. *im Supermarkt*
4. Einen Kopf Salat und ein Kilogramm Tomaten, bitte! *beim Gemüsehändler*
5. Und jetzt brauche ich noch ein Brot. *beim Bäcker*
6. Wo ist denn nur das Mineralwasser? Ich brauche zwei Flaschen. *im Supermarkt*
7. Ich möchte zwei Pfund Hackfleisch, bitte! *beim Metzger*
8. Eine Gurke und ein Pfund Kirschen, bitte! *beim Gemüsehändler*
9. Soll ich noch Joghurt kaufen? Ja, ich nehme zwei Joghurt mit nach Hause. *im Supermarkt*
10. Ich sehe, die Mutti möchte noch Käse und zehn Eier! *im Supermarkt*

Now check your answers. *Read each item again and give the correct answer.*

B14 Übung • Wo soll ich das kaufen?

Have one student at a time respond to the questions. As he or she responds, have the others list the items under the appropriate store on a shopping list.

B15 Schreibübung • Dein Einkaufszettel

Have the students work in pairs. Have them choose one of their **Einkaufszettelgespräche** and prepare it for oral presentation in class.

SECTION C

OBJECTIVES **To express feelings and emotions:** express annoyance; **to express attitudes and opinions:** ask and tell how something tastes; **to socialize:** say you want or don't want more; talk about the weather

CULTURAL BACKGROUND Germany is often rainy, and Germans generally drop everything to go outdoors when the sun is shining. Often, however, they have to go outside under inclement conditions. Munich, located at the foot of the Bavarian Alps, has a fair amount of cloudiness or rain in spring and fall and snow in winter. With the typical German worry about getting chilled, Frau Huber insists that Steffi and Florian take umbrellas and raincoats.

MOTIVATING ACTIVITY Have the students think about the way weather influences their activities. What kind of weather do they like? When do they stay home?

C1–3

Next have them imagine that they live in Germany, where it is quite cool in spring and fall and where it rains a lot. Also have them imagine they do not have a car but need to walk or use public transportation. How important would the weather report be for them? What would be the things they would listen for? What would be part of their wardrobe? Would they be influenced by bad weather or would they go on doing what they want to do?

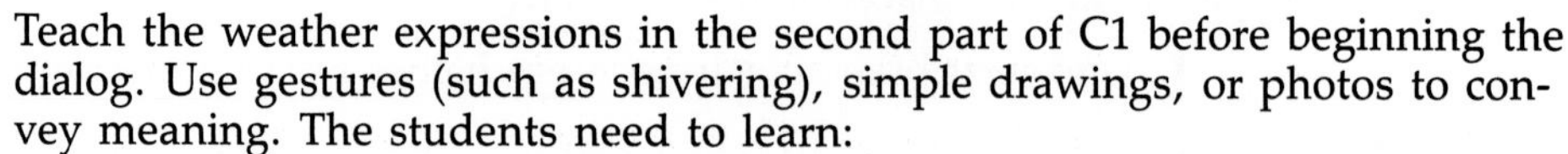

C1 Schade, es regnet.

Teach the weather expressions in the second part of C1 before beginning the dialog. Use gestures (such as shivering), simple drawings, or photos to convey meaning. The students need to learn:

—the scale: **kalt — kühl — warm — heiss**
—the basic expressions: **Die Sonne scheint. Es regnet. Es ist bewölkt.**
—how to express the idea that the weather will remain the same: **Das Wetter bleibt schön.**

Practice weather expressions related to picture 1.

Es ist kühl/kalt/bewölkt.
Es regnet.
Es regnet ab und zu.

Have the students listen to the weather report for the first picture. Ask questions: **Wie ist das Wetter hier im Foto? Ist es warm? Was sagt der Wetterbericht?** Go on to pictures 2 and 3.

Have the students listen to the first part of the dialog (left-hand side). Repeat once or twice. Work with new vocabulary: **Schau, es regnet! Das ist dumm! Das ist blöd!** Ask questions: **Warum ist Steffi sauer? Möchten die beiden zu Hause bleiben?**

Have the students listen to the second part of the dialog (right-hand side). Repeat. Ask questions such as **Was haben Steffi und Flori gegen den Regen?**

For writing practice, have the students write down all of Frau Huber's "typical mother" comments.

To practice distinguishing between **Regen** and **regnen,** give the students sentences such as the following: **Morgen soll es wieder ______. Wir haben so viel ______ im Oktober. Hast du einen ______mantel?** and so on.

C2 Übung • Fragen

As an expansion, use the map to talk about the weather in various cities. The students should use inverted word order, putting the city first each time: **In München regnet es.**

C3 Übung • Jetzt bist du dran

Have the students describe the weather with at least three phrases: **Heute ist es ______.**

Before they answer question 2, make them aware of the impersonal style of a typical weather report, with the verb omitted: **Heute heiter und warm.**

Have the students go through the year and tell what the weather is like each month in their area: **Im Januar ist es sehr kalt. Es schneit oft.** Have them use as many expressions as they can. List these expressions on an overhead transparency or a handout:

Es ist sehr kalt — kühl — warm — heiss — sehr heiss
Es ist heiter — sonnig — bewölkt
Es regnet/Es schneit/Die Sonne scheint.
immer — meistens — oft — ab und zu — selten

C4 WIE SAGT MAN DAS?

As an expansion, give the students some statements to react to with annoyance *or* with enthusiasm, such as **Wir haben heute eine Klassenarbeit.** Then let individuals make statements and have the others in the class react.

C5 Übung • Wie ist das Wetter?

Have the class keep a weather chart for a week, with one person in charge of recording the weather each day. Ask about the weather each day and have the class react to it. You may wish to continue the chart.

C6 Übung • Hör gut zu!

You will hear six statements that refer to the weather today. Listen carefully to each statement, determine if the weather is good or bad, and place your check mark in the appropriate row. For example, you hear, **Prima! Kein Regen. Heute spielen wir Basketball!** This statement indicates good weather. You place your check mark in the row labeled **gut.** Let's begin. **Fangen wir an!**

1. Das ist blöd. Dann bleiben wir zu Hause und spielen Karten. *schlecht*
2. Ja, das Wetter bleibt weiterhin schön. *gut*
3. Schau, wie dunkel es ist. Hol doch lieber einen Regenschirm! *schlecht*
4. Du, der Wetterbericht stimmt nicht. Schau mal, es ist bewölkt und es ist kalt. *schlecht*
5. Wie heiss es heute ist! Dann gehen wir schwimmen. *gut*
6. Wir brauchen den Mantel nicht. Es bleibt heute sonnig und warm. *gut*

Now check your answers. *Read each item again and give the correct answer.*

C7 DER FLORI HAT HUNGER

Make colorful picture cue cards from magazine cutouts and have them at hand. Introduce the new vocabulary through demonstration.

Ich habe grossen Hunger. Aber ich bin nicht zu Hause. Ich bin in der Stadt. Was mache ich? Ah, da ist eine Imbiss-Stube!
Hm, was soll ich essen? Eine Bratwurst oder eine Weisswurst? Oder Pizza? Nein, ich bin in München, da probiere ich Leberkäs.

Before beginning the dialog, introduce the setting.

Steffi und Florian sind in der Stadt. Es ist sechs Uhr. Sie haben Hunger. Sie suchen eine Imbiss-Stube.

Have the students listen to each part of the dialog with their books closed. Work on pronunciation:

/ŋ/	Hunger	/e:/	Leberkäs
/e:/ /ç/	Hähnchen	/o:/ /i:/	probier
/ʃt/	Stube, Imbiss-Stube	/a:/	Mineralwasser

C8–12

Ask questions: **Wer hat Hunger? Leberkäs ist eine Münchner Spezialität. Wer kennt diese Spezialität? Wer probiert den Leberkäs?**

Have the students read the dialog in pairs, using lots of expression. Ask the students questions from the menus and ads shown.

> Was kostet mehr, Pizza oder ein Wurstbrot? Was isst du lieber?
> Die Hähnchen sind gegrillt. Sind sie schon lange gegrillt?

C8

Übung • Was soll ich essen? Was soll ich trinken?

As a variation, have person B suggest something to try. Person A doesn't like the idea. Have the students use lots of expression.

> A: Was soll ich essen?
> B: Probier doch mal den Leberkäs.
> A: Den Leberkäs? Nein!

C9

ERKLÄRUNG

Work with verb pairs in short drills such as the following. Use pictures of food items to cue responses.

Was isst du?	Ich esse Fisch.
Und was esst ihr?	Wir essen auch Fisch.
Was essen wir?	Ihr esst Wurst.
Und die Leute da?	Sie essen auch Wurst.

C10

Übung • Und du?

As a variation, have one student role-play a waiter and another a restaurant patron. The "waiter" should write down the order and repeat it aloud.

> A: Ich möchte Leberkäs mit Senf und eine Fanta.
> B: Einmal Leberkäs mit Senf; eine Fanta.

Note that the students do not yet have **nehmen** in their vocabulary; be careful not to use this verb when demonstrating.

C11

WIE SCHMECKT'S?

First introduce the new vocabulary.

> Die Steffi isst Bratwurst. Die Bratwurst schmeckt gut. Hmm! Isst du noch eine Bratwurst? Nein? Hast du genug? Bist du satt?

Have the students listen to the dialog and look at the picture. Repeat. Work on pronunciation:

> /ʃm/ schmecken, er schmeckt, wie schmeckt's?
> /x/ noch eine Wurst, noch einen Leberkäs
> /u:/ genug, ich habe genug, das ist genug!
> /z/ satt, ich bin satt, bist du satt?

Ask questions: **Wo sind Steffi und Florian? Wie viele Bratwürste isst Steffi? Warum isst Florian nur einen Leberkäs?** Put the students in pairs and have them read the conversation.

C12

WIE SAGT MAN DAS?

Since all the expressions here are positive, you might give the students some negative responses. Examples are **Schmeckt nicht. Ist heute nicht gut.**

C13 Übung • Wie schmeckt's?

Concentrate on practicing masculine and feminine nouns. (Make sure that the students use the correct pronoun.)

SLOWER–PACED LEARNING Use the activity to drill all the food vocabulary in C8. First practice the words in groups by gender, adding plurals as one group; then mix the genders.

C14 ERKLÄRUNG

Put two items of the same kind on a table one by one or point to them and have the students count them in this fashion: **ein Buch — und noch ein Buch!**

C15 Übung • Möchtest du noch ein . . . ?

As a variation, reverse the order as follows:

A: Möchtest du noch einen Kaffee?
B: Ja, bitte, der Kaffee schmeckt gut!

Use the following variables:

der: Kaffee, Tee, Saft, Salat
die: Cola, Wurst, Semmel
das: Hähnchen, Eis, Wurstbrot, Ei

C16 WIE SAGT MAN DAS?

Ask the students to think about the different ways they say yes or no to offers of food in English. Then introduce the German expressions.

C17 Übung • Partnerarbeit

Before the students begin the activity, model a conversation. Ask the students to vary the responses they give.

C18 ERKLÄRUNG

Make the students aware of the difference between question and command forms, which, in the case of the **Sie**-form, is in intonation only.

Kaufst du das?	Kauf das!
Kauft ihr das?	Kauft das!
Kaufen Sie das?	Kaufen Sie das!

C19 Übung • Was passt?

CHALLENGE Have students add another command, or an explanatory statement, to the command given if that is possible.

Steffi, geh mal für mich einkaufen!
Kauf Brot und Semmeln! [or]
Ich brauche Obst und Gemüse.

C20 Übung • Was sagst du zu . . . ?

Have the students add *any* of the qualifying words to the items. To expand the activity, recycle vocabulary by using other direct objects with the verbs given: **Hol das Fleisch beim Metzger!**

ANSWERS

1. Geh bitte einkaufen! Geht bitte einkaufen! Gehen Sie bitte einkaufen!
2. (Hol/Holt/Holen Sie) das Brot beim Bäcker!
3. (Probier/Probiert/Probieren Sie) doch den Leberkäs!
4. (Iss/Esst/Essen Sie) doch die Bratwurst!
5. (Bleib/Bleibt/Bleiben Sie) lieber zu Hause!
6. (Besuch/Besucht/Besuchen Sie) doch das Nationalmuseum!

C21 Übung • Hör gut zu!

You will hear ten statements that somebody might make to Steffi, or to Steffi and Flori, or to Mrs. Huber. Listen carefully to the verb and determine who is being addressed. For example, you hear, **Probiert doch mal die Bratwurst!** You place your check mark in the row labeled **Steffi und Flori,** because the statement you heard addressed both Steffi and Flori. You can tell by the form of the verb: **probiert.** Let's begin. **Fangen wir an!**

1. Bleib zu Hause und spiel Karten! *Steffi*
2. Holen Sie das Brot bitte beim Bäcker! *Frau Huber*
3. Kaufen Sie mal den Leberkäs! Er ist ausgezeichnet. *Frau Huber*
4. Passt auf und verliert bitte das Geld nicht! *Steffi und Flori*
5. Probier doch mal das Hähnchen! Es schmeckt prima! *Steffi*
6. Iss doch bitte die Weisswurst! Oder schmeckt sie nicht? *Steffi*
7. Sagen Sie mir bitte, wo Sie die Pizza kaufen! *Frau Huber*
8. Esst bitte noch etwas und trinkt doch das Mineralwasser! Es ist gut. *Steffi und Flori*
9. Holt bitte das Brot beim Bäcker und kauft die Tomaten beim Gemüsehändler! *Steffi und Flori*
10. Besuch mal deine Grosseltern! *Steffi*

Now check your answers. *Read each item again and give the correct response.*

C22 Schreibübung • Im Restaurant

As an expansion, set up the classroom as a "restaurant." Have the students act out dialogs in small groups of a waiter and guests.

TRY YOUR SKILLS

OBJECTIVE To recombine communicative functions, grammar, and vocabulary

CULTURAL BACKGROUND Ask the students if they ever go shopping for their parents. Because shopping is frequent and is done close to home, German parents routinely send their older children shopping for them. The children know what their mothers usually buy, and often the local merchants do too. Much shopping is done in open-air markets. There is usually a market day once a week, and some markets are open every day. For one view of an open air market, see the photograph of the **Viktualienmarkt** on page 220.

1

Steffi geht mit Florian einkaufen

Have the students listen to the short narratives and conversations and read along. Then ask inferential questions starting with **Wie wissen wir, dass . . . ?** Have the students quote supporting sentences from the text.

—dass die Bäckersfrau die Steffi kennt?
—dass die Gemüsefrau gern in München wohnt?
—dass der Florian nicht mit Steffi verwandt ist?

Ask the students to imagine that Steffi goes shopping with Florian in Freiburg. What would the narratives and conversations sound like? Have the students make all necessary changes.

2

Übung • Stimmt! Stimmt nicht!

CHALLENGE Have the students make up additional items that can be answered with **Stimmt** or **Stimmt nicht.** Have the class answer the items.

3

Übung • Steffi geht einkaufen

For writing practice, have the students write a paragraph describing the shopping trip.

CHALLENGE In their descriptions, have the students state an appropriate amount of each item Steffi buys.

4

Übung • Ratespiel: Wo ist . . . ?

Since the students may not be very familiar with German cities, refer to the map on page 198 or a classroom map during the activity if necessary.

5

Übung • Werners Einkaufszettel

Tell the students to read the list to see what Werner was supposed to buy and compare it with the picture to see what he bought instead.

6

Übung • Rollenspiel: In der Imbiss-Stube

To expand the dialog, have the server come back and ask how the food tastes and have the guest respond.

7

Aussprache-, Lese- und Schreibübungen

1. As you recall, in the German diphthongs /ei/, /au/, and /ɔi/, the first element is shorter than it is in the English counterparts. Listen to the difference in these English-German word pairs: by—**bei,** house—**Haus,** boiler—**Boiler. Hör zu und wiederhole!**

/ei/ Eis, heiss, allein, scheinen, vielleicht, Fleisch, Bayern
/au/ traurig, zu Hause, einkaufen, Hauptstadt, aufpassen
/ɔi/ Deutsch, Leute, Häuser, freundlich, Flugzeug

As you remember, the German sound /ɔ/ is somewhat like the first vowel sound in the English word *awful.* However it is much shorter, and it is produced with your lips more rounded. **Hör zu und wiederhole!**

/ɔ/ Dorf, Ort, Tochter, Glockenspiel, Schloss, Sommer, sonnig, wolkig, sollen, dort, noch

/pf/ The sound /pf/, as in **Pfund,** does not exist in English. It is produced by saying the sounds /p/ and /f/ almost simultaneously: /pf/. **Hör zu und wiederhole! Pfund, Pfennig, Nymphenburg**

/ʃv/ The sound combination /ʃv/, as in **schwer,** also does not exist in English. Let's practice it. **Hör zu und wiederhole! schwer, Schwester, Schweiz, schwimmen**

2. In this section you will practice reading the words printed in your textbook on page 217. Pay attention to the following:

ei/ay **eu/äu**

1. The letter combinations **ei** and **ay** both represent the sound /ai/. The letter combinations **eu** and **äu** both represent the sound /ɔi/. **Hör zu und wiederhole! allein, Bayern, Leute, Haus, Häuser**
2. The letter **o** can be long or short. The long **o** sound is "pure"; that is, it does not glide. The sound is shorter than English long **o** and produced with your lips rounded. **Hör zu und wiederhole!**

o

   long **o** : holen, Dom, Oper, Obst, Brot, Tomate
   short **o** : Sonne, sollen, Schloss, wolkig, sonnig

3. The letter **z** is pronounced as /ts/. **Hör zu und wiederhole!**

z

   zum, zu Hause, Zimmer, Zoll, Verzeihung, Wahrzeichen, Einkaufszettel

4. The letter **w** is pronounced as /v/. **Hör zu und wiederhole!**

w

   Wurst, wissen, Wien, Wasser, Weisswurst, Wetterbericht, warm, wieder, bewölkt

3. Now close your textbook and write the sentences you hear.
1. Wir holen Wurst und Brot.
2. In Wien gehen die Leute oft in die Oper.

WAS KANNST DU SCHON?

For the second part, use photographs to review the Munich landmarks. You can use the photographs in A19, on page 204.

For the first part, have the students name as many items as they can. Use pictures of food items as cues to review vocabulary.

Have the students make up sentences beginning with **Ich bin sauer.** To review foods, play a memory game, with each person adding an item to eat: **Ich esse . . . , . . .**

WORTSCHATZ

Ask the students to make a list of all the compound words they can find in the vocabulary.

WORTSCHATZÜBUNGEN

Have the students write the words in categories: names of sights; units of measure; weather words; things to eat.

ZUM LESEN

OBJECTIVE To read for practice and pleasure

MÜNCHEN 

Have the students read the text on each page. Then discuss the pictures in relation to the text. The pictures can be used to help explain new and difficult vocabulary.

Übung • Sprich darüber!

Have the students work in small groups. Have them choose one of the following topics and see how much they can find out about it. Then have them report to the class.

1. Various architectural styles are found in and around Munich—Baroque, Renaissance, Gothic, Rococo. When did these styles flourish? What are the characteristics? How are they different from each other? Find pictures of other examples of these styles.
2. King Ludwig built many castles. What can you find out about him and these castles?
3. Make a scrapbook or a bulletin board about Munich. Collect articles, pictures, and interesting anecdotes and facts.

KAPITEL 7

Wo wohnen sie?

Where do Germans live? About 45 percent live in large cities such as Hamburg, Frankfurt, Berlin, and Munich. About 45 percent live in small cities and towns. The remaining 10 percent live in rural areas. Although society has become more mobile, many people live near the place where they were born. Big cities are made up of many different sections, each one almost like a small town. Just as in a small town, people know one another; they regularly shop at the same local stores and patronize local businesses and restaurants.

In this unit you will:

SECTION A	tell where you live, show somebody your town, ask for directions
SECTION B	shop for groceries in local stores and make suggestions about where to shop
SECTION C	talk about the weather, order food, talk about how something tastes and if you want more
TRY YOUR SKILLS	use what you've learned
ZUM LESEN	read for practice and pleasure

telling where you live, showing somebody your town, and asking for directions

The German-speaking countries are small in area, with many people living in apartments or in homes on relatively small plots of land.

A1 Wo wohnen unsere Freunde?

Grüss dich! Ich heisse Margit Dastl. Ich bin in Wien zu Hause.

Wien, die Hauptstadt von Österreich, hat 1,5 Millionen Einwohner.

Hallo! Ich bin der Jens. Ich wohne in Niebüll.

Niebüll ist eine Stadt in Schleswig-Holstein. Niebüll hat 7 000 Einwohner.

Guten Tag! Ich bin die Wiebke Nedel. Ich wohne in Neuss.

Neuss, eine Stadt in Nordrhein-Westfalen. Neuss hat 200 000 Einwohner.

Gruetzi! Ich bin der Bruno Schmidlin. Ich wohne in Zimmerwald in der Schweiz.

Die Schmidlins wohnen in Zimmerwald. Zimmerwald ist ein Dorf, ein Vorort von Bern. Bern ist die Hauptstadt der Schweiz.

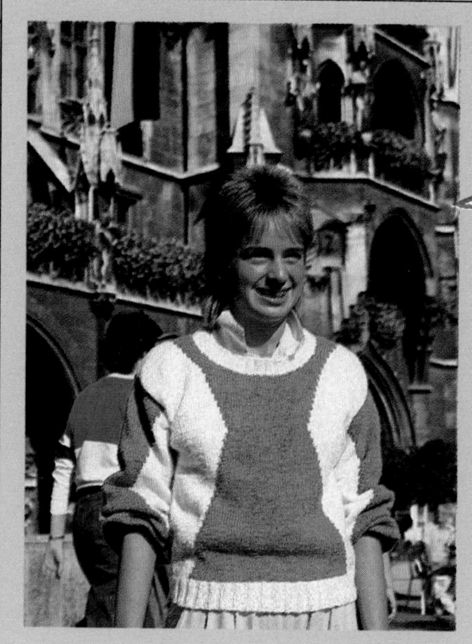

Grüss Gott! Ich bin die Steffi Huber. Ich bin 15 Jahre alt, und ich wohne hier in München.

München ist die Hauptstadt von Bayern. München ist eine Grossstadt; sie hat 1,3 Millionen Einwohner.

A2 Ein wenig Landeskunde

You know some standard greetings, such as **Hallo!, Guten Tag!, Grüss dich!** There are also many regional greetings used in different parts of the German-speaking countries. For example, in southern Germany people say: **Grüss Gott!** and in Switzerland they say: **Gruetzi!** How do you greet your friends? Would you use a different greeting if you lived in another part of the country?

A3 Übung • Mix-Match

1. Niebüll ist eine Stadt	2	eine Stadt in Nordrhein-Westfalen.
2. Neuss ist	1	in Schleswig-Holstein.
3. Wien ist die Hauptstadt	4	von Bern.
4. Zimmerwald ist ein Vorort	5	von Bayern.
5. München ist die Hauptstadt	3	von Österreich.

A4 Übung • Und du?

1. Wo wohnst du?
2. Was ist . . .?
3. Wie gross ist . . .?
4. Wo wohnen deine Grosseltern?

A5 Ein wenig Landeskunde

The Federal Republic is a federation of eleven states, called **Länder,** each one with its own state capital. The capital of the Federal Republic is Bonn. The cities of Hamburg and Bremen are states as well as cities. The city of Berlin (West) is also a state of the Federal Republic, but its status is somewhat different from that of the other states. The Federal Republic has roughly 61.5 million inhabitants.

Photo p. 194: Tottenbachstrasse im Lehel in München
Photos p. 195, top: Ein typisch friesischer Haubarg, a farm house with a high reed-covered roof (Reetdach)—the roof covers living quarters and the barn and stables; Olympic Village in Munich

1. Schleswig-Holstein, Hamburg, Bremen, Niedersachsen, Nordrhein-Westfalen, Hessen, Rheinland-Pfalz, Saarland, Baden-Württemberg, Bayern, Berlin 2. Niedersachsen/Hannover, Hessen/Wiesbaden, Rheinland-Pfalz/Mainz, Saarland/Saarbrücken, Baden-Württemberg/Stuttgart, Bayern/München, Hamburg, Bremen, Berlin

A6 Übung • Die Bundesrepublik und ihre Länder

1. Die Bundesrepublik hat elf Länder. Wie heissen sie?
2. Jedes Land hat eine Landeshauptstadt. Wie heissen sie?
   Die Landeshauptstadt von Schleswig-Holstein ist . . . Kiel
   Düsseldorf ist die Landeshauptstadt von . . . Nordrhein-Westfalen
3. Wieviel Einwohner hat Hessen? 5,6 Millionen
4. Wie heisst die Hauptstadt der BRD? Bonn
5. Die Hauptstadt der DDR ist . . . Berlin
6. Wie heisst die Hauptstadt von Österreich?
7. Die Hauptstadt der Schweiz ist . . . Bern
8. Wo ist München? Und Stuttgart?
9. Was ist Stuttgart? 6. Wien 8. in Bayern, in Baden-Württemberg 9. die Landeshauptstadt von Baden-Württemberg

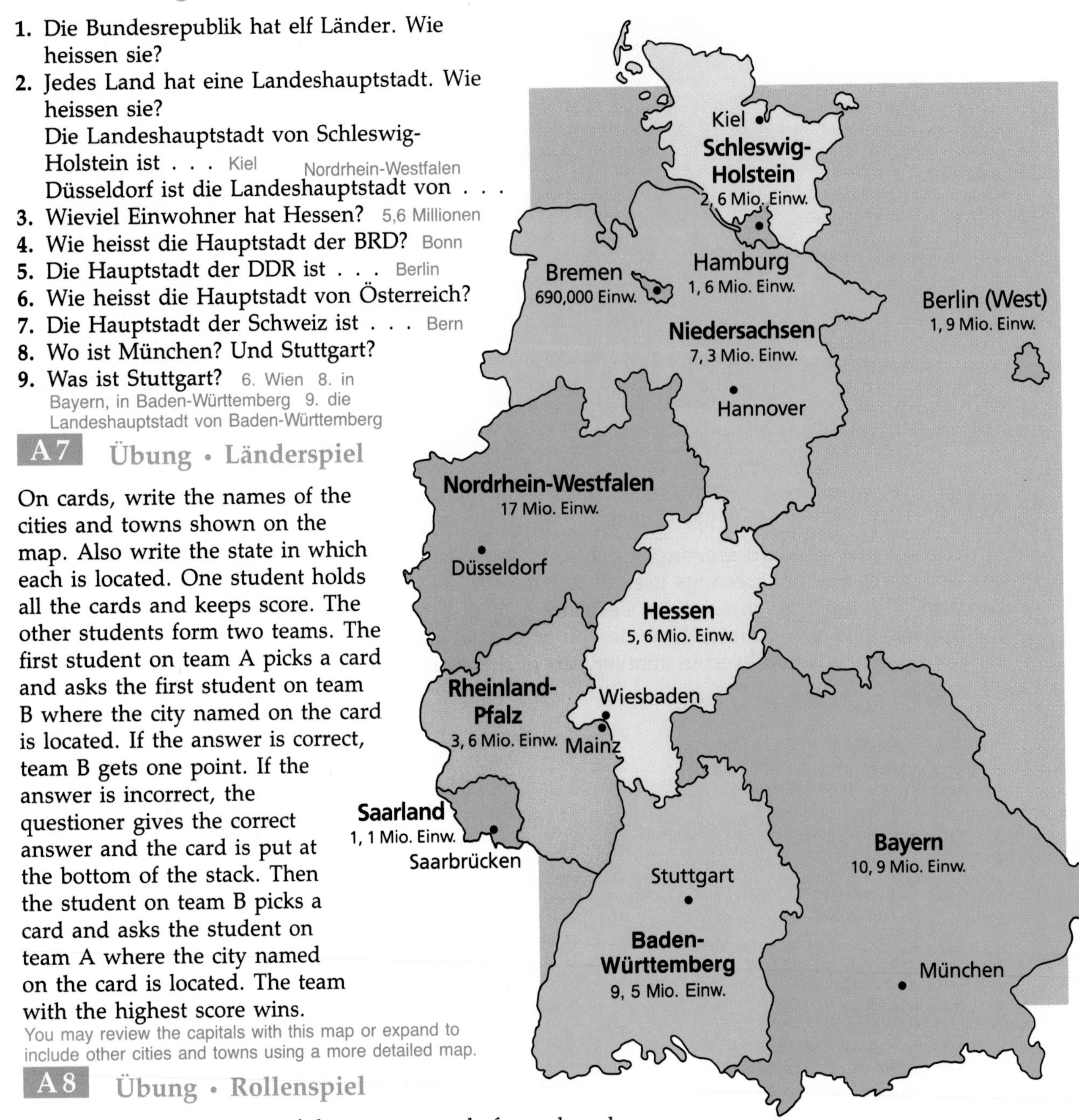

A7 Übung • Länderspiel

On cards, write the names of the cities and towns shown on the map. Also write the state in which each is located. One student holds all the cards and keeps score. The other students form two teams. The first student on team A picks a card and asks the first student on team B where the city named on the card is located. If the answer is correct, team B gets one point. If the answer is incorrect, the questioner gives the correct answer and the card is put at the bottom of the stack. Then the student on team B picks a card and asks the student on team A where the city named on the card is located. The team with the highest score wins.

You may review the capitals with this map or expand to include other cities and towns using a more detailed map.

A8 Übung • Rollenspiel

Pretend that you are one of the young people from abroad. Introduce yourself and talk about where you live, mentioning whether that place is a city, town, or village, and how big it is. Use an appropriate greeting.

A9 Schreibübung • Unsere Freunde

Write a paragraph about each of the young people from abroad.

Students should be able to recognize and identify by name the sights of Munich shown. They should not be expected to give detailed information.

A 10 IN MÜNCHEN

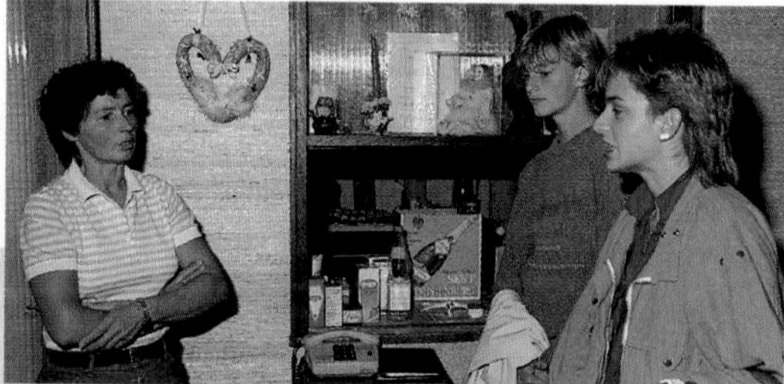
Frau Huber und ihre Tochter, die Steffi

Die Hubers wohnen in München. Sie haben eine Wohnung im Lehel.

Hubers haben Besuch, einen Jungen aus Freiburg. Der Florian kennt die Stadt nicht, und die Steffi zeigt ihm die Sehenswürdigkeiten Münchens.

Wer möchte nicht München besuchen? München ist die „heimliche Hauptstadt" Deutschlands, und jedes Jahr kommen Millionen von Besuchern aus aller Welt in das „Millionendorf" an der Isar.

Das Münchner Kindl, offizielles Wappen Münchens

Der „Alte Peter", die Peterskirche, ein Wahrzeichen Münchens

Schau, Flori! Das ist der Marienplatz und das Neue Rathaus.

GLOCKENSPIEL
CARILLON
TURM-LIFT 9.00-18.00
SAMSTAG, SONNTAG & AN FEIERTAGEN 10.00-18.00

Schau, dort oben ist das Glockenspiel!

Explain to the students that the figures on the Glockenspiel turn. When do they think this happens?

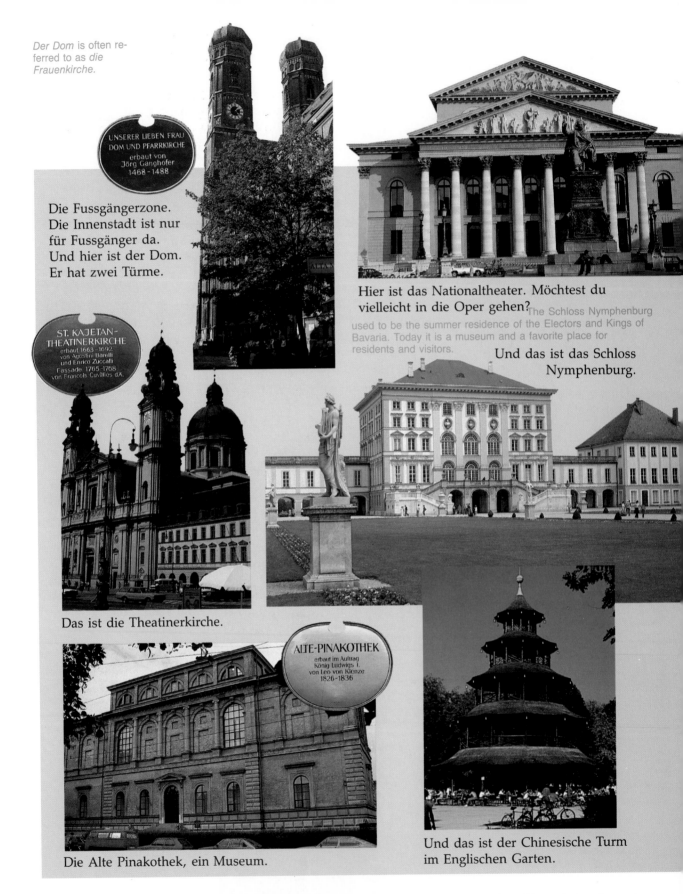

Der Dom is often referred to as *die Frauenkirche.*

Die Fussgängerzone.
Die Innenstadt ist nur für Fussgänger da.
Und hier ist der Dom.
Er hat zwei Türme.

Hier ist das Nationaltheater. Möchtest du vielleicht in die Oper gehen?

The Schloss Nymphenburg used to be the summer residence of the Electors and Kings of Bavaria. Today it is a museum and a favorite place for residents and visitors.

Und das ist das Schloss Nymphenburg.

Das ist die Theatinerkirche.

Die Alte Pinakothek, ein Museum.

Und das ist der Chinesische Turm im Englischen Garten.

In the area around the Chinesische Turm there are chairs and benches for 8000 people to gather and enjoy a meal. Many families come here during the summer. An old law permits people to bring their own food.

A 11 Übung • Mix-Match: Die Stadt München

1. Die Stadt München heisst auch	2	im Rathaus am Marienplatz.
2. Das Glockenspiel ist	10	das offizielle Wappen.
3. Hier ist der Marienplatz	1	die „heimliche Hauptstadt" Deutschlands.
4. Die Innenstadt ist nur	5	die Oper Münchens.
5. Das Nationaltheater ist	7	ein Museum.
6. Der Chinesische Turm ist	8	ein Schloss in München.
7. Die Alte Pinakothek ist	9	ein Wahrzeichen Münchens.
8. Nymphenburg heisst	4	für Fussgänger da.
9. Der Alte Peter ist	6	im Englischen Garten.
10. Das Münchner Kindl ist	3	und das Rathaus.

A 12 Ein wenig Landeskunde

Munich, the capital city of Bavaria, has over one million inhabitants and is the most popular city in Germany among both foreign visitors and native Germans.

Munich owes its origins to **Herzog Heinrich der Löwe,** *Duke Henry the Lion,* who built a bridge over the river Isar and established a customs station there in 1158. The city got its name from the monastery which was built nearby—the bridge was **bei den Mönchen.** The **Münchner Kindl,** the coat of arms of Munich, shows a monk with a stein of beer because it was the monks who started the brewery business.

Often called **das Millionendorf,** *Village of Millions,* and **Weltstadt mit Herz,** *Metropolis with Heart,* Munich has many attractive features: its location at the foot of the Alps and the Alpine lakes; its position as a capital of European art, music, theater, publishing, and fashion; its great university and its beautiful Baroque palaces and churches; its reputation for friendliness; and its beer festival—the biggest in the world—the **Oktoberfest!**

A 13 ENTSCHULDIGUNG, WO IST BITTE . . .?

Florian ist allein in der Stadt. Er möchte das Nationalmuseum sehen, aber er weiss nicht, wo es ist. Er fragt:

FLORIAN Entschuldigung! Wo ist bitte das Nationalmuseum?

MANN Keine Ahnung! Ich bin nicht von hier.

* * *

FLORIAN Verzeihung! Weisst du vielleicht, wo das Nationalmuseum ist?

JUNGE Nein, ich weiss es leider nicht.

* * *

FLORIAN Entschuldigung! Wissen Sie, wo das Nationalmuseum ist?

FRAU Moment mal, das Nationalmuseum—ja, das ist in der Prinzregentenstrasse.

A 14 WIE SAGT MAN DAS?
Asking for directions, saying you don't know

You have used „**Wo ist bitte . . .**" to ask for directions. Here are some additional ways of asking for directions and some expressions that you can use when someone asks you and you don't know the answer.

asking for directions	Wo ist bitte . . .? Wissen Sie, wo . . . ist? Weisst du vielleicht, wo . . . ist?	Where is . . ., please? Do you know where . . . is? Perhaps you can tell me where . . . is?
saying you don't know	Ich weiss es nicht. Ich weiss es leider nicht. Keine Ahnung! Ich bin nicht von hier.	I don't know. I'm sorry, I don't know. I have no idea! I'm not from here.

If you expand this to include giving directions, give the students the constructions *am* ——platz and *in der* ——*strasse* to use while practicing the functions.

A 15 Übung • Wo ist . . .?

A: Verzeihung! Wo ist bitte das Rathaus?
B: Ich weiss es leider nicht.

* * *

A: Entschuldigung! Weisst du vielleicht, wo das Rathaus ist?
B: Keine Ahnung, ich bin nicht von hier.

der	die
Dom Englische Garten Marienplatz	Alte Pinakothek Oper Theatinerkirche
das	
Nationalmuseum Nationaltheater	Rathaus Schloss Nymphenburg

A 16 ERKLÄRUNG
The Verb wissen

1. The verb **wissen,** *to know (a fact, information, etc.),* has these forms in the present tense:

ich **weiss**	wir **wissen**
du **weisst**	ihr **wisst**
er, sie, es **weiss**	sie, Sie **wissen**

2. The verb **wissen** is commonly used with the direct object **es.**

Wo ist bitte der Dom? Ich weiss **es** nicht.

3. **Wissen** can be followed by an entire clause. In such clauses, the verb is in last position.

Weiss Florian, wo der Dom **ist?** Er weiss es nicht.

Wer weiss, wo der Dom **ist?** < Ich weiss es. / Ich weiss, wo der Dom **ist.**

4. In response to a comment, the **ich**-form **ich weiss** can be used without **es.**

Niebüll hat 7 000 Einwohner. Ich weiss.

A17 Übung • Wer weiss es?

Ich weiss, wo der Dom ist. Wir . . .

Ich . . .

Wir . . . wissen, wo das Schloss Nymphenburg ist.

Florian . . . weiss, wo der Marienplatz ist.

Du . . . weisst, wo das Rathaus ist.

Ihr . . . wisst, wo der Chinesische Turm ist.

A18 Übung • Wissen Sie, wo . . .?

Du kennst München nicht, und du fragst verschiedene Passanten, wo folgende Sehenswürdigkeiten sind. Schau auf den Stadtplan!

Theatinerkirche
Nationaltheater
Alte Pinakothek
Ludwigskirche
Nationalmuseum

A: Verzeihung! Wissen Sie, wo das Nationalmuseum ist?

B: Ich weiss es nicht. *or* Moment mal! Das Nationalmuseum ist in der . . .strasse.

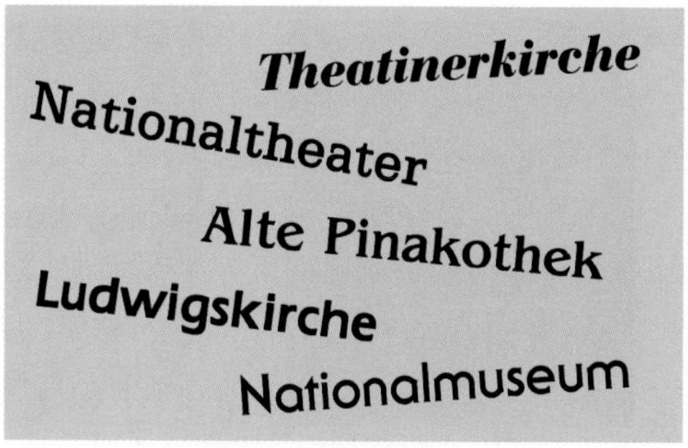

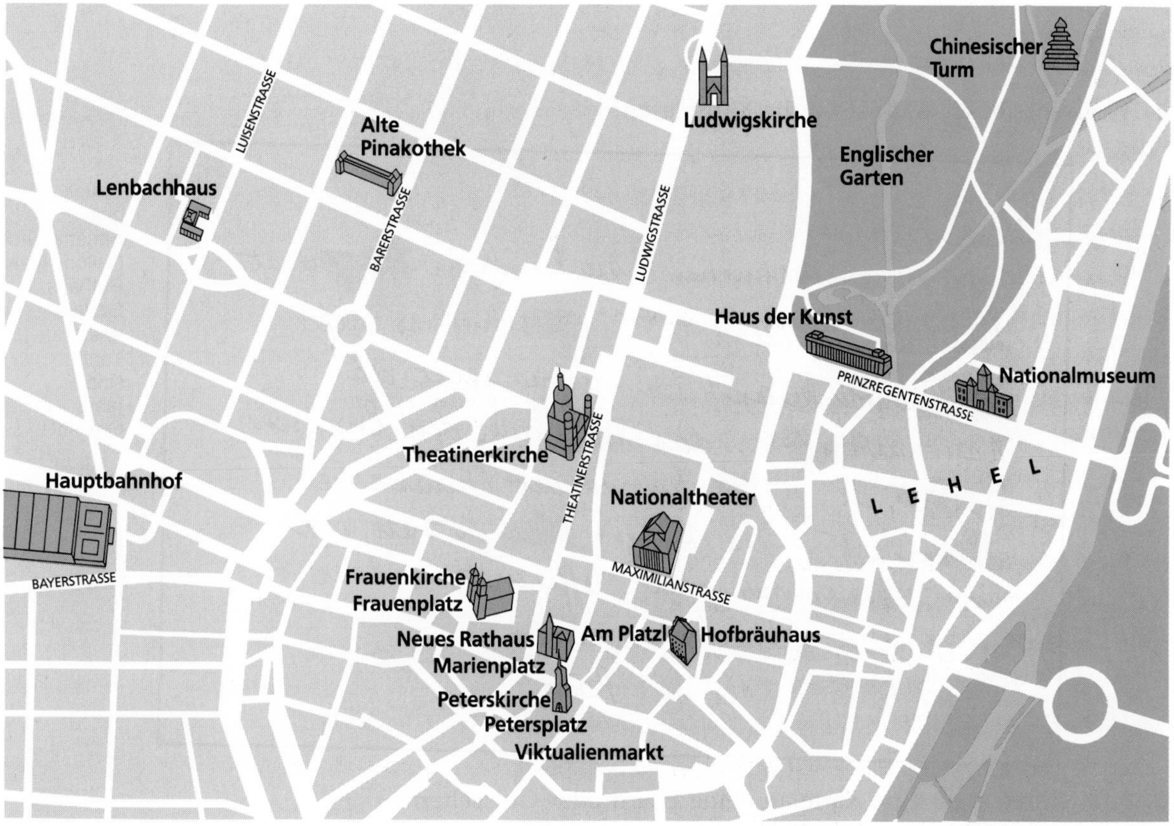

Chinesischer Turm
Ludwigskirche
Englischer Garten
Alte Pinakothek
LUISENSTRASSE
Lenbachhaus
BARERSTRASSE
LUDWIGSTRASSE
Haus der Kunst
Nationalmuseum
PRINZREGENTENSTRASSE
Theatinerkirche
THEATINERSTRASSE
Hauptbahnhof
BAYERSTRASSE
Nationaltheater
L E H E L
MAXIMILIANSTRASSE
Frauenkirche
Frauenplatz
Neues Rathaus
Marienplatz
Am Platzl
Hofbräuhaus
Peterskirche
Petersplatz
Viktualienmarkt

A 19 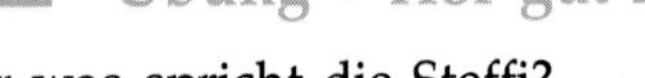 Übung • Hör gut zu!

For script and answers, see p. T141.

Über was spricht die Steffi?

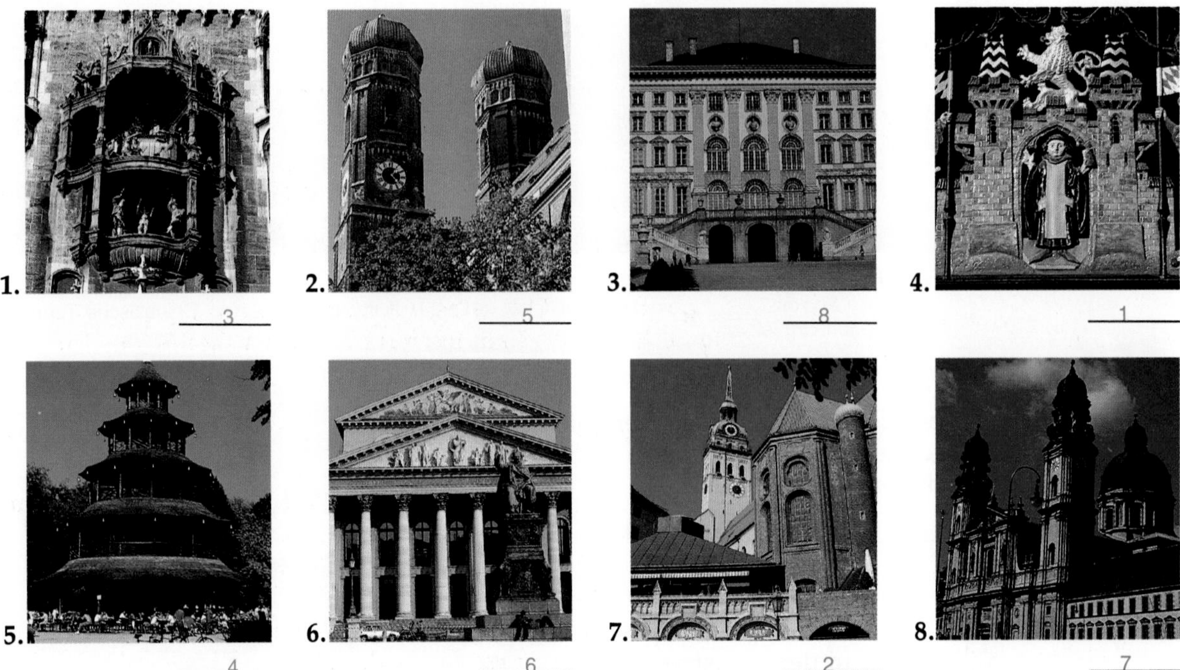

1. ___3___
2. ___5___
3. ___8___
4. ___1___
5. ___4___
6. ___6___
7. ___2___
8. ___7___

A 20 Lese- und Schreibübung • Florian schreibt nach Hause

1. Was schreibt er? Kannst du die Karte lesen?

Liebe Eltern!
Grüsse aus München! Die heimliche ___stadt Deutchlands ist toll! Es ___ hier so viele ___würdigkeiten! Ich kenne jetzt das National___, das ___haus, den Englischen ___, etc. ___ ihr, wo der Chinesische ___ ist? – Die Hubers ___ so nett, und ich ___ immer mit Steffi in die Stadt.
Herzliche ___,
Flori

Hauptstadt
gibt
Sehenswürdigkeiten
Nationaltheater
Rathaus
Garten
Wisst
Turm
sind
fahre
Grüsse

2. Jetzt schreibst du eine Karte an deine Eltern oder Grosseltern.

SECTION **B**

shopping for groceries, making suggestions about where to shop

Steffi has to go shopping for her mother. Where does she go? What does she buy?

B1

Steffi geht einkaufen

Steffis Einkaufszettel:

1 Pfd. Hackfleisch
200 g Aufschnitt
1 Brot
6 Semmeln
1 Salat
1 kg Tomaten
1 Pfd. Kirschen
1 Gurke
1 l Milch
10 Eier
1/2 Pfd. Butter
Käse, 100 g
1 Pfd. Kaffee
2 Pfd. Zucker
4 Joghurt
2 Fl. Mineralwasser

FRAU HUBER: Du, Steffi, geh doch bitte mal für mich einkaufen!

STEFFI: O.K. Was brauchst du denn?

FRAU HUBER: Schau, ich habe hier einen Zettel für dich. Aber kauf nicht alles im Supermarkt!

STEFFI: Wo soll ich das Hackfleisch kaufen?

FRAU HUBER: Kauf das Fleisch und die Wurst beim Metzger und hol das Obst und das Gemüse beim Gemüsehändler! Und kauf die Semmeln beim Bäcker! Dort sind sie immer frisch. Alles andere kaufst du im Supermarkt.

STEFFI: Gut. Ich brauche aber Geld.

FRAU HUBER: Hier sind hundert Mark. Pass bitte auf, und verlier das Geld nicht!

STEFFI: Keine Sorge! Ich pass schon auf, Mutti. Tschüs!

Was kauft Steffi beim Metzger?

ein Pfund Hackfleisch

200 Gramm Wurst, Aufschnitt

Beim Bäcker kauft sie:

ein Brot

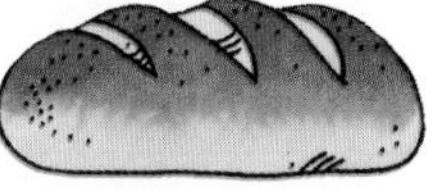

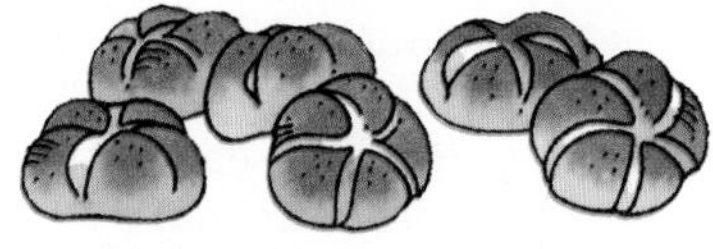

und sechs Semmeln

Was kauft sie beim Gemüsehändler? Und wieviel?

1 Kilo Tomaten

1 Pfund Kirschen

einen Kopf Salat

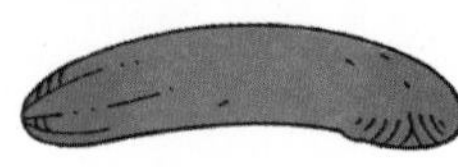
eine Gurke

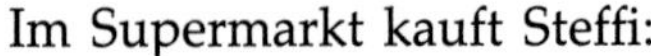

Im Supermarkt kauft Steffi:

zehn Eier

einen Liter Milch

zwei Pfund Zucker

zwei Flaschen Mineralwasser

ein Pfund Kaffee

ein halbes Pfund Butter

vier Joghurt

100 Gramm Käse

B2 Übung • Mix-Match: Steffi geht einkaufen

1. Steffi geht für ihre Mutter	6	alles andere.
2. Sie kauft nicht alles	4	beim Bäcker.
3. Das Fleisch kauft sie	3	beim Metzger.
4. Die Brötchen kauft sie	5	die Tomaten.
5. Beim Gemüsehändler kauft sie	1	einkaufen.
6. Im Supermarkt holt sie	2	im Supermarkt.

B3 Übung • Und du?

1. Wo kaufst du das Fleisch?
2. Wo kaufst du die Milch?
3. Was kaufst du im Supermarkt?

B4 WIE SAGT MAN DAS?
Making requests

One common way of making requests is to use the verb stem without the verb ending. Requests made in this way are informal and can be used with people you address with **du.** The words **doch, mal,** and **bitte** are often included.

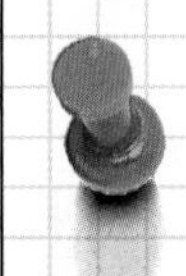

Geh doch bitte mal einkaufen!	Please go shopping.
Kauf bitte nicht alles im Supermarkt!	Please don't buy everything in the supermarket!
Hol doch das Obst beim Gemüsehändler!	Do get the fruit at the greengrocer's.
Pass bitte auf!	Please watch out!
Verlier das Geld nicht!	Don't lose the money!

B5 Übung • Wo soll ich alles kaufen?  For answers, see p. T142.

STEFFI Wo soll ich das Fleisch kaufen?
MUTTER Kauf bitte das Fleisch beim Metzger!

* * *

STEFFI Und wo soll ich das Gemüse holen?
MUTTER Hol doch bitte das Gemüse beim Gemüsehändler!

beim Metzger
beim Bäcker
beim Gemüsehändler
im Supermarkt

der	die	das	die
Aufschnitt, Salat, Käse, Kaffee, Zucker, Joghurt	Wurst, Semmel, Gurke, Tomate, Kirsche, Milch, Butter	Hackfleisch, Brot, Ei, Mineralwasser, Obst	Semmeln, Gurken Tomaten, Kirschen Eier, Brote

B6 ERKLÄRUNG
The Verb sollen

1. The verb **sollen,** *supposed to, should,* has these forms in the present tense:

ich **soll**	wir **sollen**
du **sollst**	ihr **sollt**
er, sie, es **soll**	sie, Sie **sollen**

2. **Sollen** is usually used with an infinitive that comes at the end of the sentence:

   Wo **soll** ich das Brot **kaufen?**

3. In English there are many ways of expressing **sollen.** For example:

   Wo soll ich das Brot kaufen? { *Where am I supposed to buy the bread?* / *Where should I buy the bread?* / *Where do you want me to buy the bread?* }

B7 Übung • Was soll ich kaufen? 

Variation: Move each subject to the right and repeat the exercise.

Ich soll das Brot beim Bäcker kaufen. Wir . . .

beim Bäcker
beim Metzger
beim Gemüsehändler
im Supermarkt

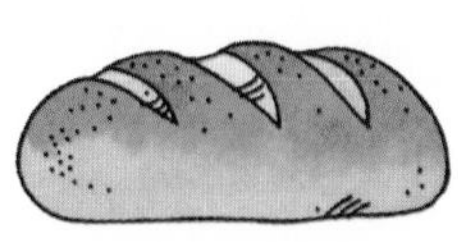

Ich . . . soll das Brot beim Bäcker kaufen.

Wir . . . sollen die Milch im Supermarkt kaufen.

Steffi . . . soll die Tomaten beim Gemüsehändler kaufen.

Ihr . . . sollt den Kaffee im Supermarkt kaufen.

Du . . . sollst den Aufschnitt beim Metzger kaufen.

Die Kinder . . . sollen die Kirschen beim Gemüsehändler kaufen.

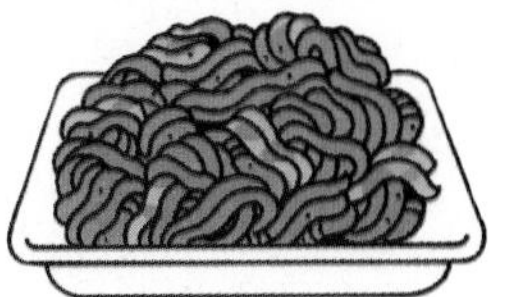

Er . . . soll das Hackfleisch beim Metzger kaufen.

B 8 Ein wenig Landeskunde

In German-speaking countries, the **Kilo** is the unit of weight. One **Kilo** has **1 000 Gramm** and is the equivalent of 2.2 American pounds. In colloquial use, the word **Pfund** is also used when referring to weight. One **Pfund** has **500 Gramm,** half a **Kilogram.** The unit of liquid measure is the **Liter.** One **Liter** also contains **1 000 Gramm** and is a little more than a quart.

B 9 Leseübung • Wie schwer ist ein Pfund?

1 kg (ein Kilogramm) = 2,2 lb.
(zwei Komma zwei amerikanische Pfund)

Das amerikanische Pfund hat nur 453 Gramm.

Das deutsche Pfund hat 500 Gramm.

1 Pfd.	(ein Pfund)	hat	500 g (Gramm)
1/2 Pfd.	(ein halbes Pfund)	hat	250 g
1/4 Pfd.	(ein viertel Pfund)	hat	125 g
3/4 Pfd.	(drei viertel Pfund)	sind	375 g
2 Pfd.	(zwei Pfund)	sind	1 000 g oder 1 kg (ein Kilogramm)

B 10 Übung • Geh mal für mich einkaufen!

A: Was brauchen wir?
B: Tomaten.
A: Und wieviel?
B: Ein Kilo.

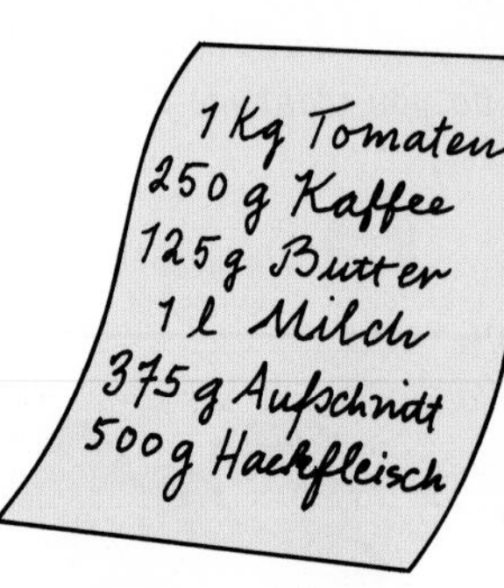

1 Kg Tomaten
250 g Kaffee
125 g Butter
1 l Milch
375 g Aufschnitt
500 g Hackfleisch

Für Ihren Campingurlaub

Aufschnitt
100 g nur **1.29**

Holzofenbrot
ca. 2000 g nur **2.89**

Original Alt-Münchner Leberkäs gebacken
100 g **–,79**

Deutscher Kopfsalat	Stck.	**–.39**
Spanische Tomaten	1 kg	**4.00**
Hohes C Orangensaft	0,7 l	**1.69**
Jakobs Kaffee	500 g	**10,60**
Deutsche Markenbutter	250 g	**2,20**
Joghurt, natur	150 g	**–,49**
Deutscher Tilsiter	100 g	**–,79**

B 11 Übung • Preisinformation

A: Du, was kostet der Kaffee im Supermarkt?
B: Ein Pfund Kaffee kostet DM 10,60.
A: Das ist preiswert!

* * *

A: Was soll ich kaufen?
B: Kauf doch bitte . . .!
A: Gut.

B 12 Übung • Was hat die Steffi alles im Netz? Rate mal!

Hier ist der Kassenzettel

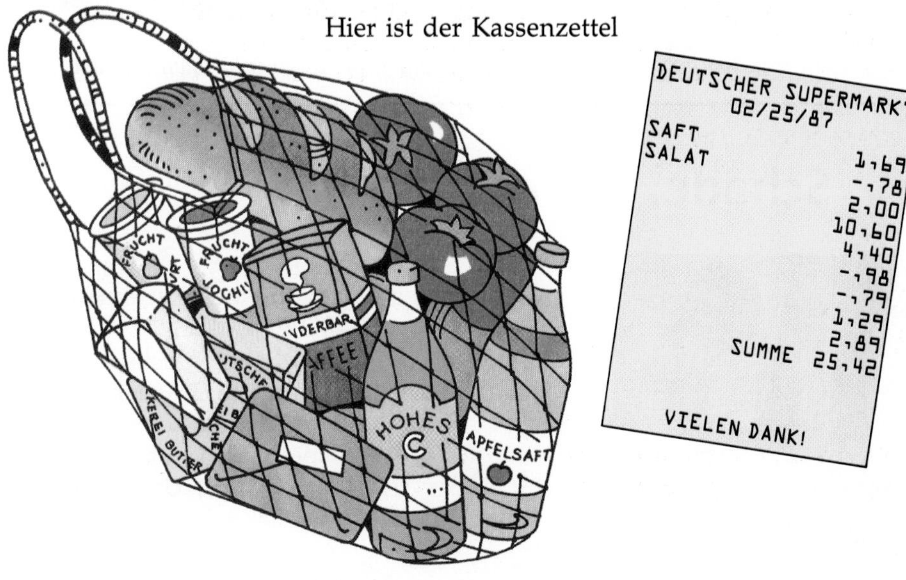

eine Flasche Saft
zwei Kopfsalat
500 g Tomaten
ein Pfund Kaffee
ein Pfund Butter
zwei Joghurt
100 g Käse (Deutscher Tilsiter)
100 g Aufschnitt
ein Holzofenbrot

B 13 Übung • Hör gut zu!

For script and answers, see p. T143.

Wo kauft die Steffi ein?

	0	1	2	3	4	5	6	7	8	9	10
beim Bäcker			✓			✓					
beim Metzger		✓						✓			
beim Gemüsehändler					✓				✓		
im Supermarkt	✓			✓			✓			✓	✓

B 14 Übung • Wo soll ich das kaufen?

Draw the grocery items mentioned in this unit on big cards—or bring in pictures of each item. One student holds up a card and asks where to buy the item pictured. Practice the following dialog with each item.

A: Wo soll ich die Tomaten kaufen?
B: Kauf sie bitte beim Gemüsehändler!
A: Wieviel Tomaten soll ich kaufen?
B: Kauf doch ein Pfund!

B 15 Schreibübung • Dein Einkaufszettel

Jetzt schreibst du einen Einkaufszettel! Du sollst acht Sachen kaufen, aber nicht alles im Supermarkt! Deine Mutter sagt dir, was du holen sollst. Schreib das Gespräch auf! Was sagt deine Mutter? Was sagst du?

SECTION C

talking about the weather, ordering in a restaurant, talking about how something tastes and if you want more

The weather doesn't look too good, but Steffi and Florian want to go into town anyway.

C1

Schade, es regnet.

FLORIAN Steffi! Was ist los? Du siehst so traurig aus.
STEFFI Ich bin sauer. —Schau, Flori, es regnet.
FLORIAN Das ist blöd! Was sollen wir jetzt machen?
FRAU HUBER Bleibt lieber zu Hause! Spielt Karten oder . . .
STEFFI Ach, Mutti!
FLORIAN Was sagt der Wetterbericht?
FRAU HUBER Es bleibt bewölkt, und es soll ab und zu regnen.
STEFFI Ach, komm, Flori! Gehen wir!
FRAU HUBER Hast du einen Regenmantel, Flori? Es ist kühl.
FLORIAN Ja, ich hole ihn schnell.
FRAU HUBER Hier sind zwei Regenschirme für euch. Und kommt nicht so spät nach Hause!
STEFFI Wir sind um 9 Uhr wieder da.
FRAU HUBER Dann viel Spass!

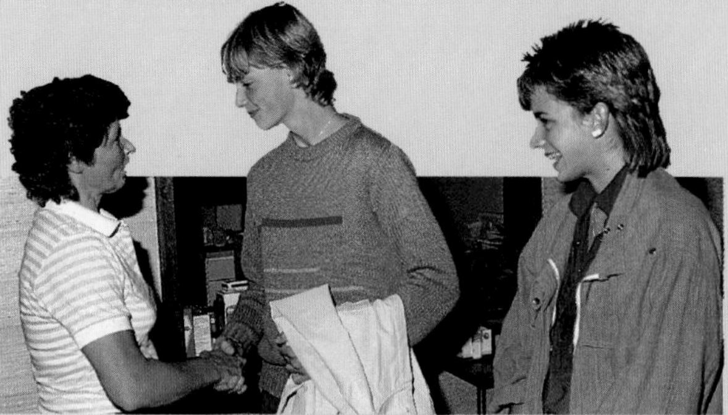

FLORIAN Danke!
STEFFI Tschüs, Mutti!

Was sagt der Wetterbericht?

Heute bewölkt und kühl, ab und zu Regen.

Es regnet. Es ist kalt.

Heiter und warm.

Die Sonne scheint.

A farm house in the Lüneburger Heide

Das Wetter bleibt schön.

Es ist sonnig und heiss.

2. Sie sollen zu Hause bleiben.
3. Es bleibt bewölkt, und es soll ab und zu regnen.

C2 Übung • Fragen

1. Warum ist Steffi sauer? Es regnet.
2. Was sollen Steffi und Flori machen? Was sagt Frau Huber?
3. Was sagt der Wetterbericht?
4. Warum holt Flori den Regenmantel?
5. Wann sind Steffi und Flori wieder da?

4. Es ist kühl. 5. um 9 Uhr

C3 Übung • Jetzt bist du dran

1. Wie ist jetzt das Wetter?
2. Was sagt der Wetterbericht?

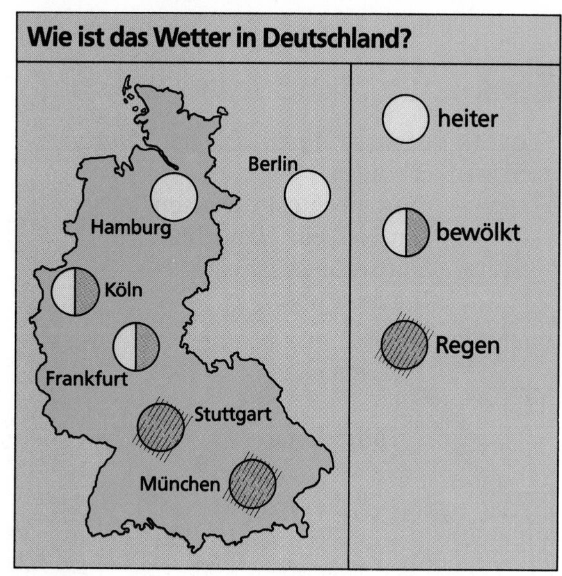

Point out that *heiter* is weather-report jargon for *schön*.

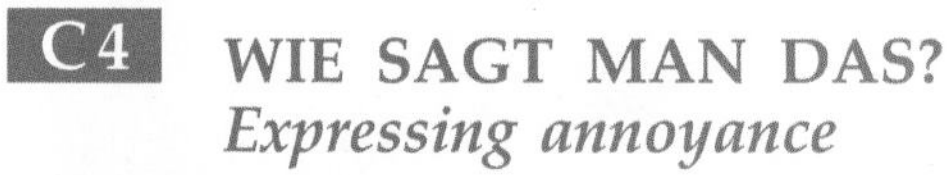

C4 WIE SAGT MAN DAS?
Expressing annoyance

You know many ways of expressing approval or enthusiasm, such as **toll!, prima!,** and so on. Here are some ways of expressing annoyance.

annoyance	Das ist (zu) blöd!	That's (really) too bad!
	Das ist (zu) dumm!	That's (really) too bad!
	Ich bin sauer.	I am annoyed.

C5 Übung • Wie ist das Wetter?

A: Wie ist das Wetter?
B: Es (ist) . . .
A: Das ist blöd!

A: Was sagt der Wetterbericht?
B: Es . . .
A: Toll! Prima!

es regnet
kühl
bewölkt
kalt
es soll regnen

es bleibt schön
es ist sonnig
es ist heiss
es bleibt warm

C6 Übung • Hör gut zu!

For script and answers, see p. T145.

Wie ist das Wetter, gut oder schlecht?

	0	1	2	3	4	5	6
gut	✓		✓			✓	✓
schlecht		✓		✓	✓		

C7 DER FLORI HAT HUNGER

FLORIAN Mensch, Steffi. Ich hab' Hunger.
STEFFI Ich auch.
FLORIAN Was möchtest du essen? Ein Eis? Ein Hähnchen?
STEFFI Dort drüben ist eine Imbiss-Stube.
FLORIAN Prima!

Probieren Sie mal den Leberkäs!

Leberkäs mit Senf	3.50
Bratwurst	2.80
Weisswurst	3.00
Wurstbrot	2.40
Fischbrot	3.50
Pizza	6.00
Mineralwasser	1.80
Kaffee	2.40
Cola	2.60

FLORIAN Was soll ich essen? Alles sieht so gut aus.
STEFFI Probier doch mal den Leberkäs[1]! Leberkäs mit Senf ist gut.
FLORIAN Und was isst du?
STEFFI Ich esse eine Bratwurst, und ich trinke ein Mineralwasser.
FLORIAN Na gut, ich probier' mal den Leberkäs, und ich trinke auch ein Wasser.

[1] **Leberkäs** is a southern German sausage specialty. It is made of beef or pork liver, pork, bacon, onion, and spices. It is baked in a loaf pan and is usually served cut in thick slices.

C8 Übung • Was soll ich essen? Was soll ich trinken?

A: Was soll ich essen?
B: Ich esse den Leberkäs.
A: Ich auch.

der/ein	die/eine	das/ein
Leberkäs Kaffee	Bratwurst Weisswurst Pizza Cola	Hähnchen Wurstbrot Mineralwasser Fischbrot Eis

essen: die/eine Bratwurst, Weisswurst, Pizza; das/ein Hähnchen, Wurstbrot, Fischbrot, E
trinken: einen Kaffee, eine Cola, e
Mineralwasser

C9 ERKLÄRUNG
The Verb essen

The verb **essen,** *to eat,* has the following forms in the present tense:

ich **esse**	wir **essen**
du **isst**	ihr **esst**
er, sie, es **isst**	sie, Sie **essen**

C10 Übung • Und du?

1. Was möchtest du mal probieren?
2. Was trinkst du? Was trinkst du gern?
3. Frag deine Klassenkameraden, was sie essen und trinken! Erzähl, was sie sagen!

C11 WIE SCHMECKT'S?

FLORIAN Wie schmeckt die Bratwurst, Steffi?
STEFFI Hm, prima! Sie schmeckt sehr gut. —Und wie ist der Leberkäs?
FLORIAN Auch gut. —Isst du noch eine Bratwurst?
STEFFI Nein, danke. Ich habe genug. Und du? Noch einen Leberkäs?
FLORIAN Nein, danke. Ich bin satt.

C12 WIE SAGT MAN DAS?
Asking and telling how something tastes

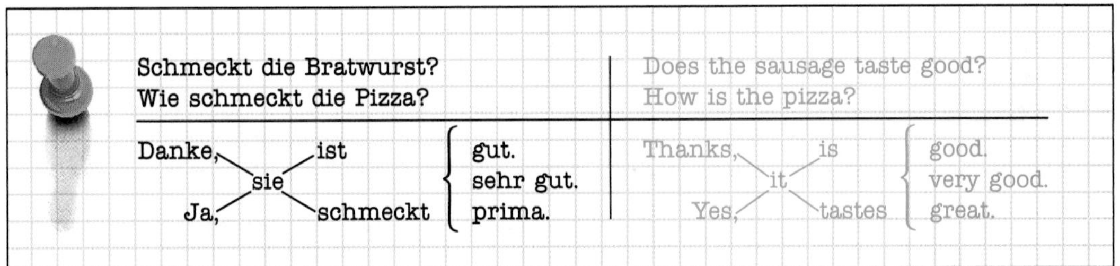

Schmeckt die Bratwurst? Wie schmeckt die Pizza?	Does the sausage taste good? How is the pizza?
Danke, / Ja, — sie — ist / schmeckt — gut. / sehr gut. / prima.	Thanks, / Yes, — it — is / tastes — good. / very good. / great.

C13 Übung • Wie schmeckt's?

A: Wie schmeckt das Hähnchen?
B: Es ist gut.

der Leberkäs, er/das Eis, es/das Fischbrot, es/das Wurstbrot, es/die Bratwurst, sie/der Senf, er

Leberkäs Eis Bratwurst Fischbrot Wurstbrot Senf

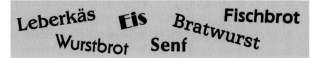

C14 ERKLÄRUNG
noch ein, *another*

The phrase **noch ein,** *another,* has the same endings as **ein.**

	Masculine	*Feminine*	*Neuter*
Nominative	**noch ein**	**noch eine**	**noch ein**
Accusative	**noch einen**		

When working with this material, be careful not to use any plural nouns.

C15 Übung • Möchtest du noch ein . . .?

1. noch ein 2. noch eine
3. noch ein 4. noch eine
5. noch ein 6. noch einen

A: Der Leberkäs schmeckt gut.
B: Möchtest du noch einen Leberkäs?

1. Das Wurstbrot schmeckt gut.
2. Die Bratwurst ist sehr gut.
3. Das Eis schmeckt toll.
4. Die Pizza ist phantastisch.
5. Das Hähnchen ist Klasse!
6. Der Kaffee ist prima.

C16 WIE SAGT MAN DAS?
Saying you want more or you don't want more

	Möchtest du noch ein Eis?	Would you like another ice cream?
saying yes	Danke, gern. Ja, bitte!	Thank you, I would (like more). Yes, please.
saying no	Nein, danke. Danke, ich bin satt. Nein, danke. Ich habe genug.	No, thank you. Thanks, I'm full. No thanks. I have enough.

C17 Übung • Partnerarbeit

Ask a classmate if he or she would like more to eat or drink. Refer to the chart in exercise C8 on page 212. Your classmate should make appropriate responses.

C18 ERKLÄRUNG
Making Suggestions Using Command Forms

One way of making a suggestion is to use the command form of the verb.

1. When suggesting something to a person you address with **du,** use the **du**-form of the verb without the ending **-st.**

Verb Form	*Command Form*	*Suggestion*
du kaufst	**kauf**	**Kauf** das Fleisch bitte beim Metzger!
du probierst	**probier**	**Probier** doch den Leberkäs!
du isst	**iss**	**Iss** doch eine Bratwurst!

2. When suggesting something to two people you address with **ihr,** use the **ihr**-form of the verb.

Verb Form	*Command Form*	*Suggestion*
ihr bleibt	**bleibt**	**Bleibt** doch zu Hause!
ihr spielt	**spielt**	**Spielt** doch Karten!
ihr esst	**esst**	**Esst** doch etwas!

3. When suggesting something to people you would address with **Sie,** use the **Sie**-form of the verb. The pronoun **Sie** is used and follows the verb.

Verb Form	*Command Form*	*Suggestion*
Sie probieren	**probieren Sie**	**Probieren Sie** mal den Leberkäs!
Sie holen	**holen Sie**	**Holen Sie** das Brot beim Bäcker!
Sie essen	**essen Sie**	**Essen Sie** doch das Hähnchen!

1. geh 2. kommt 3. probieren 4. iss 5. trink 6. verliert 7. kauf 8. besuch 9. fragen 10. such 11. spielt

C19 Übung • Was passt? 

1. Steffi, . . . mal für mich einkaufen!
2. Steffi und Flori, . . . nicht zu spät nach Hause!
3. Frau Huber, . . . Sie mal den Leberkäs!
4. Steffi, . . . doch eine Bratwurst!
5. Flori, . . . doch ein Mineralwasser!
6. Steffi und Flori, . . . bitte das Geld nicht!
7. Steffi, . . . doch bitte das Brot beim Bäcker!
8. Florian, . . . doch mal die Hubers!
9. Frau Huber, . . . Sie mal die Steffi!
10. Steffi, . . . doch mal den Regenschirm!
11. Steffi und Flori, . . . heute nicht Tennis!

essen
gehen
kaufen
kommen
probieren
trinken
verlieren
besuchen
fragen
suchen
spielen

C20 Übung • Was sagst du zu . . .?  For answers, see p. T148.

Was sollen sie tun? Sie sollen: eine Zeitung holen

Hol bitte eine Zeitung!

Holt bitte eine Zeitung!

Holen Sie bitte eine Zeitung!

1. einkaufen gehen
2. das Brot beim Bäcker holen
3. den Leberkäs probieren
4. die Bratwurst essen
5. lieber zu Hause bleiben
6. das Nationalmuseum besuchen

C21 Übung • Hör gut zu! For script and answers, see p. T148.

Mit wem sprichst du? Mit Steffi? Mit Steffi und Flori? Mit Frau Huber?

	0	1	2	3	4	5	6	7	8	9	10
Steffi		✓				✓	✓				✓
Steffi und Flori	✓				✓				✓	✓	
Frau Huber			✓	✓				✓			

C22 Schreibübung • Im Restaurant

Make up a menu and write it on poster board. Then write a dialog that takes place in a restaurant and practice it with a classmate. Use some of the following phrases.

Kellner/in	Gast 1	Gast 2
Was möchten Sie? Probieren Sie mal den . . .! Sie möchten den . . .? Möchten Sie noch einen . . .? Ist das alles? / Gut! Ja. / Nein.	Was soll ich essen? Ist der . . . gut? Ich esse . . . Haben Sie auch . . .?	Probier mal den . . .! . . . schmeckt . . .! Wie ist . . .? Und ich möchte . . .

TRY YOUR SKILLS

using what you've learned

1 Steffi geht mit Florian einkaufen

Steffi geht für ihre Mutter einkaufen, und Flori geht mit. Zuerst kaufen sie beim Bäcker ein.

—Tag, Steffi!
—Guten Tag, Frau Schmitt! Frau Schmitt, das ist der Florian Schneider, Besuch aus Freiburg.
—Soso, aus Freiburg! In Freiburg soll das Wetter immer schön sein. Stimmt das?
—Nein. Es regnet auch in Freiburg, vielleicht nicht so oft wie in München.

Steffi kauft ein Brot und acht Semmeln, und dann kaufen die beiden Obst und Gemüse beim Gemüsehändler.

—So, Steffi, was möchtest du heute?
—Eine Gurke, einen Kopf Salat und ein Pfund Kirschen.
—Hier, probier mal eine Kirsche! Ist das dein Freund, Steffi?
—Das ist Florian Schneider. Der Flori ist der Sohn von Muttis Schulfreundin.
—Woher bist du?
—Aus Freiburg.
—Und du besuchst jetzt unser schönes München. Du, da hast du eine prima Fremdenführerin. Die Steffi kennt München gut.
—Ja, das weiss ich.

Dann gehen die beiden in den Supermarkt. Hier soll Steffi ein halbes Pfund Butter und einen Liter Milch kaufen. Zuletzt gehen die beiden in den Zeitungsladen. Der Vati möchte die Abendzeitung lesen.

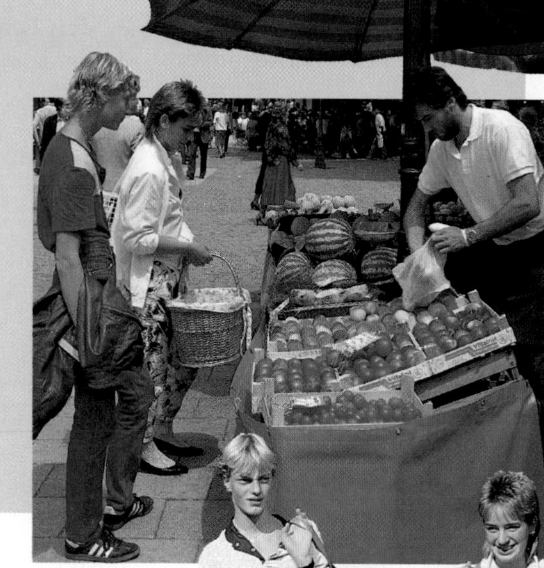

2 Übung • Stimmt! Stimmt nicht!

1. Der Florian geht für seine Mutter einkaufen. Stimmt nicht!
2. Die Steffi und der Flori kaufen zuerst beim Bäcker ein. Stimmt!
3. Die Bäckersfrau heisst Schmitt. Stimmt!
4. Sie möchte wissen, wie das Wetter in Freiburg ist. Stimmt!
5. In Freiburg regnet es so oft wie in München. Stimmt nicht!
6. Im Supermarkt kaufen sie Obst und Gemüse. Stimmt nicht!
7. Florians Mutter ist eine Schulfreundin von Steffis Mutter. Stimmt!
8. Steffi ist die Fremdenführerin—sie zeigt Florian die Stadt München.
9. Zuletzt kaufen die beiden eine Abendzeitung im Supermarkt.

8. Stimmt! 9. Stimmt nicht!

3 Übung • Steffi geht einkaufen

Steffi geht einkaufen. Sie muss folgende Sachen holen: Brötchen, Aufschnitt, Tomaten, Salat, Milch, Kaffee, Zucker und Joghurt. Beschreib Steffis Einkaufsrunde.

Steffi geht zuerst zum . . . und kauft . . . Dann geht sie . . . Bäcker Brötchen zum Metzger und kauft Aufschnitt. Dann geht sie zum Gemüsehändler und kauft Tomaten und Salat. Dann geht sie zum Supermarkt und kauft Milch, Kaffee, Zucker und Joghurt.

4 Übung • Ratespiel: Wo ist . . . ?

Practice this dialog using different cities in German-speaking countries. Then practice it using cities and towns you are familiar with in the United States.

A: Weisst du, wo Niebüll ist?
B: Na klar! Niebüll ist in Schleswig-Holstein. Niebüll ist eine Stadt; sie hat 7 000 Einwohner. *or* Ich weiss es leider nicht. *or* Keine Ahnung. *or* Frag doch mal deinen . . .

5 Übung • Werners Einkaufszettel

Was bringt Werner nach Hause?

1. Was soll Werner alles kaufen?
2. Was kauft er nicht? Butter, Kaffee, Reis, Zucker, eine Gurke
3. Was bringt er nach Hause? Milch, ein Brot, Joghurt, Pudding, Semmeln und Mineralwasser

6 Übung • Rollenspiel: In der Imbiss-Stube

Du bist in der Imbiss-Stube und möchtest etwas essen.
Ein Mitschüler ist der Kellner oder die Kellnerin.

KELLNER/IN Probieren Sie doch mal den Leberkäs!
GAST Ist er heute gut?
KELLNER/IN Ja, sehr gut!
GAST Gut, dann esse ich einen Leberkäs.

Pizza die, sie, eine
Bratwurst die, sie, eine
Hähnchen das, es, ein
Fischbrot das, es, ein

7 Aussprache-, Lese- und Schreibübungen  For script, see p. T149.

1. Listen carefully and repeat what you hear.
2. Listen, then read aloud.
   1. allein, Bayern, Leute, Haus, Häuser
   2. holen, Dom, Oper, Obst, Brot, Tomate; Sonne, sollen, Schloss, wolkig, sonnig
   3. zum, zu Hause, Zimmer, Zoll, Verzeihung, Wahrzeichen, Einkaufszettel
   4. Wurst, wissen, Wien, Wasser, Weisswurst, Wetterbericht, warm, wieder, bewölkt
3. Copy the following sentences to prepare yourself to write them from dictation.
   1. Wir holen Wurst und Brot. 2. In Wien gehen die Leute oft in die Oper.

WAS KANNST DU SCHON?

Let's review some important points you have learned in this unit.

Can you talk about where some of our friends live?
Name three of the places where our friends live and say whether each place is a city, a town, or a suburb. Wien/München, Grossstadt; Niebüll/Neuss, Stadt; Zimmerwald, Vorort
Tell where you live and what it is.

Can you identify landmarks in the city of Munich and ask for directions to get there? Entschuldigung!/Verzeihung! Wissen Sie, wo . . . ist?/Wo ist bitte . . . ? der Dom/Englische Garten/Marienplatz; die Alte Pinakothek/Oper/Theatinerkirche; das Nationalmuseum/Nationaltheater/Rathaus/Schloss Nymphenburg
Ask how to get to three landmarks in Munich.
What would you say if someone asked you directions and you did not know?
Ich weiss es (leider) nicht./Keine Ahnung! Ich bin nicht von hier.

Do you know how to go shopping for groceries?
Name two items you would buy:

1. at the bakery **2.** at the greengrocer **3.** at the supermarket

1. Brot, Semmeln 2. Salat, Gurken, Tomaten, Kirschen (Obst, Gemüse) 3. Kaffe, Käse, Eier. Milch, Zucker, Mineralwasser, Butter, Joghurt

Ask your friend to buy, in the appropriate store, each of these items you named. Use command forms.
Kauf bitte/Hol doch . . . beim Bäcker/beim Gemüsehändler/im Supermarkt!
Give the form of **sollen** that goes with each of the following subjects:

1. ich	**2.** ihr	**3.** Steffi	**4.** wir	**5.** du	**6.** Steffi und Flori
soll	sollt	soll	sollen	sollst	sollen

Can you describe the weather? Es ist schön/sonnig/heiss/warm/bewölkt/kühl/kalt/es regnet
Describe how the weather is today.

Say that the weather is bad and express annoyance. Das ist (zu) blöd/dumm!/Ich bin sauer.

Can you discuss items on a menu and talk about what you would like to order?
You are in a restaurant with a friend. Suggest three things to eat.
Iss/Probier (doch mal) den Leberkäs/eine Bratwurst/Weisswurst/Pizza/ein Hähnchen/Wurstbrot/Fischbrot
Your friend has ordered three different things. Ask how he or she likes each one. Ask your friend if he or she would like more. What would your friend say if: Wie schmeckt . . . ? Möchtest du noch ein/eine/einen . . . ?

1. he or she wanted more — Danke, gern./Ja, bitte!
2. he or she didn't want more — Nein, danke./Danke, ich bin satt/ich habe genug.

Can you suggest that someone do something?
Suggest to the following people that they try a pizza, eat another sausage, and buy a yogurt:

1. your mother	**2.** your brother and sister	**3.** your teacher
Probier eine Pizza!	Probiert doch eine Pizza!	Probieren Sie mal eine Pizza!
Iss noch eine Bratwurst!	Esst noch eine Bratwurst!	Essen Sie noch eine Bratwurst!
Kauf doch ein Eis!	Kauft doch ein Eis!	Kaufen Sie doch ein Eis!

WORTSCHATZ

SECTION A

die **Ahnung: keine Ahnung!** *I have no idea!*
allein *alone*
die **Alte Pinakothek** (see p 200)
Bayern *Bavaria*
der **Besuch** *company*
der **Besucher, -** *visitor*
der **Chinesische Turm** (see p 200)
der **Dom, -e** *cathedral*
das **Dorf, ⸚er** *village*
der **Einwohner, -** *inhabitant*
der **Englische Garten** (see p 200)
der **Fussgänger, -** *pedestrian*
die **Fussgängerzone, -n** *pedestrian mall*
das **Glockenspiel, -e** (see p 199)
die **Grossstadt, ⸚e** *big city*
Gruetzi! *hello!* (Swiss)
die **Hauptstadt, ⸚e** *capital city*
in der Prinzregentenstrasse *on Prinzregenten Street*
die **Innenstadt, ⸚e** *city center*
das **Jahr, -e** *year*
kennen *to know, be familiar with a place*
die **Kirche, -n** *church*
leider *unfortunately;* ich weiss es leider nicht *I'm sorry, I don't know*
der **Marienplatz** (see p 199)
die **Million, -en** *million*
das **Münchner Kindl** (see p 199)
das **Museum, Museen** *museum*
das **Nationaltheater** (see p 200)
das **Neue Rathaus** (see p 199)
oben: dort oben *up there*
die **Oper, -n** *opera;* in die Oper gehen *to go to the opera*
die **Peterskirche** (see p 199)
das **Schloss, ⸚er** *castle*
Schweiz: in der Schweiz *in Switzerland*
die **Sehenswürdigkeit, -en** *sight, place of interest*
die **Stadt, ⸚e** *city; town*
die **Tochter, ⸚** *daughter*
der **Turm, ⸚e** *tower*
vielleicht *maybe*
der **Vorort, -e** *suburb*
das **Wahrzeichen, -** *landmark*
das **Wappen, -** *coat of arms*
wissen *to know* (see p 202)
die **Wohnung, -en** *apartment*
zu Hause: ich bin in Wien zu Hause *I live in Vienna*

SECTION B

alles andere *everything else*
aufpassen: ich pass schon auf *I'll be careful;* pass bitte auf! please be careful!
der **Aufschnitt** *cold cuts*
der **Bäcker, -** *baker*
beim Bäcker *at the baker's*
das **Brot, -e** *bread*
die **Butter** *butter*
das **Ei, -er** *egg*
einkaufen gehen *to go shopping*
der **Einkaufszettel, -** *shopping list*
die **Flasche, -n** *bottle;* eine Flasche Mineralwasser *a bottle of mineral water*
das **Fleisch** *meat*
frisch *fresh*
das **Gemüse** *vegetable*
der **Gemüsehändler** *greengrocer*
das **Gramm** *gram;* 200 g Aufschnitt *200 grams of cold cuts*
die **Gurke, -n** *cucumber*
gut *okay, fine*
das **Hackfleisch** *chopped meat*
halb: ein halbes Pfund Butter *half a pound of butter*
holen *to get, buy*
der **Joghurt, -** *yogurt*
der **Kaffee** *coffee*
der **Käse** *cheese*
das **Kilo = Kilogramm** *kilogram;* 1 kg Tomaten *1 kilogram of tomatoes*
die **Kirsche, -n** *cherry*
der **Kopf, ⸚e** *head;* ein Kopf Salat *a head of lettuce*
der **Liter** *liter;* ein Liter Milch *a liter of milk*
der **Metzger, -** *butcher*
die **Milch** *milk*
das **Mineralwasser** *mineral water*
die **Mutti, -s** *mom*
das **Obst** *fruit*
das **Pfund** *pound;* zwei Pfund Zucker *two pounds of sugar*
der **Salat, -e** *lettuce*
die **Semmel, -n** *roll*
sollen *should, supposed to*
die **Sorge: keine Sorge** *don't worry*
der **Supermarkt, ⸚e** *supermarket*
die **Tomate, -n** *tomato*
die **Wurst, ⸚e** *sausage; cold cuts*
der **Zucker** *sugar*

SECTION C

ab und zu *now and then*
bewölkt *cloudy, overcast*
blöd *too bad!*
die **Bratwurst, ⸚e** *fried sausage*
die **Cola, -s** *cola*
das **Eis** *ice cream*
essen *to eat* (see p 212)
das **Fischbrot, -e** *fish sandwich*
genug *enough*
das **Hähnchen, -** *chicken*
heiss *hot*
heiter *fair (weather)*
Hunger haben *to be hungry*
die **Imbiss-Stube, -n** *snack bar*
kalt *cold*
kühl *cool*
der **Leberkäs** see fn p 212
los: was ist los? *what's the matter?*
mit *with*
na gut *well, okay*
nach Hause kommen *to come home*
noch ein *another*
die **Pizza, -s** *pizza*
probieren *to try;* probier mal *why don't you try*
der **Regen** *rain*
der **Regenmantel, ⸚** *raincoat*
der **Regenschirm, -e** *umbrella*
regnen: es regnet *it's raining*
satt: ich bin satt *I'm full*
scheinen *to shine*
schmecken *to taste;* wie schmeckt's? *how does it taste?*
schnell *fast, quick*
der **Senf** *mustard*
die **Sonne** *sun*
sonnig *sunny*
der **Spass: viel Spass!** *have fun!*
traurig *sad*
warm *warm*
die **Weisswurst, ⸚e** *type of sausage*
das **Wetter** *weather*
der **Wetterbericht, -e** *weather report*
wieder *again;* wir sind um 9 wieder da *we'll be back at 9*
das **Wurstbrot, -e** *sandwich made with cold cuts*
zu Hause: bleibt lieber zu Hause! *you'd better stay home!*

ZUM LESEN

The city of Munich attracts people from all over Germany and from all over the world. What makes Munich so special?

„München mag man". Was ist diese Stadt für den Besucher? Hofbräuhaus—Oktoberfest—Theater, Oper, Kunst—„Gemütlichkeit"—oder einfach Bayern?

München ist nicht nur „deutsch", München hat auch einen südlichen Charakter: griechische Säulen, italienische Renaissance-Fassaden, barocke Kirchen.

München ist gemütlich. Wer kennt nicht den Marienplatz, „die gute Stube" Münchens?

München hat seinen Viktualienmarkt. Hier gibt es alles, was Herz und Magen begehren.

Wie wär's mit einer bayrischen Brotzeit?

Inside the Asamkirche, 1743–46, the best example of the Rococo

The Antikensammlungen (mostly Greek and some Etruscan pottery)

Viktualienmarkt

Eine der berühmtesten Attraktionen Münchens ist das Oktoberfest. Rund sieben Millionen Besucher gehen Jahr für Jahr auf die „Wies'n", um hier echte Oktoberfeststimmung „live" zu erleben.

Das Oktoberfest hat heute seine Freunde überall in der Welt. Aber das Oktoberfest ist noch immer ein echtes bayrisches Traditionsfest.

Mehr als die Hälfte der Besucher sind Münchner und weitere dreissig Prozent sind Nachbarn aus dem bayrischen Umland.

Many local people appear in Tracht.

A Schweinshaxe and a Knödel is typical Bavarian fare.

Wenn man schon in München ist, so besucht man auch ein König-Ludwig-Schloss.

Neuschwanstein ist das berühmteste Schloss. Es ist im gotischen Stil nachgebaut—und ist das Muster für das Märchenschloss in Disneyland.

Schloss Herrenchiemsee steht auf einer Insel im Chiemsee. Es ist im Stil von Schloss Versailles gebaut.

Linderhof, im Rokokostil gebaut, ist das kleinste und charmanteste Schloss. Hier hat König Ludwig am liebsten gewohnt.

Ludwig II (1846–1886) was king of Bavaria from 1864 until his death in 1886. Ludwig was a patron of the arts and devotee of the composer Richard Wagner, whom he supported faithfully.

Between 1884 and 1886 King Ludwig lived in this castle on and off for a total of only about six months.

Übung • Sprich darüber!

1. München hat viel für seine Besucher. 1–2. See p. 220.
2. Die Stadt hat einen südlichen Charakter.
3. Das Oktoberfest ist weltberühmt. 3–4. See p. 221.
4. Das Fest ist noch immer ein echt bayrisches Traditionsfest.
5. Viele Touristen besuchen die Königsschlösser—und jedes Schloss ist anders. 5. See p. 222.

KAPITEL 8

1

KAPITEL 8 Auf nach München!

Wiederholungskapitel

TEACHER–PREPARED MATERIALS	UNIT RESOURCES
Overhead transparencies: typical leave-taking phrases; beverages and prices	**Übungsheft,** Unit 8 **Arbeitsheft,** Unit 8 Unit 8 Cassette Review Test 2 Transparency 21 (and 12–20)

Unit 8 contains functions, grammar, and vocabulary that the students have studied in Units 5–7. This unit provides communicative and writing practice in different situations; some of its activities lend themselves to cooperative learning. If your students require further practice, you will find additional review exercises in Unit 8 of the **Übungsheft** and the **Arbeitsheft.** On the other hand, if your students know how to use the material in Units 5–7, you may wish to omit parts of Unit 8.

OBJECTIVE To review communicative functions, grammar, and vocabulary from Units 5–7

CULTURAL BACKGROUND Train travel is much more common in Europe than in the United States. Because distances are shorter, flying is very uncommon, and even those who own cars find train travel convenient. Trains are dependable: German trains are famed for being on schedule, and all stops are announced clearly. Even very small towns are easily reachable by rail. Many trains are also fast. Train travel is especially popular among students, who often receive special rates.

MOTIVATING ACTIVITY Have the students look at the two photos on pages 224 and 225 and predict how they are connected. If necessary, ask them where Flori is on page 225 and where the train might be going **(Was meint ihr, wo . . . ?)** Tell the students to listen closely to the text to see if their prediction is right.

1

Am Bahnhof 

Have the students listen to the dialog with their books closed. Ask simple comprehension questions: **Wo wohnt Florian? Wo ist er jetzt? Wohin fährt Florian? Warum fährt er dahin?** Have the students open their books and find all the things that Mrs. Schneider as a typical mother says to Florian as he leaves on his trip. Ask the students what they think Flori has packed. Ask them about items and have them answer with **Bestimmt (nicht)** or **Wahrscheinlich (nicht).**

Hat Florian Geld mit? Ja, bestimmt.
Und Reiseschecks? Wahrscheinlich nicht.

Gastgeschenke Kamera Wörterbuch
Adressbuch Reiseführer Regenmantel
Regenschirm

Have the students, in pairs, role-play saying good-bye to someone leaving on a trip. Put key phrases on an overhead transparency. Reverse roles.

Freund oder Verwandter:	*Reisender:*
Viele Grüsse an . . .	Ja, ja.
Und schreib, bitte!	Ja, mache ich.
Telephoniere, wenn du ankommst.	
Hast du (deine Fahrkarte)?	Ja, hier ist (sie).
Gute Reise!	Danke.
	Ja, mach's gut.

2 Übung • Stimmt? Stimmt nicht?

Have the students complete the activity. Then have them correct each statement they answered with **Stimmt nicht!** according to the text.

3 Übung • Und du? Wie steht's mit dir?

Using the questions as a guide, have the students prepare a brief narrative about relatives or friends whom they go to see during their vacation. As a variation, have the students make up a story about the German's proverbial rich uncle in America. How would a German teenager tell others about his or her uncle?

4 Schreibübung

CHALLENGE Have each pair of students imagine that both of them are going on the same group trip and are conferring about what to take. Have them write out the dialog.

5 Übung • Wo hast du alles? 

Put on the board these additional places the items could be: **Hosentasche, Jackentasche, Reisetasche, Handtasche.**

SLOWER–PACED LEARNING Have the students do the activity using this shorter version:

A: Wo hast du den Reiseführer?
B: Er ist im Rucksack.

6 Übung • Wann geht der Zug? 

Have the students do the activity in pairs, choosing different desired times of arrival. You may wish to tell them whether it is Sunday or not so that they must consider this in picking a train.

7 Übung • Entschuldigung! Ich bin nicht von hier. 

Recycle phrases from B8 of Unit 5. Have the students role-play the situation in groups of four or five.

As a variation, have the students imagine that people ask them where the Munich sights are, but they don't know.

Ich bin nicht von hier.	Es tut mir leid, aber . . .
Da drüben ist die Auskunft.	
Ich bin aus Amerika. Ich weiss nicht.	

8 Übung 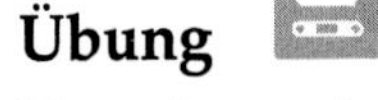

Have the students complete the activity using the foods and prices on the menu shown and these beverages and prices (put them on an overhead transparency):

Mineralwasser	1,70	Milch	1,60
Cola	2,00	Kaffee	2,80
Apfelsaft	2,25	Tee	2,50
Orangensaft	2,50		

9 Übung • Geschenke für alle

CHALLENGE As a variation, tell the students to imagine that they have a little brother and sister, who want to know what there is for them:

Hast du ein Geschenk für mich?	Pulli
Und was hast du für mich?	Buch
Was für Geschenke hast du?	Halskette
Ich will auch ein Geschenk!	Spielkarten
	Postkarte

Have the students role-play this situation in groups of three.

ANSWERS

1. Für den Opa hat er Briefmarken, für die Oma einen Pulli, für den Onkel Kurt eine Kassette, für die Tante Ella ein Buch, für die Steffi einen Taschenrechner
2. Oma, hier ist ein Pulli für dich! Onkel Kurt, hier ist eine Kassette für dich! Tante Ella, hier ist ein Buch für dich! Steffi, hier ist ein Taschenrechner für dich!

10 Schreibübung • Wer ist wer?

Have the students choose several relatives for whom they know all the information. For the ages, have them write out the numbers in words. You may wish to have the students present this information in a family tree format.

11 Übung • Klassenprojekt

As a variation, have the students report about their hometown or another American city they have visited. Have them say where the city is located, how large it is, and what sights or special features it has.

Other German-speaking Countries and Regions

Page 229

OBJECTIVE To read for cultural awareness

MOTIVATING ACTIVITY Ask your students if they know the names of countries or regions other than the Federal Republic where German is spoken. If any of them have been to one of these countries or know anything about one of them, through reading or television, for example, let them share this information with the class. Put their comments on the board or on an overhead transparency, and compare them with the information given on these pages.

THE GERMAN DEMOCRATIC REPUBLIC

CULTURAL BACKGROUND Point out to the students that in all German-speaking areas, **Hochdeutsch** is understood and used in formal situations, but regional dialects are generally used in everyday speech.

The language of the GDR is less influenced by English than that of the Federal Republic. Until fairly recently, little Western television was seen in the GDR, so that few loan words from English entered the language. The second language in East Germany is Russian, which is a required course in schools.

Background to the Photos

Pages 230–231

Pictured in the foreground are members of the **Freie Deutsche Jugend (FDJ),** the organization for educating young people in the system of the country. It was founded in 1946 and has boys and girls of all classes, beginning at age 14, as members. The young people are marching in a parade to commemorate the thirty-fifth birthday of the GDR (see banner in background). The largest celebrations in East Germany are for political events. The mural, focusing on the achievements of workers, is typical of those created for such occasions.

1. There is a strong emphasis on sports in the GDR. Training from early childhood on is state-supported. East German athletes have shown the results of this effort by excelling in international competitions.

2. Erfurt is a city of 120,000 people located at the foothills of the Thuringian Forest.

3. Monuments, such as fountains and statues, commemorating the Russian victory in the second World War are common sights in many East German cities.

6–7. The beautiful city of Dresden was known as "Florence on the Elbe" before it was destroyed in 1945. The city is now slowly being restored. For example, the **Zwinger** pictured here was once the royal palace of the kings of Saxony. Restored as an art museum, it is today a popular tourist attraction.

8. Halle, near Leipzig, is one of the leading industrial cities of East Germany. It is famous as the birthplace of the composer Handel.

LANDES-
KUNDE
2

Pages 232–233

Pages 234–235

9. The Harz Mountains region in the southwestern sector of East Germany is known for its scenic beauty and its folklore and traditions. Towns like Stolberg, which did not suffer destruction in the war, give visitors a taste of the "old" Germany.

AUSTRIA

CULTURAL BACKGROUND To most Americans, the name Austria brings to mind *The Sound of Music,* which was filmed in and near Salzburg. Austria is a small country, but there is much diversity among the states; in fact, in the German-speaking countries, regional identity often comes before national identity. The people do not always feel an association with their immediate neighbors, even within the same country. This is one reason they tend to stay in the same region where they grew up.

Background to the Photos

1. Mountainous Tyrol is a popular skiing and vacation area, especially for Germans, Dutch, and Swedes. People can ski even in the summer on glaciers.
2. Salzburg, the birthplace of Mozart, is famous for its music festivals. It also has beautiful Baroque churches and palaces.
5. As part of the strong regional identities, each region has maintained its own customs and traditional dress, as illustrated here. This region, Wachau, is a wine-growing area close to Vienna.
6. Vienna once stood next after Paris as a capital of Europe. Now that Austria and Hungary are separate and Vienna is no longer central in the country, its predominance has decreased. However, many United Nations agencies have chosen the city because of this good location between East and West.
7–8. Special attractions of the city are the Vienna Boys' Choir and the Lipizzan stallions.
9–10. Vienna is famous as a center of the arts and of fine cuisine.

SWITZERLAND

CULTURAL BACKGROUND Switzerland is bordered by France, Germany, Italy, and Austria. Because it is landlocked, this country depends on commerce with the other nations. Lacking in agriculture, the Swiss have had to develop industry in order to have items to export, such as chemicals, machinery, and watches. Although Switzerland has been a peaceful country, it has one of the world's best defense systems.

Background to the Photos

2–3. Switzerland's mountains are ideal for hiking, climbing, and skiing.
4. The country has beautiful cities, many of which are situated on rivers and lakes, such as Geneva and Zurich.
7–8. Switzerland's banking system is a profitable place to invest for both private individuals and businesses.

LIECHTENSTEIN, ALSACE, SOUTH TYROL

CULTURAL BACKGROUND Tiny Liechtenstein, sometimes referred to as a "miniature country," has its economy administrated by Switzerland. One source of revenue for the country is the beautiful stamps for which it is known. In the Alsace, both German and French are spoken. This area of France also has many German town names. Two famous cities of the Alsace are Strassburg, the seat of the **Europaparlament,** and the beautiful old city of Colmar. South Tyrol is a mountainous area known for its beautiful scenery and its wines.

Background to the Photos

1. The art collection in this castle is one of Liechtenstein's attractions.
3. This photo shows a celebration of the cattle coming back from the high pastures, where they are taken to graze during the summer. If no accidents occurred throughout the summer, the cattle are decorated with flowers for their return in the fall.

KAPITEL 8

Auf nach München!

Wiederholungskapitel

1 Am Bahnhof

Florian Schneider wohnt in Freiburg. Er ist mit seiner Mutter auf dem Bahnhof—er fährt heute mit dem Zug nach München. Dort besucht er die Hubers. Florian kennt München nicht.

FRAU SCHNEIDER	Wann bist du in München, Flori?
FLORIAN	Um Viertel nach zwei.
FRAU SCHNEIDER	Hast du alles?
FLORIAN	Ja, Mutti!
FRAU SCHNEIDER	Auch den Pass?
FLORIAN	Ich fahre nach München, Mutti!
FRAU SCHNEIDER	Hast du den Regenmantel?
FLORIAN	Warum? Das Wetter ist prima!
FRAU SCHNEIDER	Aber in München regnet es oft!
FLORIAN	Dann kaufe ich einen Regenschirm!
FRAU SCHNEIDER	Ja, und viele Grüsse an die Hubers.
FLORIAN	Mutti, hier kommt der Zug!
FRAU SCHNEIDER	Und telefoniere bitte und schreib eine Karte!
FLORIAN	Ja, ja! Tschüs, Mutti!
FRAU SCHNEIDER	Tschüs! Gute Reise!

1. Stimmt nicht!
2. Stimmt nicht!
3. Stimmt!
4. Stimmt!

2 Übung • Stimmt? Stimmt nicht?

1. Florian besucht die Schneiders in Freiburg.
2. Sein Vater bringt ihn zum Bahnhof.
3. Florian kennt München nicht.
4. Um Viertel nach zwei ist er in München.
5. Es regnet in Freiburg. Stimmt nicht!
6. Er hat einen Regenschirm. Stimmt nicht!
7. Florian soll eine Karte schreiben. Stimmt!
8. Er soll nicht telefonieren. Stimmt nicht!

3 Übung • Und du? Wie steht's mit dir?

1. Hast du Freunde oder Verwandte in Deutschland, in Österreich, in der Schweiz oder in einem anderen Staat in den USA?
2. Wer sind diese Leute? Verwandte? —Wie heissen sie?
3. Wo wohnen sie, und wo ist das?
4. Haben sie eine Wohnung? ein Haus? Wieviel Zimmer haben sie?
5. Wie findest du die Wohnung? das Haus?
6. Wie ist das Wetter dort?
7. Besuchst du sie oft? Wie oft?
8. Wie lange bleibst du dort?
9. Wie kommst du dorthin?

Photo p. 224: The tower of the Rathaus in Munich

4 Schreibübung

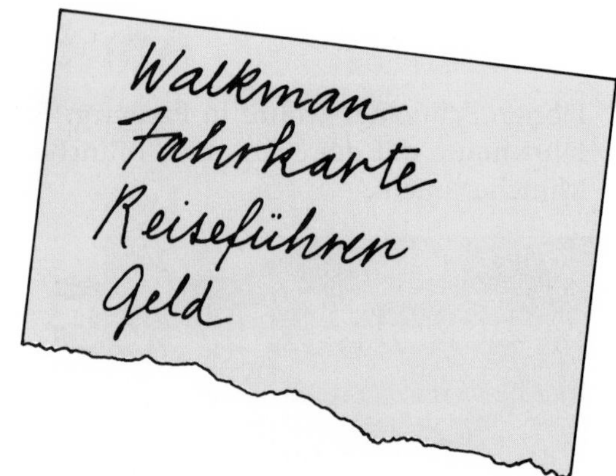

Was brauchst du für die Reise? Schreib auf, was du brauchst! Ein Klassenkamerad liest von seiner Liste und fragt dich, was du für die Reise hast. Du liest von deiner Liste und fragst ihn, was er hat.

A: Hast du den Reiseführer?
B: Ja. Und hast du den Regenmantel?
A: Ja . . .

5 Übung • Wo hast du alles?

A: Sag mal, hast du den Reiseführer?
B: Ja, er ist im Rucksack.
A: Gut. Aber pass auf und verlier ihn nicht!
B: Keine Sorge! Ich pass schon auf.

das Geld, es, es/den Regenschirm, er, ihn/die Kamera, sie, sie/die Fahrkarte, sie, sie/den Walkman, er, ihn/das Adressbuch, es, es/den Regenmantel, er, ihn/den Reiseführer, er, ihn/den Taschenrechner, er, ihn

Geld
Regenschirm
Reiseführer
Fahrkarte
Kamera
Walkman
Regenmantel
Adressbuch
Taschenrechner

6 Übung • Wann geht der Zug?

Du weisst nicht, wann der Zug geht. Du telefonierst.

A: Bahnhof Freiburg, Auskunft. Guten Tag!
B: Ich möchte nach München fahren. Wann geht da ein Zug?
A: Wann möchten Sie in München sein?
B: So um 16 Uhr.
A: O.K. Da haben wir einen Zug um 10.55. Er ist um 16.08 in München.
B: Ja, das passt prima. Vielen Dank!
A: Bitte schön! Gute Reise!

Fahrplanauszug
Sommer 1986
DB

01. Juni 1986 bis 27. September 1986

Freiburg/Breisg. → München 464 km

Verkehrszeiten über Stuttgart-Karlsruhe	ab	Zug	an	Gleis	Umsteigen in	an	ab	Zug
täglich	1.15	D 200	6.30	15	Karlsruhe	2.31	2.51	D 1163
Mo bis Sa	5.41	IC 593	10.08	18				
täglich	5.46	D 1270	11.08	18	Karlsruhe Stuttgart	7.01 8.31	7.25 8.57	D 893 IC 595
täglich	5.46	D 1270	11.20	14	Karlsruhe	7.01	7.25	D 893
täglich	6.58	E 3080	12.08	18	Stuttgart	9.46	9.57	IC 611
Mo bis Sa	7.55	IC 576	12.59	14	Karlsruhe Stuttgart	8.57 10.14	9.07 10.25	D 2751 D 795
täglich, ab Karlsruhe Kurswagen D 2753	8.55	IC 78	14.37	15	Karlsruhe	9.57	10.45	FD 211
Sonntag, ab Karlsruhe Kurswagen D 2753	9.12	D 1206	14.37	15	Karlsruhe	10.27	10.45	FD 211
täglich, ab Stuttgart nur 1.Klasse, Sonderzuschlag	10.55	IC 574	15.44	11	Karlsruhe Stuttgart	11.57 13.22	12.07 13.37	E 3009 TEE 17
täglich	10.55	IC 574	16.08	14	Karlsruhe Stuttgart	11.57 13.22	12.07 13.57	E 3009 IC 693
täglich	11.55	IC 76	16.34	19	Karlsruhe	12.57	13.05	FD 265

Angaben ohne Gewähr. Änderungen vorbehalten. Tarifangaben Stand 1.1.86

Anschlüsse von ab → nach an

1.Klasse –> 137,00 DM <–>274,00 DM Vorzugskarte <–> 220,00 DM IC Zuschlag 5,00 DM
2.Klasse –> 91,00 DM <–>182,00 DM Vorzugskarte <–> 146,00 DM

– 3 – Zugauskunft München Hbf

7 Übung • Entschuldigung! Ich bin nicht von hier.

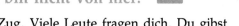

Du bist im Bahnhof und wartest auf einen Zug. Viele Leute fragen dich. Du gibst Auskunft.

A: Ich brauche ein Taxi. Weisst du vielleicht, wo die Taxis sind?
B: Die Taxis sind . . .
A: Danke!
B: Bitte! Gern geschehen.

Wo ist . . . ?
Wann geht der Bus zum Flughafen?
Wo sind . . . ?
Ich möchte Geld wechseln.
Wissen Sie, . . . ?
Ich brauche eine . . .

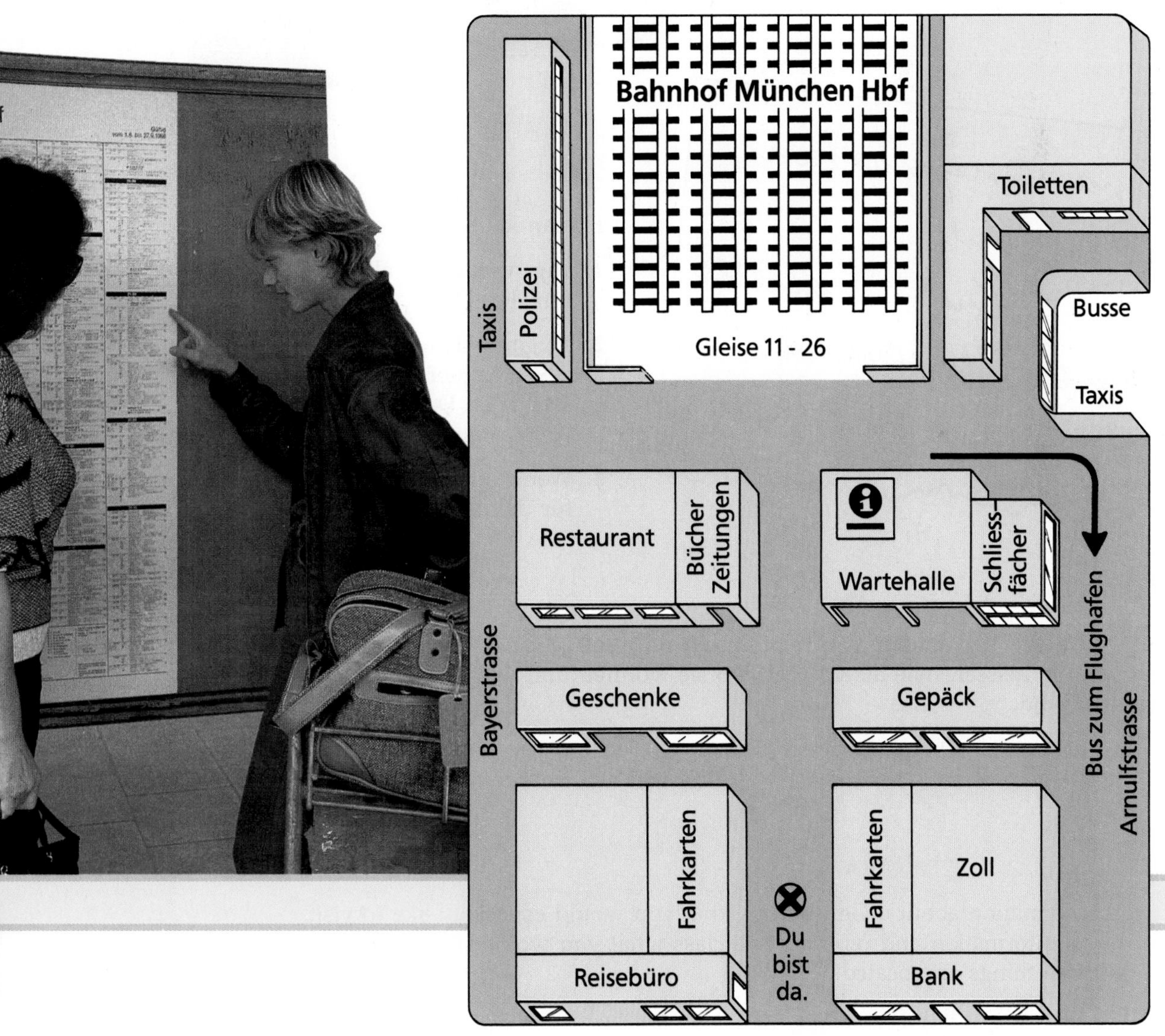

8 Übung

Du hast Hunger, und du möchtest auch etwas trinken. Im Bahnhof gibt es alles—auch einen Bäcker und einen Metzger. Da ist auch ein Restaurant, aber du gehst lieber in die Imbiss-Stube.

A: Ja, bitte?
B: Eine Bockwurst mit Senf.
A: Etwas zu trinken?
B: Einen Apfelsaft, bitte.
A: Das macht vier Mark sechzig!

Opa - Briefmarken
Oma - Pulli
Onkel Kurt - Kassette
Tante Ella - Buch
Steffi - Taschenrechner

9 Übung • Geschenke für alle

For answers, see p. T154.

Florian kauft für alle ein Geschenk.

1. Sag, was er für alle hat!
   Für den Opa . . .
2. Er gibt jedem ein Geschenk!
   A: Opa, hier sind Briefmarken für dich!
   B: Vielen Dank!
   A: Nichts zu danken.
3. Wenn du eine Reise machst, was kaufst du für deine Familie? Was sagst du?

10 Schreibübung • Wer ist wer?

Wer sind deine Verwandten? Schreib auf einen Zettel, was für Verwandte du hast, wie sie heissen, wie alt sie sind, wo sie wohnen und wie sie mit dir verwandt sind.

Ich habe einen Onkel. Er heisst John.
Er ist . . . alt. Er wohnt in . . . John ist Muttis Bruder.

11 Übung • Klassenprojekt

Collect information about a German city that you would especially like to visit. Study this information and report to the class what you would like to see and where these things are located.

Die Sehenswürdigkeiten Kölns sind . . .

LANDESKUNDE 2

Other German-speaking Countries and Regions

The German Democratic Republic

The German Democratic Republic (GDR) is located in Central Europe, with the Federal Republic to the west, Poland to the east, and Czechoslovakia to the south. The GDR is a socialist state, formed in 1949 from the Soviet-occupied zone of Germany, six months after the formation of the Federal Republic. In the GDR all decision making is in the hands of the communist party, officially known as the Socialist Unity Party (SED). Geographically, the northern and central parts of the GDR are a low-lying plain intersected by gentle ranges of hills. The southern part of the country is highland. Some of the chief cities are (East) Berlin, the capital; Leipzig, a center of printing and book trade and the site of trade fairs since 1100; Dresden, a baroque art city that has been carefully restored; and the port of Rostock on the Baltic Sea.

Die Deutsche Demokratische Republik feiert ihren 35. Geburtstag

❶ Strassengymnastik in Berlin (Ost)

❷ Vor dem Hauptbahnhof in Erfurt

❸ Freundschaftsbrunnen auf dem Alexanderplatz in Berlin (Ost)

❹ Reisende warten auf den Zug

❺ Kriegerdenkmal in Berlin (Ost)

❻ Der Zwinger in Dresden, im Barockstil gebaut, ist heute ein Kunstmuseum

❼ Die Parkanlagen des Zwingers. Besucher aus aller Welt kommen hierher, um sich die wertvolle Kunstsammlung anzusehen

❽ Kriegerdenkmal in Halle

❾ Stolberg im Harz

❿ Fussgänger in Leipzig

Austria

Austria is one of the smaller countries in Central Europe, mostly famous for its beautiful scenery, its music, and its culture. Two thirds of Austria is covered by the Alps, where skiing is the most popular sport. This country, with its beautiful mountains, lakes, historic cities, and picturesque villages, is a vacationer's dream. There are ancient abbeys, fairytale castles, and beautiful churches. Under the Habsburg rulers, Austria was the heart of a vast empire that included many different ethnic groups and nationalities. Their influence is still felt in Austria, especially in Vienna, Austria's capital.

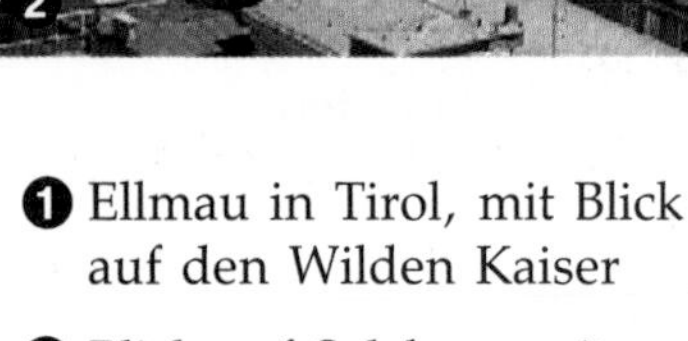

1 Ellmau in Tirol, mit Blick auf den Wilden Kaiser

2 Blick auf Salzburg mit Festung Hohensalzburg

3 Das Geburtshaus von Mozart (1756–1791) in Salzburg

4 Schilaufen in Hintertux

5 Trachtengruppe aus der Wachau

6 Opernball in Wien

7 Die Wiener Sängerknaben

8 Dressur eines Lipizzaners in der Spanischen Hofreitschule in Wien

9 Café Central in Wien, ehemaliger Treffpunkt der Wiener literarischen Gesellschaft

10 Sacher Hotel, Heimat der weltberühmten Sachertorte

Switzerland

Switzerland, with its beautiful scenery, is the most mountainous country in Europe. Besides its scenery, it is also famous for its watches and clocks, electrical equipment, precision machinery, banks, cheese, and milk chocolate. Switzerland is one of the oldest republics in the world, making democracy work in local government for seven hundred years. For more than one hundred years Switzerland has been neutral amid the wars that its neighbors fought and has been a place of safety for refugees of wars and revolutions.

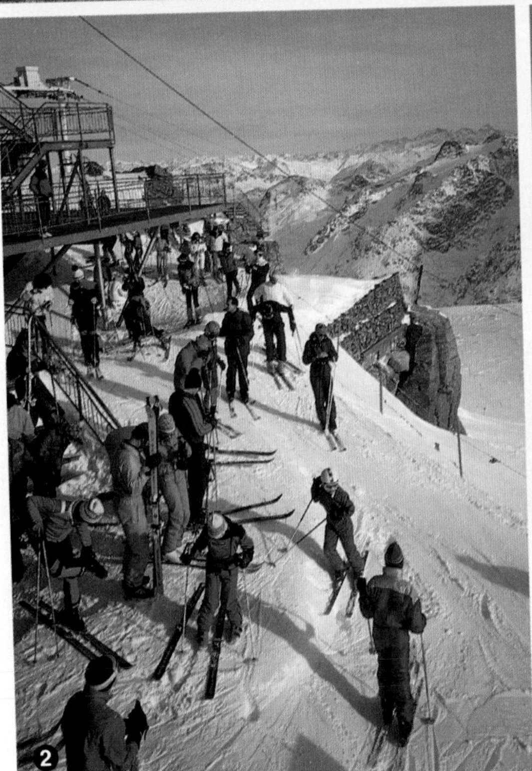

❶ Alphornbläser mit der Jungfrau (4 158 m) im Hintergrund

❷ Schilaufen in St. Moritz

❸ Bergsteigen im Berner Oberland

❹ Blick auf Zürich, grösste Stadt der Schweiz

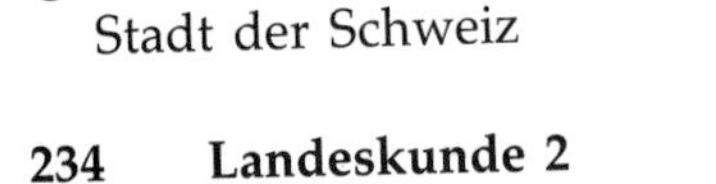

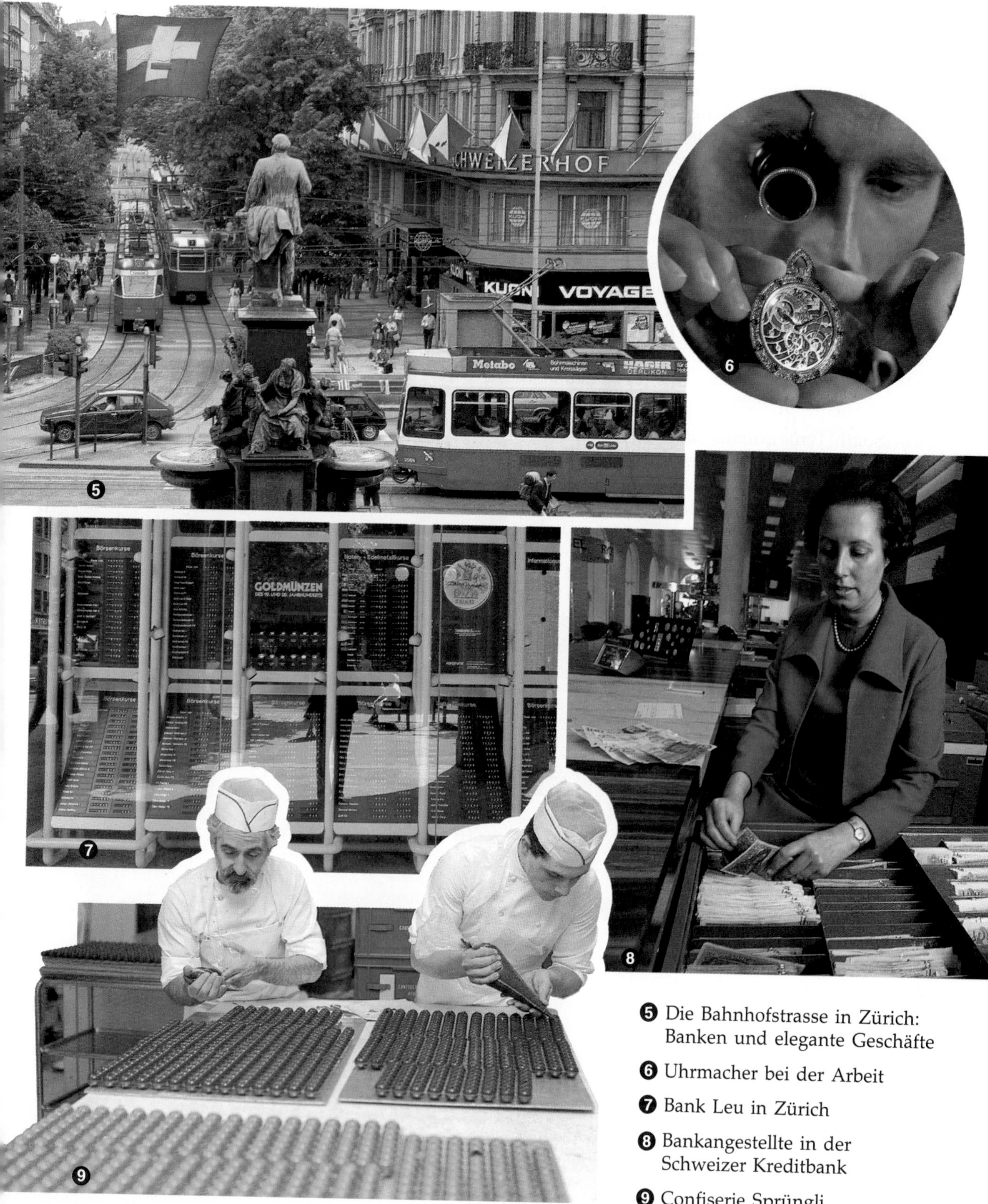

❺ Die Bahnhofstrasse in Zürich: Banken und elegante Geschäfte

❻ Uhrmacher bei der Arbeit

❼ Bank Leu in Zürich

❽ Bankangestellte in der Schweizer Kreditbank

❾ Confiserie Sprüngli

Liechtenstein, Alsace, South Tyrol

The German-speaking Principality of Liechtenstein, wedged between Switzerland and Austria, is the fourth-smallest country in the world. It is one of the most industrialized countries, and it is among those with the highest per capita income.

German is also spoken in the Alsace, a region in northeastern France at the French-German border. For hundreds of years the inhabitants have been part French and part German, and the area has long been a prize in the wars between France and Germany. The Alsace is famous for its wine and cuisine, and for its quaint medieval cities and villages.

The South Tyrol extends south of Austria to the northern Italian provinces. In 1919, South Tyrol was taken from Austria and given to Italy. Today, both Italian and German are the official languages. This Alpine area is a year-round playground for people of many countries.

❶ Schloss Vaduz, seit 1712 Wohnsitz der Prinzen von Liechtenstein

❷ Colmar mit den schönsten Fachwerkhäusern des Elsass und seiner exzellenten Küche—hier: Choucroute garnie

❸ Viehabtrieb in Südtirol

DRITTER TEIL

Karin Haupt is having a party. She invites her friends. Some accept and others decline the invitation. Karin offers her friends various things to eat and drink. They compliment her mother. At the party Karin and her friends have a good time. They listen to music, dance, tell jokes, and gossip a bit.

Your German friends like to go out. They go visiting, ride bikes, play tennis, and go into town. They go to the movies and to concerts. Sabine and Stefan want to go out together. They check the movie and concert listings and discuss what they would like to do. They talk about their favorite music groups and what kinds of films they like.

Your friends Andrea and Monika are shopping for presents—there are many birthdays and other occasions coming up. The girls go into a gift shop and also go to a clothing store, where Monika buys a sweater on sale. You read some ads suggesting presents for various occasions and learn how to express good wishes on these occasions.

Natalie and her friend Uschi are going to Austria for a few days. The villages of Fieberbrunn and St. Ulrich are popular vacation spots and offer many things to do.

KAPITEL 9

KAPITEL 9 Eine Party

Scope and Sequence

	BASIC MATERIAL	COMMUNICATIVE FUNCTIONS
SECTION A	**Karin hat eine Party (A1)**	**Socializing** • Inviting someone to a party; accepting or declining an invitation
SECTION B	**Was gibt es alles? (B1)** **Hans-Peter isst alles gern! (B4)**	**Exchanging information** • Telling what there is to eat and drink
SECTION C	**Was möchtest du? Einen Hamburger? (C1)**	**Socializing** • Offering food or drink; accepting or declining **Exchanging information** • Making negative statements
SECTION D	**So, was machen wir jetzt? (D1)** **Wie ist die Party? (D3)**	**Persuading** • Talking about things to do at a party **Socializing** • Complimenting people and complimenting someone on food
TRY YOUR SKILLS	Pronunciation /ç/, /x/, /l/, /e/, /ö/, /ü/, /R/ (review) Letter-sound correspondences **ch,** final **-ig, s, ei/ie,** final **-er** Dictation	
ZUM LESEN	**Peter Seber über deutsche Sitten** (an American teenager on German customs) **Ein Rezept: Warmer Kartoffelsalat** (a German recipe)	

WRITING A variety of controlled and open-ended writing activities appear in the Pupil's Edition. The Teacher's Notes identify other activities suitable for writing practice and suggest additional writing activities.

COOPERATIVE LEARNING Many of the activities in the Pupil's Edition lend themselves to cooperative learning. The Teacher's Notes explain some of the many instances where this teaching strategy can be particularly effective. For guidelines on how to use cooperative learning, see page T13.

GRAMMAR	CULTURE	RE–ENTRY
First and second person pronouns, accusative (A5) The verbs **anrufen, einladen,** and **vorhaben** (A7)	Planning a party and inviting your friends	Using the phone First and second person pronouns, nominative Verbs; forms of address
	Some party foods and beverages	Food and drink items Expressing likes, dislikes, and preferences Pronouns, accusative
kein, nominative and accusative case (C6) The verb **nehmen** (C9)	Accepting or declining something at a party	**Möchte-**forms Indefinite articles Days of the week; time
Possessives, nominative and accusative case (D4)	What young people do at a party Polite small talk Responding to a compliment	Suggestions and requests Expressing opinions Asking and telling how something tastes Compliments Family members
Recombining communicative functions, grammar, and vocabulary		
Reading for practice and pleasure		

TEACHER–PREPARED MATERIALS

Section A Flashcards of days of the week, times, **ja** and **nein,** names

Section B Flashcards and pictures of foods and drinks; recipes

Section C Flashcards of foods and drinks; cards saying **ja** and **nein**

Section D Flashcards of items/people in D5; compliments from D7

UNIT RESOURCES

Übungsheft, Unit 9
Arbeitsheft, Unit 9
Unit 9 Cassettes
Transparencies 22–24
Quizzes 21–24
Unit 9 Test

A1–2

OBJECTIVES **To socialize:** invite someone to a party; accept or decline an invitation

CULTURAL BACKGROUND The students in this unit are ninth-graders at the **Markgräfler Gymnasium** in Müllheim. Most of them are **Klassenkameraden,** *classmates.* In Germany, this means that they stay together as a class for years and have most of their subjects together. Consequently, they know one another very well; many of these friendships will last a lifetime.

Karin used the phone to call her friends and invite them. She probably said something like **„Du, Mutti, ich ruf mal schnell die Christine an."** German families are generally more careful about using the phone than American families are, and German teenagers are not as apt as American teenagers to spend hours on the phone.

MOTIVATING ACTIVITY Ask the students to list the different ways they might invite friends to a party. Then discuss the various ways of accepting or declining an invitation and some excuses one might give for not coming.

A1

Karin hat eine Party 

Introduce the idea of **gute Verbindung/schlechte Verbindung** by acting them out. For example, pretend to hold a phone. Looking as if you are trying desperately hard to understand, say something like **Hallo? Hallo? Ja, ich höre Sie, aber ich verstehe Sie nicht! Wir haben eine schlechte Verbindung!**

Play the cassette or read the text of the telephone conversation aloud, dividing it into manageable segments, as the students listen with their books closed. Ask such general comprehension questions as **Warum ruft die Karin bei Bergers an?** or **Kommt die Christine zur Party?** Work with the new vocabulary, in particular with the separable verbs **einladen** and **vorhaben** and with **sprechen.**

Ich habe eine Party, und ich lade Freunde ein.
Du lädst mich ein? Wie schön!
Ja, ich komme zur Party. Ich habe Zeit. Ich habe nichts vor.
Ich möchte Christine sprechen. — Christine, die Karin möchte dich sprechen.

Go through the conversation again, section by section, this time asking more specific questions, for example:

Was ist Bergers Telefonnummer?
Warum kann Christine kommen?
Wen lädt Karin noch ein?

Go on to the guests' replies on page 241. Have the students follow in their books as you play the cassette or read the replies aloud. Then have them repeat the replies after you, and finally have them read the replies aloud.

A2

Übung • Wer hat eine Party?

SLOWER–PACED LEARNING Have the students prepare a list of those who accept the invitation and a list of those who decline. After each name, have them write what the person says. You could have them do this in chart form, with captions as follows:

Wer kommt zur Party?	Was sagen sie?
Wer kommt nicht?	Was sagen sie? (Warum nicht?)

Get them started by asking questions like **Warum kann Brigitte nicht kommen?** You might have them add a third category to the lists, **Wer ist er/sie?**

A3 WIE SAGT MAN DAS?

Have the students pick out the ways of accepting or declining an invitation in A1. Also have them pick out the regrets and excuses. List these on the board or on an overhead transparency and compare the list with the one in A3.

A4 Übung • Ich lade dich ein!

CHALLENGE ACTIVITY Expand the response by having the students ask for more information; if accepting, **Ich komme gern! Um wieviel Uhr ist sie? Wen lädst du noch ein?** If declining, they should give some reason: **Es geht nicht / Ich spiele am Samstag Fussball / Ich besuche meine Tante / Ich fliege am Samstag nach Berlin.**

A5 ERKLÄRUNG

Make the students aware of the corresponding subjects and objects in English: *I call Bernd up. Bernd calls me up.* You can practice the forms with drills according to the following patterns:

> Ich rufe dich an oder du rufst mich an. Wir rufen euch an oder . . .
> Meinst du mich? — Ja, ich meine dich. Meinst du uns? . . .

A6 Übung • Jetzt bist du dran

To expand this activity, have the students add questions following the pattern. Have them ask each other, for example, **Hörst du mich? — Ja, ich höre dich.** Continue with **suchen, besuchen, fragen, verstehen,** and **sehen.**

A7 ERKLÄRUNG

Have the students go through the text in A1 and write all the sentences in which **anrufen, einladen,** and **vorhaben** are used. Then ask questions designed to elicit forms of those verbs: **Wen ruft Karin an? Hat Christine etwas vor?** and so on. When the students are comfortable with these verbs, you can have them produce sentences in which they have to use both one of the separable verbs and an object pronoun (give prompts):

> Karin ruft Bernd an (und lädt ihn ein).
> Ich rufe euch an ______.
> Wir rufen unsere Freunde an ______.
> Rufst du Christine an ______?

A8 Übung • Wen rufst du an?

SLOWER–PACED LEARNING Prepare cards with the names of various people on them: **Herr Sperling, Frau Meier, der Bernd, die Kristin, meine Eltern.** Hold up the cards at random and have the students create sentences according to the following model: you hold up the card labeled ***Bernd*** and ask, **Wer ruft an?** A student answers, **Der Bernd ruft an.** Then hold up the card labeled ***Herr Sperling*** and ask, **Wen rufst du an?** The student answers, **Ich rufe Herrn Sperling an,** and so on.

A 9 Übung • Und wen lädst du ein?

SLOWER–PACED LEARNING Using the cards prepared for A8, practice the verb **einladen.** For example, you ask, **Wen lädst du ein?** and a student answers, **Ich lade die Kristin ein.**

A 10 Übung • Alle haben etwas vor!

After you have done the basic activity, you might go through it again with the following pattern variation: the first student asks, **Hast du etwas vor?** The second one answers, **Nein, ich habe nichts vor.**

A 11 Übung • Partnerarbeit

CHALLENGE Expand the activity by re-entering vocabulary from previous units: **Soll ich — nach München fliegen? / den Taschenrechner kaufen? / Tennis spielen? / Hausaufgaben machen? / zu Hause bleiben? / den Vati fragen?**

A 12 Übung • Hör gut zu!

You will hear eight brief dialogs. In each dialog, someone is inviting someone else. The person invited either accepts or declines the invitation. Listen carefully to what is being said. For example, you hear:

A: Du, ich gehe jetzt zum Supermarkt; ich brauche Milch. Kommst du mit?
B: Ja, gern! Ich möchte einen Joghurt kaufen.

You place your check mark in the row labeled *accepting*, because the person accepted the invitation to go along. Let's begin. **Fangen wir an!**

1. A: Ich hab' am Samstag eine Party, und ich möchte dich einladen. Kommst du?
B: Schade, am Samstag hab' ich keine Zeit. *declining*
2. A: Das Wetter ist so schön, und ich möchte am Nachmittag gern in den Englischen Garten gehen. Kommst du mit?
B: Du, am Nachmittag hab' ich schon etwas vor. *declining*
3. A: Ich besuche jetzt zwei Schulkameraden, und wir hören Kassetten, prima Musikkassetten. Möchtest du mitkommen?
B: Das passt prima! Ich hab' jetzt auch nichts vor. *accepting*
4. A: Ich bin sauer. Das Wetter ist so schlecht; ich möchte jetzt am liebsten ins Museum gehen. Kommst du mit?
B: Du, es geht leider nicht. Ich hab' zwei Freunde da, und wir spielen Karten. *declining*
5. A: Ich hab' am Sonntag eine Party, und ich lade dich ein. Die Party beginnt um vier Uhr. Kommst du?
B: Na, klar! Deine Partys sind immer toll. Ich komme gern. Was soll ich mitbringen? *accepting*
6. A: Es ist so heiss. Sollen wir ein Eis essen gehen? Kommst du mit?
B: Ich komme gern. Das ist eine prima Idee! *accepting*
7. A: Ich möchte heute Tennis spielen, und ich brauche einen Partner. Möchtest du spielen?
B: Du, es geht heute leider nicht. Ich hab' schon was vor. *declining*

8. A: Ich geh' heute um elf Uhr mit Peter segeln. Das Wetter ist so schön, und morgen soll es wieder regnen. Möchtest du mitkommen?
   B: Ja, das geht. Ich hab' heute nichts vor. *accepting*

Now check your answers. *Read each dialog again and give the correct answer.*

A 13

Übung • Du möchtest eine Party haben

Remind the students that **kommst** will also change depending upon whom they are addressing.

CHALLENGE Expand the dialog by adding further lines. For example, after the second student has accepted and the first student has replied suitably, the dialog might continue as follows:

B: He, wen lädst du noch ein?
A: Den Robert.
B: Toll! Der Robert ist immer lustig! *[or]* Was?! Der Robert ist so blöd!

OBJECTIVES **To exchange information:** tell what there is to eat and drink

CULTURAL BACKGROUND Young people like to get together. Some parties are spontaneous, and everyone brings snack food. Other parties are planned ahead and are more elaborate. The generous spread at Karin's party was a cooperative effort. The parents of some of the others brought food. Some prepared their favorite recipes; one such dish was the **Gulaschsuppe.**

MOTIVATING ACTIVITY Ask the students what they eat and drink at their parties. (Have them make up lists, which they can later use for comparison.) To what extent do their parents help with the planning and the preparation of food?

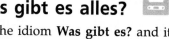

Was gibt es alles? 

Introduce the students to the idiom **Was gibt es?** and its variations (**Was gibt es alles?, Was gibt es zu essen?,** and so on). *Note:* this idiom needs to be strongly reinforced because of negative transfer from English. Students are apt to say **Was haben wir . . . ?** when they mean **Was gibt's?,** not realizing that the former means, essentially, "What's *available* to eat?"—in the refrigerator or the pantry, for example.

Introduce the material by playing the cassette or reading the text aloud as the students listen with their books closed. Stop at strategic points to ask questions and to model new vocabulary. As you present the food items, you may want to refer to the pictures on pages 238–39, 246, and 249 and to the recipe for potato salad on pages 266–67. Encourage the students to observe differences and similarities between these foods and drinks and the ones they would serve. Have them take out the lists they made up for the motivating activity and compare their lists with the ones shown here. They will probably come up with the following observations:

German	*American*
more substantial party food	snack foods, maybe pizza
sandwiches already made up	sandwiches, if any, made as needed
cheese sandwiches	cheese and crackers

B2–8

Before you have the students read the dialog themselves, work with the pronunciation of the more difficult words:

/ç/	gleich	/pf/	Apfel, Apfelsaft
/ʃ/	Gulasch	/ü:/	überhaupt, natürlich
/z/	Suppe, Saft, Salat		

B 2 Übung • Was gibt es zu essen und zu trinken?

Play a memory game; ask **Was gibt es alles?** and see how many food and drink items students can remember without looking. **Es gibt . . .**

B 3 WIE SAGT MAN DAS?

SLOWER–PACED LEARNING Have one student ask, **Was gibt es zu essen?** Go around the class having different students respond with one item each; for example, **Es gibt Kartoffelsalat.** Then do the same exercise with **trinken.**

B 4 HANS-PETER ISST ALLES GERN!

Play the cassette or read the dialog aloud. Then model and present the dialog in the usual manner. You might mention that hamburgers are popular in Germany now, and not just in American-type fast-food restaurants—they are served at home, too. American-style hamburger buns **(Hamburger-Brötchen)** are now available in many larger supermarkets.

B 5 Übung • Und du?

Do accept variations of the position of **gern.** Tell the students that **gern** can also be used before the noun. Encourage sentence variation: **Ich esse gern Bratwurst. Kartoffelsalat esse ich nicht gern. Am liebsten esse ich Hamburger.**

B 6 Übung • Partnerarbeit

SLOWER–PACED LEARNING Prepare cards with the names of food and drink items. In preparation for the dialogs in this exercise, hold up the cards at random and go around the class having students say, **Ich esse einen Hamburger. Ich trinke eine Cola.** In conjunction with each item or as a separate activity, practice the exchange **Wie schmeckt der Hamburger? — Er ist gut.**

B 7 Übung • Auf der Party

To expand this activity, re-enter food and drink items from Unit 7: **Brot, Fleisch, Gemüse, Joghurt, Käse, Milch, Tomaten, Wurst, Hähnchen, Eis,** and **Weisswurst.**

You could also have the students make a collage of the foods and beverages they like, labeling the items in German. They can use a caption such as **„Was ich gern esse (trinke)".**

B 8 Übung • Wer bekommt was?

To expand this activity and give the students further practice, add the following line after you have done the basic activity: **Ja, der Bernd bekommt die Cola.**

B 9 Übung • Was möchtest du essen und trinken? 

Do this as a role-play activity. The students play guests at a party and say what they would like to have. One student "gives" them what they ask for. As a variation, after practicing as shown in the textbook, encourage the students to use different phrases; for example: **ich möchte** or **ich esse.**

ANSWERS

1. ein Käsebrot, ein Käsebrot/eine Suppe, eine Suppe/einen Hamburger, ein Hamburger/eine Cola, eine Cola/eine Bratwurst, eine Bratwurst/eine Fanta, eine Fanta/ein Mineralwasser, ein Mineralwasser/einen Kaffee, ein Kaffee/Kartoffelsalat, Kartoffelsalat/eine Limo, eine Limo/ein Wurstbrot, ein Wurstbrot
2. ein Käsebrot, zwei Käsebrote/eine Suppe, zwei Suppen/einen Hamburger, zwei Hamburger/eine Cola, zwei Colas/eine Bratwurst, zwei Bratwürste/eine Fanta, zwei Fantas/ein Mineralwasser, zwei Mineralwasser/einen Kaffee, zwei Kaffees/Kartoffelsalat, Kartoffelsalat/eine Limo, zwei Limos/ein Wurstbrot, zwei Wurstbrote
3. ein Käsebrot, ein Käsebrot/eine Suppe, eine Suppe/einen Hamburger, ein Hamburger/eine Cola, eine Cola/eine Bratwurst, eine Bratwurst/eine Fanta, eine Fanta/ein Mineralwasser, ein Mineralwasser/einen Kaffee, ein Kaffee/Kartoffelsalat, Kartoffelsalat/eine Limo, eine Limo/ein Wurstbrot, ein Wurstbrot

   Note: Point out why certain questions and responses are in the nominative while others are in the accusative:
   1. Für mich (. . . ich nehme) einen Apfelsaft! *(accusative)*
      Hier (ist) ein Apfelsaft für dich! *(nominative)*
   2. Für uns (. . . wir nehmen) eine Cola. *(accusative)*
      Hier (sind) zwei Colas für euch! *(nominative)*
   3. Für mich (. . . ich nehme) einen Kaffee, bitte! *(accusative)*
      Bitte! Hier ist ein Kaffee für Sie! *(nominative)*

B 10 Übung • Hör gut zu! 

You will hear eight statements or questions, all referring either to food or to drink. You are at a party and your host tells you what there is to eat or drink or offers you something. Is your host talking about something to eat or something to drink? For example, you hear, **Möchtest du mal ein Käsebrot probieren?** You put your check mark in the row labeled ***zu essen,*** because food was mentioned. Let's begin. **Fangen wir an!**

1. Die Erdbeerbowle ist sehr gut. Möchtest du sie mal probieren? *zu trinken*
2. Wir haben Apfelsaft, aber vielleicht möchtest du eine Limonade. *zu trinken*
3. Hier ist eine Bratwurst für dich. Und möchtest du nicht auch mal den Kartoffelsalat probieren? Er schmeckt prima. *zu essen*
4. Ich möchte jetzt keinen Kaffee. Hast du Fanta? *zu trinken*
5. Die Wurstbrote schmecken prima. Aber jetzt probiere ich mal die Suppe. Sie sieht gut aus. *zu essen*
6. Ich esse keine Käsebrote; ich esse lieber noch eine Bratwurst. *zu essen*
7. Probier doch mal das Mineralwasser! Es ist prima. Es kommt aus Frankreich. *zu trinken*

8. Ja, was gibt es denn überhaupt? Alles sieht so gut aus. Ich probier mal eine Bratwurst und Kartoffelsalat. Ich habe einen Bärenhunger. *zu essen*

Now check your answers. *Read each item again and give the correct answer.*

B11 Schreibübung • Auf der Party

CHALLENGE Have the students write a scrambled dialog. They may work individually or in small groups. You might put some of their dialogs on the board and have the rest of the class unscramble them.

B12 Schreibübung • Projekt

If possible, you might have the party in the school cafeteria or in the home economics room and use those facilities to prepare some German foods. This would give the students the chance to put what they have been learning into practice. See the suggestions on page T177 of this Teacher's Edition under the heading **Übung: Jetzt bist du dran!**

SECTION C

OBJECTIVES **To socialize:** offer someone something to eat or drink; accept or decline what is being offered; **to exchange information:** make negative statements

CULTURAL BACKGROUND Germans drink a great deal of mineral water. There are many mineral springs in Germany, and many healing and restorative powers are attributed to them. Therefore, mineral water has always been popular with the health-conscious Germans.

In Germany, it is customary to wish one another **„Guten Appetit!"** before starting to eat. You look around, nod your head slightly at each person, and wish **„Guten Appetit!"** Others will respond with **„Danke, gleichfalls!"** *(the same to you)*

MOTIVATING ACTIVITY Make the students aware of the German custom of wishing one another **Guten Appetit.** Demonstrate how it is done and have the students compare it with American table customs.

C1 Was möchtest du? Einen Hamburger?

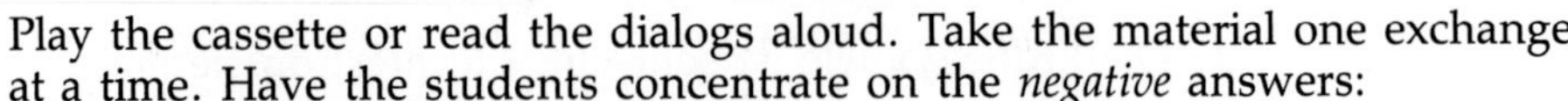

Play the cassette or read the dialogs aloud. Take the material one exchange at a time. Have the students concentrate on the *negative* answers:

Nein, keine Suppe, bitte! Und keinen Hamburger.
Du, keine Cola, bitte.
Nein, danke!
Keine Fanta.

When you go over the material a second time, ask comprehension questions:

Was hat Karin für ihre Gäste?
Isst Matthias das?
Was isst er lieber?

When the students have read the dialogs aloud as a class, you might have them act the whole conversation out, working in small groups.

C2 Übung • Und du? Wie steht's mit dir?

Have the students pretend that they are guests at Karin's party and are being offered something to eat or drink. They should accept or decline what is being offered.

C3 WIE SAGT MAN DAS?

Have the students look at C1 and pick out examples of offering, accepting, and declining something to eat or drink. Then ask them, **Möchtest du einen Kaffee?** and have them practice replying, **Nein, danke. Keinen Kaffee** or **Ja, bitte. Einen Kaffee.**

C4 Übung • Du hast eine Party!

Expand the exchange by having the students add a reason to the response: **Ja, bitte. Ich trinke Limonade gern** or **Nein, danke. Ich habe keinen Durst (Hunger).**

C5 WIE SAGT MAN DAS?

Lead the students to discover the difference between making a negative statement using **nicht** and making one using **kein.** Tell them that **nicht** negates the entire statement and usually indicates that there is a reason: you're not doing it this time, for example, because the soup is too hot or you've had enough. **Kein** indicates that you aren't in the habit of doing something, that you don't normally do it: you don't like it or it's not good for you.

C6 ERKLÄRUNG

Point out that **kein,** like **ein,** is always used before a noun. It has the same endings as **ein.** Unlike **ein,** however, **kein** has a plural form.

Work with **kein** before **Hunger** and **Durst** and before plural nouns in particular. Dialogs according to the following model should be useful.

Warum isst du nichts?	Ich habe keinen Hunger.
Warum trinkst du nichts?	Ich habe keinen Durst.
Warum kommst du nicht zur Party?	Ich habe keine Zeit.
Ich habe viele Musikkassetten. Du auch?	Nein, ich nicht. Ich habe keine Musikkassetten.

C7 Übung

Point out that the accusative is required here in the response because **ich möchte** is understood. To expand this activity, have the students, after declining in the response, add what they *would* like: **Nein, keine Suppe, bitte! Ich esse lieber eine Bratwurst.**

SLOWER–PACED LEARNING Practice a full-sentence response: **Nein, ich möchte keine Suppe, bitte.** The insertion of **ich möchte** will clarify the structure for the students.

C8 Übung

As in the preceding activity, the accusative is required in the response because **ich möchte** is understood. For expansion, after the students have declined in the response, have them add what they *would* like: **Danke, nein, keine Cola. Ich trinke lieber einen Kaffee.**

C9–12

SLOWER–PACED LEARNING Again practice a full-sentence response: **Danke, nein, ich trinke keine Cola** or **Danke, nein, ich möchte keine Cola.**

C9

ERKLÄRUNG

The verb **nehmen** not only has a stem-vowel change in the **du-** and **er/sie-** forms, but it also has a consonant change. Let the students discover these changes and tell you what they are.

C10

Übung • Jetzt bist du dran

To expand this activity, add a third person to confirm what B has said. In that case, the dialog might run as follows:

A: Was nimmst du? Eine Bratwurst vielleicht?
B: Nein, danke! Keine Bratwurst. Ich nehme ein Käsebrot.
C: Was nimmt er (sie)? Ein Käsebrot?
A: Ja, er (sie) nimmt ein Käsebrot.

CHALLENGE As a further expansion, the third person could intentionally get it wrong, leading to a continuation like the following:

C: Was nimmt er (sie)? Ein Wurstbrot?
A: Nein, er (sie) nimmt ein Käsebrot.

C11

Übung • Der Partymuffel

Have the students act this activity out, exaggerating to make it more fun. As a variation, have two **Partymuffel,** so that the friends would have to urge them using the **ihr-**form.

C12

Übung • Hör gut zu!

What would your friends like to eat or drink? Somebody is asking them, and they either accept or decline what is being offered. Listen carefully to ten brief dialogs and decide whether the second person is accepting or declining. For example, you hear **Möchtest du jetzt einen Kaffee? — Keinen Kaffee für mich, danke!** You place your check mark in the row labeled *declining,* because the person declined what was being offered. Let's begin. **Fangen wir an!**

1. Hier ist eine Limonade für dich. — Danke, aber ich habe jetzt keinen Durst. *declining*
2. Probier doch mal den Kartoffelsalat! — Ja, gern! Er sieht gut aus! *accepting*
3. Wir haben noch so viele Bratwürste! Iss doch bitte noch eine! — Ja, bitte. Sie schmecken prima. *accepting*
4. Möchtest du noch eine Bratwurst und Kartoffelsalat? — Na, klar! Ich hab' einen Bärenhunger. *accepting*
5. Ich habe noch Erdbeerbowle für dich. — Du, sie ist gut, aber jetzt nicht. Danke! *declining*
6. Möchtest du nichts mehr? Iss doch ein Brot — ein Wurstbrot oder ein Käsebrot! — Ja, bitte! Sie sehen gut aus. *accepting*
7. Wer möchte noch Salat? Oder noch ein Käsebrot? — Nichts für mich, danke! *declining*

8. Noch eine Bockwurst? Gut, nicht? — Ja, aber ich möchte jetzt nichts mehr essen. *declining*
9. Ich habe noch eine Bratwurst. Wer möchte sie? Du, ja? — Ja, gern! Das ist jetzt schon Nummer vier! *accepting*
10. Bratwurst? Bockwurst? Kartoffelsalat? Oder wer möchte jetzt Kuchen essen? Probier doch mal den Kuchen! — Du, ich habe genug. Nichts mehr für mich, danke! *declining*

Now check your answers. *Read each item again and give the correct answer.*

C13

Schreibübung • Du planst eine Party

To help the students prepare for this assignment, you might want to do it orally with the class as a whole first. You might have one student put suggestions (in the form of notes, not complete sentences) on the board or on an overhead transparency.

SECTION D

OBJECTIVES **To socialize:** talk about things to do at a party; pay compliments

CULTURAL BACKGROUND The young people at this party all know each other very well and feel at ease with one another. They dance, talk, eat, and have a good time. Videocassette recorders and video rental stores are becoming popular in Germany but are not yet as widespread as in the United States.

MOTIVATING ACTIVITY Have the students discuss briefly what they do at their parties. Compare that to the party depicted here. How are their parties similar? How are they different?

D1

So, was machen wir jetzt?

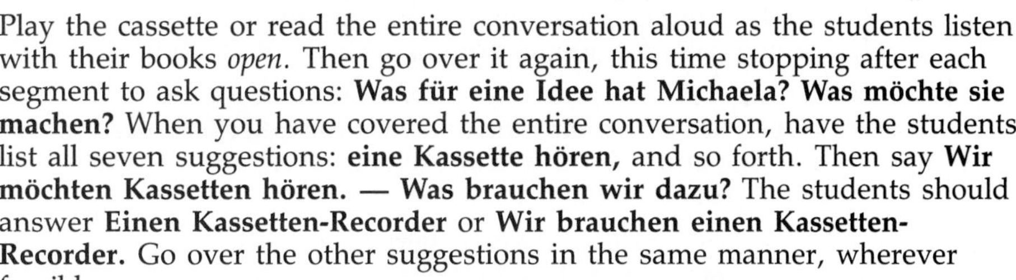

Play the cassette or read the entire conversation aloud as the students listen with their books *open*. Then go over it again, this time stopping after each segment to ask questions: **Was für eine Idee hat Michaela? Was möchte sie machen?** When you have covered the entire conversation, have the students list all seven suggestions: **eine Kassette hören,** and so forth. Then say **Wir möchten Kassetten hören. — Was brauchen wir dazu?** The students should answer **Einen Kassetten-Recorder** or **Wir brauchen einen Kassetten-Recorder.** Go over the other suggestions in the same manner, wherever feasible.

When you have the students read the conversation aloud, ask them to read it with a lot of expression, as if they were really trying to convince the others that "my idea's the best."

D2

Übung • Und du? Wie steht's mit dir?

CHALLENGE Some students may enjoy preparing jokes and riddles to present to the rest of the class. Have them work in pairs or in small groups. They will have to provide background—for example, additional vocabulary that the rest of the class needs in order to understand the jokes—before they present the jokes. Some examples follow:

- —Ein Skelett kommt zum Arzt: „Sie kommen aber wirklich spät . . . !"

D3–6

—Herr Depp sitzt in der Badewanne: „Blöde Medizin! Dreimal am Tag zehn Tropfen in warmem Wasser einnehmen!"
—Der Zoowärter ruft die Polizei an: „Wir haben einen Elefanten verloren!" — Die Polizei: „Wie sieht er denn aus?"

D3 WIE IST DIE PARTY?

Play the cassette or read the text of the comments aloud as the students listen with their books closed. See if the students get the gist of the comments:

Wie ist die Party, gut oder schlecht?
Ist Bernds Kassette gut?

Go over the material again, this time with books open, and ask more specific questions:

Wer ist nett?	Was ist gemütlich?
Wie ist das Essen?	Wer sieht phantastisch aus?

Introduce the dialogs involving Frau Haupt by playing the cassette or reading the conversation aloud as the students listen, again with their books closed. Stop after each segment and ask questions such as **Was findet Hans-Peter besonders gut?** or **Was isst Michaela sehr gern?** Afterwards have the students, working in groups of three, read the dialogs aloud.

Compliment the students and then have them compliment each other. They may do it in a simulated party setting or in any other situation they like.

D4 ERKLÄRUNG

Lead the students to discover the possessives that sound the same: **ihr** and **Ihr.** Ask them about the differences in meaning. See if they can tell you three different ways of expressing *your* in German.

D5 Übung • Auf der Party gehört

Have the students, working in pairs, act these exchanges out. You could have one pair of students present each set of exchanges to the rest of the class.

CHALLENGE Have the students vary the adjectives used in the responses. In the first and second sets of exchanges, expand the exchange by having the first person respond to the second person's remark:

A: Wie ist die Bratwurst, Bernd?
B: Frau Haupt, Ihre Bratwurst schmeckt ausgezeichnet (lecker, prima)!
A: Ach, das freut mich! (Da bin ich aber froh./Wirklich?)

For the third exchange, have the first person agree or disagree with the comment: **Ich auch. Ihre Party ist Klasse!** or **Wirklich? Ich finde ihre Party langweilig.**

D6 WIE SAGT MAN DAS?

Review the culture point made in Unit 6 about how Germans typically respond to compliments by deprecating them. Point out in particular the way Frau Haupt responds to compliments in D3. Have the students make suggestions for similar responses to other compliments in that section.

Just for fun, have the students give a complacent or boastful response to a compliment. This will also give them practice in forming and recombining independent sentences. Sample compliments and responses follow:

Du siehst gut aus.	Danke, ich weiss es. Ich sehe immer gut aus.
Die Suppe schmeckt lecker.	Ja, ich koche gut. Ja, meine Suppen schmecken immer gut.

D7 Übung • Mach doch mal ein Kompliment!

You may want to practice this exercise with the whole class first. Take each statement and see how many compliments can be made; for example, for **Der Bernd erzählt gute Witze,** the responses might be:

> Bernd, du erzählst gute Witze! *[or]*
> Du, Bernd, deine Witze sind gut! *[or]*
> Bernd, ich finde deine Witze prima!

Then have the class work in smaller groups, paying compliments and responding to them.

CHALLENGE Have the students make up statements saying something favorable about people they know. The other students reformulate these as compliments, just as in the exercise.

ANSWERS (possible)

1. Bernd, du erzählst gute Witze!
2. Frau Haupt, Ihr Kartoffelsalat ist sehr gut!
3. Karin, dein Zimmer ist gemütlich!
4. Christine, deine Kassetten sind gut!
5. Michaela, du siehst sehr hübsch aus!
6. Hans-Peter, du hast eine gute Idee!
7. Karin, deine Freunde sind lustig!
8. Karin, deine Erdbeerbowle schmeckt gut!
9. Karin, deine Eltern sind sehr nett!

D8 Übung • Hör gut zu! 

You will hear ten brief statements, each one followed by a response. Listen carefully and decide whether the response is appropriate or not appropriate. For example, you hear, **Ich möchte jetzt eine Platte hören. — Dort drüben ist der Plattenspieler.** You place your check mark in the row labeled *appropriate,* because the second statement is an appropriate response to the first one. Let's begin. **Fangen wir an!**

1. Der Kartoffelsalat schmeckt ausgezeichnet. — Das freut mich, dass er schmeckt. *appropriate*
2. Die Michaela tanzt wirklich toll. — Ja, der Plattenspieler ist ausgezeichnet. *not appropriate*
3. Wie findest du Karins Freundin, die Christine? — Ihre Eltern sind so nett. *not appropriate*
4. Der Bernd erzählt prima Witze. — Was?! Ich finde sie blöd. *appropriate*
5. Wo habt ihr euren Kassetten-Recorder? — Warum? Möchtest du einen Film sehen? *not appropriate*
6. Wie schmeckt der Kuchen? — Er ist wirklich ausgezeichnet. *appropriate*

D9– SKILLS 3

7. Wer ist denn der Tanzpartner von Christine? Er tanzt wirklich toll. — Das ist ein Klassenkamerad. *appropriate*
8. Möchtest du mal eine Bratwurst? — Ja, wirklich? Schmeckt sie auch? *not appropriate*
9. Der Bernd sieht gut aus. Aber ich finde ihn arrogant. — Wirklich? Ich finde ihn sehr nett. *appropriate*
10. Was möchtest du jetzt tun? Musik hören und tanzen? Oder Witze erzählen? — Der Kartoffelsalat schmeckt gut. *not appropriate*

Now check your answers. *Read each item again and give the correct answer.*

D9 **Schreibübung • Wie ist die Party?**

As a variation, have the students, working in groups, write dialogs in which two or more people are discussing the party they are attending. Some of these could be performed in front of the class.

TRY YOUR SKILLS

OBJECTIVE To recombine communicative functions, grammar, and vocabulary

CULTURAL BACKGROUND In Germany, young people can buy printed party invitations at the store; however, they frequently prefer to make their own. These homemade invitations are often humorous. Some young people like to collect them as mementos, sometimes posting them on the wall as decorations.

1 **Bernd schreibt eine Einladungskarte**

Play the cassette or read the invitation aloud as the students listen with their books open. Have them look at the invitation for differences between the German and the American ways of writing the date, time, address, and telephone number. You might put some more dates, times, and addresses on the board to give the students extra practice in correlating the way these items are written with the way they are spoken; for example:

$18^{\underline{30}}$ Uhr	achtzehn Uhr dreissig
den 17. Feb.	den siebzehnten Februar
Bahnhofstr. 27	Bahnhofstrasse siebenundzwanzig

2 **Übung • Du rufst den Bernd an. Gehst du oder gehst du nicht?**

Have the students role-play this activity. One student plays the part of Bernd. Other students take turns calling him up and responding to his party invitation.

CHALLENGE Expand the conversation. Have the students ask for more details about the party or discuss other subjects, such as school or sports and activities.

3 **Schreibübung • Wann ist deine Party?**

Have the students work in groups of three to five. Each group should write an invitation, make a guest list, and write what they are having to eat and drink. Have each group write the things required; then have a representative for the group read the results to the class. The class could vote on which party they would most like to attend.

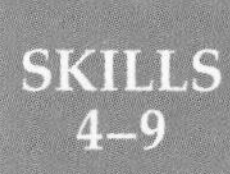

4 Leseübung • Karins Party ist toll!

Read this paragraph aloud to the class or play the cassette. Ask comprehension questions after the students have listened to it twice through. Then use it as a dictation.

5 Übung • Meine Partys sind auch toll!

SLOWER–PACED LEARNING Do this as a class exercise, using the board or an overhead projector. Discuss what changes are to be made and why they should/must be made. Then have the students write the paragraph in the first person.

6 Leseübung • Ein Durcheinander

CHALLENGE Have the students retell what the mix-up is about. They should avoid using **dass.** For example, they might retell it as follows:

> Bernd fragt Karin, wo sein Hamburger ist. Karin glaubt, Hans-Peter isst seinen (Bernds) Hamburger. Aber Hans-Peter sagt, er isst Bernds Hamburger nicht.

7 Übung • Rollenspiel

CHALLENGE After the students have practiced these dialogs in groups of three, acting them out and exaggerating for fun, have them continue past the point at which the dialogs end:

> BERND Ja, wo ist denn mein Hamburger? *[or]*
> Wer isst denn meinen Hamburger?
> HANS-PETER Ich weiss nicht.
> KARIN Schau, Bernd, hier ist noch ein Hamburger für dich!

ANSWERS
first dialog
mein, dein, sein Wurstbrot/meine, deine, seine Gulaschsuppe/mein, deinen, seinen Kartoffelsalat/meine, deine, seine Bratwurst
second dialog
mein, dein, deinen, seinen Apfelsaft/meine, deine, deine, seine Limonade/mein, dein, dein, sein Mineralwasser/mein, dein, deinen, seinen Kaffee

8 Übung • Was gehört zusammen?

CHALLENGE Have the students think of their own rejoinders to the questions and statements on the left, or have them think of appropriate questions or comments to elicit the responses on the right.

9 Übung • Mix-Match

First practice this orally with the class and then assign it as written homework. The students could be required to add words to make more combinations with these two verbs.

SKILLS 10–13

10 Übung • Karin geht für die Party einkaufen

As a variation, write a dialog with the class. Karin and her mother are discussing what to serve at the party and they are making up their shopping list. Then Karin's mother tells her where to buy the various items. This scene could be acted out in front of the class or in small groups.

11 Übung • Im Lokal

Have the students draw one big menu to display in front of the class or make smaller menus to be distributed. They may copy the menu in the textbook and add other food and drink items they have had: **Bratwurst, Hamburger, Leberkäs,** and **Kaffee,** for example. Turn the class into a "restaurant." A few students will play waiters and waitresses while the others, sitting in small groups at tables, play customers. Act out the dialogs. The students may order from the big menu or from the smaller ones that the waiter or waitress gives them.

12 Übung • Was sagen sie?

Have the students describe each picture and then say what the people pictured might be saying. They could also make humorous suggestions.

CHALLENGE Have the students make up a little story as background for each picture, giving more information about the young people pictured: name, age, school, hobbies and interests, friends, and so on.

13 Aussprache-, Lese- und Schreibübungen 

1. In this section, you will be reviewing some familiar sounds. First you will hear a group of words with the **ich**-sound. **Hör zu und wiederhole!**

/ç/ gleich, endlich, natürlich, mich, vielleicht, freundlich, lustig, gemütlich, Brötchen, Kirche, Küche, furchtbar

Now you will hear a group of words containing the **ach**-sound. **Hör zu und wiederhole!**

/x/ Kuchen, Besuch, doch, Tochter

Next you will hear a group of words containing the /l/ sound. **Hör zu und wiederhole!**

/l/ Limonade, lecker, Platte, Film, Apfelsaft, Gulaschsuppe, gleich, klingeln, einladen, erzählen, endlich, natürlich, Ratespiel

Now you will hear several groups of words containing the sounds /e/, /ö/, and /ü/. **Hör zu und wiederhole!**

/e/ Käse, Bärenhunger, lädt ein, erzählen, später, Städte, Bäcker;
/ö/ schön, Brötchen, Schlösser, Dörfer; Gemüse, natürlich, überhaupt,
/ü/ Sehenswürdigkeit, gemütlich, hübsch, Küche

Now you will hear a group of words that contains the sound /R/. **Hör zu und wiederhole!**

/R/ Ruhe, Ratespiel, Recorder, anrufen, diskutieren, bringen, Käsebrot, Bärenhunger, Kartoffelsalat, Partner, furchtbar, Freund, sprechen, prima, froh, das freut mich

2. In this section, you will practice reading the words printed in your textbook on page 261. Pay attention to the following:

1. The letter combination **ch** represents an **ich**-sound after the vowels, **e, i (ie), ä, ö,** and **ü;** after the diphthongs **ei** and **eu (äu);** and after consonants. The letter combination **-ig** at the end of a word is also pronounced /iç/ **(ich).** The letter combination **ch** represents an **ach-**sound after the vowels **a, o,** and **u** and after the diphthong **au. Hör zu und wiederhole!**

   ch **-ig** schlecht, Kirche, möchte, vielleicht, traurig; nach, noch, Buch, auch; Fach — Fächer, Buch — Bücher
2. The letter **s** has the sound of *z* as in *zebra* at the beginning of a word or syllable when it is followed by a vowel; in other positions, **s** is voiceless and sounds like *s* as in *post.* **Hör zu und wiederhole!**

   s Salat, Suppe, sein, Käse, Musik, Apfelsaft
3. The letter combination **ei** represents the sound /ai/ as in **mein.** The letter combination **ie** represents the sound /i:/ as in **hier.** You must learn to react quickly to these combinations when you encounter them. **Hör zu und wiederhole!**

   ie/ei hier, dein, Wien, wieder, heiss, vier, fliegen, gleich, leider, Spiel, vielleicht
4. In the final position of words of more than one syllable, the letter combination **-er** represents a vowel sound, the sound /ʌ/, which is similar to the vowel sound you hear at the end of the English word *sofa.* **Hör zu und wiederhole!**

   -er unser, euer, später, lecker, Hunger, Spieler, Partner, Recorder

3. Now close your textbooks and write the sentences you hear.
1. Unser Salat ist wieder lecker.
2. Ich fliege auch gleich weiter.
3. Ich möchte auch drei Bücher.
4. Das Spiel ist leider wieder in Wien.

WAS KANNST DU SCHON?

SECTION A

If the students need more practice, vary the date in the invitation: Sunday at 4:00 P.M., Friday at 8:00 P.M. Have them practice the different ways of accepting and declining the invitation.

SECTION B

As the students take turns telling what there is to eat and drink, have the other students write the items in their notebooks. One student could list the items on the board. For more practice and review, have students comment on each line as it is mentioned:

A: Es gibt Leberkäs.
B: Leberkäs? Prima, ich esse Leberkäs gern!

SECTION C

Using the list compiled in the preceding section, have the students practice offering food and drink to their classmates. The classmate to whom something is offered should accept or decline. For variation, practice this activity with the circle game, previously described in the **Was kannst du schon?** section of Unit 3. The student in the inner circle offers the student facing him or her in the outer circle something to eat or drink. That student accepts or declines. Then the inner circle moves to the right and the outer circle stays where it is, creating a new set of partners.

SLOWER–PACED LEARNING Have the students, working in small groups, write down at least six compliments you might pay to someone at a party. The compliments may be directed at different people. They could then share them with the class. As each compliment is read, a student might volunteer an appropriate response.

WORTSCHATZ

Have the students list all the food and drink items in the **Wortschatz.** Have them pick out the words that are close to their English equivalents or that have been taken over directly from English.

WORTSCHATZÜBUNGEN

Have the students, working individually, write down their findings. Then correct the papers with the entire class, one student recording the answers on the board. The students may then enter the answers in the **Wortschatz** section of their notebooks.

ZUM LESEN

OBJECTIVE To read for practice and pleasure

PETER SEBER ÜBER DEUTSCHE SITTEN 

Allow the students to read each section silently first. Then play the cassette or read the section aloud. On a second reading, ask questions about the content of the section, at first fairly general ones: **Was ist manchmal für Peter ein Problem? Was vergisst er meistens?** Then zero in on the specific cultural differences, section by section, eliciting them by questions such as the following:

— Was sagen die Deutschen, wenn sie sich die Hand geben?
— Wer schüttelt die Hand? Nur Männer oder auch Frauen?
— Wen muss man siezen? Wen kann man duzen?
— In welcher Hand halten die Deutschen die Gabel, in der linken oder in der rechten? Und die Amerikaner?
— Wann essen wir unser grosses, warmes Essen in Amerika? Und die Deutschen? Wann essen sie es? Was ist besser für die Gesundheit?

Have the students list these differences, formulating them as **man-**sentences: **Man bringt etwas mit, man schüttelt sich die Hand, man hält die Gabel in der linken Hand,** and so forth.

You might have the students, working in groups of three, illustrate these cultural differences by acting them out. Give them some direction, such as **Zeige, wie man in Deutschland richtig isst!** They could also draw pictures, using their **man-**sentences as captions, to illustrate the customs.

SLOWER–PACED LEARNING Have the students tell briefly in English what each section is about. They should not translate. Let them discover the words and expressions most important for understanding the gist of the section. Explain the meaning of any they don't understand. Help them to derive meaning from context, using the information they do understand.

Übung • Stimmt! Stimmt nicht!

First have the students try to do this exercise without referring to the reading selection. Then have them correct the statements that are not true. At this point, they may refer to the selection if necessary.

EIN REZEPT: WARMER KARTOFFELSALAT 

See how many unfamiliar words the students can figure out by looking at the pictures.

CHALLENGE The style of the text under the pictures is typical of a German cookbook. Have the students rewrite the instructions using the **Sie-**form: **Waschen Sie und kochen Sie die Kartoffeln!** Sometimes they will have to add words: **Schneiden Sie die Kartoffeln in Scheiben!** Point out the seperable-prefix verbs.

Übung • Jetzt bist du dran!

If possible, make this potato salad with your class—perhaps for the party mentioned in B12. Perhaps you could arrange to use the home economics facilities with your class. Be sure to have all the ingredients and utensils on hand. You might be able to have **Bratwurst** or **Leberkäs** to go with the potato salad. The utensils:

ein Topf mit Deckel	eine Schüssel	Messlöffel
ein Sieb	eine Pfanne	Salatbesteck
ein scharfes Messer	ein Messbecher	

KAPITEL 9
Eine Party

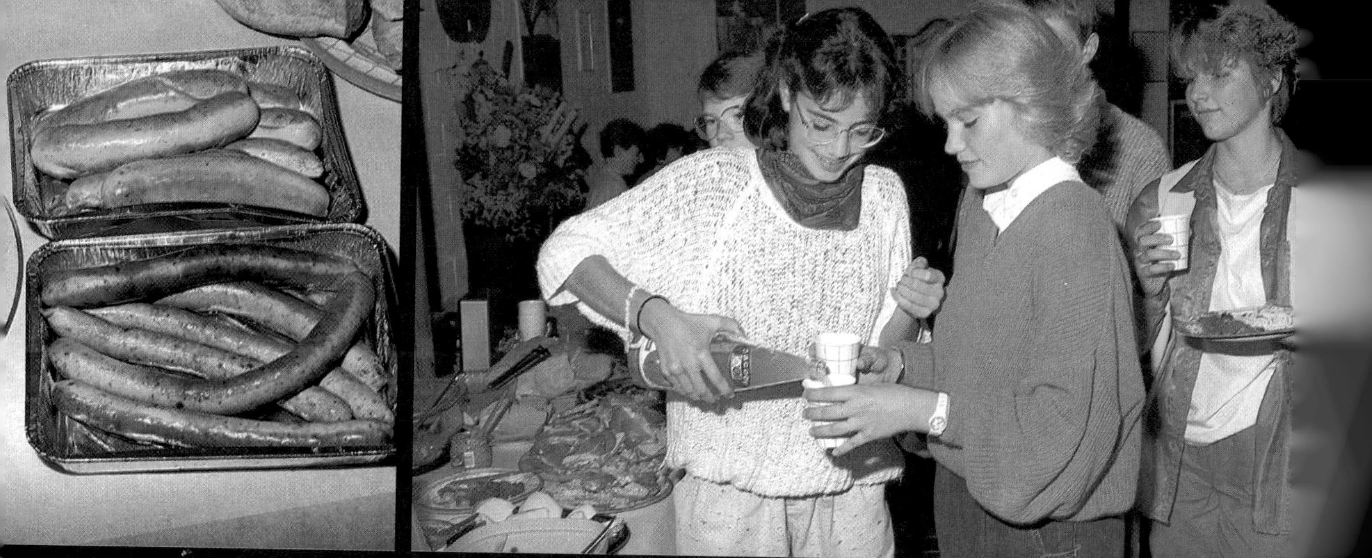

Parties are fun to give and fun to go to. Young people are always ready for an impromptu get-together, but a really good party takes planning. Whom do you invite? What do you serve to eat and drink? What kinds of activities should you plan?

In this unit you will:

SECTION A	invite someone to a party and accept or decline an invitation
SECTION B	tell about what there is to eat and drink
SECTION C	offer someone something to eat and drink and accept or decline what is being offered
SECTION D	talk about things to do at a party and pay compliments
TRY YOUR SKILLS	use what you've learned
ZUM LESEN	read for practice and pleasure

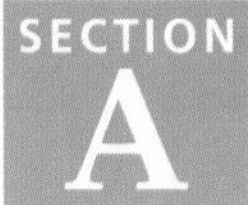

inviting someone to a party; accepting or declining an invitation

Karin is having a party. She has made her guest list and is calling her friends. What does she say? How do her friends respond? What would you say if you were invited?

A1

Karin hat eine Party

KARIN Drei—fünf—neun—null—eins—vier. (Es klingelt.)

FRAU BERGER Berger. Ja, hallo! Ich höre Sie, aber ich verstehe Sie nicht. Hallo, wer ist denn da?

(Klick.) (Es klingelt wieder.)

FRAU BERGER Hier Berger.

KARIN Guten Tag, Frau Berger! Hier ist die Karin. Ist die Christine da?

FRAU BERGER Ach, du bist's Karin! Jetzt verstehe ich dich gut. Moment mal! . . . Christine! Die Karin möchte dich sprechen!

CHRISTINE Grüss dich, Karin! Wie geht's? Was gibt's?

KARIN Du, hör zu! Ich hab' am Samstag eine Party, und ich möchte dich einladen. Kommst du?

CHRISTINE Ja, gern! Am Samstag hab' ich nichts vor. Um wieviel Uhr?

KARIN Um sieben.

CHRISTINE Das ist prima! Wen lädst du denn noch ein?

KARIN Die Michaela, den Bernd, . . .

CHRISTINE Wirklich? Du, ich bringe meine Musikkassetten, ja?

KARIN Toll! Dann bis Samstag. Tschüs!

CHRISTINE Tschüs! Und vielen Dank!

Karin ruft jetzt ihre Freunde und Freundinnen an. Wer kommt? Wer kommt nicht?

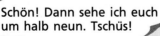

Ja, ich komme gern!

Michaela, eine Schulfreundin

Ach, das ist schade. Samstag geht es leider nicht.

Uwe, ein Klassenkamerad

Was? Du hast eine Party, und du lädst mich ein? Toll!

Hans-Peter, Michaelas Freund

Du, es geht leider nicht. Samstag hab' ich schon etwas vor.

Brigitte, eine Klassenkameradin

Um sieben Uhr geht's nicht. Aber wir kommen etwas später, so um halb neun, O.K.?

Lisa und Heidi, Karins Kusinen

Na, klar! Samstag habe ich nichts vor, das passt prima!

Bernd, ihr Tennispartner

Schön! Dann sehe ich euch um halb neun. Tschüs!

Nein, Samstag hab' ich leider keine Zeit. Schade!

Klaus, ein Klassenkamerad

1. Karin. Sie sagt: „Ich habe am Samstag eine Party, und ich möchte dich einladen. Kommst du?" 2. Christine, Michaela, Hans-Peter, Lisa, Heidi und Bernd kommen. 3. Uwe, Brigitte und Klaus kommen nicht.

A2 Übung • Wer hat eine Party?

1. Wer hat eine Party? Was sagt sie?
2. Wer kommt? Was sagen sie?
3. Wer kommt nicht? Was sagen sie?

A3 WIE SAGT MAN DAS?
Accepting and declining an invitation

accepting an invitation	Ja, gern! Ja, ich komme gern! Na, klar! Das passt prima!	Sure, I'd love to! Yes, I'd love to come! Well, of course! That suits me fine!
declining an invitation	Es geht nicht. Samstag geht es nicht.	I can't. I can't on Saturday.
regrets	Das ist schade! Es geht leider nicht.	That's too bad! I'm sorry, I can't.
excuses	Ich habe schon etwas vor. Ich habe keine Zeit.	I already have something planned. I have no time.

A4 Übung • Ich lade dich ein!

Invite six classmates to your party on Saturday. Which classmates accept, which ones decline your invitation? What does each one say?

A: Ich habe am Samstag eine Party. Kommst du?
B: Ja, . . . *or* Nein, . . .

A5 ERKLÄRUNG
First and Second Person Pronouns, Accusative Case

1. You know the subject pronouns **ich** and **wir, du** and **ihr** and **Sie.** Since these are subject pronouns, they are in the nominative case.
2. Each of these pronouns has an accusative case form you use when the pronoun functions as a direct object or as an object of a preposition such as **für.**

Pronoun as Subject (Nominative Case)			*Pronoun as Direct Object (Accusative Case)*		
Ich **Du**	rufe rufst	Bernd an.	Bernd ruft	**mich** **dich**	an.
Wir **Ihr**	rufen ruft			**uns** **euch**	
Sie	rufen			**Sie**	

A6 Übung • Jetzt bist du dran 

Du sprichst zuerst mit einem Freund, dann mit zwei Klassenkameraden, mit deiner Deutschlehrerin und mit zwei Lehrern.

Du möchtest ihn oder sie etwas fragen.
Was sagst du?
Ich möchte dich etwas fragen.
Ich möchte euch etwas fragen.
Ich möchte Sie etwas fragen.
Ich möchte Sie etwas fragen.

ein Freund

zwei Klassenkameraden

1. Du verstehst ihn oder sie nicht.
2. Du möchtest ihn oder sie einladen.
3. Du möchtest ihn oder sie morgen anrufen.
4. Du kennst ihn oder sie gut.
5. Du findest ihn oder sie prima!

1. Ich verstehe dich/euch/Sie/Sie nicht.
2. Ich möchte dich/euch/Sie/Sie einladen.
3. Ich möchte dich/euch/Sie/Sie morgen anrufen.
4. Ich kenne dich/euch/Sie/Sie gut.
5. Ich finde dich/euch/Sie/Sie prima.

die Deutschlehrerin

zwei Lehrer

A7 ERKLÄRUNG
The Verbs anrufen, einladen, vorhaben

1. The verbs **anrufen,** *to call on the telephone,* **einladen,** *to invite,* and **vorhaben,** *to plan to do,* belong to a group of verbs that have a separable prefix: **an**rufen, **ein**laden, **vor**haben. In the present tense, the prefix is separated from the verb and used at the end of the sentence. In addition, the verb **einladen** changes its stem vowel from **a** to **ä** in the **du**-form and in the **er/sie**-form.

anrufen				einladen				vorhaben			
Ich	**rufe**	Bernd	**an.**	Ich	**lade**	Karin	**ein.**	Ich	**habe**	was	**vor.**
Du	**rufst**		**an.**	Du	**lädst**		**ein.**	Du	**hast**		**vor.**
Er, Sie	**ruft**		**an.**	Er, Sie	**lädt**		**ein.**	Er, Sie	**hat**		**vor.**
Wir	**rufen**		**an.**	Wir	**laden**		**ein.**	Wir	**haben**		**vor.**
Ihr	**ruft**		**an.**	Ihr	**ladet**		**ein.**	Ihr	**habt**		**vor.**
Sie	**rufen**		**an.**	Sie	**laden**		**ein.**	Sie	**haben**		**vor.**

2. The verb **einladen** does not change the stem vowel in the command form.

Du, Karin, **lad** doch die Christine **ein!**

A8 Übung • Wen rufst du an?

A: Rufst du den Bernd an?
B: Ja, ich rufe ihn an.

A: Und Bernds Freundin?
B: Ja, ich rufe sie auch an.

1. Und den Amerikaner aus New York? ihn
2. Und mich? dich
3. Und uns? euch
4. Und Christines Freund? ihn

A 9 Übung • Und wen lädst du ein?

A: Lädst du die Michaela ein?
B: Ja, ich lade sie ein.

A: Und Michaelas Freund?
B: Ja, ich lade ihn auch ein.

1. Und den Amerikaner aus New York? ihn
2. Und uns? euch
3. Und mich? dich
4. Und Karins Freundin? sie

A 10 Übung • Alle haben etwas vor!

A: Hast du etwas vor?
B: Ja, ich habe leider etwas vor.

1. Hat Bernd etwas vor? er hat
2. Und Bernds Schwester? sie hat
3. Und die Eltern? sie haben
4. Und ihr? wir haben

A 11 Übung • Partnerarbeit

Du fragst einen Mitschüler, was du machen sollst!

A: Was soll ich machen? Soll ich . . .
B: Ja, lad doch die Michaela ein!

Probier doch den Leberkäs!
Lad doch den Lehrer ein!
Hol doch das Eis!
Frag doch deine Mutter!
Trink doch eine Limo!
Geh doch zu Karins Party!
Ruf doch den Bernd an!
Bring doch die Musikkassetten!

die Michaela einladen?
den Leberkäs probieren?
den Lehrer einladen?
das Eis holen?
meine Mutter fragen?
zu Karins Party gehen?
eine Limo trinken?
den Bernd anrufen?
die Musikkassetten bringen?

A 12 Übung • Hör gut zu!

For script and answers, see p. T162.

Sagen deine Freunde ja oder nein?

	0	1	2	3	4	5	6	7	8
accepting	✓			✓		✓	✓		✓
declining		✓	✓		✓			✓	

A 13 Übung • Du möchtest eine Party haben

Deine Party ist am Samstag. Ruf die folgenden Leute an und lad sie ein: einen Freund, zwei Klassenkameradinnen, deinen Deutschlehrer. Schreib die Gespräche auf!

A: Ich habe am Samstag eine Party, und ich lade . . . ein. Kommst . . .?
B: . . .
A: . . .

SECTION B

telling what there is to eat and drink

Karin's friends are arriving at the party. They are hungry and already asking about the food! Let's hear and see what Karin and her mother have prepared for the guests to eat and drink. Think about what you would offer your guests at a party at your house.

B1 Was gibt es alles?

HEIDI Du, Karin! Wir haben Hunger. Wann essen wir?
KARIN Gleich!
HEIDI Was gibt es überhaupt?
KARIN Es gibt eine Suppe—eine Gulaschsuppe—Kartoffelsalat, Hamburger, Bratwurst, Wurstbrote und Käsebrote . . . und natürlich auch Kuchen.
HEIDI Und zu trinken?
KARIN Schau! Wir haben Erdbeerbowle[1], Limonade, Fanta, Cola, Mineralwasser, . . . äh . . . Apfelsaft, und die Mutti macht auch einen Kaffee.
HEIDI Prima! Wann geht's endlich los? Ich habe einen Bärenhunger!

Was hast du für mich?
Für dich? Einen Apfelsaft.

Was gibt's zu essen? Wer hat Hunger?

Suppe Hamburger Käsebrote BRATWURST Kartoffelsalat Kuchen Wurstbrote

Und was gibt's zu trinken? Wer hat Durst?

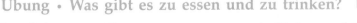

Mineralwasser Fanta Apfelsaft Limonade Erdbeerbowle Cola Kaffee

B2 Übung • Was gibt es zu essen und zu trinken?

A: Was gibt's zu essen?
B: Es gibt . . . Suppe, Hamburger, Käsebrote, Kartoffelsalat, Kuchen, Wurstbrote, Bratwurst.
A: Toll! Wann geht's los?

A: Und was gibt's zu trinken?
B: Wir haben . . . Mineralwasser, Fanta, Apfelsaft, Limonade, Erdbeerbowle, Cola, Kaffee.
A: Du, ich hab' Durst!

[1]Karin made a strawberry punch for her friends with fresh strawberries, raspberry syrup, and lemon flavored soda.

B3 WIE SAGT MAN DAS?
Saying what there is to eat and drink

Was gibt's zu essen?	What's there to eat?
Was gibt's zu trinken?	What's there to drink?
Es gibt . . .	There is / There are . . .
Wir haben . . .	We have . . .

B4 HANS-PETER ISST ALLES GERN! 

Hans-Peter is always hungry and he likes everything! What do you like to eat and drink?

KARIN Was isst du? Einen Hamburger?
HANS-PETER Natürlich! Ich esse Hamburger gern.
KARIN Für wen ist die Limonade?
HANS-PETER Für mich.
KARIN Was, du trinkst Limo?
HANS-PETER Na und?! Ich trinke Limo gern.

B5 Übung • Und du?

1. Was isst du gern? Was trinkst du gern?
2. Was isst du nicht gern?
3. Was isst und trinkst du am liebsten?
4. Frag deine Klassenkameraden und deine Lehrerin oder deinen Lehrer, was sie gern essen und trinken!
5. Erzähl, was sie sagen!

B6 Übung • Partnerarbeit 

You and a classmate are at Karin's party. Practice the following dialogs, using the list on the right. Make necessary changes.

A: Isst du einen Hamburger?
B: Nein, ich esse Hamburger nicht gern.
A: Isst du lieber ein Wurstbrot?
B: Ja, Wurstbrote esse ich gern!

* * *

A: Ich habe Durst. Ich trinke einen Apfelsaft. Was trinkst du?
B: Ich trinke lieber Mineralwasser.
A: Du trinkst immer nur Mineralwasser.
B: Na und? Mineralwasser schmeckt gut.

der / ein	die / eine	das / ein
Apfelsaft	Bratwurst	Käsebrot
Hamburger	Cola	Mineralwasser
Kaffee	Erdbeerbowle	Wurstbrot
Kartoffel-salat	Fanta	
	Limonade	
	Suppe	

B7 Übung • Auf der Party

Write what you like to eat and drink, choosing from the list on the preceding page. Then write what a friend of yours likes.

Ich esse gern . . . (Robert) isst gern . . .

B8 Übung • Wer bekommt was?

A: Ist die Cola für den Bernd?
B: Ja, die Cola ist für ihn.

1. Ist der Apfelsaft für die Heidi? für sie
2. Ist das Käsebrot für den Hans-Peter? für ihn
3. Ist die Limonade für die Kinder? für sie
4. Ist der Hamburger für die Lisa? für sie
5. Ist der Kartoffelsalat für die Karin? für sie
6. Ist der Kaffee für die Eltern? für sie

B9 Übung • Was möchtest du essen und trinken?  For answers, see p. T165.

Du hast eine Party. Deine Freunde haben Hunger und Durst. Was möchten deine Freunde und was möchte dein Lehrer essen und trinken? Was sagen sie? Was sagst du?

1. eine Klassenkameradin

Für mich einen Apfelsaft!

Hier, ein Apfelsaft für dich!

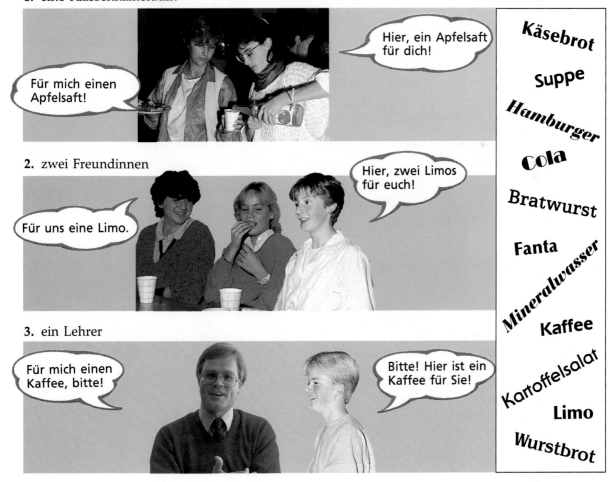

2. zwei Freundinnen

Für uns eine Limo.

Hier, zwei Limos für euch!

3. ein Lehrer

Für mich einen Kaffee, bitte!

Bitte! Hier ist ein Kaffee für Sie!

Käsebrot
Suppe
Hamburger
Cola
Bratwurst
Fanta
Mineralwasser
Kaffee
Kartoffelsalat
Limo
Wurstbrot

B 10 Übung • Hör gut zu!

For script and answers, see p. T165.

Du bist auf einer Party. Was gibt es zu essen und zu trinken?

	0	1	2	3	4	5	6	7	8
zu essen	✓			✓		✓	✓		✓
zu trinken		✓	✓		✓			✓	

B 11 Schreibübung • Auf der Party

1. Wir haben Hunger! Was gibt es zu essen? 2. Es gibt Suppe, Bratwurst und Kartoffelsalat. 3. Prima! 4. Es gibt auch Kuchen. 5. Toll! Kuchen esse ich immer gern! 6. Wir haben Durst! Was gibt es zu trinken? 7. Wir haben Erdbeerbowle, Fanta und Limonade. 8. Wann essen wir? 9. Gleich!

1. Schreib einen Dialog!

Wir haben Hunger! Was gibt es zu essen?
Es gibt auch Kuchen.
Gleich!
Wir haben Durst! Was gibt es zu trinken?
Toll! Kuchen esse ich immer gern!
Prima!
Wann essen wir?
Es gibt Suppe, Bratwurst und Kartoffelsalat.
Wir haben Erdbeerbowle, Fanta und Limonade.

2. Karin und ihre Mutter bringen das Essen. Wer bekommt was? Schreib auf, was Karins Mutter fragt und was Karin antwortet!

der Bernd—die Bratwurst

Bekommt der Bernd die Bratwurst?
Ja, sie ist für ihn.

1. der Hans-Peter—das Käsebrot es, für ihn
2. die Heidi—den Apfelsaft er, für sie
3. die Lisa—den Hamburger er, für sie
4. die Kinder—die Limonade sie, für sie
5. der Bernd—den Kartoffelsalat er, für ihn

B 12 Schreibübung • Projekt

1. Plan a class party.
2. Design and draw a decorative menu for your party.
3. Make a shopping list.

offering someone something to eat and drink, accepting or declining what is being offered

Karin is offering her friends various things to eat and drink. Let's hear what everyone would like to have. What about you? What would you like?

C1 Was möchtest du? Einen Hamburger? 

KARIN Was möchtest du, Matthias? Hm? Eine Gulaschsuppe? Einen Hamburger?
MATTHIAS Nein, keine Suppe, bitte! Und keinen Hamburger. Ich . . . äh . . . esse eine Bratwurst.

KARIN Und was nimmst du, Christine? Ein Wurstbrot, vielleicht?
CHRISTINE Ja, bitte!
KARIN Und eine Cola?
CHRISTINE Du, keine Cola, bitte. Ich nehme Mineralwasser.

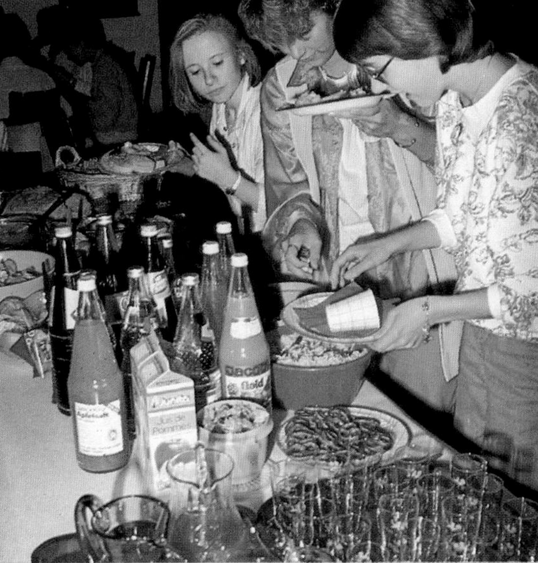

HANS-PETER Und ich nehme einen Hamburger, eine Bratwurst, ein Wurstbrot . . .
KARIN Noch was?
HANS-PETER Nein, danke!
KARIN Na, dann guten Appetit!

Zwiebelkuchen

Leberkäs

MICHAELA Herr Haupt, was trinken Sie? Eine Limo? Eine Fanta? Erdbeerbowle?
HERR HAUPT Keine Fanta. Hm, ich trinke einen Kaffee.

C2 Übung • Und du? Wie steht's mit dir?

1. Was möchtest du? Eine Suppe?
2. Möchtest du einen Hamburger?
3. Oder möchtest du eine Limo?
4. Was isst du gern?
5. Und was trinkst du?

C3 WIE SAGT MAN DAS?
Accepting or declining something to eat or drink

accepting	Ja, bitte! Ja, gern!	Yes, please. Yes, I'd love some.
declining	Nein, danke! Keinen Kaffee für mich, danke!	No thanks. No coffee for me, thanks.

C4 Übung • Du hast eine Party!

Was möchten deine Gäste essen und trinken? Was sagen sie?

A: Möchtest du eine Limonade?
B: . . . *or* . . .

einen Apfelsaft
eine Fanta
eine Bockwurst
ein Wurstbrot
eine Suppe
eine Cola
eine Limonade
eine Erdbeerbowle
eine Bratwurst
einen Kaffee

C5 WIE SAGT MAN DAS?
Making negative statements

You already know that **nicht** is used to make negative statements. To negate a noun, use the word **kein.**

negating the entire statement	Ich esse die Suppe nicht. Ich trinke die Cola nicht.	I am not eating the soup. I am not drinking the cola.
negating noun phrases	Ich esse keine Suppe. Ich trinke keinen Kaffee.	I do not eat soup. I do not drink coffee.

Kein can have slightly different meanings in a sentence. What do you notice about the following examples?

Ich trinke keinen Kaffee.	*I do not drink coffee.*
Ich esse kein Wurstbrot, ich esse ein Käsebrot.	*I am not eating a sandwich with cold cuts; I am eating a cheese sandwich.*

C6 ERKLÄRUNG
kein, *Nominative and Accusative Case*

1. The word **kein** has the same endings as **ein.**

	Nominative			*Accusative*		
Masculine	Ist das Das ist	**ein** **kein**	Hamburger? Hamburger.	Ich esse Ich esse	**einen** **keinen**	Hamburger. Hamburger.
Feminine	Ist das Das ist	**eine** **keine**	Erdbeerbowle? Erdbeerbowle.	Ich trinke Ich trinke	**eine** **keine**	Erdbeerbowle. Erdbeerbowle.
Neuter	Ist das Das ist	**ein** **kein**	Käsebrot? Käsebrot.	Ich esse Ich esse	**ein** **kein**	Käsebrot. Käsebrot.
Plural	Sind das Das sind	 **keine**	Bratwürste? Bratwürste.	Ich esse Ich esse	 **keine**	Bratwürste. Bratwürste.

2. Kein is also used before some nouns that have no determiner in the corresponding positive phrase.

Sie hat Durst.	Sie hat keinen Durst.	*She's not thirsty.*
Ich habe Hunger.	Ich habe keinen Hunger.	*I'm not hungry.*
Das macht Spass.	Das macht keinen Spass.	*That's no fun.*
Hast du Zeit?	Nein, ich habe keine Zeit.	*No, I don't have time.*

C7 Übung

Du isst ja überhaupt nichts!

A: Was möchtest du? Eine Suppe?
B: Nein, keine Suppe, bitte!

1. einen Hamburger? keinen
2. ein Käsebrot? kein
3. Bratwürste? keine
4. Kartoffelsalat? keinen
5. ein Wurstbrot? kein
6. eine Gulaschsuppe? keine

C8 Übung

Du trinkst ja nichts!

A: Was trinkst du? Eine Cola?
B: Danke, nein, keine Cola!

1. einen Kaffee? keinen
2. eine Fanta? keine
3. ein Mineralwasser? kein
4. einen Apfelsaft? keinen
5. eine Limonade? keine

C9 ERKLÄRUNG
The Verb nehmen

The verb **nehmen,** *to take,* has the following forms in the present tense:

ich **nehme**	wir **nehmen**
du **nimmst**	ihr **nehmt**
er, sie, es **nimmt**	sie, Sie **nehmen**

C10 Übung • Jetzt bist du dran

1. You're having a party. Ask various classmates what they would like to eat or drink and make suggestions. Your classmates do not care for what you suggest but would like something else.
   A: Was nimmst du? Eine Bratwurst vielleicht?
   B: Nein, danke! Keine Bratwurst. Ich nehme ein Käsebrot.
2. Now practice offering something to two classmates.
3. Offer your teacher something to eat or drink.

C11 Übung • Der Partymuffel

Was sagt der Partymuffel?

Was sagen seine Freunde?

Ich komme nicht.
Ich esse keine Bratwurst.
Ich trinke keine Cola.
Ich möchte den Kuchen nicht probieren.
Ich tanze nicht.
Ich gehe jetzt.
Komm doch!
. . . . . . !

Iss doch eine Bratwurst!
Trink doch eine Cola!
Probier doch den Kuchen!
Tanz doch!
Bleib doch!

C12 Übung • Hör gut zu!

For script and answers, see p. T168.

Was möchten deine Freunde essen und trinken? Was möchten sie nicht essen und trinken?

	0	1	2	3	4	5	6	7	8	9	10
accepting			✓	✓	✓		✓			✓	
declining	✓	✓				✓		✓	✓		✓

C13 Schreibübung • Du planst eine Party

Write a paragraph telling about a party you are planning. Tell the day and time, whom you are inviting, and what you are going to have to eat and drink.

Ich habe am Samstag um . . .

talking about things to do at a party, paying compliments

What are our friends doing at their party? What would you like to do if you were there?

D1 So, was machen wir jetzt?

So, was machen wir jetzt? Wer hat eine Idee?

MICHAELA Ich möchte Hans-Peters Kassette hören. —Wo habt ihr euren Kassetten-Recorder?
CHRISTINE Karin, wo hast du deinen Plattenspieler? Ich möchte eine Platte hören.
HANS-PETER Wo ist die Musik? Ich möchte tanzen.

UWE Ich möchte einen Film sehen. —Habt ihr einen Video-Recorder?
BERND Einen Film sehen? Du spinnst! —Möchtet ihr lieber einen Witz hören?

Ruhe! Der Bernd erzählt einen Witz!

Mensch, Bernd! Deine Witze sind blöd!

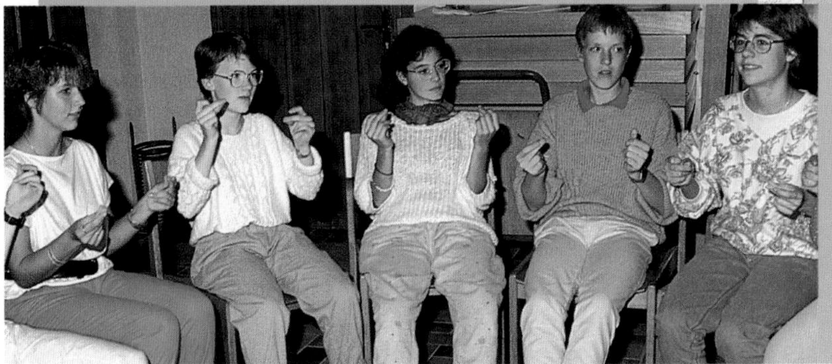

HEIDI Ich habe eine Idee: wir spielen jetzt ein Ratespiel!
LISA Ein Ratespiel? Ich möchte lieber diskutieren.

D2 Übung • Und du? Wie steht's mit dir?

1. Was machst du, wenn du eine Party hast?
2. Frage deine Klassenkameraden, was sie machen!
3. Jetzt fragst du deinen Lehrer oder deine Lehrerin!
4. Was machst du gern? Was machst du am liebsten?
5. Was machst du nicht? Warum nicht?
6. Hast du einen Video-Recorder?
7. Hast du Video-Filme oder mietest du sie?
8. Kennst du einen Witz? Möchtest du ihn erzählen?

Kassetten hören
tanzen
Musik hören
Witze erzählen
einen Film sehen
diskutieren
Ratespiel spielen
essen und trinken

D3 WIE IST DIE PARTY?

Karin, deine Eltern sind so nett!

He, Bernd! Deine Kassette ist furchtbar!

Ich finde euer Haus so gemütlich.

Klasse Party!

Das Essen ist Spitze!

Lecker!

Ist das die Michaela? Wer ist denn ihr Tanzpartner? Uwe? Er tanzt wirklich toll!
Die Michaela sieht phantastisch aus!
Tolle Musik!

Michaela und Hans-Peter finden das Essen prima. Was sagen sie?

HANS-PETER	Frau Haupt, Ihr Kartoffelsalat schmeckt ausgezeichnet.
FRAU HAUPT	Wirklich? Ist er gut?
HANS-PETER	Ganz prima!
FRAU HAUPT	Da bin ich aber froh.
MICHAELA	Ihre Wurstbrote sehen lecker aus.
FRAU HAUPT	Ja, schmecken sie auch?
MICHAELA	Und wie!
FRAU HAUPT	Das freut mich.

D4 ERKLÄRUNG
Possessives, Nominative and Accusative Case

The words **mein, dein, sein, unser, euer, ihr** are called possessives. They have the same endings as the indefinite article **ein** and are often called **ein**-words.

The following is a summary chart of the possessives showing all nominative and accusative forms used before masculine, feminine, neuter, and plural nouns.

	before a masculine noun		*before a neuter noun*	*before feminine & plural nouns*
	Nominative	*Accusative*	*Nominative & Accusative*	*Nominative & Accusative*
my	**mein**	**meinen**	**mein**	**meine**
your	**dein**	**deinen**	**dein**	**deine**
his	**sein**	**seinen**	**sein**	**seine**
her	**ihr**	**ihren**	**ihr**	**ihre**
our	**unser**	**unseren**	**unser**	**unsere**
your	**euer**	**eueren**	**euer**	**euere**
their	**ihr**	**ihren**	**ihr**	**ihre**
your	**Ihr**	**Ihren**	**Ihr**	**Ihre**

D5 Übung • Auf der Party gehört

Ihr Kartoffelsalat, Ihre Wurstbrote (schmecken), Ihr Ka[illegible] Ihre Limonade, Ihr Apfelsaft, Ihre Gulaschsuppe

Wie ist die Bratwurst, Bernd?

Frau Haupt, Ihre Bratwurst schmeckt ausgezeichnet!

der Kartoffelsalat? die Wurstbrote?
der Kaffee? die Limonade?
der Apfelsaft? die Gulaschsuppe?

Du, wie findest du meine Schwester?

Ich finde deine Schwester sehr nett.

Wie findest du Karins Party?

Ich finde ihre Party Klasse!

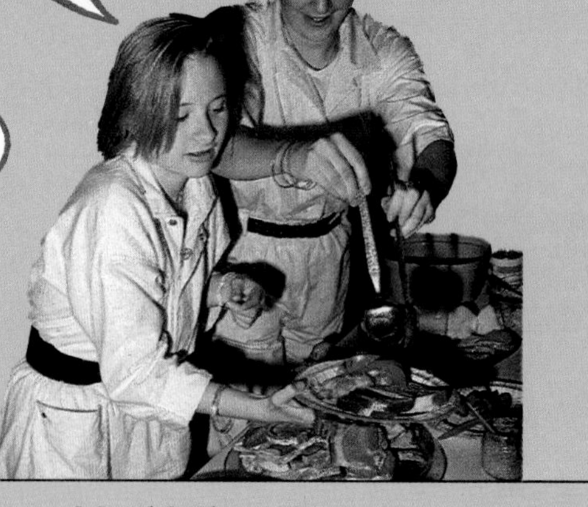

meinen Bruder? meine Kusine?
meine Eltern? meinen Freund?
meine Lehrerin? meine Geschwister?

Musik? Platten?
Tanzpartner? Video-Recorder?
Freunde?

deinen Bruder, deine Kusine, deine Eltern, deinen Freund, deine Lehrerin, deine Geschwister

ihre Musik, ihre Platten, ihren Tanzpartner, ihren Video-Recorder, ihre Freunde

D6 WIE SAGT MAN DAS?

Complimenting people, complimenting someone on food

In Unit 6 you learned how to pay a compliment and to respond to a compliment. Here are some more ways of complimenting.

complimenting people	Du siehst gut aus. Er tanzt wirklich toll. Deine Eltern sind so nett.	You look good. He really dances well. Your parents are so nice.
complimenting someone on food	Ihr Kuchen ist ausgezeichnet. Die Suppe schmeckt lecker. Ich finde Ihren Kaffee gut.	Your cake is excellent. The soup tastes delicious. I think your coffee is good.

Look at the dialogs on page 255. How does Frau Haupt respond to the compliments? What would you say if someone complimented you?

D7 Übung • Mach doch mal ein Kompliment!

For answers, see p. T171.

Du siehst, dass die Karin gut tanzt. Was sagst du? Und was sagt Karin?

A: Karin, du tanzt wirklich toll!
B: Meinst du?

1. Der Bernd erzählt gute Witze.
2. Frau Haupts Kartoffelsalat ist sehr gut.
3. Karins Zimmer ist gemütlich.
4. Christines Kassetten sind gut.
5. Michaela sieht sehr hübsch aus.
6. Der Hans-Peter hat eine gute Idee.
7. Karins Freunde sind lustig.
8. Karins Erdbeerbowle schmeckt gut.
9. Karins Eltern sind sehr nett.

ausgezeichnet
nett
Spitze!
gut
tanzt gut
gemütlich
prima
sieht hübsch aus
Klasse!
lustig
toll

Hast du sie gern?
Findest du?
Ja? Ist sie gut?
Ja, wirklich?
Schmeckt er auch?
Meinst du?

D8 Übung • Hör gut zu!

For script and answers, see p. T171.

Listen to the statement. Is the one that follows appropriate or not?

	0	1	2	3	4	5	6	7	8	9	10
appropriate	✓	✓			✓		✓	✓		✓	
not appropriate			✓	✓		✓			✓		✓

D9 Schreibübung • Wie ist die Party?

Pretend you are at a party at a classmate's house. Write a paragraph commenting on the party. Mention the food, company, music, and anything else that comes to mind.

TRY YOUR SKILLS

using what you've learned

1 Bernd schreibt eine Einladungskarte

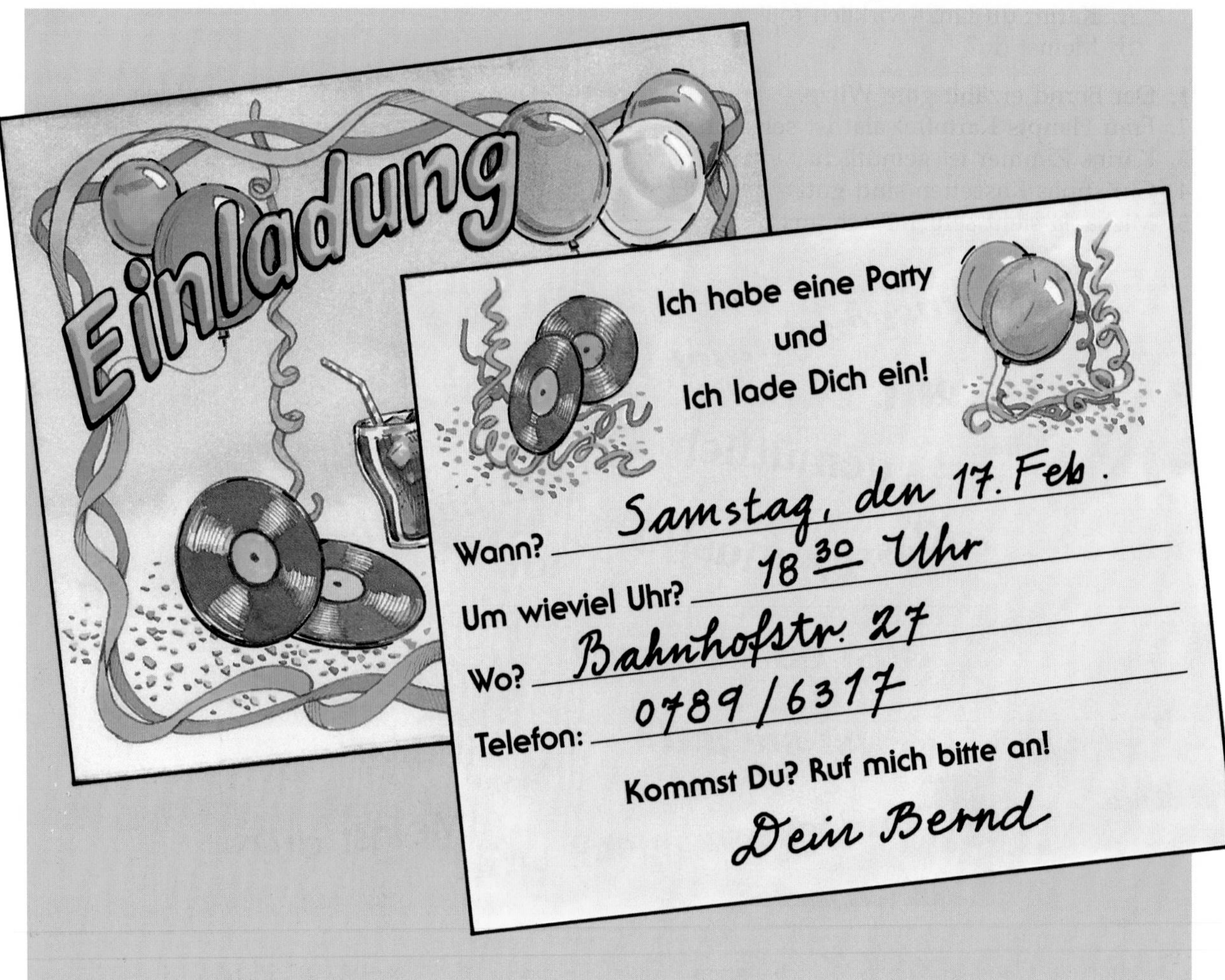
Einladung
Ich habe eine Party
und
Ich lade Dich ein!
Wann? Samstag, den 17. Feb.
Um wieviel Uhr? 18 30 Uhr
Wo? Bahnhofstr. 27
Telefon: 0789/6317
Kommst Du? Ruf mich bitte an!
Dein Bernd

2 Übung • Du rufst den Bernd an. Gehst du oder gehst du nicht?

Du Hallo, Bernd! Du hast eine Party und lädst mich ein! Toll!
Bernd Na klar! Kommst du?
Du Ja, . . . *or* Nein, . . .

3 Schreibübung • Wann ist deine Party?

Du hast auch eine Party. Schreib eine Einladungskarte! Wen lädst du ein? Schreib eine Gästeliste! Was gibt es alles zu essen und zu trinken? Schreib eine Einkaufsliste! Was kann man alles auf einer Party tun? Schreib eine Liste mit Ideen!

4 Leseübung • Karins Party ist toll!

Karins Partys sind immer toll. Sie lädt nette Jungen und Mädchen ein. Leider kommt ihre Freundin Katja nicht, sie hat schon etwas vor. Das ist schade, denn sie ist die beste Tänzerin. Karins Mutter macht wieder ihren guten Kartoffelsalat, und Karin macht ihre Erdbeerbowle. Das Essen und die Getränke sind wirklich lecker. Karin hat einen neuen Plattenspieler. Ihr Freund Bernd bringt seine „tollen" Platten mit, aber Karin findet seine Musik furchtbar.

5 Übung • Meine Partys sind auch toll!

1. The preceding passage describes Karin's party in the third person. After you have read the text carefully, pretend that this is your party and that you are talking about it.

   Meine Partys sind immer . . .

   meine Partys/ich lade/meine Freundin Katja/meine Mutter/ich mache/meine Erdbeerbowle/ich habe/mein Freund Bernd/ich finde

2. Make up questions about the passage on Karin's party and ask a classmate to answer them.

   Wie sind Karins Partys? Wen . . . lädt sie ein? Wer kommt nicht? Warum nicht? Warum ist das Schade? Was macht Karins Mutter? Was macht Karin? Wie sind das Essen und die Getränke? Was hat Karin? Was bringt Karins Freund Bernd? Wie findet Karin seine Musik?

6 Leseübung • Ein Durcheinander 

Bernd Mensch, Karin! Wo ist mein Hamburger?
Karin Ich glaube, der Hans-Peter isst deinen Hamburger.
Hans-Peter Was? Ich . . . ich esse seinen Hamburger? —Nein!!!

Hans-Peter Mensch, Christine, wo ist meine Fanta?
Christine Deine Fanta? —Die Michaela trinkt deine Fanta.
Michaela Was? Ich? Ich trinke seine Fanta? —Nein!!!

7 Übung • Rollenspiel 

For answers, see p. T173.

You and your classmates take the roles of Bernd, Karin, Hans-Peter, Christine, and Michaela. Practice the dialogs above, substituting the following items:

Wurstbrot, Apfelsaft, Gulaschsuppe, Limonade
Kartoffelsalat, Mineralwasser, Bratwurst, Kaffee

8 Übung • Was gehört zusammen?

Match the statements on the left with appropriate responses on the right.

1. Was möchtest du, einen Hamburger?
2. Ich habe eine Party, und ich lade dich ein. Kommst du?
3. Wen lädst du noch ein?
4. Ich habe Durst.
5. Was gibt es zu essen?
6. Kommt ihr?
7. Ihr Kartoffelsalat ist ausgezeichnet, Frau Haupt.
8. Was gibt es zu trinken?
9. Christine! Hier ist die Karin!

6 **a.** Das geht leider nicht. Wir haben was vor.
8 **b.** Es gibt Apfelsaft, Fanta, Cola und Mineralwasser.
4 **c.** Möchtest du eine Cola?
9 **d.** Grüss dich, Karin! Was gibt's?
2 **e.** Ja, ich komme gern.
3 **f.** Den Bernd, die Michaela und die Heidi.
5 **g.** Wir haben Bratwurst, Käsebrote und Wurstbrote.
1 **h.** Nein, danke. Ich habe keinen Hunger.
7 **i.** Dann bin ich aber froh.

9 Übung • Mix-Match

Wieviel Sätze kannst du machen?

Karin lädt meine Kusine am Wochenende ein.

wer?		wen?	wann? wie oft?	
ich wir Karin	lade rufe laden rufen lädt ruft	dich euch meine Kusine meinen Freund ihre Freundin	am Wochenende einmal in der Woche um sieben Uhr immer	an ein

10 Übung • Karin geht für die Party einkaufen

Karin braucht noch ein paar Sachen für die Party. Schau auf den Einkaufszettel!

Karins Einkaufszettel:

Für den Kuchen braucht sie . . . Zucker, Eier, Butter
Für den Kartoffelsalat braucht sie . . . Kartoffeln
Für die Hamburger braucht sie . . . Hackfleisch, Semmeln
Für die Wurst- und Käsebrote braucht sie . . . Aufschnitt, Käse, Brot

Karins Mutter sagt ihr, wo sie alles kaufen soll:

Kauf die Kartoffeln beim . . .! Gemüsehändler
Hol . . .! die Semmeln beim Bäcker!

Hol das Hackfleisch beim Metzger!
Hol den Aufschnitt auch beim Metzger!
Hol das Brot beim Bäcker!

Hol den Käse, den Zucker, die Eier und die Butter im Supermarkt!

11 Übung • Im Lokal

Du bist mit einem Klassenkameraden in der Stadt. Ihr habt Hunger und Durst und geht in eine Imbiss-Stube.

1. A: Du, was gibt's denn hier?
   B: Schau, hier gibt's . . .
   A: Prima!

eine Portion
eine Portion
eine Portion

2. A: Was nimmst du?
   B: Eine Limo.
   A: Gut. Eine Limo für dich und einen Apfelsaft für mich.

3. A: Fräulein!
   FRÄULEIN: Ja, bitte?
   A: Eine Limo und einen Apfelsaft, bitte.
   FRÄULEIN: Noch etwas?
   A: Nein, danke!

ein Spezi
ein Apollinaris
ein-einen
einen

...auch zum Mitnehmen ...		
Pommes frites	Portion	1.70
Sauerkraut	"	1.20
Kartoffelsalat . . .	"	1.20
Bier-hell	0,5 l	2.30
Weißbier	0,5 l	2.50
Pils	0,33 l	2.–
Radlermaß	1 l	4.40
Cola, Fanta, Spezi, . .	0,33 l	1.60
Apollinares	0,33 l	1.60
Apfel-u. Orangen-Saft	0,2 l	1.60
Zitronenlimonade . .	0,5 l	2.–

4. FRÄULEIN: Eine Limo für Sie und . . .
   A: Nein, ich bekomme keine Limo, ich bekomme den Apfelsaft.
   FRÄULEIN: Entschuldigung!

5. FRÄULEIN: So, wer bekommt den Apfelsaft?
   A: Der Apfelsaft ist für mich, und mein Freund bekommt die Limo.

12 Übung • Was sagen sie?

Der Hamburger schmeckt gut.

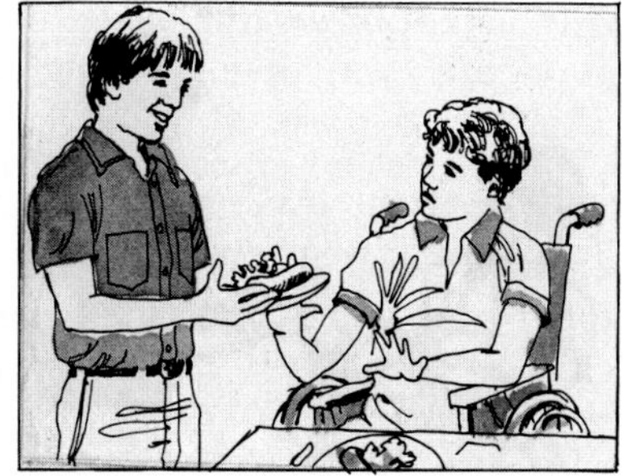

Nein, danke. Nichts für mich.

Die Musik ist toll!

13 Aussprache-, Lese- und Schreibübungen

For script, see p. T174.

1. Listen carefully and repeat what you hear.
2. Listen, then read aloud.
   1. schlecht, Kirche, möchte, vielleicht, traurig; nach, noch, Buch, auch; Fach—Fächer, Buch—Bücher
   2. Salat, Suppe, sein, Käse, Musik, Apfelsaft
   3. hier, dein, Wien, wieder, heiss, vier, fliegen, gleich, leider, Spiel, vielleicht
   4. unser, euer, später, lecker, Hunger, Spieler, Partner, Recorder
3. Copy the following sentences to prepare yourself to write them from dictation.
   1. Unser Salat ist wieder lecker.
   2. Ich fliege auch gleich weiter.
   3. Ich möchte auch drei Bücher.
   4. Das Spiel ist leider wieder in Wien.

WAS KANNST DU SCHON?

Let's review some important points you have learned in this unit.

Can you invite someone to a party?
You are having a party on Saturday at 7 o'clock. Call the following people and invite them to the party: Ich habe am Samstag um sieben eine Party, und ich möchte . . .

1. a friend **2.** two classmates **3.** your teacher 1. dich einladen 2. euch einladen 3. Sie einladen. Kommst du/Kommt ihr/Kommen Sie?

Do you know how to accept or decline a party invitation?
A classmate has just invited you to a party.

1. Accept the invitation.
2. Decline the invitation.
3. Decline the invitation and make an excuse.

1. Ja, (ich komme) gern!/Na, klar!/Das passt prima! 2. Samstag geht es nicht/es geht nicht. 3. Es geht leider nicht. Ich habe schon etwas vor/Ich habe keine Zeit.

Can you tell someone what there is to eat and drink?
You are having a party. Tell your guests what you have to eat and drink.

Es gibt/Wir haben . . . Suppe/Hamburger/Käsebrote/Kartoffelsalat/Kuchen/Wurstbrote/Bratwurst/Mineralwasser/Fanta/Apfelsaft Limo(nade)/Erdbeerbowle/Cola/Kaffee

Do you know how to offer someone something to eat and drink?
Offer a friend each of the following things:

eine Bratwurst, Erdbeerbowle, ein Wurstbrot, Mineralwasser
Möchtest du/Trinkst du/Nimmst du . . ?

Do you know how to accept or decline something to eat and drink?
You have just been offered some cake. Give two ways of accepting and two ways of declining. Ja, bitte! Ja, gern!
Nein, danke! Keinen Kuchen für mich, danke!

Can you make negative statements?
Make each of the following statements negative:

1. Er isst die Suppe.
2. Wir haben Zeit.
3. Er möchte einen Hamburger.
4. Ich habe Hunger.
5. Du bekommst Apfelsaft.
6. Das macht Spass.

1. Er isst die Suppe nicht. 2. Wir haben keine Zeit. 3. Er möchte keinen Hamburger. 4. Ich habe keinen Hunger. 5. Du bekommst keinen Apfelsaft. 6. Das macht keinen Spass.

Can you talk about things to do at a party?
Name six things you like to do at a party. Ich . . . gern. esse/trinke/tanze/diskutiere/höre Musik, Kassetten/erzähle Witze/spiele Ratespiele/sehe Filme

Can you pay someone a compliment?
Compliment your friend's mother on the following things:

Kartoffelsalat, Kuchen, Gulaschsuppe Frau . . . , Ihr . . . schmeckt gut/lecker/ausgezeichnet! Ihr Kartoffelsalat/Kuchen/Ihre Erdbeerbowle

Compliment Karin on her party.
Karin, deine Party ist toll!/Spitze!/Klasse!

WORTSCHATZ

SECTION A

anrufen *to call up* (see p 243)
bringen *to bring*
einladen *to invite* (see p 243)
etwas *something;* etwas später *a little later*
der **Freund, -e** *boyfriend*
gehen: es geht nicht *I can't*
gut *well*
hör zu! *listen!*
kein, keine *no, not any*
klingeln: es klingelt *the phone rings*
noch: wen lädst du noch ein? *who else are you inviting?*
passen: das passt prima *that suits me fine*
schon *already*
schön! *good! great!*
die **Schulfreundin, -nen** *friend from school* (f)
so um halb neun *around 8:30*
später *later*
sprechen: die Karin möchte dich sprechen *Karin would like to talk to you*
Uhr: um wieviel Uhr? *at what time?*
verstehen *to understand*
vorhaben *to have plans* (see p 243)
was gibt's? *what's up?*
wie geht's? *how are you?*

SECTION B

der **Apfelsaft, ¨e** *apple juice*
der **Bärenhunger: ich habe einen Bärenhunger!** *I'm hungry as a bear!*
der **Durst: Durst haben** *to be thirsty*
die **Erdbeerbowle, -n** *strawberry punch*
es gibt *there is . . .*
die **Fanta** *orange-flavored soda*
gleich *right away*
die **Gulaschsuppe, -n** *goulash soup*
der **Hamburger, -** *hamburger*
der **Kartoffelsalat, -e** *potato salad*
das **Käsebrot, -e** *cheese sandwich*
der **Kuchen, -** *cake*
die **Limonade** *flavored soda*
los: wann geht's endlich los? *when are we finally going to get going?*
na und?! *so what?*
natürlich *of course*
die **Suppe, -n** *soup*
überhaupt *in any case;* was gibt es überhaupt? *what are we having anyway?*
was gibt es alles? *what do you have?*

SECTION C

Appetit: guten Appetit! *enjoy your meal!*
die **Limo = Limonade** *lemon soda*
na, dann *well then*
nehmen *to take* (see p 252)

SECTION D

ausgezeichnet *excellent*
dein, deine *your* (sing)
diskutieren *to discuss*
die **Eltern** (pl) *parents*
erzählen *to tell*
euer, euere *your* (pl)
der **Film, -e** *film, movie*
freuen: das freut mich *I'm glad*
froh *happy, glad;* da bin ich aber froh! *I'm glad to hear that!*
furchtbar *terrible, awful*
ganz prima! *really great!*
die **Idee, -n** *idea*
ihr, ihre *her; their*
Ihr, Ihre *your* (formal)
der **Kassetten-Recorder, -** *cassette recorder*
lecker *delicious*
die **Musik** *music*
die **Platte, -n** *record*
der **Plattenspieler, -** *record player*
das **Ratespiel, -e** *guessing game*
Ruhe! *quiet!*
sein, seine *his; its*
spinnen: du spinnst! *you're crazy!*
tanzen *to dance*
der **Tanzpartner, -** *dance partner*
und wie! *and how!*
unser, unsere *our*
der **Video-Recorder, -** *video recorder*
der **Witz, -e** *joke*

1. anrufen (sep), bringen, einladen (sep,vc), verstehen, vorhaben (sep), nehmen (vc), diskutieren, erzählen, tanzen
2. verstehen, Kartoffelsalat, Limonade, natürlich, überhaupt, Appetit, ausgezeichnet, diskutieren, erzählen, Idee, Kassetten-Recorder, Musik
3. Schulfreundin, Apfelsaft, Bärenhunger, Erdbeerbowle, Gulaschsuppe, Kartoffelsalat, Käsebrot, Kassetten-Recorder, Plattenspieler, Ratespiel, Tanzpartner, Video-Recorder

WORTSCHATZÜBUNGEN

1. Make a list of all the verbs in the **Wortschatz.** Which ones have a separable prefix? Which ones have a vowel change in the second and third person?
2. Write down all words that are not stressed on the first syllable. Pronounce each one.
3. How many compound words can you find in the **Wortschatz?**

ZUM LESEN

Peter Seber über deutsche Sitten 

Peter Seber, der junge Amerikaner aus New York, ist schon drei Wochen bei den Nedels in Neuss. Zwei Schüler interviewen den Peter heute für die Schülerzeitung in Wiebkes Schule.

Was für Probleme hast du hier? Was findest du anders als° in Amerika?
Wie findest du unsere Musik?

„Ach, du, das Händeschütteln ist manchmal ein Problem für mich. Ich weiss oft nicht, ob ich zuerst die Hand geben soll oder nicht°. Und meistens vergesse ich es ganz°.

Auch beim Siezen und Duzen° gibt es oft Probleme. Manchmal sage ich ‚du' zu einem Lehrer, und dann lacht die ganze Klasse. Und ich habe beim Essen Schwierigkeiten°. Warum halten alle Deutschen immer die Gabel° in der linken Hand? Das ist einfach noch zu schwer für mich. Aber ich übe°, und eines Tages kann ich auch so essen wie die meisten Deutschen: die Gabel in der linken Hand und das Messer° in der rechten."

---

die Sitte *custom;* **anders als** *different than;* **ob . . . nicht** *whether I should hold out my hand first or not;* **vergesse ich es ganz** *I forget it completely;* **beim Siezen und Duzen** *when saying* **Sie** *or* **du;** **Schwierigkeiten** *difficulties;* **die Gabel** *fork;* **üben** *to practice;* **das Messer** *knife*

„Das Essen ist hier auch anders. Die meisten Leute haben ein grosses, warmes Essen zu Mittag und essen dann kalt zu Abend°. Wir machen das umgekehrt°! Und alle grillen hier. Ich finde das Wort ‚Grillfest' lustig. Wiebkes Vater sagt, es kommt aus Amerika! Und hier gibt es so viele Wurstsorten°. Man sagt, über 1 400!"

„Ja, und ich finde es prima, dass die Leute hier viel tanzen. Die Schüler besuchen alle eine Tanzschule—das ist anders als bei uns. Hier lernt man nicht nur Disko-Tanzen, sondern man lernt auch die traditionellen Tänze, den Walzer, den Tango und so weiter°. Und das finde ich prima."

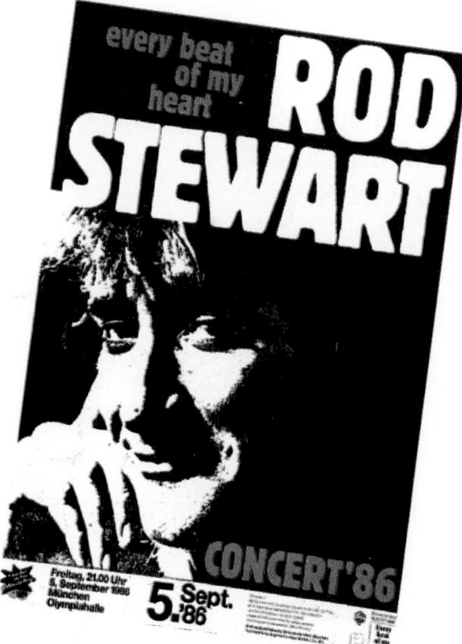

„Nur ist die Musik hier nicht viel anders als zu Hause. Ihr kennt hier alle unsere amerikanischen Gruppen, und ihr kennt die Texte oft besser als wir—und sogar° in englisch. Ich finde aber viele deutsche Gruppen und Sänger auch toll, die Spider Murphy Gang, den Maffay und besonders° die Nina Hagen."

„Und wenn man hier auf eine Party geht, bringt man immer etwas mit°, Blumen°, Schokolade. Wenn Wiebkes Eltern zu einer Party gehen, bringen sie oft eine Flasche Wein mit. Ich finde, dass die meisten Leute hier Blumen gern haben, und man kauft hier viel mehr Blumen als bei uns."

---

zu Abend *in the evening;* **umgekehrt** *the other way around;* **die Wurstsorten** *types of cold cuts and sausages;* **und so weiter** *and so forth;* **sogar** *even;* **besonders** *especially;* **mit** *along;* **die Blumen** *flowers*

Übung • Stimmt! Stimmt nicht!

1. Peter gibt immer zuerst die Hand. Stimmt nicht!
2. Er muss „Sie" zum Lehrer sagen. Stimmt!
3. Die Deutschen essen mit der Gabel in der rechten Hand. Stimmt nicht!
4. Peter möchte nie lernen, wie die Deutschen essen. Stimmt nicht!
5. Die Deutschen essen gern gegrillte Würste. Stimmt!
6. Die jungen Deutschen lernen die traditionellen Tänze nicht. Stimmt nicht!
7. In Deutschland hört man viel amerikanische Musik. Stimmt!
8. Die jungen Deutschen kennen die Texte nicht. Stimmt nicht!
9. Die Deutschen haben Blumen gern. Stimmt!
10. Wenn man eingeladen ist, bringt man immer etwas mit. Stimmt!

Ein Rezept:

Warmer Kartoffelsalat

(für 6–8 Personen)

Zutaten:

9 mittelgrosse Kartoffeln
½ Pfund Speck
1 Zwiebel
¼ Tasse Essig
¼ Tasse Wasser
½ Teelöffel Salz
¼ Teelöffel Pfeffer

1. Die Kartoffeln waschen und kochen.

2. Das Wasser abgiessen.

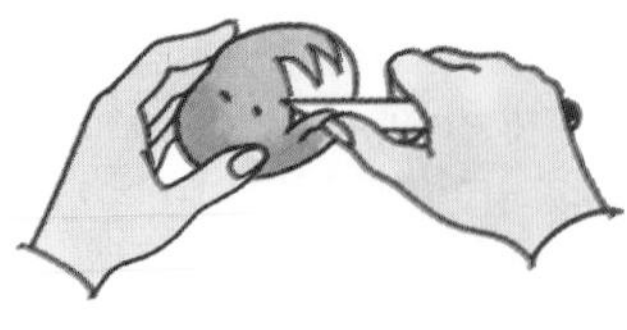

3. Die Kartoffeln schälen.

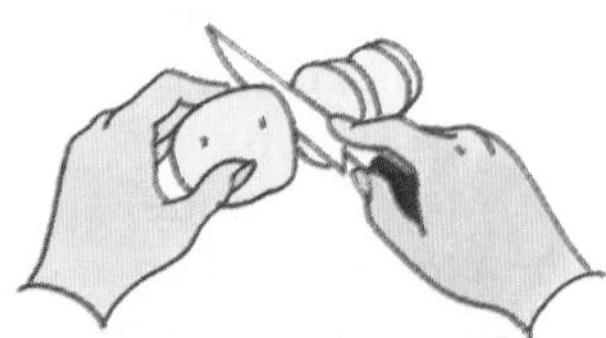

4. In Scheiben schneiden.

5. Die Kartoffelscheiben in eine Schüssel geben.

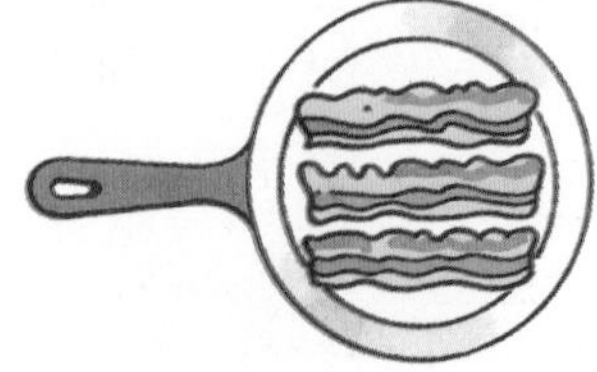

6. Den Speck bräunen.

7. Auf Papier legen.

8. In kleine Stücke schneiden.

9. Die Zwiebel in kleine Stücke schneiden.

10. Die Zwiebel im Fett vom Speck bräunen.

11. Essig, Wasser, Salz und Pfeffer zugeben. 1-2 Minuten rühren.

12. Die heisse Sosse über die Kartoffeln giessen.

13. Den Speck dazugeben.

14. Alles gut mischen.

Guten Appetit!

Übung • Jetzt bist du dran!

Before you attempt to make the German potato salad, make sure you can follow all the steps correctly. In this list, the steps are all mixed up. Place them in the proper order by referring to the pictures and captions.

Add the bacon pieces to the salad.	13	10	*Brown the onions in bacon fat.*
Drain the bacon on paper towels.	7	5	*Put the potato slices in a bowl.*
Peel the potatoes.	3	4	*Cut the potatoes in slices.*
Wash and boil the potatoes.	1	12	*Pour the hot sauce over the potatoes.*
Cut the onion into small pieces.	9	8	*Cut the bacon in small pieces.*
Brown the bacon.	6	14	*Mix everything.*
Add vinegar, water, salt and pepper. Stir.	11	2	*Drain the potatoes.*

KAPITEL 10

KAPITEL 10 Gehen wir aus!

Scope and Sequence

	BASIC MATERIAL	COMMUNICATIVE FUNCTIONS
SECTION A	**Was macht unsere Jugend? (A1)** **Hast du etwas vor, Sabine? (A6)** **Wie geht's? (A8)**	**Exchanging information** • Discussing what you do in your free time **Socializing** • Asking and responding to "How are you?" **Persuading** • Making suggestions for going out
SECTION B	**Konzert oder Kino? (B1)** **Was für Filme siehst du gern? (B3)** **Was für Filme sind das? (B7)**	**Expressing attitudes** • Making choices about where to go • Discussing types of movies **Expressing feelings** • Expressing preference or indifference
SECTION C	**Was für Filme mögt ihr? (C1)**	**Expressing feelings and emotions** • Expressing whether you like or dislike someone or something
SECTION D	**Was hast du gestern abend gemacht? (D1)**	**Exchanging information** • Talking about what you did
TRY YOUR SKILLS	Pronunciation /e:/, /o:/, /u:/, /l/, /ɔ/ (review) Letter-sound correspondences **j, z, ng** Dictation	
ZUM LESEN	**Die Prominenten kommen auch nach Deutschland** (young people talk about their favorite stars and groups) **Stars, die heute beliebt sind** (favorite German rock singers)	

WRITING A variety of controlled and open-ended writing activities appear in the Pupil's Edition. The Teacher's Notes identify other activities suitable for writing practice and suggest additional writing activities.

COOPERATIVE LEARNING Many of the activities in the Pupil's Edition lend themselves to cooperative learning. The Teacher's Notes explain some of the many instances where this teaching strategy can be particularly effective. For guidelines on how to use cooperative learning, see page T13.

GRAMMAR	CULTURE	RE–ENTRY
The verbs **können** and **wollen** (A14) The verbs **fahren, radfahren,** and **ausgehen** (A17)	Young people going out	Talking about interests Sports and activities; when and how often Greetings Inviting someone Expressing enthusiasm Suggestions/preferences
The verb **anfangen** (B5) **welcher, welche, welches,** nom. and acc. (B14) **was für ein?** nominative and accusative case (B17)	Concerts and movies in Germany Going to the movies in Germany	Expressing likes, dislikes, and preferences Expressing enthusiasm or regret Time
The verb **mögen** (C5)	Movie and concert ads	Expressing (dis)agreement Extending an invitation; accepting or declining
The conversational past tense (D3)		Verbs Sports and activities **haben, sein** (pres. tense) Days of the week
Recombining communicative functions, grammar, and vocabulary		
Reading for practice and pleasure		

TEACHER–PREPARED MATERIALS

Section A Flashcards of activities and frequency expressions in A3; humorous pictures (responses to **Wie geht's?**); sports and activities pictures; page from a weekly planner

Section B Movie, theater, and concert ads; cards with names of movies, singers, or groups; toy clock

Section C Flashcards of adjectives in C10

Section D Flashcards of verbs, past participles, sports and activities

UNIT RESOURCES

Übungsheft, Unit 10
Arbeitsheft, Unit 10
Unit 10 Cassettes
Transparencies 25–27
Quizzes 25–28
Unit 10 Test

OBJECTIVES **To exchange information:** discuss what you do in your free time; **to persuade:** make and accept or reject suggestions for going out

CULTURAL BACKGROUND In Germany, many students finish their schooling at the age of fifteen and go into training programs that prepare them for jobs in various trades. Other young people finish secondary school at age sixteen and enter training programs for semiprofessional jobs in such areas as banking, insurance, and industry. Still other young people attend the **Gymnasium,** an academic secondary school with a college-preparatory program.

Apprentices, **Lehrlinge,** have more time and money at their disposal than high school students do. High school students have to depend on allowances, gifts from relatives, and income from occasional small jobs. Apprentices attend more sports events; high school students are more likely to attend a play, a concert of classical music, or an opera. Both groups love movies and rock concerts.

MOTIVATING ACTIVITY Before starting Section A, have the students think about what they do when they go out. Where do they go? What do they do? Do they go in pairs or in groups? Do they always go around with the same people or does it vary? Are these friends from school? From work? From the neighborhood? Write the answers briefly on the board or on an overhead transparency.

A1

Was macht unsere Jugend? 

Before you introduce the new text, clarify the following three terms, which are often mixed up or misspelled:

jung	*young*
der Junge, -n	*boy, young man*
die Jugend	*youth, young people* (as a group)
der Jugendliche, -n	*young person, teenager*

Also introduce some of the new vocabulary or concepts, in particular **Zeit verbringen, Sportveranstaltung, zusammen, Kino,** and **Stadtbummel,** by modeling them and acting them out. For example, to illustrate **Stadtbummel,** you might say:

> Wir gehen in die Stadt und gehen langsam durch die Stadt. Wir bummeln. Wir machen einen Stadtbummel. Wir sehen uns die Schaufenster an von Boutiquen und Geschenkläden. Wir bummeln weiter. Wir gehen in eine Imbiss-Stube oder ein Café. Ein Stadtbummel ist prima und kostet nicht viel.

Then introduce the text by playing the cassette or reading the text aloud. Take the material section by section and have the students listen with their books open or closed according to the level of difficulty of that section. Stop to ask comprehension questions after the introductory part and after each interview; for example:

> Was fragt die Reporterin? *(introduction)*
> Wohnt sie in der Stadt oder in einem Vorort? *(first interview)*
> Wie gross ist die Clique? *(second interview)*
> Hat sie viele Freunde oder Freundinnen? *(third interview)*
> Was meint er mit „Wir machen nur einen Stadtbummel"? *(fourth interview)*

When you have gone through the entire selection, have the students draw up a chart with the possible activities running vertically and the interview subjects running horizontally. Compare; who shares interests?

A2

Übung • Rollenspiel

Have the students take turns playing the roles of the interviewer and the four students. First each student may read the text in response to the question. Then see how much they can remember without referring to the textbook. The interviewer should inject some questions and comments: **Wirklich? Macht das Spass? Wie oft machst du das?** You might want to assign sections to individual students and give them time to prepare.

A3

Übung • Frag deine Klassenkameraden!

This activity gives the students many choices. You might want to have them work in small groups first, asking each other the questions and practicing answers. Then the activity could be done with the whole class. At this point, more spontaneous answers should be expected.

SLOWER–PACED LEARNING Work on the questions individually, eliciting a number of different responses for each one. **Was machst du? Ich gehe aus. Ich gehe ins Kino. Ich besuche Freunde.**

A4

Übung • Und du? Wie steht's mit dir?

This activity can also be done as a written exercise. Have the students write the answers in paragraph form. Remind them to vary the word order, not to start every sentence with the subject.

A5

Übung • Klasseninterview

Prepare questionnaires as shown in the textbook or have the students prepare them. The students should work in groups of three to five. They can take turns asking the questions, but all students should write down the information for each person who answers. A representative from each group should then report to the class.

A6

HAST DU ETWAS VOR, SABINE?

In general, young people in Germany tend to do things in groups. They often have a "clique" of several friends with whom they like to do things. German teenagers do date, but it is not as commonplace as in the United States, nor does dating start at as young an age. When young people go out together in Germany, the boy does not automatically pay. It is usually understood that it is "Dutch treat."

Play the cassette or read the dialog as the students listen with their books closed. Follow the usual procedure. When the students have role-played the parts and are comfortable with the exchange, have them ad-lib the situation without any script. Give them some guidance, such as:

> (name of a student), ask whether (name of another student) already has plans.
> (second student), say that you have no plans.
> (first student), make some suggestions.
> (second student), react to the suggestions.

A7 Übung • Jetzt fragst du!

SLOWER–PACED LEARNING Elicit various possibilities for what to do and list them on the board or an overhead transparency. Ask each question in combination with several suggestions before going on to the next: **Möchtest du ins Theater gehen? Möchtest du schwimmen gehen? Möchtest du . . . ?**

A8 WIE GEHT'S?

Present and model these responses to the question **„Wie geht's?"** Act out the response and have the students guess it. Then have the students act the responses out for their classmates to guess.

A9 WIE SAGT MAN DAS?

You may want to tell the students how to ask "And how are *you*?" after they have answered. They should learn **Und wie geht's dir? Und wie geht's euch? Und wie geht's Ihnen?** only lexically. They will learn more dative case forms later.

A10 Übung • Grüss dich! Wie geht's?

CHALLENGE Try to expand the dialog by having the students give more information: **Wie geht's? — Prima! Ich habe heute keine Hausaufgaben!** or **Schlecht! — Warum? — Ich habe eine Vier in Mathe.**

A11 WIE SAGT MAN DAS?

The students should go back to A6 and pick out all the suggestions in the text. Have them write the suggestions in their notebooks.

A12 Übung • Und was willst du tun?

The students should work in groups. Have them start off with each one listing what he or she would like to do. Then have them practice the dialogs as directed.

CHALLENGE The students keep the dialog going as long as possible by not agreeing immediately. They have to come up with different suggestions and excuses.

A13 Übung • Ja, gehen wir . . . !

Bring in pictures that suggest various activities, or have the students do so. As you or a student holds up a picture for the class to see, the students take turns making "let's" suggestions based on the picture.

A14 ERKLÄRUNG

Remind the students of the verb **sollen.** Let them discover similarities in form and usage with **können** and **wollen.** How are **können** and **wollen** different from **sollen?**

Note: There will be positive transfer from English to German in the case of **können,** especially with **kann,** and to a lesser extent with **kannst;** there will be strong negative transfer from English in the case of **wollen,** in particular with the forms **will** and **willst.** The students will want to use **will** for *will* rather than *want.* Thus, in the case of **können,** the plural forms are more difficult for the students, but in the case of **wollen,** the singular forms are more difficult and will require more practice in skill-getting and skill-using activities.

A 15 Übung • Was willst du tun? Was kannst du machen? 

As a variation, for each numbered item, pick one activity pictured and do the following exchanges based on it:

1. A: Was willst du tun? Willst du ins Kino gehen?
B: Ja, gehen wir ins Kino! *[or]* Nein, lieber nicht.
2. A: Kannst du Tennis spielen?
B: Ja, ich kann Tennis spielen. Spielen wir doch Tennis! *[or]* Nein, ich kann nicht Tennis spielen.

A 16 Schreibübung • Versteckte Sätze

CHALLENGE Expand this activity by adding vocabulary from previous units to the last two columns: **zu Hause bleiben, Hausaufgaben machen, eine Party haben, einkaufen gehen.** This also gives practice with verb phrases. Personalizing the names in the first column by using the names of class members will also add interest.

A 17 ERKLÄRUNG

Point out that **fahren** means both *to drive,* literally, and *to go* (in a vehicle, as a passenger). Write these sentences on the board and discuss their English equivalents with the students:

Ich fahre in die Stadt.	*I'm going into town.*
	I'm driving into town.
Ich fahre mit dem Bus.	*I'm going by bus.*
	I'm taking the bus.

Fahren and **radfahren** have a stem-vowel change in the **du-** and the **er/sie-** forms but not in the singular command form. Ask the students if they can think of another verb of this kind **(einladen)**.

A 18 Übung • Was macht ihr jetzt?

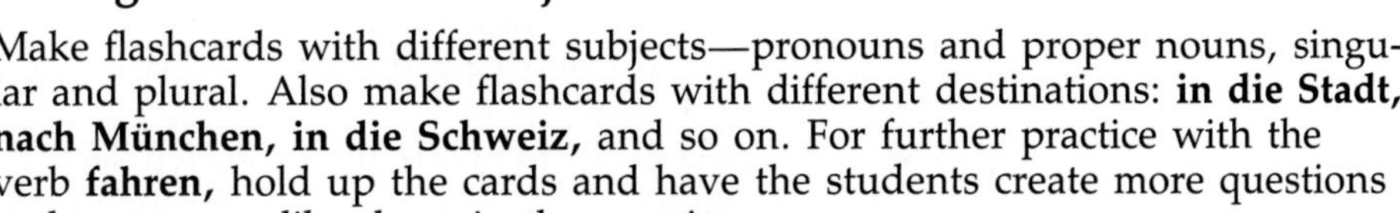

Make flashcards with different subjects—pronouns and proper nouns, singular and plural. Also make flashcards with different destinations: **in die Stadt, nach München, in die Schweiz,** and so on. For further practice with the verb **fahren,** hold up the cards and have the students create more questions and statements like those in the exercise.

A 19 Übung • Was machst du jetzt?

SLOWER–PACED LEARNING Use the subject cards prepared for A18 to give more practice with the verb **radfahren.**

A 20 Übung • Wann? Wie oft?

CHALLENGE Expand the activity by adding the line: **Und was macht sie?** The students supply a response, such as **Sie geht in eine Disko.**

A21–25

A 21 Übung • Was können wir tun?

SLOWER–PACED LEARNING Prepare for this exercise by having the students make some suggestions using **können: Ich kann ins Kino gehen** or **Wir können radfahren.** You may want to write these on the board. One student then reads the **ich kann/wir können** suggestion, while another student uses the command form: **Ja, geh doch ins Kino!** or **Geht doch ins Kino!** Have the students refer to the following activity for ideas, if necessary.

A 22 Übung • Mix-Match

Make this a class discussion or have the students work in groups of three to five. They need not limit themselves to the suggestions and excuses listed.

A 23 Übung • Was sagst du? Was sagen deine Mitschüler?

You may first read these questions to the class and have them write responses. Then go over the results with the whole class.

CHALLENGE Have the students make up more questions to ask each other. Divide the class into two teams. Have one team ask the questions, while the other team answers. The two teams should alternate at this.

A 24 Übung • Partnerarbeit: Hast du was vor?

This activity may also be used for dictation practice. Have the students draw a calendar page as shown in the exercise or provide one yourself. Dictate activities and times for various days, mentioning the date also. Have the students write the information correctly on the calendar page.

A 25 Übung • Hör gut zu!

You will hear ten brief statements. Each one is followed by a response. Listen carefully and decide whether the response is appropriate or not. For example, you hear, **Du, der Jochen geht nie aus. Er bleibt immer nur zu Hause und liest!** followed by the response **— Das find' ich blöd. So langweilig!** You place your check mark in the row labeled *appropriate*, because the second statement follows logically—it makes sense in light of the first one. Let's begin. **Fangen wir an!**

1. Die Jungen und Mädchen gehen ins Kino, ins Konzert und zu Sportveranstaltungen. — Du hast recht, sie haben keine Interessen; sie sind Freizeitmuffel. *not appropriate*
2. Sag mal, wie verbringst du deine Freizeit? — Danke, ich habe schon was vor. *not appropriate*
3. Ich gehe meistens am Wochenende ins Kino. Ich sehe Filme gern. — Ich auch. Besonders, wenn sie gut und spannend sind. *appropriate*
4. Wie verbringst du deine Freizeit? Gehst du oft aus, ins Kino, ins Konzert? — Nein, lieber nicht. Ich habe heute keine Zeit. *not appropriate*
5. Komm, wir gehen ins Kino! Es gibt einen super Film im Tivoli, einen Action-Film. — Mensch, toll! Das ist eine prima Idee! *appropriate*
6. Gehst du denn immer aus? Ins Kino? Ins Konzert? — Du, ich bin auch gern zu Hause. Ich habe viele Bücher und lese gern. *appropriate*

7. Ich gehe gern mit Freunden in die Stadt. Wir machen einen Stadtbummel, gehen in ein Café und essen Eis. — Gehst du gern mit Freunden in die Stadt? *not appropriate*
8. Es ist heute so langweilig. Alle haben am Wochenende etwas vor. — Dann können wir zusammen etwas tun. Was meinst du? *appropriate*
9. Du, ich will am Wochenende in ein Konzert gehen. Möchtest du mitgehen? — Das passt prima. Ich habe nichts vor. *appropriate*
10. Ich gehe Freunde besuchen; wir gehen ins Kino, wir spielen Tennis, wir gehen in Konzerte. — Ach, wie langweilig! Könnt ihr nicht zusammen etwas tun? *not appropriate*

Now check your answers. *Read each item again and give the correct answer.*

A 26 Schreibübung • Was macht Ulrike heute?

For variation, have the students make up questions based on this paragraph. Have them write both the questions and the answers.

A 27 Schreibübung • Was hast du vor?

Have the students work individually to write the conversations. Then they may pair off and correct each other's work, eventually producing a joint effort. You could then call on pairs of students to present some of the conversations to the class.

OBJECTIVES **To express attitudes and opinions:** make choices about where to go when you go out; express preference or indifference

CULTURAL BACKGROUND American movies and movie stars as well as American music groups and performers are well known and popular in German-speaking countries. Although tickets for rock concerts are very expensive, the concerts are well attended, indeed often sold out. Movie tickets come in different price ranges, depending on where you sit. The first few rows are the least expensive. In cities the large movie theaters have been divided into several smaller ones, as in the United States.

MOTIVATING ACTIVITY Ask the students to name some films, actors and actresses, music groups, and performers from German-speaking countries. Have they seen any German films, and if so, were they actually shown in the original German, with subtitles, or were they dubbed? Do the groups and performers sing in German or in English? If any of the students have album covers with song texts in German, have them bring those in to share with the class.

Konzert oder Kino? 

Ask the students, in German, if they recognize any of the performers listed on the concert schedule. Which ones do they like? Which ones don't they like? Point out that starting times are listed according to the 24-hour system.

Play the cassette or read the dialog aloud as the students listen with their books open, looking at the newspaper listing. Break the dialog into two parts. Ask such questions as:

Welche Gruppe hat Sabine am liebsten?
Warum gehen sie nicht ins Konzert?
Was meint ihr, ist Sabine sehr traurig, dass sie nicht ins Konzert gehen?

Have the students read the conversation as given in the book and then do it again, substituting their own preferences as to music groups and their own curfew times.

B2 Übung • Und du? Wie steht's mit dir?

First go through the questions with the whole class. The students may need help pronouncing American names in German. Then you could have them work in groups of three to five. They should ask one another the questions and record the results to share with the class.

CHALLENGE Have the students, this time working *without* scripts, practice the dialog in B1. They should substitute their own favorite singers and groups.

B3 WAS FÜR FILME SIEHST DU GERN?

Explain that titles of American movies may be rendered quite differently in German. See if the students can figure out the English titles of the movies listed: ***Der Mann mit zwei Gehirnen*** *(The Man with Two Brains);* ***Zwölf Uhr mittags*** *(High Noon);* ***Jenseits von Afrika*** *(Out of Africa);* ***Piranha 2; Das Boot*** *(The Boat).*

Germans have long had a fascination with the American West. The famous German writer Karl May wrote many novels about the American West, and Winnetou and Old Sure Hand are familiar characters to generations of Germans. Numerous movies have been made based on these stories.

Introduce the dialog by playing the cassette or reading the text aloud as the students listen. The students should go on to practice the dialog in pairs. As soon as they have absorbed the phrases, have them practice it substituting film titles and genres of their own choosing, making an error similar to the one Stefan makes. Also have them read and interpret the movie listings:

Wo spielt *Zwölf Uhr mittags?*
Wie oft spielt *Der Mann mit zwei Gehirnen?* Wann fängt der Film an?
Es ist 17 Uhr und ich möchte ins Kino gehen. — Was kann ich sehen?

B4 Übung • Wie steht's mit dir?

To expand this activity, have the students bring in some American movie timetables. Have them say what movie is playing where and have them give the starting times, both as written and according to the 24-hour system.

B5 ERKLÄRUNG

Help the students discover where the vowel changes occur. What other verbs have they learned with these vowel changes? **(einladen, fahren,** and **radfahren)**

B6 Übung • Frag deine Klassenkameraden!

SLOWER–PACED LEARNING Prepare flashcards with different subjects: **Ich, du, der Film, wir, ihr, die Ferien.** Also prepare cards with various time expressions: **jetzt, am Montag, im Sommer.** Hold up the cards and have the students create statements, questions, and commands: **Du fängst jetzt an. Fängst du jetzt an? Fang doch jetzt an!**

B7 WAS FÜR FILME SIND DAS?

This basic material provides students with the vocabulary to talk about their preferences in types of movies. As an additional motivating activity, have them name some current films and say what type of film each one is: ***Beverly Hills Cop* mit Eddie Murphy ist eine Komödie.** This could be expanded, with another student disagreeing: **Ach, Quatsch, das ist ein Action-Film!** The first student could then agree or disagree: **Stimmt! Du hast recht!** or **Stimmt nicht!**

B8 Übung • Jetzt bist du dran

Students should take turns asking each other what style of film each of the ones shown in B7 is. See how many they can remember without looking. Then, referring to the poster on page 280, ask them which film is playing at each theater and what type of film it is. This could also be done in pairs or in small groups of three to five.

B9 Übung • Kennst du den Film?

As an expansion, have one student write the different genres of film on the board. As the other students ask about films, he or she writes the name of the film in the appropriate column.

B10 WIE SAGT MAN DAS?

Remind the students that they learned to express preference when they were talking about sports and hobbies. To refresh their memories, ask some questions; for example:

> Was spielst du besonders gern?
> Was machst du am liebsten?
> Was sammelst du lieber, Briefmarken oder Münzen?
> Was isst du besonders gern?
> Was trinkst du lieber, Milch oder Saft?

B11 Übung • Was willst du tun?

SLOWER–PACED LEARNING Do this exercise with the entire class in preparation for working in smaller groups. Refer to the posters on pages 279 and 280. Ask members of the class what they would like to do. If they need help, give them some choices or make suggestions: **Was siehst du lieber, den Western oder die Komödie mit Steve Martin? / Ich sehe Western gern. Du auch?**

B12 Übung • Was hast du lieber?

To expand this activity and review vocabulary, have the students write down two each of their favorite sports, hobbies, foods, drinks, and school subjects on cards. Then they should hold up the cards and ask a classmate: **Was spielst du lieber? Was isst du lieber?** and so on. (For the school subjects, make it **Was hast du lieber?**)

KAPITEL 10

B13–19

B 13 WIE SAGT MAN DAS?

Have the students look at the basic materials on pages 279 and 280. Tell them to pick out examples of **welch-** and **was für ein** and to examine the context in which they are used. Ask the students why they think **welch-** has different endings.

B 14 ERKLÄRUNG

Make students aware of the similarities of these endings to those of the definite and indefinite articles. Have them write lists with all three:

Nominative			*Accusative*		
der	ein	welch**er**	de**n**	ein**en**	welch**en**
di**e**	ein**e**	welch**e**	di**e**	ein**e**	welch**e**
da**s**	ein	welch**es**	da**s**	ein	welch**es**
di**e**	—	welch**e**	di**e**	—	welch**e**

B 15 Schreibübung • Welche Form von welch-?

Look at the statements and questions with the students. Ask them to determine whether the information asked for is in the nominative or accusative case. How does this influence the ending on **welch-?** As a variation, have the students write out the questions and then work with a partner, one student reading the question and the other reading the answer. The questions could also be used for dictation.

B 16 Schreibübung • Schreib Fragen!

To expand this exercise, have the students work in pairs and ask each other the questions they have written. The student answering may refer to the posters on pages 279 and 280.

B 17 ERKLÄRUNG

SLOWER–PACED LEARNING As preparation, review the indefinite articles. Hold up vocabulary cards and ask questions designed to elicit forms of the indefinite article, such as:

— Was kaufst du? (einen Bleistift, eine Kassette, . . .)
— Was brauchst du? (einen Bleistift, eine Kassette, . . .)
— Wer ist das? (Das ist ein Freund, eine Klassenkameradin, . . .)

B 18 Schreibübung • Welche Form von was für ein?

Look at the statements and questions with the students. Ask them to determine whether the information asked for is in the nominative or the accusative case. How does this influence the ending on **was für ein?** As a variation, have the students write out the questions and then work with a partner, one student reading the question and the other reading the answer. The questions could also be used for dictation.

B 19 Schreibübung • Schreib Fragen!

To expand this activity, have the students work in pairs and ask each other the questions they have written. The student who answers may refer to the posters on pages 279 and 280.

ANSWERS

2. 1. Was für eine Gruppe ist Sunsplash?
   2. Welche Gruppe hört ihr heute?
   3. Was für ein Konzert gibt es in der Olympiahalle?
   4. Welches Konzert hört ihr?
   5. Was für Filme sind *Zwölf Uhr mittags* und *Rio Bravo*?
   6. Was für einen Film siehst du um 19 Uhr?

B 20 **Ein wenig Landeskunde**

German film in recent years has become much more widely known. Have the students look in newspapers and magazines and bring in the names of German films, filmmakers, and stars—also articles about them, if available. Do a bulletin board on German film.

SECTION C

OBJECTIVES **To express feelings and emotions:** express whether you like or dislike someone or something

CULTURAL BACKGROUND Germans enjoy the same types of movies that Americans do. Almost all "big" movies are shown in Germany and are very popular. Most Germans have a view of the United States formed by American television programs shown on German television and by the many American films playing in German movie theaters. With this in consideration, ask your students how they think Germans might view America and Americans. Can they get an accurate picture from television and the movies? How do your students picture Germany and Germans? What formed their opinions, aside from what they have learned from you and from this textbook?

MOTIVATING ACTIVITY This section talks about tastes in films. Discuss likes and dislikes briefly in English. Ask the students what kinds of films they like and dislike and have them give reasons.

C1 **Was für Filme mögt ihr?** 

Work with the ways of saying *like* in German. Put a conversation like the following on the board or on an overhead transparency:

A: Möchtest du einen Abenteuerfilm sehen?
B: Ja, ich mag Abenteuerfilme. Ich sehe sie gern.
A: Magst du Robert Redford und Meryl Streep?
B: Ja, ich mag sie gern.
A: *Jenseits von Afrika* spielt im Roxi. Möchtest du ihn sehen?
B: Ja, gern.

Discuss the difference between *like* and *would like* in English. Which is more general in its applications? More specific? Ask the students which word, **mag** or **möchte,** corresponds to the idea of "would like."

Introduce the interviews by playing the cassette or reading the interviews aloud, one at a time. The students will probably get the gist of the interviews without trouble, since there is no new vocabulary except for **grausam** and **hassen.** Ask such questions as the following:

— Warum möchte der Junge den Film *Der Mann mit zwei Gehirnen* sehen?
— Warum sagt Stefan: „Wirklich? Sie mögen Science-fiction-Filme?"
— Warum mögen die Mädchen keine Kriegsfilme?

Then have the students, working in groups of three to five (some of the students can double up on parts), act out the interviews. Ask them to be as expressive as possible, registering an intonation of surprise upon learning that the teacher likes science fiction films and of distaste at the thought of war films: . . . ***grausam!* Ich *hasse* sie!**

C2 Übung • Beanworte die Fragen!

SLOWER–PACED LEARNING Have the students respond in short-answer form first; then have them answer in complete sentences:

1. Welchen Film sieht der Schüler heute? — *Den Mann mit zwei Gehirnen.* Er sieht *Den Mann mit zwei Gehirnen.*
2. Wie ist der Film? — Lustig. Der Film ist lustig.

C3 WIE SAGT MAN DAS?

Point out to the students that the phrase **gern haben** and the verb **mögen** both mean *to like*. The phrase **gern mögen** also means *to like* but is a little stronger. Have the students look at the dialogs in C1 and pick out the sentences expressing liking and disliking.

C4 Übung • Und du?

For expansion, have the students write more questions asking about different groups, stars, specific movies, and types of movies. Go around the class, giving each student the opportunity to ask you or a classmate one of the questions.

C5 ERKLÄRUNG

Ask the students to point out changes in the forms of **mögen.** What other verbs have they learned that follow the same or a similar pattern? **(sollen, wollen, können)** What is the same about **sollen?** (no ending in the **ich-** and **er/sie-**forms) What is different? (no stem-vowel change in the singular as in **mögen, wollen,** and **können**)

Practice a few sentences with **mögen** and another infinitive: **Warum mögt ihr nicht ins Kino gehen? — Wir mögen diesen Film nicht sehen. Er ist zu grausam.** Note that when **mögen** is used with another infinitive, it is usually in negative sentences.

C6 Übung • Alle mögen die Gruppe

To expand this activity and give the students further practice with the forms of **mögen,** add the line: **Wirklich? Ihr mögt die Gruppe?**

C7 Übung • Keiner mag den Film

CHALLENGE Have the students try to add a further response to the first exchange. They may use **mögen** or **nicht mögen** in the response.

A: Geht ihr in *Piranha 2?*
B: Nein, wir mögen den Film nicht.
A: Ich mag den Film auch nicht. *[or]*
Wirklich? Ich mag Action-Filme gern.

C8 Übung • Versteckte Sätze

For expansion, you could have the students do one or more of the following:

1. Add an item in the third column.
2. Add an appropriate infinitive at the end of each sentence they form: **Stefan mag die Gruppe aus England besonders gern hören.**
3. Personalize column one with the names of class members. When a statement is made about that student, he or she should respond, either agreeing or disagreeing with the statement: **Anne mag den Falco nicht. — Das stimmt. Ich mag ihn nicht.** or **— Das stimmt nicht. Ich mag ihn gern.**

C9 Übung • Was magst du am liebsten? 

Mention that **Lieblings-** is a noun prefix meaning *favorite.* A noun prefix can be combined with many nouns. Have the students try to write this activity on their own. Then go over it together in class. Write the nouns in each sentence on the board; then combine those nouns with **Lieblings-: die Stadt — meine Lieblingsstadt.**

CHALLENGE Have the students write a list of their own favorites: **Mein Lieblingssport ist . . . , mein Lieblingsfach ist . . .**

ANSWERS

1. München ist meine Lieblingsstadt. Welche Stadt magst du am liebsten?
2. Die Gruppe Supercharge ist meine Lieblingsgruppe. Welche Gruppe magst du am liebsten?
3. Café Krone ist mein Lieblingscafé. Welches Café magst du am liebsten?
4. Horrorfilme sind meine Lieblingsfilme. Was für Filme magst du am liebsten?
5. Mau-Mau ist mein Lieblingskartenspiel. Welches Kartenspiel magst du am liebsten?

C10 Übung • Wie findest du die Gruppe? den Film? das Konzert?

This exercise gives the students further opportunity to express their own likes, dislikes, and preferences. They may work in pairs or in small groups of three to five students. They should ask one another how they like various groups, movies, and stars. They may refer to pages 279, 280, and 281 if necessary. They may also expand the exchange by responding to the answer: **Du magst die Scorpions nicht? Wie kannst du das sagen? Die Scorpions sind toll!**

C11 Übung • Umfrage

Take a poll in the class. Have one student write the names of various groups, films, and stars on the board, as dictated by the class. Then the student asks in German how many like each one and how many dislike each one, counting the show of hands and recording the results next to each name. Add up the results and have the students write lists entitled **Unsere Lieblingsgruppen, Unsere Lieblingsfilme,** and **Unsere Lieblingsstars.** An attractive poster could be made for the bulletin board.

C12 Übung • Hör gut zu!

You will hear ten statements, some expressing likes and some expressing dislikes. For example, you hear, **Ich sehe Filme gern, auch wenn sie schlecht sind.** You place your check mark in the row labeled *likes*. Let's begin. **Fangen wir an!**

1. Science-fiction-Filme sind spannend. Ich finde sie interessant, und ich mag sie gern. *likes*
2. Kriegsfilme sind meistens traurig und oft grausam. Ich hasse sie. *dislikes*
3. Abenteuerfilme sind meine Lieblingsfilme. *likes*
4. Western sind spannend. Ich sehe sie am liebsten. *likes*
5. Horrorfilme mag ich nicht. Ich finde sie blöd. *dislikes*
6. Ich möchte gern einen Film sehen, einen Liebesfilm, aber ich mag die Schauspieler nicht. *dislikes*
7. Action-Filme mag ich am liebsten. Sie sind spannend und phantasievoll. *likes*
8. Ich finde Liebesfilme blöd. Sie können oft gut sein, aber ich finde sie langweilig und oft schmalzig. *dislikes*
9. Am liebsten mag ich Film-Komödien. Sie sind lustig. *likes*
10. Western können oft so schön sein — aber ich finde sie dumm. Sie können manchmal brutal sein. *dislikes*

Now check your answers. *Read each item again and give the correct answer.*

C13 Schreibübung • Schreib zwei Dialoge!

SLOWER–PACED LEARNING Do this exercise orally in class first. Say each direction and have the students volunteer what should be said: **Ein Freund** (or insert a student's name) **fragt, ob du ins Kino gehen willst.** A student supplies: **Willst du ins Kino gehen?** As a variation, do this as a directed dialog:

(student's name), frag (another student's name), ob er ins Kino gehen will.
(second student), sag (first student), dass du gern gehst.
(first student), frag ihn/sie, was er/sie sehen möchte.
(second student), sag (first student), dass du *Jenseits von Afrika* gern sehen möchtest!
(first student), sag (second student), dass du den Film auch gern siehst!

C14 Übung • Und du?

Have the students work in pairs or in small groups. They should select what they would like to do from the ads and make suggestions to each other, accepting or rejecting each one. They can make excuses; express opinions, likes, dislikes, and preferences; and ask each other for more information—for example, as to where the event is playing or taking place. In the latter case, other students look the information up.

OBJECTIVE **To exchange information:** talk about what you did

CULTURAL BACKGROUND In this section students learn to talk about past events. The most common way to express past time in conversation is to use the **Perfekt** (the conversational past). This is especially true in southern Germany and in Austria and Switzerland. In northern Germany—and in general in more formal situations—the simple past is also heard in conversation. At this point, however, the students will be learning only the conversational past.

MOTIVATING ACTIVITY The students will be learning to express what happened in the past in the context of telling what they did. Ask them to think of the different ways they tell in English what they did. Write them on the board: *What did you do last night? I went to the movies.*

D1 **Was hast du gestern abend gemacht?** 

Play the cassette or read the conversations aloud, one by one, as the students listen with their books open. Reinforce each one immediately with questions. Ask the students to answer in complete sentences, so that they will be forced to use the past tense. Some sample questions follow:

Wann ist Herbert ins Kino gegangen?
Was hat er gesehen?
Ist Karin ins Kino gegangen?
Was hat Wiebke gemacht?

Ask the students to tell you two things they did the night before. These may be invented, because they will have to use the phrases from D1—not all of which will be appropriate.

D2 **Übung • Mix-Match**

After going through this exercise at least once, have the students cover the past participles and see how many sentences they can complete without looking. You could also do this orally. You say the sentence, pausing for the students to supply the past participle. Also have the students write the sentences.

D3 **ERKLÄRUNG**

Have the students look at D3. What do they notice about the verb? How many parts does it have? Which part changes to match the subject? Where does the second part come in the sentence?

Read the explanation of the conversational past tense with the students. Ask them what they notice about the past participles. (some end in **-t,** some in **-en**) Ask them to name the infinitive form for each past participle. How does the infinitive differ from the past participle?

D4 **Übung • Was hast du gestern abend gemacht?** 

In preparation for this activity, have the students supply the appropriate infinitive to go with each word or phrase on the right: **ein Buch lesen, einen prima Film sehen.**

Have the students say the sentences, supplying the correct form of **haben** or **sein** and an appropriate word or phrase from the right. Do this at

D5–8

least once. Then see if the students can say the sentence given only the cues on the right. For additional practice, have the students write these sentences from dictation.

D5 Übung • Wer hat was gemacht?

SLOWER–PACED LEARNING Before doing the exercise as shown, go through the exercise using the same subject for each picture cue: **Wir sind ins Kino gegangen. Wir haben Tennis gespielt. Wir haben Eis gegessen, . . .** Then use the second subject with each picture cue, and so on.

D6 Übung • Hör gut zu!

You will hear ten statements, some of which refer to the present and some to the past. For example, you hear, **Ich habe am Wochenende einen prima Film gesehen.** You place your check mark in the row labeled *conversational past,* because the statement you heard referred to the past. Let's begin. **Fangen wir an!**

1. Ich habe viele Interessen. Ich gehe oft aus, ich habe Hobbys, und ich lese viel. *present*
2. Ich habe meine Freunde besucht, und wir haben Kassetten gehört. *conversational past*
3. Wir haben einen Stadtbummel gemacht und Eis gegessen. *conversational past*
4. Wir gehen oft zusammen aus — in Kinos, in Konzerte, zu Sportveranstaltungen. *present*
5. Wir sind ins Kino gegangen und haben einen prima Film gesehen. *conversational past*
6. Am Wochenende schwimmen wir, und wir spielen Tennis oder Squash. *present*
7. Wir sind in die Stadt gefahren und haben dort etwas gegessen. *conversational past*
8. Wir haben zwei Stunden Tennis gespielt, und dann haben wir eine Limonade getrunken. *conversational past*
9. Ich habe viele Freunde. Ich besuche sie oft; wir hören Musik und spielen Karten. *present*
10. Ich bin zu Hause geblieben und habe ein Buch gelesen. *conversational past*

Now check your answers. *Read each item again and give the correct answer.*

D7 Übung • Und du? Wie steht's mit dir?

The students may need some help in saying what they did. Discuss the activities and write some of the most common ones on the board: **Ich habe ferngesehen. Ich habe gearbeitet.**

D8 Schreibübung • Was hast du gestern abend gemacht?

The students may need to refer to the activities written on the board for the preceding exercise. After they have written the exercise, they should exchange papers. Ask what they did on each day of the week: **Wer hat am Montag einen Film gesehen?** Students holding papers with this activity listed for Monday raise their hands: **Der Peter hat am Montag einen Film gesehen.**

TRY YOUR SKILLS

OBJECTIVE To recombine communicative functions, grammar, and vocabulary

1

Brief an einen Brieffreund

Give the students time to read this letter silently. They should take notes, listing briefly some of the topics Ulli mentions:

— was wir im Sommer machen können
— Kino, Oper, Theater, Gartenpartys, Diskothek, Johannisfeuer
— Freunde und Freundinnen
— was sie machen, wenn sie ausgehen
— Rockkonzerte

After the students have had time to read the letter and take notes, go over the letter together in class. List the topics on the board. Have the students point out any passages they had trouble understanding; before explaining, see if another student can help. Ask comprehension questions:

1. Was gibt es im Juli?
2. Was für Filme mag Ulli am liebsten?
3. Wer ist Uschi?
4. Was macht sie gern? Macht Ulli das auch gern?
5. Was für Partys haben Ulli und seine Freunde im Sommer?
6. Was machen sie alles auf diesen Partys?
7. Geht Ulli gern in die Diskothek?
8. Was gibt es am 21. Juni?
9. Was sagt Ulli über seine Freunde?
10. Was für Karten will Ulli schon kaufen?

2

Übung • Jetzt bist du dran

The students should use the notes they prepared for Skills 1 as a guide. If necessary, have them write more detailed notes in English in preparation for the first part of the activity.

SLOWER–PACED LEARNING Go through the letter with the students. Help them to form simple sentences based on the contents of the letter:

— Mein Brieffreund schreibt, was wir machen können, wenn ich im Juli komme.
— Wir können ins Theater gehen.
— Ulli geht gern in die Diskothek.
— Er hat nette Freunde.
— Ulli möchte jetzt schon Karten für ein Rockkonzert kaufen.
— Im Sommer sind sie schnell ausverkauft.

Write the sentences on the board and have the students copy them in their notebooks.

3

Schreibübung • Was schreibt Ulli? Was schreibst du?

Students should work in groups of three to five to do both parts of this activity. A representative from each group should read the results to the class for comment and correction.

ANSWERS

1. Ulli schreibt, was sie machen können, wenn John im Juli kommt. Es gibt ein internationales Filmfest. Sie können viele interessante Filme sehen. Ulli geht einmal in der Woche ins Kino. Er mag Action-Filme am liebsten. Ullis Schwester Uschi geht lieber in die Oper, aber Ulli findet Opern langweilig. Er geht gern ins Theater. Im Sommer haben sie viele Gartenpartys. Sie grillen, spielen Musik und tanzen. In der Nähe von Ulli ist auch eine Diskothek. Ulli geht gern dorthin. Im Juni gibt es immer ein grosses Johannisfeuer und ein Feuerwerk. Ullis Freunde und Freundinnen sind nett. Sie gehen oft zusammen aus. Sie bummeln durch die Stadt, oder sie gehen in ein Café und diskutieren. Ulli schickt John Prospekte für die Rockkonzerte im Juli. Er kann schon aussuchen, was er hören will. John soll schreiben, und Ulli kauft schon die Karten.

4 Übung • Telefongespräch

Have the students work in pairs. Suggest that they first make a list of possibilities and means of transportation. Then they should discuss what time and how much money they will need.

5 Übung • Klassenprojekte

Try to find ads from German magazines and newspapers to show the students. They may also get ideas from the photos of posters in this unit.

6 Übung • Ratespiel

If possible, bring in some more examples of German titles of American films. Ask the students why they think the titles are sometimes so different in each language.

7 Übung • Was sagen die Jungen und Mädchen? 

SLOWER–PACED LEARNING Have the students draw up lists of ideas on their own, in English, in preparation for working in groups. Then have them work in groups of three to five to develop the conversations.

8 Übung • In der Freizeit

Ask the students what other items they would like to add to the questionnaire and help them with vocabulary if necessary. Have one student write the items on the board and record the results while another student asks questions. A group of students could compile the results and report to the class.

9 Übung • Deine Eltern fragen dich

The students should have fun acting out this scene. Have them prepare in groups of three to five. Select several students (or ask for volunteers) to present the scene to the rest of the class. As a challenge, encourage the students to expand the dialog.

10 Aussprache-, Lese- und Schreibübungen 

1. You will hear a number of words with the long vowel sounds /e:/, /o:/, and /u:/. **Hör zu und wiederhole!**

/e:/ /e:/ Café, Theater, kegeln, gelesen, gesehen
/o:/ /o:/ Kino, Disko
/u:/ /u:/ tun, Jugend, Naturfilm, brutal

Now you will hear some words with the /l/ sound. **Hör zu und wiederhole!**

/l/ Film, also, glauben, wollen, welch-, brutal, schmalzig, Jugendliche, Clique, Stadtbummel, kegeln, Schauspieler, Lieblingsgruppe, sensationell, phantasievoll, miserabel, geblieben, gelesen, gespielt, Sportveranstaltung

Now you will hear a group of words with the sound /ɔ/. **Hör zu und wiederhole!**

/ɔ/ Sport, besonders, wollen, Reporter, Konzert, Rockkonzert

2. In this section, you will practice reading the words printed in your textbook on page 293. **Hör zu und wiederhole!**
   j Jugend, Jugendliche, jenseits; **z** Konzert, Freizeit, Zeitung, schmalzig; **ng** singen, Sänger, anfangen, gegangen, verbringen, Zeitung, Lieblingsstar

3. Now close your textbook and write the sentences you hear.
   1. Jugendliche lesen auch die Zeitung.
   2. Wir sind ins Konzert gegangen.
   3. Der Sänger ist mein Lieblingsstar.
   4. Wie verbringen wir unsere Freizeit?

WAS KANNST DU SCHON?

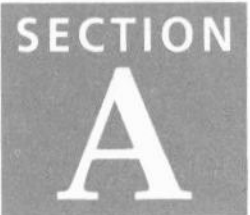

For further practice, have the students also ask each other questions:

Willst du ins Kino gehen?
Kannst du heute in die Stadt fahren?

Be sure the students understand how to use **welch-?** and **was für ein?** Have them write a few questions with each, both in the nominative and the accusative cases, and have them also write an appropriate answer for each question.

Write the names of some movies, movie stars, popular groups, and performers on the board. Have the students react to them using **mögen, nicht mögen,** and **gern haben.**

To be sure the students have learned the new past participles in this unit, ask them such questions as: **Willst du den Film *Das Boot* sehen?** They respond, **Ich habe den Film schon gesehen.** Ask similar questions using the verbs **lesen, gehen, besuchen, machen, hören, spielen, essen, trinken, bleiben,** and **fahren.**

WORTSCHATZ

Have the students find items in the vocabulary list that belong to the following categories and write them down.

1. places to go
2. things to do
3. adjectives to describe movies
4. verbs

WORTSCHATZÜBUNGEN

Have the students work individually and write down their findings. Then correct the papers with the entire class.

ZUM LESEN

DIE PROMINENTEN KOMMEN AUCH NACH DEUTSCHLAND

Allow sufficient time for the students to read pages 296 and 297 silently. Then play the cassette or read the text aloud. Ask questions that tie the individual commentaries together:

— Annemarie Mai sagt: „Wenn man die Musik von Supertramp hört, kann man gut nachdenken. — Was sagen die anderen Jugendlichen? Was kann man bei der Musik tun?
— Die Texte sind auch sehr wichtig. Was finden die Jugendlichen an den Texten von diesen Gruppen gut?
  Supertramp   Police   Peter Maffay
  Bob Marley   AC/DC
— Musikgruppen kommen und gehen. Heute ist eine Gruppe sehr beliebt, in ein paar Monaten kann sie vergessen sein. Welche von diesen Gruppen sind heute populär? Was meinst du, warum?

STARS, DIE HEUTE BELIEBT SIND 

After the students have read the text and listened to the cassette or you have read the text aloud, ask short questions to check comprehension: **Wer ist Nina Hagen? Woher kommt sie? Was nennt man sie?** and so on.

CHALLENGE Have several students take the roles of the stars featured on pages 298 and 299. They should introduce themselves to the class and talk about themselves, basing the talk on the information given in the textbook and any information they know or can find out.

Alternatively, you can have the students play "school newspaper reporter interviewing famous rock star." They could first prepare lists of questions in committees of three and then pair off to act the interview out.

Übung • Jetzt bist du dran!

Have the students discuss their likes and dislikes in popular music—the groups and performers they like, the ones they like best, and the ones they don't like. Encourage them to react to one another's choices.

Übung • Umfrage

Have the students write their favorite group from the United States on a sheet of paper and their favorite from another country on a second sheet. Have volunteers compile the results and make a final list for display.

Übung • Klassenprojekt

Have the students look through magazines, both American and German, and find articles on more German groups and individual stars.

KAPITEL 10
Gehen wir aus!

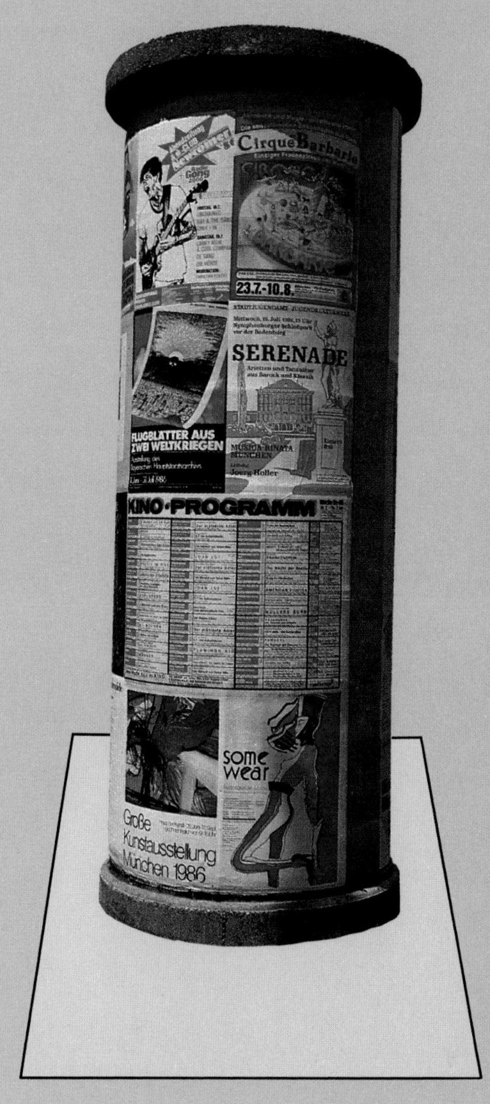

There are many different activities to choose from when you go out. Should you go to a movie or a concert or a sports event? You discuss the choices, decide on an activity, and make your plans.

In this unit you will learn to:

SECTION **A**	discuss what you do in your free time, make and accept or reject suggestions for going out
SECTION **B**	make choices about where to go when you go out, express preference and indifference
SECTION **C**	express whether you like or dislike something or someone
SECTION **D**	talk about what you did
TRY YOUR SKILLS	use what you've learned
ZUM LESEN	read for practice and pleasure

For teaching suggestions, see the Teacher's Notes preceding this unit, pp. T178–199.

SECTION
A

discussing what you do in your free time, making and accepting or rejecting suggestions for going out

Young people like to go out. Where do German teenagers go and what do they do? The following interview will tell you some of the things young Germans do in their free time. How does it compare with what you do?

A1 Was macht unsere Jugend?

Wie verbringst du deine Freizeit?

Unsere Jugendlichen: sie haben Geld, sie gehen aus, sie haben viele Interessen. Man sieht sie in Kinos, Konzerten und Sportveranstaltungen: sie sind keine Freizeitmuffel!—Was machen unsere Freunde? Wie verbringen sie ihre Freizeit? Wohin gehen sie? Was tun sie? Fragen wir mal!

Ja, ich gehe oft aus, zwei- oder dreimal in der Woche. Ich fahre in die Stadt, äh . . . ich gehe ins Kino, ins Theater, tja . . . und manchmal in ein Konzert. Oder ich besuche Freunde. Dann gehen wir zusammen aus.

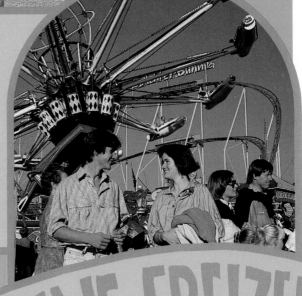

KEINE FREIZEIT

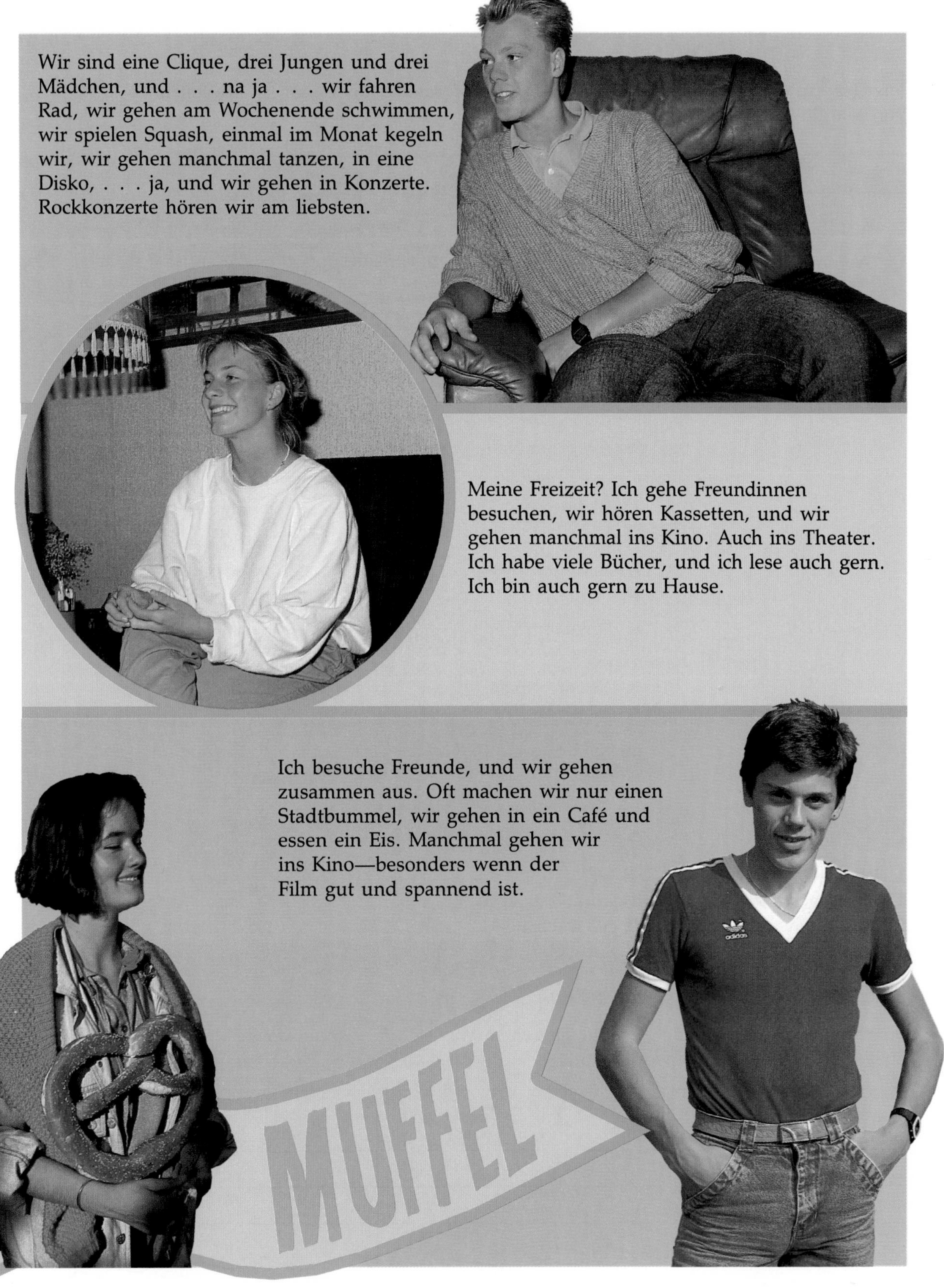

Wir sind eine Clique, drei Jungen und drei Mädchen, und . . . na ja . . . wir fahren Rad, wir gehen am Wochenende schwimmen, wir spielen Squash, einmal im Monat kegeln wir, wir gehen manchmal tanzen, in eine Disko, . . . ja, und wir gehen in Konzerte. Rockkonzerte hören wir am liebsten.

Meine Freizeit? Ich gehe Freundinnen besuchen, wir hören Kassetten, und wir gehen manchmal ins Kino. Auch ins Theater. Ich habe viele Bücher, und ich lese auch gern. Ich bin auch gern zu Hause.

Ich besuche Freunde, und wir gehen zusammen aus. Oft machen wir nur einen Stadtbummel, wir gehen in ein Café und essen ein Eis. Manchmal gehen wir ins Kino—besonders wenn der Film gut und spannend ist.

A2 Übung • Rollenspiel

Jetzt bist du ein Reporter oder eine Reporterin. Mitschüler übernehmen die Rollen von Margit, Jens, Kristin und Bruno. Du interviewst sie.

A3 Übung • Frag deine Klassenkameraden!

Wohin gehst du?
Was machst du?

Wie verbringst du deine Freizeit?

Wann gehst du aus?
Wie oft gehst du aus?

ins Kino gehen	***einmal***
ausgehen	***selten***
gern lesen	***in der Woche***
schwimmen gehen	***nie***
Eis essen	***manchmal***
tanzen gehen	***im Monat***
Squash spielen	***dreimal***
kegeln	***meistens***
Musik hören	***am Wochenende***
in ein Konzert gehen	***immer***
Freunde besuchen	***am Samstag***
ins Theater gehen	***oft***
in die Stadt fahren	***am Sonntag***
gern zu Hause sein	***zweimal***
in ein Café gehen	
einen Stadtbummel machen	
in eine Disko gehen	

A4 Übung • Und du? Wie steht's mit dir?

1. Wie verbringst du deine Freizeit?
2. Was machst du? Wohin gehst du?
3. Wann gehst du aus? Wie oft gehst du aus?

A5 Übung • Klasseninterview

Frag fünf Klassenkameraden, wohin sie gehen, was sie tun, wann oder wie oft sie ausgehen! Schreib die Antworten auf!

Name	wohin?	was?	wann?	wie oft?
1.				
2.				
3.				

A6 HAST DU ETWAS VOR, SABINE? 

Stefan runs into Sabine, a former classmate of his. They haven't seen each other in a while, and Stefan suggests that they do something together this afternoon or evening.

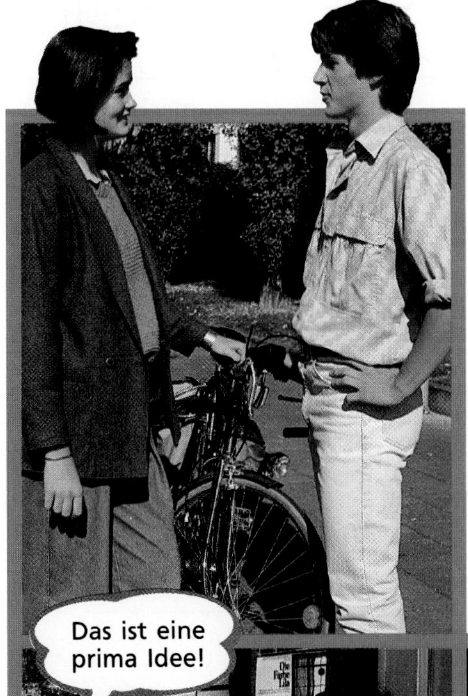

STEFAN	Sabine! Hallo!
SABINE	Stefan! Ja, grüss dich! Wie geht's denn?
STEFAN	Danke, prima! Mensch, das ist toll! Was machst du jetzt? Hast du etwas vor?
SABINE	Nö[1]. Warum?
STEFAN	Dann können wir zusammen etwas tun, ja?
SABINE	Prima! —Also, was machen wir?
STEFAN	Nun ja, wir können . . . wir können in die Stadt fahren und einen Stadtbummel machen. Oder willst du lieber in ein Café gehen? Eis essen?
SABINE	Mensch, toll! Klasse!

Gehen wir ins Kino! Es gibt einen prima Film im Roxi!

Oder möchtest du in ein Konzert gehen? In ein Rockkonzert?

A7 Übung • Jetzt fragst du!

Was möchten deine Klassenkameraden machen? Wie antworten sie?

1. Möchtest du . . .?
2. Willst du lieber . . .?
3. Wir können . . .
4. Gehen wir . . .!

---

[1]In casual German, **nö** is often used instead of **nein.**

A8 WIE GEHT'S?

Prima!

Gut, danke.

Nicht schlecht.

So lala.

Schlecht.

Miserabel!

A9 WIE SAGT MAN DAS?
Asking and responding to "How are you?"

Wie geht's? Wie geht's denn?	How are you? / How's it going? Say, how are things?
Ach, prima! Danke, gut! Nicht schlecht. So lala. Schlecht. Miserabel!	Oh, great! Fine, thanks. Not bad. So-so. Bad. Miserable!

A10 Übung • Grüss dich! Wie geht's? 

Begrüss deine Klassenkameraden und frag, wie es geht!

A: Grüss dich, Peter!
B: Tag, Monika! Wie geht's?
A: Danke, gut.

A11 WIE SAGT MAN DAS?
Making suggestions

How do you make suggestions? In Unit 5 you learned the **möchte**-forms. You can also use the forms of the verbs **wollen,** *to want to,* and **können,** *can,* expressing possibility. The **wir**-forms of most verbs, the *let's*-form, can also be used.

making suggestions	Möchtest du ins Kino gehen?	Would you like to go to the movies?
asking for someone's wishes	Willst du ins Kino gehen?	Do you want to go to the movies?
expressing possibility	Wir können ins Kino gehen.	We can go to the movies.
"let's" suggestion	Gehen wir doch ins Kino!	Let's go to the movies.

A 12 Übung • Und was willst du tun? 

1. You have the day off. Discuss with several classmates what you might do together. You make a suggestion, and a classmate either accepts or rejects your idea.

   A: Wir können in die Stadt fahren.
   B: . . .

2. After your classmate rejects your suggestion, he or she suggests something else. Now it's your turn to say whether or not you like the idea. Accept or reject your classmate's suggestion.

   A: Willst du einen Stadtbummel machen?
   B: Wie langweilig! Ich möchte heute lieber Tennis spielen.
   A: Mensch! Das ist eine prima Idee!

A 13 Übung • Ja, gehen wir . . . !

A: Möchtest du ins Kino gehen?
B: Ja, gehen wir ins Kino!

ins Kino, ins Konzert, in ein Café, in eine Disko

A 14 ERKLÄRUNG
The Verbs können *and* wollen

1. The verbs **können** and **wollen** have the following forms in the present tense:

können	wollen
ich **kann**	ich **will**
du **kannst**	du **willst**
er, sie, es **kann**	er, sie, es **will**
wir **können**	wir **wollen**
ihr **könnt**	ihr **wollt**
sie, Sie **können**	sie, Sie **wollen**

2. **Können** and **wollen** are usually used with an infinitive that comes at the end of the sentence. If the meaning of that infinitive is clear, it can be left out.

Wir können in die Stadt fahren.	*We can go to town.*
Du, ich kann heute nicht (in die Stadt fahren).	*I can't (go to town) today.*

A 15 Übung • Was willst du tun? Was kannst du machen? 

ins Kino gehen, eine Kassette hören, radfahren, ins Konzert gehen, Tennis spielen, schwimmen gehen

1. 1. Du willst ins Kino gehen. Du willst eine Kassette hören. Du . . .
2. Wir wollen ins Kino gehen. Wir wollen . . .
3. Ihr (wollt) 4. Mein Vetter (will) 5. Deine Freunde (wollen) 6. Ich (will)

2. 1. Du kannst ins Kino gehen. Du . . .
2. Wir können . . .
3. Ihr (könnt) 4. Mein Bruder (kann) 5. Deine Freunde (können) 6. Ich (kann)

Fussball spielen

A 16 Schreibübung • Versteckte Sätze

Wieviel Sätze kannst du machen? Schreib zehn Sätze!

Herbert will am Wochende ins Kino gehen.

ich	kann	am Wochenende	einen Stadtbummel	besuchen
Katrin	können	am Samstag	Freunde	fahren
wir	möchte	einmal in der Woche	in die Stadt	gehen
Herbert	möchten	immer	in eine Disko	hören
die Jungen und Mädchen	will	manchmal	ins Kino	machen
	wollen	selten	Kassetten	spielen
du	willst	nie	Rad	
ihr	wollt	meistens	tanzen	
			Tennis	

Possible answers: Ich möchte am Wochenende in die Stadt fahren. Herbert kann nie tanzen gehen. Wir wollen einmal in der Woche Rad fahren. Ihr wollt immer Freunde besuchen.

A 17 ERKLÄRUNG
The Verbs fahren, radfahren, *and* ausgehen

1. The verbs **fahren,** *to go (by vehicle),* and **radfahren,** *to bicycle,* have a stem-vowel change in the **du-** and **er/sie-**forms. In addition, **radfahren** is a verb with a separable prefix. Note that **Rad** is capitalized when it is separated from **fahren.**

fahren			radfahren			
Ich Du Er, sie	**fahre** **fährst** **fährt**	in die Stadt.	Ich Du Er, sie	**fahre** **fährst** **fährt**	gern	**Rad.**

2. **Fahren** and **radfahren** do not have a stem-vowel change in the singular command form.

Fahr doch in die Stadt! **Fahr** mal **Rad!**

3. The verb **ausgehen,** *to go out,* is also a verb with a separable prefix.

Gehst du heute **aus?**
Ich **gehe** am Wochenende **aus.**

A 18 Übung • Was macht ihr jetzt?

A: Was macht ihr jetzt?
B: Wir fahren jetzt in die Stadt.

A: Und was macht Sabine?
B: Sie fährt jetzt auch in die Stadt.

1. Und du? ich fahre
2. Und deine Geschwister? sie fahren
3. Und der Stefan? er fährt
4. Und ihr? wir fahren

A 19 Übung • Was machst du jetzt?

A: Was machst du jetzt?
B: Ich fahre jetzt Rad.

A: Und Stefan?
B: Er fährt jetzt auch Rad.

1. Und ihr? wir fahren
2. Und Sabine? sie fährt
3. Und deine Geschwister? sie fahren
4. Und du? ich fahre

A 20 Übung • Wann? Wie oft?

A: Wie oft geht Katrin aus? einmal in der Woche?
B: Ja, sie geht einmal in der Woche aus.

1. Und der Stefan? am Samstag?
2. Und du? am Wochenende?
3. Und deine Freunde? immer?
4. Und dein Bruder? zweimal im Monat?
5. Und ihr zwei? selten?

1. Er geht am Samstag aus. 2. Ich gehe am Wochenende aus. 3. Meine Freunde gehen immer aus. 4. Mein Bruder geht zweimal im Monat aus. 5. Wir gehen selten aus.

A 21 Übung • Was können wir tun?

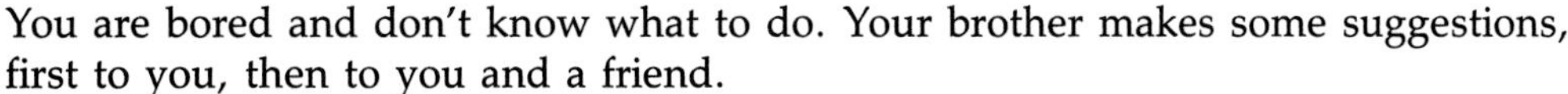

You are bored and don't know what to do. Your brother makes some suggestions, first to you, then to you and a friend.

1. Geh doch ins Kino! Fahr . . .!
2. Geht doch ins Kino! Fahrt . . .!

A 22 Übung • Mix-Match

Discuss what you can do together with your classmates and with your teacher. Choose suggestions and responses from below.

Du, (Brian), willst du . . .?
Du, (Barbara), kannst du heute . . .?
Was macht ihr jetzt? Wollt ihr . . .?
(Frl. Seifert), können Sie heute . . .?

in die Stadt fahren	*Das find' ich blöd.*
ins Kino gehen	Ich habe schon was vor.
in ein Café gehen	*Nein, lieber nicht.*
einen Stadtbummel machen	Das ist eine prima Idee!
radfahren	*Ach, wie langweilig!*
Kassetten hören	Das geht jetzt nicht.
den (Jens) besuchen	*Mensch, toll!*
einen Film sehen	Ich kann leider nicht.
Karten spielen	*Ich habe heute keine Zeit.*
Tennis spielen	Super! Schade!
Windsurfen	*Nein, das macht keinen Spass.*

A 23 Übung • Was sagst du? Was sagen deine Mitschüler?

1. What would you say if someone asked you the following questions?

1. Wie geht's?
2. Hast du heute was vor?
3. Was machst du heute?
4. Können wir zusammen was tun?
5. So, was machen wir?
6. Wann fährst du in die Stadt?
7. Was machst du dort?
8. Machst du einen Stadtbummel?
9. Willst du radfahren?
10. Was machst du am liebsten?

2. Now ask some of your classmates the previous questions.

A 24 Übung • Partnerarbeit: Hast du was vor?

FEBRUAR	
	21 Mo
Fastnacht 15 00 Party bei Sven	22 Di
Aschermittwoch	23 Mi
19 00 Kegeln	24 Do
	25 Fr
Nachmittag: Stadtbummel mit Gitta	26 Sa
15 00 Kino	27 So

Make a weekly planner. Write down what you are going to do on four different days. Indicate the activity and specific times. Don't let your classmates see your entries. Now select a partner. Call your partner up and invite him or her to the four activities. Your partner responds according to the entries on his or her calendar. If your partner is free, he or she accepts. If not, agree on another date. Then it is your partner's turn to invite you.

A 25 Übung • Hör gut zu!

For script and answers, see p. T184.

Listen to the statement. Is the one that follows appropriate or not?

	0	1	2	3	4	5	6	7	8	9	10
appropriate	✓			✓		✓	✓		✓	✓	
not appropriate		✓	✓		✓			✓			✓

A 26 Schreibübung • Was macht Ulrike heute?

Ulrike tells you what she plans to do today. You repeat it to a friend. Write what you would say.

Ulrike: Ich fahre heute in die Stadt. Ich will einen Stadtbummel machen, und ich möchte meine Tante besuchen. Wir wollen zusammen einen Film sehen. Dann wollen wir in ein Café gehen. Am liebsten gehen wir ins Café Krone. Ich finde es dort sehr gemütlich. Um neun Uhr will ich wieder zu Hause sein.

Du erzählst: Ulrike fährt . . . heute in die Stadt. Sie will . . . und sie möchte ihre Tante besuchen. Sie wollen . . . Dann wollen sie . . . gehen sie . . . Ulrike (sie) findet . . . will sie . . .

A 27 Schreibübung • Was hast du vor?

Using the suggestions and responses in Exercise A22, write five short conversations.

SECTION **B**

making choices about where to go when you go out, expressing preference and indifference

Stefan and Sabine cannot quite decide whether to go to a concert or a movie. The ads in the paper help them make up their minds.

B1 Konzert oder Kino?

KONZERTE „live"
JAZZ ROCK SOUL ACTION
Fr. 17.10. CIRCUS KRONE
SALSA FESTIVAL mit Eddie Palmieri Orchestra, Salsa Picante, und Celia Cruz & Tito Puente Orchestra 20.00
Fr. 17.10. ALABAMAHALLE
SCORPIONS Monsters of Rock, mit Ozzy Osbourne, Bon Jovi, Warlock 20.30
Fr. 17.10. OLYMPIAHALLE
QUEEN Die Englische Rockgruppe
VORGRUPPE: Craaft Eine deutsche Band auf dem Sprung in die US-Charts 20.00
Sa. 18.10. OLYMPIAHALLE
FALCO Der österreichische Popstar 20.00
Sa. 18.10. CIRCUS KRONE
REGGAE SUNSPLASH mit Black Uhuru, The Wailers, Dennis Brown & Guests 20.00
Sa. 18.10. ALABAMAHALLE
SUPERCHARGE Die sagenhafte Rhythm'n Blues Band 20.30

STEFAN Du, Sabine, willst du ins Kino gehen oder lieber in ein Konzert?
SABINE Ach, Stefan, das ist mir gleich. Du, schauen wir doch mal in die Zeitung!
SABINE Hier, Konzerte!
STEFAN Wer singt?
SABINE Da ist der Falco . . . welchen Sänger hörst du gern?
STEFAN Ich habe viele gern. Schau, Sabine, die Gruppe ist toll!
SABINE Welche Gruppe?
STEFAN Die Scorpions. Hörst du die Gruppe gern?
SABINE Mensch, das ist meine Lieblingsgruppe! Was für Gruppen hast du am liebsten?
STEFAN Ich höre alle Rockgruppen gern.
SABINE Ich auch, aber die Scorpions höre ich besonders gern. Schade, die Konzerte fangen so spät an. Ich soll um 10 Uhr zu Hause sein.
STEFAN Dann gehen wir ins Kino, ja?
SABINE Gut!

B2 Übung • Und du? Wie steht's mit dir?

1. Gehst du lieber ins Kino oder in ein Konzert?
2. Welchen Sänger oder welche Sängerin hörst du gern?
3. Wie heissen deine Lieblingssänger?
4. Welche Gruppe hörst du gern? Wie heisst deine Lieblingsgruppe?
5. Welche Gruppe möchtest du nicht hören? Warum nicht?
6. Wann fangen die Konzerte an?

B3 WAS FÜR FILME SIEHST DU GERN? 

Was für Filme siehst du gern?

Wie heisst dein Lieblingsstar?

SABINE Hm, *Zwölf Uhr mittags*—was für ein Film ist das?
STEFAN Das ist ein Western. Hast du Western gern?
SABINE Nicht besonders.
STEFAN Schau, *Piranha 2*. Ich glaube, das ist ein Naturfilm.
SABINE Ach, Quatsch! Das ist ein Action-Film und kein Naturfilm.

KINO KINO KINO

Mathäser–Filmpalast
16.00 und 18.45 Steve Martin
Der Mann mit 2 Gehirnen

Theatiner–Film
20.00 Gary Cooper
Zwölf Uhr mittags

Tivoli
17.00 u. 20.00 Sidney Pollack
Jenseits von Afrika

Royal-Filmpalast
13 / 15 / 17 / 19 Uhr
Piranha 2

Gloria
14.00 / 16.30 / 19.00
Das Boot

B4 Übung • Wie steht's mit dir?

1. Welchen Film möchtest du sehen? Warum?
2. Wo spielt der Film? (im . . .)
3. Wann fangen die Filme an?

B5 ERKLÄRUNG
The Verb anfangen

1. The verb **anfangen,** *to begin,* is a verb with a separable prefix. It also has a vowel change in the **du-** and **er/sie-**forms.

Ich Du Er, sie	**fange** **fängst** **fängt**	um 2 Uhr	**an.**	Wir Ihr Sie	**fangen** **fangt** **fangen**	um 2 Uhr	**an.**

2. The singular command form does not have a vowel change: **Fang** doch **an!**

B6 Übung • Frag deine Klassenkameraden!

1. Frag, wann die Filme und die Konzerte anfangen! Wann fängt . . . an?
2. Frag deine Klassenkameraden, wann ihre (Mathestunden) anfangen! Wann fängt deine Mathestunde an?
3. Frag sie, wann sie ihre Hausaufgaben machen! Wann machst du deine Hausaufgaben?

B7 WAS FÜR FILME SIND DAS?

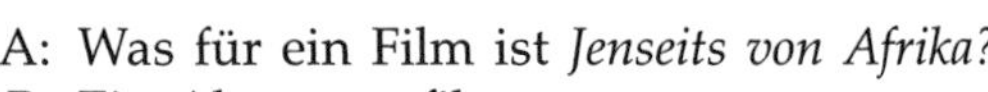

A: Was für ein Film ist *Jenseits von Afrika?*
B: Ein Abenteuerfilm.
A: Kennst du die Schauspieler?
B: Na klar!

A: Was für ein Film ist . . .
B: . . . ist ein . . .

Jenseits von Afrika

ein Abenteuerfilm

Zwölf Uhr mittags

ein Western

Das Boot

ein Kriegsfilm

Der Mann mit 2 Gehirnen

eine Komödie

Werwolf in London

ein Horrorfilm

Piranha 2

ein Action-Film

Aliens

ein Science-fiction-Film

Liebesgeschichte

ein Liebesfilm

B 8 Übung • Jetzt bist du dran

1. Was für Filme siehst du gern? Warum?
2. Was für ein Film ist *Das Boot?* ein Kriegsfilm
3. Und *Jenseits von Afrika?* ein Abenteuerfilm
4. Welcher Film spielt im Mathäser? Was für ein Film ist das? etc. (Schau auf das Kinoplakat auf Seite 280!)
   Der Mann mit zwei Gehirnen; eine Komödie

B 9 Übung • Kennst du den Film?

Schreib den Titel von einem Film in grossen Buchstaben auf ein Blatt Papier! Zeig deinen Klassenkameraden den Titel und frag:

—Kennt ihr den Film?
—Was für ein Film ist das?
—Siehst du . . . filme gern?

B 10 WIE SAGT MAN DAS?
Expressing preference and indifference

You already know the words **lieber** and **am liebsten.** Here are some other ways of expressing preference.

expressing preference	Ich höre Rock lieber. Ich sehe Western am liebsten. Ich höre Rockgruppen besonders gern. Das ist meine Lieblingsgruppe. Das ist mein Lieblingsstar.	I prefer rock. I like westerns best of all. I especially like to listen to rock groups. That's my favorite group. That's my favorite star.
expressing indifference	Das ist mir gleich.	It's all the same to me.

B 11 Übung • Was willst du tun?

Now you and your friend are deciding what to do. You are standing in front of a **Plakatsäule.** Ask your friend what he or she prefers to do. Take turns making suggestions, accepting some, rejecting others, and then finally agreeing on something.

B 12 Übung • Was hast du lieber?

In large letters, write the title of your favorite film on one sheet of paper and your favorite group on another sheet. Ask a classmate which one he or she would like to see or hear. After your classmate expresses an opinion, make an appropriate comment.

B 13 WIE SAGT MAN DAS?
Asking for information

specific information	**Welcher Film spielt heute?** Which (What) film is playing today?	*Das Boot.*
categories of things	**Was für Filme siehst du gern?** What kind of films do you like to see?	Action-Filme.

B 14 ERKLÄRUNG
welcher? welche? welches?, *Nominative and Accusative Case*

The interrogative **welcher? (welche?, welches?)**, *which*, can be used in front of nouns: **welcher?** is used before a masculine noun, **welches?** before a neuter noun, and **welche?** before a feminine or plural noun.

Der Film ist toll. —Welcher Film ist toll?
Die Gruppe ist Spitze! —Welche Gruppe ist Spitze?
Das Konzert ist Klasse! —Welches Konzert ist Klasse?
Die Gruppen sind prima! —Welche Gruppen sind prima?

	Masculine	*Feminine*	*Neuter*	*Plural*
Nominative	**welcher?**	**welche?**	**welches?**	**welche?**
Accusative	**welchen?**			

B 15 Schreibübung • Welche Form von welch-?

1. Im Gloria spielt *Das Boot.* — ____ Film spielt im Gloria? welcher
2. Ich sehe heute *Jenseits von Afrika.* — ____ Film siehst du heute? welchen
3. Wir hören heute das Salsa Festival. — ____ Konzert hörst du? welches
4. Supercharge beginnt schon um 20 Uhr. — ____ Konzert beginnt schon um 20 Uhr? welches
5. Ich höre die Gruppe Queen gern. — ____ Gruppe hörst du gern? welche
6. Die Gruppe Reggae Sunsplash spielt heute. — ____ Gruppe spielt heute? welche
7. Die Konzerte beginnen um 20 Uhr. — ____ Konzerte beginnen um 20 Uhr? welche
8. Die Scorpions spielen in der Alabama-Halle. — ____ Gruppe spielt in der Alabama-Halle? welche
9. Die Gruppe Queen ist aus England. — ____ Gruppe ist aus England? welche
10. Das Falco Konzert beginnt um 19 Uhr. — ____ Konzert beginnt um 19 Uhr? welches

B 16 Schreibübung • Schreib Fragen!

Look at the ads on pages 279 and 280 and write eight questions similar to the ones you have been asking in Exercise B15. Begin each question with a form of **welcher.**

B 17 ERKLÄRUNG
was für ein?, *Nominative and Accusative Case*

The interrogative **was für ein?**, *what kind of (a)?*, introduces questions that ask about categories of things.

Was für ein Film ist das?	Ein Horrorfilm.
Was für eine Gruppe spielt?	Eine Gruppe aus England.
Was für ein Konzert ist das?	Ein Rockkonzert.
Was für Filme siehst du gern?	Naturfilme und Action-Filme.

	Masculine	*Feminine*	*Neuter*	*Plural*
Nominative	**was für ein?**	**was für eine?**	**was für ein?**	**was für?**
Accusative	**was für einen?**	**was für eine?**	**was für ein?**	**was für?**

B 18 Schreibübung • Welche Form von was für ein?

1. *Zwölf Uhr mittags* ist ein Western. ——— Film ist *Zwölf Uhr mittags?* was für ein
2. Wir sehen heute einen Kriegsfilm. ——— Film seht ihr heute? was für einen
3. Ich höre am liebsten ein Rockkonzert. ——— Konzert hörst du am liebsten? was für ein
4. Ich sehe gern Western und Action-Filme. ——— Filme siehst du gern? was für
5. Ich höre am liebsten Pop- und Rockkonzerte. ——— Konzerte hörst du am liebsten? was für
6. Queen ist eine Rockgruppe. ——— Gruppe ist Queen? was für eine
7. *Piranha 2* ist ein Action-Film. ——— Film ist *Piranha 2?* was für ein

B 19 Schreibübung • Schreib Fragen!

1. Look at the ads on pages 279 and 280 and write five questions similar to the ones you have been asking in Exercise B18. Begin each question with a form of **was für ein?**
2. Schreib Fragen mit **welcher** oder **was für ein!** For answers, see p. T188.

A: *Piranha 2* ist ein Abenteuerfilm.
B: Was für ein Film ist *Piranha 2?*

A: Ich sehe den Film *Jenseits von Afrika.*
B: Welchen Film siehst du?

1. Sunsplash ist eine Reggae Gruppe.
2. Wir hören heute die Gruppe Queen.
3. In der Olympiahalle gibt es ein Rockkonzert.
4. Wir hören das Konzert in der Alabama-Halle.
5. *Zwölf Uhr mittags* und *Rio Bravo* sind Western.
6. Ich sehe den Western um 19 Uhr.

B 20 Ein wenig Landeskunde

American movies are very popular in Germany. Most movies are dubbed into German. However, larger cities usually have at least one movie theater that shows foreign movies with the original sound track.

All movies are rated, and movie ads give the ratings in the form of age limits: **ab 12 Jahre, ab 14 Jahre,** and so on.

SECTION C — expressing whether you like or dislike someone or something

Stefan is interviewing different people for his school paper. Let's hear what kind of movies these people like and dislike, and why. What are your likes and dislikes when it comes to movies?

C1 Was für Filme mögt ihr?

STEFAN Welchen Film möchtest du heute sehen?
SCHÜLER Moment mal, . . . wie heisst er denn? Der Film mit Steve Martin! —Ach, ja! *Der Mann mit zwei Gehirnen.*
STEFAN Der Film ist lustig. Magst du Steve Martin?
SCHÜLER Ich mag ihn gern.
STEFAN Ich auch.

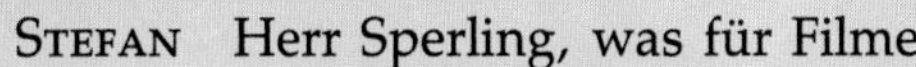

STEFAN Herr Sperling, was für Filme mögen Sie?
HERR SPERLING Ich? Am liebsten mag ich Science-fiction-Filme.
STEFAN Wirklich? Sie mögen Science-fiction-Filme?
HERR SPERLING Ja. Ich finde sie interessant und oft sehr spannend.

STEFAN Was für Filme mögt ihr zwei?
MÄDCHEN 1 Wir mögen Liebesfilme, Action-Filme—nur keine Kriegsfilme.
STEFAN Warum mögt ihr keine Kriegsfilme?
MÄDCHEN 2 Kriegsfilme finde ich grausam und traurig.
MÄDCHEN 1 Ich hasse sie.

C2 Übung • Beantworte die Fragen!

1. Welchen Film sieht der Schüler heute?
2. Wie ist der Film?
3. Magst du Steve Martin?
4. Was für Filme mag Herr Sperling?
5. Was für Filme mag er am liebsten? Warum?
6. Was für Filme mögen die beiden Mädchen?
7. Was für Filme finden sie grausam?

1. Den Mann mit zwei Gehirnen. (Point out that the definite article is usually changed according to the function of the title in the sentence.) 2. lustig 3. ja/nein 4. Science-fiction-Filme
5. Science-fiction-Filme, er findet sie interessant und oft sehr spannend.
6. Liebesfilme, Action-Filme 7. Kriegsfilme

C3 WIE SAGT MAN DAS?
Saying you like or dislike someone or something

You have been expressing likes and dislikes using **gern** and **nicht gern** with various verbs. Here are some more ways of saying you like or dislike someone or something.

liking	Ich mag den Film. Ich mag Steve Martin.	Ich habe den Film gern. Ich mag Steve Martin gern.
disliking	Ich mag Kriegsfilme nicht. Ich mag den Schauspieler nicht.	Ich habe Kriegsfilme nicht gern. Ich mag den Schauspieler nicht gern.
strong disliking	Ich hasse Kriegsfilme. Ich hasse den Schauspieler.	

C4 Übung • Und du? 

1. Wie findest du die Gruppe Queen?
2. Wie findest du Falco?
3. Wie findest du den Film *Jenseits von Afrika?*
4. Wie findest du Robert Redford?
5. Wie findest du Abenteuerfilme?

C5 ERKLÄRUNG
The Verb mögen

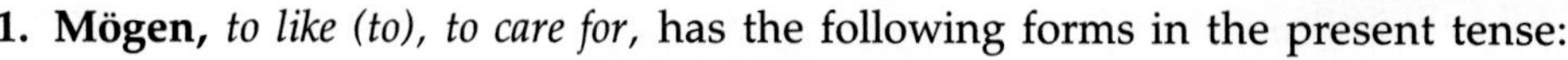

1. **Mögen,** *to like (to), to care for,* has the following forms in the present tense:

ich **mag**	wir **mögen**
du **magst**	ihr **mögt**
er, sie, es **mag**	sie, Sie **mögen**

2. An infinitive may also be used together with the **mag-**forms.

   Welche Gruppe **magst** du nicht **hören?** *Which group don't you want to hear?*

C6 Übung • Alle mögen die Gruppe 

A: Warum hört ihr die Scorpions?
B: Wir mögen die Gruppe.

A: Und du?
B: Ich mag die Gruppe auch.

1. Und Sabine? sie mag
2. Und die Schüler? sie mögen
3. Und ihr? wir mögen
4. Und Stefan? er mag

C7 Übung • Keiner mag den Film 

A: Geht ihr in *Piranha 2?*
B: Nein, wir mögen den Film nicht.

A: Und Sabine?
B: Sabine mag den Film auch nicht.

1. Und die Schüler? sie mögen
2. Und Stefan? er mag
3. Und ihr? wir mögen
4. Und du? ich mag

C8 Übung • Versteckte Sätze

Wieviel Sätze kannst du machen?

Die Schüler mögen Horrorfilme nicht.

ich du Stefan Katrin ihr die Schüler	mögen mögt mag magst	die Gruppe aus England die Rockgruppe Horrorfilme Steve Martin	am liebsten besonders gern lieber nicht

Possible answers: Ich mag Steve Martin nicht. Du magst die Gruppe aus England besonders gern. Katrin mag die Rockgruppe lieber. Die Schüler mögen Horrorfilme am liebsten.

C9 Übung • Was magst du am liebsten?

For answers, see p. T191.

Rephrase each statement using **Lieblings-**. Then write a question.

Ich spiele Tennis am liebsten.
Tennis ist mein Lieblingsspiel. Welches Spiel magst du am liebsten?

1. Ich besuche die Stadt München am liebsten.
2. Ich höre die Gruppe Supercharge am liebsten.
3. Ich gehe am liebsten in das Café Krone.
4. Ich sehe Horrorfilme am liebsten.
5. Ich habe das Kartenspiel Mau-Mau am liebsten.

C10 Übung • Wie findest du die Gruppe? den Film? das Konzert?

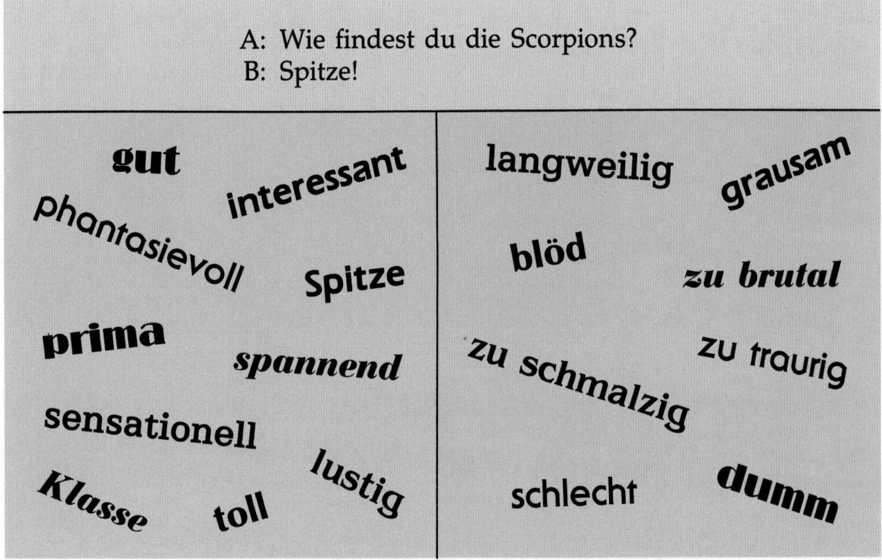

A: Wie findest du die Scorpions?
B: Spitze!
gut
interessant
phantasievoll
Spitze
prima
spannend
sensationell
lustig
Klasse
toll
langweilig
grausam
blöd
zu brutal
zu schmalzig
zu traurig
schlecht
dumm

C11 Übung • Umfrage

1. Mach eine Liste von Filmen und Musikgruppen, die du gern oder nicht gern hast! Frag deine Klassenkameraden, wie sie den Film oder die Gruppe finden!
2. Frag deine Mitschüler, was für Filme, Musikgruppen oder Konzerte sie mögen oder nicht mögen und warum! Frag auch deinen Lehrer!

C12 Übung • Hör gut zu!

For script and answers, see p. T192.

Wer mag das? Wer mag das nicht?

	0	1	2	3	4	5	6	7	8	9	10
likes	✓	✓		✓	✓			✓		✓	
dislikes			✓			✓	✓		✓		✓

C13 Schreibübung • Schreib zwei Dialoge!

1. Ein Freund fragt, ob du ins Kino gehen willst. Du sagst, dass du gern gehst. Du fragst, was er sehen möchte, und du sagst, dass du den Film auch gern siehst.
2. Ein Freund fragt, ob du ins Kino gehen möchtest. Du sagst, dass es geht, dass du Zeit hast. Du fragst, welchen Film er sehen möchte. Aber du hast den Film nicht gern, und du sagst, warum du ihn nicht sehen magst.

C14 Übung • Und du?

SECTION D talking about what you did

D1 Was hast du gestern abend gemacht? 

LEHRER Herbert, was hast du gestern abend gemacht?
HERBERT Ich bin ins Kino gegangen.
LEHRER Was hast du gesehen?
HERBERT *Jenseits von Afrika.* Ein prima Film!

LEHRER Und du, Karin? Was hast du gemacht?
KARIN Ich habe Freunde besucht, und wir haben Karten gespielt.

LEHRER Und du, Wiebke?
WIEBKE Ich bin zu Hause geblieben. Ich habe ein Buch gelesen.

D2 Übung • Mix-Match

1. Was hast du . . .?
2. Ich bin ins Kino . . .
3. Ich habe *Jenseits von Afrika* . . .
4. Ich habe Freunde . . .
5. Wir haben Karten . . .
6. Ich bin zu Hause . . .
7. Ich habe ein Buch . . .

4 besucht.
6 geblieben.
2 gegangen.
7 gelesen.
1 gemacht?
3 gesehen.
5 gespielt.

D3 ERKLÄRUNG
The Conversational Past Tense

1. In the conversational past tense, two verb forms are used: the present tense forms of the verbs **haben** or **sein** and a form of the main verb, called a past participle. The past participle is in last position.

	Helping Verb		*Past Participle*
Ich	**habe**	ein Buch	**gelesen.**
Er	**ist**	ins Kino	**gegangen.**

2. Here are some conversational past tense forms of verbs you have been using in this unit. Most past participles are used with the helping verb **haben.** Note especially those used with **sein.**

hat besucht	**hat gesehen**	**ist gegangen**
hat gemacht	**hat gelesen**	**ist geblieben**
hat gehört	**hat gegessen**	**ist gefahren**
hat gespielt	**hat getrunken**	

3. Can you name the infinitive forms of the past participles listed in this chart?

D4 Übung • Was hast du gestern abend gemacht?

A: Was hast du gestern abend gemacht?
B: Ich habe . . . *or* Ich bin . . .

1. Ich . . . habe . . . gelesen.
2. Ich . . . habe . . . besucht.
3. Ich . . . bin . . . geblieben.
4. Ich . . . bin . . . gefahren.
5. Ich . . . bin . . . gegangen.
6. Ich . . . habe . . . gesehen.
7. Ich . . . habe . . . gehört.
8. Ich . . . habe . . . gemacht.

1 ein Buch
6 einen prima Film
8 einen Stadtbummel
2 Freunde
4 in die Stadt
5 ins Kino
7 Musik
3 zu Hause

D5 Übung • Wer hat was gemacht?

Wir sind ins Kino gegangen.

1. Wir . . . sind ins Kino gegangen.

2. Die Jungen . . . haben Tennis gespielt.

3. Hans . . . hat Eis gegessen.

4. Ich . . . habe Kassetten gehört.

5. Ihr . . .? seid ins Theater gegangen?

6. Du . . .? hast ein Buch gelesen?

7. Karin . . . ist in ein Café gegangen.

8. Wir . . . sind ins Konzert gegangen.

D6 Übung • Hör gut zu!

For script and answers, see p. T194.

Is it in the present or is it in the conversational past?

	0	1	2	3	4	5	6	7	8	9	10
Present		✓			✓		✓			✓	
Convers. Past	✓		✓	✓		✓		✓	✓		✓

D7 Übung • Und du? Wie steht's mit dir?

1. Was hast du gestern abend gemacht?
2. Was haben deine Freunde gemacht?
3. Was hat dein Klassenkamerad gemacht?

D8 Schreibübung • Was hast du gestern abend gemacht?

Schreib auf, was du letzte Woche an jedem Abend und am Wochenende gemacht hast:

Am Montag . . .

TRY YOUR SKILLS

using what you've learned

Having a pen pal in a foreign country can be a rewarding experience. Many students who have pen pals end up visiting them. Here, Ulli tells his American pen pal, John, about the different things they will be doing together when John comes to Germany. As you read Ulli's letter, think of what you would like to do and see and where you would like to go in Munich.

1 Brief an einen Brieffreund

München, den 28. Mai

Lieber John!

Danke für Deinen Brief und die Briefmarken. Sie sind schön, und ich habe diese Marken noch nicht.

Ich schreibe heute, was wir machen können, wenn Du im Juli kommst. Im Juli haben wir ein Filmfest, ein internationales Filmfest. Da können wir viele interessante Filme sehen: Filme aus Frankreich, Ungarn, aus den USA natürlich, aus Deutschland, Italien, usw. Du gehst doch gern ins Kino, oder nicht? Ich gehe einmal in der Woche. Am liebsten mag ich Action-Filme. Und Du? Was für Filme magst Du am liebsten?

Meine Schwester, die Uschi, geht lieber in die Oper. Aber das ist nichts für mich. Ich finde Opern langweilig. Aber wir können auch ins Theater gehen. Sie spielen jetzt „Don Carlos", ein Stück von Schiller.

Im Sommer haben wir auch viele Gartenpartys. Diese Partys sind immer sehr lustig. Wir grillen, spielen tolle Musik und tanzen.

Und in der Nähe von uns ist eine Diskothek. Gehst Du gern in Diskotheken? Ich finde sie toll. Dort kannst Du Typen sehen - - und die Musik ist Klasse!

Es ist schade, dass Du nicht schon im Juni kommen kannst. Am 21. Juni, am längsten Tag im Sommer, haben wir in der Nähe immer ein grosses Johannisfeuer und ein ganz tolles Feuerwerk.

Meine Freunde und Freundinnen sind auch nett. Du hast sie bestimmt gern. Wir gehen oft zusammen aus: wir bummeln durch die Stadt, oder wir gehen in ein Café und diskutieren über alle möglichen Probleme.

Ich schicke Prospekte für die Rockkonzerte im Juli. Du kannst schon jetzt aussuchen, was Du hören willst. Und schreibe bald, dann kaufe ich schon die Karten. Viele Konzerte sind schnell ausverkauft. Wie Du siehst, spielen die meisten Gruppen in der Alabamahalle - - ja, wir haben eine Alabamahalle hier in München! Findest Du das nicht lustig?

Alles Gute und viele Grüsse, auch an Deine Eltern,

Dein Ulli

[1]**Johannisfeuer** is a huge bonfire in celebration of midsummer night.

2 Übung • Jetzt bist du dran

1. You have just received this letter from Ulli. In English, tell your friends who don't study German the gist of what he has written.
2. In German, tell a classmate what Ulli has written.
3. Pretend that you are about to visit Ulli in Germany. Tell your classmates what you and Ulli are going to do.

3 Schreibübung • Was schreibt Ulli? Was schreibst du? For answers, see p. T195.

1. Write a summary of Ulli's letter, using third person verb forms. Your letter may begin like this:

   Ulli dankt John für den Brief und die Briefmarken. Er hat diese Marken noch nicht. Ulli schreibt, was sie . . .

2. Now pretend the German student Ulli is coming to visit you. Tell him all about your friends and the things that you can do together when he comes to see you.

4 Übung • Telefongespräch

A student from Germany is visiting friends in your neighborhood. You have met this student at a party, and now you are inviting him or her to go out with you. You have not decided yet where to go and what to do, and you are discussing various possibilities, including: Use present tense forms.

—where you will go
—how to get there
—what time you will be there
—how much money you will need

5 Übung • Klassenprojekte

1. Choose a film that you have seen recently and design an ad for it in German.
2. Bring in a movie ad or a concert ad from your newspaper. Tell the class what kind of concert or film it is, why you like it, and when it begins.

6 Übung • Ratespiel

Amerikanische Filme in Deutschland haben meistens einen deutschen Titel. Der Titel ist oft ein wenig anders als der amerikanische. Rate mal: wie heissen diese Filme wohl auf englisch?

Zwölf Uhr mittags (mit Gary Cooper) ist . . . High Noon
Reise nach Indien Passage to India
Der Mann mit 2 Gehirnen (mit Steve Martin) The Man with Two Brains
Der weisse Hai Jaws
Odyssee im Weltraum 2001—A Space Odyssey
Für eine Handvoll Dollar (mit Clint Eastwood) A Fistful of Dollars
Nur Samstagnacht (mit John Travolta) Saturday Night Fever
Der Herr der Ringe Lord of the Rings

7 Übung • Was sagen die Jungen und Mädchen?

Es ist Freitag. Die Schule ist aus. Die Jungen und Mädchen machen Pläne für das Wochenende. Was sagen sie?

In der Freizeit

wollen 10- bis 19jährige Jugendliche am liebsten

Sport treiben	46%
Lesen	31%
Musik hören	20%
Tanzen	8%
Fernsehen	9%
Kino gehen	1%
Basteln	8%
Wandern, spazierengehen	10%
Handarbeiten	5%

8 Übung • In der Freizeit

Eine Umfrage zeigt, wie die 10- bis 19jährigen Jugendlichen ihre Freizeit verbringen. Sprich darüber mit deinen Klassenkameraden, und mach eine ähnliche Umfrage in deiner Klasse und mit deinen Freunden! Vergleiche die beiden Umfragen!

9 Übung • Deine Eltern fragen Dich

Es ist Samstag abend. Du willst ausgehen, und du fragst deine Eltern.

DU Ich möchte jetzt in die Stadt fahren.
DEINE ELTERN Ja, (Peter), du gehst wieder aus?
DU . . .
DEINE ELTERN Wohin gehst du?
DU . . .
DEINE ELTERN Was machst du dort?
DU . . .
DEINE ELTERN Und wann kommst du nach Hause?
DU . . .
DEINE ELTERN Das ist sehr spät!
DU . . .

10 Aussprache-, Lese- und Schreibübungen

For script, see p. T196.

1. Listen carefully and repeat what you hear.
2. Listen, then read aloud.
   Jugend, Jugendliche, jenseits; Konzert, Freizeit, Zeitung, schmalzig;
   singen, Sänger, anfangen, gegangen, verbringen, Zeitung, Lieblingsstar
3. Copy the following sentences to prepare yourself to write them from dictation.
   1. Jugendliche lesen auch die Zeitung.
   2. Wir sind ins Konzert gegangen.
   3. Der Sänger ist mein Lieblingsstar.
   4. Wie verbringen wir unsere Freizeit?

WAS KANNST DU SCHON?

Let's review some important points you have learned in this unit.

Can you tell what you do in your free time? Ich gehe . . . aus/ins Kino/schwimmen/tanzen/in ein Konzert/ins Theater/in ein Café/in eine Disko
Mention six of your activities. Ich lese/kegle/höre Musik/besuche Freunde/mache einen Stadtbummel/spiele . . .

Can you suggest some things to do with a friend?
You and a friend want to do something together. Make six suggestions. Use **können, wollen,** and the *let's*-form. Possible answers: Wir können ins Kino gehen. Willst du in die Stadt fahren? Gehen wir doch ins Konzert!

SECTION B

Can you tell what kinds of movies you like and don't like? Possible answers are given below.
Mention four kinds of movies and tell if you like or dislike each one. Tell which kind you prefer and which kind you like most of all. Give some reasons why. Ich sehe . . . (nicht) gern/lieber/am liebsten. Ich finde . . . toll. Ich hasse . . . Ich finde sie lustig/interessant/spannend/grausam/traurig.

Can you discuss which movie or concert you and a friend would like to go to?
Ask a friend which movie he or she would like to see. Welchen Film möchtest du sehen?

Ask what kind of concert he or she would like to hear. Was für ein Konzert möchtest du hören?

SECTION C

Can you say you like certain things or people and dislike others?
Name two movies and two movie stars you like and two you dislike. Use **mögen, nicht mögen,** and **gern haben.**
Ich mag den Film/den Schauspieler . . . (nicht).
Ich habe . . . gern.

Can you talk about what you did?
Tell what you did yesterday evening. Gestern abend habe ich/bin ich . . . ein Buch gelesen/einen Film gesehen/einen Stadtbummel gemacht/Freunde besucht/in die Stadt gefahren/ins Kino gegangen/Musik gehört/zu Hause geblieben/ . . . gespielt
Tell what the following people did:

1. your sister
   Meine Schwester hat/ist . . .
2. your parents
   Meine Eltern haben/sind . . .
3. you and your friend
   Mein(e) Freund(in) und ich haben/sind . . .

B. Liebesfilme/Abenteuerfilme/Western/Komödien/Kriegsfilme/Action-Filme/Horrorfilme/Science-fiction-Filme

WORTSCHATZ

SECTION A

also *well then*
ausgehen *to go out* (see p 276)
besonders *especially*
das **Café, -s** *café;* in ein Café gehen *to go to a café*
die **Clique, -n** *clique*
die **Disko, -s** *disco;* in eine Disko gehen *to go to a disco*
fahren *to go, drive, ride;* in die Stadt fahren *to go into town* (see p 276)
fragen wir mal! *let's ask*
die **Freizeit** *free time, leisure time*
der **Freizeitmuffel, -** *person who doesn't know what to do with free time*
gut, danke *fine, thanks*
das **Interesse, -n** *interest*
die **Jugend** *youth, young people*
die **Jugendlichen** (pl) *young people*
kegeln *to bowl*
das **Kino, -s** *movies;* ins Kino gehen *to go to the movies;* gehen wir ins Kino! *let's go to the movies!*
können *can, be able to* (see p 275)
das **Konzert, -e** *concert;* ins Konzert gehen *to go to a concert*
man *one, you (in general), people*
miserabel *miserable*
na ja *oh, well*
nö = nein *no* (casual)
nun ja *well, yes*
radfahren: wir fahren Rad *we go bike riding*
das **Rockkonzert, -e** *rock concert*
so lala *so-so*
spannend *exciting*
die **Sportveranstaltung, -en** *sports event*
Squash *squash*
der **Stadtbummel, -** *stroll through the city;* einen Stadtbummel machen *to take a stroll through the city*
das **Theater, -** *theater;* ins Theater gehen *to go to the theater*
tun *to do*
verbringen *to spend (time)*
wenn *when, if*
wollen *to want to* (see p 275)
zu Hause *at home*
zusammen *together*

SECTION B

der **Abenteuerfilm, -e** *adventure film*
der **Action-Film, -e** *action film*
anfangen *to start* (see p 280)
gern haben *to like*
glauben *to think, believe*
gleich: das ist mir gleich *it's all the same to me*
die **Gruppe, -n** *group*
der **Horrorfilm, -e** *horror film*
ja? *okay?*
die **Komödie, -n** *comedy*
der **Kriegsfilm, -e** *war film*
der **Liebesfilm, -e** *love story*
Lieblings- *favorite*
die **Lieblingsgruppe, -n** *favorite group*
der **Lieblingsstar, -s** *favorite star*
der **Naturfilm, -e** *nature film*
Quatsch! *nonsense!*
der **Sänger, -** *singer*
schauen *to look;* in die Zeitung schauen *to look in the newspaper*
der **Schauspieler, -** *actor*
der **Science-fiction-Film, -e** *science fiction film*
singen *to sing*
was für *what kind of (a)*
welch- *which*
der **Western, -** *western*
die **Zeitung, -en** *newspaper*
zu *too*

SECTION C

brutal *brutal*
dumm *dumb, stupid*
grausam *cruel*
hassen *to hate*
heisst: wie heisst er denn? *what's it called again?*
mögen *to like;* gern mögen *to like* (see p 286)
phantasievoll *imaginative*
schmalzig *schmaltzy*
sensationell *sensational*
warum? *why?*

SECTION D

gestern abend *last night*

1. ausgehen, fahren, kegeln, können, radfahren, verbringen, wollen, anfangen, glauben, schauen, singen, hassen, mögen

WORTSCHATZÜBUNGEN

a. ausgehen, radfahren, anfangen

1. Make a list of all the verbs in the **Wortschatz**. Which ones have a separable prefix? Which ones have a vowel change in the second and third person? Which ones change their forms in the first, second, and third person? c. ausgehen, fahren, kegeln, radfahren, verbringen, anfangen, glauben, schauen, singen

b. fahren, radfahren, anfangen

2. Write down all the nouns that contain the word **Film.** Abenteuerfilm, Action-Film, Horrorfilm, Kriegsfilm, Liebesfilm, Naturfilm, Science-fiction-Film
3. **Lieblings-** is a noun prefix meaning *favorite.* Look at the **Wortschatz** and pick out all the nouns you can combine with it. Café, Disko, Kino, Theater, Gruppe, Sänger, Schauspieler, Zeitung
4. List all the words taken from English. Disko, Reporterin, Rockkonzert, Squash, Action-Film, Horrorfilm, Science-fiction-Film, Western

ZUM LESEN

Die Prominenten kommen auch nach Deutschland

Alle grossen Sänger und Musikgruppen aus dem Ausland kommen hierher—ihre Konzerte sind immer gleich ausverkauft°.

Die deutschen Jungen und Mädchen kennen die meisten Sänger und Gruppen aus dem Ausland. Die Hitliste zeigt euch, welche Sänger und Gruppen jetzt beliebt° sind.

Und ihr könnt auch einige Kommentare lesen. Junge Leute haben uns gesagt, wie sie einige Sänger und Musikgruppen finden. Was meint ihr? Habt ihr die gleiche Meinung° oder eine andere?

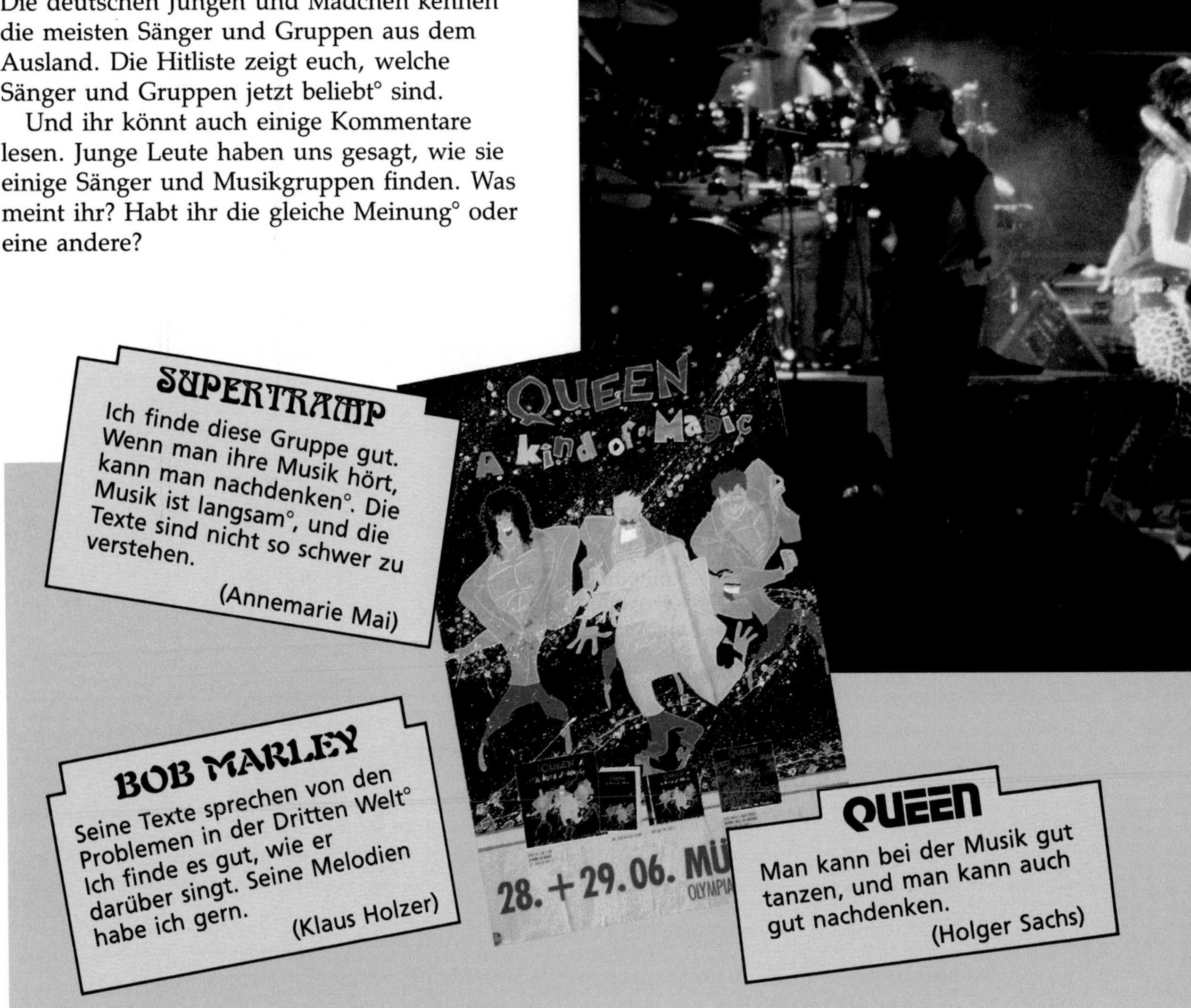

SUPERTRAMP
Ich finde diese Gruppe gut. Wenn man ihre Musik hört, kann man nachdenken°. Die Musik ist langsam°, und die Texte sind nicht so schwer zu verstehen.
(Annemarie Mai)
QUEEN
A kind of Magic
28. + 29.06. MÜ
OLYMPIA
BOB MARLEY
Seine Texte sprechen von den Problemen in der Dritten Welt°. Ich finde es gut, wie er darüber singt. Seine Melodien habe ich gern.
(Klaus Holzer)
QUEEN
Man kann bei der Musik gut tanzen, und man kann auch gut nachdenken.
(Holger Sachs)

---

ausverkauft *sold out;* **beliebt** *popular;* **die gleiche Meinung** *the same opinion;* **nachdenken** *to think about*
langsam *slow;* **in der Dritten Welt** *in the Third World*

POLICE

Die Gruppe Police habe ich sehr gern. Sie macht gute Musik. Ihre Texte sind anspruchsvoll°.

(Silke Mahler)

AC/DC

Diese Gruppe ist einfach toll! Totale Spitze! Ihre Musik ist anders als von anderen Heavy-Metall-Gruppen. Gut finde ich auch die Texte von AC/DC. Sie sind fast° alle über ihr eigenes Leben°.

(Hans Krug)

PETER MAFFAY

Er schreibt Songs—man kann dabei träumen°. Seine Songs haben auch Sinn°. Viele Texte sind so, wie es heute in der Welt ist.

(Ulla Strass)

OZZY OSBOURNE

Ozzy's Live-Shows sind Spitze! Perfekte Light-Shows, grosser Sound und eine technisch brillante Band!

(Helga Breuer)

Hitliste der Klasse 9b

(nach Gruppen/Interpreten)

1. AC/DC
2. Queen
   Peter Maffay
3. Police
4. Falco
5. Scorpions
   Ozzy Osbourne
6. Pink Floyd
7. Bob Marley
8. Supertramp

---

anspruchsvoll *stimulating;* **fast** *almost;* **über ihr eigenes Leben** *about their own life;* **träumen** *to dream;* **Sinn** *meaning*

Stars, die heute beliebt sind

Nina Hagen, eine deutsche Sängerin von Weltrang, kommt aus Berlin. Man nennt sie die Rocklady oder die Rock-Walküre. Nina gibt Konzerte in der ganzen Welt, in Italien, Frankreich, Österreich, Norwegen, Kanada, in den USA und in Südamerika.

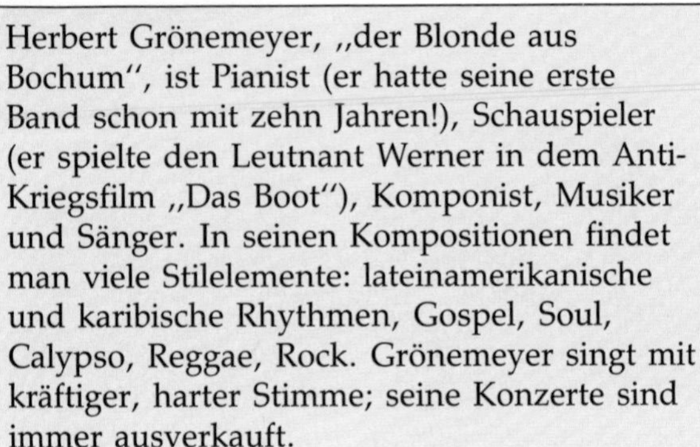

Herbert Grönemeyer, „der Blonde aus Bochum“, ist Pianist (er hatte seine erste Band schon mit zehn Jahren!), Schauspieler (er spielte den Leutnant Werner in dem Anti-Kriegsfilm „Das Boot“), Komponist, Musiker und Sänger. In seinen Kompositionen findet man viele Stilelemente: lateinamerikanische und karibische Rhythmen, Gospel, Soul, Calypso, Reggae, Rock. Grönemeyer singt mit kräftiger, harter Stimme; seine Konzerte sind immer ausverkauft.

In Deutschland ist er ein Super-Star, der Rocksänger Peter Maffay. Seine Konzerte sind immer ausverkauft, sein Publikum kommt aus allen Generationen: Oma, Opa, Mutter, Vater, Tochter und Sohn. Seine Musik und seine Texte sind für alle interessant.

Falco, der Hit-Interpret, heisst eigentlich Johann Hölzel. Er ist Österreicher und kommt aus Wien. Falco steht mit „Rock me Amadeus" nach den USA nun auch in England in den Charts auf Platz „Eins". Diesen Herbst startet Falco zu einer 18-Städte-Tournee.

Übung • Jetzt bist du dran!

1. Welche Gruppen oder Sänger und Sängerinnen kennst du und welche kennst du nicht?
2. Welche Gruppen oder Interpreten hörst du gern? Welche hörst du nicht gern?
3. Wie heissen deine Lieblingsgruppen oder Lieblingssänger?

Übung • Umfrage

Welches ist eure Hitliste? Macht eine Umfrage in der Klasse:

Unsere Hitliste: Gruppen aus den USA
Unsere Hitliste: Gruppen aus anderen Ländern

Schreibübung • Klassenprojekt

Jeder von euch schreibt ein kurzes Resümee von einer Gruppe oder von einem Sänger oder einer Sängerin. Lest dann in der Klasse vor, was ihr geschrieben habt und besprecht eure Arbeiten!

KAPITEL 11 Geschenke kaufen
Scope and Sequence

	BASIC MATERIAL	COMMUNICATIVE FUNCTIONS
SECTION A	**Geschenke für Freunde und Familie (A1)**	**Expressing attitudes and opinions** • Discussing what to give as a present; asking for advice on what to give
SECTION B	**Im Kaufhaus (B1)** **Haben Sie den Pulli vielleicht in Blau? (B9)**	**Socializing** • Getting someone's attention **Exchanging information** • Conversing with a salesperson; talking about colors
SECTION C	**Geschenkideen (C1)** **Wann hast du Geburtstag? (C9)** **Wann hast du Geburtstag? Oder Namenstag? (C10)** **Was hast du ihm geschenkt? (C16)**	**Exchanging information** • Saying the seasons and months • Giving the date **Socializing** • Expressing good wishes
TRY YOUR SKILLS	Pronunciation /a:/, /e:/, /o:/, /u:/, /ü:/; /ei/, /au/, /ɔi/; /ç/, /x/, /l/ Letter-sound correspondences **d, g, b, z, w, s, v, r** Dictation	
ZUM LESEN	**Ein Gewohnheitsmensch** (a short story about a pair of new shoes)	

WRITING A variety of controlled and open-ended writing activities appear in the Pupil's Edition. The Teacher's Notes identify other activities suitable for writing practice and suggest additional writing activities.

COOPERATIVE LEARNING Many of the activities in the Pupil's Edition lend themselves to cooperative learning. The Teacher's Notes explain some of the many instances where this teaching strategy can be particularly effective. For guidelines on how to use cooperative learning, see page T13.

GRAMMAR	CULTURE	RE–ENTRY
Indirect objects; dative case forms of possessives (A4) The verb **geben** (A7)	Buying presents	Gift items Possessives Family members The verb **sollen**
dieser, jeder, nominative and accusative case (B3) **der, die, das** used as demonstrative pronouns (B11)	Types of stores and store hours	Talking about prices Numbers Saying please/thank you Saying you don't know Expressing enthusiasm **dieser, jeder, welcher**
Third person pronouns, dative case (C5) More past participles (C17)	Occasions for giving gifts; gifts to give a host or hostess	Making suggestions Expressing likes Seasons of the year The conversational past
Recombining communicative functions, grammar, and vocabulary		
Reading for practice and pleasure		

TEACHER–PREPARED MATERIALS

Section A Pictures of gifts; ads from newspapers, magazines or catalogs; flashcards, family members; calendar

Section B Pictures of clothing items; price tags; color cards

Section C Pictures of gifts; flashcards and pictures of special occasions; calendars; flashcards of verbs, past participles

UNIT RESOURCES

Übungsheft, Unit 11
Arbeitsheft, Unit 11
Unit 11 Cassettes
Transparencies 28–30
Quizzes 29–31
Unit 11 Test

A1–2

SECTION A

OBJECTIVES **To express attitudes and opinions:** discuss what to give as a present and ask for advice on what to give

CULTURAL BACKGROUND Young people in the German-speaking countries are very aware of birthdays, anniversary dates, and dates of other special occasions. They know this not only for immediate family members, but very often for the extended family and circle of closest friends. One reason for this awareness is the fact that most forms and documents ask for the names and dates of birth of parents as well as grandparents. Young people are usually expected to attend family celebrations. This is possible because families for the most part still live close to each other or at least in the same area.

It is customary to give gifts on special occasions in Germany, even if only small ones. Books are especially popular gift items, and book stores usually carry a large selection of gift books in every price range and on every subject. Candy and flowers are traditionally popular gifts. From early childhood on, young people are encouraged to do something special on important occasions—to make something, to perform a musical piece, or to recite a poem.

MOTIVATING ACTIVITY Ask your students what special occasions they celebrate in their families. How do they celebrate? What presents do they give? Do they know the dates of birth and anniversary dates of family members and close friends?

A1

Geschenke für Freunde und Familie

Bring in pictures of various articles presented in A1 or, if possible, the actual articles. Act out the dialog, demonstrating meaning through gestures, pointing, and pictures. Ask the question **Was schenke ich meinem Vater?,** leaving out **bloss.** Then ask it again *with* **bloss,** emphasizing the word and expressing exasperation. Hold up the articles or pictures of articles, asking various students for their opinions: **Eine Brieftasche, vielleicht? Was meinst du?** The students might answer with:

Ja, eine Brieftasche! Ja, prima Idee!
Ich weiss nicht. Keine Ahnung!

Ask the students: **Welche Geschenke gibst du gern? Welche Geschenke bekommst du gern?**

Re-enter previously learned adjectives such as **schön, super, schick, hübsch,** and **toll.** Have the students respond to statements and questions:

Soll ich meinem Vater eine Brieftasche schenken?
— Ja, die Brieftasche ist schön.
Hier, ein Buch für meine Schwester. Sie liest gern.
— Das Buch sieht interessant aus.

A2

Übung • Im Schaufenster

This activity is designed to give practice with the new vocabulary, first practicing plural forms, then the new nouns with indefinite articles in the accusative, and finally with the definite articles in the nominative. Have the students look at the items and prices on pages 302–303, or make a poster with magazine pictures to display them. Be sure to include prices.

As a variation, use the definite article in the second exchange to give practice in the accusative; then use the indefinite article in the third exchange to give practice with the nominative.

SLOWER–PACED LEARNING First go around the class, asking students at random: **Was kaufst du?** Each student gives two items: **Ich kaufe eine Brieftasche und ein Armband.** Then have the students work in pairs. One student asks what each item pictured costs. The second student answers. Then have them reverse roles.

A3 Übung • Merkspiel: Was für Geschenke kaufst du?

As an expansion, encourage students to include other vocabulary they have learned. Some examples are **Taschenrechner, Kuli, Wörterbuch, Spielkarten, Musikkassette, Adressbuch, Kamera, Reiseführer, Reisetasche, Regenschirm.**

A4 ERKLÄRUNG

The dative case is introduced here through possessives in a natural, easy-to-practice context. At this point, limit the use of the dative to these possessives. Ask the students to look at A1 and pick out the phrases that express "to" or "for" someone. Ask them to observe the endings on the possessives in these phrases. Together with the students, look at the chart on page 304. Ask them to point out spelling differences between the possessives in the dative and those in the nominative and accusative. You might want to write them on the board or on an overhead transparency.

Write the following three questions on the board. Write the answer only to the first question. Ask the students to provide the answers for questions two and three. What similarity do they see between the interrogatives and the possessives in the answers?

Wer ist das?	Mein Vater.
Wen fragst du?	(Meinen Vater.)
Wem schenkst du das Buch?	(Meinem Vater.)

A5 Übung • Was kauft Andrea für ihre Familie und Freunde?

SLOWER–PACED LEARNING For more practice and to highlight the dative form, change lines two and three of the dialog to the following:

B: *Wem* kauft sie ein Buch?
A: Ihrem Bruder.

A6 Übung • Was schenkst du alles?

To expand the activity and practice more possessive forms, have the students pretend they are addressing a brother and sister. Have them vary the dialog as follows:

A: Ich habe ein Buch für meinen Vater. Was schenkt ihr eurem Vater?
B: Vielleicht schenken wir unserem Vater auch ein Buch.

A7 ERKLÄRUNG

Ask the students to name some other verbs they have learned that have a stem vowel change from **e** to **i** in the **du-** and **er/sie-** forms. **(essen, nehmen)**

A8 Übung • Frag mal deine Klassenkameraden und deine Lehrer!

First do this activity with the whole class. If some students have difficulty

A9–12

coming up with the gift ideas, ask other students to make suggestions. **Du kannst deinen Eltern eine Kassette schenken. Ein Buch, vielleicht. Ich schenke meinen Eltern gewöhnlich Blumen.** Then have the students work in cooperative learning groups of three to five and ask each other the questions in this activity. They may refer to pages 302 and 303 in the textbook.

A 9 Übung • Mix-Match: Wem schenkst du was?

CHALLENGE Personalize the first column with names of class members. Then to the last column add some gift suggestions that might be humorous to give to certain people in column three:

eine Brille	ein Flugticket nach Alaska	einen Hund
ein Flugzeug	ein Rock-und-Roll-Poster	einen Video-Recorder
eine Gurke	einen Audi	ein Schloss

A 10 Übung • Hör gut zu!

You will hear ten statements. Some contain an indirect object and some don't. For example, you hear, **Die Monika kauft ihrem Vater gewöhnlich ein Buch.** You place your check mark in the row labeled *ja,* indicating that the statement you heard contained an indirect object. Let's begin. **Fangen wir an!**

1. Was soll ich nur meinen Grosseltern kaufen? *ja*
2. Ich kaufe ein Radio und vielleicht einen Kassetten-Recorder. *nein*
3. Die Andrea schenkt ihrer Mutter immer Parfüm. *ja*
4. Ich kaufe meinen Eltern einen Strauss Blumen. *ja*
5. Das Portemonnaie ist für meinen Bruder. *nein*
6. Meine Schwester hat keine Armbanduhr. *nein*
7. Wir geben unserer Oma eine Schachtel Pralinen. *ja*
8. Du, die Pralinen sind für meinen Opa. *nein*
9. Ich schenke meinem Freund meistens eine Musikkassette. *ja*
10. Wir kaufen unseren Geschwistern immer Bücher. *ja*

Now check your answers. *Read each item again and give the correct answer.*

A 11 Schreibübung • Deine Geschenkliste

Put names of gift items, including ones suggested in the text and teacher's notes for A9, on cards. On another set of cards, put words for relatives. Have the students draw cards in pairs, one drawing from each pile, and use the words drawn to create questions and responses: **Was schenkst du (deiner Mutter)? Ich schenke meiner Mutter (einen Hund).** For added interest, this could be done as a competition. The team making the least mistakes wins.

A 12 WIE SAGT MAN DAS?

Point out the role of words **bloss** and **nur** in the questions in the first box. Read the questions first matter-of-factly without **bloss** and **nur,** then with more expression, including **bloss** and **nur.** Ask the students what they notice. How are the sets of questions different? How is this difference expressed in English? *(What on earth . . . , whatever should I . . .)*

A 13

Übung • Was soll ich bloss schenken?

Have the students work in pairs or in small cooperative learning groups. Point out that not all items work with **gewöhnlich** and **meistens** and adjustments have to be made. For example, they might say **Ich habe meiner Mutter eine Kamera gekauft** or **Ich will meiner Tante einen Regenschirm kaufen. Sie braucht einen Regenschirm.**

As a variation, combine the presents and persons differently than shown, for example, **Ich kaufe meinem Vater meistens Pralinen. Er isst Pralinen gern.** This is also a good opportunity to re-enter other vocabulary from preceding units: **Ich kaufe meinem Bruder einen Taschenrechner. Er ist nicht gut in Mathe.**

CHALLENGE Encourage the students to think of different reasons to give a particular present or not to:

Sie liest gern.	Sie hat schon einen Kalender.
Er mag Pralinen nicht.	Ich kaufe immer Blumen.

OBJECTIVES **To socialize:** get someone's attention; **to exchange information:** converse with a salesperson; talk about colors

CULTURAL BACKGROUND Germans shop for clothing in small specialty stores and in large department stores. But no matter where they shop, they can expect professional help and attention because all salespeople are professionally trained as such. Germans tend to find one or two stores they like and shop there almost exclusively. They often have a certain salesperson to whom they always go. Sales personnel often establish a regular clientele.

MOTIVATING ACTIVITY Ask the students where they shop for clothes. Do they go to the same stores regularly? Are they always waited on by the same salesperson?

B 1

Im Kaufhaus

Bring in pictures of the clothing items to be presented in this section and attach prices to them. Also make a sign with a price crossed out and a lower price written below it. Present the dialog and model the new vocabulary. You might pretend to be a salesperson pointing out various items and prices to a customer; or you could be a customer shopping with a friend, commenting on items and prices. With the aid of the pictures and gestures, make the distinction between **dieser** and **jeder.** Point to a T-shirt, for example, and say **Dieses T-Shirt kostet nur acht Mark.** Then point to a picture of a display of shirts and say **Jedes Hemd kostet zwölf Mark.** Gradually involve the students by asking them questions that require them to repeat the name of the item. For example, point to a picture of a blouse with a price tag and say: **Entschuldigung! Was kostet die Bluse? (Die Bluse kostet . . .)**

B 2

Übung • Was kaufst du?

This activity provides practice with the new vocabulary, requiring the students to use the definite and indefinite articles, nominative and accusative case, singular and plural. Note that **dieser** and **jeder** are not yet practiced here.

First go around the class having each student fill in an item from the chart on the right: **Ich kaufe ein Hemd. Ich kaufe einen Pulli,** and so on. Do each statement or question in this way. Then have the students cover the chart. Go around the class for each statement or question, this time holding up a picture of an item with the price tag as a cue.

Finally, do little exchanges that would take place in a shopping situation. Ask the students questions to elicit the answer in the activity or ask the question as stated and require an answer:

1. Was kaufst du?
Ich kaufe einen Pulli.
2. Wie teuer ist der Pulli?
Der Pulli kostet 18 Mark.
3. Sind die Pullis im Angebot?
Ja, die Pullis sind im Angebot. Sie kosten heute nur 18 Mark.
4. Möchten Sie den Pulli?
Ja, ich möchte den Pulli. *[or]* Nein, ich möchte den Pulli nicht.

B3 ERKLÄRUNG

As in B1, again make the distinction between **dieser** and **jeder** using pictures and gestures. Emphasize the ending vocally: **dies*er* Mantel, jed*es* Hemd.** Ask the students to listen carefully and tell you what they hear. Have them point out the various endings. Then have them look at B1 and pick out all examples of **dies-, jed-,** and **all-.** Why do they think the endings are different? How are these words similar to the definite articles? Have one student write the definite articles, nominative and accusative case, on the board. Ask two other students to write the forms of **dies-** and **jed-** next to the definite articles. The rest of the class should write the information in their notebooks. Then check and correct the results. Finally, read the explanation with the class.

B4 Übung • Im Kaufhaus

Play the cassette or model these dialogs for the students. Then have them work in pairs, practicing the dialogs with the items pictured and reversing roles periodically.

ANSWERS
1. 1. dieser, jeder Mantel 2. dieser, jeder Pulli 3. dieses, jedes Hemd 4. diese, jede Mütze 5. dieses, jedes Halstuch 6. diese, jede Bluse 7. diese, alle Schuhe 8. diese, jede Hose 9. dieses, jedes T-Shirt 10. diese, jede Krawatte
2. 1. dieser, jeden Mantel, ihn 2. dieser, jeden Pulli, ihn 3. dieses, jedes Hemd, es 4. diese, jede Mütze, sie 5. dieses, jedes Halstuch, es 6. diese, jede Bluse, sie 7. diese, alle Schuhe, sie 8. diese, jede Hose, sie 9. dieses, jedes T-Shirt, es 10. diese, jede Krawatte, sie
3. 1. der, diesen Mantel 2. der, diesen Pulli 3. das, dieses Hemd 4. die, diese Mütze 5. das, dieses Halstuch 6. die, diese Bluse 7. die, diese Schuhe 8. die, diese Hose 9. das, dieses T-Shirt 10. die, diese Krawatte

B5 Übung • Merkspiel

SLOWER–PACED LEARNING Hold up pictures of items as cues. If necessary, start off by providing the definite article for each new item that is added, but require the students to remember the gender of previously mentioned items.

B6 WIE SAGT MAN DAS?

Briefly have the students practice getting the attention of a salesperson. Have them take turns playing each role. This may be done humorously; for example, the customer may have to try repeatedly because the salesperson is ignoring him or her.

B7 Übung • Verkaufsgespräch

CHALLENGE Have the students work in pairs and expand the conversation, asking more questions and making appropriate comments. This activity can also be done in cooperative learning groups of three or four students. In this case, the customer is shopping with one or two friends. The customer might ask their opinion, and they might make comments and ask more questions.

B8 Ein wenig Landeskunde

The issue of store hours in Germany is a controversial one. Because of the shorter store hours, people who work find that they do not have enough time to shop. On Saturdays, especially "long Saturdays," the stores are extremely crowded, making shopping difficult and unpleasant. Stores are not open longer because it is felt that it would be unfair to store personnel to require them to work evenings and weekends. In Germany, all salespeople have gone through a formal apprenticeship program in which they have been professionally trained for the occupation of salesperson. Germans are used to being waited on by salespeople who know what they are talking about and can give thorough, professional information about the products they are selling. It is against the law to hire someone who has not had this training. The pool of part-time help consisting of housewives, students, and people looking for a second job to supplement income is not available in Germany as it is in this country.

B9 HABEN SIE DEN PULLI VIELLEICHT IN BLAU?

Follow the usual procedure. Model the dialog using sweaters cut out of red and blue construction paper, or use pictures. Repeat the dialog, substituting another item of clothing and other colors. You might point to something one of the students is wearing and use that.

To practice different colors, point out some of the colors students are wearing: **Der Brian trägt heute Dunkelblau und Weiss.** Have students say the color they are wearing: **Ich trage heute . . .** Give vocabulary for additional colors if necessary: **Lila, Rosarot, Purpurrot, Orange.** Be sure to elicit only the colors—students cannot yet say **Ich trage einen blauen Pulli.**

B10 Übung • Und du? Wie steht's mit dir?

As a variation, have the students guess each other's favorite colors, and yours: **(Rot) ist deine/Ihre Lieblingsfarbe.** They should respond with

Stimmt! or **Stimmt nicht!** As an expansion, ask them to tell the favorite colors of family members or of friends: **Onkel Kurts Lieblingsfarbe ist Hellblau.**

B 11 ERKLÄRUNG

Have the students look at the dialog in B9 and pick out all the definite articles. They will notice that some are not followed by nouns. See if anyone can tell you how these are used in the sentence. They are used as pronouns, and they are called demonstrative pronouns. Now read the explanation with the students. Be sure to emphasize the demonstrative pronouns in the examples as you read them.

B 12 Übung • Was sagt die Verkäuferin? Was sagst du?

SLOWER–PACED LEARNING First do the exercise substituting the definite article for **dieser** in the first line of the exchange: **Der Pulli ist hübsch, nicht?** Then do the exercise as written.

B 13 Übung • Was?! Du kaufst alles?

SLOWER–PACED LEARNING Follow the suggestion given in the notes to B12. For further practice as well as review, add items from Section A and from preceding units.

B 14 Übung • Hör gut zu!

For this exercise, open your textbook to page 311. Look at the objects shown in Excercise B14. You will hear ten statements. On your answer sheet, write the number of the statement under the object shown. **Fangen wir an!**

1. Dieses Hemd sieht toll aus. Was kostet es?
2. Entschuldigung! Haben Sie diesen Mantel auch in Braun?
3. Ja, dieser Pulli ist wirklich sehr schick. Ich nehme ihn.
4. Ich weiss nicht: soll ich diese Hose kaufen oder nicht? Was meinst du?
5. Nein, danke. Diese Brieftasche kostet zu viel.
6. Ich finde dieses Halstuch sehr schön. Die Farbe ist so toll!
7. Eine Mütze für zwanzig Mark ist zu teuer.
8. Fräulein! Was kostet die Halskette dort drüben, bitte?
9. Das Portemonnaie ist schick. Ich mag nur die Farbe nicht.
10. Gut, ich nehme die Bluse, ja, die in Grün. Grün ist meine Lieblingsfarbe.

Now check your answers. The numbers in the first row should read, from left to right, *2, 6, 10, 8, 1;* in the second row, *3, 9, 4, 7, 5.*

B 15 Schreibübung • Was darf es sein, bitte?

Have the students work in pairs or in cooperative learning groups of three to five. After the students have written dialogs and practiced them with each other, ask for two volunteers to come to the front of the class. One is to take the role of the salesperson, the other the role of the customer. Tell the student who is playing the customer the item he or she would like to buy (it could be any of the new clothing items) and have the students act out a spontaneous buying situation.

SECTION C

OBJECTIVES **To exchange information:** say the seasons and months; give the date; **to socialize:** express good wishes

CULTURAL BACKGROUND In traditionally Catholic areas of Germany such as Bavaria and the Rhineland, many people observe their name day (see C10). Name days commemorate saints and people from Biblical times, for whom people are often named. Many German calendars list name days, and most people are aware of theirs even if they do not celebrate it.

MOTIVATING ACTIVITY Ask your students what they say in English to express congratulations and good wishes on special occasions. List the expressions on the board. Tell the students they will learn what to say on such occasions in German.

C1 Geschenkideen

The third person dative pronouns are introduced here in the context of an ad in a German magazine. Together with the students, look at page 312. Read each gift suggestion. In the one top left **(Zum Muttertag? Schenken Sie ihr Parfüm!)**, ask the students, **Wer ist das? Was bedeutet „ihr"? „Ihr" ist die Mutter—Zum Muttertag schenken Sie Ihrer Mutter Parfüm!**

Do this for each picture. For **Weihnachten** and **Geburtstag,** ask who **ihm** and **ihr** *could* be **(Freund, Schwester).** After you have gone through all the pictures in this fashion, ask the students for the English equivalents—*Give her perfume! Buy him a wallet! Give them flowers!*

Also present the expressions of good wishes. Model and have the students repeat the general expressions—**Alles Gute, Gute Wünsche,** and **Herzliche Glückwünsche.** Then give them little situations and have them express appropriate good wishes: **Zum Muttertag schenkst du deiner Mutter Blumen. Was sagst du?**

C2 Ein wenig Landeskunde

Ask your students if their parents bring a gift when they go visiting. If they do, what do they bring? Are there vending machines for flowers in their neighborhoods?

C3 Was sagt die Reklame?

CHALLENGE Have the students work in pairs or in cooperative learning groups of three to five and have them prepare brief TV commercials to present to the class. Each group selects one person to present the commercial. Encourage the students to use all the vocabulary they have learned. For example:

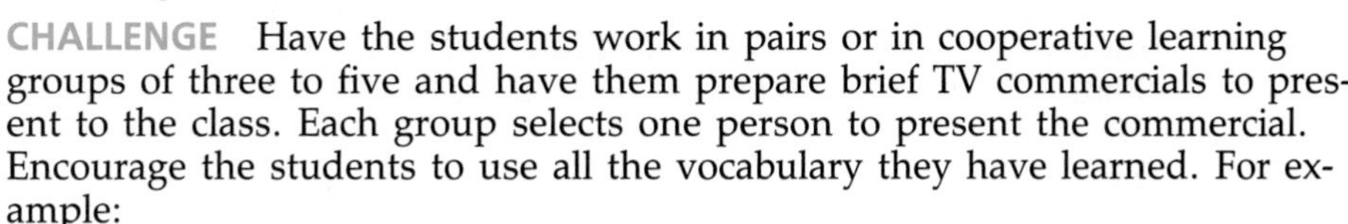

> Ihr Freund hat bald Geburtstag. Was sollen Sie nur schenken? Sie haben keine Ahnung! Sie brauchen eine Idee! Macht er gern Sport! Schenken Sie ihm ein Buch über Sport! Kommt er immer zu spät? Kaufen Sie ihm eine Armbanduhr! Geht er nicht gern aus? Kaufen Sie ihm einen Video-Recorder! Oder vielleicht ein Radio. Schauen Sie, hier haben wir ein Radio! Dieses Radio ist prima! Und was kostet es? Nur dreihundert Mark!

C4–8

The students should bring pictures or the actual articles they are advertising. The presentations may be serious or humorous. The use of adjectives preceding the noun should be avoided—encourage the students to use sentences such as **Ein Buch über Sport ist doch interessant.** Suggest phrases in which no adjective ending is required: **Ein prima Geschenk! Eine super Idee!**

C4 Übung • Was schenkst du?

SLOWER–PACED LEARNING Go around the class changing only one element of the sentence. For example, **Was schenkst du deinem Bruder zum Geburtstag?** A student answers **Zum Geburtstag schenke ich meinem Bruder ein T-Shirt.** The next student answers the same question, supplying a different gift item. After this pattern has been practiced, do the same changing only the recipient and finally the occasion.

C5 ERKLÄRUNG

Have the students observe similarities in the endings of the dative possessives and the pronouns. Have them look at C1 and pick out all examples of dative pronouns. What are the corresponding English pronouns? What similarities do they see? **(ihm—him, ihr—her)**

C6 Übung • Was soll ich bloss schenken?

Have the students work in pairs to practice these dialogs. They should be careful to make all the necessary adjustments in the dialogs as they make key changes.

CHALLENGE Have the students vary the last line of each dialog. For example, they might say **Ach, nein. Er braucht keine Krawatte** or **Meinst du? Parfüm ist so teuer.**

ANSWERS

1. meinen Eltern, ihnen, sie haben/meinem Vater, ihm, er/meiner Mutter, ihr, sie/meiner Freundin, ihr, sie/meinem Freund, ihm, er/ meinen Geschwistern, ihnen, sie haben/meinem Bruder, ihm, er/ meiner Schwester, ihr, sie
2. meinen Eltern, ihnen, sie mögen/meinem Vater, ihm, er/meiner Mutter, ihr, sie/meiner Freundin, ihr, sie/meinem Freund, ihm, er/ meinen Geschwistern, ihnen, sie mögen/meinem Bruder, ihm, er/ meiner Schwester, ihr, sie

C7 Übung • Mutter hat für alle eine Geschenkidee

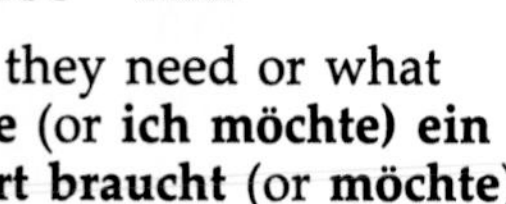

As an expansion, have members of the class say what they need or what they would like. For example, Robert says, **Ich brauche** (or **ich möchte) ein Radio.** Another student reports to the class: **Der Robert braucht** (or **möchte**) **ein Radio.** The class responds in unison: **Gut, dann schenken wir ihm ein Radio!**

C8 Übung • Was schenkst du?

CHALLENGE Have the *students* add items to the exercise, for example:

> Die Mary lernt Französisch. — Dann kannst du ihr ein Wörterbuch schenken.
> Der Thomas sammelt Briefmarken. — Dann kannst du ihm Briefmarken (oder ein Buch über Briefmarken) schenken.

C9 WANN HAST DU GEBURTSTAG?

Go around the class having each student say in what season and in what month his or her birthday is. Note that the students cannot yet say on what *day*. Tell the students that if they bought a wall calendar in Austria, **Januar** would be written **Jänner** and **Februar** would be written **Feber.** Sing the song **„Und wer im Januar geboren ist".**

C10 WANN HAST DU GEBURTSTAG? ODER NAMENSTAG?

Students are introduced to ordinals here in order to express when their birthday is. They should just learn these phrases and not use ordinals in any other way. Do have the students observe the endings of ordinals **(-ten, -sten)** and spelling differences **(dritten)** compared with cardinal numbers.

C11 Übung • Und du? Wie steht's mit dir?

Bring in a calendar on which different holidays are noted, including name days and various religious holidays, depending on what your students will want to express. Ask additional questions; for example, **Wann fängt Chanukah an?**

C12 WIE SAGT MAN DAS?

You may wish to give some additional expressions of good wishes: **Frohe Ostern! Alles Gute zum neuen Jahr! Alles Gute zum Valentinstag!** There is no real German equivalent for Thanksgiving. A church holiday called **Erntedankfest** is celebrated on the first Sunday in October, but mainly in the countryside. It is not celebrated nationwide. To wish American students a happy Thanksgiving, you could say **Ein frohes Fest!**

C13 Übung • Was sagst du . . .

To expand the activity, add other holidays as mentioned in the notes to C12. Give the students the opportunity to practice expressing various kinds of good wishes to each other. Take advantage of the chance to practice these expressions at appropriate times during the year.

C14 Übung • Hör gut zu!

For this exercise, open your textbook to page 316. Look at the objects depicted in C14. You will hear ten statements. On your answer sheet, write the number of the statement under the object shown. **Fangen wir an!**

1. Meinem Vater schenke ich zum Vatertag eine Schachtel Pralinen. Er isst Pralinen gern.
2. Zum Geburtstag kaufe ich meiner Mutter ein Buch über Tennisspielen. Sie liest gern.
3. Am siebten Juni haben meine Grosseltern ihren Hochzeitstag. Ich möchte ihnen zwei Platten kaufen; sie hören Musik gern.
4. Zum Namenstag schenke ich meinem Bruder eine Schultasche. Er braucht eine. Seine alte Schultasche ist kaputt.
5. Am zehnten Juni hat mein Bruder Geburtstag. Ich möchte ihm eine Uhr kaufen. Er weiss nie, wie spät es ist.

C15–18

6. Meiner Schwester schenke ich zum Namenstag ein Portemonnaie. Hoffentlich verliert sie dann ihr Geld nicht mehr.
7. Zu Weihnachten schenke ich meinem Freund ein Wörterbuch. Hoffentlich bekommt er dann in Englisch gute Noten.
8. Meiner Mutter schenke ich eine Vase zum Muttertag. Sie hat immer so viele Blumen, und sie weiss manchmal nicht, wo sie sie hintun soll.
9. Mein Freund bekommt zum Geburtstag eine Brieftasche. Er fliegt weg, und er braucht eine Brieftasche für seinen Pass und sein Flugticket.
10. Ich bekomme zum Geburtstag ein Fahrrad. Ich kann dann mit dem Rad in die Schule fahren. Ich brauche nicht mehr mit dem Bus zu fahren.

Now check your answers. The numbers in the first row should read, from left to right, *4, 9, 2, 10, 8;* in the second row, *1, 5, 7, 3, 6.*

C15 Schreibübung • Wer hat Geburtstag?

Ask for a show of hands as to whose birthday falls in this month. (Suggestions for making a class birthday calendar are on page 321 in the student textbook.) Ask them the day and ask what they want: **Was möchtest du zum Geburtstag haben?** Write the names, days, and wishes on the board. Have the rest of the class make some other gift suggestions, and write them on the board as well. Then have the students write a dialog as directed, working individually or in pairs. They should exchange dialogs and practice them with each other.

C16 WAS HAST DU IHM GESCHENKT?

Tell the students that German calendars are often printed with the numbers running down, as shown on this page. Have the students practice using both **haben** and **sein** when talking about special days: **Wann ist dein Geburtstag gewesen? Wann hast du deinen Namenstag gehabt? — Ich habe im Januar Geburtstag gehabt. Mein Namenstag ist am vierten Mai gewesen.**

C17 ERKLÄRUNG

Remind the students that the conversational past is a way of talking about past events. Have them look at the exchanges in C16 and point out the conversational past forms. How many parts does each verb have? Where does each part appear in the sentence? Which part changes? Why? What is the infinitive of each verb? See if anyone can read the exchanges in C16 in the present.

Have the students look at the verbs listed in the explanation. Have them tell you the infinitive for each past participle. Write both on the board. What changes do the students observe?

C18 Übung • Was haben alle gekauft?

SLOWER–PACED LEARNING Go through each item pictured with one subject before going on to the next number: **Ich habe ein Portemonnaie gekauft. Ich habe einen Strauss Blumen gekauft.**

C19 **Übung • Und du? Wie steht's mit dir?**

For additional practice, prepare cards with the nouns **Mutter, Vater, Schwester, Bruder, Grosseltern, Lehrer, Freund,** and **Freundin.** Prepare a second set of cards with names of gift items from this unit and preceding ones. Have two students stand in front of the class; each one picks a card at random and holds it up. Seated students take turns saying sentences in the conversational past using these cues: **Ich habe meiner Mutter einen Strauss Blumen geschenkt (gekauft, gegeben).**

TRY YOUR SKILLS

OBJECTIVE To recombine communicative functions, grammar, and vocabulary

CULTURAL BACKGROUND It is customary to send cards for special occasions in Germany but not to the extent that it is in the United States. Children and young people are expected to sign birthday cards and letters to relatives. They are most certainly expected to send thank-you notes for gifts they have received.

1 **Karin hat Geburtstag**

Have the students listen to the text and read along. Have them point out the expressions of good wishes. What phrase gives you a clue as to what Karin's letter to her Aunt Dora is about? **(Vielen Dank)** Have the students observe the greeting and the closing on the cards and on the letter. How does Karin write the date on her letter? What precedes the date? Have the students practice writing some dates in this manner.

2 **Übung • Beantworte die Fragen!**

You might have the students first work individually to answer these questions, briefly writing down their answers. Then go over the questions and answers with the whole class. If any students had difficulty answering the questions, help them to find clues and work out meaning.

3 **Schreibübung • Jetzt bist du dran**

SLOWER–PACED LEARNING Students may use Karin's thank-you note as a model. Have them insert the appropriate city, date, and persons. Encourage them and, if necessary, help them to think of other gifts and make appropriate comments. Elicit suggestions from class members.

CHALLENGE Have the students try to make the thank-you note different from Karin's. Also have them make the letter longer and more newsy.

4 **Übung • Probleme mit Geschenken!**

Have the students work in pairs or in cooperative learning groups of three to five. They should try to keep the conversation going as long as possible, making various suggestions, accepting and rejecting ideas, and finally coming up with a gift list that fits within the budget specified. Have one student in each group record the results.

SKILLS 5–10

5 Übung • Farbenspiel: Ich seh' etwas, was du nicht siehst . . .

Students who enjoy art projects could make a poster showing the different colors on the color wheel. They should label the colors in German. Display the poster on a bulletin board or hang it on the wall.

6 Übung • Wenn ich Geld hätte . . .

Have the students first think about this activity. They might jot down names of family members and friends and what they would buy for them. The pictured items are just suggestions. Then the students might work in small groups, discussing their thoughts and what they have jotted down. A representative from each group should take notes and report to the class.

7 Übung • Rollenspiel: Auf einer Auktion 

Act out this auction in class. Before starting the auction, spread out the items and have each person tell what the item is he or she has brought and say something about it: **Es ist alt, hübsch, schön.** Help them with a few additional words such as **wertvoll, einmalig, sehr kostbar.** They might also say what they would like to start the bidding at: **Wir fangen mit 5 Mark an!** Have students take turns playing the auctioneer, with all students bidding.

8 Übung • Wie passen die Sätze zusammen? 

CHALLENGE Have the students cover the left column. Using the words on the right, have them see how many sentences/questions they can write.

9 Übung • Klassenprojekt: Ein Geburtstagskalender

Ask for volunteers for this project. Have one or two students design the page for each month, doing it either of the two ways illustrated. Fill out each page with the class. If there is room, display all the pages. If not, display the current month. You might also have students make a family birthday calendar, filling in the birthdays of their own friends and relatives.

10 Aussprache-, Lese- und Schreibübungen 

/a:/, /e:/, /o:/ /u:/, /ü:/

1. The following words review the long vowel sounds /a:/, /e:/, /o:/, /u:/, and /ü:/. **Hör zu und wiederhole!**
   Vater, Radio, Idee, geben, gewesen, Hose, Bluse, Blume, Uhr, grün, Parfüm

/ei/ /au/ /ɔi/

These words review the diphthongs /ei/, /au/, and /ɔi/. **Hör zu und wiederhole!**
   Reisebuch, Hochzeit, Weihnachten, meinen, vielleicht, weiss; Strauss, glauben, gekauft, grau, blau, braun; teuer, Sträusse

/ç/ /x/

These words review the **ich**-sound and the **ach**-sound. **Hör zu und wiederhole!**
   gewöhnlich, vielleicht, fröhlich, herzlich, Reisebuch, Hochzeit, Schachtel, Halstuch, Weihnachten

/l/

These words review the /l/ sound. **Hör zu und wiederhole!**
   Kalender, Halskette, Schachtel, Pralinen, Blume, Pulli, Bluse, Mantel, Lieblingsfarbe, glauben, bald, gewöhnlich, vielleicht, blau,

gelb, hellblau, dunkelblau, bloss, herzlich, Glückwünsche, fröhlich, alles Gute

2. In this section you will practice reading the words in your textbook on page 321.

d g b 1. First you will read words with **d, g,** and **b. Hör zu und wiederhole!**
Armband, sag, ich glaub', Hemd, gelb, Vatertag, bald, gehabt

z 2. Now you will read some words with **z. Hör zu und wiederhole!**
Mütze, Hochzeit, schwarz, herzlich, zum

w 3. Now you will read some words with **w. Hör zu und wiederhole!**
Krawatte, Weihnachten, gewesen, gewöhnlich, weiss, schwarz, warum, Witz

s 4. Now you will read some words with **s. Hör zu und wiederhole!**
Halskette, Hose, diese, weiss, gewesen, bloss, Bluse, Vase, Strauss

v 5. Now you will read some words with **v. Hör zu und wiederhole!**
Vatertag, vielleicht, verbringen, verstehen, verlieren; Video, Vase

r 6. Now you will read some words with **r. Hör zu und wiederhole!**
braun, darf, Krawatte, teuer, nur, schwarz, Farbe, rot, Reisebuch, fröhlich, grün, Radio, dieser, Armbanduhr, Muttertag, Portemonnaie, Strauss, Uhr, herzlich, Kalender, grau, Geburtstag, Vatertag, jeder, Parfüm, Brieftasche, Pralinen, am dritten, am ersten, Quarzuhr

3. Now close your textbook and write the sentences you hear.

1. Ich glaub', das Hemd ist gelb.
2. Diese Hose ist zu teuer.
3. Die Krawatte hab' ich zu Weihnachten bekommen.
4. Herzliche Glückwünsche zum Geburtstag!

WAS KANNST DU SCHON?

If the students need more practice, use the cards prepared as suggested in the notes to C19 as cues. Hold up a card naming a person and a card naming a gift item. Ask questions such as **Was schenkst du? Wem schenkst du das? Was schenkst du deiner Mutter?**

Students could work in pairs to act out these situations. For additional practice, do directed dialogs. For example:

—Du bist im Kaufhaus. Die Verkäuferin sieht dich nicht. Was sagst du? Was sagt die Verkäuferin?
—Du siehst einen schönen Mantel. Frag die Verkäuferin, was der Mantel kostet! Sag dem Kunden, er kostet 80 Mark!
—Frag die Verkäuferin, ob sie den Mantel auch in Dunkelblau hat! Sag dem Kunden, nein, du hast den Mantel nur in Grün!

If the students do not know these dates, have them ask their parents or make them up. In the final part of this section, another holiday could be substituted for Christmas.

WORTSCHATZ

WORTSCHATZ

Have the students find items on the vocabulary list that belong to the following categories and write them down.

1. items of clothing
2. other gift items
3. colors
4. months of the year
5. special occasions
6. expressions of good wishes

WORTSCHATZÜBUNGEN

Have the students work individually and write down their findings. Then correct papers with the entire class. Have them write these words in their notebooks.

ZUM LESEN

ZUM LESEN

OBJECTIVE To read for practice and pleasure

EIN GEWOHNHEITSMENSCH 

Allow sufficient time for the students to read the entire story silently. Then play the cassette or read the story aloud. Next have the students read the story one section at a time. Pause after each of the sections to check comprehension. Ask questions in German about the content. Accept short answers, since the main objective is to read with fluency and comprehension. For example, after the first section you might ask: **Was für ein Mann ist Herr Neuschuh? Wo kauft er seine Sachen? Was sagt er über die Mode?**

SLOWER–PACED LEARNING Have the students tell briefly in English what happens in each section. Do not ask them to translate, however. Explain the meaning of any word or expression that hinders comprehension.

Übung • Let's take a closer look

Have the students do these questions individually first, examining the text and writing down the answers. Then go over the answers together in class.

ANSWERS

1. Er ist nett, höflich, pünktlich, immer korrekt, gut angezogen. Er kauft seine Sachen in den besten Geschäften, aber er macht sich wenig aus der Mode.

2. pünktlich = punctual; korrekt = correct, proper; besten = best; klassischen = classical; Stil = style; kommen = come; England = England; Italien = Italy; Morgen = morning; neue = new; alle = all; ein Paar = a pair; hier = here; Braun = brown; das letzte Paar = the last pair; perfekt = perfect; Modell = model; recht = right; Interesse = interest; Minute = minute; jung = young; grotesk = grotesque; wunderbar = wonderful; „in" = "in"; Karton = carton; Kreditkarte = credit card. *Other answers possible.*
3. Herr Neuschuh: „Nein, kein Interesse." Die Verkäuferin holt die Schuhe und sagt: „Hier ist Ihr neues Modell!" Herr Neuschuh: „Ich habe eine Verabredung." Verkäuferin: „Sehen Sie, das ist genau Ihre Marke." Herr Neuschuh: „Nun, ich danke Ihnen. Ich komme nach meiner Verabredung zurück." Verkäuferin: „Das macht zweihundertfünfundvierzig Mark." Herr Neuschuh: „Aber ich will diese Schuhe nicht!" Verkäuferin: „Soll ich die Schuhe in einen Karton packen, oder . . . " Herr Neuschuh: „Nein, ich . . . " Verkäuferin: „Zahlen Sie bar oder mit einem Euro-Scheck? Oder mit Kreditkarte?"
4. He feels ridiculous: „Ich fühle mich lächerlich in diesen Schuhen." Verkäuferin: „Ganz im Gegenteil! Diese Schuhe machen Sie jung!" Herr Neuschuh: „Ich sehe grotesk aus." Verkäuferin: „Nein, wunderbar."

Übung • Was meinst du?

Discuss the word **schmeicheln** with the students. Give them some examples. What is the difference between **ein Kompliment machen** and **schmeicheln?**

Have the students give simple answers to these questions. For 2, for example, they might say **Er kann nicht nein sagen** or **Er mag die Schuhe** or **Er findet, er sieht doch elegant aus.** Give the students additional words if necessary and help them with any vocabulary in the questions they might not understand.

Übung • Und du? Wie steht's mit dir?

You might want to assign these questions for homework to give the students time to think about them. Have the students prepare for a discussion in class the next day.

Übung • Klassenprojekte

Have pairs of students take turns reading the scene in the shoe store. Have them listen to the cassette once more, or model the scene for them. Give them time to prepare and encourage them to read with appropriate expression.

CHALLENGE The remaining projects provide challenge activities for the students. Have them choose the scene they would like to work on and form groups. Each group should write a dialog cooperatively and then select group members to perform the scene for the class.

KAPITEL 11

Geschenke kaufen

Birthdays and anniversaries, Christmas, and other holidays are occasions for buying gifts for family and friends. It is sometimes difficult, however, to find appropriate gifts, and the advice of friends is often appreciated. What do young people in the German-speaking countries buy and give as presents—the same type of things you do?

In this unit you will:

SECTION A	discuss buying presents for family and friends, ask for advice on what to give
SECTION B	get a salesperson's attention and ask about price and color of specific items
SECTION C	make suggestions for presents for special occasions and express good wishes
TRY YOUR SKILLS	use what you've learned
ZUM LESEN	read for practice and pleasure

For teaching suggestions, see the Teacher's Notes preceding this unit, pp. T200–217.

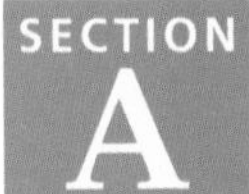

buying presents for family and friends, thinking about what to give, and asking for advice

Special occasions are coming up and presents have to be bought. On a stroll down a popular shopping street, Andrea and Monika pass a store that sells presents and souvenirs.

A1 Geschenke für Freunde und Familie

ANDREA Was schenke ich bloss meinem Vater? Er hat bald Geburtstag. Was meinst du? Hast du eine Idee? Was schenkst du gewöhnlich deinem Vater?

MONIKA Ach, ich kaufe meinem Vater meistens ein Buch. Er hat Reisebücher gern.

ANDREA Hm, der Vati hat schon so viele Bücher! — Du, und was gebe ich meinen Grosseltern? Sie haben bald goldene Hochzeit.

MONIKA Schau, Andrea, hier gibt es so viele Geschenke!

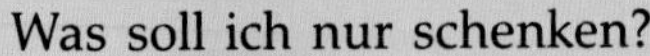

Was soll ich nur schenken?

DM 10,–

Eine Brieftasche?

DM 25,–

Ein Portemonnaie? Dieses Portemonnaie ist schick!

DM 40,–

Ein Radio, vielleicht?

DM 28,–

Parfüm? Dieses Parfüm ist toll!

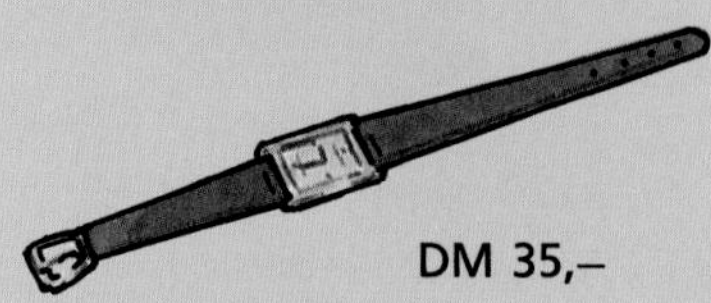

DM 35,–

Eine Armbanduhr, eine Quarzuhr?

DM 8,–

Einen Kalender?

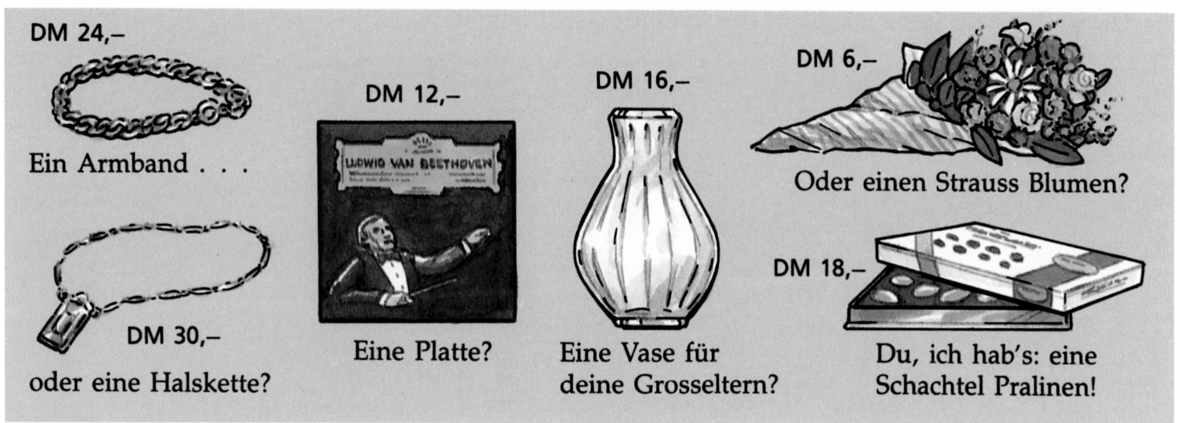
DM 24,–
Ein Armband . . .
DM 12,–
LUDWIG VAN BEETHOVEN
DM 16,–
DM 6,–
Oder einen Strauss Blumen?
DM 30,–
oder eine Halskette?
Eine Platte?
Eine Vase für
deine Grosseltern?
DM 18,–
Du, ich hab's: eine
Schachtel Pralinen!

A2 Übung • Im Schaufenster 

Let's take a look in the store window.

A: Was gibt es hier?
B: Hier gibt es Brieftaschen, . . . Portemonnaies, Radios, Parfüms, Armbanduhren, Kalender, Armbänder, Blumen, Halsketten, Platten, Vasen, Pralinen

A: Was kaufst du alles?
B: Ich kaufe eine Brieftasche, . . .

A: Was kostet das alles?
B: Die Brieftasche kostet zehn Mark, . . . das Portemonnaie, das Radio, das Parfüm, die Armbanduhr, der Kalender, das Armband, der Strauss Blumen, die Halskette, die Platte, die Vase, die Schachtel Pralinen

A3 Übung • Merkspiel: Was für Geschenke kaufst du?

MONIKA Ich kaufe ein Portemonnaie.
STEFAN Ich kaufe ein Portemonnaie und einen Kalender.
ANDREA Ich kaufe ein Portemonnaie, einen Kalender und ein . . .

A4 ERKLÄRUNG
Indirect Objects, Dative Case Forms of Possessives

1. The following sentences include a noun phrase you have not used up to now. This noun phrase signals the indirect object, which expresses the idea of "to someone" or "for someone." In German, the idea of "to someone" or "for someone" can be expressed by using dative case forms.

   Ich kaufe **meiner Schwester** eine Platte. — *I'm buying a record for my sister.* / *I'm buying my sister a record.*

   Ich gebe **meinen Brüdern** Bücher. — *I give my brothers books.* / *I give books to my brothers.*

2. In English, the indirect object is signaled by word order: I'm giving *my dad a wallet.* The same idea can be expressed by a prepositional phrase: I'm buying a record *for my sister.* In German, the indirect object is signaled by the form of the determiner **meinem, meiner, meinen,** etc. It is sometimes signaled by the noun itself:
   a. Nouns that add **-n** or **-en** in the accusative case (see page 140) also add these endings in the dative singular: **mein Klassenkamerad—meinem Klassenkameraden.**
   b. The dative plural of almost all nouns ends in **-n: seine Brüder—seinen Brüdern.** If the nominative plural form already ends in **-n,** there is no change in the dative plural form: **unsere Eltern—unseren Eltern.**

(continued)

3. The dative case forms of the possessives are listed below.

before masculine & neuter nouns	*before feminine nouns*	*before plural nouns*
meinem	**meiner**	**meinen**
deinem	**deiner**	**deinen**
seinem	**seiner**	**seinen**
ihrem	**ihrer**	**ihren**
unserem	**unserer**	**unseren**
euerem	**euerer**	**eueren**
ihrem	**ihrer**	**ihren**
Ihrem	**Ihrer**	**Ihren**

4. To ask the questions *to whom?* or *for whom?*, the dative form **wem?** is used.

Wem	kauft sie Pralinen?	*For whom is she buying fancy chocolates?*
Wem	schenkt sie ein Buch?	*To whom is she giving a book?*

A5 Übung • Was kauft Andrea für ihre Familie und Freunde?

A: Ihr Bruder bekommt ein Buch.
B: Wie bitte?
A: Sie kauft ihrem Bruder ein Buch.

1. Ihre Freundin bekommt Parfüm. ihrer
2. Ihr Vater bekommt ein Portemonnaie. ihrem
3. Ihre Geschwister bekommen Bücher. ihren Geschwistern
4. Ihr Freund bekommt ein Poster. ihrem
5. Ihre Kusine bekommt eine Halskette. ihrer
6. Ihr Opa bekommt Pralinen. ihrem

A6 Übung • Was schenkst du alles?

A: Ich habe ein Buch für meinen Vater.
B: Vielleicht schenke ich meinem Vater auch ein Buch.

1. Ich habe eine Vase für meine Oma. meiner
2. Ich habe eine Armbanduhr für meinen Freund. meinem
3. Ich habe Pralinen für meine Eltern. meinen
4. Ich habe ein Armband für meine Schwester. meiner
5. Ich habe Kassetten für meine Freunde. meinen Freund
6. Ich habe eine Platte für meinen Vetter. meinem

A7 ERKLÄRUNG
The Verb geben

The verb **geben** has the following forms in the present tense. Note the vowel change from **e** to **i** in the **du-** and **er/sie**-forms.

ich **gebe**	wir **geben**
du **gibst**	ihr **gebt**
er, sie, es **gibt**	sie, Sie **geben**

A8 Übung • Frag mal deine Klassenkameraden und deine Lehrer!

1. Was gibst du deinen Eltern?
2. Was gibst du deinen Geschwistern?
3. Was gebt ihr euern Grosseltern?
4. Frau (Meier), was geben Sie Ihren Kindern?

A 9 Übung • Mix-Match: Wem schenkst du was?

Ich kaufe meinem Vater gewöhnlich ein Buch.

ich	gebe	meinem Vater	gewöhnlich	ein Buch
wir	gibt	ihren Eltern	immer	eine Armbanduhr
Andrea	geben	seiner Schwester	meistens	Parfüm
Peter	kaufe	unseren Grosseltern	vielleicht	einen Strauss Blumen
die Kinder	kauft	seinem Opa		eine Schachtel Pralinen
	kaufen	seinen Eltern		eine Platte
	schenke	ihrer Tante		einen Kalender
	schenkt	ihren Geschwistern		eine Halskette
	schenken	meiner Mutter		ein Portmonnaie

A 10 Übung • Hör gut zu!

For script and answers, see p. T204.

Does the sentence have an indirect object or not?

		0	1	2	3	4	5	6	7	8	9	10
sentence has an indirect object	ja	✓	✓		✓	✓			✓		✓	✓
	nein			✓			✓	✓		✓		

A 11 Schreibübung • Deine Geschenkliste

Make a list of your family members including some aunts, uncles, and cousins, and write what you might give each one as a present.

Ich schenke meiner Mutter . . .,
meinem Onkel (Fred) . . .

Now exchange lists with a classmate and take turns telling the class what is on your classmate's list.

(Bob) schenkt seiner Mutter . . .
Er schenkt seinem Vetter (David) . . .

Vati, vielen Dank für den Computer!

A 12 WIE SAGT MAN DAS?

Wondering what to give, asking for advice

wondering what to give	Was schenke ich bloss meinem Vater?	What on earth should I give my father?
	Was gebe ich nur meiner Mutter?	What can I give to my mother?
	Was soll ich kaufen?	What should I buy?
asking for advice	Was meinst du?	What do you think?
	Hast du eine Idee?	Do you have an idea?

A13 Übung • Was soll ich bloss schenken?

You ask different classmates for advice on what to buy for various people.

A: Was schenk' ich bloss meiner Freundin? Was meinst du? Hast du eine Idee?
B: Hm. Ich kaufe meiner Freundin gewöhnlich ein Buch.
A: Ja! Vielleicht ein Buch!

* * *

A: Du, Peter!
B: Ja?
A: Was kann ich bloss meiner Kusine schenken?
B: Deiner Kusine? —Ich kaufe meiner Kusine meistens eine Platte. Sie hat Platten gern.
A: Ach, sie hat schon so viele Platten.

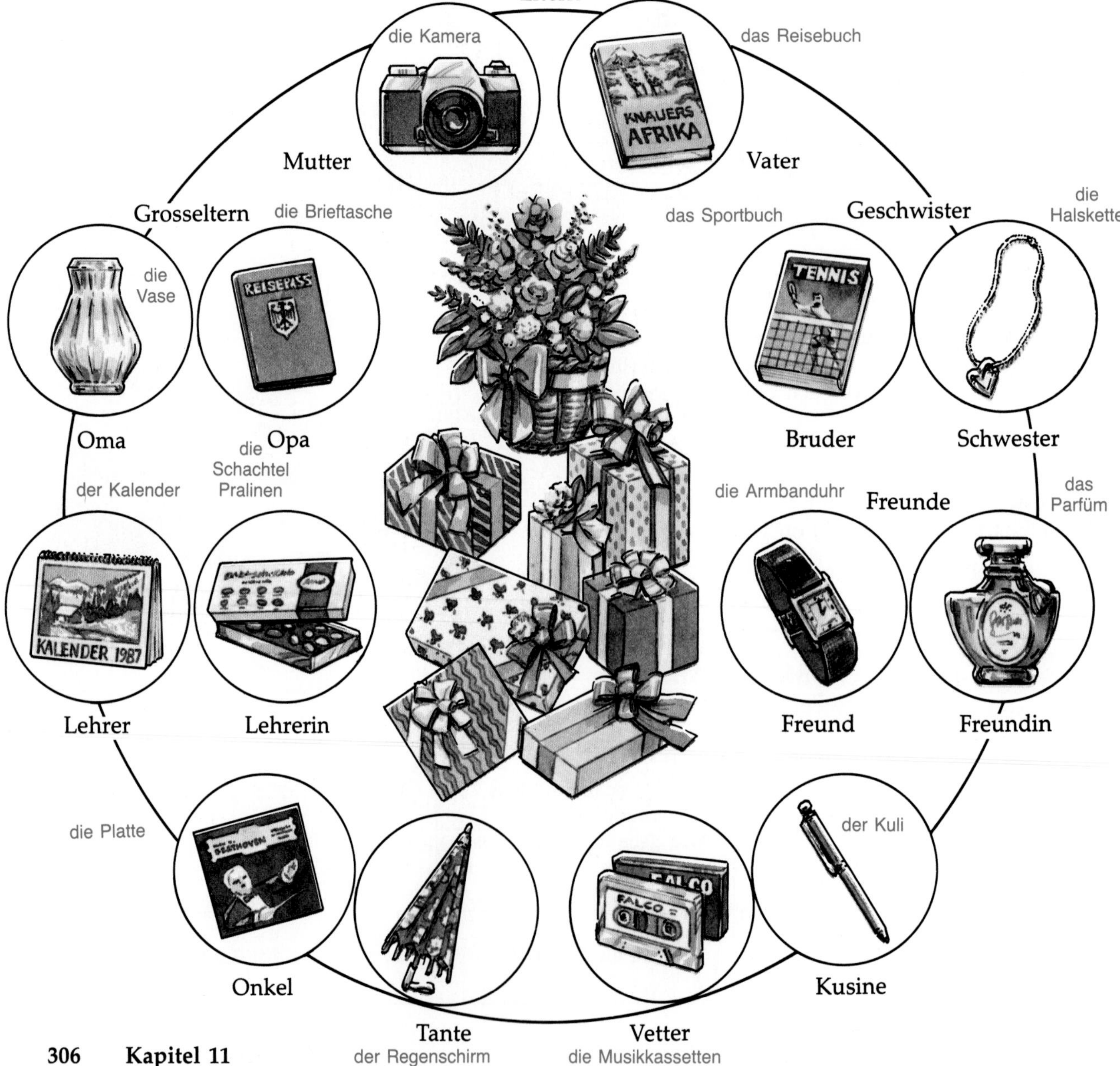

SECTION B

getting a salesperson's attention and asking about price and color of specific items

Andrea and Monika are in a department store. Some items don't have a price tag. Andrea asks the salesperson how much various items cost. Which items would you buy?

B1

Im Kaufhaus

ANDREA	Fräulein!
VERKÄUFERIN	Ja, bitte? Was darf es sein?
ANDREA	Wie teuer ist dieser Pulli, bitte?
VERKÄUFERIN	Die Pullis sind heute im Angebot. Jeder Pulli kostet achtzehn Mark.
ANDREA	Danke!
VERKÄUFERIN	Bitte schön!

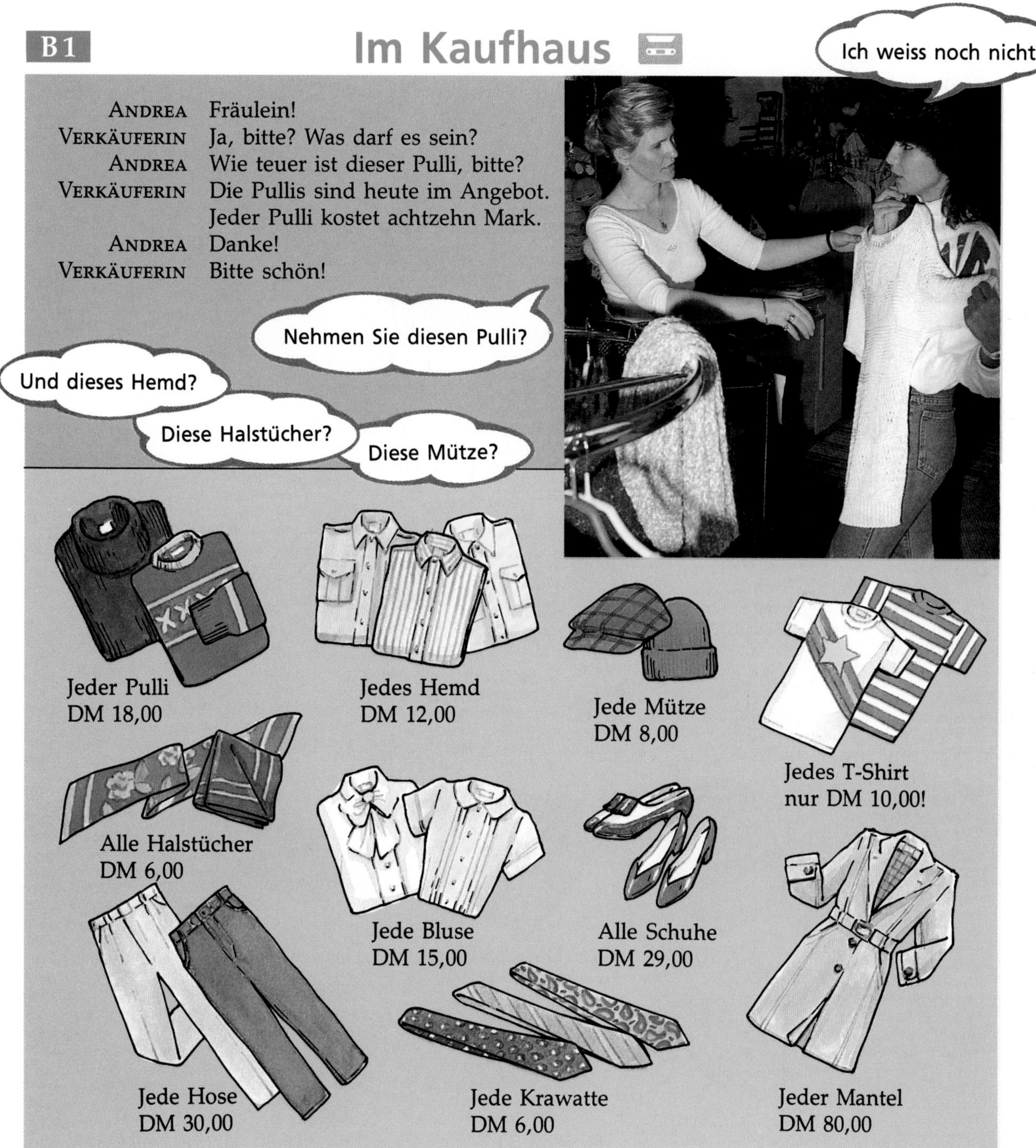

B2 Übung • Was kaufst du?

1. Ich kaufe ein . . .
2. Wie teuer ist der . . .?
3. Sind die . . . im Angebot?
4. Ich möchte den . . .

den einen	die eine	das ein	die —
der	**die**	**das**	**die**
Pulli s Mäntel	Mütze n Bluse n Hose n Krawatte n	Hemd en Halstüch er T-Shirt s	Schuhe

B3 ERKLÄRUNG
dieser, jeder: *Nominative and Accusative Case*

1. **Dieser, diese, dieses,** *this, these,* are called demonstratives, because they are used to point to specific items.

Wie teuer ist dieser Pulli? — *How much is this sweater?*
Diese Hemden sind teuer. — *These shirts are expensive.*

Dieser has the following forms in the nominative and the accusative cases:

	Masculine	*Feminine*	*Neuter*	*Plural*
Nominative	**dieser**	**diese**	**dieses**	**diese**
Accusative	**diesen**			

2. **Jeder, jede, jedes,** *each, every,* and the plural form **alle,** *all,* have the same endings as **dieser.**

Jeder Mantel kostet DM 80. — *Every coat costs 80 Marks.*
Alle Mäntel kosten DM 80. — *All coats cost 80 Marks.*

	Masculine	*Feminine*	*Neuter*	*Plural*
Nominative	**jeder**	**jede**	**jedes**	**alle**
Accusative	**jeden**			

B4 Übung • Im Kaufhaus  For answers, see p. T206.

Practice the conversations on the next page, using each item pictured.

dieser Mantel

1. DM 80,-

dieser Pulli

2. DM 18,-

dieses Hemd
3. DM 12,-

diese Mütze
4. DM 8,-

dieses Halstuch
5. DM 6,-

6. DM 15,-
diese Bluse

7. DM 29,-
diese Schuhe

8. DM 30,-
diese Hose

9. DM 12,50
dieses T-Shirt

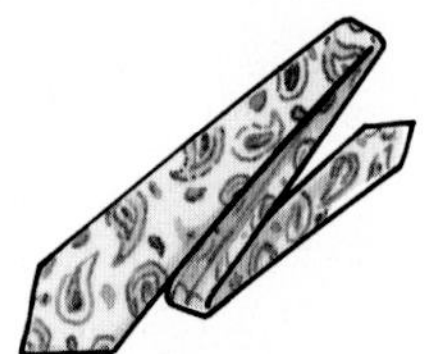
10. DM 6,-
diese Krawatte

1. A: Wie teuer ist dieser Mantel, bitte?
   B: Jeder Mantel kostet achtzig Mark.
   A: Das ist zu teuer!
2. A: Fräulein, was kostet dieser Mantel, bitte?
   B: Sie bekommen jeden Mantel für achtzig Mark.
   A: Ja, dann nehme ich ihn.
3. A: Der Mantel ist toll (prima, Spitze, schön)!
   B: Möchtest du diesen Mantel?
   A: Ich weiss noch nicht.

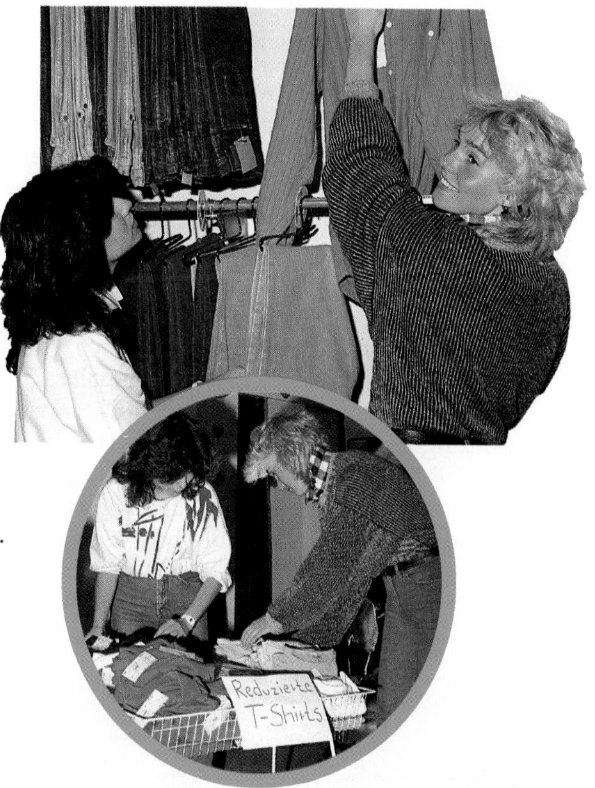

B5 Übung • Merkspiel

Wir gehen einkaufen.

MONIKA Ich möchte diesen Pulli.
STEFAN Ich möchte diesen Pulli und dieses T-Shirt.
ANDREA Ich möchte diesen Pulli, dieses T-Shirt und . . .

B6 WIE SAGT MAN DAS?
Getting someone's attention

The words **Entschuldigung!** and **Verzeihung!** can be used to get someone's attention. In a store you can also use **Fräulein** to get the attention of a saleswoman. The salesperson will usually respond with **Ja, bitte? Was darf es sein?** *May I help you?*

getting someone's attention in general	Entschuldigung! Verzeihung!	Excuse me!
getting the attention of a saleswoman	Fräulein!	Miss!
salesperson's response	Ja, bitte? Was darf es sein?	Yes, may I help you?

B7 Übung • Verkaufsgespräch 

You are a salesperson in a department store. Your classmate is a customer asking about prices of items on his or her shopping list.

KUNDE Verzeihung!
VERKÄUFER/IN Ja, bitte?
KUNDE Wie teuer ist dieser Pulli, bitte?
VERKÄUFER/IN Jeder Pulli kostet zwanzig Mark.
KUNDE Danke!
VERKÄUFER/IN Bitte schön!

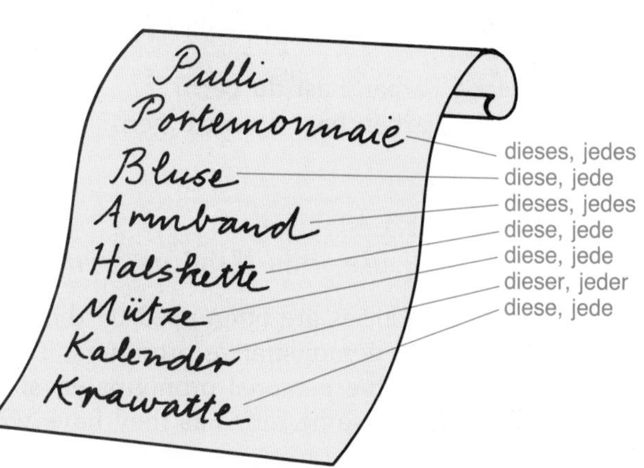

Pulli
Portemonnaie
Bluse
Armband
Halskette
Mütze
Kalender
Krawatte
dieses, jedes
diese, jede
dieses, jedes
diese, jede
diese, jede
dieser, jeder
diese, jede

B 8 Ein wenig Landeskunde

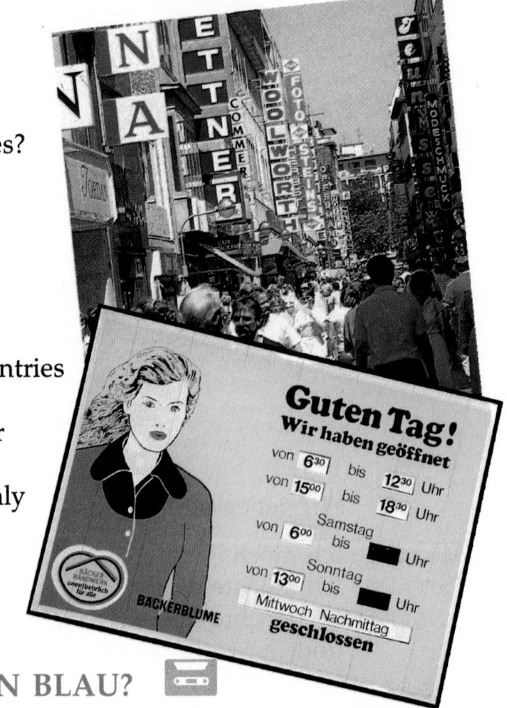

What kind of stores are there in German-speaking countries? There are smaller specialty stores—for example, **Bekleidungsgeschäfte,** *clothing stores,* **Plattenläden,** *record stores,* **Buchhandlungen,** *book stores,* and **Blumengeschäfte,** *florist shops.* There are large **Kaufhäuser,** *department stores,* and many areas now have a modern and attractive **Einkaufszentrum,** *shopping mall.*

Shopping hours are shorter in the German-speaking countries than in the United States. Small stores, except for those in downtown sections of cities, are usually closed for an hour or two at lunchtime. Almost all stores close by 6:30 P.M., including grocery stores. On Saturdays, stores are open only until 2 P.M., although once a month many cities have **„einen langen Samstag,"** *a long Saturday,* during which stores are open until 6. All stores are closed on Sundays.

B 9 HABEN SIE DEN PULLI VIELLEICHT IN BLAU?

VERKÄUFERIN Der Pulli ist hübsch, nicht?
MONIKA Ja, der ist sehr schön. Nur mag ich Rot nicht. Haben Sie den vielleicht in Blau? Blau ist meine Lieblingsfarbe.
VERKÄUFERIN Ich glaube, ja. —Hier ist dieser Pulli in Blau.
MONIKA Gut, den nehme ich. Das Blau ist toll.

Wir haben auch dieses Hemd in vielen Farben:

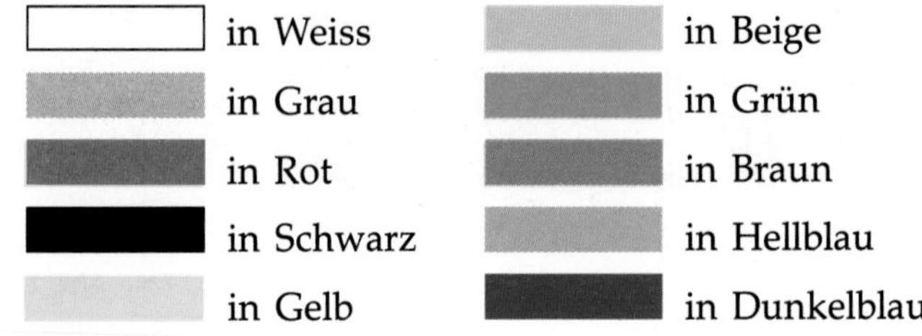

B 10 Übung • Und du? Wie steht's mit dir?

1. Welche Farben hast du gern?
2. Welche Farben hast du nicht gern?
3. Was ist deine Lieblingsfarbe?

B 11 ERKLÄRUNG
der, die, das *Used as Demonstrative Pronouns*

The definite articles are often used by themselves, that is, without a noun. When used this way, they are called demonstrative pronouns. They function as pronouns, but they have more emphasis than the personal pronouns **er, sie,** and **es.** When used as pronouns, the definite articles have the same forms as they have when used as definite articles.

<table>
<tr><th></th><th>Masculine</th><th>Feminine</th><th>Neuter</th><th>Plural</th></tr>
<tr><td>Nominative</td><td>der</td><td rowspan="2">die</td><td rowspan="2">das</td><td rowspan="2">die</td></tr>
<tr><td>Accusative</td><td>den</td></tr>
</table>

Dieser Pulli ist hübsch, nicht? *This sweater is pretty, isn't it?*	Ja, **der** ist sehr schön. *Yes, it is very nice.*
Möchten Sie **diesen Pulli?** *Would you like this sweater?*	Ja, **den** nehme ich. *Yes, that's the one I'll take.*

B12 Übung • Was sagt die Verkäuferin? Was sagst du? 

A: Dieser Pulli ist hübsch, nicht?
B: Ja, der ist sehr schön.

1. diese Schuhe sind . . . ? die
2. dieses Hemd? das
3. dieser Mantel? der
4. dieses T-Shirt? das
5. diese Mütze? die
6. dieses Halstuch? das

B13 Übung • Was?! Du kaufst alles? 

A: Möchten Sie diesen Mantel?
B: Ja, den nehme ich.

1. diese Bluse? die
2. diese Schuhe? die
3. dieses Hemd? das
4. diesen Pulli? den
5. diese Hose?
6. diesen Kalender? den

B14 Übung • Hör gut zu!  For script and answers, see p. T208.

Über was sprechen die beiden?

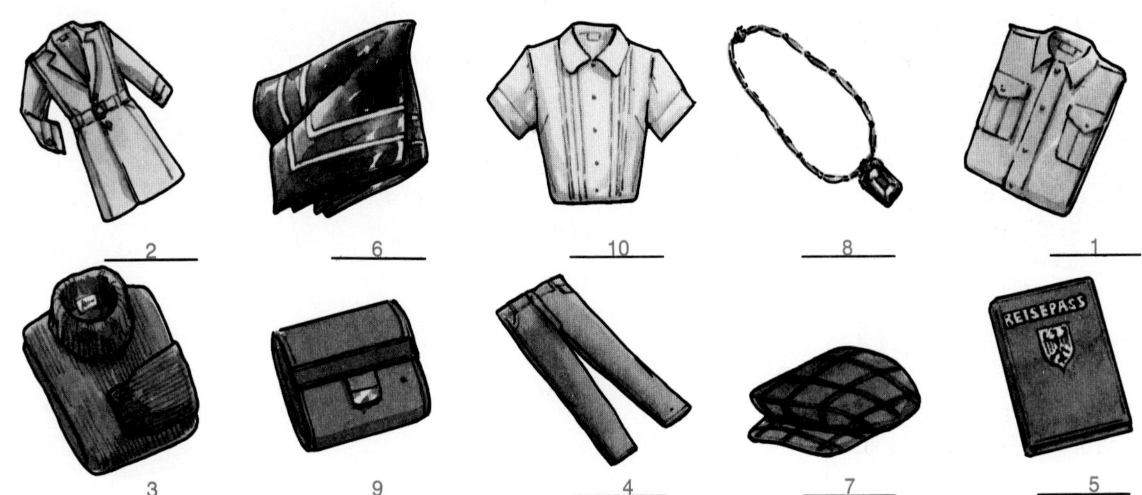

B15 Schreibübung • Was darf es sein, bitte?

Schreibe ein Verkaufsgespräch! Du bist in einem Kaufhaus, und du möchtest etwas kaufen, einen Mantel vielleicht. Du fragst die Verkäuferin, wie teuer die Mäntel sind und ob sie im Angebot sind. Die Verkäuferin zeigt dir einen Mantel. Du findest ihn schick, aber du möchtest eine andere Farbe. Übe dein Gespräch mit einem Klassenkameraden!

making suggestions for presents for special occasions and expressing good wishes on these occasions

There are many special occasions throughout the year when we buy presents, and ads in magazines can give us ideas for special gifts.

C1 Geschenkideen

Was schenken Sie ihm?
Was geben Sie ihr?

Zum Vatertag alles Gute!

Zum Muttertag? Schenken Sie ihr Parfüm!

Zum Vatertag? Kaufen Sie ihm ein Portemonnaie!

Alles Gute zum Muttertag!

Gute Wünsche zum Hochzeitstag!

Zum Hochzeitstag? Schenken Sie ihnen Blumen!

Herzliche Glückwünsche zum Geburtstag!

Zum Geburtstag? Geben Sie ihm ein T-Shirt!

Zu Weihnachten? Schenken Sie ihr eine Uhr!

Fröhliche Weihnachten!

C2 Ein wenig Landeskunde

Occasions for giving gifts in German-speaking countries are pretty much the same as in the United States: birthday, Christmas, anniversary, Mother's Day, and Father's Day, to mention a few. It is also customary to give a gift when visiting someone. Flowers, which Germans are especially fond of, are often given as a gift. Some flower shops even have a vending machine outside so that people can purchase a bouquet even if the store is closed—for example, on a Sunday. Many people buy a gift box of candy or a bottle of wine. It is also customary to bring a bar of chocolate for each child in the family.

Herzliche Wünsche zum Namenstag
Zum Geburtstag alles Gute!

C3 Was sagt die Reklame? 

Zum Geburtstag?
Schenken Sie ihr eine Armbanduhr!
Zum Geburtstag?
Zum Namenstag?
Zum Muttertag?
Zum Vatertag?
Zum Hochzeitstag?
Zu Weihnachten?
Schenken Sie
ihm
ihr
ihnen
Sport

C4 Übung • Was schenkst du?

1. Zum Geburtstag schenke ich meinem Bruder ein T-Shirt.
2. Zum Namenstag schenke ich meiner Mutter ein Buch.
3. Zu . . .

C5 ERKLÄRUNG
Third Person Pronouns, Dative Case

The dative case forms of the third person pronouns are **ihm, ihr,** and **ihnen.** They refer to noun phrases in the dative case.

		Indirect Object: Dative Case		*Dative Pronoun*	
Masculine	Was schenkst du	**deinem Vater?**	Ich schenke	**ihm**	Blumen.
Feminine		**deiner Freundin?**		**ihr**	
Plural		**deinen Eltern?**		**ihnen**	

C6 Übung • Was soll ich bloss schenken?

For answers, see p. T210.

A: Was soll ich nur meinem Vater schenken?
B: Schenk ihm doch eine Krawatte!
A: Prima Idee. Er hat Krawatten gern.

* * *

A: Was gebe ich bloss meiner Freundin?
B: Gib ihr doch Parfüm!
A: Gut! Sie mag Parfüm.

Wem?	**Eltern Vater Mutter Freundin Freund Geschwister Bruder Schwester**
Was?	**Krawatte Blumen Schachtel Pralinen Platte Musikkassette Halstuch Buch**

C7 Übung • Mutter hat für alle eine Geschenkidee

A: Die Monika braucht einen Pulli.
B: Gut, dann schenken wir ihr einen Pulli.

1. Der Stefan braucht ein T-Shirt. ihm
2. Die Kinder brauchen Tennisschuhe. ihnen
3. Die Andrea braucht eine Bluse. ihr
4. Der Vater braucht eine Brieftasche. ihm
5. Die Ingrid braucht ein Portemonnaie. ihr
6. Paul und Jörg brauchen ein Wörterbuch. ihnen

C8 Übung • Was schenkst du?

Was kann man diesen Personen zum Geburtstag schenken? Hast du eine Idee?

A: Die Monika hört gern Musik.
B: Die Monika hört gern Musik? Dann kannst du ihr eine Musikkassette schenken.

1. Frl. Seifert mag Blumen.
2. Die Kinder lesen gern.
3. Der Markus verliert immer sein Geld.
4. Die Monika fotografiert gern.
5. Der Jens ist schlecht in Mathe.

1. ihr einen Strauss Blumen
2. ihnen ein Buch
3. ihm ein Portemonnaie
4. ihr eine Kamera
5. ihm einen Taschenrechner

C9 WANN HAST DU GEBURTSTAG? 

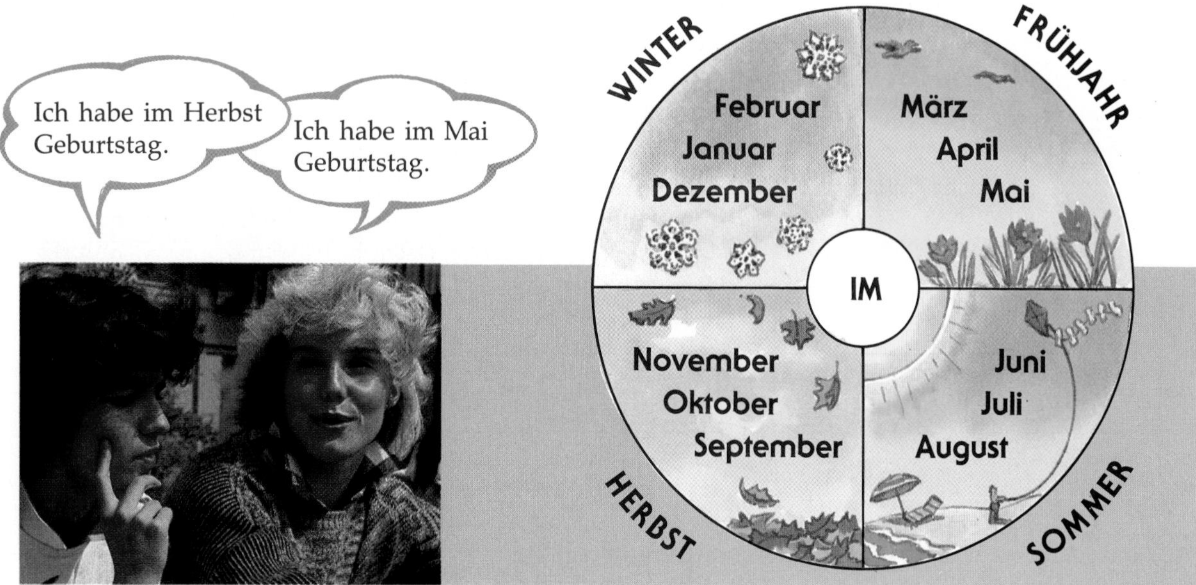

C10 WANN HAST DU GEBURTSTAG? ODER NAMENSTAG?

To say on what day your birthday is, you have to know some ordinal numbers, which are used in a phrase with **am.**

am 1. = am ersten
am 2. = am zweiten
am 3. = am dritten
am 4. = am vierten
am 5. = am fünften
am 6. = am sechsten
am 7. = am siebten
am 8. = am achten
am 9. = am neunten
am 10. = am zehnten
am 11. = am elften
am 12. = am . . .

am 20. = am zwanzigsten
am 21. = am einundzwanzigsten
am 22. = am zweiundzwanzigsten

Ich habe am vierten Mai Geburtstag.

Namenstage im Juli
10. Erich/Erika
13. Margarete
15. Heinrich
24. Christine
25. Jakob
26. Anne Marie
29. Martha
Gratulieren Sie mit Blumen

C11 Übung • Und du? Wie steht's mit dir?

1. Wann hast du Geburtstag?
2. Wann ist dein Namenstag?
3. Wann haben deine Eltern Geburtstag?
4. Und deine Geschwister?
5. Wann ist Muttertag?
6. Wann ist Vatertag?
7. Wann beginnen die Ferien?
8. Wann ist Weihnachten?
9. Wann haben deine Freunde Geburtstag?
10. Wann haben sie ihren Namenstag?

C12 WIE SAGT MAN DAS?
Expressing good wishes

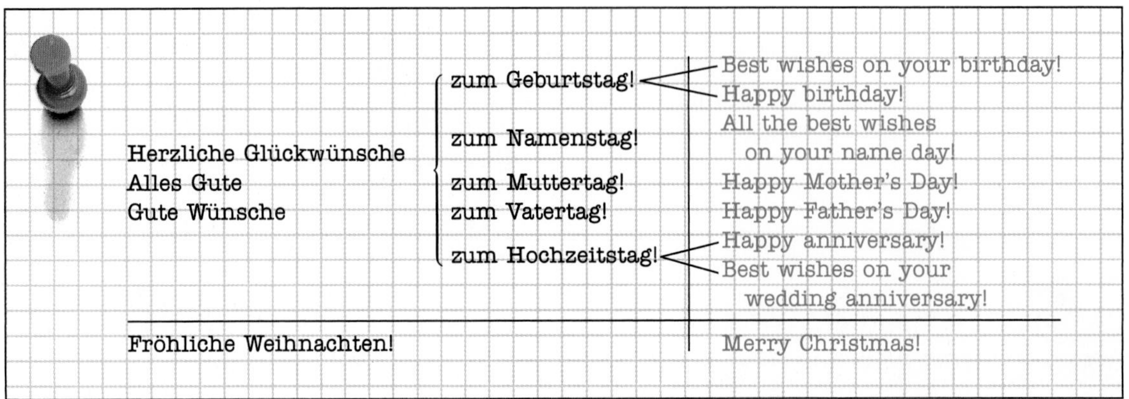

Herzliche Glückwünsche Alles Gute Gute Wünsche	zum Geburtstag!	Best wishes on your birthday! Happy birthday!
	zum Namenstag!	All the best wishes on your name day!
	zum Muttertag!	Happy Mother's Day!
	zum Vatertag!	Happy Father's Day!
	zum Hochzeitstag!	Happy anniversary! Best wishes on your wedding anniversary!
Fröhliche Weihnachten!		Merry Christmas!

C13 Übung • Was sagst du . . . 

1, 3–6. Herzliche Glückwünsche zum . . . !

1. zum Muttertag?
2. am 25. Dezember?
3. zum Geburtstag?
4. zum Hochzeitstag?
5. zum Vatertag?
6. zum Namenstag?

2. Fröhliche Weihnachten!

 C14 Übung • Hör gut zu!  For script and answers, see p. T211.

Wem schenkst du was?

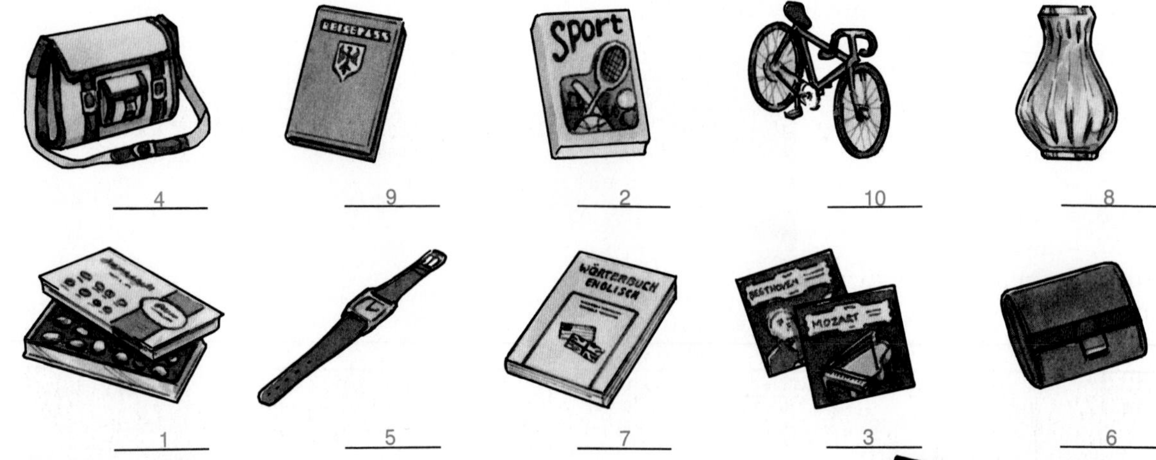

C15 Schreibübung • Wer hat Geburtstag?

1. Wer in der Klasse hat in diesem Monat Geburtstag? Du hast für jeden ein anderes Geschenk. Schreibe das Gespräch auf, und übe es mit einem Klassenkameraden!

   A: Der Fritz hat am achten Geburtstag. Was schenkst du ihm?
   B: Vielleicht ein T-Shirt.
   A: Was?! Du gibst ihm ein T-Shirt?
   B: Warum nicht?

2. Entwirf für jedes Geburtstagskind eine Geburtstagskarte!

Zum Geburtstag alles Gute und recht viel Glück!

C16 WAS HAST DU IHM GESCHENKT?

—Du, sag, wann hat dein Bruder Geburtstag gehabt?
—Am zweiten Mai.
—Was hast du ihm gekauft?
—Einen Pulli.

—Wann ist dein Namenstag gewesen?
—Am achten April.

—Was hast du deinen Eltern geschenkt?
—Ich habe ihnen eine Schachtel Pralinen gegeben.

C17 ERKLÄRUNG
More Past Participles

1. Here are the conversational past tense forms of some verbs you have been using in this unit.

hat gegeben	**ist gewesen**
hat gekauft	
hat geschenkt	
hat gehabt	

2. Can you name the infinitive forms of the past participles listed in this chart?

C18 Übung • Was haben alle gekauft? 

Ich habe ein Portemonnaie gekauft.

1. Ich . . . habe ein Portemonnaie gekauft.
2. Die Mädchen . . . haben einen Strauss Blumen gekauft.
3. Monika . . . hat ein Buch gekauft.
4. Wir . . . haben eine Armbanduhr gekauft.
5. Du . . . ? hast einen Pulli gekauft?

C19 Übung • Und du? Wie steht's mit dir?

1. Hast du schon Geburtstag gehabt?
2. Wann ist dein Namenstag gewesen?
3. Was hast du deinen Freunden zum Geburtstag geschenkt?
4. Was hast du deinem Bruder gegeben? Und deinem Vater? Und . . .
5. Was hast du alles für die Ferien gekauft?

TRY YOUR SKILLS

using what you've learned

On special occasions it is nice to remember friends and family with gifts and cards. When somebody remembers you and sends a gift, you write a thank-you note.

1 Karin hat Geburtstag 

Karin bekommt zum Geburtstag viele Geburtstagskarten.

Liebe Karin,
Zum Geburtstag alles Gute! Dein Oliver

Wir gehen am 23. Mai in ein Rockkonzert. Kommst du mit? Tschüs!

Liebe Karin! den 3. Mai
Herzliche Glückwünsche zum Geburtstag und alles Gute,
Deine Tante Dora

P.S. Ein Geschenk ist unterwegs.

Liebe Karin!
Alles Gute zum Geburtstag!
Deine Kusine Annegret

Ich komme am 2. Juni mit Mutti nach Wien. Dann gehen wir zusammen aus... ins Kino, Kaffee trinken...

Karin schreibt an Tante Dora.

Liebe Tante Dora! Wien, den 10 Mai
Vielen Dank für die Karte und die Geschenke zum Geburtstag. Die Quartzuhr ist toll! Ich brauche eine Uhr. Und die Musikkassette ist Spitze! Die Spider Murphy Gang ist meine Lieblingsgruppe.
Wie geht's? Wann besuchst Du uns? Viele Grüsse, auch an Onkel Heinz und an Babsie und Rolf.
Deine Karin

2 Übung • Beantworte die Fragen!

1. Wer hat Geburtstag? Karin
2. Wer schickt eine Geburtstagskarte? Oliver, Tante Dora, ihre Kusine Annegret
3. Was für Geschenke bekommt sie? eine Quarzuhr, eine Musikkassette
4. Wer sind Babsie und Rolf? Babsie ist Karins Kusine, Rolf ist ihr Vetter.

3 Schreibübung • Jetzt bist du dran

1. It is your best friend's birthday. Design and write a birthday card.
2. Your grandmother sent you a birthday card and a gift. Write a thank-you note. Comment on why you like the gift.

4 Übung • Probleme mit Geschenken!

Dein Vater, deine Freundin und deine Oma haben diesen Monat Geburtstag. Drei Geburtstage! Du brauchst drei Geschenke. Du hast aber nur vierzig Mark. Was kannst du kaufen? Du sprichst mit einem Freund darüber.

A: Du, ich brauche . . .
B: . . .

Ich habe nur vierzig Mark.
Was kann ich (ihm) kaufen?
Was meinst du?
Kauf (ihm) doch eine . . .
Was kostet . . .?
Nein, das ist zu teuer.
Hast du eine Idee?
Das ist eine prima Idee.
Was willst du (ihm) schenken?

12,-
die/eine Platte

20,-
der/einen Taschenrechner

18,-
das/ein Buch

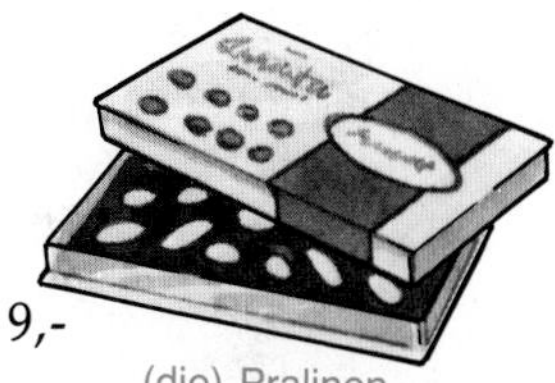
9,-
(die) Pralinen

13,-
das/ein Halstuch

6,-
die/eine Krawatte

8,-
das/ein T-Shirt

7,-
der/einen Kalendar

5 Übung • Farbenspiel: Ich seh' etwas, was du nicht siehst . . .

MONIKA Ich seh' etwas, was du nicht siehst, und es ist blau.
STEFAN Meinst du mein Hemd?
MONIKA Nein!
ULLI Peters T-Shirt?
MONIKA Nein!
JOCHEN Meinen Pulli?
MONIKA Jaaa! —So, Jochen, jetzt bist du dran!

6 Übung • Wenn ich Geld hätte . . .

Du hast viel Geld gewonnen und willst deinen Verwandten und Freunden schöne Geschenke kaufen. Was kaufst du? Was sagst du?

> Ich schenke meinem Bruder ein Sportrad. Er braucht ein Rad. *or* Er fährt gern Rad. *or* Er möchte ein Rad haben.

Ein Klassenkamerad erzählt, was du alles kaufst.

> Der Paul kauft seinem Bruder ein Sportrad. Sein Bruder braucht ein Rad. *or* Sein Bruder fährt gern Rad. *or* Sein Bruder möchte ein Rad haben.

7 Übung • Rollenspiel: Auf einer Auktion

You and your classmate are at an auction. Each student should bring at least one item (or a picture of an item) to class. Take turns offering items for sale. Praise each item, using expressions such as **toll, Spitze, Klasse.**

AUKTIONÄR	Hier ist eine Halskette. Diese Halskette ist sehr alt. —Was bieten Sie°?
KÄUFER	Ich finde diese Halskette Spitze. Ich biete zwei Mark.
AUKTIONÄR	Zwei Mark. Wer bietet mehr?
KÄUFER	Drei Mark.
AUKTIONÄR	Zwei Mark, drei Mark für diese Halskette. Wer bietet mehr?
KÄUFER	Vier Mark.
AUKTIONÄR	Vier Mark! Zum ersten, zum zweiten—und zum dritten! Verkauft für vier Mark!

8 Übung • Wie passen die Sätze zusammen?

1.	Was schenke ich nur	6	achtzehn Mark.
2.	Ich kaufe meinem Vater	7	auch in Grün?
3.	Was schenkst du jetzt deiner Freundin	8	dein Parfüm?
4.	Ich schenke der Monika eine Platte. Sie	2	gewöhnlich ein Buch.
5.	Meine Grosseltern haben morgen	5	ihren Hochzeitstag.
6.	Jeder Pulli kostet heute	10	im Oktober.
7.	Haben Sie diesen Pulli	9	meine Lieblingsfarbe.
8.	Du riechst so gut. Ist das	1	meinem Freund?
9.	Das Blau ist schön. Blau ist	4	hört gern Musik.
10.	Ich habe im Herbst Geburtstag,	3	zum Geburtstag?

Was bieten Sie? *What's your bid?*

9 Übung • Klassenprojekt: Ein Geburtstagskalender

Wer hat wann Geburtstag? Entwirf für deine Klasse einen Geburtstagskalender! Für jeden Monat frage deine Klassenkameraden: Wer hat im (Januar) Geburtstag? Alle, die in diesem Monat Geburtstag haben, sagen an welchem Tag, und du schreibst die Namen auf den Kalender.

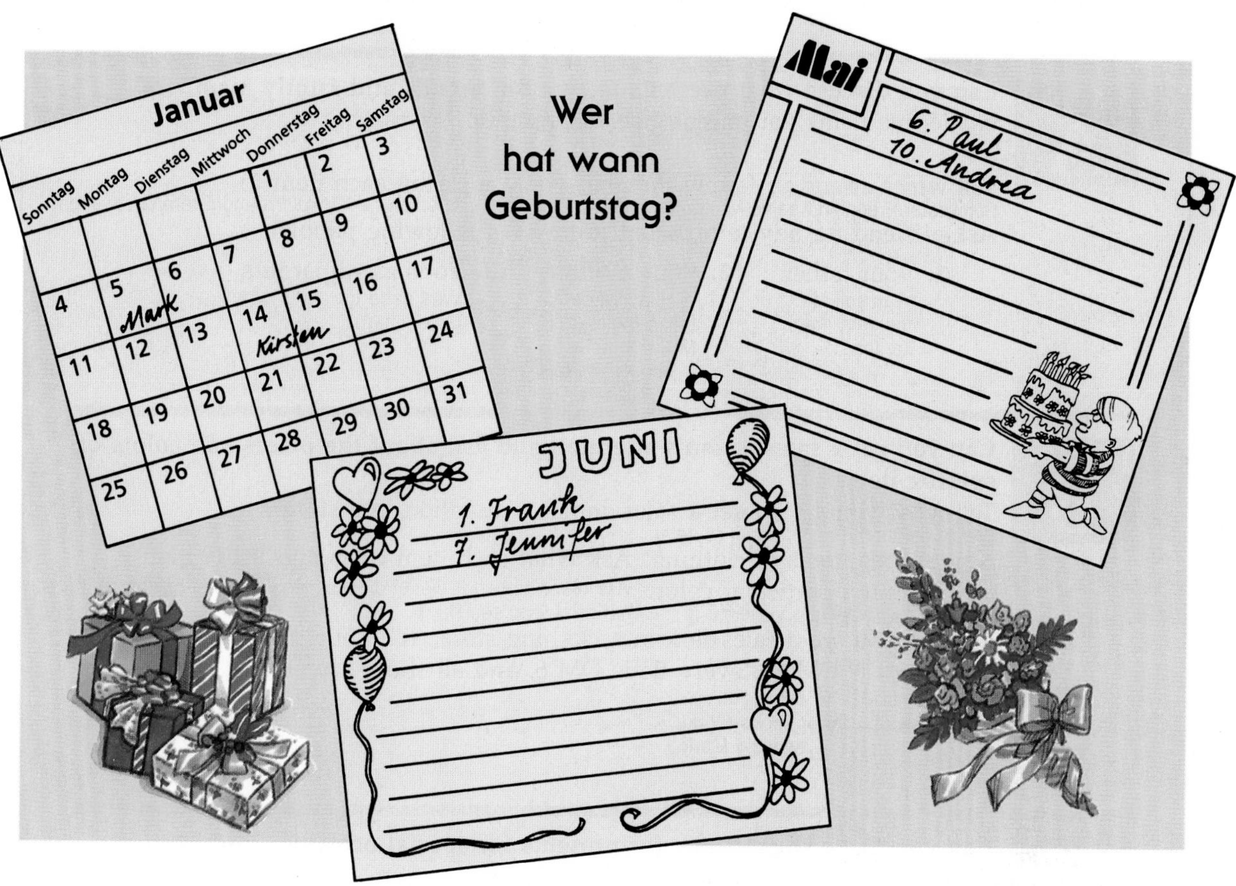

10 Aussprache-, Lese- und Schreibübungen

For script, see p. T214.

1. Listen carefully and repeat what you hear.

2. Listen, then read aloud.
1. Armband, sag, ich glaub', Hemd, gelb, Vatertag, bald, gehabt
2. Mütze, Hochzeit, schwarz, herzlich, zum
3. Krawatte, Weihnachten, gewesen, gewöhnlich, weiss, schwarz, warum, Witz
4. Halskette, Hose, diese, weiss, gewesen, bloss, Bluse, Vase, Strauss
5. Vatertag, vielleicht, verbringen, verstehen, verlieren; Video, Vase
6. braun, darf, Krawatte, teuer, nur, schwarz, Farbe, rot, Reisebuch, fröhlich, grün, Radio, dieser, Armbanduhr, Muttertag, Portemonnaie, Strauss, Uhr, herzlich, Kalender, grau, Geburtstag, Vatertag, jeder, Parfüm, Brieftasche, Pralinen, am dritten, am ersten, Quarzuhr

3. Copy the following sentences to prepare yourself to write them from dictation.
1. Ich glaub', das Hemd ist gelb.
2. Diese Hose ist zu teuer.
3. Die Krawatte hab' ich zu Weihnachten bekommen.
4. Herzliche Glückwünsche zum Geburtstag!

WAS KANNST DU SCHON?

Let's review some important points you have learned in this unit.

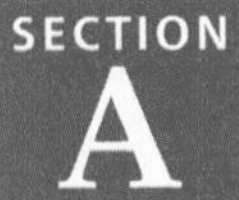

Can you discuss what presents to buy for friends and family members?

Name five items you might give as presents. See below.

Tell which friend or family member you are giving each item to.
Schwester/Freundin/Kusine/Mutter/Oma/Tante/Vetter/Opa/Vater/Bruder/Onkel/Freund/Eltern/Grosseltern

Ask a friend for advice on what to buy the following people:

1. your father
Was soll ich meinem Vater kaufen?

2. your mother
Was schenke ich bloss meiner Mutter?

3. your grandparents
Was gebe ich nur meine Grosseltern?

Can you get a salesperson's attention and ask about the prices and colors of specific items?

Tell what you say to get a saleswoman's attention in a store.
Entschuldigung!/Verzeihung!/Fräulein!

Name three items of clothing. Ask what each item costs and if the item is available in a particular color. Wie teuer ist (sind) dieser/dieses/diese . . . ? (For items, see B2, p. 308.)
Haben sie den/das/die vielleicht in . . . ? (For colors, see B9, p. 310.)

Pretend you are a salesclerk in a clothing store. Tell your customer that every coat is DM 80, every tie is DM 6, and all shoes are DM 20.
Jeder Mantel kostet achtzig Mark.
Jede Krawatte kostet sechs Mark.
Alle Schuhe kosten zwanzig Mark.

Can you make suggestions for presents for special occasions and express good wishes on those occasions?

Give the month and day of your mother's birthday, of your father's birthday, and of your grandparents' wedding anniversary. Say what you are going to give them. Meine Mutter/Mein Vater hat am . . . Geburtstag./Meine Grosseltern haben am . . . ihren Hochzeitstag. Ich schenke ihr/ihm/ihnen . . .

How do you express good wishes on the following occasions?

1. birthday **2.** anniversary **3.** Christmas **4.** Mother's Day

3. Fröhliche Weihnachten!
1., 2., 4. Herzliche Glückwünsche/Alles Gute/Gute Wünsche zum Geburtstag/ Hochzeitstag/Muttertag!

A friend is asking for advice on what to give to his or her mother, brother, grandparents, and teacher for Christmas. Make suggestions for each one.
Schenk ihr/ihm/ihnen doch . . . !

A. Brieftasche/Buch/Portemonnaie/Armband/Pralinen/Halskette/Radio/Kalendar/Parfüm/Blumen/Platte/Armbanduhr/Poster/Musikkassetten/Vase

WORTSCHATZ

SECTION A

das **Armband, ¨er** *bracelet*
die **Armbanduhr, -en** *wristwatch*
bald *soon*
bloss: was schenke ich bloss meinem Vater? *what on earth should I give my father?*
die **Blume, -n** *flower*
die **Brieftasche, -n** *passport case*
dies- *this, these*
geben *to give* (see p 304)
der **Geburtstag, -e** *birthday;* er hat Geburtstag *it's his birthday*
gewöhnlich *usually*
die **Hochzeit: goldene Hochzeit** *golden wedding anniversary*
ich hab's! *I have it!*
der **Kalender, -** *calendar*
meinen *to think, be of the opinion;* was meinst du? *what do you think?*
nur: was soll ich nur schenken? *what should I give?*
das **Parfüm, -s** *perfume*
das **Portemonnaie, -s** *wallet*
die **Praline, -n** *fancy chocolate*
die **Quarzuhr, -en** *quartz clock, watch*
das **Radio, -s** *radio*
das **Reisebuch, ¨er** *travel book*
die **Schachtel, -n** *box;* eine Schachtel Pralinen *a box of fancy chocolates*
schenken *to give (as a gift)*
schick *chic*
der **Strauss, ¨e** *bouquet;* ein Strauss Blumen *a bouquet of flowers*
die **Vase, -n** *vase*

SECTION B

das **Angebot: im Angebot** *on sale*
das **Beige** *the color beige*
das **Blau** *the color blue;* in Blau *in blue*
die **Bluse, -n** *blouse*
das **Braun** *the color brown*
das **Dunkelblau** *the color dark blue*
die **Farbe, -n** *color;* in vielen Farben *in many colors*
das **Gelb** *the color yellow*
glauben: ich glaube, ja *I think so*
das **Grau** *the color grey*
das **Grün** *the color green*
das **Halstuch, ¨er** *scarf*
das **Hellblau** *the color light blue*
das **Hemd, -en** *shirt*
die **Hose, -n** *pants*
ja, bitte? *yes, may I help you?*
jed- *each, every*
das **Kaufhaus, ¨er** *department store;* im Kaufhaus *in the department store*
die **Krawatte, -n** *tie*
die **Lieblingsfarbe, -n** *favorite color*
der **Mantel, ¨** *coat*
die **Mütze, -n** *cap*
noch nicht *not yet;* ich weiss noch nicht *I don't know yet*
der **Pulli, -s** *sweater*
das **Rot** *the color red;* in Rot *in red*
der **Schuh, -e** *shoe*
das **Schwarz** *the color black*
teuer *expensive*
das **T-Shirt, -s** *t-shirt*
was darf es sein? *may I help you?*
das **Weiss** *the color white*
wie teuer ist *how much is*

SECTION C

alles Gute zum . . . *all the best wishes on . . .*
am ersten *on the first;* am ersten Mai *on May 1st* (see p 315)
April *April*
August *August*
Dezember *December*
Februar *February*
der **Geburtstag: herzliche Glückwünsche zum Geburtstag!** *happy birthday!* ich habe im Mai Geburtstag *my birthday is in May;* zum Geburtstag *for (your) birthday*
die **Geschenkidee, -n** *gift idea*
herzliche Glückwünsche zum . . . *happy . . .*
der **Hochzeitstag, -e** *wedding anniversary;* zum Hochzeitstag *for (your) anniversary*
Januar *January;* im Januar *in January*
Juli *July*
Juni *June*
Mai *May*
März *March*
der **Muttertag** *Mother's Day;* zum Muttertag *for Mother's Day*
der **Namenstag, -e** *name day;* zum Namenstag *for (your) name day*
November *November*
Oktober *October*
die **Reklame** *ad*
sag, . . . *say, . . .*
September *September*
die **Uhr, -en** *clock, watch*
der **Vatertag** *Father's Day;* zum Vatertag *for Father's Day*
Weihnachten *Christmas;* fröhliche Weihnachten! *merry Christmas!* zu Weihnachten *for Christmas*
der **Wunsch: gute Wünsche zum . . .** *best wishes on . . .*

WORTSCHATZÜBUNGEN

1. Make a list of all the compound nouns.
   Armband, Armbanduhr, Brieftasche, Geburtstag, Hochzeit, Quarzuhr, Reisebuch, Dunkelblau, Halstuch, Hellblau, Kaufhaus, Lieblingsfarbe, Geschenkidee, Hochzeitstag, Muttertag, Namenstag, Vatertag, Weihnachten
2. Which words are borrowed from other languages such as English and French?
   Portemonnaie, Radio, T-Shirt, Parfüm, Praline
3. The colors are listed in the **Wortschatz** as nouns and are therefore capitalized. When used as adjectives, they are spelled the same way but are not capitalized. Write the colors as nouns and as adjectives.

Beige, Blau, Braun, Dunkelblau, Gelb, Grau, Grün, Hellblau, Rot, Schwarz. The colors should also be written lowercase.

ZUM LESEN

Ein Gewohnheitsmensch

Herr Neuschuh ist ein netter Mann. Er ist höflich°, pünktlich, immer korrekt. Er ist auch immer gut angezogen°: er kauft seine Sachen in den besten Geschäften°. Aber er macht sich wenig aus der Mode°. „Die Mode", so sagt er, „ist nur für die Jugend." Herr Neuschuh liebt den klassischen Stil. Seine Anzüge° kommen aus England, seine Krawatten kommen aus Frankreich und seine Schuhe aus Italien. Jeden Morgen, bevor Herr Neuschuh zur Arbeit geht, bürstet er seinen Anzug und putzt° seine Schuhe. Er ist ein schicker Herr°.

Nun, eines Tages möchte Herr Neuschuh ein Paar neue Schuhe. Er geht in das Schuhgeschäft, wo er immer seine Schuhe kauft. Dort kennt er alle Verkäufer.

„Guten Tag, Herr Neuschuh! Was darf es heute sein?"

„Ist Frl. Seidel nicht da?"

„Frl. Seidel ist gestern in Urlaub gegangen°."

„Ach, so was! —Nun, das macht nichts°. Ich möchte ein Paar Schuhe."

„Welche Marke°?"

„Diese hier."

ein Gewohnheitsmensch *a creature of habit;* **höflich** *polite;* **gut angezogen** *well-dressed;* **das Geschäft** *store;* **er macht sich wenig aus der Mode** *he doesn't pay much attention to fashion, to what's in style;* **der Anzug** *suit;* **putzen** *to clean, polish;* **ein schicker Herr** *a smartly-dressed gentleman;* **in Urlaub gehen** *to go on vacation;* **das macht nichts** *it doesn't matter;* **die Marke** *make*

Herr Neuschuh zieht seine Schuhe aus°.
„Welche Grösse° haben Sie?"
„Dreiundvierzig."
„Diese Grösse haben wir, aber nicht in Schwarz."
„Nicht in Schwarz?"
„Nein, nur in Braun. Sie haben das letzte Paar in Schwarz. Dieses Modell gibt es jetzt nicht mehr."
„Warum nicht? Es ist doch ein perfektes Modell!"
„Ja, Sie haben recht, ein perfektes Modell. Aber die Mode ändert sich°."
„Ach, die Mode! Immer diese Mode!"
„Möchten Sie ein anderes° Modell anprobieren?"
„Nein, nie!"
„Wir haben aber sehr schöne Modelle. Möchten Sie sie nicht sehen?"
„Nein, kein Interesse."

Aber es ist zu spät. Die Verkäuferin ist schon weg, die Schuhe suchen. Herr Neuschuh wartet°, wütend°: „Ach, diese neue Verkäuferin! Warum ist Frl. Seidel ausgerechnet gestern° in Urlaub gegangen? —So, ich geh' jetzt. Hier bekomme ich doch nichts."
In diesem Moment kommt die Verkäuferin zurück.
„Herr Neuschuh, hier ist Ihr neues Modell!"
„Entschuldigung, mein Fräulein, aber ich habe jetzt keine Zeit."
„Nur eine Minute! Warten Sie doch!"
„Ich habe eine Verabredung°."
„Sehen Sie, das ist ganz genau° Ihre Marke."
„Na gut!"

Herr Neuschuh probiert die Schuhe an; rot, weich°, das neuste Modell. Und aus Italien. Wie immer.
„Laufen Sie doch ein wenig umher°! —Sie sehen prima aus. Ausgezeichnet!"
„Ich fühle mich lächerlich° in diesen Schuhen."

---

ausziehen *to take off;* **die Grösse** *size;* **die Mode ändert sich** *style changes;* **ein anderes** *another;* **warten** *to wait;* **wütend** *furious;* **ausgerechnet gestern** *yesterday of all days;* **die Verabredung** *appointment;* **ganz genau** *exactly;* **weich** *soft;* **laufen Sie doch ein wenig umher!** *why don't you walk around a little;* **ich fühle mich lächerlich** *I feel ridiculous*

„Zahlen° Sie bar° oder mit einem Euro-Scheck? Oder mit Kreditkarte?"

Hier steht nun Herr Neuschuh auf der Strasse mit seinen neuen Schuhen. Er betrachtet sich° in einem Schaufenster°. „Lächerlich! . . . Lächerlich!" Was mache ich jetzt bloss mit den Schuhen? Ach, ich hab's! Der Willibald hat bald Geburtstag—er hat auch Grösse 43."

Zwei Monate sind vergangen°, und Herr Neuschuh hat seinem Bruder die Schuhe noch immer nicht gegeben. Er hat seine alten Schuhe weggeworfen°, und er trägt° jetzt seine neuen Schuhe jeden Tag, auch in die Arbeit! Er hat sich an die Schuhe gewöhnt°. Jetzt ist er ein neuer Mann. Jetzt ist er ein Modemensch°!

„Ganz im Gegenteil°!" Diese Schuhe machen Sie jung!"

„Ich sehe grotesk aus."

„Nein, wunderbar!"

„Sie schmeicheln° mir, mein Fräulein."

„Wir haben dieses Modell auch in Grün, in Gelb, in . . ."

„Aber nicht in Schwarz?"

„Nein, Herr Neuschuh, nicht in Schwarz. Die Mode, wissen Sie. Das sind heute die Farben—diese Farben sind ‚in'".

„Nun, ich danke Ihnen. Ich komme nach meiner Verabredung zurück."

„Das macht zweihundertfünfundvierzig Mark."

„Aber ich will diese Schuhe nicht!"

„Soll ich die Schuhe in einen Karton packen, oder . . ."

„Nein, ich . . ."

---

ganz im Gegenteil *just the opposite;* **schmeicheln** *to flatter;* **zahlen** *to pay;* **bar** *cash;* **er betrachtet sich** *he looks at himself;* **das Schaufenster** *show window;* **vergangen** *past;* **wegwerfen** *to throw away;* **tragen** *to wear;* **er hat sich an die neuen Schuhe gewöhnt** *he got used to the new shoes;* **ein Modemensch** *a man of style*

Übung • Let's take a closer look For answers, see p. T216.

1. How can you tell what kind of a person Herr Neuschuh is? What words and phrases tell you?
2. There are quite a few words in this story that are very close to English in both spelling and meaning. Make a list of them with their English counterparts.
3. The saleswoman does not seem to hear what Herr Neuschuh says, or perhaps she just chooses to ignore him. Point out some examples of this—what does Herr Neuschuh say? How does the saleswoman respond?
4. How does Herr Neuschuh feel in the new shoes? How does he describe himself? What does the saleswoman say to convince him to buy the shoes?

Übung • Was meinst du?

1. Die Verkäuferin schmeichelt Herrn Neuschuh. Was sagt sie? Meinst du, sie glaubt das wirklich?
2. Warum kauft Herr Neuschuh die Schuhe?
3. Nach zwei Monaten hat Herr Neuschuh die Schuhe immer noch—und er trägt sie auch. Was meinst du? Hat er sich an die Schuhe gewöhnt? Mag er die Schuhe jetzt? Ist er irgendwie anders geworden?

Übung • Und du? Wie steht's mit dir?

1. Bist du ein „Modemensch", oder machst du dir wenig aus der Mode?
2. Wieso weisst du, was gerade Mode ist? Wie entscheidest du dich, wenn du etwas kaufst? Was ist für dich wichtig?
3. Wo kaufst du ein? Kaufst du gern in kleinen Geschäften ein oder in grossen Kaufhäusern? Lässt du dich gern von dem Verkäufer oder von der Verkäuferin beraten? Gehst du allein einkaufen, oder nimmst du gern jemanden mit? Wen am liebsten?

Übung • Klassenprojekte

1. Act out the scene in the shoe store as it is written. Then work out some other scenes—in teams or as a class—in which:
   a. Herr Neuschuh doesn't buy the shoes
   b. another salesclerk waits on him who isn't so assertive
   c. the salesclerk he usually goes to, Frl. Seidel, is there
2. Write a dialog between Herr Neuschuh and his brother as Herr Neuschuh presents the shoes to him on his birthday.
3. Pretend you are a friend of Herr Neuschuh's and you see him for the first time wearing his new shoes. What do you think? What do you say? What does he say? Write a dialog.

KAPITEL 12 Ferien in Österreich

Wiederholungskapitel

TEACHER–PREPARED MATERIALS	UNIT RESOURCES
Travel folders from vacation areas in Austria; typical Austrian items, or pictures; postcards from Austria	**Übungsheft,** Unit 12 **Arbeitsheft,** Unit 12 Unit 12 Cassette Review Test 3 Transparency 31 (and 22–30) Final Test Proficiency Tests 2 and 3

Unit 12 contains functions, grammar, and vocabulary that the students have studied in Units 9–11. This unit provides communicative and writing practice in different situations; some of its activities lend themselves to cooperative learning. If your students require further practice, you will find additional review exercises in Unit 12 of the **Übungsheft** and the **Arbeitsheft.** On the other hand, if your students know how to use the material in Units 9–11, you may wish to omit parts of Unit 12.

OBJECTIVE To review communicative functions, grammar, and vocabulary from Units 9–11

CULTURAL BACKGROUND Austria is one of the favorite vacation spots for Germans. There are many little villages where people can find inexpensive accommodations in private homes, in **Pensionen,** and in village inns. The picture on page 328 shows **St. Jakob** in Tyrol. The mountain on the right is the **Kitzbüheler Horn.** On the other side of the mountain is the famous ski resort, **Kitzbühel.** The picture shown on page 329 is a **Bauernhaus** in **St. Jakob,** the home of the Reiter family. Like many other farmers in the village, this family rents rooms to vacationers throughout the year. People come to hike, to climb the surrounding mountains, to swim, and to go boating and fishing in the summer, and to ski (both downhill and cross country), go sledding and go winter hiking on specially packed trails.

MOTIVATING ACTIVITY Ask the students where they like (or would like) to vacation, and why. Then ask for their reactions to the pictures on pages 328 and 329. Do they think they would like to go to Austria? What do they think it might be like?

1 Natalie macht Pläne für die Ferien

Have the students listen to the narrative with their books closed. Ask simple comprehension questions such as **Was möchte Natalie machen? Warum ruft sie die Uschi an?** Have the students open their books and look at the photos. Discuss the photos in relation to the text. For example, ask about the bottom photo **Wohin fahren die Leute?** (Point out the sign and explain **Grenzübergang**—this line of cars is going across the border into Austria.)

2 Übung • Ruf doch mal die Uschi an!

Have the students work in pairs, with one student taking the role of Natalie, the other of Uschi. (Boys' names may be substituted.) Natalie tells Uschi her plans. Uschi consults her calendar and discusses dates with Natalie.

SLOWER–PACED LEARNING To prepare the students for working in pairs, take the role of Natalie and guide the conversation. (You might begin, **Ich möchte gern am 11. oder am 18. Juli nach Österreich fahren. Fährst du mit?**) After the students have practiced with you, have them do the activity independently.

CHALLENGE After the students have done the activity as shown, have them make up their own **Monatskalender.** Again, have them work in pairs and see if they can find a time to take a vacation trip together.

3 Übung • Wohin?

St. Ulrich and **Fieberbrunn** are two other scenic villages in Tyrol. They attract vacationers both summer and winter. Have the students locate these two villages on a map showing Germany, Austria, and Switzerland. What well-known cities and resorts are close by? Bring in travel folders from vacation areas in Austria or ask students to find information and pictures to show the class, and perhaps make a bulletin board display.

Have the students answer the questions by looking at the pictograms:

> Wir können mit dem Bus nach St. Ulrich fahren. Dort können wir im Sommer segeln, windsurfen, angeln, schwimmen und Minigolf spielen. Im Winter können wir Schi laufen. Wir können mit dem Zug nach Fieberbrunn fahren. Im Sommer können wir schwimmen, kegeln, reiten, Golf spielen und Filme sehen. Im Winter können wir auch kegeln und Filme sehen, und natürlich können wir Schi laufen.

Then have the students do the dialog below the pictograms. Have them work in pairs.

4 Übung • Was brauchst du noch?

As a variation, give the students the following cues and have them name the appropriate item:

> A: Fotografierst du gern?
> B: Ja, ich brauche meine Kamera. *[or]* Ja, ich nehme meine Kamera mit.
>
> In Österreich regnet es viel. Fährst du nach Österreich?
> Hörst du gern Musik? Willst du wandern gehen?
> In Österreich ist es auch im Sommer oft kühl.

CHALLENGE Play a game in which one student makes a statement or asks a question like the ones listed above and another student must respond with an appropriate item. Re-enter previously learned vocabulary.

5 Leseübung • Was macht ihr in der Freizeit?

Have the students work in groups of three to practice this dialog. Franz should ask questions about what the girls like to do; the girls should mention various sports and activities. They should expand the dialog by commenting on each other's interests and reacting to comments:

> FRANZ Geht ihr auch tanzen?
> USCHI Ja, manchmal.
> FRANZ Ich gehe oft tanzen. Ich tanze gern!
> USCHI Wo kannst du tanzen? Gehst du in die Disko?
> FRANZ Ja, wir haben hier eine prima Disko. Die Musik ist toll!

6 Übung • So, was machen wir? 

Have the students look at the posters on this page and make suggestions for what to do and where to go. This could be done with the whole class as a review activity. Then have the students work in pairs or small groups, making suggestions, commenting, rejecting some, accepting others, and finally deciding on what to do.

7 Übung • Im Geschenkladen 

Use the picture next to the dialog for some gift items to substitute in the conversation. If possible, bring in typically Austrian items, such as a **Tiroler Hut** or a **Dirndlkleid,** or pictures of those items.

8 Übung • Im Café Troger 

Tell the students that **Jause** (on the menu) is an Austrian word for a small, light meal or between-meal snack. Have the students act out this restaurant scene in small groups. One student takes the role of the waiter or waitress, and others order something to eat and drink from the menu. After getting what they have ordered, they might ask each other how it tastes and if anyone wants more.

9 Schreibübung • Eine Karte

If possible, bring in postcards from Austria. As a project, you might ask students to make postcards by cutting out pictures from magazines, travel sections from newspapers, or travel folders and pasting them on oaktag cut into a postcard shape. Have them write home on these cards about their vacation.

10 Übung • Wieder zu Hause

Note that the students are limited as to what activities they can talk about in the conversational past. Steer them toward the verbs **sehen, spielen, essen, trinken,** and **kaufen,** for which they know the past participles. For example, you could refer them to the menu and the gift shop pictured on this page.

Festivals and Holidays

OBJECTIVE To read for cultural awareness

MOTIVATING ACTIVITY Ask the students to think of the holidays and special days or seasons they celebrate. Make a list on the board in chronological sequence throughout the year. Then, to the right of this list, fill in important German holidays beside the appropriate month. The following are some of the most important:

Neujahrstag (New Year's Day) (New Year's Eve = **Silvesternacht**)	January 1
Heilige Drei Könige (Epiphany)	January 6 (in **Baden-Württemberg** and **Bayern**)
Karfreitag (Good Friday)	
Ostersonntag, Ostermontag (Easter)	
Tag der Arbeit (Labor Day)	May 1
Christi Himmelfahrt (Ascension Day)	
Pfingstsonntag, Pfingstmontag (Whitsuntide/Pentecost)	7 weeks following Easter
Fronleichnam (Corpus Christi)	(in **Baden-Württemberg, Bayern** [in Catholic areas], **Hessen, Nordrhein-Westfalen, Rheinland-Pfalz, Saarland**)
Tag der Deutschen Einheit (Day of German Unity)	June 17 (similar to U.S. Indence Day—established after the uprising of the population in the GDR in 1953)
Mariä Himmelfahrt (Assumption Day)	August 15 (in **Bayern** [Catholic areas] and **Saarland**)
Allerheiligen (All Saint Day)	November 1 (in **Baden-Württemberg, Bayern, Nordrhein-Westfalen, Rheinland-Pfalz, Saarland**)
Buss- und Bettag (Repentance Day)	November 16
Erster und zweiter Weihnachtstag	December 25–26

Although Germans have more holidays than we do, holidays that occur on fixed days are never moved to the next Friday or Monday. Some popular celebrations that are not official holidays are **Karneval** (January 7 to the beginning of Lent) and **Nikolaus Tag** (December 6).

CULTURAL BACKGROUND Germans in general like to celebrate, and they do this in many different ways. In addition to the national holidays, there are a number of regional ones, like the wine festivals held in wine-growing regions in late summer and autumn. (The largest is the **Wurstmarkt** in **Bad Dürkheim.**) Many small towns have a **Jahrmarkt** with an amusement fair. Celebrations may last only a day or a weekend, or they may be quite long, like the nine-week carnival season. They may be frequent or infrequent, like the **Landshuter Hochzeit** (see page 336) occurring every four years or the **Oberammergau** Passion Play that occurs only once every ten years and attracts people from all over the world.

Background to the Photos

Karneval is celebrated primarily in three German areas, around the cities of **Köln, Mainz,** and **München,** as well as in Swabia, where it is called **Fasnet.** Each of these areas lends its own style to the celebration.

Page 333

1–2. These religious celebrations commemorate events in the life of Jesus Christ.

Pages 334–35

3–4. Secular traditions such as Easter eggs are also popular at Eastertime. Easter in Germany is a special time for children and often a time of family vacations, since the children have two weeks off from school and working adults have a long weekend, with both Good Friday and Easter Monday being national holidays.

6. Dancing around the maypole is a tradition to usher in the "merry" month of May. Much is made of it when a new maypole is put up (wooden ones must be replaced every few years), or when a maypole is stolen or other mischief occurs. Maypoles are decorated with symbols representing the trades practiced in the village.
7. This open-air worship service is a memorial day celebration honoring those who died in combat.

Pages 336–37

1. Riflemen's associations usually play a part in the traditional festivals of their town. There are also special **Schützenfeste.**
2. Usually, individual towns in a wine-growing region have their own festivities and elect their own **Weinkönigin.**
3. The "Goat Auction" in **Deidesheim** is a well-known folk festival.
4. Many German festivals are based on events in history or folklore. The **Landshuter Hochzeit** commemorates a famous wedding between a Polish princess and the son of a Bavarian duke. For four weeks, the entire town is decorated and the people wear medieval costumes. The wedding festivities are reenacted, complete with a parade, jousting tournaments, and the like. The trade guilds, which date back to those times, take an active part in the celebration.
5. In addition to being popular with adults from all over, the **Oktoberfest** offers entertainment for children. Parents often bring their children—there are special shows and booths for them.

Pages 338–39

1. The German St. Nicholas, as well as looking somewhat different from the Santa Claus we know, traditionally comes on a sled and leaves goodies in one shoe that each child has left on the windowsill.
2. Most large cities and towns have a Christmas market, which attracts people to the downtown area. Merchants have booths with gift items or hot refreshments for sale. Another famous **Christkindlmarkt** is in **Nürnberg.**
3. Although putting candles on the Christmas tree strikes most Americans as dangerous, this practice is very common in Germany. The tree is not left lit when no one is in the room, and in general is not up as long as Christmas trees in American homes. If candles are not used, the tree traditionally has white lights. However, the colorful American tree-decorating style is becoming more popular, especially among youngsters. Some German homes today have two trees—a traditional one for the parents and one to satisfy the children, hung, for example, with colored lights and faddish ornaments.

LANDESKUNDE 3

4. In this New Year's Eve tradition, each person melts a small piece of lead and drops it into cold water. Whatever object the emerging shape resembles is taken to symbolize the fortunes of the year to come.
5. A church is a special place to celebrate. Large cities usually have one main church or cathedral, which is often a tourist attraction. People go there to attend a mass or a service in special surroundings. Traditionally, churches are an important part of the landscape of a city—in downtown Munich, no building may be erected that stands higher than 36 meters, to preserve the silhouette of the churches in the skyline.
6. **Klein-Walsertal** is part of Austria, but the only access to it is through part of Germany.
7. An **Abiturklasse** is a special group. It is usually much smaller than a high school graduating class in the United States, since only part of the class going on to high school attends **Gymnasium.** Most **Abitur** classes take a class trip before graduation, often to a destination abroad.

Page 340

1. This old tradition is a "test" of the couple's ability to work together. It is said that if they successfully guide the saw through the log, they will be able to steer their way through whatever they confront in life.
2. Unlike in the United States, it is not customary in Germany to throw rice as the newlyweds leave. Other wedding traditions differ also: for example, showers are not given, although gifts may be delivered on the eve of the wedding. This evening is called **Polterabend,** after the tradition of breaking old pots in front of the bride's door or window. The noise was said to avert bad luck, as long as the bride swept up the fragments by herself! In Germany, a civil marriage is obligatory. It is performed in advance of the church wedding.

KAPITEL 12

Ferien in Österreich

Wiederholungskapitel

For teaching suggestions, see the Teacher's Notes preceding this unit, pp. T218–T220.

1 Natalie macht Pläne für die Ferien

Die Ferien beginnen am 28. Juni. Natalie möchte gern wegfahren, nach Österreich. Aber sie weiss noch nicht, mit wem. Viele Freundinnen haben schon etwas vor. Da hat sie eine Idee. Sie ruft jetzt mal die Uschi an. Vielleicht kann sie mitfahren.

2 Übung • Ruf doch mal die Uschi an!

Natalie möchte gern am 11. oder am 18. Juli wegfahren und vier oder fünf Tage bleiben. Geht's? Kann die Uschi mitfahren? Was sagt Natalie? Was sagt Uschi? Hier ist Uschis Monatskalender:

JULI					
Sonntag	27	4	11 } Tenniskurs	18 Stadtfest	25
Montag	28	5	12 } Tenniskurs	19	26
Dienstag	29 Geburtstagsparty f. Sabine	6	13 } Tenniskurs	20 Vatis Geburtstag	27 Rockkonzert
Mittwoch	30	7	14	21	28
Donnerstag	1 Kino!	8	15 Grosseltern kommen	22	29 Ferien mit Eltern
Freitag	2	9	16	23	30 ↓
Samstag	3	10 Fussballspiel aus Mexiko	17	24 Sommerfest	31 ↓

3 Übung • Wohin?

Wohin wollt ihr fahren? Da sind zum Beispiel Fieberbrunn und St. Ulrich, zwei Feriendörfer in Tirol, in Österreich.

mit der Bahn; mit dem Bus

1. Wie kommt ihr nach Fieberbrunn? Nach St. Ulrich?
2. Was könnt ihr dort alles machen?
3. Wohin möchtest du lieber fahren?
4. Was ist dein Lieblingssport?

segeln, Windsurfen, Schi laufen, angeln, schwimmen, Minigolf spielen.

ÖSTERREICH
TIROL
St. Ulrich
835 m
Am Pillersee

FIEBERBRUNN
in den Kitzbüheler Alpen
AUSTRIA
TIROL

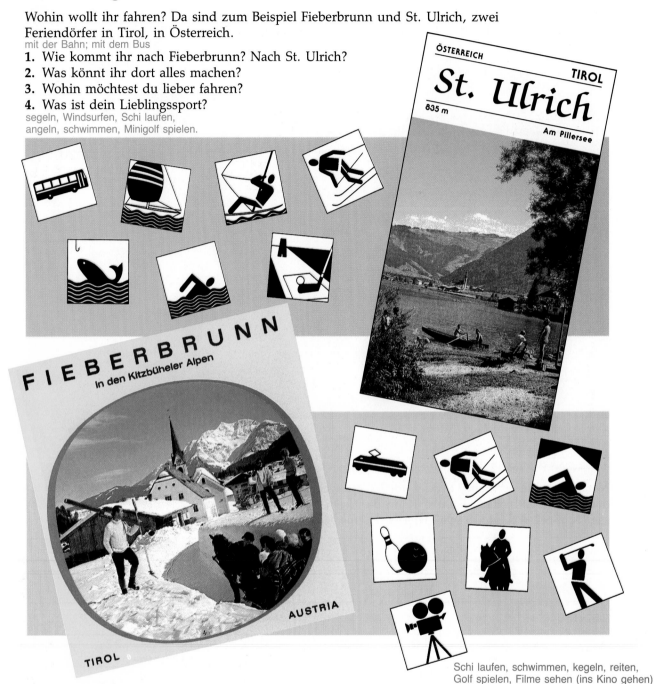

Schi laufen, schwimmen, kegeln, reiten, Golf spielen, Filme sehen (ins Kino gehen)

Und jetzt diskutiert, wohin ihr fahren wollt und warum!

A: Du, ich will lieber nach St. Ulrich fahren.
B: Warum?
A: Dort können wir . . .
B: Das stimmt. Aber in . . .

4 Übung • Was brauchst du noch?

Du machst jetzt Ferien. Deine Mutter fragt dich, was du noch brauchst. Sie nennt sechs verschiedene Dinge. Du brauchst sie nicht. Was sagst du?

A: Brauchst du einen Regenschirm?
B: Nein, ich brauche keinen Regenschirm. Es . . .

einen, keinen Pullover — Es ist nicht kalt./einen, keinen Regenschirm — Es regnet nicht./eine, keine Kamera — Ich fotografiere

nicht./eine, keine Kassette — Ich habe keinen Walkman./einen, keinen Reiseführer — Ich fahre nicht nach Österreich. *or* Ich habe schon einen Reiseführer./—, keine Wanderstiefel — Ich wandere nicht.

5 Leseübung • Was macht ihr in der Freizeit?

Natalie und Uschi spielen Minigolf. Und da spielt auch ein Junge. Er sieht nett aus. Er heisst Franz.

FRANZ Ihr spielt aber nicht oft Minigolf!
USCHI Das stimmt. Spielen wir so schlecht?
FRANZ Das möchte ich nicht sagen!! Spielt ihr Tennis . . . was macht ihr denn gewöhnlich in der Freizeit?
NATALIE Wir gehen schwimmen, wir wandern . . .
FRANZ Geht ihr auch tanzen?
USCHI Ja, manchmal.

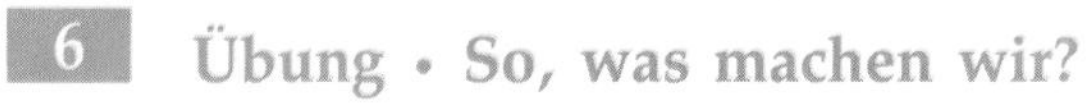

6 Übung • So, was machen wir?

Franz lädt die Mädchen ein. Gehen sie mit oder nicht?

A: So, gehen wir zusammen in die Disko?
B: . . . *or* . . .

7 Übung • Im Geschenkladen 

In St. Ulrich gibt es zwei Souvenirläden. Hier kannst du Geschenke für deine Eltern, Geschwister und Freunde kaufen.

A: Was kauf' ich bloss meiner Mutti?
B: Schau, die Blusen!
A: Die sind sehr schön, aber viel zu teuer.
B: Dann kauf ihr doch einen Kalender aus Österreich!
A: Du, das ist eine prima Idee!

* * *

A: Haben Sie dieses Halstuch auch in Blau?
B: Nein, leider nicht. Nur in Rot.
A: Schade. Blau ist meine Lieblingsfarbe.

8 Übung • Im Café Troger

Ihr habt einen Dorfbummel gemacht, und ihr möchtet jetzt etwas essen und trinken. Ihr geht ins Café Troger[1].

A: Was darf's sein, bitte?
B: Ein Eis für mich.
C: Und ein Wurstbrot für mich.
A: Ja, gern!

* * *

A: Für wen ist das Wurstbrot?
C: Für mich.
A: Guten Appetit!
C: Danke!

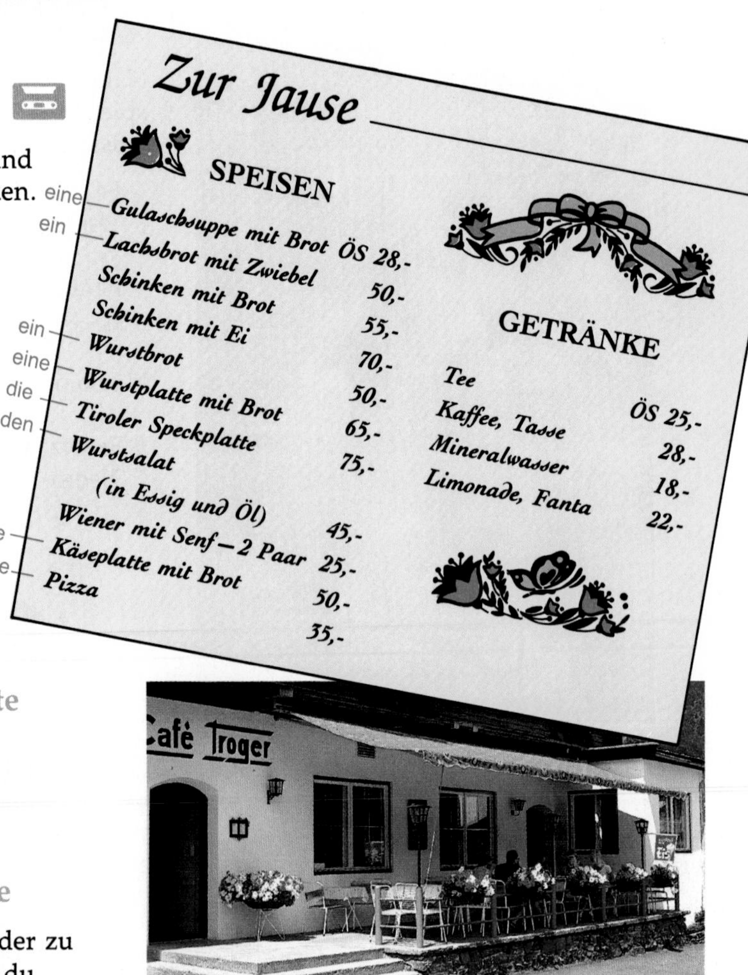

Zur Jause

SPEISEN

eine — Gulaschsuppe mit Brot ÖS 28,-
ein — Lachsbrot mit Zwiebel 50,-
Schinken mit Brot 55,-
Schinken mit Ei 70,-
ein — Wurstbrot 50,-
eine — Wurstplatte mit Brot 65,-
die — Tiroler Speckplatte 75,-
den — Wurstsalat (in Essig und Öl) 45,-
die — Wiener mit Senf – 2 Paar 25,-
eine — Käseplatte mit Brot 50,-
Pizza 35,-

GETRÄNKE

Tee ÖS 25,-
Kaffee, Tasse 28,-
Mineralwasser 18,-
Limonade, Fanta 22,-

9 Schreibübung • Eine Karte

Schreib eine Karte nach Hause!

10 Übung • Wieder zu Hause

Eure Ferien sind zu Ende. Ihr seid wieder zu Hause. Du erzählst deinen Eltern, was du gesehen und gemacht hast.

---

[1]Note that the prices on the menu are in Austrian schillings. ÖS 50,- reads: fünfzig Schilling.

LANDESKUNDE 3

Festivals and Holidays

It is said that in Germany festivals are as numerous as the days of the year. This is no exaggeration! Wherever you go, there is always something going on—a popular festival, a religious feast, a folk-dance, a historical or costume parade, or simply some occasion for public merrymaking. The calendar of festivities begins with carnival, a season that starts on the seventh of January and lasts until Lent, 40 days before Easter. It is celebrated mostly in the Catholic areas. The Rhenish carnival turns Cologne, Düsseldorf, and Mainz upside down. During the famous "Fasching," its Bavarian counterpart, Munich celebrates. The Swabian "Fasnet" conjures up the ghosts and demons of old in the strange dance of bell-jingling masks.

❶ Fastnacht in Rottweil, Schwaben

❷ Lustige Maske

❸ Rosenmontag in Köln; keiner arbeitet, alle feiern Karneval auf der Strasse

❹ Kinderfasching

The celebration of Easter week begins on Palm Sunday, seven days before Easter Sunday. Good Friday is a national holiday, and Easter week climaxes with Easter, a joyous celebration. Colorful Easter eggs and the Easter Bunny are part of the tradition for younger children.

❶ Palmsonntag-Umzug in Tirol

❷ Auferstehungsfeier an Ostersonntag in Wattens, Tirol

❸ Mädchen mit Ostereiern

❹ Ostereibrunnen in der Fränkischen Schweiz, Bayern

The advent of spring is celebrated in many different ways, depending upon the region. During springtime, one of the most impressive religious feasts in predominantly Catholic parts is Corpus Christi Day.

❺ Frühlingsanfang in Franken: der Winter wird offiziell verbrannt

❻ Am ersten Mai: Maibaumtanz im Westerwald

❼ Bergmesse in St. Jakob, Tirol

❽ Fronleichnamsprozession in einem bayrischen Dorf

During the summer and early fall there are innumerable local festivals throughout the country, festivals in which young and old participate and which uphold local and often century-old traditions.

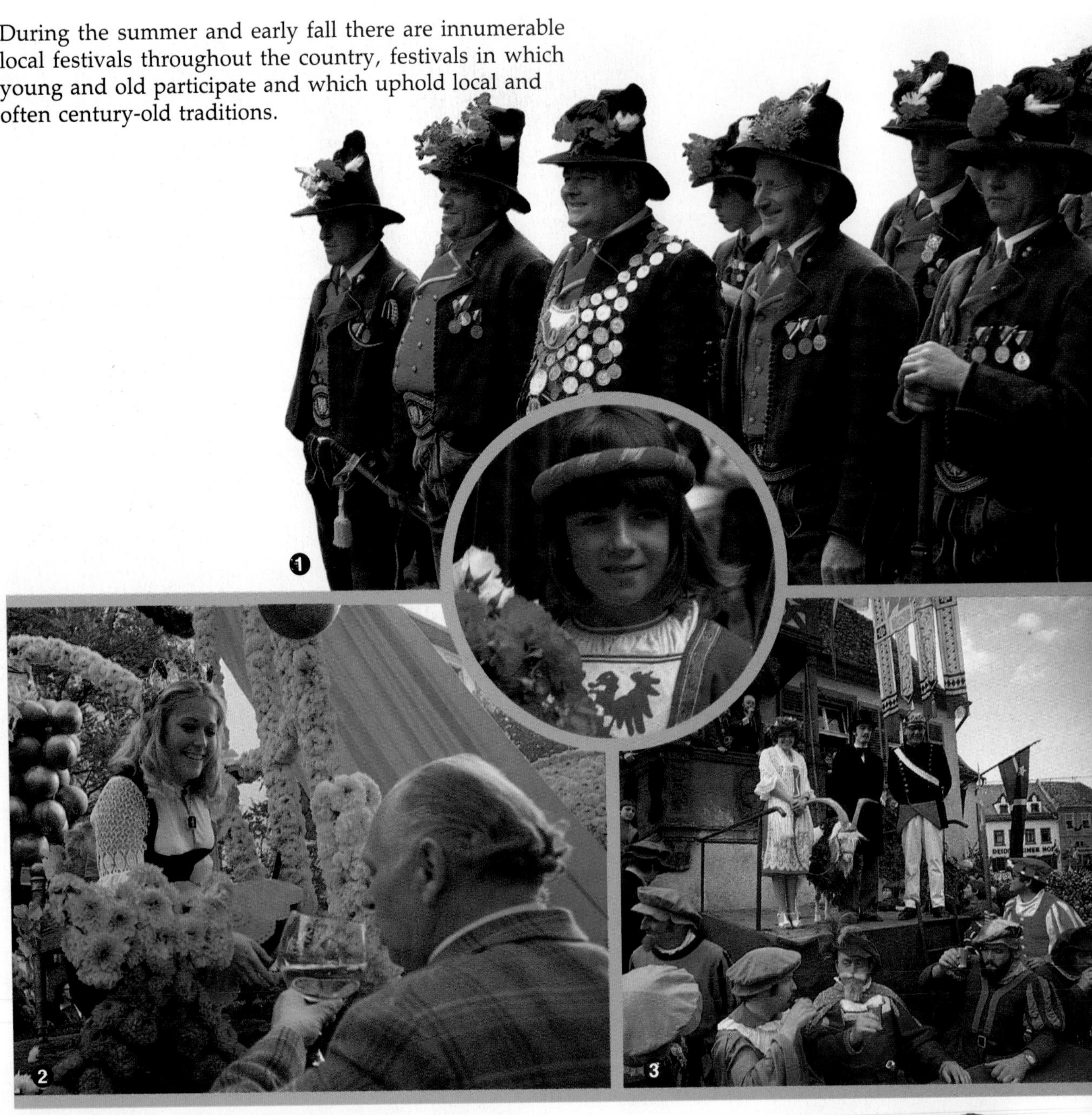

❶ Gebirgsschützen im Chiemgau, Bayern

❷ Die Deutsche Weinkönigin

❸ Weinfest in Deidesheim an der Deutschen Weinstrasse

❹ Landshuter Hochzeit: alle vier Jahre feiert Landshut die Fürstenhochzeit, die 1475 stattgefunden hat

❺ Ende September, Anfang Oktober findet das grösste Volksfest statt, das Münchner Oktoberfest, das an die Prinzenhochzeit von 1813 erinnert; hier ein Bierzelt, in dem 7 000 Menschen Platz finden

❻ Ein Kettenkarussell, grosser Spass für jung und alt

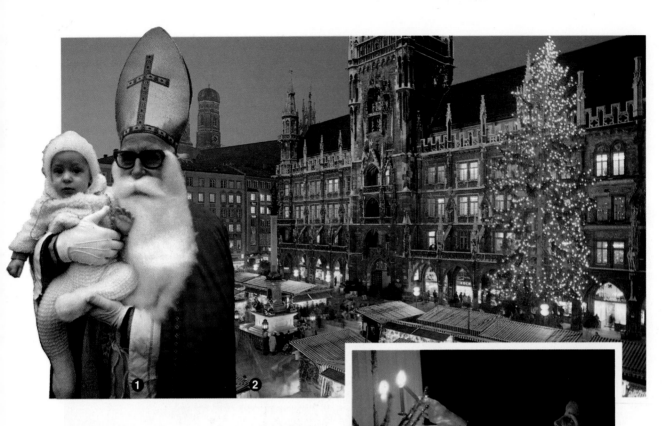

Many of the world's most cherished Christmas traditions are of German or Austrian origin. It was in the Black Forest that evergreen trees were first decorated and used as a part of Christmas. The Christmas season begins on Advent, the fourth Sunday before Christmas. Many families display colorful Advent calendars with little windows, one for each day of the season. An evergreen wreath with four candles is made, and every Sunday until Christmas one more candle is lighted. Father Christmas, or St. Nicholas, brings gifts to the children on the sixth of December. During this joyous season many cities have colorful outdoor Christmas markets. Christmas Eve is celebrated by the lighting of the Christmas tree, exchanging gifts, and attending a midnight church service. New Year's Eve brings the holiday season to an exuberant end with fireworks and traditional balls.

❶ Sankt Nikolaus

❷ Christkindlmarkt auf dem Marienplatz in München

❸ Weihnachtsbaum mit Kerzen

❹ Bleigiessen an Sylvester bringt Glück!

Among all the public festivals and holidays there are many special occasions celebrated within the family, such as birthdays, baptisms, first communion, confirmation, graduations, weddings, and anniversaries.

5 Eine Taufe

6 Heilige Kommunion (im Klein-Walsertal, Österreich)

7 Abiturklasse

8 Kinder-Geburtstag

9 Der Opa feiert seinen achtzigsten Geburtstag

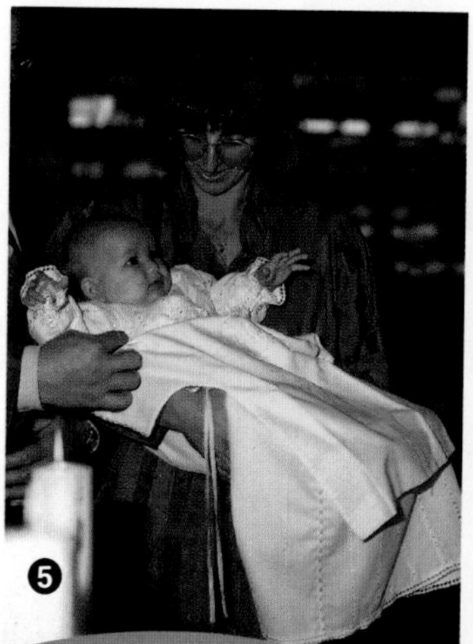

❶ Ein alter Hochzeitsbrauch: das junge Paar sägt Holz (Wernigerode, DDR)

❷ Eine weisse Hochzeitskutsche

❸ Gratulation zum 25jährigen Betriebsjubiläum

❹ Sie gedenken der Toten—auf dem Friedhof in St. Jakob, Tirol

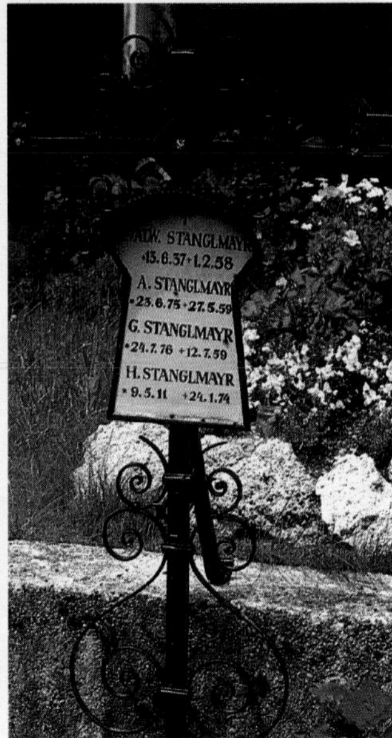

FOR REFERENCE

SUMMARY OF FUNCTIONS

The term *functions* can be defined as what you do with language—what your purpose is in speaking. As you use this textbook, you will find yourself in a number of situations—in a store, in a restaurant, at a party, at the airport, in a new city. How do you "function" in these situations? How do you ask about prices in a store, order a meal in a restaurant, compliment your host at a party, greet arriving friends at an airport, or ask for directions in an unfamiliar city? You need to know certain basic functional expressions.

Here is a list of functions accompanied by the expressions you have learned to communicate them. The number of the unit in which the expressions were introduced is followed by the section letter and number in parentheses.

SOCIALIZING

Saying hello

1 (A3) Guten Morgen!
Guten Tag!
short forms: Morgen!
Tag!
informal: Hallo!
regional: Grüss dich!

7 (A1) Grüss Gott!
Gruetzi!

Saying goodbye

1 (A3) Auf Wiedersehen!
short form: Wiedersehen!
informal: Tschüs!
Tschau!
Bis dann!

5 (C6) Bis gleich!

Addressing people

1 (A1) *first name*

1 (A7) Herr + *last name*
Frau + *last name*
Fräulein + *last name*

3 (A4) *with* du
(A15) *with* Ihr
(A19) *with* Sie

Introducing someone

6 (A3) Peter, das ist + *name*

Introducing yourself

6 (A3) Ich heisse . . .
Ich bin der / die + *first name*
Ich bin ein Freund von + *name*

Responding to an introduction

6 (A3) Guten Tag, + *name*
Hallo, + *first name*
Grüss dich, + *first name.* Wie geht's?

Asking "How are you?"

10 (A9) Wie geht's?
Wie geht's denn?

Responding to "How are you?"

10 (A9) Ach, prima!
Danke, gut!
Nicht schlecht.
So lala.
Schlecht.
Miserabel.

Welcoming people

6 (A1) Willkommen in . . .!
Schön, dass du hier bist!

Getting someone's attention

2 (B25) Du, (Jens), . . .
Schau!
Schau, (Jens)!
Schau mal!
Schau mal, (Jens)!
Entschuldigung!

5 (B1) Verzeihung!

11 (B6) Fräulein!

Greeting a customer in a store or restaurant

11 (B1) Ja, bitte? Was darf es sein?

Saying please

2 (B8) Bitte!

Saying thank you

2 (B8) Danke!

6 (B16) Tausend Dank!
Vielen Dank!

Responding to thank you

2 (B8) Bitte!

5 (B1) Gern geschehen!

5 (C13) Bitte sehr!

6 (B16) Bitte schön!
Nichts zu danken.

Making a phone call:

answering the phone

5 (C11) *last name*
Hier + *last name*

person calling

Hier + *name*
Hier ist + *name*

ending a phone conversation

Auf Wiederhören!
Tschüs!
Bis gleich!

Extending an invitation

9 (A1) Ich möchte dich einladen. Kommst du?

Accepting an invitation

9 (A3) Ja, gern!
Ja, ich komme gern.
Na, klar!
Das passt prima!

Declining an invitation

9 (A3) Es geht nicht.
(Samstag) geht es nicht.

Expressing regrets

9 (A3) Das ist schade!
Es geht leider nicht.

Making excuses

9 (A3) Ich habe schon was vor.
Ich habe keine Zeit.

Offering something to eat or drink

7 (C16) Möchtest du . . .?

9 (C1) Nimmst du . . .?
Essen Sie . . .?
(Ein Wurstbrot), vielleicht?

Accepting something to eat or drink

9 (C3) Ja, bitte!
Ja, gern!

Declining something to eat or drink

9 (C3) Nein, danke.
Keinen (Kaffee) für mich, danke!

Saying what you would like to eat or drink

9 (C1) Ich möchte . . .
Ich nehme . . .
Für mich einen . . .

Offering more or another

7 (C14) (Möchtest du) noch ein . . .?
Isst du noch ein . . .?

9 (C1) Nimmst du noch ein . . .?

10 (A6) Willst du noch ein . . .?

Accepting an offer

7 (C16) Danke, gern.
Ja, bitte!

Saying you don't want more to eat or drink

7 (C16) Nein, danke.
Danke, ich bin satt.
Nein, danke. Ich habe genug.

Complimenting someone

6 (B3) Ich finde (dein Zimmer) toll!
(Das Wohnzimmer) sieht gemütlich aus.

9 (D6) Du siehst (gut) aus.
(Du) tanzt wirklich (toll).
Deine Eltern sind (so nett).

Complimenting someone on food or drink

9 (D6) Ihr (Kuchen) ist ausgezeichnet.
(Die Suppe) schmeckt lecker.
Ich finde Ihren (Kaffee) gut.

Responding to compliments

6 (B3) Ja, wirklich?
Findest du?

6 (C1) Meinst du?

9 (D3) Da bin ich aber froh.
Das freut mich.

Expressing good wishes

2 (C10) Viel Glück!

5 (B1) Schöne Ferien!

5 (C13) Guten Flug!

7 (C1) Viel Spass!

9 (C1) Guten Appetit!

11 (C12) Herzliche Glückwünsche zum . . .!
Alles Gute zum . . .!
Gute Wünsche zum . . .!
Fröhliche Weihnachten!

Saying you don't understand

1 (D14) Wie bitte?
Woher?
Wer?
Der (Stefan)?
Ich?

9 (A1) Ich verstehe dich nicht.

EXCHANGING INFORMATION

Asking someone his or her name
1 (B5) Wie heisst du?
1 (D16) Wie heissen Sie?

and giving yours
1 (B5) Ich heisse . . .

Asking someone else's name
1 (B5) Wie heisst er / sie?

and giving it
Er / sie heisst . . .

Asking who someone is
1 (B9) Wer ist das?

Identifying people and places
1 (B9) Das ist . . .
7 (A10) Das ist . . . / Hier ist . . .

Asking someone his or her age
1 (C7) Wie alt bist du?

and giving yours
Ich bin (15).
Ich bin (15) Jahre alt.

telling someone else's age
Er / sie ist (15) Jahre alt.

Asking someone where he or she is from
1 (D4) Woher bist du?

and saying where you are from
Ich bin aus . . .

saying where someone else is from
Er / sie ist aus . . .

Asking someone about his or her interests
3 (A7) Was machst du?
Machst du (Sport)?
Spielst du (Fussball)?
Hast du Hobbys?

Saying where you live
7 (A1) Ich wohne in (Wien).
Ich bin in (Wien) zu Hause.

Answering questions
1 (D8) Ja, . . .
Nein, . . .
3 (A1) Na, klar!
9 (B4) Natürlich!

Asking for directions
5 (B3) Wo ist bitte . . .?
Wo ist . . . , bitte?
7 (A14) Weisst du, wo . . . ist?
Weisst du vielleicht, wo . . . ist?

Giving directions
5 (B3) . . . ist hier / da / hier rechts / da links!
Geradeaus!
Da drüben! / Dort drüben!
Dort drüben, rechts!

Saying you don't know
2 (B20) Ich weiss nicht.
7 (A14) Ich weiss es nicht.
Ich weiss es leider nicht.
Keine Ahnung!
Ich bin nicht von hier.
11 (B1) Ich weiss noch nicht.

Eliciting agreement, affirmation
6 (C1) Meinst du nicht?
9 (A1) Ja?
11 (B9) Nicht?

Asking about appearance
6 (C3) Wie sieht . . . aus?

describing appearance
. . . sieht (gut) aus.
. . . ist (gross, schlank).

Inquiring about prices
2 (B16) Was kostet . . .?
11 (B1) Wie teuer ist . . .?

Asking what there is (to eat)
9 (B3) Was gibt's zu (essen)?

and telling what there is
Es gibt . . .
Wir haben . . .

Asking for specific information
10 (B13) Welcher (Film) spielt heute?

Asking about categories of things
10 (B13) Was für (Filme) siehst du gern?

Saying that you don't do something in general or usually
3 (A14) Ich (segle) nicht.
(B3) Ich (spiele) nie (Fussball).
9 (C5) Ich (esse) keine (Suppe).

Saying you are not going to do something specifically or at the present time
9 (C5) Ich (esse) (die Suppe) nicht.

Talking about the past
10 (D1) Was hast du gemacht?
Gestern bin ich ins Kino gegangen.

EXPRESSING ATTITUDES AND OPINIONS

Expressing agreement
2 (D1) Ja, . . .
Ja, das ist (blöd).
3 (C7) Stimmt!
Das finde ich auch.
6 (C9) Du hast recht.
Ich auch.

7 (B1) Gut.
O.K.

7 (C7) Na, gut.

9 (A1) Schön!

11 (B9) Ich glaube, ja.

Expressing disagreement

3 (C7) Stimmt nicht!
Das finde ich nicht.

6 (C9) Das ist Geschmackssache.

Contradicting, correcting

2 (B20) Unsinn! Das ist . . .

10 (B3) Quatsch! Das ist kein . . .

Asking for an opinion

3 (C3) Wie findest du . . .?

11 (A12) Was meinst du?
Hast du eine Idee?

Giving an opinion

3 (C3) Ich finde . . . (toll).

Wondering what to give

11 (A12) Was schenke ich bloss meinem (Vater)?
Was gebe ich nur meiner (Mutter)?
Was soll ich kaufen?

Asking for advice

7 (C1) Was sollen wir machen?

11 (A12) Was meinst du?
Hast du eine Idee?

Giving advice

7 (C1) Bleibt lieber zu Hause!

11 (C1) Schenken Sie ihm ein . . .!

Asking about someone's wishes

9 (C1) Was möchtest du?
Was nimmst du?

10 (A11) Willst du (ins Kino gehen)?

Expressing wishes

5 (B11) Ich möchte (Briefmarken kaufen).

10 (A6) Ich will (in die Stadt fahren).

Expressing intention

5 (B11) Ich möchte . . .

9 (C1) Ich esse . . . / trinke . . . / nehme . . .

10 (A6) Ich will . . .

Asking how something tastes

7 (C12) Schmeckt (der, die, das) . . .?
Wie schmeckt (der, die, das) . . .?

9 (D5) Wie ist (der, die, das) . . .?

Telling how something tastes

7 (C12) Danke, (er, sie, es) ist . . .
Danke, (er, sie, es) schmeckt . . .

9 (D3) Und wie!

EXPRESSING FEELINGS AND EMOTIONS

Expressing surprise

3 (C7) Was?!
Wirklich?

6 (C9) Meinst du?

Expressing liking

3 (C11) Ich (spiele) gern (Gitarre).

10 (C3) Ich mag . . .
Ich mag . . . gern.
Ich habe . . . gern.

Expressing dislike

3 (C11) Ich (spiele) nicht gern (Fussball).

10 (C3) Ich habe . . . nicht gern.
Ich mag . . . nicht.
Ich mag . . . nicht gern.

Expressing strong dislike

10 (C3) Ich hasse . . .

Expressing preference

3 (C11) Ich (spiele) lieber . . .

10 (B10) Ich (höre) . . . lieber.
Ich (höre) . . . besonders gern.

Expressing strong preference

3 (C11) Ich (spiele) am liebsten . . .

10 (B10) Ich (sehe) . . . am liebsten.
Das ist mein(e) Lieblings . . .

Expressing indifference

9 (B4) Na und?!

10 (B10) Das ist mir gleich.

Responding to good news

2 (D5) Gut!
Prima!
Phantastisch!
Toll!

Responding to bad news

2 (D5) Blöd!
Das ist nicht so gut.
Das ist schlecht.
Schade!

Expressing enthusiasm

2 (A1) Toll!

3 (C1) Ich finde . . . interessant!
. . . ist Klasse / Spitze / super / prima / phantastisch / toll!
. . . macht Spass!

6 (B11) Mensch!

9 (A1) Schön!

9 (D3) Und wie!

Expressing lack of enthusiasm

3 (C1) Ich finde . . . blöd.
. . . ist langweilig.

10 (B3) Ich mag . . . nicht besonders.

Expressing annoyance

7 (C4) Das ist blöd / dumm!
Das ist zu blöd / dumm!
Ich bin sauer.

Expressing regret

9 (A3) Das ist schade.
Es geht leider nicht.

Expressing relief

5 (B1) Gott sei dank!

5 (C6) Endlich!

PERSUADING: GETTING SOMEONE TO DO SOMETHING

Making requests

7 (B4) Geh doch bitte mal (einkaufen)!
Kauf bitte nicht alles beim . . .!
Hol doch (das Obst) beim . . .!

Giving commands

7 (B4) Pass bitte auf!
Verlier das Geld nicht!

Making suggestions

7 (C7) Probier doch mal den . . .!

10 (A11) Möchtest du ins (Kino) gehen?
Willst du ins (Kino) gehen?
Gehen wir doch ins (Kino)!

11 (C1) Kaufen Sie . . .!
Schenken Sie ihm . . .!

Expressing possibility

10 (A11) Wir können ins (Kino) gehen.

Giving advice

7 (C1) Bleibt lieber zu Hause!

11 (C1) Kaufen Sie . . .!
Schenken Sie ihm . . .!

GRAMMAR SUMMARY

DETERMINERS

In German, nouns can be grouped into three classes or genders: masculine, feminine, and neuter. There are words that tell you the gender of a noun. One of these is called the definite article. In English there is one definite article: *the.* In German there are three, one for each gender: **der, die,** and **das.**

Gender:	MASCULINE	FEMININE	NEUTER
Noun Phrase:	**der Junge** *the boy* **der Ball** *the ball*	**die Mutter** *the mother* **die Kassette** *the cassette*	**das Mädchen** *the girl* **das Haus** *the house*

Other words can be used with a noun instead of the definite article. Examples of these words in English are *a, this, that, my,* and *every.* These words and the definite article are called determiners. They help to make clear, or determine, which person or thing you mean—for example, whether you are talking about *this book, my book,* or just any book. A determiner plus a noun is called a noun phrase.

DEFINITE ARTICLES

	NOMINATIVE	ACCUSATIVE
Masculine	**der**	**den**
Feminine	**die**	**die**
Neuter	**das**	**das**
Plural	**die**	**die**

DIESER–WORDS

The determiners **dieser, jeder, welcher,** and **alle** are called **dieser**-words because their endings are the same as those of **dieser.** Note that the endings of the **dieser**-words are very similar to those of the definite articles.

dieser	*this, that*
jeder	*each, every*
alle	*all*
welcher	*which, what*

	NOMINATIVE	ACCUSATIVE	NOMINATIVE	ACCUSATIVE	NOMINATIVE	ACCUSATIVE
Masculine	**dieser**	**diesen**	**jeder**	**jeden**	**welcher**	**welchen**
Feminine	**diese**	**diese**	**jede**	**jede**	**welche**	**welche**
Neuter	**dieses**	**dieses**	**jedes**	**jedes**	**welches**	**welches**
Plural	**diese**	**diese**	**alle**	**alle**	**welche**	**welche**

INDEFINITE ARTICLES

The determiner **ein,** *a, an,* is called an indefinite article. There is no plural form of **ein.** You must use words like **viele,** *many,* **einige,** *some,* **mehrere,** *several,* which you will learn later.

	NOMINATIVE	ACCUSATIVE
Masculine	**ein**	**einen**
Feminine	**eine**	**eine**
Neuter	**ein**	**ein**
Plural	—	—

THE NEGATIVE DETERMINER *KEIN*

The negative determiner **kein,** *no, not, not any,* has the same endings as **ein.** Note that **kein** has a plural form.

	NOMINATIVE	ACCUSATIVE
Masculine	**kein**	**keinen**
Feminine	**keine**	**keine**
Neuter	**kein**	**kein**
Plural	**keine**	**keine**

POSSESSIVES

	BEFORE MASCULINE NOUNS			BEFORE FEMININE NOUNS		BEFORE NEUTER NOUNS		BEFORE PLURAL NOUNS	
	NOM	ACC	DAT	NOM & ACC	DAT	NOM & ACC	DAT	NOM & ACC	DAT
my	mein	meinen	meinem	meine	meiner	mein	meinem	meine	meinen
your	dein	deinen	deinem	deine	deiner	dein	deinem	deine	deinen
his	sein	seinen	seinem	seine	seiner	sein	seinem	seine	seinen
her	ihr	ihren	ihrem	ihre	ihrer	ihr	ihrem	ihre	ihren
our	unser	unseren	unserem	unsere	unserer	unser	unserem	unsere	unseren
your	euer	eueren	euerem	euere	euerer	euer	euerem	euere	eueren
their	ihr	ihren	ihrem	ihre	ihrer	ihr	ihrem	ihre	ihren
your	Ihr	Ihren	Ihrem	Ihre	Ihrer	Ihr	Ihrem	Ihre	Ihren

Commonly used short forms for unseren: unsren *or* unsern *for* unsere: unsre
eueren: euren *or* euern euere: eure

for unserem: unsrem *or* unserm *for* unserer: unsrer
euerem: eurem *or* euerm euerer: eurer

NOUN PLURALS

Noun gender and plural forms are not always predictable. Therefore, you must learn each noun together with its article (**der, die, das**) and with its plural form. As you learn more nouns, however, you will discover certain patterns. Although there are always exceptions to these patterns, you may find them helpful in remembering the plural forms of many nouns.

Most German nouns form their plurals in one of five ways. Some nouns add endings in the plural; some add endings and/or change the sound of the stem vowel in the plural, indicating the sound change with the umlaut (¨). Only the vowels **a, o, u** and the diphthong **au** can take the umlaut. If a noun has an umlaut in the singular, it keeps the umlaut in the plural. Most German nouns fit into one of the following plural groups:

Group:	I	II	III	IV	V
Ending:	–	–e	–er	–(e)n	–s
Umlaut:	*sometimes*	*sometimes*	*always*	*never*	*never*

1. Nouns in Group I do not have any ending in the plural. Sometimes they take an umlaut. NOTE: There are only two feminine nouns in this group: **die Mutter** and **die Tochter.**

der Bruder, die Brüder
der Garten, die Gärten
der Lehrer, die Lehrer
der Mantel, die Mäntel
der Onkel, die Onkel
der Schüler, die Schüler
der Vater, die Väter

die Mutter, die Mütter
die Tochter, die Töchter

das Fräulein, die Fräulein
das Mädchen, die Mädchen
das Poster, die Poster
das Zimmer, die Zimmer

2. Nouns in Group II add the ending **-e** in the plural. Sometimes they take an umlaut. NOTE: There are many one-syllable words in this group.

der Bleistift, die Bleistifte
der Freund, die Freunde
der Pass, die Pässe
der Sohn, die Söhne
der Witz, die Witze

die Stadt, die Städte

das Jahr, die Jahre
das Spiel, die Spiele
das Stück, die Stücke

3. Nouns in Group III add the ending **-er** in the plural. They always take an umlaut wherever possible, that is when the noun contains the vowels **a, o,** or **u,** or the diphthong **au.** NOTE: There are no feminine nouns in this group. There are many one-syllable words in this group.

das Buch, die Bücher
das Dorf, die Dörfer
das Fach, die Fächer
das Haus, die Häuser
das Land, die Länder

4. Nouns in Group IV add the ending **-en** or **-n** in the plural. They never add an umlaut. NOTE: There are many feminine nouns in this group.

der Angestellte, die Angestellten
der Herr, die Herren
der Junge, die Jungen

der Kamerad, die Kameraden
der Name, die Namen
der Vetter, die Vettern

die Briefmarke, die Briefmarken
die Familie, die Familien
die Farbe, die Farben
die Frau, die Frauen
die Karte, die Karten
die Klasse, die Klassen

die Küche, die Küchen
die Schwester, die Schwestern
die Tante, die Tanten
die Wohnung, die Wohnungen
die Zahl, die Zahlen
die Zeitung, die Zeitungen

Feminine nouns ending in **-in** add the ending **-nen** in the plural.

die Freundin, die Freundinnen
die Lehrerin, die Lehrerinnen
die Verkäuferin, die Verkäuferinnen

5. Nouns in Group V add the ending **-s** in the plural. They never add an umlaut. NOTE: There are many words of foreign origin in this group.

der Kuli, die Kulis — das Auto, die Autos
die Kamera, die Kameras — das Hobby, die Hobbys

PRONOUNS

PERSONAL PRONOUNS

		NOMINATIVE	ACCUSATIVE	DATIVE
Singular				
1st person		ich	mich	mir
2nd person		du	dich	dir
	m.	er	ihn	ihm
3rd person	*f.*	sie	sie	ihr
	n.	es	es	ihm
Plural				
1st person		wir	uns	uns
2nd person		ihr	euch	euch
3rd person		sie	sie	ihnen
Formal Address		Sie	Sie	Ihnen

DEFINITE ARTICLES AS DEMONSTRATIVE PRONOUNS

The definite articles can be used as demonstrative pronouns, giving more emphasis to the sentences than the personal pronouns **er, sie, es.** Note that the demonstrative pronouns have the same forms as the definite articles.

	NOMINATIVE	ACCUSATIVE
Masculine	der	den
Feminine	die	die
Neuter	das	das
Plural	die	die

INTERROGATIVES

INTERROGATIVE PRONOUNS

Nominative	**wer?** *who?*	**was?** *what?*
Accusative	**wen?** *whom?*	**was?** *what?*
Dative	**wem?** *to, for whom?*	

SUMMARY OF INTERROGATIVES

wann?	*when?*	**wo?**	*where?*	**welche?**	*which? what?*
warum?	*why?*	**woher?**	*from where?*	**was für (ein)?**	*what kind of (a)?*
wie?	*how?*	**wohin?**	*to where?*		
wieviel?	*how much? how many?*				

WAS FÜR (EIN)?

	NOMINATIVE	ACCUSATIVE
Masculine	**Was für ein** Lehrer ist er?	**Was für einen** Lehrer hast du?
Feminine	**Was für eine** Platte ist das?	**Was für eine** Platte kaufst du?
Neuter	**Was für ein** Radio ist das?	**Was für ein** Radio hast du?
Plural	**Was für** Instrumente sind hier?	**Was für** Instrumente spielt ihr?

WORD ORDER

The verb is in first position in	*questions that do not begin with an interrogative:* Trinkst du Kaffee? Spielst du Fussball? *suggestions using command forms:* Geht doch ins Kino!
The verb is in second position in	*statements:* Wir spielen Tennis. Am Wochenende spiele ich Fussball. *questions that begin with an interrogative:* Wohin fahrt ihr? Was spielst du gern?
The verb is in last position in	*clauses following* **wissen:** Ich weiss, wo der Dom ist.

POSITION OF *NICHT* IN A SENTENCE

Er fragt seinen Vater		**nicht.**	*as near the end as possible to negate entire sentence*
Ich rufe ihn	**nicht**	an.	*before a separable prefix*
Er kommt	**nicht**	heute. (Er kommt morgen.)	*before any part of a sentence you want to negate, contrast, emphasize*
Ich wohne	**nicht**	in Berlin.	*before part of a sentence answering the question* wo?

VERBS

PRESENT TENSE VERB FORMS

INFINITIVES:		spiel -en	mogel -n	find -en	heiss -en
PRONOUNS		stem + ending	stem + ending	stem + ending	stem + ending
I	ich	spiel **-e**	mogl **-e**	find **-e**	heiss **-e**
you	du	spiel **-st**	mogel **-st**	find **-est**	heiss **-t**
he, she	er, sie	spiel **-t**	mogel **-t**	find **-et**	heiss **-t**
we	wir	spiel **-en**	mogel **-n**	find **-en**	heiss **-en**
you	ihr	spiel **-t**	mogel **-t**	find **-et**	heiss **-t**
they	sie	spiel **-en**	mogel **-n**	find **-en**	heiss **-en**
you (formal)	Sie	spiel **-en**	mogel **-n**	find **-en**	heiss **-en**

Note the following exceptions in the preceding chart:

a. Verbs ending in **-eln (mogeln, segeln)** drop the "**e**" of the ending **-eln** in the **ich**-form: **ich mogle,** and add only **-n** in the **wir-, sie-,** and **Sie**-form. These forms are always identical with the infinitive: **mogeln, wir mogeln, sie mogeln, Sie mogeln.**

b. Verbs with a stem ending in **-d** or in **-t,** such as **finden,** add **-est** in the **du**-form, and **-et** in the **er-** and **ihr**-forms: **du findest, er findet, ihr findet.**

c. All verbs with stems ending in an "**s**" sound **(heissen)** add only **-t** in the **du**-form: **du heisst.**

d. In speaking, the **ich**-form is often used without the ending **-e: ich spiel', ich frag'.** The omission of the **-e** is shown in writing by an apostrophe.

VERBS WITH A STEM–VOWEL CHANGE

There are a number of verbs in German that change their stem vowel in the **du-** and **er/sie-**form. Some verbs, such as **nehmen,** have a consonant change as well. There is no way to predict these verbs, so you must learn each one individually.

	e → i			e → ie		a → ä		
	essen	**geben**	**nehmen**	**lesen**	**sehen**	**anfangen**	**einladen**	**fahren**
ich	esse	gebe	nehme	lese	sehe	fange an	lade ein	fahre
du	**isst**	**gibst**	**nimmst**	**liest**	**siehst**	**fängst** an	**lädst** ein	**fährst**
er, sie	**isst**	**gibt**	**nimmt**	**liest**	**sieht**	**fängt** an	**lädt** ein	**fährt**
wir	essen	geben	nehmen	lesen	sehen	fangen an	laden ein	fahren
ihr	esst	gebt	nehmt	lest	seht	fangt an	ladet ein	fahrt
sie, Sie	essen	geben	nehmen	lesen	sehen	fangen an	laden ein	fahren

THE VERBS *HABEN, SEIN, WISSEN*

	haben	sein	wissen
ich	habe	bin	weiss
du	hast	bist	weisst
er, sie, es	hat	ist	weiss
wir	haben	sind	wissen
ihr	habt	seid	wisst
sie	haben	sind	wissen
Sie	haben	sind	wissen

SOME MODAL VERBS

The verbs **können, mögen** (and the **möchte**-forms), **sollen,** and **wollen** are usually used with an infinitive that comes at the end of the sentence. If the meaning of that infinitive is clear, it can be left out.

	können	**mögen**	**sollen**	**wollen**	**möchte**-forms
ich	kann	mag	soll	will	möchte
du	kannst	magst	sollst	willst	möchtest
er, sie, es	kann	mag	soll	will	möchte
wir	können	mögen	sollen	wollen	möchten
ihr	könnt	mögt	sollt	wollt	möchtet
sie	können	mögen	sollen	wollen	möchten
Sie	können	mögen	sollen	wollen	möchten

VERBS WITH SEPARABLE PREFIXES

Some verbs have separable prefixes. A separable prefix is a prefix that is sometimes separated from the main verb.

	INFINITIVE: **anfangen**
ich fange an	Ich **fange** jetzt **an.**
du fängst an	Wann **fängst** du **an?**
er, sie, es fängt an	**Fängt** er immer zuerst **an?**
wir fangen an	Wir **fangen** nicht zuerst **an.**
ihr fangt an	Warum **fangt** ihr nicht **an?**
sie fangen an	Sie **fangen** morgen nach der Schule wieder **an.**

Here is a list of verbs with separable prefixes and similar verbs.

abheben	auspacken	kennenlernen
anfangen	aussehen	radfahren
anrufen	einladen	
ausgehen	vorhaben	

COMMAND FORMS

	bleiben	**essen**	**anfangen**
Persons you address			
with **du** (*sing*)	bleib!	iss!	fang an!
with **ihr** (*pl*)	bleibt!	esst!	fangt an!
with **Sie** (*sing* & *pl*)	bleiben Sie!	essen Sie!	fangen Sie an!
let's form	bleiben wir!	essen wir!	fangen wir an!

Here are some other command forms you have learned:

anrufen	**ausgehen**	**einladen**	**erzählen**	**holen**	**kaufen**
ruf an!	geh aus!	lad ein!	erzähl!	hol!	kauf!
ruft an!	geht aus!	ladet ein!	erzählt!	holt!	kauft!
rufen Sie an!	gehen Sie aus!	laden Sie ein!	erzählen Sie!	holen Sie!	kaufen Sie!
rufen wir an!	gehen wir aus!	laden wir ein!	erzählen wir!	holen wir!	kaufen wir!

radfahren	schauen	schenken	verlieren	versuchen
fahr Rad! fahrt Rad! fahren Sie Rad! fahren wir Rad!	schau! schaut! schauen Sie! schauen wir!	schenk! schenkt! schenken Sie! schenken wir!	verlier! verliert! verlieren Sie! verlieren wir!	versuch! versucht! versuchen Sie! versuchen wir!

Verbs with stem vowel changes:

geben	nehmen	sehen
gib! gebt! geben Sie! geben wir!	nimm! nehmt! nehmen Sie! nehmen wir!	sieh! seht! sehen Sie! sehen wir!

THE CONVERSATIONAL PAST

German verbs are divided into two groups: weak verbs and strong verbs. Weak verbs usually follow a regular pattern, such as the English verb forms *play—played—has played.* Strong verbs usually have irregularities, like the English verb forms *run—ran—has run* or *go—went—has gone.*

The conversational past tense of weak and strong verbs consists of the present tense of **haben** or **sein** and a form called the past participle, which is usually in last position in the clause or sentence.

Die Schüler	**haben**	ihre Hausaufgaben schon	**gemacht.**
Sabine	**ist**	gestern zu Hause	**geblieben.**

Here is a list of past participles you have been using in this textbook. Note that:

1. The past participle of most weak verbs is formed by putting the prefix **ge-** before the present tense **er**-form, which ends in **-t.** The ending **-t** tells you that the verb is weak. (**gemacht, gehört, gekauft**)
2. Verbs with an inseparable prefix (a prefix never separated from the verb stem) do not add **ge-** in the past participle. (**besuchen, hat besucht**)
3. The past participle of many strong verbs is formed by putting the prefix **ge-** before the infinitive of the verb. However, the past participles of most strong verbs have a stem vowel different from the stem vowel of the infinitive. In addition, there may be consonant changes. Some strong verbs have special forms in the past participle, for example, the verb **sein.**

You have learned the following past participles:

Weak Verbs		Strong Verbs	
INFINITIVE	PAST PARTICIPLE	INFINITIVE	PAST PARTICIPLE
besuchen	hat **besucht**	bleiben	ist **geblieben**
hören	hat **gehört**	essen	hat **gegessen**
kaufen	hat **gekauft**	fahren	ist **gefahren**
machen	hat **gemacht**	geben	hat **gegeben**
schenken	hat **geschenkt**	gehen	ist **gegangen**
spielen	hat **gespielt**	haben	hat **gehabt**
		lesen	hat **gelesen**
		sehen	hat **gesehen**
		sein	ist **gewesen**
		trinken	hat **getrunken**

PRINCIPAL PARTS OF STRONG VERBS

This list includes all strong verbs listed in the **Wortschatz** sections of this textbook. Weak verbs with separable prefixes, stem vowel changes, or other irregularities are also listed. Past participles formed with **sein** are indicated. All other past participles on this list are formed with **haben.** Usually only one English meaning of the verb is given. Other meanings may be found in the German-English Vocabulary.

The past participles considered active, that is, the ones you learned in Units 10 and 11, are in heavy type.

INFINITIVE	PRESENT (stem vowel change and/or separable prefix)	PAST PARTICIPLE	MEANING
abheben	er hebt ab	abgehoben	*to lift (the receiver)*
anfangen	er fängt an	angefangen	*to start*
anrufen	er ruft an	angerufen	*to call up*
ausgehen	er geht aus	ist ausgegangen	*to go out*
aussehen	er sieht aus	ausgesehen	*to look, appear*
beginnen		begonnen	*to begin*
bekommen		bekommen	*to get, receive*
bleiben		**ist geblieben**	*to stay*
bringen		gebracht	*to bring*
einladen	er lädt ein	eingeladen	*to invite*
essen	er isst	**gegessen**	*to eat*
fahren	er fährt	**ist gefahren**	*to drive, ride*
finden		gefunden	*to find, think*
fliegen		ist geflogen	*to fly*
geben	er gibt	**gegeben**	*to give*
gehen		**ist gegangen**	*to go*
gewinnen		gewonnen	*to win*
haben	er hat	**gehabt**	*to have*
heissen		geheissen	*to be called*
kennen		gekannt	*to know*
kommen		ist gekommen	*to come*
können	er kann	gekonnt	*to be able to*
lesen	er liest	**gelesen**	*to read*
mögen	er mag	gemocht	*to like*
nehmen	er nimmt	genommen	*to take*
radfahren	er fährt Rad	ist radgefahren	*to go bike riding*
scheinen		geschienen	*to shine*
schwimmen		ist geschwommen	*to swim*
sehen	er sieht	**gesehen**	*to see*
sein	er ist	**ist gewesen**	*to be*
singen		gesungen	*to sing*
sprechen	er spricht	gesprochen	*to speak*
stehen		gestanden	*to stand*
trinken		**getrunken**	*to drink*
tun		getan	*to do*
verbringen		verbracht	*to spend (time)*
verlieren		verloren	*to lose*
verstehen		verstanden	*to understand*
vorhaben	er hat vor	vorgehabt	*to have planned*
wissen	er weiss	gewusst	*to know*
wollen	er will	gewollt	*to want*

PRONUNCIATION

Pronunciation and reading exercises are found in the Try Your Skills section of each unit, with the exception of the review units.

			as in:
Kapitel (p. 53)	1	The **ich**-sound (/ç/)	ich, dich, Mädchen
		The **ach**-sound (/x/)	acht, achtzehn, auch
		The /l/ sound	alt, elf, Lehrer
Kapitel (p. 85)	2	Long vowels	da, dem, vier, du
		Short vowels: the sound /ɔ/	kosten, toll, von
		The /ü/ sound	für, fünf, Glück
		The /ö/ sound	blöd, Österreich, Wörterbuch
Kapitel (p. 113)	3	The sounds /R/ and /ʌ/	frei, Rad, lieber
		The diphthongs /ai/, /au/, /ɔi/	ein, sauer, neun
		The sound /ʃ/	Schule, spät, Bleistift
Kapitel (p. 159)	5	The /l/ sound (review)	Köln, Zoll, Kilometer
		The **ach**-sound (review)	nach, Schliessfach, besuchen
		The /ü/ sound (review)	Reiseführer, Münze, zurück
		The /ö/ sound (review)	Köln, möchte
Kapitel (p. 187)	6	Long vowels (review)	Bahn, gehen, wie, Oma, Flug
		The sounds /R/ and /ʌ/ (review)	Bruder, Zimmer, Keller
		Long **ä** (/ä:/, /e:/)	Mädchen, Bäder
		The sound /t/	Mutter, bitte, Tante
Kapitel (p. 217)	7	The diphthongs /ei/, /au/, /ɔi/ (review)	Eis, Hauptstadt, Leute
		The sound /ɔ/ (review)	Dorf, Schloss, wolkig
		The sound /pf/	Pfund, Pfennig
		The sound /ʃv/	schwer, Schwester, Schweiz
Kapitel (p. 261)	9	The **ich**-sound (review)	gleich, mich, gemütlich
		The **ach**-sound (review)	Kuchen, Buch
		The /l/ sound (review)	Platte, einladen
		The umlaute **ä, ö,** and **ü** (review)	Käse, schön, hübsch
		The sound /R/ (review)	Ruhe, anrufen
Kapitel (p. 293)	10	Long vowels /e:/, /o:/, /u:/ (review)	gesehen, Kino, Jugend
		The /l/ sound (review)	also, wollen, miserabel
		The sound /ɔ/ (review)	Sport, besonders, Konzert
Kapitel (p. 321)	11	Long vowels /a:/, /e:/, /o:/, /u:/, and /ü:/ (review)	Vater, geben, Hose, Bluse, grün
		The diphthongs /ei/, /au/, /ɔi/ (review)	weiss, glauben, Sträusse
		The **ich**-sound (review)	gewöhnlich, herzlich
		The **ach**-sound (review)	Schachtel, Weihnachten
		The /l/ sound (review)	Kalender, Blume, fröhlich

NUMBERS

0	null	14	vierzehn	50	fünfzig
1	eins	15	fünfzehn	60	sechzig
2	zwei	16	sechzehn	70	siebzig
3	drei	17	siebzehn	80	achtzig
4	vier	18	achtzehn	90	neunzig
5	fünf	19	neunzehn	100	hundert
6	sechs	20	zwanzig	101	hunderteins
7	sieben	21	einundzwanzig	102	hundertzwei
8	acht	22	zweiundzwanzig	103	hundertdrei
9	neun	23	dreiundzwanzig	200	zweihundert
10	zehn	24	vierundzwanzig	201	zweihunderteins
11	elf	30	dreissig	300	dreihundert
12	zwölf	31	einunddreissig	400	vierhundert
13	dreizehn	40	vierzig	1000	tausend

ENGLISH EQUIVALENTS

The following are the English equivalents of the basic material in each section of every unit, with the exception of review units. They are not literal translations, but represent what a speaker of English would say in the same situation.

1 NEW FRIENDS

A1 Hello! Goodbye!
Hi, Steffi!
Hi, Andreas!
Hi, Stefan!
Hello, Michael!
Morning, Natalie!
Good morning!
Bye!
Bye! So long!
See you later!
Goodbye!

A5 Mr., Mrs., Miss
Good morning, Mr. Sperling.
Hello, Antje.

Hello, Mrs. Meier.
Hi, Michael.

Bye, Miss Seifert.
Goodbye.

B1 What's your name?
Hi! My name is Andreas. What's your name?
My name is Natalie.

And what's your name? My name is _____.

B3 What's the boy's name? What's the girl's name?
What's the boy's name?
His name is Stefan.

And the girl? What's her name?
Her name is Sabine.

B8 Who is that?
Who is that?
That's Stefan.

And who is that?
That is Mr. Sperling, the teacher.

Who is that?
That's Sabine.
And that's Mrs. Meier, the teacher.

Mr. Sperling, the German teacher.
Mrs. Meier, the German teacher

C1 How old are you?
How old are you?
I'm thirteen years old.

How old is Sabine?
Sabine is fifteen.

And how old is Stefan?
Stefan is fifteen too.

How old are Ulrike and Michael?
They are also fifteen years old.

And how old are you? I'm _____.

D1 Where are you from?
My name is Jens Kröger. I am sixteen years old. I'm from Niebüll, from Germany.

I'm Wiebke Nedel. I'm fifteen. I am also from Germany, from Neuss.

My name is Dastl, Margit Dastl. I am fourteen. I'm from Vienna, from Austria.

My name is Bruno Schmidlin. I'm fifteen. I am from Switzerland, from Zimmerwald.

I am Kurt Langer. I'm fifteen too. I'm from the DDR, from Dresden.

And where are you from? From Kansas City? From Harrisburg? Dallas? I'm from _____.

D7 Yes or no?
Jörg asks Jens:
Is your name Michael?
No, my name is Jens.
Are you from Niebüll?
Yes.

Jörg asks Lars:
Is that Jens?
Yes.
Is his name Nedel?
No, his name is Kröger.
Is he from Niebüll?
Yes, he's from Niebüll.

D13 I beg your pardon?
I'm from Liechtenstein.
From where?

What's your name?

Me? My name is . . .

That's Hans-Helmut Kurtmeyer.
I beg your pardon? Who is that?

How old is Stefan?
Stefan? —He's fifteen.

D16 What is your name? Where are you from?
Are you the German teacher?
No, I'm the math teacher.

Is your name Müller?
My name is Fischer.

Where are you from?
From Munich.

2 SCHOOL

A1 How do you get to school?
A: Look, here comes Jens on his moped!
B: Great!
A: How do you get to school?
B: Me? I come by bus. And you?
A: On foot.

Margit comes by streetcar.
Jens comes by moped.
Miss Seifert comes by car.
Wiebke comes by bike.
Who walks?

B1 School Supplies

JENS	Excuse me! How much is the dictionary, please?
SALESWOMAN	The dictionary? —Thirteen marks.
JENS	And how much is the pocket calculator?
SALESWOMAN	Eighteen marks.
JENS	I beg your pardon?
SALESWOMAN	Eighteen marks.
JENS	Great, only eighteen marks! And how much is the cassette?
SALESWOMAN	Six marks.
JENS	Thank you.
SALESWOMAN	You're welcome.

B12 How much are the school supplies? They cost . . .
books, 8 marks; pocket calculators, 18 marks;
posters, 5 marks; pencils, 1 mark;
cassettes, 6 marks; ballpoint pens, 4 marks

B20 Hey, where is the dictionary?
Hey, Jens, where is the dictionary?
It's over there. Look, Kristin, there!

Hey, Kristin, the pocket calculator's gone.
Nonsense! It's there.

Jens, where is the cassette?
Isn't it there? —Take a look, Kristin! Here it is.

Excuse me, Mrs. Meier. Where are the posters, please?
I don't know. Aren't they there?
No, they're gone.
Gone? Take a look. They are over there.

C1 Which subjects do you have today?

MRS. KRÖGER	Which subjects do you have today?
JENS	I have math, history, —wait a minute! Look, here is my class schedule. Today is Tuesday?
MRS. KRÖGER	Yes.
JENS	I have German at eight o'clock, at a quarter to nine math. Then I have English and history.
MRS. KRÖGER	When do you have physics?
JENS	On Friday.

Jens goes to high school in Niebüll. He has school from Monday to Friday. Jens has Saturdays off. School begins at eight o'clock and is over at one.

What subjects does he have? Here is Jens' class schedule.

C7 When does Jens have math?
at one o'clock / at one
at two o'clock / at two
What time is it? It is . . .
nine o'clock
nine-oh-five / five after nine
nine-ten / ten after nine
nine-fifteen / a quarter after nine
nine-twenty
nine twenty-five
nine-thirty / half past nine
nine thirty-five
nine-forty
nine forty-five / a quarter of ten
nine-fifty / ten of ten
nine fifty-five / five of ten

C10 What do you have now?
What do you have now?
We have bio now. And you?
Math. We're having a test.
Well then, good luck!

Jörg and Kristin are classmates. They are in the ninth grade, the 9a.

Mona and Lars are also classmates. They are in the ninth grade too, in the other section, the 9b.

D1 Homework and grades

Jens is doing his homework. He's doing math. In math Jens is not so good. What marks does he have in math? A four, a three, and a four. Here are Jens' grades.

KRISTIN Hey, Jens, what do you have in German?
JENS A two.
KRISTIN That's great! A two in German. Fantastic!
JENS Yes, that's good, but I only have a four in math. Dumb!
KRISTIN Yes, that's bad. Too bad!

What do you have?
A one!
Great! Terrific!
Dumb! Too bad!

D7 Is bio hard?

Do you have a one in bio?
Yes, biology is easy.

You have algebra?
Yes.
Is algebra hard?
No, algebra isn't hard. It's easy.

3 LEISURE TIME

A1 Leisure Time: Sports and Hobbies

INTERVIEWER What's your name?
JENS My name is Jens.
INTERVIEWER How old are you?
JENS Sixteen.
INTERVIEWER What do you do in your free time?
JENS Well, I visit friends, I listen to music cassettes, I . . .

Jens visits friends. They listen to music cassettes.

INTERVIEWER Do you participate in sports?
JENS Yes. I swim and I play tennis.

Jens swims and he plays tennis.

INTERVIEWER Do you play soccer too?
JENS Of course!

Jens plays soccer too.

INTERVIEWER Do you play an instrument?
JENS Yes, I play guitar.

He plays guitar.

INTERVIEWER Do you also have hobbies?
JENS I collect stamps and I play chess.

Jens collects stamps.

A11 And what do you do?

INTERVIEWER And what do you do? Do you participate in sports too?
GÜNTER We play basketball.

The girls are sailing.
The boys are playing hockey.
The students are playing basketball.

INTERVIEWER Do you have hobbies?
GÜNTER Yes, I collect coins.
INTERVIEWER And you, Kurt?
KURT I do too.

Günter and Kurt collect coins.

The four classmates are playing cards. The game is called Mau-Mau.

INTERVIEWER What are you playing?
KRISTIN Mau-Mau.
INTERVIEWER Really? Who's winning?
KRISTIN Jens and Jörg.
JENS As always.
KRISTIN But you're cheating. As always.
JENS What?! We're not cheating. You're losing and you're sore. Ha ha!

B1 When do you participate in sports?

What do you do in the summer? In fall? In the winter? In the spring?

URSEL In the summer I play tennis and I swim.
PETER In the fall I play soccer.
HANS In the winter I play ice hockey and I ski.
KARIN In the spring I play basketball.

Jörg, what do you do on the weekend?
On the weekend I play soccer.

On Sunday
on the weekend

B3 How often do you do sports?

Petra: "I seldom play tennis. Well, sometimes in the summer. In the winter I often play basketball."

Michael: "I participate in sports four times a week. Once a week, usually on Wednesday, I play tennis. On the weekend I play soccer and I swim twice a week."

once	a day
twice	a week
three times	a month
four times	a year (in the summer)

C1 Soccer is great!

INTERVIEWER What do you do, Margit? Do you participate in sports?
MARGIT I do gymnastics.
INTERVIEWER Really?
MARGIT Yes, gymnastics is fun!

INTERVIEWER Jörg, you play soccer?
JÖRG Yes, soccer is great.
INTERVIEWER Do you play tennis too?
JÖRG No. I think tennis is boring.

INTERVIEWER Wiebke, what do you do in your free time?
WIEBKE I read a lot.
INTERVIEWER That's interesting. What do you read?
WIEBKE Novels, books about sports, fantasy books . . . they're terrific!
INTERVIEWER What do you think of comics?
WIEBKE Dumb!

C6 True! Not true!

A: Soccer is great!
B: True!

A: How do you like the cassette?
B: Super! It's terrific!
A: Really? I think it's dumb.

A: You collect stamps?
B: Yes. Collecting is fun.
A: What? I don't think so.

A: Playing cards is boring.
B: I think so too.

A: Sailing is boring too.
B: That's not so! Sailing is great!

C10 What do you like to do?

I don't like to sail.
I like to do gymnastics.
I rather play soccer.
I like being lazy best of all.

5 OFF TO COLOGNE!

A1 Off to Germany!

The plane to Frankfurt is filled to capacity. Germans are flying back to Germany, Americans are visiting friends and relatives or going on vacation.

HANS Are you staying in Frankfurt?
PAUL No, I'm flying on to Munich.

JULIA Where are you going?
PETER To Cologne.

JOHN What are you going to do in Germany?
MARY I'm visiting friends.

JOE How long are you staying?
BOB Four weeks.

A7 What does Peter need for the trip?

PETER Dad, where's my flight ticket? And the travel guide?
VATI Peter, I have your passport, your flight ticket, and the travel guide here.
PETER Great! Thanks, Dad! And where are the traveler's checks? I need money too.
VATI That's right. Here are the traveler's checks. Do you have everything now? What else do you need?

I need the Walkman, the music cassettes, the address book, the dictionary, the camera, the film, and the playing cards.

Who is Peter?
Peter Seber is an American. He is 15 years old and lives in New York. Peter's father is from Austria, his mother is from California.

The Sebers have friends in Germany, the Nedel family in Neuss. Peter is going to visit the Nedels. Tomorrow he flies to Frankfurt and from there on to Cologne.

A10 What are you looking for? Whom do you ask?

What are you looking for, Peter?
My passport. Who has my passport?
Hey, I'll just ask Dad.

B1 Peter in Frankfurt

The plane lands in Frankfurt. The passengers go through the passport control, they get their luggage, and they go through customs.

OFFICIAL Passport, please.
PETER Here you are.
OFFICIAL How long are you staying?
PETER Four weeks.
OFFICIAL Good. And have a nice vacation!
PETER Thank you.

JULIA Do you have everything?
PETER My travel bag is missing!
JULIA Look, there it is!
PETER Thank God!

Peter has nothing to declare. He goes through by the green symbol.

left right straight ahead
Where is the information counter, please?
Over there, on the left.

PETER Excuse me! Where is the information counter, please?
BOY Over there, on the left.
PETER Thanks.
BOY You're welcome. My pleasure.

PETER Excuse me! Where are the lockers, please?
WOMAN Here, to your right.
PETER Thank you.
WOMAN You're welcome.

B8 What do the travelers say?
I'm looking for the information counter. I would like to ask something.

I'm looking for the restaurant. I would like something to eat and drink.

I'm looking for the post office. I would like to make a phone call and buy stamps.

I'm looking for the bank. I would like to exchange money.

I'm looking for the gift shop. I would like to buy a present.

B15 How does Peter get to Neuss?
JULIA How are you getting to Neuss, Peter?
PETER From Frankfurt to Cologne by plane and from Cologne to Neuss by car.
JULIA How far is it from Frankfurt to Cologne?
PETER Just a minute! —Look, 189 kilometers! That's about 120 miles.

by plane
by train
by car

C1 Peter changes money
PETER I would like to change 50 dollars.
BANK TELLER How much, please?
PETER 50 dollars.
BANK TELLER Into D-marks?
PETER Yes, please.
BANK TELLER The exchange rate today is DM 2,34.
PETER Not bad.
BANK TELLER That makes 117 marks.
PETER Thank you.
BANK TELLER You're welcome! And have a nice vacation!
PETER Thanks.

C2 German Money
There are bills:
a 10-mark bill, a 20-mark bill, a 50-mark bill, a 100-mark bill

there are coins:
a penny, five pennies, a one-mark piece, a 5-mark piece

C6 Telephoning is not hard
Telephoning in Germany is really not hard. You lift the receiver, put coins in the phone and dial the number. That's all.

but sometimes . . .
all the phone booths are occupied . . .
or the phone is out of order
Finally! But . . . Busy!
Peter tries once more. (sound you hear when making a call and it is ringing)

PETER 0 3 4 3 1 6 4 2 3
MRS. NEDEL Nedel speaking.
PETER Hello, Peter Seber speaking.
MRS. NEDEL It's you, Peter! Where are you?
PETER In Frankfurt. At the airport.
MRS. NEDEL Oh, I see. And you'll be in Cologne at 1:10?
PETER Yes, as planned. I'm on flight LH 368.
MRS. NEDEL Good! We'll be there on time. See you soon! Bye.
PETER Goodbye.
MRS. NEDEL Goodbye.

C13 When does the flight to Cologne leave?
This is the monitor.

PETER When does the flight to Cologne leave? I'm on Flight LH 368.
INFORMATION Flight LH 368 to Cologne at 12:40. Gate B 10.
PETER Thank you.
INFORMATION You're welcome. Have a good flight!

6 AT THE NEDELS'

A1 Friends and Relatives
MR. NEDEL So, Peter, we're here. Now you're going to meet a lot of people. Poor Peter!
PETER Oh, that's not so bad.

WIEBKE Peter, these are my grandparents—Mr. and Mrs. Graf—my grandpa, my grandma.
PETER Hello, Mrs. Graf. Hello, Mr. Graf.
MR. GRAF Welcome to Neuss!
PETER Thank you.

WIEBKE My uncle and my aunt, Jürgen and Christa Wolf.
PETER Hello!

WIEBKE This is my brother and my sister—my brother Philipp and my sister Ulrike.
PETER Hello, Philipp! How are you?
PHILIPP Nice that you're here.

WIEBKE And that's my dog Beppo.

WIEBKE This is my cousin Julian.
PETER Hi, Julian.

WIEBKE And my cousin Alice, Ali.
PETER Hello, Ali.

My name is Markus. I'm a friend of Wiebke's.
Hi, Markus.

My name is Monika. I'm a friend of Wiebke's.
Hello, Monika.

I'm Antje, a classmate.
Hello, Antje.

I'm a classmate of Wiebke's. My name is Jochen.
So, how are you?

B1 Peter thinks the house is great!

PETER Hey, Wiebke, I think your house is great!
WIEBKE Do you think so?
PETER It's big, modern . . . How many rooms do you have?
WIEBKE Would you like to see the house?
PETER Yes, I would like to.
WIEBKE Come on! I'll show it to you.

WIEBKE We have six rooms, a kitchen . . .
PETER How modern it is!

WIEBKE A living room . . .
PETER It looks so cozy!
WIEBKE You think so?
PETER Yes, very cozy.

WIEBKE A dining room, . . . A bathroom and two toilets, one downstairs and one upstairs.
PETER So big and bright!

WIEBKE Downstairs we have a basement too.
PETER Fantastic for a party!

WIEBKE And here is the guest room. This is your room now.
PETER How nice!

WIEBKE Four bedrooms, and this is my room.
PETER Small but great!

WIEBKE Look, we have a garden too. And here we have a garage and a car, an Audi.

B11 Peter has a present for all the Nedels

Peter unpacks his backpack. All the Nedels get a present.

PETER Here's a necklace for Wiebke.
WIEBKE Great! Thanks a lot, Peter!
PETER Don't mention it.

PETER And here I have a pocket calculator for Philipp.
PHILIPP Boy, terrific! Thanks a million!

PETER And here's a book for Ulrike.
ULRIKE Thanks, Peter.
PETER You're welcome.

There's still more on Peter's list.

C1 Do you know Wiebke's friends?

Antje is small, blond, and slim. She is very pretty.

MARKUS Antje is so attractive.
JOCHEN You think so? That's a matter of taste. I find her pretty.
MARKUS Really?

That's Markus. He's tall, dark, he wears glasses.

ALI Markus is good-looking, isn't he?
ANTJE Yes, that's true. I think he's intelligent.
ALI Do you think so?

Jochen has dark-blond hair.

ANTJE Boy, is Jochen ever boring!
WIEBKE What?! I don't think so. I think he's nice.
ANTJE Nice, yes—but boring!
WIEBKE That's not true!

Monika is brunette.

PHILIPP Monika is very friendly, don't you think so?
JOCHEN You're right. She's funny and I think she's very nice.
PHILIPP I do too.

7 WHERE DO THEY LIVE?

A1 Where do our friends live?

Hi! My name is Margit Dastl. I live in Vienna.

Vienna, the capital of Austria, has 1.5 million inhabitants.

Hello! I'm Jens. I live in Niebüll.
Niebüll is a town in Schleswig-Holstein.
Niebüll has 7,000 inhabitants.

Hello! I'm Wiebke Nedel. I live in Neuss.
Neuss, a city in Nordrhein-Westfalen.
Neuss has 200,000 inhabitants.

Hi! I'm Bruno Schmidlin. I live in Zimmerwald in Switzerland.
The Schmidlins live in Zimmerwald.
Zimmerwald is a village, a suburb of Bern.
Bern is the capital of Switzerland.

Hello! I'm Steffi Huber. I'm 15 years old, and I live here in Munich.
Munich is the capital of Bavaria. Munich is a big city: it has 1.3 million inhabitants.

A10 In Munich

Mrs. Huber and her daughter Steffi.

The Hubers live in Munich. They have an apartment in Lehel.

The Hubers have company, a boy from Freiburg. Florian doesn't know the city and Steffi shows him the places of interest in Munich.

Who wouldn't like to visit Munich?
Munich is the "secret capital" of Germany, and every year millions of visitors come from all over the world to the "village of millions" on the Isar River.

The "Münchner Kindl," official emblem of Munich

The "Alte Peter," St. Peter's Church, a Munich landmark

Look, Flori! That's the Marienplatz and the New City Hall.

Look, up there is the Glockenspiel!

The pedestrian mall. The inner city is only for pedestrians. And here is the cathedral. It has two towers.

Here is the National Theater. Would you perhaps like to go to the opera?

And that's Nymphenburg Castle.

That's the Theatinerkirche.

The Alte Pinakothek, a museum.

And that's the Chinese Tower in the English Garden.

A13 Excuse me. Where is . . . , please?

Florian is alone in the city. He would like to see the National Museum, but he doesn't know where it is. He asks:

FLORIAN Excuse me. Where is the National Museum, please?
MAN I have no idea! I'm not from here.
FLORIAN Excuse me. Perhaps you can tell me where the National Museum is?
BOY No, I'm sorry, I don't know.
FLORIAN Pardon me. Do you know where the National Museum is?
WOMAN Just a minute, the National Museum—oh, yes, that's on Prinzregenten Street.

B1 Steffi goes shopping

MRS. HUBER Steffi, would you please go shopping for me?
STEFFI Okay. What do you need?
MRS. HUBER Look, I have a list here for you. But don't buy everything at the supermarket.
STEFFI Where should I buy the chopped meat?
MRS. HUBER Buy the meat and the cold cuts at the butcher's and get the fruit and the vegetables at the greengrocer's. And buy the rolls at the bakery. They're always fresh there. Buy everything else at the supermarket.
STEFFI Okay. But I need money.
MRS. HUBER Here are 100 marks. Please be careful and don't lose the money!
STEFFI Don't worry! I'll be careful, Mom. Bye!

What does Steffi buy at the butcher's?
a pound of chopped meat
200 grams of cold cuts

At the bakery she buys:
a loaf of bread and six rolls

What does she buy at the greengrocer's?
And how much?
1 kilo of tomatoes, 1 pound of cherries, a head of lettuce, a cucumber

At the supermarket Steffi buys:
ten eggs, a liter of milk, two pounds of sugar, two bottles of mineral water, a pound of coffee, half a pound of butter, four yogurts, 100 grams of cheese

C1 Too bad, it's raining.

FLORIAN Steffi! What's the matter? You look so sad.

STEFFI I'm annoyed. —Look, Flori, it's raining.
FLORIAN That's too bad. What should we do now?
MRS. HUBER You'd better stay home. Play cards or . . .
STEFFI Oh, Mom!
FLORIAN What does the weather report say?
MRS. HUBER It's going to stay cloudy and it's supposed to rain now and then.
STEFFI Oh, come on, Flori! We'll go anyway.
MRS. HUBER Do you have a raincoat, Flori? It's cool.
FLORIAN Yes, I'll get it right away.
MRS. HUBER Here are two umbrellas for you. And don't come home so late.
STEFFI We'll be back at 9 o'clock.
MRS. HUBER Well then, have fun!
FLORIAN Thanks.
STEFFI Bye, Mom!

What does the weather report say?
Today cloudy and cool, occasional rain.
It's raining. It's cold.

Fair and warm.
The sun is shining.

The weather will stay nice.
It's sunny and hot.

C7 Flori is hungry

FLORIAN Boy, Steffi. I'm hungry.
STEFFI Me too.
FLORIAN What would you like to eat? An ice cream? A grilled chicken?
STEFFI Over there is a snack bar.
FLORIAN Great!

FLORIAN What should I eat? Everything looks so good.
STEFFI Why don't you try the Leberkäs? Leberkäs with mustard is good.
FLORIAN And what are you eating?
STEFFI I'm eating a Bratwurst and I'm drinking mineral water.
FLORIAN Okay, I'll try the Leberkäs and I'll drink mineral water too.

C11 How does it taste?

FLORIAN How's the Bratwurst, Steffi?
STEFFI Hm, great! It tastes very good. — And how's the Leberkäs?
FLORIAN It's good too. —Will you have another Bratwurst?
STEFFI No, thanks. I have enough. And you? Another Leberkäs?
FLORIAN No, thanks. I'm full.

9 A PARTY

A1 Karin has a party

KARIN Three—five—nine—zero—one—four. (It's ringing.)
MRS. BERGER Berger. Hello! I can hear you but I can't understand you. Hello, who's there?

(Click.) (It rings again.)

MRS. BERGER Here Berger.
KARIN Hello, Mrs. Berger. This is Karin. Is Christine there?
MRS. BERGER Oh, it's you, Karin! Now I can understand you well. Just a minute. . . . Christine! Karin would like to talk to you!
CHRISTINE Hi, Karin! How are you? What's up?
KARIN Listen! I'm having a party on Saturday and I would like to invite you. Can you come?
CHRISTINE I'd love to. I don't have anything planned for Saturday. What time?
KARIN At seven.
CHRISTINE That's great! Who else are you inviting?
KARIN Michaela, Bernd, . . .
CHRISTINE Really? Hey, I'll bring my cassettes, o.k.?
KARIN Great! Till Saturday, then. Bye!
CHRISTINE Bye! And thanks a lot.

Karin now calls up her friends. Who's coming? Who's not coming?

Yes, I'd love to come!
Michaela, a friend from school

Oh, that's too bad. Saturday I can't.
Uwe, a classmate

What? You're having a party and you're inviting me? Great!
Hans-Peter, Michaela's boyfriend

Oh, I can't. I already have something to do on Saturday.
Brigitte, a classmate

We can't at seven. But we can come a little later, around 8:30, okay?

Good! Then I'll see you at 8:30. Bye!
Lisa and Heidi, Karin's cousins

Well, of course! I am free on Saturday, that suits me fine!
Bernd, her tennis partner

No, Unfortunately I have no time on Saturday. Too bad!
Klaus, a classmate

B1 What's there to eat and drink?

HEIDI Hey, Karin! We're hungry. When are we going to eat?
KARIN Right away!
HEIDI What are we having anyway?
KARIN There's soup—a goulash soup—potato salad, hamburgers, bratwurst, sandwiches with cold cuts, and cheese sandwiches . . . and of course cake, too.
HEIDI And to drink?
KARIN Look! We have strawberry punch, lemonade, fanta, cola, mineral water, . . . uh . . . apple juice, and my mother's making coffee too.
HEIDI Great! When are we finally going to get started? I'm hungry as a bear!

What do you have for me?
For you? Apple juice.

What's there to eat? Who's hungry?
Soup, hamburgers, cheese sandwiches, bratwurst, potato salad, cake, and sandwiches with cold cuts.

And what's there to drink? Who's thirsty?
Mineral water, Fanta, apple juice, lemon soda, strawberry punch, cola, coffee

B4 Hans-Peter likes to eat everything!

KARIN What are you having to eat? A hamburger?
HANS-PETER Of course! I like hamburgers.
KARIN Who's the lemonade for?
HANS-PETER For me.
KARIN What, you're drinking lemonade?
HANS-PETER So what?! I like lemonade.

C1 What would you like? A hamburger?

KARIN What would you like, Matthias? Hm? Goulash soup? A hamburger?
MATTHIAS No, no soup, please. And no hamburger. I'll . . . ah . . . take a bratwurst.
KARIN And what are you having, Christine? A sandwich with cold cuts, maybe?
CHRISTINE Yes, please.
KARIN And a cola?
CHRISTINE No cola, please. I'll take mineral water.
HANS-PETER And I'll have a hamburger, a bratwurst, a sandwich with cold cuts . . .
KARIN Anything else?
HANS-PETER No, thanks.
KARIN Well, then, enjoy your meal!
MICHAELA Mr. Haupt, what would you like to drink? Lemon soda? Fanta?
MR. HAUPT Not fanta. Hm, I'll drink some coffee.

D1 So, what will we do now?

So, what will we do now? Who has an idea?

MICHAELA I would like to hear Hans-Peter's cassette. —Where do you have your cassette recorder?
CHRISTINE Karin, where do you have your record player? I would like to hear a record.
HANS-PETER Where's the music? I want to dance!
UWE I would like to see a film. —Do you have a video recorder?
BERND See a film? You're crazy! Would you rather hear a joke?

Quiet! Bernd is going to tell a joke!

Boy, Bernd! Your jokes are dumb!

HEIDI I have an idea: now we'll play a guessing game!
LISA A guessing game? I'd rather have a discussion.

D3 How's the party?

Karin, your parents are so nice!
Hey, Bernd! Your cassette is terrible!
I think your house is so cozy.
Great party!
The food is terrific!
Delicious!

Is that Michaela? Who is she dancing with?
Uwe? He really dances well!
Michaela looks fantastic!
Great music!

Michaela and Hans-Peter think the food is great. What do they say?

HANS-PETER Mrs. Haupt, your potato salad tastes excellent.

MRS. HAUPT	Really? Is it good?
HANS-PETER	Really great!
MRS. HAUPT	Then I'm happy.
MICHAELA	Your sandwiches with cold cuts look delicious.
MRS. HAUPT	Oh, and do they also taste good?
MICHAELA	And how!
MRS. HAUPT	I'm glad.

10 LET'S GO OUT!

A1 What do our young people do?

Our young people: they have money, they go out, and they have many interests. You see them at the movies, at concerts, and at sports events: they know what to do with their free time! —What do our friends do? How do they spend their leisure time? Where do they go? What do they do? Let's ask!

Well, I go out a lot, two or three times a week. I go into the city, ah . . . I go to the movies, to the theater, . . . and sometimes to a concert. Or I visit friends. Then we go out together.

We're a clique, three boys and three girls, and . . . well . . . we ride bikes, we go swimming on the weekend, we play squash, once a month we bowl, sometimes we go dancing, to a disco, . . . well, and we go to concerts. We like rock concerts best.

My leisure time? I go to visit friends, we listen to cassettes, and sometimes we go to the movies. Also to the theater. I have lots of books, and I like to read too. I also enjoy staying at home.

I visit friends and we go out together. Often we just take a stroll through the city, we go to a café, and we eat some ice cream. Sometimes we go to the movies—especially if the film is good and exciting.

A6 Are you planning to do something, Sabine?

STEFAN	Sabine! Hello!
SABINE	Stefan! Well, hi! How are you?
STEFAN	Thanks, terrific! Boy, this is great! What are you doing now? Are you doing anything?
SABINE	No. Why?
STEFAN	Then we can do something together, okay?
SABINE	Great! —Well then, what should we do?
STEFAN	Well, we can . . . we can go to the city and walk around. Or would you rather go to a café? Have some ice cream?
SABINE	Boy, that's great! Terrific!

Let's go to the movies! There's a good film at the Roxi.

Or would you like to go to a concert? To a rock concert?

A8 How are you?

Great!
Fine, thanks.
Not bad.
So-so.
Bad.
Miserable! Terrible!

B1 Concert or Movie?

STEFAN	Hey, Sabine, do you want to go to the movies or would you rather go to a concert?
SABINE	Oh, Stefan, it's the same to me. Hey, let's take a look in the paper.
SABINE	Here, concerts.
STEFAN	Who's singing?
SABINE	There's Falco . . . which singer do you like?
STEFAN	I like a lot of them. Look, Sabine, this group is terrific!
SABINE	Which group?
STEFAN	The Scorpions. Do you like the group?
SABINE	Wow, that's my favorite group! What groups do you like best?
STEFAN	I like all rock groups.
SABINE	Me too, but I especially like the Scorpions. Too bad that the concerts start so late. I'm supposed to be home at 10 o'clock.
STEFAN	Then let's go to the movies, okay?
SABINE	Good!

B3 What kind of films do you like to see?

SABINE	What kind of films do you like to see?
STEFAN	Who is your favorite star?
SABINE	Hm, *High Noon*—what kind of a film is that?
STEFAN	That's a western. Do you like westerns?
SABINE	Not especially.
STEFAN	Look, *Piranha 2*. I think that's a nature film.
SABINE	Oh, don't be silly! That's an action film, not a nature film!

B7 What kind of films are they?

What kind of film is *Out of Africa?*
An adventure film.
Do you know the actors?
Of course!

What kind of film is . . . ?
. . . is a . . .

Out of Africa
an adventure film

High Noon
a western

The Boat
a war movie

The Man with Two Brains
a comedy

Werewolf in London
a horror movie

Piranha 2
an action film

Aliens
a science fiction movie

Liebesgeschichte
a romance

C1 What kind of films do you like?

STEFAN Which film would you like to see today?
STUDENT Just a minute . . . what's it called again? The film with Steve Martin. —Oh, yes! *The Man with Two Brains.*
STEFAN That film is funny. Do you like Steve Martin?
STUDENT I like him a lot.
STEFAN Me too.

STEFAN Mr. Sperling, what kind of movies do you like?
MR. SPERLING Me? I like science fiction movies best of all.
STEFAN Really? You like science fiction movies?
MR. SPERLING Yes. I think they're interesting and often very exciting.

STEFAN What kind of movies do you two like?
1ST GIRL We like love stories, action films—just no war movies.
STEFAN Why don't you like war movies?
2ND GIRL I think war movies are cruel and sad.
1ST GIRL I hate them.

D1 What did you do last night?

TEACHER Herbert, what did you do last night?
HERBERT I went to the movies.
TEACHER What did you see?
HERBERT *Out of Africa.* A terrific movie!

TEACHER And you, Karin? What did you do?
KARIN I visited friends and we played cards.

TEACHER And you, Wiebke?
WIEBKE I stayed home. I read a book.

11 BUYING PRESENTS

A1 Presents for Friends and Family

ANDREA What on earth should I give my father? He has a birthday soon. What do you think? Do you have an idea? What do you usually give your father?
MONIKA Oh, I buy my father a book most of the time. He likes travel books.
ANDREA Hm, Dad already has so many books. And what should I give my grandparents? Their golden wedding anniversary is coming up.
MONIKA Look, Andrea, there are so many presents.

What should I give?
A passport case?
A wallet? This wallet is chic.
A radio, perhaps?
Perfume? This perfume is great!
A wristwatch, a quartz watch?
A calendar?
A bracelet . . . or a necklace?
A record?
A vase for your grandparents?
Or a bouquet of flowers?
Hey, I have it: a box of fancy chocolates!

B1 In the Department Store

ANDREA Miss!
SALESPERSON Yes? May I help you?
ANDREA How much is this sweater, please?
SALESPERSON The sweaters are on sale today. Every sweater is 18 marks.
ANDREA Thank you!
SALESPERSON You're welcome.

Are you taking this sweater?
And this shirt? these scarves? this cap?
I don't know yet.

Every sweater, every shirt, every cap
Every T-shirt only 10 marks!
All scarves, every blouse, all shoes, every pair of pants, every tie, every coat

B9 Do you have this sweater in blue, perhaps?

SALESPERSON This sweater is pretty, isn't it?
MONIKA Yes, it's very nice. Only I don't like red. Do you perhaps have it in blue? Blue is my favorite color.
SALESPERSON I think so. Here is this sweater in blue.
MONIKA Good, I'll take it. The blue is great!

We also have this shirt in many colors:
in white, in grey, in red
in black, in yellow, in beige
in green, in brown
in light blue, in dark blue

C1 Gift Ideas

What are you going to give him?
What are you giving her?

For Mother's Day? Give her perfume.
Happy Mother's Day!

For Father's Day? Buy him a wallet.
Happy Father's Day!

For an anniversary? Give them flowers.
Best wishes on your anniversary!

For his birthday? Give him a T-shirt.
Happy Birthday!

For Christmas? Give her a watch.
Merry Christmas!

C9 When is your birthday?

My birthday is in the fall.
My birthday is in May.

C10 When is your birthday? Or your Name Day?

My birthday is on May 4.

C16 What did you give him?

—Hey, tell me, when was your brother's birthday?
—On May 2.
—What did you buy him?
—A sweater.

—When was your name day?
—On the eighth of April.

—What did you give your parents?
—I gave them a box of chocolates.

GERMAN-ENGLISH VOCABULARY

This vocabulary includes almost all words in this textbook, both active and passive. Active words and phrases are those introduced in basic material and listed in the **Wortschatz** sections of the units. You are expected to know and be able to use active vocabulary. All other words—those appearing in the Introduction, in exercises, in optional and visual material, in the Try Your Skills and **Zum Lesen** sections, in the review units, and in the pictorial **Landeskunde** sections—are considered passive. Passive vocabulary is for recognition only. The meaning of passive words and phrases can usually be understood from context or may be looked up in this vocabulary.

With some exceptions, the following are not included: most proper nouns, forms of verbs other than the infinitive, and forms of determiners other than the nominative.

Nouns are listed with definite article and plural form, when applicable. The numbers in the entries refer to the unit where the word or phrase first appears. A number in black, heavy type indicates that the word or phrase has been actively introduced in that unit. Passive vocabulary is followed by numerals in light type.

The following abbreviations are used in this vocabulary: adj (adjective), pl (plural), pp (past participle), sep (separable prefix), sing (singular), and s. th. (something).

A

ab *from, starting at,* **4;** *leaves, departs,* 5; ab und zu *now and then,* **7**
der **Abend:** zu Abend *in the evening,* 9
die **Abendzeitung, -en** *evening paper,* 7
der **Abenteuerfilm, -e** *adventure film,* **10**
aber *but,* **2**
abgiessen (sep) *to drain,* 9
abheben (sep) *to lift,* **5**
die **Abiturklasse, -n** *graduating class*
die **Abkürzung, -en** *abbreviation,* 4
ABR = Amtliches Bayrisches Reisebüro *Bavarian State Travel Bureau,* 8
ach: ach so! *oh, I see!* **5;** ach, Mutti! *oh, Mom!* **7**
acht *eight,* **1**
Achtung! *attention!* 2
achtzehn *eighteen,* **1**
achtzig *eighty,* **5**
der **Action-Film, -e** *action film,* **10**
ADAC = Allgemeiner Deutscher Automobil-Club *German Automobile Club*
das **Adressbuch, ¨er** *address book,* **5**
ähnlich *similar,* 10
die **Ahnung:** keine Ahnung! *I have no idea!* **7**
Algebra *algebra,* **2**
alle *all; everyone,* **5;** alle drei Jahre *every three years*
allein *alone,* **7**
alles *everything; all,* **5;** alles andere *everything else,* **7;** alles Gute zum . . . *all the best wishes on . . .,* **11;** das ist alles *that's all,* **5**
der **Alphornbläser, -** *alpenhorn player*
als *than,* 7
also *well then,* **10**
alt *old,* **1**
der **Altar, ¨e** *altar*
das **Alter** *age,* 3
ältest- *oldest*
am: am ersten *on the first,* **11;** am ersten Mai *on May first,* **11;** am Freitag *on Friday,* **2;** am Main *on the Main River;* am Sonntag *on Sunday,* **3;** am Tag *(times) a day,* **3;** am Wochenende *on the weekend,* **3**
der **Amerikaner, -** *American* (person), **5;** er ist Amerikaner *he's an American,* **5**
amerikanisch *American* (adj), 3
an *to,* 3; *arrives,* 5; an der Isar *on the Isar (River),* **7**
ander-: eine andere *another,* 10; in anderen Städten *in other cities,* 5; in einem anderen Staat *in another state,* 8
die **andern** *the others,* 4
ändern: sich ändern *to change,* 5
anders *different,* 7
der **Anfang, ¨e** *beginning;* Anfang Oktober *beginning of October*
anfangen (sep) *to start,* **10**
das **Angebot:** im Angebot *on sale,* **11;** unser Schul-Spezial-Angebot *our school special offer,* 2
angezeigter: angezeigter Betrag *the amount shown,* 5
angezogen: gut angezogen *well-dressed,* 11
der **Ankauf** *purchase, buying,* 5
anprobieren (sep) *to try on,* 11
anrufen (sep) *to call up,* **9**
die **Anschlüsse** (pl) *connections,* 8
anspruchsvoll *stimulating,* 10
die **Antwort, -en** *answer,* 10
antworten *to answer,* 9
die **Anzeige, -n** *ad,* 3
der **Anzug, ¨e** *(man's) suit,* 11
der **Apfel, ¨** *apple,* 6
der **Apfelsaft, ¨e** *apple juice,* **9**
Apollinaris *brand name of a mineral water,* 9
der **Apparat, -e** *phone,* **5**
Appetit: guten Appetit! *enjoy your meal!* **9**

der **April** *April,* **11**
die **Arbeit, -en** *work,* 5; bei der Arbeit *at work;* nach der Arbeit *after work*
arbeiten *to work,* 6
arm: armer Peter! *poor Peter!* **6**
das **Armband, ¨-er** *bracelet,* **11**
die **Armbanduhr,-en** *wristwatch,* **11**
arrogant *arrogant,* **6**
der **Artikel, -** *article* (grammar), 1; *article for a newspaper or magazine,* 2
Aschenputtel *Cinderella,* 6
Aschermittwoch *Ash Wednesday,* 10
die **Attraktion, -en** *attraction,* 7
attraktiv *attractive,* **6**
auch *also,* **1;** ich auch *me too,* **3**
der **Audi, -s** *Audi* (a German-made car), **6**
auf *on,* **6;** *to,* 9; auf dem Marktplatz *at the market;* auf der Party *at the party,* 9; auf nach . . . *off to . . .,* **5;** auf Wiederhören! *goodbye* (on the phone), **5;** auf Wiedersehen! *goodbye!* **1;** schau auf die Karte! *look at the map,* 1
die **Auferstehungsfeier** *celebration of the Resurrection*
aufgebaut: ist aufgebaut worden *was built up,* 5
aufpassen: ich pass schon auf *I'll be careful,* **7;** pass bitte auf! *please be careful!* **7**
der **Aufschnitt** *cold cuts,* **7**
aufschreiben (sep) *to write down,* 8
der **Auftrag:** im Auftrag *commissioned by,* 7
das **Auge, -n** *eye,* 2
der **Augenblick:** im selben Augenblick *at the same moment,* 5
der **August** *August,* **11**
die **Auktion, -en** *auction,* 11
das **Au-pair-Mädchen, -** *mother's helper,* 6
aus *from,* **1;** *out, over,* **2;** *out of,* 4; aus der Schweiz *from Switzerland,* **1;** die Schule ist aus *school's out, over,* **1**
das **Ausflugsschiff, -e** *excursion boat*
der **Ausgang, ¨-e** *exit,* **5**
ausgehen (sep) *to go out,* **10**
ausgezeichnet *excellent,* **9**
die **Auskunft** *information,* **5;** an der Auskunft *at the information desk,* 5
das **Ausland** *abroad, foreign country,* 10
das **Auslandsgespräch, -e** *telephone call to a foreign country,* 5
auspacken (sep) *to unpack,* 6; er packt den Rucksack aus *he unpacks his backpack,* **6**
aussehen (sep) *to look (like), appear,* **6;** gut aussehen *to look good; to be handsome, pretty, attractive,* **6**
die **Ausspracheübung, -en** *pronunciation exercise,* 1
aussprechen (sep) *to pronounce,* 6
aussuchen (sep) *to choose,* 10
ausverkauft *sold out,* 10
auswählen (sep) *to choose, select,* 2
ausziehen (sep) *to take off,* 11
das **Auto, -s** *car,* **6;** mit dem Auto *by car,* **2**
der **Autor, -en** *author,* 3

B

der **Bäcker, -** *baker,* 1, **7**
die **Bäckersfrau, -en** *baker's wife,* 7
das **Bad, ¨-er** *bathroom,* **6**
die **Badener Weinstrasse** *scenic road winding through the wine-growing region of the state of Baden*
die **Bahn:** mit der Bahn *by train,* **5**
der **Bahnhof, ¨-e** *railroad station,* 8; am Bahnhof *at the station,* 8; auf dem Bahnhof *at the station,* 8
die **Bahnhofsmission** *Traveler's Aid Society,* 8
die **Bahnpolizei** *railroad police,* 8
bald *soon,* **11**
der **Balkon, -s** *balcony,* 6
der **Ball, ¨-e** *ball,* 6; sie geht auf einen Ball *she goes to a ball,* 6
die **Banane, -n** *banana*
die **Bank, -en** *bank,* **5**
der **Bankangestellte, -n** *bank teller,* **5**
bar *cash,* 11; zahlen Sie bar? *will you pay cash?* 11
der **Bärenhunger:** ich habe einen Bärenhunger! *I'm as hungry as a bear!* **9**
barock *Baroque,* 7
der **Bart, ¨-e** *beard; mustache,* 5
Basel *Basel,* **1**
Basketball *basketball,* **3**
das **Basteln** *doing crafts and hobbies,* 10
der **Bau:** 1. Bau *first construction,* 7
das **Bauernbrot, -e** *dark peasant bread*
der **Baum, ¨-e** *tree*
Bayern *Bavaria,* **7**
bayrisch *Bavarian* (adj), 7; das bayrische Umland *Bavarian countryside surrounding Munich,* 7
der **Beamte, -n** *official,* **5**
bedeuten *to mean,* 5
begehren *to desire,* 7
beginnen *to begin,* 10
beginnt *begins,* **2**
begrüssen *to greet*
bei *by, with,* 6; *at,* 9; bei den Nedels *at the Nedels',* **6;** bei Gabi *at Gabi's house,* 5; bei Grün *by the green* (symbol), **5;** bei uns *in our country, at home,* 9
die **beiden** *the two of them,* 5
das **Beige** *the color beige,* **11**
beim: beim Bäcker *at the baker's,* **7**
das **Beispiel, -e** *example,* 5; zum Beispiel *for example,* 5
bekommen *to get, receive,* **6**
Belgien *Belgium,* 1
beliebt *popular,* 10
beraten: sich beraten lassen *to get advice,* 11
der **Berg, -e** *mountain*
die **Bergmesse, -n** *mass celebrated on top of a mountain*
das **Bergsteigen** *mountain climbing*
Bern *Bern,* 1
berücksichtigen *to consider, take into consideration,* 5
berühmt *famous,* 7
beschreiben *to describe,* 6
die **Beschreibung, -en** *description,* 6
besetzt *occupied,* **5;** *busy* (a phone), **5**
besonders *especially,* **10**
besprechen *to discuss,* 10
besser *better,* 6
best- *best,* 9
bestimmt *surely,* 10
der **Besuch** *company,* **7**
besuchen *to visit,* **3;** Freunde besuchen *to visit friends,* **3**
der **Besucher, -** *visitor,* **7**
betrachten *to look, observe,* 11; er betrachtet sich *he looks at himself,* 11
der **Betrag:** angezeigter Betrag *the amount shown,* 5
bevor *before,* 11
bewölkt *cloudy, overcast,* **7**
die **Bibel** *Bible,* 6
das **Bier** *beer,* 9
das **Bierzelt, -e** *tent at a beer festival or carnival where you drink beer and eat*
das **Bild, -er** *picture,* 2
das **Bilder-Quiz** *picture quiz,* 3
die **Bio** *short for* Biologie, **2**
die **Biologie** *biology,* **2**
bis *to,* 6; bis dann! *see you later,* **1;** bis gleich *see you soon,* **5;** von . . . bis *from . . . to,* **1**
bisher *until now,* 2
bisschen: ein bisschen *a little,* 6
bist: du bist *you are* **1;** du bist's *it's you,* **5**
bitte *please,* **2;** *you're welcome,* **2;** bitte! *here you are!* **5;** bitte schön! *you're welcome,* **6;** bitte sehr! *you're welcome,* **5**
bitten: darf ich mal bitten? *may I have this dance?* 9
das **Blatt, ¨-er** *sheet (of paper),* 10
das **Blau** *the color blue,* **11;** in Blau *in blue,* **11**
bleiben *to stay,* **5**
das **Bleigiessen** *pouring lead* (a custom on New Year's Eve—the shape the lead takes tells you something about the new year)
der **Bleistift, -e** *pencil,* **2**
der **Blick, -e** *view;* mit Blick auf *with a view of*
blöd *stupid, dumb,* **2;** das ist blöd! *that's too bad!* **7**
blond *blond,* **6**

bloss: was schenke ich bloss meinem Vater? *what on earth should I give my father?* **11**
die **Blume, -n** *flower,* **11**
die **Blumenfrau, -en** *flower lady*
die **Bluse, -n** *blouse,* **11**
BMW = Bayerische Motorenwerke *Bavarian Motor Works* (BMW is a German-made car)
der **Bodensee** *Lake Constance*
Bord: an Bord *on board,* 5
böse *mean, bad, wicked,* 6
die **Bratwurst, ¨-e** *fried sausage,* **7**
brauchen *to need,* **5**
das **Braun** *the color brown,* **11**
bräunen *to brown,* 9
das **Braunkohlenwerk, -e** *brown-coal mine*
BRD = Bundesrepublik Deutschland *Federal Republic of Germany,* 1
die **Bremer-Stadtmusikanten** (pl) *The Bremen Town Musicians,* 6
der **Brief, -e** *letter,* 1
der **Briefeinwurf** *letter drop,* 5
der **Brieffreund, -e** *pen pal,* 1
die **Briefmarke, -n** *stamp,* **3**
das **Briefmarkensammeln** *stamp collecting,* 3
die **Brieftasche, -n** *passport case,* **11**
die **Brille, -n** *glasses,* **6**
bringen *to bring,* **9**
BRK = das Bayrische Rote Kreuz *Bavarian Red Cross,* 8
das **Brot, -e** *bread,* **7**
die **Brotzeit** *between-meal snack or light meal* (Bavarian), 7
der **Bruder, ¨** *brother,* **6**
brünett *brunette,* **6**
der **Brunnen, -** *well,* 6
brutal *brutal,* **10**
das **Buch, ¨-er** *book,* **6**
der **Büchermuffel, -** *person who doesn't like books,* 3
die **Buchhandlung, -en** *book store,* 4
der **Buchstabe, -n** *letter* (of the alphabet), 10
bummeln *to stroll,* 10
die **Bundesrepublik** *Federal Republic,* 1
die **Bundesrepublik Deutschland** *Federal Republic of Germany,* 1
bürsten *to brush,* 11
der **Bus:** mit dem Bus *by bus,* **2**
der **Butt, -e** *flounder,* 3
die **Butter** *butter,* **7**

C

das **Café, -s** *café,* 10; in ein Café gehen *to go to a café,* **10**
der **Charakter** *character,* 7
charmanteste *most chaming,* 7
der **Chinesische Turm** *name of a well-known sight in Munich,* **7**
der **Christkindlmarkt** *Christmas market*
die **Clique, -n** *clique,* **10**
die **Cola, -s** *cola,* **7**
die **Colonie, -n** *colony, settlement,* 5
die **Comics** (pl) *comics,* **3**
der **Computer, -** *computer,* 3
das **Computerspiel, -e** *computer game,* 3
die **Confiserie, -n** *candy shop*

D

da *there; here,* **2;** da drüben *over there,* **2;** da kommt *here comes,* **2;** wir sind da *we'll be there,* **5;** *we're here,* **6**
das **Dach, ¨-er** *roof*
damit *so that,* 6
Dänemark *Denmark,* 1
Dank: tausend Dank! *thanks a million!* **6;** vielen Dank! *thanks a lot!* **6**
danken *to thank,* **6;** danke! *thanks! thank you!* **2;** nichts zu danken *don't mention it,* **6**
dann *then,* **2**
darf: darf ich mal bitten? *may I have this dance?* 9; was darf es sein? *may I help you?* **11**
darüber: sprechen wir darüber! *let's talk about it,* 7, 10
das *the; that,* **1;** das ist *that is,* **1;** das sind *that makes, that comes to,* **5;** *these are,* **6**
dass *that,* **6**
dazugeben (sep) *to add to it,* 9
DDR = Deutsche Demokratische Republik *German Democratic Republic,* **1**
das **Deckenfresko, -ken** *ceiling fresco*
dein, deine *your* (sing), **6**
denken *to think,* 5
denn (particle), **5;** *because,* 9
der *the,* **1**
deutsch- *German* (adj), 9; das deutsche Geld *German money,* **5**
das **Deutsch** *German* (language), **2**
der **Deutsche, -n** *German* (person), **5**
die **Deutsche Demokratische Republik** *German Democratic Republic,* 1
Deutschland *Germany,* **1**
der **Deutschlehrer, -** *German teacher* (m), **1**
die **Deutschlehrerin, -nen** *German teacher* (f), **1**
der **Devisenkurs, -e** *rate of exchange,* 5
der **Dezember** *December,* **11**
der **Dialog, -e** *dialog,* 5, 10
dich *you* (sing), 1, **9**
dick *fat,* 6
der **Dicke, -n** *fat one,* 6
die *the,* **1**
der **Dienstag, -e** *Tuesday,* **2**
dies- *this, these,* **11**
das **Ding, -e** *thing,* 12
dir *you* (sing), 7; wie steht's mit dir? *what about you?* 2
die **Disko, -s** *disco,* **10;** in eine Disko gehen *to go to a disco,* **10**
das **Disko-Tanzen** *disco dancing,* 9
die **Diskothek, -en** *discothèque,* 10
diskutieren *to discuss,* **9**
DM *abbreviation for Deutsche Mark,* **2**
die **D-Mark** = Deutsche Mark *German monetary unit,* **5**
doch (particle), 5; du kommst doch aus Denver, ja? *you do come from Denver, don't you?* 5
der **Dollar, -** *dollar,* **5**
der **Dom, -e** *cathedral,* **7**
die **Donau** *Danube River*
der **Donnerstag, -e** *Thursday,* **2**
das **Dorf, ¨-er** *village,* **7**
der **Dorfbummel** *stroll through the village,* 12
dort *there,* **2;** dort drüben *over there,* **2**
dorthin (to) there, 8; wie kommst du dorthin? *how do you get there?* 8
das **Drachenfliegen** *hang gliding,* 3
dran: jetzt bist du dran *now it's your turn,* 1
drei *three,* **1**
dreimal *three times,* **3**
dreissig *thirty,* 2, **5**
dreizehn *thirteen,* **1**
die **Dressur** *training*
dritt-: in der Dritten Welt *in the Third World,* 10; zum ersten, zum zweiten, zum dritten! *going, going, gone!* 11
drüben: da drüben *over there,* **2;** dort drüben *over there,* **2**
das **Drücken:** durch Drücken der grünen Taste *by pressing the green button,* 5
dtv = Deutscher Taschenbuch Verlag *German paperback publisher*
du *you* (sing), **1;** du, . . . *hey, . . .,* **2**
dumm *dumb, stupid,* 6, **10**
der **Dummkopf, ¨-e** *dummy,* 6
dunkel *dark,* **6**
das **Dunkelblau** *the color dark blue,* 11
dunkelblond *dark blond,* **6**
durch *through,* **5**
das **Durcheinander** *confusion, mix-up,* 9
der **Durst:** Durst haben *to be thirsty,* **9**
das **Duzen** *addressing someone with* du, 9

E

echt *real, genuine,* 7
ehemalig *former*
das **Ei, -er** *egg,* **7**
eigen- *own,* 10; aus eigener Metzgerei *from our own butcher shop,* 7
eigentlich *actually,* 10
der **Eigentümer, -** *owner*
ein, eine *a, an,* **2, 3**
einfach *simple, easy,* 1; *simply,* 7

eingeladen *invited,* 9
einige *several, some,* 3
einkaufen (sep) *to shop,* 7; einkaufen gehen *to go shopping,* **7**
die **Einkaufsliste, -n** *shopping list,* 9
die **Einkaufsrunde** *shopping trip* (from store to store), 7
der **Einkaufszettel, -** *shopping list,* **7**
einladen (sep) *to invite,* **9**
die **Einladungskarte, -n** *invitation,* 9
einmal *once,* **3;** *someday,* 9
eins *one,* **1;** eine Eins *a one* (see note, p 51), **2**
der **Einwohner, -** *inhabitant,* **7**
das **Eis** *ice cream,* **7**
das **Eishockey** *ice hockey,* **3**
das **Eistanzen** *ice dancing,* 3
elf *eleven,* **1**
das **Elsass** *Alsace-Lorraine*
die **Eltern** (pl) *parents,* 6, **9**
das **Ende** *end;* Ende gut, alles gut! *all's well that ends well,* 5; Ende September *end of September;* zu Ende *over,* 12
endlich *finally,* **5**
englisch *English* (adj), 4
Englisch *English* (language), **2**
der **Englische Garten** *well-known public park in Munich,* **7**
entscheiden *to decide,* 11; wie entscheidest du dich? *how do you decide?* 11
Entschuldigung! *excuse me,* **2**
entwirf: entwirf eine Geburtstagskarte! *design a birthday card,* 11
er *he; it,* **2**
erbaut *built,* 5
die **Erdbeerbowle, -n** *strawberry punch,* **9**
die **Erdkunde** *geography,* 4
erhalten *preserved,* 5
erinnern an *to commemorate*
die **Erklärung, -en** *explanation,* 1
erleben *to experience,* 7
erst: am ersten *on the first,* **11;** am ersten Mai *on May first* (see p 271), **11;** ihr erstes Kind *her first child,* 6; zum ersten, zum zweiten, zum dritten! *going, going, gone!* 11
erwarten *to expect,* 5
erzählen *to tell,* **9;** erzähl mal *tell,* 2
es *she; it,* **2;** es gibt *there is, there are,* **5**
essen *to eat,* **5, 7**
das **Essen** *food; eating; meal,* 9; beim Essen *while eating, at meals,* 9
der **Essig** *vinegar,* 9
das **Esszimmer, -** *dining room,* **6**
etwa *about, approximately,* 5
etwas *something,* **5;** etwas später *a little later,* **9;** etwas unfreundlich *a little unfriendly,* 6
euch *you* (pl), 5
euer, eure *your* (pl), **9**
Europa *Europe,* 1
der **Euro-Scheck, -s** *checking service providing members with checks that can be cashed in many European countries,* 11
die **Expressannahme** *express (baggage) check,* 8
die **Express-Ausgabe** *express pickup,* 8

F

das **Fach, ¨er** *subject,* **2**
das **Fachwerkhaus, ¨er** *half-timbered house*
fahren *to go, drive, ride,* **10;** in die Stadt fahren *to go into town,* **10**
der **Fahrplan, ¨e** *(train) schedule, timetable,* 5
der **Fahrplanauszug, ¨e** *excerpt from a train schedule,* 8
fällt *falls,* 6
die **Familie, -n** *family,* **5;** die Familie Nedel *the Nedel family,* **5**
die **Fanta** *orange-flavored soda,* **9**
das **Fantasy-Buch, ¨er** *fantasy book,* **3**
die **Farbe, -n** *color,* **11;** in vielen Farben *in many colors,* **11**
das **Farbenspiel, -e** *color game,* 11
die **Fassade, -n** *front of a building,* 7
fast *almost,* 10
die **Fastnacht** *Shrove Tuesday,* 10
faulenzen *to lie around, be lazy,* **3**
der **Februar** *February,* **11**
fehlen *to be missing,* **5**
feiern *to celebrate*
der **Feiertag, -e** *holiday*
die **Ferien** (pl) *vacation,* **5;** Ferien machen *to go on vacation,* **5;** schöne Ferien! *have a nice vacation!* **5**
das **Feriendorf, ¨er** *resort town,* 12
das **Fernsehen** *watching TV,* 10
das **Fest, -e** *festival,* 7
der **Festspielort, -e** *town having a festival or pageant*
die **Festung, -en** *fortress*
das **Fett** *fat,* 9
das **Feuerwerk** *fireworks,* 10
die **Figur, -en** *figure,* 3
der **Film, -e** *(camera) film,* **5;** *film (movie),* **9**
das **Filmfest, -e** *film festival,* 10
das **Finanzzentrum, -zentren** *financial center*
finden *to find, think, have the opinion about s.th.,* **3;** das finde ich nicht *I don't think so,* **3;** findest du? *do you think so?* **6;** ich finde mich nett *I think I'm nice,* 6; wie findest du . . .? *how do you like . . .? what do you think of . . .?* **3**
das **Fischbrot, -e** *fish sandwich,* **7**
der **Fischer, -** *fisherman,* 1
der **Fischerhafen, ¨** *fishing port*
der **Fk-Schalter** = Fahrkartenschalter *ticket counter,* 8
Fl. = Flasche *bottle,* 7
die **Flasche, -n** *bottle,* **7;** eine Flasche Mineralwasser *a bottle of mineral water,* **7**
das **Fleisch** *meat,* **7**
fliegen *to fly,* **5**
fliessen *to flow*
der **Flug, ¨e** *flight,* **5;** guten Flug! *have a good flight!* **5**
der **Flügelbahnhof, ¨e** *wing of main train station, used for commuter trains,* 8
der **Flughafen, ¨** *airport,* **5**
der **Flugplan, ¨e** *flight schedule,* 5
der **Flugplatz, ¨e** *airport,* 5
das **Flugticket, -s** *airplane ticket,* **5**
das **Flugzeug, -e** *airplane,* **5**
der **Flur, -e** *hall,* 6
der **Fluss, ¨e** *river*
folgende *following,* 7
der **Fotoapparat, -e** *camera*
fotografieren *to photograph,* 11
die **Frage, -n** *question,* 10
fragen *to ask,* **5;** fragen wir mal *let's ask,* **10;** ich frag' mal . . . *I'll just ask . . .,* **5**
Franken *Franconia*
fränkisch: die Fränkische Schweiz *Franconian Switzerland (part of Franconia having many lakes)*
Frankreich *France,* 1
Französisch *French (language),* 5
die **Frau, -en** *Mrs.,* **1;** *woman,* 5
das **Fräulein, -** *Miss,* **1**
frei *off,* **2;** er hat frei *he has off, he has no school,* **2**
der **Freitag, -e** *Friday,* **2**
die **Freizeit** *free time, leisure time,* **10;** in deiner Freizeit *in your free time,* **3**
der **Freizeitmuffel, -** *person who doesn't know what to do with free time,* **10**
die **Fremdenführerin, -nen** *tour guide* (f), 7
das **Fresko, Fresken** *fresco*
freuen: das freut mich *I'm glad,* **9**
der **Freund, -e** *friend,* 3; *boyfriend,* **9**
die **Freundin, -nen** *girl friend,* **6**
freundlich *friendly,* **6**
frisch *fresh,* **7**
Frl. = Fräulein *Miss,* **1**
froh *happy, glad,* **9;** da bin ich aber froh! *I'm glad to hear that!* **9**
fröhlich: fröhliche Weihnachten! *Merry Christmas!* **11**
die **Fronleichnamsprozession, -en** *Corpus Christi Day procession*
der **Frosch, ¨e** *frog,* 6
der **Froschkönig** *The Frog Prince,* 6
das **Frühjahr** *spring,* 3; im Frühjahr *in the spring,* **3**
der **Frühlingsanfang** *beginning of spring*
die **Fuggerei** *trading company run by the Fugger family in the 16th century*
fühlen *to feel,* 11
das **Fundbüro, -s** *lost-and-found department,* 8

fünf *five,* **1**
fünfunddreissig *thirty-five,* **2**
fünfundfünfzig *fifty-five,* **2**
fünfundvierzig *forty-five,* **2**
fünfundzwanzig *twenty-five,* **2**
fünfzehn *fifteen,* **1**
fünfzig *fifty,* **2**
für *for,* **5**
furchtbar *terrible, awful,* **9**
die **Fürstenhochzeit, -en** *royal wedding*
der **Fuss:** am Fusse *at the foot of;* ich komme zu Fuss in die Schule *I walk to school,* **2;** zu Fuss *on foot,* **2**
Fussball *soccer,* **3**
der **Fussgänger, -** *pedestrian,* **7**
die **Fussgängerzone, -n** *pedestrian mall,* 7

G

die **Gabel, -n** *fork,* 9
ganz *whole, entire,* 6; *completely, entirely,* 9; ganz allein *all alone,* 6; ganz genau *exactly,* 11; ganz prima! *really great!* **9;** im ganzen Land *in the whole country,* 6
gar: gar nicht *not at all,* 3
die **Garage, -n** *garage,* **6**
der **Garten, ⸚** *garden,* **6**
die **Gartenparty, -s** *garden party,* 10
der **Gärtner, -** *gardener,* 1
der **Gast, ⸚e** *guest,* 7
der **Gastbruder, ⸚** *host brother,* 6
die **Gästeliste, -n** *guest list,* 9
das **Gästezimmer, -** *guest room,* **6**
die **Gastfamilie, -n** *host family*
die **Gaststätte, -n** *restaurant,* 8
gebacken (pp) *baked,* 7
gebaut *built,* 7; man hat lange an diesem Dom gebaut *they worked on building this cathedral for a long time,* 5
geben *to give,* **11;** es gibt *there is, there are,* **5**
der **Gebirgsschütze, -n** *mountain marksman*
das **Geburtshaus, ⸚er** *house of birth*
der **Geburtstag, -e** *birthday,* **11;** er hat Geburtstag *it's his birthday,* **11;** ich habe im Mai Geburtstag *my birthday is in May,* **11;** herzliche Glückwünsche zum Geburtstag! *happy birthday!* **11;** zum Geburtstag *for (your) birthday,* **11**
der **Geburtstagskalender, -** *birthday calendar,* 11
die **Geburtstagskarte, -n** *birthday card,* 11
das **Geburtstagskind, -er** *birthday child,* 11
die **Gedächtniskirche, -n** *Memorial Church*
das **Gegenteil, -e** *opposite,* 11; ganz im Gegenteil *just the opposite,* 11
gegrillt *grilled, barbecued,* 9
gehen *to go,* **5;** der Apparat geht nicht *the phone is out of order,* **5;** es geht nicht *I can't,* **9;** geht's? *is it possible?* 12; sie gehen in die achte Klasse *they're in the eighth grade,* **2;** wie geht's? *how are you?* **9**
das **Gehirn, -e** *brain,* 10
gehören: was gehört zusammen? *what belongs together?* 9
gehört: auf der Party gehört *heard at the party,* 9
die **Geigenbauerstadt, ⸚e** *town of violin makers*
das **Gelb** *the color yellow,* **11**
das **Geld** *money,* **5;** das deutsche Geld *German money,* **5**
das **Gemüse** *vegetable,* **7**
der **Gemüsehändler, -** *greengrocer,* **7**
gemütlich *cozy, comfortable,* **6**
die **Gemütlichkeit** *friendly, relaxed atmosphere,* 7
genau *exact,* 11; ganz genau *exactly,* 11
genug *enough,* **7**
genutzt: kann genutzt werden *can be used,* 5
die **Geographie** *geography,* **2**
das **Gepäck** *baggage,* **5**
die **Gepäckannahme** *baggage check,* 8
die **Gepäckausgabe** *baggage pickup,* 8
gerade *just now, at the moment,* 3
geradeaus *straight ahead,* **5**
gern *gladly,* 3; gern geschehen! *my pleasure!* **5;** gern haben *to like,* **10;** gern (machen) *to like (to do),* **3;** ja, gern *yes, I'd like to,* **6;** nicht gern (machen) *to not like (to do),* **3**
gesagt: junge Leute haben uns gesagt *young people told us,* 10
die **Gesamtausgabe, -n** *complete edition,* 6
das **Geschäft, -e** *store,* 11
das **Geschenk, -e** *present,* **5**
die **Geschenkidee, -n** *gift idea,* **11**
der **Geschenkladen, ⸚** *gift shop,* **5**
die **Geschenkliste, -n** *gift list,* 11
die **Geschichte, -n** *history,* **2;** *story,* 5
geschlossen *closed,* 5, 12
die **Geschmackssache** *a matter of taste,* **6**
geschrieben (pp) *written,* 10
die **Geschwister** (pl) *brothers and sisters,* **6**
die **Gesellschaft, -en** *society*
das **Gespräch, -e** *conversation,* 5; *call,* 5; schreib das Gespräch auf! *write the conversation down,* 7
gestern abend *last night,* **10**
die **Getränke** (pl) *drinks,* 9
gewinnen *to win,* **3**
der **Gewohnheitsmensch, -en** *creature of habit,* 11
gewöhnlich *usually,* **11**
gewöhnt: er hat sich an die Schuhe gewöhnt *he got used to the shoes,* 11
gewonnen (pp) *won,* 11
gibt: es gibt *there is, there are,* **5;** was gibt's? *what's up?* **9**
das **Giebelhaus, ⸚er** *house with gables*
giessen *to pour,* 9
die **Gitarre, -n** *guitar,* **3**
glauben *to think, believe,* **10;** ich glaube, ja *I think so,* **11**
gleich *right away,* **9;** *same,* 10; es ist mir gleich *it's all the same to me,* **10**
das **Gleis, -e** *track,* 8
das **Glockenspiel, -e** *set of bells and mechanical figures often put in clock towers to play when the hour strikes,* **7**
das **Glück** *luck;* viel Glück *good luck!* **2**
die **Glückwünsche** (pl) *best wishes,* **11;** herzliche Glückwünsche zum . . . *best wishes on (your) . . ., happy . . .,* **11**
GmbH = Gesellschaft mit beschränkter Haftung *company with limited liability*
golden- *golden,* 6
gotisch *Gothic,* 7
der **Gott:** Gott bring mich durch diesen Tag! *God, let me survive this day!* 4; Gott sei Dank! *thank God!* **5**
g = Gramm *gram,* **7**
das **Gramm** *gram,* **7;** 200 g Aufschnitt *200 grams of cold cuts,* **7**
gratulieren *to congratulate,* 11
das **Grau** *the color grey,* **11**
grausam *cruel,* **10**
griechisch *Greek* (adj), 7
grillen *to barbecue,* 9
gross *big; tall,* **6**
die **Grösse, -n** *size,* 11
die **Grosseltern** (pl) *grandparents,* **6**
die **Grossmutter, ⸚** *grandmother,* 6
die **Grossstadt, ⸚e** *big city,* **7**
grösst- *biggest*
der **Grossvater, ⸚** *grandfather,* 6
grotesk *grotesque,* 11
Gruetzi! *hello!* (Swiss), **7**
das **Grün** *the color green,* **11**
die **Gründung:** bei Gründung der Colonie *at the founding of the colony,* 5
die **Gruppe, -n** *group,* **10**
der **Gruss, ⸚e** *greeting,* 6; viele Grüsse *best regards,* 1, 8; viele Grüsse an *best regards to,* 8
grüss dich! *hi!* **1**
die **Gulaschsuppe, -n** *goulash soup,* **9**
die **Gurke, -n** *cucumber,* **7**
gut *good,* **2;** *okay,* **5;** *okay, fine,* **7;** *well,* **9;** gut, danke *fine, thanks,* **10;** guten Appetit! *enjoy your meal!* **9;** guten Flug! *have a good flight!* **5;** guten Morgen! *good morning!* **1;** guten Tag! *hello!* **1;** hör gut zu! *listen carefully,* 1
Gute: alles Gute zum . . . *all the best wishes for . . .,* **11**
Güte: ach, du meine Güte! *oh, for*

goodness' sake! 5

das **Gymnasium, Gymnasien** *type of German secondary school,* 2

die **Gymnastik:** Gymnastik machen *to do gymnastics,* **3**

H

das **Haar, -e** *hair,* 5

haben *to have,* **2;** ich hab's! *I have it!* **11**

das **Hackfleisch** *chopped meat,* **7**

haha! *ha ha!* 3

das **Hähnchen, -** *chicken,* **7**

der **Hai, -e** *shark,* 10

halb: ein halbes Pfund Butter *a half a pound of butter,* **7;** halb zehn *nine-thirty,* **2**

die **Hälfte** *half,* 7

hallo! *hi!* **1**

der **Halm, -e** *blade, piece*

die **Halskette, -n** *necklace,* **6**

das **Halstuch, ⸚er** *scarf,* **11**

halten *to hold,* 9

der **Hamburger, -** *hamburger,* **9**

die **Hand, ⸚e** *hand,* 5; in der Hand *in his hand,* 5

das **Handarbeiten** *doing needlework,* 10

das **Händeschütteln** *shaking hands,* 9

die **Handgepäckaufbewahrung** *carry-on luggage consignment,* 8

hängen: warum hängt ihr Haar herunter? *why is her hair hanging down?* 6

hart *hard,* 6, 10

der **Hase, -n** *hare,* 6

hassen *to hate,* **10**

hässlich *ugly,* 6

hatte *had,* 10

hätte *would have*

die **Hauptstadt, ⸚e** *capital city,* **7**

das **Haus, ⸚er** *house,* **6;** er schreibt nach Hause *he writes home,* 7; nach Hause kommen *to come home,* **7;** zu Hause *at home,* 9

die **Hausaufgaben** (pl) *homework,* **2;** er macht Hausaufgaben *he's doing homework,* **2**

die **Hausfassade, -n** *house front*

Hbf = Hauptbahnhof *main train station,* 8

heben: du hebst den Hörer ab *you lift the receiver,* **5**

das **Heft, -e** *notebook,* **2**

die **Heide, -n** *heath, moor*

die **Heidschnucke, -n** *moorland sheep*

die **Heilige Kommunion** *Holy Communion*

die **Heimat** *home*

heimlich: die heimliche Hauptstadt Deutschlands *the secret capital of Germany,* **7**

heiss *hot,* **7**

heissen *to be called,* **1;** er heisst Jens *his name is Jens,* **1;** ich heisse *my name is,* **1;** wie heisst du? *what's your name?* **1;** wie heisst er denn? *what's it called again?* **10**

heiter *fair (weather),* **7**

helfen *to help,* 6

hell *light,* **6**

das **Hellblau** *the color light blue,* **11**

das **Hemd, -en** *shirt,* **11**

der **Herbst** *fall,* 3; im Herbst *in the fall,* **3**

Herr *Mr.,* **1**

herunterhängen (sep) *to hang down,* 6

das **Herz, -en** *heart,* 7

herzlich: herzliche Glückwünsche zum (Geburtstag) *best wishes on your (birthday), happy (birthday),* **11;** herzliche Grüsse *sincerely, best regards,* 6

hessisch *Hessian,* 6

heute *today,* **2**

die **Hexe, -n** *witch,* 6

hier *here,* **2;** hier Nedel *Nedel speaking,* **5**

hierherkommen (sep) *to come here,* 10

hin: da gehen wir mal hin *we'll go there sometime,* 5

der **Hintergrund** *background*

das **Hobby, -s** *hobby,* **3**

höchster: Deutschlands höchster Berg *Germany's highest mountain*

die **Hochzeit, -en** *wedding;* goldene Hochzeit *golden wedding anniversary,* **11**

der **Hochzeitstag, -e** *wedding anniversary,* **11;** zum Hochzeitstag *for (your) anniversary,* **11**

Hockey *hockey,* **3**

das **Hofbräuhaus** *a famous beer hall in Munich,* 7

höflich *polite,* 11

holen *to fetch, pick up,* **5;** *to get,* **7**

das **Holstentor** *Holsten Gate*

der **Holzschnitt, -e** *woodcut,* 6

hören *to listen,* **3;** *to hear,* 5; hör gut zu! *listen carefully!* 1; hör zu! *listen!* **9**

der **Hörer, -** *telephone receiver,* **5**

der **Horrorfilm, -e** *horror film,* **10**

das **Hörspiel, -e** *radio play*

die **Hose, -n** *pants,* **11**

hübsch *pretty,* **6**

der **Hubschrauber, -** *helicopter,* 2

der **Hund, -e** *dog,* **6**

hundert *hundred,* **5**

hunderteins *a hundred one,* **5**

der **Hunger:** Hunger haben *to be hungry,* **7**

I

ich *I,* **1;** ich? *me?* **1**

die **Idee, -n** *idea,* **9**

identifizieren *to identify,* 4

der **Igel, -** *hedgehog, porcupine,* 6

ihm *him,* 7

Ihnen *you,* 11

ihr *you* (pl), **2**

ihr, ihre *her; their,* **9**

Ihr, Ihre *your* (formal), **9**

im = in dem *in the,* **5**

die **Imbiss-Stube, -n** *snack bar,* **7**

immer *always,* **3;** noch immer nicht *still (did) not,* 11

in *in,* **2;** *into,* **5;** in der Prinzregentenstrasse *on Prinzregenten Street,* **7**

Indien *India,* 10

das **Inlandsgespräch, -e** *telephone call within the country,* 5

die **Innenstadt, ⸚e** *center of the city,* **7**

die **Insel, -n** *island,* 7

das **Instrument, -e** *instrument,* **3**

interessant *interesting,* **3**

das **Interesse, -n** *interest,* **10**

der **Interpret, -en** *interpreter (of a song),* 10

das **Interview, -s** *interview,* 3

interviewen *to interview,* 9

der **Interviewer, -** *interviewer,* **3**

irgendwie *somehow,* 11

die **Isar** *Isar River,* 7

ist *is,* **1**

Italien *Italy,* 10

italienisch *Italian* (adj), 7

J

ja *yes,* **1;** ja? *okay?* **10;** ja, bitte? *yes, may I help you?* **11**

das **Jahr, -e** *year,* **7;** im Jahr *(times) a year,* **3;** Jahr für Jahr *year after year,* 7

das **Jahreszeugn.** = Jahreszeugnis, -se *report card,* 2

das **Jahrhundert, -e** *century*

jährig: die 10- bis 19jährigen *10- to 19-year-olds,* 10

der **Januar** *January,* **11;** im Januar *in January,* **11**

die **Jause, -n** *snack, small meal (Austrian),* 12

die **Jeans-Tasche, -n** *denim bag,* 2

jed- *each, every,* **11**

jemand *someone,* 6

jetzt *now,* **2**

der **Joghurt, -** *yogurt,* **7**

die **Jugend** *youth, young people,* **10**

die **Jugendlichen** (pl) *young people,* **10**

der **Juli** *July,* **11**

jung *young,* 5

der **Junge, -n** *boy,* **1**

der **Juni** *June,* **11**

K

der **Kaffee** *coffee,* **7**

der **Kaiser:** der Wilde Kaiser *mountain range in Tirol*

der **Kalender, -** *calendar,* **11**

Kalifornien *California,* **5**

kalt *cold,* **7**

die **Kamera, -s** *camera,* **5**

Kanada *Canada,* 10

das **Kapitel, -** *chapter,* 1

karibisch *Caribbean,* 10

der **Karneval, -e** *carnival, Mardi Gras*

die **Karte, -n** *map,* 1; *card,* **3;** *ticket,*

10; Karten spielen *to play cards,* **3**
das **Kartenspielen** *playing cards,* **3**
die **Kartoffel, -n** *potato,* 9
der **Kartoffelsalat, -e** *potato salad,* **9**
die **Kartoffelscheiben** (pl) *potato slices,* 9
der **Karton, -s** *carton, box,* 11
das **Karwendelgebirge** *Karwendel Mountains*
der **Käse** *cheese,* **7**
das **Käsebrot, -e** *cheese sandwich,* **9**
die **Käseplatte, -n** *platter with assorted cheeses,* 12
der **Kassenzettel, -** *cash register receipt,* 7
die **Kassette, -n** *cassette,* **2**
der **Kassetten-Recorder, -** *cassette recorder,* **9**
kaufen *to buy,* **5;** wo kauft Steffi ein? *where does Steffi shop?* 7
das **Kaufhaus, ⸚er** *department store,* **11;** im Kaufhaus *in the department store,* **11**
kegeln *to bowl,* **10**
kehrt: zurückkehren (sep) *to return,* 4
kein, keine *no, not any,* **9;** keine Sorge *don't worry,* **7**
keiner *no one,* 10
der **Keller, -** *basement, cellar,* **6**
der **Kellner, -** *waiter,* 7
die **Kellnerin, -nen** *waitress,* 7
kennen *to know,* **6;** *to know, be familiar with a place,* **7**
kennenlernen (sep) *to meet, get to know,* **6;** du lernst viele Leute kennen *you're going to meet a lot of people,* **6**
die **Kerze, -n** *candle*
kg = Kilogramm *kilogram,* **7**
das **Kilo** *short for* Kilogramm, **7;** 1 kg Tomaten *1 kilogram of tomatoes,* **7**
das **Kilogramm, -** *kilogram,* **7**
der **Kilometer, -** *kilometer,* **5**
das **Kind, -er** *child,* 6
der **Kinderfasching** *children's carnival, children's Mardi Gras*
das **Kino, -s** *movies,* **10;** gehen wir ins Kino! *let's go to the movies!* **10;** ins Kino gehen *to go to the movies,* **10**
das **Kinoplakat, -e** *movie poster,* 10
die **Kirche, -n** *church,* **7**
die **Kirsche, -n** *cherry,* **7**
klar *clear,* 6; na klar! *well, of course!* **3**
die **Klasse, -n** *class; grade,* **2;** Klasse! *great!* **3**
die **Klassenarbeit, -en** *test,* **2**
der **Klassenkamerad, -en** *classmate,* **2**
die **Klassenkameradin, -nen** *classmate* (f), **6**
das **Klassenprojekt, -e** *class project,* 1
klassisch *classical,* 6, 11
das **Klavier, -e** *piano,* 4
klein *small; short,* **6**
klick *click,* 9
klingeln: es klingelt *the phone rings,* **9**
kochen *to cook,* 9
Köln *Cologne,* **5**
das **Komma, -s** *comma,* 7
kommen *to come,* **2;** komm! *come on!* **6;** kommen nach *to get to,* **5;** wie kommt er in den Turm? *how does he get into the tower?* 6
der **Kommentar, -e** *commentary, remarks,* 10
die **Komödie, -n** *comedy,* **10**
das **Kompliment, -e** *compliment,* 9; ein Kompliment machen *to pay a compliment,* 9
der **Komponist, -en** *composer,* 10
die **Komposition, -en** *composition,* 10
der **Konflikt, -e** *conflict,* 6
der **König, -e** *king,* 7
das **König-Ludwig-Schloss, ⸚er** *castle built by King Ludwig of Bavaria,* 7
das **Königsschloss, ⸚er** *royal castle,* 7
der **Königssohn, ⸚e** *king's son,* 6
die **Königstochter, ⸚** *princess, king's daughter,* 6
können *can, be able to,* **10**
das **Konzert, -e** *concert,* 10; ins Konzert gehen *to go to a concert,* **10**
der **Kopf, ⸚e** *head;* ein Kopf Salat *a head of lettuce,* **7**
korrekt *correct, proper,* 11
korrespondieren *to correspond,* 4
der **Körper, -** *body,* 4
kosten *to cost,* 2; was kosten? *how much are?* **2**
kostet: was kostet? *how much is?* **2**
kräftig *strong,* 10
krank *sick,* 5
die **Krawatte, -n** *tie,* **11**
die **Kreditbank** *bank*
die **Kreditkarte, -n** *credit card,* 11
der **Kriegsfilm, -e** *war film,* **10**
die **Krone, -n** *crown,* 6
die **Küche, -n** *kitchen,* **6**
der **Kuchen, -** *cake,* **9**
die **Kugel, -n** *ball,* 7
kühl *cool,* **7**
der **Kuli, -s** *ballpoint pen,* **2**
die **Kunst** *art,* 2
der **Kurort, -e** *health resort town*
der **Kurs, -e** *rate of exchange,* **5**
der **Kurswagen, -** *through car (of a train),* 8
kurz *short,* 10
kurzfristig *on short notice,* 5
die **Kusine, -n** *cousin* (f), **6**
küssen *to kiss,* 6

L

lachen *to laugh,* 9
das **Lachsbrot, -e** *smoked salmon (lox) sandwich,* 12
die **Ladeaufsicht** *loading supervisor,* 8
der **Laden, ⸚** *store,* 2
die **Lampe, -n** *lamp*
das **Land, ⸚er** *country,* 1; *state,* **6**
landen *to land,* **5**
das **Länderspiel, -e** *name-the-state game,* 7
die **Landeshauptstadt, ⸚e** *state capital,* 7
die **Landeskunde** *culture,* 1; ein wenig Landeskunde *a little culture,* 1
lange *long,* 5; *for a long time,* 5
langsam *slowly,* 4
längst: am längsten Tag *on the longest day,* 10
langweilig *boring,* **3**
lässt: lässt du dich gern von dem Verkäufer beraten? *do you like to get advice from the salesperson?* 11
Latein *Latin,* **2**
lateinamerikanisch *Latin American,* 10
laufend *continuously,* 7
der **Lautsprecher, -** *loudspeaker,* 5
das **Leben** *life,* 4; langsam kehrt Leben in meinen Körper zurück *slowly life is returning to my body,* 4
der **Leberkäs** (see fn p 212) **7**
lecker *delicious,* **9**
legen auf *to lay on,* 9
der **Lehrer, -** *teacher* (m), **1**
die **Lehrerin, -nen** *teacher* (f), **1**
leicht *easy,* **2**
leider *unfortunately,* **7;** ich weiss es leider nicht *I'm sorry, I don't know,* **7**
lernen *to learn,* 3
lesen *to read,* **3**
das **Lesen** *reading,* 3; zum Lesen *for reading,* 1
die **Leseübung, -en** *reading exercise,* 1
letzt- *last,* 10
die **Leute** (pl) *people,* **6**
der **Leutnant, -s** *second lieutenant,* 10
lieben *to love,* 11
lieber (machen) *to prefer (to do),* **3;** ich spiele lieber Fussball *I'd rather play soccer,* **3**
lieber (m), liebe (f) *dear,* 3
der **Liebesfilm, -e** *love story,* 10
Lieblings- (pref) *favorite,* **10**
das **Lieblingsfach, ⸚er** *favorite subject,* 4
die **Lieblingsfarbe, -n** *favorite color,* **11**
die **Lieblingsgruppe, -n** *favorite group,* **10**
der **Lieblingsstar, -s** *favorite star,* **10**
liebsten: am liebsten (machen) *to like (to do) most of all,* **3**
Liechtenstein *Liechtenstein,* 1
liegen *to lie,* 1
liest: was liest du? *what do you read?* **3**
lila *purple,* 10
die **Limo** = Limonade *lemon soda,* **9**
die **Limonade** *lemon soda,* **9**
link- *left,* 9; in der linken Hand *in the left hand,* 9
links *left, on the left,* **5**
der **Lipizzaner, -** *type of horse*
die **Liste, -n** *list,* 8
l = Liter *liter,* **7**
der **Liter, -** *liter,* **7;** ein Liter Milch *a liter of milk,* **7**

literarisch *literary*
das **Lokal, -e** *restaurant,* 9
los: wann geht's endlich los? *when are we finally going to get going?* **9;** was ist los? *what's the matter?* **7**
der **Lücken-Dialog, -e** *dialog with blanks to be filled in,* 3
der **Luftkurort, -e** *high-altitude or mountain resort*
die **Lüftlmalerei** *the tradition of painting scenes on houses*
lustig *merry, funny,* **6**

M

machen *to do,* **3;** er macht sich wenig aus *he doesn't care much about,* 11; was machst du? *what are you doing? what do you do?* **3**
macht: er macht Mathe *he's doing math,* **2**
das **Mädchen, -** *girl,* **1**
mag: München mag man *people like Munich,* 7
der **Magen, ¨** *stomach,* 7
der **Mai** *May,* **11**
der **Maibaumtanz** *dance around the Maypole*
mal (particle); ich frag' mal den Vati *I'll just ask Dad,* **5**
man *one, you (in general), people,* **10;** man spricht Deutsch *German is spoken,* 1; wie sagt man das? *how do you say that?* 1
manchmal *sometimes,* **3**
der **Mann, ¨er** *man,* 6, 7
der **Mantel, ¨** *coat,* **11**
das **Manuskript, -e** *manuscript,* 6
das **Märchen, -** *fairy tale,* 6
das **Märchenbuch, ¨er** *book of fairy tales,* 6
der **Märchenfilm, -e** *fairy-tale film,* 6
die **Märchenkassette, -n** *cassette recording of fairy tales,* 6
das **Märchenschloss, ¨er** *fairy-tale castle,* 7
das **Märchensymbol, -e** *symbol found in a fairy tale,* 6
der **Marienplatz** *square in front of the city hall in Munich,* **7**
die **Mark, -** *mark* (German monetary unit), **2;** eine Mark *one mark,* **2;** eine Mark zehn *one mark and 10 pennies,* **2;** zwei Mark *two marks,* 2
die **Marke, -n** *stamp,* 10; *make, brand,* 11
der **Marktplatz, ¨e** *marketplace*
der **März** *March,* **11**
die **Maschine, -n** *plane,* **5**
die **Maske, -n** *mask*
die **Mathe** *math,* **2**
das **Mathematikbuch, ¨er** *math book*
der **Mathematiklehrer, -** *math teacher,* **1**
die **Mathestunde, -n** *math class,* 10
die **Mauer, -n** *wall,* 5
Mau-Mau *card game similar to crazy eights,* **3**
mehr *more,* **6;** mehr als *more than,* 7
die **Meile, -n** *mile,* **5**
mein, meine *my,* **6**
meinen *to think, be of the opinion,* **11;** *to mean,* 11; meinst du? *do you think so?* **6;** meinst du mein Hemd? *do you mean my shirt?* 11; meinst du nicht? *don't you think so?* **6;** was meinst du? *what do you think?* 6
die **Meinung, -en** *opinion,* 3
die **meisten** *most,* 9
meistens *mostly,* **3;** *most of the time,* 9
die **Melodie, -n** *melody,* 10
der **Mensch, -en** *person;* Mensch! *boy! wow!* **6**
das **Merkspiel, -e** *memory game,* 5
das **Messer, -** *knife,* 9
der **Metzger, -** *butcher,* **7**
die **Metzgerei, -en** *butcher shop,* 7
der **Miesmacher, -** *grouch,* 6
mieten *to rent,* 9
die **Milch** *milk,* **7**
die **Million, -en** *million,* **7**
das **Millionendorf** *village of millions,* 7
das **Mineralwasser** *mineral water,* **7**
die **Minute, -n** *minute,* 9
mir: mit mir *with me,* 6
mischen *to mix,* 9
miserabel *miserable,* **10**
mit *with,* **7;** *along,* 7; mit dem Auto *by car,* **2;** mit dem Bus *by bus,* **2;** mit dem Moped *on (his) moped,* **2;** mit dem Rad *by bicycle,* **2;** mit der Strassenbahn *by streetcar,* **2;** mit zehn Jahren *at the age of 10,* 10
mitbringen (sep) *to bring along,* 9
mitfahren (sep) *to go along,* 12
mitgehen (sep) *to go along,* 7, 12
mitnehmen (sep) *to take along,* 9, 11; zum Mitnehmen *take-out,* 11
der **Mitschüler, -** *classmate (m),* 1
der **Mittag:** zu Mittag *at noon,* 9
mittelgross *medium-sized,* 9
mitten in *in the middle of,* 1
die **Mitternacht** *midnight,* 10
der **Mittwoch** *Wednesday,* **2**
möchten *would like to,* **5**
die **Mode** *fashion,* 11
das **Modell, -e** *model, style,* 11
der **Modemensch, -en** *person of style,* 11
modern *modern,* **6**
mogeln *to cheat,* **3**
mögen *to like,* **10;** gern mögen *to like a lot,* **11**
möglich *possible,* 10
der **Moment:** Moment mal! *wait a minute!* **2**
der **Monat, -e** *month,* 11; im Monat *(time) a month,* **3**
der **Monatskalender, -** *monthly calendar,* 12
der **Monitor, Monitoren** *monitor,* 5
der **Montag** *Monday,* **2**
das **Moped, -s** *moped,* 2; mit dem Moped *on (his) moped,* **2**
morgen *tomorrow,* **5**
der **Morgen, -** *morning,* 11; Morgen! *morning!* **1**
der **Müller, -** *miller,* 1
die **Müllerstochter, ¨** *miller's daughter,* 6
München *Munich,* **1**
der **Münchner, -** *person from Munich,* 7
das **Münchner Kindl** *official emblem of Munich,* **7**
die **Münze, -n** *coin,* **3**
das **Museum, Museen** *museum,* **7**
die **Musik** *music,* **2, 9**
musikalisch *musical,* 6
der **Musiker, -** *musician,* 10
die **Musikkassette, -n** *music cassette,* **3;** Musikkassetten hören *to listen to music cassettes,* **3**
müssen *must, have to,* **10**
das **Muster, -** *model,* 7
die **Mutter, ¨** *mother,* **5**
der **Muttertag** *Mother's Day,* **11;** zum Muttertag *for Mother's Day,* **11**
die **Mutti, -s** *mom,* **7**
die **Mütze, -n** *cap,* **11**

N

na *well,* **2;** na, dann *well then,* **9;** na gut *well, okay,* **7;** na ja *oh well,* **10;** na klar! *of course!* **3;** na und?! *so what?* **9**
nach *after, past,* **2;** to, **5;** *according to,* **10;** kommen nach *to get to,* **5;** nach Hause kommen *to come home,* 7
der **Nachbar, -n** *neighbor,* 1
nachdenken (sep) *to think about,* 10
nachgebaut *built in imitation of,* 7
der **Nachmittag, -e** *afternoon,* 5; am Nachmittag *in the afternoon,* 6; heute nachmittag *this afternoon,* 5
nachschauen (sep) *to check,* **5**
die **Nacht, ¨e** *night,* 6; in der Nacht *in the night,* 6
die **Nähe:** in der Nähe von uns *near where we live,* 10
der **Name, -n** *name,* **2**
der **Namenstag, -e** *name day,* **11;** zum Namenstag *for (your) name day,* **11**
das **Nationaltheater** *National Theater,* **7**
der **Naturfilm, -e** *nature film,* **10**
natürlich *of course,* **9**
nehmen *to take,* **9**
nein *no,* **1**
nennen *to call,* 10; *to name,* 12
nett *nice,* **6;** er sagt nie etwas Nettes *he never says anything nice,* 6
das **Netz, -e** *net shopping bag,* 7
neu *new,* 1; neue Freunde *new friends,* **1**

der **Neubau, -ten** *new building*
neun *nine,* **1**
neunzehn *nineteen,* **1**
neunzig *ninety,* **5**
neuste: das neuste Modell *the latest model,* 11
nicht *not,* **2;** nicht? *don't you think so?* **6**
nichts *nothing,* **5**
nie *never,* **3**
die **Niederlande** (pl) *the Netherlands,* 1
nö = nein *no* (casual), **10**
noch *still,* **5;** noch ein *another,* **7;** noch einmal *again, once more,* **5;** noch immer *still,* 7; noch mehr *still more,* 6; noch nicht *not yet,* **11;** noch nie *never yet,* 6; was brauchst du noch? *what else do you need?* **5;** was machen sie noch? *what else do they do?* 3; wen lädst du noch ein? *who else are you inviting?* **9**
Norddeutschland *Northern Germany,* 6
das **Nordfriesenhaus, ⸚er** *North Frisian house*
Norditalien *Northern Italy,* 1
nördlich *north,* 1
Nördlicher Ladehof *north loading platform,* 8
Nordrhein-Westfalen *state in Germany,* **7**
die **Nordseeinsel, -n** *island in the North Sea*
das **Nordtor:** das Römische Nordtor *Roman North Gate,* 5
Norwegen *Norway,* 10
die **Note, -n** *grade, mark,* **2**
der **November** *November,* **11**
null *zero,* **1**
die **Nummer, -n** *number,* **5**
nun: nun ja *well, yes,* **10**
nur *only,* **2;** was soll ich nur schenken? *what on earth should I give?* **11**
nutzen *to use,* 5

O

ob *if, whether,* 5
oben *upstairs,* **6;** dort oben *up there,* **7**
das **Oberland** *highland*
die **Oberschule, -n** *high school,* **2;** er geht auf die Oberschule *he goes to high school,* **2**
das **Obst** *fruit,* **7**
oder *or,* **1**
offiziell *official,* 7
oft *often,* **3**
O. K. *okay,* **7**
der **Oktober** *October,* **11**
die **Oktoberfeststimmung** *mood, atmosphere of the Oktoberfest,* 7
das **Öl** *oil,* 12
die **Oma, -s** *grandma,* **6**
der **Onkel, -** *uncle,* **6**
der **Opa, -s** *grandpa,* **6**
die **Oper, -n** *opera,* **7;** in die Oper gehen *to go to the opera,* **7**
der **Opernball, ⸚e** *opera benefit ball*
der **Orangensaft, ⸚e** *orange juice,* 7
ordentlich *neat, orderly,* 6
das **Original:** im Original *in the original (language),* 3
Ost *East,* 1
das **Osterei, -er** *Easter egg*
der **Ostereibrunnen** *Easter egg well*
Österreich *Austria,* **1**
der **Österreicher, -** *Austrian* (person), 10
der **Ostersonntag** *Easter Sunday*
ostfriesisch *East Frisian*
Ostfriesland *East Frisia*
östlich *east,* 1

P

paar: ein paar *a few,* 9
das **Paar, -e** *pair,* 11; ein Paar Schuhe *a pair of shoes,* 11
packen *to pack,* 5
der **Palmsonntag** *Palm Sunday*
das **Papier** *paper,* 9
die **Parallelklasse, -n** *class of the same grade,* **2**
das **Parfüm, -s** *perfume,* **11**
der **Parkplatz, ⸚e** *parking lot,* 8
der **Partner, -** *partner,* 1
die **Partnerarbeit** *teamwork,* 1
die **Party, -s** *party,* **6**
der **Pass, ⸚e** *passport,* **5**
die **Passanten** (pl) *passers-by,* 7
passen *to fit,* 2; das passt prima! *that suits me fine!* **9**
die **Passkontrolle** *passport control,* **5**
die **Pause, -n** *break, recess,* **2**
perfekt *perfect,* 10
die **Person, -en** *person,* 9
die **Personenfähre, -n** *passenger ferry*
die **Peterskirche** *famous church in Munich,* **7**
die **Pfarrkirche, -n** *parish church,* 7
Pfd. = Pfund *pound,* **7**
der **Pfeffer** *pepper,* 9
der **Pfennig, -e** *penny,* **5**
die **Pflanze, -n** *plant*
das **Pfund** *pound,* **7;** zwei Pfund Zucker *two pounds of sugar,* **7**
phantasievoll *imaginative,* **10**
phantastisch *fantastic, great,* **2**
philosophieren *to philosophize,* 3
das **Photo, -s** *photo,* 6
Physik *physics,* **2**
das **Piktogramm, -e** *pictogram,* 5
Pils *type of beer,* 9
die **Pinakothek:** Alte Pinakothek *name of a famous art museum in Munich,* **7**
die **Pizza, -s** *pizza,* **7**
die **Plakatsäule, -n** *large, round pillar with posters advertising various events,* 10
planen *to plan,* **5**
die **Platte, -n** *record,* **9**
der **Plattenspieler, -** *record player,* **9**
der **Platz, ⸚e** *place, spot,* 10; Platz finden *to find a seat*
die **Pommes frites** (pl) *French fries,* 9
populär *popular,* 3
das **Portemonnaie, -s** *wallet,* **11**
die **Post** *post office,* 5
das **Postamt, ⸚er** *post office,* **5**
das **Poster, -** *poster,* **2**
die **Postkarte, -n** *postcard,* 1
die **Praline, -n** *fancy chocolates,* **11;** eine Schachtel Pralinen *a box of fancy chocolates,* **11**
der **Preis, -e** *price,* 2
die **Preisinformation** *price information,* 7
preiswert *reasonable,* 7
prima! *great!* **2**
der **Prinz, -en** *prince,* 6
die **Prinzenhochzeit** *prince's wedding*
probieren *to try,* **7;** probier doch mal den . . . *why don't you try the . . .* **7**
das **Problem, -e** *problem,* 9
das **Promenadenkonzert, -e** *concert on a promenade*
der **Prominente, -n** *celebrity,* 10
der **Prospekt, -e** *flyer, ad,* 10
das **Prozent, -e** *percent,* 7
das **Publikum** *audience,* 10
der **Pulli, -s** *sweater (pullover),* **11**
pünktlich *on time, punctual,* **5**
putzen *to clean,* 11

Q

die **Quarzuhr, -en** *quartz clock,* **11**
Quatsch! *nonsense!* **10**

R

das **Rad;** mit dem Rad *by bike,* **2;** wir fahren Rad *we go bike riding,* **10**
das **Radio, -s** *radio,* **11**
die **Radlermass** *combination of beer and lemon soda,* 9
raten *to guess,* 1; rat mal! *take a guess!* 1
das **Ratespiel, -e** *guessing game,* 1, **9**
das **Rathaus, ⸚er** *city hall,* 4; am Rathaus *next to the city hall,* 4; das Neue Rathaus *New City Hall,* **7**
die **Rathausfassade, -n** *front of the city hall*
der **Räuber, -** *robber,* 6
rausziehen (sep) *to pull out*
die **Realschule, -n** *type of German secondary school,* 4
recht- *right,* 9; in der rechten (Hand) *in the right (hand),* 9
recht haben *to be right,* **6**
rechts *right, on the right,* **5**
reduziert *reduced,* 2
das **Reetdach, ⸚er** *thatched roof*
der **Regen** *rain,* **7**
der **Regenmantel, ⸚** *raincoat,* **7**
der **Regenschirm, -e** *umbrella,* **7**

regieren *to reign, rule,* 6
regnen: es regnet *it's raining,* 7
die **Reise, -n** *trip,* **5**; gute Reise! *have a good trip!* 8
das **Reisebuch, ⸚er** *travel book,* **11**
der **Reiseführer, -** *travel guide,* **5**
der **Reisende, -n** *traveler,* **5**
der **Reisescheck, -s** *traveler's check,* **5**
die **Reisetasche, -n** *travel bag,* **5**
die **Reitschule, -n** *riding school*
die **Reklame, -n** *ad,* 2, **11**
die **Religion** *religion,* **2**
der **Reporter, -** *reporter* (m), 10
die **Reporterin, -nen** *reporter* (f), 10
die **Residenz, -en** *(prince's) residence*
der **Rest, -e** *remains, ruins,* 5
das **Restaurant, -s** *restaurant,* **5**
das **Rezept, -e** *recipe,* 9
der **Rhein** *Rhine River,* 5; am Rhein *cn the Rine,* 5
das **Rheinland** *Rhineland*
das **Rockkonzert, -e** *rock concert,* **10**
die **Rock-Walküre** *rock Valkyrie (Valykrie = figure from Norse mythology),* 10
der **Rokokostil** *Rococo style,* 7
das **Rollenspiel** *role-playing,* 2
der **Roman, -e** *novel,* **3**
der **Römer, -** *Roman* (person)
das **Römisch-Germanische Museum** *Roman-Germanic Museum,* 5
der **Rosenmontag** *Monday before Lent*
das **Rot** *the color red,* **11**; in Rot *in red,* **11**
Rotkäppchen *Little Red Riding Hood,* 6
der **Rucksack, ⸚e** *knapsack, backpack,* **6**
rufen: er ruft an *he calls up,* 5
die **Ruhe:** Ruhe! *quiet!* **9**; in Ruhe *not rushed,* 2
rühren *to stir,* 9
die **Ruine, -n** *ruin*
rund *around, about,* 7

S

die **Sache, -n** *thing, item,* 7
die **Sachertorte, -n** *special chocolate cake originated at the Hotel Sacher in Vienna*
sagen *to say,* **5**; sag, . . . *say, . . .,* **11**; sag mal, . . . *tell me, . . .,* 8
sagenhaft *sensational,* 10
der **Salat, -e** *lettuce,* **7**
das **Salz** *salt,* 9
sammeln *to collect,* **3**
das **Sammeln** *collecting,* **3**
der **Samstag** *Saturday,* **3**
der **Sänger, -** *singer,* **10**
die **Sängerin, -nen** *singer* (f), 10
der **Sängerknabe:** die Wiener Sängerknaben *Vienna Choir Boys*
satt: ich bin satt *I'm full,* **7**
der **Satz, ⸚e** *sentence,* 9
sauer *sore, annoyed,* **3**
die **Säule, -n** *pillar,* 7
die **S-Bahn** (Stadtbahn) *metropolitan rapid transit,* 8

der **Science-fiction-Film, -e** *science-fiction film,* **10**
Schach *chess,* **3**
die **Schachtel, -n** *box,* 11; eine Schachtel Pralinen *a box of fancy chocolates,* **11**
schade! *too bad!* **2**
der **Schäfer, -** *shepherd*
der **Schaffner, -** *fare collector*
schälen *to peel,* 9
die **Schallplatte, -n** *record,* 4
die **Schalterhalle, -n** *area where ticket counters are located,* 8
schauen *to look,* **10**; in die Zeitung schauen *to look in the newspaper,* **10**; Peter schaut nach *Peter checks,* **5**; schau! *look!* **2**; schau auf die Karte! *look at the map,* 1; schau mal! *look! take a look!* **2**
das **Schaufenster, -** *shop window,* 11
der **Schauspieler, -** *actor,* **10**
die **Scheibe, -n** *slice;* in Scheiben schneiden *to slice,* 9
der **Schein, -e** *bill,* **5**; ein 10-Mark-Schein *a ten-mark bill,* **5**
scheinen *to shine,* **7**
schenken *to give (as a gift),* **11**
Schi: ich laufe Schi *I go skiing,* **3**
schick *chic,* **11**
schicken *to send,* 10
das **Schiff, -e** *ship, boat,* 5
das **Schilaufen** *skiing*
das **Schild, -er** *sign,* 5
der **Schinken** *ham,* 12
schlafen *to sleep,* 6
das **Schlafzimmer, -** *bedroom,* **6**
schlampig *sloppy,* 6
schlank *slim,* **6**
schlecht *bad,* **2**
Schleswig-Holstein *state in Northern Germany,* **7**
das **Schliessfach, ⸚er** *locker,* **5**
schlimm *bad,* **6**
das **Schloss, ⸚er** *castle,* 6, **7**; Schloss Nymphenburg *Nymphenburg Castle,* **7**
schmalzig *schmaltzy,* **10**
schmecken *to taste,* **7**; wie schmeckt's? *how does it taste?* **7**
schmeicheln *to flatter,* 11
Schneewittchen *Snow White,* 6
schneiden *to cut,* 9
schnell *fast, quick,* **7**
die **Schokolade, -n** *chocolate,* 9
schon *already,* **9**
schön *nice; pretty, beautiful,* **6**; schön! *good! great!* **9**; schön, dass du da bist *nice that you're here,* **6**; schöne Ferien! *have a nice vacation!* **5**
die **schönste, -n** *most beautiful,* 6
Schreck: ach du Schreck! *horrors!* 5
schreiben *to write,* 1; bitte schreib mir! *please write to me,* 1; schreib das Gespräch auf! *write the conversation down,* 7; schreiben an *to write to,* 7; wer schreibt uns? *who will write to us?* 3
die **Schreibgeräte** (pl) *writing instruments,* 2
die **Schreibübung, -en** *writing exercise,* 1
die **Schreibwaren** (pl) *writing supplies,* 4
das **Schreibwarengeschäft, -e** *stationery store,* 2
der **Schuh, -e** *shoe,* **11**
das **Schuhgeschäft, -e** *shoe store,* 11
der **Schuhmacher, -** *shoemaker,* 1
der **Schulanfang** *beginning of school,* 2
die **Schule, -n** *school,* **2**
der **Schüler, -** *student, pupil,* **3**
die **Schülerzeitung, -en** *school newspaper,* 2
die **Schulfreundin, -nen** *friend from school* (f), **9**
die **Schulsachen** (pl) *school supplies,* **2**
die **Schultasche, -n** *school bag,* **2**
der **Schulweg** *way of getting to school,* 4
die **Schulwoche** *the school week,* 4
die **Schüssel, -n** *bowl,* 9; in eine Schüssel geben *to put in a bowl,* 9
Schwaben *Swabia*
das **Schwarz** *the color black,* **11**
der **Schwarzwald** *Black Forest*
Schwarzwälder: Schwarzwälder Schinken *Black Forest ham*
die **Schweiz** *Switzerland,* **1**; in der Schweiz *in Switzerland,* **7**
schwer *difficult,* **2**; *heavy,* 7
die **Schwester, -n** *sister,* **6**
die **Schwierigkeit, -en** *difficulty,* 9
schwimmen *to swim,* **3**
das **Schwimmen** *swimming,* 3
sechs *six,* **1**
sechzehn *sixteen,* **1**
sechzig *sixty,* **2**
segeln *to sail,* **3**
das **Segeln** *sailing,* **3**
sehen *to see,* **6**
die **Sehenswürdigkeit, -en** *place of interest, sight,* **7**
sehr *very,* **6**
sein, seine *his; its,* **5, 9**
seit *since*
die **Seite, -n** *page,* 5
selb-: im selben Augenblick *at the same moment,* 5
selten *seldom,* **3**
die **Semmel, -n** *roll,* **7**
der **Senf** *mustard,* **7**
sensationell *sensational,* **10**
der **September** *September,* **11**
sichtbar *visible,* 5
sie *she, it; they,* **2**
Sie *you* (formal), **1, 3**
sieben *seven,* **1**
siebzehn *seventeen,* **1**
siebzig *seventy,* **5**
das **Siezen** *addressing someone with* Sie, 10
singen *to sing,* **10**
der **Sinn** *meaning,* 10

die **Sitte, -n** *custom,* 9
sitzen *to sit,* 5
so *so,* **2;** *so, well then,* **6;** ach, so was! *well, of all things!* 11; so la la so-so, **10;** so um halb sechs *around 5:30,* **9**
das **Sofa, -s** *sofa*
sogar *even,* 9
der **Sohn, ⸚e** *son,* 7
sollen *should, to be supposed to,* **7**
der **Sommer, -** *summer,* 3; im Sommer *in the summer,* **3**
sondern *but,* 9; nicht nur . . . sondern auch *not only . . . but also,* 9
der **Sonnabend** *Saturday,* **2**
sonnabends *Saturdays, on Saturdays,* **2**
die **Sonne** *sun,* **7**
sonnig *sunny,* **7**
der **Sonntag** *Sunday,* **3**
sonst: ein Tag wie sonst *a day like any other,* 3
die **Sorge:** keine Sorge *don't worry,* **7**
soso *well, well,* 7
die **Sosse, -n** *sauce,* 9
die **Sozialwohnung, -en** *government-supported housing*
spanisch *Spanish* (adj)
spannend *exciting,* **10**
der **Spass** *fun,* 3; Gymnastik macht Spass *gymnastics is fun,* **3;** viel Spass! *have fun!* **7**
spät *late,* 10; wie spät ist es? *what time is it?* **2;** später *later,* **9;** bis später *see you later,* 5
spazierengehen (sep) *to go for a walk,* 10
der **Speck** *bacon,* 9
die **Speckplatte:** Tiroler Speckplatte *plate of Tyrolean bacon,* 12
das **Spezi, -s** *combination of cola and lemon soda,* 9
die **Spezialität, -en** *specialty,* 7
der **Spiegel, -** *mirror,* 6; in den Spiegel schauen *to look in the mirror,* 6
das **Spieglein, -** *little mirror,* 6
das **Spiel, -e** *game,* **3**
spielen *to play,* **3**
die **Spielkarten** (pl) *playing cards,* **5**
spinnen *to spin,* 6; du spinnst! *you're crazy!* **9**
Spitze! *terrific!* **3**
der **Sport** *gym,* **2;** Sport machen *to participate in a sport, to do sports,* **3;** Sport treiben *to participate in sports,* 10
der **Sport- und Hobbyfreund, -e** *sport and hobby enthusiast,* 3
der **Sport- und Hobbymuffel, -** *person who doesn't like sports or hobbies,* 3
das **Sportbuch, ⸚er** *book about sports,* **3**
sportlich *sporty,* 6
das **Sportrad, ⸚er** *10-speed bike,* 11
die **Sportveranstaltung, -en** *sports event,* **10**

die **Sprache, -n** *language,* 3; der deutschen Sprache *of the German language,* 3
sprechen *to speak, talk,* 3; die Karin möchte dich sprechen *Karin would like to talk to you,* **9;** sie sprechen Will Baden aus wie Bill Barton *they pronounce Will Baden like Bill Barton,* 5; sprechen wir darüber! *let's talk about it,* 6
sprich: sprich darüber! *talk about it,* 10; sprich mich nicht an! *don't talk to me,* 4
sprichst: du sprichst mit *you are talking to,* 9
spricht: man spricht Deutsch *German is spoken,* 1; über was spricht Steffi? *what is Steffi talking about?* 7
Squash *squash,* **10**
der **Staat, -en** *state,* 8
die **Stadt, ⸚e** *city; town,* **7**
der **Stadtbummel, -** *stroll through the city,* **10;** einen Stadtbummel machen *to take a stroll through the city,* **10**
der **Stadtbus, -se** *city bus,* 6
der **Stadtplan, ⸚e** *city map,* 7
starten zu *to start on,* 10
stattfinden (sep) *to take place*
stattgefunden: hat stattgefunden *took place*
der **Steckbrief, -e** *resumé,* 4
stecken *to stick, put,* **5**
stehen *to stand,* 5; da steht noch mehr auf Peters Zettel *there's still more on Peter's list,* **6;** wie steht's? *how are things?* 9; wie steht's mit dir? *what about you?* 2
stellt: Wiebke stellt ihre Familie vor *Wiebke introduces her family,* 6
sterben *to die,* 4; lieber Gott, lass mich sterben! *dear God, let me die!* 4
die **Stiefmutter, ⸚** *stepmother,* 6
der **Stil, -e** *style,* 7, 11
das **Stilelement, -e** *element of (one's) style,* 10
die **Stimme, -n** *voice,* 10
stimmt: stimmt! *that's right! true!* **3;** stimmt nicht! *that's not so! not true!* **3**
das **Stövchen, -** *candle warmer*
die **Strasse, -n** *street,* 3
die **Strassenbahn:** mit der Strassenbahn *by streetcar,* **2**
der **Strauss, ⸚e** *bouquet,* 11; ein Strauss Blumen *a bouquet of flowers,* **11**
das **Stroh** *straw,* 6
die **Stube, -n** *room,* 7; die gute Stube *parlor, living room,* 7; Sacher Stube *Café Sacher*
St. = Stück *piece, item,* 4; Bleistifte (10 St.) *10 pencils,* 4
das **Stück, -e** *piece, item,* 2, 9; *play,* 10; ein Fünf-Mark-Stück *a five-mark piece,* **5**

der **Stundenplan, ⸚e** *class schedule,* **2**
suchen *to look for,* **5**
Südamerika *South America,* 10
südlich *south,* 1; *southern,* 7
Südlicher Ladehof *south loading platform,* 8
Südtirol *South Tyrol,* 1
die **Summe** *sum, total,* 7
super! *super! terrific!* **3**
der **Supermarkt, ⸚e** *supermarket,* **7;** im Supermarkt *in, at the supermarket,* **7**
die **Suppe, -n** *soup,* **9**
das **Sylvester** *New Year's Eve*
das **Symbol, -e** *symbol,* 6
sympathisch *likeable, nice,* **6**

T

die **Tabelle, -n** *table, chart,* 5
der **Tag, -e** *day,* 3; am Tag *(times) a day,* **3;** eines Tages *one day,* 11; guten Tag! *hello!* **1;** Tag! *hello! hi!* **1**
täglich *daily, every day,* 3, 10
die **Tante, -n** *aunt,* **6**
der **Tanz, ⸚e** *dance,* 9
tanzen *to dance,* **9**
das **Tanzen** *dancing,* 4
die **Tänzerin, -nen** *dancer* (f), 9
der **Tanzpartner, -** *dance partner,* **9**
die **Tanzschule, -n** *dancing school,* 9
der **Taschenrechner, -** *pocket calculator,* **2**
die **Tasse, -n** *cup,* 9
die **Taste, -n** *(push) button,* 5
die **Taufe, -n** *baptism*
tausend *thousand,* **6;** tausend Dank! *thanks a million!* **6**
das **Taxi, -s** *taxi,* 5
technisch *technically,* 10
der **Tee** *tea,* 12
der **Teelöffel, -** *teaspoon,* 9
das **Teeservice, -** *tea set, service*
der **Teil, -e** *part,* 1
das **Telefon, -e** *telephone,* **5**
das **Telefongespräch, -e** *telephone conversation,* 10
telefonieren *to make a phone call,* **5**
das **Telefonieren** *telephoning,* **5**
die **Telefonnummer, -n** *telephone number,* 1
die **Telefonzelle, -n** *telephone booth,* **5**
das **Tennis** *tennis,* **3**
teuer *expensive,* **11;** wie teuer ist es? *how much is it?* **11**
der **Text, -e** *text, words (to a song),* 9
das **Theater, -** *theater,* **10;** ins Theater gehen *to go to the theater,* **10**
Tirol *Tyrol*
der **Titel, -** *title,* 10
tja *hm* **3**
die **Tochter, ⸚** *daughter,* **7**
die **Toilette, -n** *toilet; bathroom,* **6;** *restroom,* **5**
toll! *great!* **2**
die **Tomate, -n** *tomato,* **7**

das **Tor, -e** *gate,* **5**
der **Tourist, -en** *tourist,* 7
die **Tournee, -s** *tour,* 10
die **Tracht, -en** *traditional costume*
die **Trachtengruppe, -n** *group in traditional costume*
traditionell *traditional,* 9
das **Traditionsfest, -e** *traditional festival,* 7
trägt *wears,* 11
träumen *to dream,* 10
die **Traumfabrik** *dream factory,* 10
traurig *sad,* **7**
der **Treffpunkt, -e** *meeting place*
treiben: Sport treiben *to participate in sports,* 10
das **Treppenhaus, ¨er** *staircase*
trinken *to drink,* **5**
tropisch *tropical*
trotzdem *anyway, in spite of,* **7**
tschau! *bye! so long!* **1**
die **Tschechoslowakei** *Czechoslovakia,* 1
tschüs! *bye! so long!* **1**
das **T-Shirt, -s** *T-shirt,* **11**
tun *to do,* **10**
der **Turm, ¨e** *tower,* **7**
tüt: tüt, tüt *sound heard when you make a call and it rings,* 5
der **Typ, -en** *character,* 10
typisch *typical*

U

die **U-Bahn** = Untergrundbahn *subway,* 4; mit der U-Bahn *by subway,* 4
üben *to practice,* 9
das **Üben** *practice, practicing,* 1
über *about,* 1; *over,* 5
überall *everywhere, all over,* 7
überhaupt *in any case,* **9;** du isst ja überhaupt nichts! *why, you're not eating anything at all!* 9; was gibt es überhaupt? *what are we having, anyway?* **9**
übernehmen *to take on,* 10
die **Übung, -en** *exercise, activity, practice,* 1
die **Uhr, -en** *clock, watch,* **11;** neun Uhr dreissig *nine-thirty,* **2;** neun Uhr fünf *nine-oh-five,* **2;** neun Uhr zehn *nine-ten,* **2;** um wieviel Uhr? *at what time?* **9**
der **Uhrmacher, -** *watchmaker*
um *at,* **2;** *in order to,* 7; so um *around, about,* 8; um acht Uhr *at eight o'clock,* **2;** um eins *at one,* **2;** um 1172 *around 1172,* 5
die **Umfrage, -n** *survey, poll,* 3
umgekehrt *the other way round,* 9
umherlaufen (sep) *to walk around,* 11
das **Umland** *surrounding area,* 7
umsteigen (sep) *to change (trains),* 8
der **Umzug, ¨e** *parade*
und *and,* **1;** und wie! *and how!* **9**

unfreundlich *unfriendly,* 6
Ungarn *Hungary,* 10
ungefähr *about, approximately,* **5**
die **Universitätsstadt, ¨e** *university town*
unmöglich *impossible,* 2
die **Unordnung** *mess, disorder,* 2; so eine Unordnung! *what a mess!* 2
unrealistisch *unrealistic,* 6
uns *us,* 3
unser, unsere *our,* **7, 9**
der **Unsinn:** Unsinn! *nonsense!* **2**
unsympathisch *unpleasant, not nice,* **6**
unten *downstairs,* **6**
unterwegs *on the way,* 11
der **Urlaub, -e** *vacation,* 11
usw. = und so weiter *etc., and so forth,* 8

V

die **Vase, -n** *vase,* **11**
der **Vater, ¨** *father,* **5**
der **Vatertag** *Father's Day,* **11;** zum Vatertag *for Father's Day,* **11**
der **Vati, -s** *dad,* **5**
verabredet: wie verabredet *as planned,* **5**
die **Verabredung, -en** *appointment,* 11
verbrannt *burned*
verbringen *to spend (time),* **10**
die **Vereinigten Staaten** (pl) *United States,* 1
vergangen *past (time),* 11
vergessen *to forget,* 9
vergleichen *to compare,* 10
der **Verkauf** *sale, selling,* 5
die **Verkäuferin, -nen** *salesperson,* **2**
das **Verkaufsgespräch, -e** *conversation with a salesperson,* 11
verkauft! *sold!* 11
verlieren *to lose,* **3**
verrückt *crazy,* 7
verschieden *different, various,* 7, 12
verstanden: hast du verstanden? *did you understand?* 5
versteckt: versteckte Sätze *hidden sentences,* 3
verstehen *to understand,* **9**
versuchen *to try,* **5**
verwandt *related,* 8; wie sind sie verwandt mit dir? *how are they related to you?* 8
der **Verwandte, -n** *relative,* **5**
Verzeihung! *excuse me!* **5**
verzollen *to declare at customs,* **5**
der **Vetter, -n** *cousin* (m), **6**
der **Video-Recorder, -** *video recorder,* **9**
der **Viehabtrieb** *driving cattle down from the mountain*
viel *much, a lot,* **3;** viel Glück! *good luck!* **2**
viele *many,* **6;** viele Grüsse *best regards,* 1
der **Vielfrass** *glutton,* 9

vielleicht *maybe,* **7**
vier *four,* **1**
viermal *four times,* **3**
das **Viertel:** Viertel nach neun *a quarter after nine,* **2**
vierzehn *fourteen,* **1**
vierzig *forty,* **2**
der **Viktualienmarkt** *colorful open market in Munich,* 7
das **Volksfest, -e** *fair, festival*
voll *full,* **5;** voll besetzt *completely occupied,* **5**
vollschlank *heavyset,* **6**
vom = von dem *from the,* 9
von *by,* 3; *from,* **5;** *of,* **6;** ein Freund von Wiebke *a friend of Wiebke's,* **6;** von . . . bis *from . . . to,* **1;** von dort *from there,* **5**
vor *before, of,* **2;** *in front of, outside of*
vorhaben (sep) *to have plans,* **9**
vorlesen (sep) *to read aloud,* 10
der **Vorname, -n** *first name,* 1
der **Vorort, -e** *suburb,* **7**
die **Vorschau** *preview,* 10
vorstellen (sep) *to introduce,* 6
der **Vortrag, ¨e** *presentation,* 2
VW = Volkswagen *a German-made car*

W

die **Wachau** *valley of the Danube in Austria*
wählen *to dial,* **5**
die **Währung, -en** *currency,* 5
das **Wahrzeichen, -** *landmark,* **7**
der **Wald, ¨er** *forest, woods,* 6
der **Walkman** *Walkman,* **5**
der **Walzer** *waltz,* 9
die **Wand, ¨e** *wall,* 6
wandern *to wander, hike,* 6
das **Wandern** *hiking,* 10
wann? *when?* **2**
das **Wappen, -** *coat of arms, emblem,* **7**
wär's: wie wär's mit *how about,* 7
warm *warm,* **7**
die **Wartehalle, -n** *waiting room,* **5**
warten *to wait,* 5; warten auf *to wait for,* 5, 8
der **Wartesaal, -säle** *waiting room,* 8
warum? *why?* **10**
was? *what?* **2;** was?! *what?!* **3;** ach, so was! *well, of all things!* 11; was darf es sein? *may I help you?* **11;** was für? *what kind of (a)?* **10;** was gibt's? *what's up?* **9;** was gibt es alles? *what's there to eat and drink?* **9;** was kosten? *how much are?* **2;** was kostet? *how much is?* **2;** was machst du? *what are you doing? what do you do?* **3**
waschen *to wash,* 9
die **Waschmaschine, -n** *washing machine*
das **Wasser** *water,* 9
das **Wasser** = Mineralwasser *mineral water,* **9**

wechseln *to change, exchange,* **5;** Geld wechseln *to exchange money from one currency to another,* **5**
die **Wechselstube, -n** *currency exchange office,* 8
weg *gone,* **2**
wegen *because of,* 5; wegen Störung geschlossen *closed—out of order,* 5
wegfahren (sep) *to go away,* 12
wegwerfen (sep) *to throw away,* 11
weich *soft,* 11
das **Weihnachten** *Christmas,* **11;** fröhliche Weihnachten *Merry Christmas,* **11;** zu Weihnachten *for Christmas,* **11**
der **Weihnachtsbaum, ⸚e** *Christmas tree*
der **Wein, -e** *wine,* 9; eine Flasche Wein *a bottle of wine,* 9
der **Weinberg, -e** *vineyard*
das **Weinfest, -e** *wine festival*
die **Weinkönigin, -nen** *wine queen*
die **Weinstrasse, -n** *road through wine-growing villages*
weiss: ich weiss nicht *I don't know,* **2**
das **Weiss** *the color white,* **11**
das **Weissbier** *type of beer,* 9
die **Weisswurst, ⸚e** *type of sausage,* **7**
weit *far,* **5**
weiter *further, on,* **5;** ich fliege weiter nach *I'm flying on to,* **5;** und so weiter *and so forth,* 9
weitere: für weitere Gespräche *for additional calls,* 5
welch- *which,* **10**
welche *which, what,* **2**
die **Welt** *world;* aus aller Welt *from all over the world,* 7
der **Weltatlas, -se** *world atlas,* 4
weltberühmt *world-famous,* 7
die **Weltmeisterschaft, -en** *world championship,* 10
der **Weltrang:** von Weltrang *world-class,* 10
der **Weltraum** *outer space,* 10
wem? *(to, for) whom?* 7
wen? *whom?* **5**
wenig: ein wenig *a little,* 1
wenn *when, if,* **10**
wer? *who?* **1**
werden: kann genutzt werden *can be used,* 5
der **Western, -** *western,* **10**
Westfalen *Westphalia*
westlich *west,* 1
die **Wette, -n** *bet,* 6
das **Wetter** *weather,* **7**
der **Wetterbericht, -e** *weather report,* **7**
wichtig *important,* 11
wie *such as,* 3; *as, like,* **5;** wie? *how?* **1;** wie bitte? *I beg your pardon?* **1;** wie geht's? *how are you?* **9;** wie heisst du? *what's your name?* **1;** wie immer *as always,* **3;** wie kommst du in die Schule? *how do you get to school?* **2;** wie lange? *how long?* **5;** wie oft? *how often?* **3;** wie spät ist es? *what time is it?* **2;** und wie! *and how!* **9**
wieder *again,* **7;** wir sind um 9 wieder da *we'll be back at 9,* **7**
das **Wiederholungskapitel, -** *review unit (chapter),* 4
das **Wiedersehen:** auf Wiedersehen! *goodbye!* **1;** Wiedersehen! *bye!* **1**
Wien *Vienna,* **1**
der **Wiener, -** *type of frankfurter sausage,* 12
Wies'n = Wiese *fairgrounds,* 7; auf die Wies'n gehen *to go to the Oktoberfest,* 7
wieso? *how?* 11
wieviel? *how much?* **5;** *how many?* **6**
Willkommen: Willkommen in Neuss! *welcome to Neuss!* **6**
das **Windsurfen** *wind surfing,* 3
der **Winter** *winter,* 3; im Winter *in the winter,* **3**
wir *we,* **2**
wird: wird offiziell verbrannt *is officially burned*
wirklich *really,* **5;** wirklich? *really?* **3**
wissen *to know (a fact, information),* **7**
der **Witz, -e** *joke,* **9**
wo? *where?* **2**
die **Woche, -n** *week,* **5;** in der Woche *(times) a week,* **3**
woher? *from where?* **1;** woher bist du? *where are you from?* **1**
wohin? *to where?* **5**
wohl *probably,* 10
wohnen *to live,* **5**
das **Wohnhaus, ⸚er** *house*
der **Wohnsitz, -e** *residence*
die **Wohnung, -en** *apartment,* **7**
der **Wohnungsplan, ⸚e** *floor plan of an apartment,* 6
das **Wohnzimmer, -** *living room,* **6**
der **Wolf, ⸚e** *wolf,* 6
wollen *to want to,* **10**
das **Wort, ⸚er** *word,* 9
das **Wörterbuch, ⸚er** *dictionary,* **2**
der **Wortschatz** *vocabulary,* 1
die **Wortschatzübung, -en** *vocabulary exercise, practice,* 1
wunderbar *wonderful,* 11
der **Wunsch:** gute Wünsche zum *best wishes on,* **11**
würde *would*
die **Wurst, ⸚e** *sausage; cold cuts,* **7**
das **Wurstbrot, -e** *sandwich made with cold cuts,* **7**
die **Wurstplatte, -n** *platter with an assortment of cold cuts,* 7
der **Wurstsalat, -e** *meat salad made with various cold cuts cut into strips and an oil and vinegar dressing,* 12
die **Wurstsorte, -n** *type of cold cuts or sausages,* 9
wütend *furious,* 11

Z

die **Zahl, -en** *number,* **1**
zahlen *to pay,* 11
zehn *ten,* **1**
zeigen *to show,* **6;** ich zeig es dir *I'll show it to you,* **6**
die **Zeit** *time,* **2**
die **Zeitschrift, -en** *magazine,* 3
die **Zeitung, -en** *newspaper,* **10**
der **Zeitungsladen, ⸚** *paper store,* 7
der **Zensurenspiegel** *grade record,* 2
das **Zepter, -** *scepter,* 6
der **Zettel, -** *list, slip of paper,* **6**
das **Zimmer, -** *room,* **6**
die **Zitronenlimonade** *carbonated lemon drink,* 9
der **Zoll** *customs,* **5**
zu *to,* **5;** *too,* **10;** *for,* **11;** zu Fuss *on foot,* **2;** zu Hause *at home,* **10;** bleibt lieber zu Hause *you'd better stay home,* **7;** ich bin in Wien zu Hause *I live in Vienna,* **7;** zu Weihnachten *for Christmas,* **11**
der **Zucker** *sugar,* **7**
zuerst *first,* 7
die **Zugauskunft** *train information,* 8
zugeben (sep) *to add,* 9
zuletzt *last of all,* 7
zum: zum Bahnhof *to the station,* 8; zum Geburtstag *for (someone's) birthday,* **11;** alles Gute zum Geburtstag! *best wishes on (your) birthday!* **11;** herzliche Glückwünsche zum Geburtstag! *happy birthday!* **11**
Zürich *Zurich,* 1
zurück *back,* **5**
zurückkehren (sep) *to return,* 4
zusammen *together,* **10**
die **Zutaten** (pl) *ingredients,* 9
zwanzig *twenty,* **1**
zwei *two,* **1**
zweihundert *two hundred,* **5**
zweihunderteins *two hundred one,* **5**
zweimal *twice,* **3**
zweit-: zum ersten, zum zweiten, zum dritten! *going, going, gone!* 11
der **Zwerg, -e** *dwarf,* 6
die **Zwiebel, -n** *onion,* 9
zwischen *between,* 1
zwölf *twelve,* **1**

ENGLISH-GERMAN VOCABULARY

This vocabulary includes all the words in the **Wortschatz** sections of the units. These words are considered active—you are expected to know them.

Idioms are listed under the English word you would be most likely to look up. German nouns are listed with definite article and plural ending, when applicable. The number after each German word or phrase refers to the unit in which it is first introduced. To be sure of using the German words and phrases in correct context, refer to the units in which they appear.

A

a *eine,* 2; *ein,* 3
able: to be able to *können,* 10
about *ungefähr,* 5
action film *der Action-Film, -e,* 10
actor *der Schauspieler, -,* 10
address book *das Adressbuch, ⸚er,* 5
adventure film *der Abenteuerfilm, -e,* 10
after *nach,* 2
again *wieder,* 7; *noch einmal,* 5
agree: as agreed on *wie verabredet,* 5
ahead: straight ahead *geradeaus,* 5
airplane *das Flugzeug, -e,* 5
airport *der Flughafen, ⸚,* 5
algebra *Algebra,* 2
all *alle; alles,* 5
alone *allein,* 7
already *schon,* 9
also *auch,* 1
always *immer,* 3; as always *wie immer,* 3
am: I am *ich bin,* 1
American (person) *der Amerikaner, -,* 5; he's an American *er ist Amerikaner,* 5
an *ein,* 3; *eine,* 2
and *und,* 1
anniversary (wedding) *der Hochzeitstag, -e,* 11; for (your) anniversary *zum Hochzeitstag,* 11; golden wedding anniversary *goldene Hochzeit,* 11
another *noch ein,* 7
anyway *trotzdem,* 7; what are we having, anyway? *was gibt es überhaupt?* 9
apartment *die Wohnung, -en,* 7
appear *aussehen,* 6
apple juice *der Apfelsaft, ⸚e,* 9
approximately *ungefähr,* 5
April *der April,* 11
are: you are *du bist,* 1; they are *sie sind,* 1
around *um,* 9; around 8:30 *so um halb neun,* 9
arrogant *arrogant,* 6
art *die Kunst,* 2
as *wie,* 5
ask *fragen,* 5
at *um,* 2; at eight o'clock *um acht Uhr,* 2; at one *um eins,* 2; at what time? *um wieviel Uhr?* 9
attractive *attraktiv,* 6
Audi (German car) *der Audi, -s,* 6
August *der August,* 11
aunt *die Tante, -n,* 6
Austria *Österreich,* 1
awful *furchtbar,* 9

B

back *zurück,* 5; we'll be back at 9 *wir sind um 9 wieder da,* 7
backpack *der Rucksack, ⸚e,* 6
bad *schlecht,* 2; *schlimm,* 6; too bad! *schade!* 2; *blöd!* 7
bag: travel bag *die Reisetasche, -n,* 5
baggage *das Gepäck,* 5
baker *der Bäcker, -,* 7; at the baker's *beim Bäcker,* 7
ballpoint *der Kuli, -s,* 2
bank *die Bank, -en,* 5
bank teller *der Bankangestellte, -n,* 5
basement *der Keller, -,* 6
basketball *Basketball,* 3
bathroom *das Bad, ⸚er,* 6; *die Toilette, -n,* 5
Bavaria *Bayern,* 7
beautiful *schön,* 6
bedroom *das Schlafzimmer, -,* 6
before *vor,* 2
begin *beginnen,* 2
beige *beige,* 11; the color beige *das Beige,* 11
believe *glauben,* 11
best: best wishes *alles Gute,* 11; best wishes on . . . *gute Wünsche zum* . . . 11; all the best wishes on . . . *alles Gute zum* . . . 11
bicycle *das Rad, ⸚er,* 2; by bicycle *mit dem Rad,* 2; to go bicycle riding *radfahren,* 10; we go bike riding *wir fahren Rad,* 10
big *gross,* 6
bill *der Schein, -e,* 5; a 10-mark bill *ein 10-Mark-Schein,* 5
bio *Bio,* 2
biology *Biologie,* 2
birthday *der Geburtstag, -e,* 11; happy birthday! *herzliche Glückwünsche zum Geburtstag!* 11; my birthday is in May *ich habe im Mai Geburtstag,* 11; for (your) birthday *zum Geburtstag,* 11; it's his birthday *er hat Geburtstag,* 11
black *schwarz,* 11; the color black *das Schwarz,* 11
blond *blond,* 6
blouse *die Bluse, -n,* 11
blue *blau,* 11; the color blue *das Blau,* 11; in blue *in Blau,* 11; dark blue *dunkelblau,* 11; light blue *hellblau,* 11
book *das Buch, ⸚er,* 6; address book *das Adressbuch, ⸚er,* 5; book about sports *das Sportbuch, ⸚er,* 3
booth: phone booth *die Telefonzelle, -n,* 5
boring *langweilig,* 3
bottle *die Flasche, -n,* 7; a bottle of mineral water *eine Flasche Mineralwasser,* 7
bouquet *der Strauss, ⸚e,* 11; a bouquet of flowers *ein Strauss Blumen,* 11
bowl *kegeln,* 10
box *die Schachtel, -n,* 11; a box of fancy chocolates *eine Schachtel Pralinen,* 11
boy *der Junge, -n,* 1; boy! *Mensch!* 6
boyfriend *der Freund, -e,* 9
bracelet *das Armband, ⸚er,* 11
bread *das Brot, -e,* 7
bring *bringen,* 9
brother *der Bruder, ⸚,* 6; brothers and sisters *die Geschwister* (pl), 6
brown *braun,* 11; the color brown *das Braun,* 11
brunette *brünett,* 6
brutal *brutal,* 10
bus *der Bus, -se,* 2; by bus *mit dem Bus,* 2
busy (a phone) *besetzt,* 5
but *aber,* 2
butcher *der Metzger, -,* 7

butter *die Butter,* 7
buy *kaufen,* 5
by: by bicycle *mit dem Rad,* 2; by bus *mit dem Bus,* 2; by car *mit dem Auto,* 2; by moped *mit dem Moped,* 2; by streetcar *mit der Strassenbahn,* 2
bye! *tschau!* 1; *tschüs!* 1; *Wiedersehen!* 1

C

café *das Café, -s,* 10; to go to a café *in ein Café gehen,* 10
cake *der Kuchen, -,* 9
calculator: pocket calculator *der Taschenrechner, -,* 2
calendar *der Kalender, -,* 11
California *Kalifornien,* 5
call up *anrufen,* 9
called: what's it called again? *wie heisst er denn?* 10
camera *die Kamera, -s,* 5
can *können,* 10; I can't *es geht nicht,* 9
cap *die Mütze, -n,* 11
capital city *die Hauptstadt, ¨e,* 7
car *das Auto, -s,* 6; by car *mit dem Auto,* 2
cards *die Karten* (pl), 3; playing cards *die Spielkarten* (pl), 5
careful: I'll be careful *ich pass' schon auf,* 7; please be careful! *pass bitte auf!* 7
case: in any case *überhaupt,* 9
cassette *die Kassette, -n,* 2; music cassette *die Musikkassette, -n,* 3
cassette recorder *der Kassetten-Recorder, -,* 9
castle *das Schloss, ¨er,* 7
cathedral *der Dom, -e,* 7
center (of the city) *die Innenstadt, ¨e,* 7
change *wechseln,* 5
cheat *mogeln,* 3
check: traveler's check *der Reisescheck, -s,* 5; Peter checks *Peter schaut nach,* 5
cheese *der Käse,* 7; cheese sandwich *das Käsebrot, -e,* 9
cherry *die Kirsche, -n,* 7
chess *Schach,* 3
chic *schick,* 11
chicken *das Hähnchen, -,* 7
chocolates fancy chocolate candy *die Praline, -n,* 11; a box of fancy chocolates *eine Schachtel Pralinen,* 11
chopped meat *das Hackfleisch,* 7
Christmas *Weihnachten,* 11; for Christmas *zu Weihnachten,* 11; Merry Christmas! *fröhliche Weihnachten!* 11
church *die Kirche, -n,* 7
city *die Stadt, ¨e,* 7; big city *die Grossstadt, ¨e,* 7; capital city *die Hauptstadt, ¨e,* 7
class *die Klasse, -n,* 2; class of the same grade *die Parallelklasse, -n,* 2
classmate (m) *der Klassenkamerad, -en,* 2
classmate (f) *die Klassenkameradin, -nen,* 2
clique *die Clique, -n,* 10
clock *die Uhr, -en,* 11
cloudy *bewölkt,* 7
coat *der Mantel, ¨,* 11
coat of arms *das Wappen, -,* 7
coffee *der Kaffee,* 7
coin *die Münze, -n,* 3
cola *die (das) Cola, -s,* 7
cold *kalt,* 7
cold cuts *der Aufschnitt,* 7; *die Wurst, ¨e,* 7; sandwich made with cold cuts *das Wurstbrot, -e,* 7
collect *sammeln,* 3
collecting *Sammeln,* 3
Cologne *Köln,* 5
color *die Farbe, -n,* 11; in many colors *in vielen Farben,* 11
come *kommen,* 2; come on! *komm!* 6; that comes to *das sind,* 5
comedy *die Komödie, -n,* 10
comics *Comics* (pl), 3
company *der Besuch,* 7
concert *das Konzert, -e,* 10; to go to a concert *ins Konzert gehen,* 10
cool *kühl,* 7
cost *kosten,* 2
cousin (m) *der Vetter, -n,* 6
cousin (f) *die Kusine, -n,* 6
cozy *gemütlich,* 6
crazy: you're crazy! *du spinnst!* 9
cruel *grausam,* 10
cucumber *die Gurke, -n,* 7
customs *der Zoll,* 5; to declare at customs *verzollen,* 5

D

dad *der Vati, -s,* 5
dance *tanzen,* 9
dancing partner *der Tanzpartner, -,* 9
dark *dunkel,* 6; dark blond *dunkelblond,* 6
daughter *die Tochter, ¨,* 7
day *der Tag, -e,* 3; (times) a day *am Tag,* 3
December *der Dezember,* 11
declare (at customs) *verzollen,* 5
delicious *lecker,* 9
department store *das Kaufhaus, ¨er,* 11; in the department store *im Kaufhaus,* 11
dial *wählen,* 5
dictionary *das Wörterbuch, ¨er,* 2
difficult *schwer,* 2
dining room *das Esszimmer, -,* 6
disco *die Disko, -s,* 10; to go to a disco *in eine Disko gehen,* 10
discuss *diskutieren,* 9
do *machen,* 2, 3; *tun,* 10; he's doing math *er macht Mathe,* 2; what are you doing? *was machst du?* 3; what do you do? *was machst du?* 3
dog *der Hund, -e,* 6
dollar *der Dollar, -,* 5
downstairs *unten,* 6
drink *trinken,* 5
drive *fahren,* 10
dumb *blöd,* 2; *dumm,* 10

E

each *jed-,* 11
easy *leicht,* 2
eat *essen,* 5
egg *das Ei, -er,* 7
else: who else are you inviting?: *wen lädst du noch ein?* 9
emblem *das Wappen, -,* 7
English *Englisch,* 2
enjoy: enjoy your meal! *guten Appetit!* 9
enough *genug,* 7
especially *besonders,* 10
every *jeder (-e, -es),* 11
everything *alles,* 5; everything else *alles andere,* 7
excellent *ausgezeichnet,* 9
exchange *wechseln,* 5
exciting *spannend,* 10
excuse: excuse me! *Entschuldigung!* 2; *Verzeihung!* 5
exit *der Ausgang, ¨e,* 5
expensive *teuer,* 11

F

fair (weather) *heiter,* 7
fall *der Herbst,* 3; in the fall *im Herbst,* 3
familiar to be familiar with a place *kennen,* 7
family *die Familie, -n,* 5; the Nedel family *die Familie Nedel,* 5
fantastic *phantastisch,* 2
fantasy book *das Fantasy-Buch, ¨er,* 3
fast *schnell,* 7
father *der Vater, ¨,* 5
Father's Day *der Vatertag,* 11; for Father's Day *zum Vatertag,* 11
favorite *Lieblings-,* 10; favorite color *die Lieblingsfarbe, -n,* 11; favorite group *die Lieblingsgruppe, -n,* 10; favorite star *der Lieblingsstar, -s,* 10
February *der Februar,* 11
fetch *holen,* 5, 7
film *der Film, -e,* 5, 10
finally *endlich,* 5
find *finden,* 3
fine *gut,* 7; fine, thanks *gut, danke,* 10
first: on the first *am ersten,* 11; on May 1st *am ersten Mai,* 11
fish sandwich *das Fischbrot, -e,* 7
flight *der Flug, ¨e,* 5; have a good flight! *guten Flug!* 5
flower *die Blume, -n,* 11
fly *fliegen,* 5
foot: on foot *zu Fuss,* 2
for *für,* 5
four *vier;* four times *viermal,* 3
free time *die Freizeit,* 3; in your free time *in deiner Freizeit,* 3; person who does not know what to do with free time *der Freizeitmuffel, -,* 10

fresh *frisch, 7*
Friday *der Freitag, 2*; on Friday *am Freitag, 2*
friend *der Freund, -e, 3*; girlfriend *die Freundin, -nen, 6*; girlfriend from school *die Schulfreundin, -nen, 9*
friendly *freundlich, 6*
from *aus, 1; von, 1, 5*
fruit *das Obst, 7*
full *voll, 5*; I'm full *ich bin satt, 7*
fun *der Spass, 3*; gymnastics is fun *Gymnastik macht Spass, 3*; have fun! *viel Spass! 7*
funny *lustig, 6*
further *weiter, 5*

G

game *das Spiel, -e, 3*
garage *die Garage, -n, 6*
garden *der Garten, ⸚, 6*
geography *Geographie, 2*
German (language) *Deutsch, 2*
German (person) *der Deutsche, -n, 2*
German Democratic Republic *Deutsche Demokratische Republik (DDR), 1*
Germany *Deutschland, 1*
get *bekommen, 6; holen, 7*; get to *kommen nach, 5*; how do you get to school? *wie kommst du in die Schule? 2*
gift *das Geschenk, -e, 5*
gift shop *der Geschenkladen, ⸚, 5*
girl *das Mädchen, -, 1*
girlfriend *die Freundin, -nen, 6*
give *geben, 11*; give as a gift *schenken, 11*; what should I give? *was soll ich nur schenken? 11*
glad *froh, 9*; I'm glad *das freut mich, 9*; I'm glad to hear that *da bin ich aber froh, 9*
glasses *die Brille, -n, 6*
go *gehen, 5*; when are we going to get going? *wann geht's los? 9; fahren, 10*; to go into the city *in die Stadt fahren, 10*; to go out *ausgehen, 10*
gone *weg, 2*
good *gut, 2*; good luck! *viel Glück! 2*; good! *schön! 9*
goodbye! *auf Wiedersehen! 1*; (on the phone) *auf Wiederhören! 5*
good morning! *Guten Morgen! 1*
goulasch soup *die Gulaschsuppe, -n, 9*
grade *die Note, -n, 2; die Klasse, -n, 2*
gram *das Gramm, 7*; 200 grams of cold cuts *200 Gramm Aufschnitt, 7*
grandma *die Oma, -s, 6*
grandpa *der Opa, -s, 6*
grandparents *die Grosseltern* (pl), *6*
great! *prima! 2; toll! 2; Klasse! 3; schön! 9*
green *grün, 11*; the color green *das Grün, 11*; by the green symbol *bei Grün, 5*
greengrocer *der Gemüsehändler, -, 7*
grey *grau, 11*; the color grey *das Grau, 11*
group *die Gruppe, -n, 10*
guessing game *das Ratespiel, -e, 9*
guest room *das Gästezimmer, -, 6*
guitar *die Gitarre, -n, 3*
gymnastics *Gymnastik, 3*; to do gymnastics *Gymnastik machen, 3*

H

half *halb, 7*; half a pound of butter *ein halbes Pfund Butter, 7*
hamburger *der Hamburger, -, 9*
handsome *gut aussehen, 6*; he is handsome *er sieht gut aus, 6*
happy *froh, 9*; happy . . . *herzliche Glückwünsche zum . . ., 11*
hate *hassen, 10*
have *haben, 11*; I have it! *ich hab's! 11*; what do you have? *was gibt es alles? 9*
have to *müssen, 10*
he *er, 2*
head *der Kopf, ⸚e, 7*; a head of lettuce *ein Kopf Salat, 7*
heavyset *vollschlank, 6*
hello! *hallo!; Tag!; guten Tag! 1; Gruetzi!* (Swiss), *7*
help: may I help you? *was darf es sein? 11*; yes, may I help you? *ja, bitte? 11*
her *ihr, ihre, 9*
here *hier, 2*; here comes *da kommt, 2*; here you are! *bitte! 5*
hey, . . . *du, . . ., 2*
hi! *grüss dich!; hallo!; Tag! 1*
high school *die Oberschule, -n, 2*; he goes to high school *er geht auf die Oberschule, 2*
his *sein, seine, 5, 9*
history *Geschichte, 2*
hm *tja, 3*
hobby *das Hobby, -s, 3*
hockey *Hockey, 3*
home: at home *zu Hause, 10*; to come home *nach Hause kommen, 7*; you'd better stay home *bleibt lieber zu Hause! 7*
homework *die Hausaufgaben* (pl), *2*; he's doing homework *er macht Hausaufgaben, 2*
horror film *der Horrorfilm, -e, 10*
hot *heiss, 7*
house *das Haus, ⸚er, 6*
how *wie, 1*; and how! *und wie! 9*; how long? *wie lange? 5*; how many? *wieviel? 6*; how much? *wieviel? 5*; how much are . . .? *was kosten . . .? 2*; how much is . . .? *was kostet . . .? 2*; how often? *wie oft? 3*; how old are you? *wie alt bist du? 1*
hungry: to be hungry *Hunger haben, 7*; I'm hungry as a bear! *ich habe einen Bärenhunger! 9*

I

ice cream *das Eis, 7*
ice hockey *Eishockey, 3*
idea *die Idee, -n, 9*; I have no idea *keine Ahnung! 7*; idea for a gift *die Geschenkidee, -n, 11*
if *ob, 5; wenn, 10*
imaginative *phantasievoll, 10*
in *in, 2*; in the *im, 5*; they're in the ninth grade *sie gehen in die neunte Klasse, 2*
information *die Auskunft, 5*
inhabitant *der Einwohner, -, 7*
instrument *das Instrument, -e, 3*
interest *das Interesse, -n, 10*
interesting *interessant, 3*
interviewer *der Interviewer, -, 3*
into *in, 5*
invite *einladen, 9*
is: he is *er ist, 1*; she is *sie ist, 1*
it *er, 2; sie, 2; es, 2*
its *sein, seine, 9*

J

January *der Januar, 11*; in January *im Januar, 11*
joke *der Witz, -e, 9*
juice: apple juice *der Apfelsaft, ⸚e, 9*
July *der Juli, 11*
June *der Juni, 11*
just: I'll just ask . . . *ich frag' mal . . ., 5*; let's ask *fagen wir mal! 10*

K

kilogram *das Kilo = Kilogramm, 7*; 1 kilogram of tomatoes *1 kg Tomaten, 7*
kilometer *der Kilometer, -, 5*
kind: what kind of (a) *was für, 10*
kitchen *die Küche, -n, 6*
knapsack *der Rucksack, ⸚e, 6*
know *kennen, 6; wissen, 7*; I don't know *ich weiss nicht, 2*; I don't know yet *ich weiss noch nicht, 11*

L

land *landen, 5*
landmark *das Wahrzeichen, -, 7*
last: last night *gestern abend, 10*
later *später, 9*; a little later *etwas später, 9*
Latin *Latein, 2*
lazy: to lie around, be lazy *faulenzen, 3*
left *links, 5*; on the left *links, 5*
lemon soda *die Limonade, -n, 9; die Limo, -s, 9*
lettuce *der Salat, -e, 7*; a head of lettuce *ein Kopf Salat, 7*
lift *abheben, 5*; you lift the receiver *du hebst den Hörer ab, 5*
light *hell, 6*
like *mögen, 10; gern mögen, 10*; to like (to do) *gern (machen), 3*; to like (to do) most of all *am liebsten (machen), 3*; to not like (to do) *nicht gern (machen), 3*; how do you like . . .?

wie findest du . . .? 3; would like to *möchten,* 5; yes, I'd like that *ja, gern,* 6; *gern haben,* 10
like *wie,* 5
likeable *sympathisch,* 6
list *der Zettel, -,* 6
listen (to) *hören,* 3; listen! *hör zu!* 9
liter *der Liter,* 7; a liter of milk *ein Liter Milch,* 7
live *wohnen,* 5; I live in Vienna *ich bin in Wien zu Hause,* 7
living room *das Wohnzimmer, -,* 6
locker *das Schliessfach, ¨er,* 5
look *schauen,* 5; to look in the newspaper *in die Zeitung schauen,* 10; look! *schau!* 2; *schau mal!* 2; to look (like) *aussehen,* 6; to look good *gut aussehen,* 6
look for *suchen,* 5
lose *verlieren,* 3
lot: a lot *viel,* 3
love story *der Liebesfilm, -e,* 10
luck: good luck! *viel Glück!* 2

M

mall: pedestrian mall *die Fussgängerzone, -n,* 7
many *viele,* 6
March *der März,* 11
mark *die Note, -n,* 2; *die Mark,* 2; German mark *Deutsche Mark (die D-Mark),* 5
math *Mathe,* 2
math teacher *der Mathematiklehrer, -,* 2
matter: what's the matter? *was ist los?* 7
May *der Mai,* 11
maybe *vielleicht,* 7
me? *ich?* 1; me too *ich auch,* 3
meat *das Fleisch,* 7; chopped meat *das Hackfleisch,* 7
meet *kennenlernen,* 6; you're going to meet a lot of people *du lernst viele Leute kennen,* 6
mention: don't mention it *nichts zu danken,* 6
merry *lustig,* 6; Merry Christmas *fröhliche Weihnachten,* 11
mile *die Meile, -n,* 5
milk *die Milch,* 7
million *die Million, -en,* 7; thanks a million! *tausend Dank!* 6
mineral water *das Mineralwasser,* 7
minute: wait a minute! *Moment mal!* 2
miserable *miserabel,* 10
Miss *Fräulein,* 1
missing: to be missing *fehlen,* 5
modern *modern,* 6
mom *die Mutti, -s,* 7
Monday *der Montag, -e,* 2; on Monday *am Montag,* 2
money *das Geld,* 5; German money *das deutsche Geld,* 5
monitor *der Monitor,* 5
month *der Monat, -e,* 3; (times) a month *im Monat,* 3
moped *das Moped, -s,* 2; by moped *mit dem Moped,* 2
more *mehr,* 6; once more *noch einmal,* 5; still more *noch mehr,* 6
most: to like (to do) most of all *am liebsten (machen),* 3
mostly *meistens,* 3
mother *die Mutter, ¨,* 5
Mother's Day *der Muttertag,* 11; for Mother's Day *zum Muttertag,* 11
movie *der Film, -e,* 9
movies *das Kino, -s,* 10; to go to the movies *ins Kino gehen,* 10
Mr. *Herr,* 1
Mrs. *Frau,* 1
much *viel,* 3
Munich *München,* 1
museum *das Museum, Museen,* 7
music *die Musik,* 2
music cassette *die Musikkassette, -n,* 3
must *müssen,* 10
mustard *der Senf,* 7
my *mein, meine,* 6

N

name *der Name, -n,* 2; his name is *er heisst,* 1; my name is *ich heisse,* 1; her name is *sie heisst,* 1; what's . . . name? *wie heisst . . .?* 1; is your name . . .? *heisst du . . .?* 1
name day *der Namenstag, -e,* 11; for (your) name day *zum Namenstag,* 11
nature film *der Naturfilm, -e,* 10
need *brauchen,* 5
never *nie,* 3
newspaper *die Zeitung, -en,* 10
nice *nett,* 6; *sympathisch,* 6; *schön,* 6; nice that you're here *schön, dass du da bist,* 6; not nice *unsympathisch,* 6
night: last night *gestern abend,* 10
nine *neun,* 1; nine-thirty *halb zehn,* 2
ninth grade *die neunte Klasse,* 2
no *nein,* 1; *kein, keine,* 9
nonsense! *Unsinn!* 2; *Quatsch!* 10
not *nicht,* 2; to not like (to do) *nicht gern (machen),* 3; not any *kein, keine,* 9
notebook *das Heft, -e,* 2
nothing *nichts,* 5
novel *der Roman, -e,* 3
November *der November,* 11
now *jetzt,* 2; now and then *ab und zu,* 7
number *die Zahl, -en,* 1; the numbers from zero to twenty *die Zahlen von null bis zwanzig,* 1; the numbers from 5 to 60 *die Zahlen von 5 bis 60,* 2

O

occupied *besetzt,* 5
October *der Oktober,* 11
of *von,* 6; a quarter of nine *Viertel vor neun,* 2; of course! *na klar!* 3; *natürlich!* 9
off *frei;* he has off, he has no school *er hat frei,* 2; off to *auf nach,* 5
official *der Beamte, -n,* 5
often *oft,* 3; how often? *wie oft?* 3
oh: oh, well *na ja,* 10
okay *O.K.,* 7; *gut,* 7; okay? *ja?* 10
old *alt,* 1
on *weiter,* 5; *auf,* 6
once *einmal,* 3
one *eins,* 2; (the grade of) one *eine Eins,* 2; *man,* 10
only *nur,* 2
opera *die Oper, -n,* 7; to go to the opera *in die Oper gehen,* 7
opinion: to have the opinion about *finden,* 3; *meinen,* 11
or *oder,* 1
our *unser, unsere,* 9
out *aus,* 2; school is out *die Schule ist aus,* 2; out of order *(der Apparat) geht nicht,* 5
over *aus,* 2; school is over *die Schule ist aus,* 2; over there *da drüben,* 2
overcast *bewölkt*

P

pants *die Hose, -n,* 11
pardon: I beg your pardon? *wie bitte?* 1
party *die Party, -s,* 6
passport *der Pass, ¨e,* 5; passport control *die Passkontrolle,* 5
passport case *die Brieftasche, -n,* 11
past: five past nine *fünf nach neun,* 2
pedestrian *der Fussgänger, -,* 7
pedestrian mall *die Fussgängerzone, -n,* 7
pen (ballpoint) *der Kuli, -s,* 2
pencil *der Bleistift, -e,* 2
penny *der Pfennig, -e,* 5
people *die Leute* (pl), 6; people in general *man,* 10
perfume *das Parfüm, -s,* 11
phone *der Apparat, -e,* 5; the phone is out of order *der Apparat geht nicht,* 5
phone booth *die Telefonzelle, -n,* 5
physics *Physik,* 2
pick up *holen,* 5
piece: a five-mark piece *ein fünf-Mark-Stück,* 5
pizza *die Pizza, -s,* 7
plan *planen,* 5
plane *die Maschine, -n,* 5
plans: to have plans *etwas vorhaben,* 9
play *spielen,* 3
playing cards *die Spielkarten* (pl), 5; *Kartenspielen,* 3
please *bitte,* 2
pleasure: my pleasure! *gern geschehen!* 5
pocket calculator *der Taschenrechner, -,* 2
poor: poor Peter! *armer Peter!* 6
post office *die Post,* 5
poster *das Poster, -,* 2
potato salad *der Kartoffelsalat, -e,* 9
pound *das Pfund,* 7; two pounds of sugar *zwei Pfund Zucker,* 7

prefer *lieber,* 3; to prefer (to do) *lieber (machen),* 3
present *das Geschenk, -e,* 5
pretty *hübsch; schön,* 6; she is pretty *sie sieht gut aus,* 6
punctual *pünktlich,* 5
pupil *der Schüler, -,* 3
put *stecken,* 5

Q

quarter: a quarter after nine *Viertel nach neun,* 2
quartz watch *die Quarzuhr, -en,* 11
quick *schnell,* 7
quiet! *Ruhe!* 9

R

radio *das Radio, -s,* 11
rain *der Regen,* 7; it's raining *es regnet,* 7
raincoat *der Regenmantel, ̈,* 7
rather *lieber,* 3; I'd rather play soccer *ich spiele lieber Fussball,* 3
read *lesen,* 3; what do you read? *was liest du?* 3
really *wirklich,* 5; really? *wirklich?* 3; really great! *ganz prima!* 9
receive *bekommen,* 6
receiver (phone) *der Hörer, -,* 5; you lift the receiver *du hebst den Hörer ab,* 5
recess *die Pause, -n,* 2
record *die Platte, -n,* 9
record player *der Plattenspieler, -,* 9
red *rot,* 11; in red *in Rot,* 11; the color red *das Rot,* 11
relative *der Verwandte, -n,* 5
religion *Religion,* 2
reporter *der Reporter, -* (m), 10; *die Reporterin, -nen* (f), 10
restaurant *das Restaurant, -s,* 5
restroom *die Toilette, -n,* 5
ride *fahren,* 10
right *rechts,* 5; on the right *rechts,* 5; right away *gleich,* 9; that's right! *stimmt!* 3; to be right *recht haben,* 6
ring *klingeln,* 9; the phone rings *es klingelt,* 9
rock concert *das Rockkonzert, -e,* 10
roll *die Semmel, -n,* 7
room *das Zimmer, -,* 6

S

sad *traurig,* 7
sail *segeln,* 3
sailing *Segeln,* 3
sale: on sale *im Angebot,* 11
salesperson *die Verkäuferin, -nen,* 2
same: it's all the same to me *das ist mir gleich,* 10
Saturday *der Samstag, -e,* 3; *der Sonnabend, -e,* 2; on Saturday *am Sonnabend,* 2; (on) Saturdays *sonnabends,* 2
sausage *die Wurst, ̈e,* 7; fried sausage *die Bratwurst, ̈e,* 7
say *sagen,* 5; say, . . . *sag, . . .,* 11
scarf *das Halstuch, ̈er,* 11
schedule: class schedule *der Stundenplan, ̈e,* 2
schmaltzy *schmalzig,* 10
science-fiction film *der Science-fiction-Film, -e,* 10
school *die Schule, -n,* 2; high school *die Oberschule, -n,* 2; he goes to high school *er geht auf die Oberschule,* 2; how do you get to school? *wie kommst du in die Schule?* 2
school supplies *die Schulsachen* (pl), 2
see *sehen,* 6; oh, I see! *ach so!* 5; see you later! *bis dann!* 1; see you soon! *bis gleich!* 5
seldom *selten,* 3
sensational *sensationell,* 10
September *der September,* 11
she *sie; es,* 2
shine *scheinen,* 7
shirt *das Hemd, -en,* 11
shoe *der Schuh, -e,* 11
shopping: to go shopping *einkaufen gehen,* 7
shopping list *der Einkaufszettel, -,* 7
short *klein,* 6
should *sollen,* 7; what on earth should I give my father? *was schenke ich bloss meinem Vater?* 11
show *zeigen,* 6; I'll show it to you *ich zeig' es dir,* 6
sight *die Sehenswürdigkeit, -en,* 7
sing *singen,* 10
singer *der Sänger, -,* 10
sister *die Schwester, -n,* 6; brothers and sisters *die Geschwister* (pl), 6
ski: I go skiing *ich laufe Schi,* 3
slim *schlank,* 6
slip (of paper) *der Zettel, -,* 6
small *klein,* 6
snack bar *die Imbiss-Stube, -n,* 7
so *so,* 2; so long! *tschüs! tschau!* 2; so what?! *na und?* 9
soccer *Fussball,* 3
something *etwas,* 5
sometimes *manchmal,* 3
soon *bald,* 11; see you soon! *bis gleich!* 5
sore *sauer,* 3
so-so *so lala,* 10
soup *die Suppe, -n,* 9
speak: (Nedel) speaking *hier (Nedel),* 5
spend (time) *verbringen,* 10
spite: in spite of *trotzdem,* 7
spring *das Frühjahr,* 3; in the spring *im Frühjahr,* 3
sport *der Sport,* 3; sports *der Sport,* 3; to participate in a sport, to do sports *Sport machen,* 3
sports event *die Sportveranstaltung, -en,* 10
squash *Squash,* 10
stamp *die Briefmarke, -n,* 3
start *anfangen,* 10
stay *bleiben,* 5
stick *stecken,* 5
still *noch,* 5; still more *noch mehr,* 6
straight: straight ahead *geradeaus,* 5
strawberry punch *die Erdbeerbowle, -n,* 9
street *die Strasse, -n,* 7; on Prinzregenten Street *in der Prinzregentenstrasse,* 7
streetcar *die Strassenbahn, -en,* 2; by streetcar *mit der Strassenbahn,* 2
stroll: stroll through the city *der Stadtbummel, -,* 10; to take a stroll through the city *einen Stadtbummel machen,* 10
student *der Schüler, -,* 3
stupid *blöd,* 2; *dumm,* 10
subject *das Fach, ̈er,* 2
suburb *der Vorort, -e,* 7
sugar *der Zucker,* 7
suit: that suits me fine *das passt prima,* 9
summer *der Sommer, -,* 3; in the summer *im Sommer,* 3
sun *die Sonne,* 7
Sunday *der Sonntag, -e,* 3; on Sunday *am Sonntag,* 3
sunny *sonnig,* 7
super! *super!* 3
supermarket *der Supermarkt, ̈e,* 7
supposed to *sollen,* 7
sweater *der Pulli, -s,* 11
swim *schwimmen,* 3
Switzerland *die Schweiz,* 1; from Switzerland *aus der Schweiz,* 1; in Switzerland *in der Schweiz,* 7

T

take *nehmen,* 9
talk *sprechen,* 9; Karin would like to talk to you *die Karin möchte dich sprechen,* 9
tall *gross,* 6
taste *schmecken,* 7; how does it taste? *wie schmeckt's?* 7; that's a matter of taste *das ist Geschmackssache,* 6
teacher *der Lehrer, -* (m), 1; *die Lehrerin, -nen* (f), 1; German teacher *der Deutschlehrer, -,* 1
telephone *das Telefon, -e,* 5; to telephone, make a phone call *telefonieren,* 5
telephone receiver *der Hörer, -,* 5
telephoning *Telefonieren,* 5
tell *erzählen,* 9
teller *der Bankangestellte, -n,* 5
tennis *Tennis,* 3
terrible *furchtbar,* 9
terrific! *Spitze!* 3
test *die Klassenarbeit, -en,* 2
thank *danken,* 5; thank goodness! *Gott sei Dank!* 5; thank you *danke,* 2
thanks *danke,* 2; fine, thanks *gut, danke,* 10; thanks a lot! *vielen Dank!* 6; thanks a million! *tausend Dank!* 6
that *das,* 1; that comes to *das sind,* 5; that's . . . *das ist . . .* 1; *dass,* 6
the *der, die, das,* 1

theater *das Theater, -,* 10; to go to the theater *ins Theater gehen,* 10
their *ihr, ihre,* 9
then *dann,* 2; now and then *ab und zu,* 7
there *da, dort,* 2; over there *da drüben, dort drüben,* 2; there is, there are *es gibt,* 5; up there *dort oben,* 7; we'll be there *wir sind da,* 5; we're here *wir sind da,* 6
these *dies-,* 11; these are *das sind,* 6
they *sie,* 2
think *finden,* 3; *meinen,* 6; *glauben,* 10; do you think so? *findest du? meinst du?* 6; don't you think so? *meinst du nicht?* 6; I don't think so *das finde ich nicht,* 3; I think so *ich glaube, ja,* 11; what do you think? *was meinst du?* 11; what do you think about . . .? *wie findest du . . .?* 3
thirsty: to be thirsty *Durst haben,* 9
this *dies-,* 11
thousand *tausend,* 6
three *drei,* 3; three times *dreimal,* 3
through *durch,* 5
Thursday *der Donnerstag,* 2; on Thursday *am Donnerstag,* 2
ticket (plane) *das Flugticket, -s,* 5
tie *die Krawatte, -n,* 11
time *die Zeit, -en,* 5; at what time? *um wieviel Uhr?* 9; free time *die Freizeit,* 3; in your free time *in deiner Freizeit,* 3; on time *pünktlich,* 5; what time is it? *wie spät ist es?*
times: three times *dreimal,* 3; four times *viermal,* 3
to *nach; zu,* 5; off to *auf nach,* 5
today *heute,* 2
together *zusammen,* 10
toilet *die Toilette, -n,* 5
tomato *die Tomate, -n,* 7
tomorrow *morgen,* 5
too *zu,* 10; me too *ich auch,* 3
tower *der Turm, ⸚e,* 7
train *die Bahn,* 5; by train *mit der Bahn,* 5
travel bag *die Reisetasche, -n,* 5
travel book *das Reisebuch, ⸚er,* 11
travel guide *der Reiseführer, -,* 5
traveler *der Reisende, -n,* 5
traveler's check *der Reisescheck, -s,* 5
trip *die Reise, -n,* 5
true! *stimmt!* 3; not true! that's not so! *stimmt nicht!* 3
try *versuchen,* 5; *probieren,* 7; why don't you try . . . *probier doch mal . . .* 7
T-shirt *das T-Shirt, -s,* 11
Tuesday *der Dienstag,* 2; on Tuesday *am Dienstag,* 2
twice *zweimal,* 3

U

umbrella *der Regenschirm, -e,* 7
uncle *der Onkel, -,* 6
understand *verstehen,* 9
unfortunately *leider,* 7; I'm sorry, I don't know *ich weiss es leider nicht,* 7
unpack *auspacken,* 6; he unpacks his backpack *er packt den Rucksack aus,* 6
unpleasant *unsympathisch,* 6
up: up there *dort oben,* 7; what's up? *was gibt's?* 9
upstairs *oben,* 6
usually *gewöhnlich,* 11

V

vacation *die Ferien* (pl), 5; have a nice vacation! *schöne Ferien!* 5; to go on vacation *Ferien machen,* 5
vegetable *das Gemüse,* 7
very *sehr,* 6
video recorder *der Video-Recorder, -,* 9
Vienna *Wien,* 1
village *das Dorf, ⸚er,* 7
visit *besuchen,* 3
visitor *der Besucher, -,* 7

W

wait: wait a minute! *Moment mal!* 2
waiting room *die Wartehalle, -n,* 5
Walkman *der Walkman,* 5
wallet *das Portemonnaie, -s,* 11
want *wollen,* 10
war film *der Kriegsfilm, -e,* 10
warm *warm,* 7
watch *die Uhr, -en,* 11; wristwatch *die Armbanduhr, -en,* 11
we *wir,* 2
weather *das Wetter,* 7
weather report *der Wetterbericht, -e,* 7
Wednesday *der Mittwoch,* 2; on Wednesday *am Mittwoch,* 2
week *die Woche, -n,* 5; (times) a week *in der Woche,* 3
weekend *das Wochenende, -n,* 3; on the weekend *am Wochenende,* 3
welcome: welcome to . . .! *Willkommen in . . .!* 6; you're welcome *bitte,* 2; *bitte sehr,* 5; *bitte schön,* 6
well *na,* 2; *gut,* 9; well, okay *na gut,* 7; well then *so,* 6; *na, dann,* 9; *also,* 10; well, yes *nun ja,* 10
western *der Western, -,* 10
what? *was?* 2; *welche?* 2; what?! *was?!* 3
when? *wann?* 2; *wenn?* 10
where? *wo?* 2; from where? *woher?* 1; to where? *wohin?* 5; where are you from? *woher bist du?* 1
whether *ob,* 5
which *welch-,* 10
white *weiss,* 11; the color white *das Weiss,* 11
who? *wer?* 1; who's that? *wer ist das?* 1
whom? *wen?* 5
why? *warum?* 10
win *gewinnen,* 3
winter *der Winter, -,* 3; in the winter *im Winter,* 3
with *mit,* 7
worry: don't worry *keine Sorge,* 7
wow! *Mensch!* 6
wristwatch *die Armbanduhr, -en,* 11

Y

year *das Jahr, -e,* 1; thirteen years old *dreizehn Jahre alt,* 1; (times) a year *im Jahr,* 3
yellow *gelb,* 11; the color yellow *das Gelb,* 11
yes *ja,* 1
yet: not yet *noch nicht,* 11; I don't know yet *ich weiss noch nicht,* 11
yogurt *der Joghurt,* 7
you *du,* 1; *Sie* (formal), 1; *ihr, Sie* (pl), 2; (in general) *man,* 10; it's you! *du bist's!* 5
young people *die Jugend; die Jugendlichen* (pl), 10
your *dein, deine* (sing), 6; *euer, eure* (pl), 9; *Ihr, Ihre* (formal), 9
youth *die Jugend,* 10

V

vase *die Vase, -n,* 11

GRAMMAR INDEX

ABBREVIATIONS

acc	*accusative*	nom	*nominative*
comm	*command*	pers	*person*
conv past	*conversational past*	plur	*plural*
dat	*dative*	prep	*preposition*
def	*definition*	pres	*present*
def art	*definite article*	pron	*pronoun(s)*
dir obj	*direct object*	ques	*question(s)*
indef art	*indefinite article*	sep pref	*separable prefix*
indir obj	*indirect object*	sing	*singular*
inf	*infinitive*	subj	*subject*
interr	*interrogative*		

15: (c)Elizabeth Opalenik/Stock Market; (b)Julius Fekete/Stock Market; **16:** (t)Courtesy *Beitung und Herold;* (b) Culver; **17:** Bettmann Archive; **18:** (l)Culver; (c) Culver; (r)German Information Center; **22:** (t)Maggie Steber/Stock Boston; (b)German Information Center; **23:** (tl)Dagmar Fabricius/Stock Boston; (tr)Ted Horowitz/Stock Market; (c) Courtesy of CMA–German Agricultural Marketing Board; (2nd from b)Courtesy Mercedes-Benz; (b)Courtesy Braun; **24:** (tl)Paolo Koch/Photo Researchers; (tr)Joachim Messerschmidt/Leo de Wys; (cl)Gabe Palmer/Stock Market; (cr)Rick Browne/Stock Boston; (bl)Arthur Grace/Stock Boston; (br)Gabe Palmer/Stock Market; **25:** (tr)Tomas Sennett/Magnum; (c)Brownie Harris/Stock Market; (bl)Chris Sorensen/Stock Market; (br)Homer Sykes/Woodfin Camp; **34:** (tr)Abbott/Leo de Wys; (2nd row l)Ted Horowitz/Stock Market; (3rd row l)Robin Schwartz/International Stock Photo; (b, 3rd from l)Nancy Brown/Image Bank; (b, 2nd from r)Gabe Palmer/Stock Market; (br)S. Niedorf/Image Bank; **38:** (cl)Abbott/Leo de Wys; (cr)Ted Horowitz/Stock Market; **53:** Shostal Associates; **70:** (br)Ted Horowitz/Stock Market; **95:** (tl)Clyde Smith/Peter Arnold; (c)Werner Müller/Peter Arnold; (tr)Werner Müller/Peter Arnold; (bl)Jon Feingersh/Stock Market; (br)Tom King/Image Bank; **104:** (br)© World Copyright 1986 by Rolf Kauka and Erich Pabel Verlag GmbH; **119:** (t)*Max und Moritz,* the complete edition, by Wilhelm Busch. Pestalozzi Verlag; (cl)© 1966 and 1952 Walt Disney Productions. Deutsche Übersetzung: © 1970 Walt Disney Productions. Erschienen im Delphin Verlag, Stuttgart and Zurich; (c)© Dargaud Editeur 1969; (cr)*Der Struwwelpeter,* the complete edition, by Dr. Heinr. Hoffman. Pestalozzi Verlag; **125:** (t)Joachim Messerschmidt/Leo de Wys; **127:** (cl)Wolfgang Kunz/Bilderberg; **128:** (cr)Steve Vidler/Leo de Wys; (b)Porterfield/Chickering/Photo Researchers; **129:** (tl)Milan Horacek/Bilderberg; (tr)Milan Horacek/Bilderberg; (bl)Walter Schmidt/Peter Arnold; (br)Dagmar Fabricius/Stock Boston; **134:** Lufthansa Airlines; **135:** (tr)Lufthansa Airlines; (bl)Lufthansa Airlines; **143:** Lufthansa Airlines; **144:** (t)Lufthansa Airlines; **145** (r)Volker Corell; **158:** Lufthansa Airlines; **168:** (tc)Lawrence Fried/Image Bank; (tr)Lawrence Fried/Image Bank; (cr)Nancy Brown/Image Bank; **191:** (b)Culver; **210:** (bl)Porges/Peter Arnold; (bc)Lothar Reupert/Image Bank; (br)Lisl Dennis/Image Bank; **229:** Thomas Höpker/Woodfin Camp; (insert)Thomas Höpker/Anne Hamann; **230:** (tl oval)Thomas Höpker/Anne Hamann; (tr)Jim Cartier/Photo Researchers; (cl) J. Kappelmeyer/Leo de Wys; (cr)Rudi Meisel/Visum/Woodfin Camp; (b)Yada Claassen/Stock Boston; **231:** (tl)Thomas Höpker/Anne Hamann; (tr)Tom McHugh/Photo Researchers; (cl)Thomas Höpker/Anne Hamann; (cr)Thomas Höpker/Anne Hamann; (b)Tom McHugh/Photo Researchers; **232:** (cr)Fred McKinney/Stock Market; (b)Vera Bradshaw/Photo Researchers; **233:** (t)Cornell Capa/Magnum; (tr insert)Thomas Höpker/Anne Hamann; (cr)Thomas Höpker/Anne Hamann; (bl)John Mason/Stock Market; (br)Claudia Parks/Stock Market; **234:** (t)Dallas & John Heaton/Click Chicago; (cl)Claudia Parks/Stock Market; (cr)Swiss National Tourist Office; (b)Swiss National Tourist Office; **235:** (tl)Fred Mayer/Anne Hamann; (tr circle)Cottom Coulson/Woodfin Camp; (cl)Fred Mayer/Anne Hamann; (cr)Paolo Koch/Photo Researchers; (b)Fred Mayer/Anne Hamann; **236:** (t)J. Mahl/Leo de Wys; (t insert)James Sugar/Photo Researchers; (cr)Weiss-Rapho/Photo Researchers; (b)Ossi Baumeister/Anne Hamann; **240:** (t)George Ancona/International Stock Photo; **243:** (bl)Ted Horowitz/Stock Market; (bc)Abbott/Leo de Wys; (br)Jonas/Leo de Wys; **247:** (bl)Jonas/Leo de Wys; **248:** (l)Peter Russell Clemens/International Stock Photo; **255:** (cl)Peter Russell Clemens/International Stock Photo; **256** (tl)Peter Russell Clemens/International Stock Photo; **281:** (tr)Museum of Modern Art Film Stills Library; (cl)Kobal Collection; (center)Globe Photos; (cr)Kobal Collection; (bl)Kobal Collection; (bc)Kobal Collection; (br)Kobal Collection; **285:** (t)Globe Photos; (c)Kobal Collection; (b)Universal Pictures; **296:** D. Fineman/Sygma; **297:** T. Westenberger/Sygma; **298:** (1)Reporta/New Eyes: (r)Gurlitt/Gamma-Liason; **299:** (l)Gamma-Liason; (r)Lothar Lange/New Eyes; **313:** (b)K. McCunnall/Leo de Wys; **333:** (t)Owen Franken/Stock Boston; (c oval)Francisco Hidalgo/Image Bank; (bl)Michael Rosenfeld/Image Bank; (br)Horst Schäfer/Peter Arnold; **334:** (tl)H. Gritscher/Peter Arnold; (tr)H. Gritscher/Peter Arnold; (bl)Wolfgang Kunz/Bilderberg; (br)Horst Schäfer/Peter Arnold; **335:** (tl)Horst Schäfer/Peter Arnold; (tr)Horst Schäfer/Peter Arnold; (b)Horst Schäfer/Peter Arnold; **336:** (t)Hans Madej/Bilderberg; (cr)Michael Engler/Bilderberg; **337:** (t)J. Messerschmidt/Leo de Wys; (b)F. Damm/Leo de Wys; **338:** (t)F. Damm/Leo de Wys; (tl insert)Horst Schäfer/Peter Arnold; (c)Owen Franken/Stock Boston; (b)F. P. Wartenberg/New Eyes; **339:** (tl)Silvestris GmbH; (tr)Horst Schäfer/Peter Arnold; (c 2nd from b)Grotty/New Eyes; **340:** (tl)L. Freed/Magnum; (tr)Volker Corell; (c)Silvestris GmbH.

ART CREDITS: Bert Dodson **164, 165, 324, 325, 326** Eldon Doty **321** Don Dyen **36, 42, 45, 50, 51, 78, 84, 94, 101, 106, 111, 140, 157, 181, 187, 215, 252, 261, 305** Tonia Hampson **205, 206, 207, 208, 209, 266, 267** Diane Dawson Hearn **192, 193** Steven Schindler **39, 40, 79, 89, 97, 98, 107, 108, 182, 183, 274** Lauren Simeone **64, 66, 67, 81, 97, 142, 171, 185, 258, 276, 290, 302, 303, 306, 307, 308, 311, 312, 313, 314, 315, 316, 317, 319, 320, 321, 331**

8
9
C 0
D 1
E 2
F 3
G 4
H 5
I 6
J 7